W9-CNF-501

Introduction to LAW ENFORCEMENT and CRIMINAL JUSTICE

TENTH EDITION

Introduction to LAW ENFORCEMENT and CRIMINAL JUSTICE

KÄREN MATISON HESS, PH.D.

President, Institute for Professional Development
Former Instructor, Normandale Community College
Bloomington, Minnesota

CHRISTINE HESS ORTHMANN, M.S.

Orthmann Writing and Research
Rosemount, Minnesota

with contributions from Henry Lim Cho, M.A.

Australia • Brazil • Japan • Korea • Mexico • Singapore • Spain • United Kingdom • United States

Introduction to Law Enforcement and Criminal Justice, Tenth Edition

Kären Matison Hess and Christine Hess Orthmann

Vice President, Career and Professional Editorial: Dave Garza

Director of Learning Solutions: Sandy Clark

Senior Acquisitions Editor: Shelley Esposito

Managing Editor: Larry Main

Product Manager: Anne Orgren

Editorial Assistant: Danielle Klahr

Vice President, Career and Professional Marketing: Jennifer Baker

Marketing Director: Deborah S. Yarnell

Marketing Manager: Erin Brennan

Marketing Coordinator: Erin Deangelo

Production Director: Wendy Troeger

Production Manager: Mark Bernard

Senior Content Project Manager: Betty Dickson

Senior Art Director: Joy Kocsis

Photo Researcher: Terri Wright Design, www.terriwright.com

Production Service: Sara Dovre Wudali, Buuji, Inc.

For product information and technology assistance, contact us at
Cengage Learning Customer & Sales Support, 1-800-354-9706

For permission to use material from this text or product,
submit all requests online at **www.cengage.com/permissions**
Further permissions questions can be e-mailed to
permissionrequest@cengage.com

Library of Congress Control Number: 2010933641

ISBN-13: 978-1-111-13890-5

ISBN-10: 1-111-13890-7

Delmar
5 Maxwell Drive
Clifton Park, NY 12065-2919
USA

Cengage Learning is a leading provider of customized learning solutions with office locations around the globe, including Singapore, the United Kingdom, Australia, Mexico, Brazil, and Japan. Locate your local office at: **international.cengage.com/region**

Cengage Learning products are represented in Canada by Nelson Education, Ltd.

To learn more about Delmar, visit **www.cengage.com/delmar**

Purchase any of our products at your local college store or at our preferred online store **www.Cengagebrain.com**

Printed in the United States of America
1 2 3 4 5 6 7 14 13 12 11 10

BRIEF CONTENTS

CONTENTS

SECTION II:

CONTEMPORARY LAW ENFORCEMENT 119

PREFACE

Law enforcement and criminal justice in the United States have evolved tremendously since the country was founded over 200 years ago. Actually, the changes that have occurred in the past three decades alone are impressive.

Most of you were not yet born when the first edition of this text was published in 1979. Students studying law enforcement at that time were not exposed to the breadth and depth of topics you are about to explore. The inaugural edition of this book had no mention of the Internet, cybercrime, phishing or identity theft. Coverage of drugs did not include methamphetamine, Ecstasy or prescription drug abuse. There were no sections devoted to terrorism, school shootings or hate crimes. Students did not learn about use-of-force continuums, how to interact with the media or how to communicate with immigrant populations and increasingly diverse communities. Acronyms such as BAC, DUI, CAD, GIS, MIS, IEDs, WMDs, HIV and AIDS were meaningless. Concepts such as racial profiling, accreditation and community policing had not yet taken shape. Clearly, the issues facing students of law enforcement and criminal justice have changed substantially during the past 30 years.

Introduction to Law Enforcement and Criminal Justice was written to present an overview of the field and the numerous complexities within it. It also seeks to instill an appreciation for those who "serve and protect" our society and an understanding of this exciting, challenging profession. The future of our lawful, democratic society depends largely on those currently in the field of criminal justice and those preparing to enter it. Law enforcement officers have awesome power and tremendous responsibilities that must be met under constantly changing circumstances and in a way that protects individual rights and society's rights simultaneously—a tremendous challenge.

When we wrote the first edition of this text over 30 years ago, law enforcement seemed more predictable and faced different challenges than it does now. In the 1970s law enforcement was focused on restoring its image after the disturbances and civil unrest of the 1960s. It saw organized crime as a major national threat. Crime fighting was its most obvious mission. Victims were seen primarily as sources of information. AIDS, crack cocaine, drive-by shootings and children shooting children, domestic violence and terrorism were not perceived as problems. The first edition contained no chapters on community policing, problem solving, juveniles or victims because these were not priorities. The beginnings of community policing could be seen, however, in the discussions of team policing and community service—helping citizens help themselves. The first edition also had no chapters on courts or corrections, focusing solely on the law enforcement component of the criminal justice system.

This current edition recognizes the interrelationships of the components of the criminal justice system and the need for coordination among them. As you learn about law enforcement, you will find three recurring themes in this text. The first theme is that of community or service orientation to law enforcement and the critical importance of partnerships, viewing citizens as co-producers of justice. A second theme is that of police officers as peace officers as well as crime fighters and a concern for not only criminal justice but social justice as well. The third theme is that of police officers' discretion in their role as gatekeepers to the criminal justice system. Each chapter in the text serves as an overview of an area that could be expanded into an entire course.

MAJOR FEATURES—CONTEXT THEMES

Not unexpectedly, the text begins with chapters that provide needed background (Section I). Our present system of law enforcement did not just magically appear. It has evolved slowly, shaped by numerous factors, including social and political influences. Chapter 1 describes the evolution of law enforcement and the criminal justice system from its ancient roots to the present system. Chapter 2 describes the laws all U.S. citizens are expected to obey and how they came to be. Chapter 3 explores crime in the United States: what types of crimes are occurring and theories about why, who commits crime and the effect it has on victims. This section provides the context within which to understand contemporary U.S. policing: its history and traditions, the laws under which it operates and which it enforces as well as the individuals who choose to disobey the laws and their victims. Policing is, at its heart, about people.

Section II helps you understand the traditional organization and functions of law enforcement, most of which can still be found within our law enforcement agencies. First, an overview of the organization, goals, characteristics and culture is presented (Chapter 4). This is followed by a discussion of the general functions of most agencies, patrol and traffic (Chapter 5), and the specialized assignments frequently found in larger agencies, such as investigators, SWAT teams, school resource officers and reserve officers (Chapter 6). The section ends with a discussion of the current approaches to policing being used throughout the county—community policing, problem-solving policing, intelligence-led policing and evidence-based policing (Chapter 7).

Section III explores important challenges to the profession in the 21st century. It begins with a discussion of the challenge of policing within the law, apprehending criminals without violating their constitutional rights (Chapter 8). Next, the challenges posed by gangs and drugs, problems that have overshadowed the previous concern with organized crime, are presented (Chapter 9). This is followed by an examination of the latest threat to our country—terrorism (Chapter 10). Then significant issues involved in policing are described, including discretion, discrimination, racial profiling, use of force, pursuit, liability, corruption and ethics (Chapter 11). The section concludes with a discussion of departmental issues, including recruiting and retaining officers, civilian review boards, sexual harassment, unions, moonlighting, privatization of law enforcement, accreditation and professionalism (Chapter 12).

The final section places law enforcement into the context of the criminal justice system, examining its role with the other two components of the criminal justice system, the courts and corrections. The need for collaboration and cooperation among the three components has become an important focus during the past decade. Chapter 13 describes the U.S. court system, its structure, key players, critical stages, the trial itself and the role of the law enforcement officer in the court system. Chapter 14 explains the U.S. corrections system, its purposes, components, alternatives and issues, including that of capital punishment. Both Chapters 13 and 14 also explain these two components within the juvenile justice system.

NEW TO THIS EDITION

This tenth edition has been completely updated, with most sources cited being published between 2007 and 2010. Included are 35 new terms, 20 new Supreme Court cases and more than 450 new cites. The InfoTrac assignments have been replaced with assignments from the Gale Emergency Services Database, and the Internet assignments have been revised. Specific changes within each chapter include the following:

- Chapter 1—A Brief History:
  - Added brief info on Pinkerton (early detectives) and new info on first women officers
  - Added discussion of paradigms, paradigm shifts and an emerging fourth era of policing
  - Added discussion of five strategies operating in contemporary policing
  - Added significant dates in policing to Figure 1.4
- Chapter 2—Our Laws:
  - Added 2008 ruling in *District of Columbia v. Heller* that the Second Amendment affirms individual's right to possess firearms for traditional lawful purposes
  - Added 2009 ruling in *Melendez-Diaz v Massachusetts* that it is a violation of the Sixth Amendment for a prosecutor to submit a chemical drug test report without the testimony of the scientist
- Chapter 3—Crime:
  - Added homelessness to hate crime discussion
  - Brought classical and positivist theories of crime into 21st century with current prevailing theories—self-control vs. strain
  - Included developments in adopting the National Incident-Based Reporting System (NIBRS)
- Chapter 4—Contemporary Policing
  - Expanded discussion of 10-codes to balance the controversy
  - Expanded discussion of dispatchers, including Next Generation 911: NG911
  - New discussions of records and the accountability model

- Chapter 5—Patrol:
  - Added discussion of self-initiated tasks
  - Added to discussion on enforcing traffic laws, use of cell phones and texting
  - Added brief discussion of boating under the influence
  - Added new technologies used in patrol, including in traffic enforcement
- Chapter 6—Specialized Roles:
  - Added Supreme Court case requiring that laboratory analysts who performed test appear in court to testify
  - Added National Sheriffs' Association (NSA) report on the need to reform forensics
  - Added controversial issues related to DNA analysis
- Chapter 7—Community Policing:
  - Cut community policing discussion by almost one-third to make room for data-driven strategies
  - Added three new sections on data-driven policing (CompStat policing, intelligence-led policing and evidence-based policing)
  - Added Safe City Program and Data-Drive Approaches to Crime and Traffic Safety (DDACTS)
  - Changed chapter title to reflect the change in content
  - New opening chapter quote
  - New discussion questions to balance new topics covered in the chapter
- Chapter 8—Policing within the Law:
  - Added discussion of detention—continuum from simple stop to arrest
  - Added paragraph on the exclusionary rule and fruit of the poisonous tree doctrine
  - Added new terms: detention, exclusionary rule, investigatory stop
  - Added new Supreme Court cases:
    - *Virginia v. Moore*—probable cause to arrest
    - *Arizona v. Gant*—limits authority to search a vehicle incident to arrest
    - *Arizona v. Johnson*—the right to frisk vehicle passengers with reasonable suspicion
    - *Michigan v. Fisher*—emergency entrance to protect a person from himself
    - *Florida v. Powell*—discretion in the working of the *Miranda* warning
    - *Maryland v. Shatzer*—*Miranda* warning lasts for 14 days
- Chapter 9—Gangs and Drugs:
  - Expanded the discussion on legalization/decriminalization of drugs
  - Condensed information on gangs and drugs
  - Added the Mexican drug wars, violent victimization of gang members, more recent research on G.R.E.A.T. and D.A.R.E., changing nature of gangs

- Chapter 10—Terrorism and Homeland Security:
  - Added a discussion of radicalization
  - Added attack at Ft. Hood, and the foiled terrorist plot of a militant Christian group to kill law enforcement officers
  - Added several national initiatives including the revised National Information Management System (NIMS), the National Response Framework (NRF), and the National Emergency Communication Plan (NECP)
  - Added the Suspicious Activities Report (SAR) Initiative and the importance of SARs
  - Added Los Angeles Police Department's National Counter-Terrorism Academy (NCTA) and Hydra training simulator
- Chapter 11—Police Conduct:
  - Added the *Garrity* Rule, and officers' rights; the 329(g) program on oversight of state and local immigration laws; and added the controversial Arizona immigration legislation
  - Added 9th Circuit Court of Appeals 2009 case of *Brady v. McPherson* limiting use of the TASER in that district, with implications for law enforcement officers throughout the country
- Chapter 12—Becoming a Law Enforcement Professional:
  - Added *Ricci v. DeStephano* (2009) upholding Whites in a reverse discrimination ruling
  - Added H.R.413: The Public Safety Employer-Employee Cooperation Act of 2009 and the Americans with Disabilities Amendments Act (2009)
- Chapter 13—Courts:
  - Added an in-depth discussion of plea bargaining
  - Added a brief explanation of expert testimony
  - Expanded the discussion of sentencing
  - Added a discussion of felony versus misdemeanor courts and the huge overload on misdemeanor court defense attorneys
  - Added a brief section on courtroom security and the implications for law enforcement officers
- Chapter 14—Corrections:
  - Eliminated some of the historical material
  - Focused more on reentry
  - Added pretrial services
  - Added need for swift and certain sanctions in probation and parole—the Ohio and California studies—and the need for graduated sanctions

HOW TO USE THIS TEXT

Introduction to Law Enforcement and Criminal Justice is more than a text. It is a learning experience requiring your active participation to obtain the best results.

You will get the most out of the book if you first familiarize yourself with the total scope of law enforcement: read and think about the subjects listed in the table of contents. Then follow five steps for each chapter to achieve triple-strength learning:

1. Read the objectives at the beginning of each chapter, stated in the form of "Do You Know?" questions. This is your *first* exposure to the key concepts of the text. The following is an example of this format:

   ### Do You Know . . .

   - What the basic instrument of government is?

   Review the key terms and think about their meaning in the context of law enforcement.

2. Read the chapter, underlining or taking notes if that is your preferred study style. Pay special attention to all information set apart in the text with a graphic symbol. This is your *second* exposure to the chapter's key concepts. The following is an example of this format:

   The U.S. Constitution is the basic instrument of government and the supreme law of the United States.

   The key concepts of each chapter are emphasized in this manner. Also pay attention to all words in bold print. All key terms will be in bold print when they are first used and defined.

3. Read the summary carefully. This will be your *third* exposure to the key concepts. By this point you should have internalized the information.
4. To make sure you have learned the information, when you have finished reading a chapter reread the list of objectives given at the beginning of that chapter to make certain you can answer each question. If you find yourself stumped, find the appropriate material in the chapter and review it. Often these questions will be used as essay questions during testing.
5. Review the key terms to be certain you can define each. These also are frequently used as test items.

Note: The material selected to be highlighted using the triple-strength learning instructional design includes only the chapter's key concepts. While this information is certainly important in that it provides a structural foundation for understanding the topic(s) discussed, you cannot simply glance over the "Do You Know?" highlighted boxes and summaries and expect to have mastered the chapter. You are also responsible for reading and understanding the material that surrounds these basics—the "meat" around the bones, so to speak.

The text also provides an opportunity for you to apply what you have learned or to go into specific areas in greater depth through discussion questions, Gale Emergency Services database assignments and Internet assignments. Complete each of these areas as directed by the text or by your instructor. Be prepared to share your findings with the class. Good reading and learning!

An extensive package of supplemental aids is available for instructor and student use with this edition of *Introduction to Law Enforcement and Criminal Justice.*

FOR THE INSTRUCTOR

- **CourseMate Website** Access this book-specific site through your Single Sign-on (SSO) login. The password-protected companion website for instructors provides the instructor's manual, test bank, and PowerPoint slides online, as well as providing access to the CourseMate website for students. CourseMate includes:
    - an interactive eBook
    - interactive teaching and learning tools including:
        - Study Guide
        - Quizzes
        - Flashcards
        - Critical thinking questions
        - and more
    - Engagement Tracker, a first-of-its-kind tool that monitors student engagement in the course.
- **ExamView® Computerized Testing** Create, deliver and customize tests and study guides, both in print and online, in minutes with this easy-to-use assessment and tutorial system. ExamView® offers both a Quick Test Wizard and an Online Test Wizard that guide you step-by-step through the process of creating tests, while the unique "WYSIWYG" capability allows you to see the test you are creating on the screen exactly as it will print or display online. You can build tests of up to 250 questions using 12 question types. Using ExamView®'s complete word-processing capabilities, you can enter an unlimited number of new questions or edit existing questions. The updated test bank includes multiple-choice questions, true/false questions, fill-in-the-blank questions, and essay questions.
- **Instructor's Resource Manual with Test Bank** The updated and revised Instructor's Resource Manual for the Tenth Edition provides a detailed outline, key terms and concepts, discussion topics and student activities, recommended readings, critical thinking questions and testing suggestions that will help time-pressed teachers more effectively communicate with their students while allowing them to strengthen coverage of course material.
- **Microsoft® PowerPoint® Slides** These handy, ready-to-use PowerPoint slides, created for each chapter of *An Introduction to Law Enforcement and*

Criminal Justice, Tenth Edition, will save you time in preparing engaging lectures and presentations for your course.

- **The Wadsworth Criminal Justice Media Library** So many exciting resources—so many great ways to enrich your lectures and spark discussion of the material in this text! Contact your Cengage Learning representative to access this customizable, interactive source of videos, simulations and more. View a demo at http://cengagesites.com/academic/assets/emarketing/cjml/index.html.

FOR THE STUDENT

- **CourseMate Website** To access additional course materials including CourseMate, please visit www.cengagebrain.com. At the CengageBrain.com home page, search for the ISBN of your title (from the back cover of your book) using the search box at the top of the page. This will take you to the product page where these resources can be found. CourseMate includes:
  - an interactive eBook, with highlighting, note taking and search capabilities
  - interactive teaching and learning tools including:
    - Study Guide
    - Quizzes
    - Flashcards
    - Critical thinking questions
    - and more
- **Careers in Criminal Justice and Related Fields: From Internship to Promotion, 6th Edition** This comprehensive text provides you with the invaluable information you need to help you enter and succeed in the field of criminal justice—from finding an internship to identifying the right criminal justice profession for you.
- **Careers in Criminal Justice Website** View a demo at academic.cengage.com/criminal justice/careers This unique website helps students investigate the criminal justice career choices that are right for them with the help of several important tools:
    - *Career Profiles* Video testimonials from a variety of practicing professionals in the field as well as information on many criminal justice careers, including job search strategies.
    - *Links for Reference* Direct links to federal, state, and local agencies where students can get contact information and learn more about current job opportunities.

ACKNOWLEDGMENTS

First, we must acknowledge Henry M. Wrobleski (1922–2007), the original lead author for the first six editions of this text. Henry was the former coordinator of the Law Enforcement Program at Normandale Community College, Bloomington, Minnesota. He was a respected author, lecturer, consultant and expert witness with 30 years of experience in law enforcement. He was also the dean of instruction for the Institute for Professional Development and a graduate of the FBI Academy. Other Cengage texts Mr. Wrobleski coauthored are *Introduction to Private Security,* 4th ed., and *Police Operations,* 3rd ed. He is truly missed.

We would like to thank the reviewers for the tenth edition: Megan Cole, Brown College; Elizabeth DeValve, Fayetteville State University; Chad Rosa, Kaplan University and MSB/Globe University; Christine L. Stymus, Bryant & Stratton College; and Robert F. Vodde, Fairleigh Dickinson University.

For their valuable suggestions for the previous editions of *Introduction to Law Enforcement and Criminal Justice,* thank you to Constance M. Bennett, Seminole Community College; Kenneth Bowser, Westfield State College; Robert Brode, College of the Canyons; Roger Brown, Golden Valley Lutheran College; Steven Brown, East Tennessee State University; William Castleberry, University of Tennessee–Martin; Lisa Kay Decker, Indiana State University; Vincent Del Castillo, John Jay College of Criminal Justice; Elizabeth DeValve, Fayetteville State University; Rita Dorsey, Shelby Community College; David G. Epstein, Brunswick Junior College; Chris W. Eskridge, University of Nebraska; Larry Gaines, Eastern Kentucky University; James N. Gilbert, University of Nebraska; Larry A. Gould, Northern Arizona University; George Green, Mankato State University; Martin A. Greenberg, Ulster County Community College; Edmund Grosskopf, Indiana State University; Daniel Gunderson, Chippewa Valley Technical College; Burt C. Hagerman, Oakland Community College; Hill Harper, Valdosta State University; Larry W. Hensel, Tallahassee Community College; Thomas Hinze, Riverland Community College; Robert G. Huckabee, Indiana State University; Robert Ingram, Florida International University; Robert R. Ives, Rock Valley College; Paul H. Johnson, Murray State University; William Kelly, Auburn University; William R. King, Bowling Green State University; Leonard Luzky, Ocean City College; Sidney A. Lyle, Odessa College; Michael Moberly, Southern Illinois University at Carbondale; Glen Morgan, Lincolnland Community College; M. G. Neithercutt, California State University—Hayward; James E. Newman, Police Academy, Rio Hondo Community College; Darek Niklas, Rhode Island College; E. W. Oglesby, Fullerton College; Charles Ousley, Seminole State College; Joseph Polanski,

Sinclair Community College; Frank Post, Fullerton College; James W. Robinson, Louisiana State University–Eunice; Steve Rugger, University of South Carolina Upstate; Jack Spurlin, Missouri Southern College; James Stinchcomb, Miami Dade Community College; Jack Taylor, Oscar Rose Junior College; Gary W. Tucker, Sinclair Community College; Larry Tuttle, Palm Beach Junior College; Lawrence Trostle, University of Anchorage; Myron Utech, University of Wisconsin at Eau Claire; Tim Vieders, Niagara County Community College; Robert C. Wadman, Weber State University; James Walsh, Mount San Jacinto College; Douglas Watson, Northern Essex Community College; David A. Wilson, Turnbull Police Department; Dawn B. Young, Bossier Parish Community College; and Gay A. Young, Johnson County Community College.

Any errors in the text are, however, the sole responsibility of the authors.

Thank you also to Bobbi Peacock, our photo consultant; Terri Wright, our photo researcher; Tim Hess, our leadership and management consultant; and to our production team at Delmar, Cengage Learning: Senior Acquisitions Editor Shelley Esposito; Product Manager Anne Orgren; Editorial Assistant Danielle Klahr; and Senior Content Project Manager Betty Dickson; as well as Sara Dovre Wudali, production editor at Buuji, Inc.; and our family and colleagues for their support and assistance throughout the evolution of this text.

ABOUT THE AUTHORS

Kären Matison Hess, Ph.D., has written extensively in the field of law enforcement and criminal justice. She has been a member of the English department at Normandale Community College as well as the president of the Institute for Professional Development. She is also a member of the Academy of Criminal Justice Sciences (ACJS), the American Correctional Association (ACA), the Bloomington Crime Prevention Association, the International Association of Chiefs of Police (IACP), the International Law Enforcement Educators and Trainers Association (ILEETA), the Justice Research and Statistics Association (JRSA), the National Council of Teachers of English (NCTE), and the Police Executive Research Forum. In addition she is a member of and fellow in the Textbook and Academic Authors' Association (TAA), as well as a member of the TAA Foundation Board of Directors.

Other Cengage texts Dr. Hess has coauthored are *Constitutional Law*, 4th edition; *Corrections in the 21st Century: A Practical Approach*; *Criminal Investigation*, 9th edition; *Criminal Procedure*; *Introduction to Private Security*, 5th edition; *Juvenile Justice*, 5th edition; *Management and Supervision in Law Enforcement*, 6th edition; *Community Policing: Partnerships for Problem Solving*, 6th edition; *Police Operations*, 5th edition; and *Careers in Criminal Justice and Related Fields: From Internship to Promotion*, 6th edition.

Christine Hess Orthmann, M.S., has been writing and researching in various aspects of criminal justice for over 20 years. She has been the indexer, writer of the Instructor's Manuals and the test banks for the Hess texts until 2003. She is a coauthor of *Corrections for the 21st Century; Criminal Investigation*, 9th edition; *Community Policing: Partnerships for Problem Solving,* 6th edition; *Police Operations*, 5th edition; *Constitutional Law,* 4th edition; *Management and Supervision in Law Enforcement,* 5th edition; and *Juvenile Justice,* 5th edition. Orthmann is a member of the Text and Academic Authors Association (TAA), the Academy of Criminal Justice Sciences (ACJS), the American Society of Criminology (ASC), and the National Criminal Justice Honor Society (Alpha Phi Sigma), as well as a reserve officer with the Rosemount (Minnesota) Police Department.

ABOUT THE CONTRIBUTOR

Henry Lim Cho holds an M.A. in Human Services with an emphasis on Criminal Justice Leadership from Concordia University—St. Paul, Minnesota. He has worked in the field of criminal justice for over 10 years, having held positions in private security, as a community service officer, police officer and detective. He currently holds the rank of Sergeant with the Rosemount (Minnesota) Police Department. Sgt. Cho has experience as a use-of-force instructor and a crime scene investigator. His professional memberships include the Minnesota Police and Peace Officer's Association, International Association of Identification—Minnesota Chapter, Minnesota Sex Crimes Investigator Association, High Technology Crime Investigation Association, National White Collar Crime Center, and Fraternal Order of Police. Sgt. Cho has been published in the *Minnesota Police Journal*, has appeared as a profile contributor in *Introduction to Law Enforcement and Criminal Justice*, 9th edition, and is a contributor to *Police Operations*, 5th edition.

SECTION I

THE EVOLUTION OF LAW ENFORCEMENT AND CRIMINAL JUSTICE

The criminal justice system is a vital part of our society and a complex amalgamation of three major components: law enforcement, courts and corrections. Each component acts independently and interdependently as the total system functions. Law enforcement, as the first point of contact with citizens, serves as the gatekeeper to this system, which has grown and evolved exponentially since our country was founded.

To illustrate how massive this system has become, the Bureau of Justice Statistics reports the United States spent a record $214 billion in 2006 for police protection, corrections and legal activities, an increase of 5.1 percent since 1982. Police protection accounted for about $98 billion, about $46 billion went for judicial and legal services, and about $68 billion was spent on corrections. In 2006 the nation's federal, state and local justice systems employed about 2.4 million people, remaining relatively stable over the last 10 years despite a growth in our population. About 45 percent of these employees were in police protection, 20 percent in were employed in judicial and legal capacities, and 35 percent worked in corrections ("Employment and Expenditure," 2010). The criminal justice system costs taxpayers billions of dollars, employs millions of people, deals with the lives of millions of people who break the law and the lives of their victims and often involves matters of life and death.

This first section of the text provides the background necessary to understand contemporary law enforcement and its role within the criminal justice system and American society. Chapter 1 describes how law enforcement has evolved from ancient times to the present. It traces the development of important federal agencies that provide assistance to law enforcement and that also rely on local law enforcement to fulfill their missions. Of special importance in the 21st century is the establishment of the Department of Homeland Security.

Chapter 2 explains how our system of laws evolved and the important roles of the U.S. Constitution and the Bill of Rights in this evolution. Several amendments in the Bill of Rights guide how law enforcement functions and what it can and cannot do. The inherent conflict between individual rights and the needs of the country symbolized in the scales of justice and the resulting need for balancing crime control and due process are one focus of this chapter.

Chapter 3 details what has historically been the focus of law enforcement: crime. Controlling crime has been a challenge since our country was founded. Although our forefathers sought freedom, they also had a firm belief in law and order. This chapter looks at the types of crime found in our country today and at various theories of crime causation. The chapter also describes those who break the law as well as the effect crime has on its victims. The change in focus from punishing offenders to involving victims and the community to bring about community justice is explained and sets the stage for the remaining chapters of the text.

CHAPTER 1

A Brief History: The Evolution of Law and Our Criminal Justice System

> The farther backward you can look, the farther forward you are likely to see.
>
> —Winston Churchill

This abandoned building, initially constructed for visiting Scottish nobility, was the location chosen by Sir Robert Peel for the newly created London Police. This structure became known the world over as Scotland Yard, as immortalized by A. Conan Doyle in his Sherlock Holmes mysteries.

Do You Know . . .

- When and why law enforcement began?
- The significance of the tithing system, the Frankpledge system, Leges Henrici, the Magna Carta, the parish constable system, and the Watch and Ward system?
- The origins of features of our criminal justice system, such as general alarms and citizen's arrests? The offices of constable, sheriff and justice of the peace?
- The origins of local responsibility for law enforcement? Division of offenses into felonies and misdemeanors? Jury by peers and due process? Paid law enforcement officers? Women in law enforcement?
- What significant contributions Sir Robert Peel made to law enforcement?
- Where and when the first police department was established in England and what it was called?
- What systems of law enforcement were brought from England to colonial New England and the South?
- When and where the first modern American police force began and what it was modeled after?
- What the vigilante movement was and why it occurred?
- When and how federal and state law enforcement agencies originated in the United States?
- Who the chief law enforcement officer at the federal level is?
- What the first modern state police agency was and when it was established?
- What the five levels of law enforcement are? What additional form of law enforcement operates in the United States?
- What three eras of policing traditionally have been identified? The main characteristics of each?
- What effect the spoils system had in the 1900s?
- What the Pendleton Act accomplished?
- What the Equal Employment Opportunity Act prohibits?
- What fourth era of policing is emerging? The impetus behind it?

Can You Define?

Bow Street Runners
community era
constable
Frankpledge system
hue and cry
hundreds
law
Leges Henrici
lex talionis
Magna Carta
paradigm
parish
parish constable system
political era
proactive
professional model
rattle watch
reactive
reeve
reform era
regulators
riot act
sheriff
shire-reeve
shires
slave patrols
spoils system
tithing
tithing system
vigilante
Watch and Ward

INTRODUCTION

The heritage of law enforcement is a source of pride, as well as a guide to avoiding mistakes in the future. Specific dates and events are not as important as acquiring a sense of the sequence or chronology of how present-day laws and our system of law enforcement came into existence. **Law** is a body of rules for human conduct enforced by imposing penalties for their violation. Technically, laws are made and passed by the legislative branches of our federal, state, county and city governments. They are based on customs, traditions, mores and current need.

law

A body of rules for human conduct enforced by imposing penalties for their violation.

Law implies both prescription (rule) and enforcement by authority. In the United States, those who enforce the laws are *not* the same as those who make them. Historically, in other countries, this was not the case. Often rulers both made and enforced the laws.

THE CHAPTER AT A GLANCE

This chapter begins with a discussion of primitive and ancient law and its influence on the development of English law and law enforcement. Next is an overview of the evolution of law enforcement in England, and how the criminal justice system developed in the United States after the early colonists arrived. This is followed by a description of the various federal, state, county, local and tribal agencies established over the years. Next the overlap in these agencies is discussed, followed by a description of the three eras of policing traditionally identified: the political era, the reform era, and the community era, as well as a discussion of the emergence of a fourth era—the beginnings of the post-9/11 era alternately referred to as the era of homeland security or the intelligence-led policing (ILP) era. The chapter concludes with a brief recap of important dates in police history.

PRIMITIVE AND ANCIENT LAW

Law enforcement can be traced back to the cave dwellers, who were expected to follow certain rules or face banishment or death. The customs depicted in early cave-dwelling drawings may represent the beginning of law and law enforcement.

The prehistoric social order consisted of small family groups living together as tribes or clans. Group living gave rise to customs everyone was expected to observe. The tribe's chief had executive, legislative and judicial powers and often appointed tribe members to perform special tasks, such as serving as a bodyguard or enforcing edicts. Crimes committed against individuals were handled by the victim or the victim's family. The philosophy of justice was retaliatory: punish the offender. A person who stole the game from a neighbor's traps could expect to pay for the crime by being thrown into a pot of boiling oil or a cage of wild beasts. Other common punishments for serious offenses were flaying, impalement, burning at the stake, stoning, branding, mutilation and crucifixion.

A system of law and law enforcement began earlier than 2000 BC as a means to control human conduct and enforce society's rules. Keeping the peace was the responsibility of the group.

The earliest record of ancient people's need to standardize rules and methods of enforcement to control human behavior dates back to approximately 2300 BC, when the Sumerian rulers Lipitshtar and Eshumma set standards on what constituted an offense against society. A hundred years later, the Babylonian King Hammurabi established rules for his kingdom designating not only offenses but punishments as well. Although the penalties prescribed were often barbaric by today's standards, the relationship between the crime and the punishment is of interest (Figure 1.1). The main principle of the Code of Hammurabi was that "the strong shall not injure the weak." Hammurabi originated the legal principle of ***lex talionis***—an eye for an eye.

lex talionis
An eye for an eye.

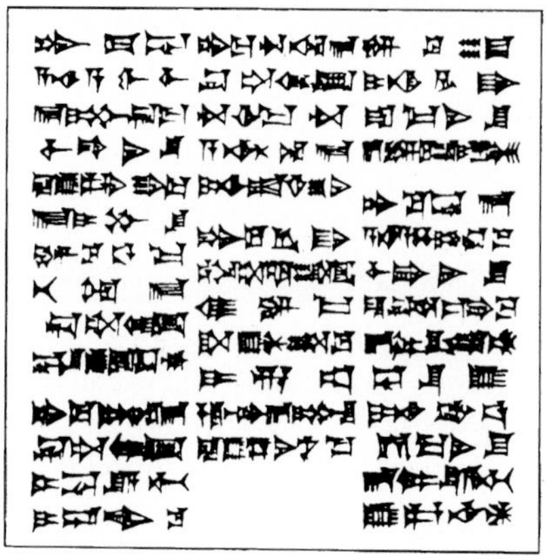

If a builder builds a house for a man and does not make its construction firm and the house collapses and causes the death of the owner of the house—that builder shall be put to death. If it causes the death of a son of the owner—they shall put to death a son of that builder. If it causes the death of a slave of the owner—he shall give the owner a slave of equal value. If it destroys property he shall restore whatever it destroyed and because he did not make the house firm he shall rebuild the house which collapsed at his own expense. If a builder builds a house and does not make its construction meet the requirements and a wall falls in—that builder shall strengthen the wall at his own expense.

FIGURE 1.1 From the Code of Hammurabi (2200 BC)

SOURCE: Masonry Institute, 55 New Montgomery Street, San Francisco, CA 94105. Reprinted with permission.

Egypt

The first accounts of a developing court system came from Egypt in approximately 1500 BC. The court system was presided over by judges appointed by the pharaoh. About 1000 BC in Egypt, public officers performed police functions. Their weapon and symbol of authority was a staff topped by a metal knob engraved with the king's name. The baton carried by the modern police officer may have its origin in that staff.

Greece

The Greeks had an impressive form of law enforcement called the *ephori*. Each year at Sparta, a body of five *ephors* was elected and given almost unlimited powers as investigator, judge, jury and executioner. These five men also presided over the Senate and Assembly, ensuring that their rules and decrees were followed. From the Greek philosopher Plato, who lived from 427 to 347 BC, came the idea that punishment should serve a purpose other than simple retaliation.

Rome

Like the Greeks, the Romans had a highly developed system to administer justice. The Twelve Tables, the first written laws of the Roman Empire, were drawn up by 10 of the wisest men in Rome in 451 and 450 BC and were fastened to the speakers' stand in the Roman Forum. The tables dealt with legal procedures, property ownership, building codes, marriage customs and punishment for crimes.

At about the time of Christ, the Roman emperor Augustus chose members from his military to form the Praetorian Guard to protect the palace and the Urban Cohort to patrol the city. Augustus also established the Vigiles of Rome. Initially assigned as firefighters, they were eventually given law enforcement responsibilities. As the first civilian police force, the Vigiles sometimes kept the peace very ruthlessly. The word *vigilante* derives from these Vigiles.

Another important contribution from the Roman Empire was the Justinian Code. Justinian I, ruler of the eastern Roman Empire from AD 527 to 565, collected all existing Roman laws. They became known as the *Corpus Juris Civilis*, meaning "body of law."

ENGLISH LAW AND LAW ENFORCEMENT

The beginnings of just laws and social control were destroyed during the Dark Ages as the Roman Empire disintegrated. Germanic invaders swept into the old Roman territory of Britain, bringing their own laws and customs. These invaders intermarried with those they conquered, the result being the hardy Anglo-Saxon.

The Anglo-Saxons and the Tithing System

The Anglo-Saxons grouped their farms around small, self-governing, self-policed villages. When criminals were caught, the punishment was often severe. Sometimes, however, the tribe would let offenders prove innocence through battle or through testimony by other tribe members willing to swear that the accused was innocent. Additionally, the tribe sometimes allowed criminals to pay a fine for committing a crime or to work off the debt.

Over time, the informal family groupings became more structured. Alfred the Great (AD 849 to 899) established that all freemen belonged to an association binding them with a certain group of people. If one person in the group committed a crime and was convicted, all group members were responsible for the person's fine. Consequently all group members were careful to see that no one in the group broke the law. Every male, unless excused by the king, was enrolled in a group of 10 families known as a **tithing**. To maintain order they had a chief tithingman who was the mayor, council and judge in one. Society was so basic that it enforced only two laws: laws against murder and theft.

The **tithing system** established the principle of collective responsibility for maintaining local law and order.

Any victim or person who discovered a crime would put out the **hue and cry**, for example, "Stop, thief!" Those hearing the cry would stop what they were doing and help capture the suspect.

The hue and cry may be the origin of the general alarm and the citizen's arrest.

When capture was made, the suspect was brought before the chief tithingman, who determined innocence or guilt plus punishment. Theft was often punished by working off the loss through bondage or servitude—the basis for civil law, restitution for financial loss (Lunt, 1938).

If a criminal sought refuge in a neighboring village, that village was expected to return the criminal for punishment. This cooperation among villagers eventually resulted in the formation of **hundreds**, groups of 10 tithings. The top official of the hundred was called a **reeve**.

The hundreds also elected a **constable** to lead them in pursuit of any law breakers. The constable was the first English police officer and had charge of the community's weapons and horses. Finally, the hundreds were consolidated into **shires** or counties. The head of the shire was called the **shire-reeve**, the forerunner of our county sheriff.

---

tithing
In Anglo-Saxon England, a unit of civil administration consisting of 10 families; established the principle of collective responsibility for maintaining law and order.

tithing system
Established the principle of collective responsibility for maintaining local law and order by organizing families into groups of 10 families known as tithings.

hue and cry
A shout by a citizen who witnessed a crime, enlisting the aid of others in the area to chase and catch the offender; may be the origin of the general alarm and the citizen's arrest.

hundreds
Groups of 10 tithings.

reeve
The top official of a hundred.

constable
An elected official of a hundred, responsible for leading the citizens in pursuit of any lawbreakers; the first English police officer and, as such, in charge of the weapons and horses of the entire community.

shires
Counties in England.

shire-reeve
The top official of a shire (county); the forerunner of our county sheriff.

The shire-reeve, a word that evolved into *sheriff*, acted as both police officer and judge, traveling from hundred to hundred. The shire-reeve had the power of *posse comitatus*, meaning he could gather all the men of a shire together to pursue a lawbreaker, a practice that was the forerunner of our posse.

The Norman Frankpledge System

In 1066 William the Conqueror, a Norman, invaded and conquered England. As king of the conquered nation, William was too concerned about national security to allow the tithings to keep their system of home rule. He established 55 military districts, each headed by a Norman shire-reeve who answered directly to the crown. The Normans modified the tithing system into the **Frankpledge system**.

Frankpledge system

Norman modification of the tithing system requiring loyalty to the king's law and mutual local responsibility in maintaining the peace.

The Frankpledge system required loyalty to the king's law and mutual local responsibility of all free Englishmen to maintain the peace.

William also decided that shire-reeves should serve only as police officers. He selected his own judges, who traveled around and tried cases, forerunners of our circuit judges, in effect separating the law enforcement and judicial roles.

The Twelfth Century

William's son, Henry I, ruled England from 1100 to 1135 and issued the **Leges Henrici**, establishing arson, robbery, murder and crimes of violence as being against the king's peace. This set the precedent that for certain crimes a person is punished by the state rather than by the victim.

Leges Henrici

A document that made law enforcement a public matter and separated offenses into felonies and misdemeanors.

The Leges Henrici made law enforcement a public matter and separated offenses into felonies and misdemeanors.

Henry I's reign was followed by many years of turmoil, which lasted until Henry II became king in 1154.

Henry II established the jury system.

Henry II's jury system, called an inquisition, required people to give information to a panel of judges who determined guilt or innocence.

For the next 100 years, kings appointed enforcement officers to meet their needs. When John became king in 1199, he abused his power by demanding more military service from the feudal class, selling royal positions to the highest bidder and increasing taxes without obtaining consent from the barons—actions all contrary to feudal custom. In addition, John's courts decided cases according to his wishes, not according to law.

In 1213 a group of barons and church leaders met to call for a halt to the king's injustices. They drew up a list of rights they wanted King John to grant them. After the king refused on two separate occasions, the barons raised an army and forced him to meet their demands. On June 15, 1215, King John signed the Magna Carta.

The Magna Carta

Our modern system of justice owes much to the Magna Carta, a decisive document in the development of England's constitutional government.

The **Magna Carta**, a precedent for democratic government and individual rights, laid the foundation for requiring rulers to uphold the law; forbade taxation without representation; required due process of law, including trial by jury; and provided safeguards against unfair imprisonment.

Magna Carta
A decisive document in the development of constitutional government in England that checked royal power and placed the king under the law (1215).

The Magna Carta contained 63 articles, most requiring the king to uphold feudal law. Article 13 restored local control to cities and villages, a fundamental principle of American law enforcement. Another article declared that no freeman should be imprisoned, deprived of property, sent out of the country or destroyed except by the lawful judgment of peers or the law of the land. The concept of due process of law, including trial by jury, developed from this article.

The Next 500 Years

Several interesting developments in law enforcement occurred in the following centuries. In 1285 King Edward I established a curfew and night watch program that allowed for the gates of Westminster, then capital of England, to be locked, keeping the city's occupants in and unwanted persons out. Bailiffs were hired as night watchmen to enforce the curfew and guard the gates. Edward I also mandated that groups of 100 merchants be responsible for keeping peace in their districts, again making law enforcement a local responsibility. This system of law enforcement, called the **Watch and Ward**, provided citizens protection 24 hours a day, with the day shift called *ward* and the night shift called *watch*. Within the contemporary law enforcement community, the night shift is still referred to as the "dogwatch."

Watch and Ward
A system of law enforcement that was used to protect citizens 24 hours a day; the day shift was called the *ward* and the night shift was called the *watch*.

An ever-increasing population and a trend toward urbanization led law enforcement to become truly a collective responsibility. If a man's next-door neighbor broke the law, the man was responsible for bringing the lawbreaker before the shire-reeve. The hundred decided yearly who would be responsible for maintaining law and order, with responsibility rotated among community members. Inevitably some people paid other members to serve in their place, beginning a system of deputies paid to be responsible for law and order. The paid deputy system was then formalized so that those whose turn it was to pay met and appointed the law enforcers. The abuse of citizen duty to serve as watchmen was pervasive, however, and led to petty thieves and town drunks serving as watchmen.

During the 14th century, the shire-reeve was replaced by the justice of the peace.

The justice of the peace was assisted by the constables and three or four men knowledgeable of the country's laws. At first the justice of the peace was involved in both judicial matters and law enforcement, but later his powers became strictly judicial. The justice of the peace eventually became the real power of local government (Lunt, 1938).

With the passing of feudal times and the rise in the church's power, the unit of local government in rural areas progressed from the hundred to the **parish**, the area

parish
The area in which people who worshipped in a particular parish church lived.

in which people who worshipped in a particular church lived. Each year the parish appointed a parish constable to act as their law officer. This system of maintaining law and order in rural Britain lasted from the Middle Ages until the 18th century.

parish constable system

An early system of law enforcement used primarily in rural areas.

During the Middle Ages, the **parish constable system** was used for rural law enforcement; the Watch and Ward system was used for urban law enforcement.

Developments in urban England required a different system of law enforcement. With urbanization came commerce, industry and a variety of buildings usually made of wood because England was primarily forest land. For fire prevention purposes the town guild appointed men who patrolled at night on fire watch. They assumed the coincidental responsibility of preventing people from breaking into houses and shops.

Although the Watch and Ward system was primitive and ineffective, it was adequate until the Industrial Revolution (1750) began. About the same time, famine struck the rural areas, and large numbers of people moved from the country into the towns seeking work in weaving and knitting mills and in factories. Many, however, failed to find work, and England experienced much unemployment, poverty and crime.

In addition, political extremists often incited mobs to march on Parliament. The government had no civil police force to deal with mob violence, so it would order a magistrate to read the **riot act**, permitting the magistrate to call in the military to quell the riot. This is the forerunner of today's gubernatorial authority to call out a state's National Guard in times of rioting or violent strikes.

riot act

An order permitting the magistrate to call in the military to quell a riot.

The use of a military force to repress civil disobedience did not work very well. Soldiers hesitated to fire on their own townspeople, and the townspeople, who actually paid the soldiers' wages, resented being fired on by soldiers they had hired to protect them.

In addition to unemployment, poverty and resentment against the use of military force, the invention of gin and whiskey in the 17th century and the subsequent increase in the liquor trade also caused a rise in violent crimes and theft. Because many constables were employed in the liquor trade, they often did not enforce regulations governing taverns and inns. Furthermore the London watchmen were highly susceptible to bribes and payoffs.

Henry Fielding and the Bow Street Runners

In 1748 Henry Fielding, lawyer, playwright and novelist, was appointed chief magistrate of Bow Street in policeless London. Fielding fought for social and criminal reform. He defied the law by discharging prisoners convicted of petty theft, giving reprimands in place of the death penalty and exercising general leniency.

Fielding wrote and published pamphlets and books about London's poverty-stricken inhabitants and the causes of crime, calling for an understanding and lessening of their suffering. He also urged that magistrates be paid a salary rather than depending on fees and fines for their income.

During this time thieves and robbers moved freely in London's streets, looting and rioting. Although such riots inevitably brought soldiers, they sometimes did not arrive for two or three days. Fielding suggested that citizens join together, go into the streets and trace the perpetrators of crime and instigators of mob violence *before* they committed crimes or caused destruction. Such views made Fielding one of the earliest advocates of crime prevention.

Fielding was also instrumental in establishing the **Bow Street Runners**, the first detective unit in London. This amateur volunteer force, under Fielding's direction, swept clean the Bow Street neighborhood. When these runners proved successful, other units were organized. Foot patrols of armed men guarded the city's streets, and a horse patrol combated highway robbery on the main roads as far as 25 miles from Bow Street.

Bow Street Runners

The first English detective unit; established in London by Henry Fielding in 1750.

Although the Bow Street Runners and patrols greatly improved control in the Bow Street area, other parts of London were overwhelmed by the impact of the Industrial Revolution. Machines were taking the place of many jobs, causing unemployment and poverty. The cities were developing into huge slums, and the crime rate soared. Children were often trained to be thieves, and for the first time in England's history, juvenile delinquency became a problem. Developments in England had a great influence on the juvenile justice system that would later develop in the United States. Citizens began carrying weapons, and the courts used long-term prison sentences, resulting in overcrowded jails and prisons. Punishments were also severe, with more than 160 crimes punishable by death.

Despite the rampant crime, however, most Londoners resisted an organized police force, seeing it as restricting their liberty. They had fought hard to overcome the historical abuse of military power by English kings and resisted any return to centralized military power. Then, in 1819 and 1820, two contrasting incidents helped people change their minds. The first was the Peterloo Massacre, an attack by armed soldiers on a meeting of unemployed workers that left 11 people dead and hundreds injured. This incident vividly illustrated the danger of using soldiers to maintain peace. In contrast, in the second incident, the Bow Street Runners broke up a conspiracy to murder a number of government officials. When the conspirators were executed, people saw that actions by professional peacekeepers could prevent a major insurrection.

In addition to rampant crime, Parliament was also concerned about poverty, unemployment and general conditions. Five parliamentary commissions of inquiry met in London between 1780 and 1820 to determine what should be done about the public order. It was not until Sir Robert (Bobbie) Peel was appointed Home Secretary that the first constructive proposal was brought before Parliament.

Peelian Reform

Sir Robert Peel, often referred to as the "father of modern policing," proposed a return to the Anglo-Saxon principle of individual community responsibility for preserving law and order.

Peel's principles for reform called for local responsibility for law and order; appointed, paid civilians to assume this responsibility; and standards for these individuals' conduct and organization. His proposals led to the organization of the Metropolitan Police of London in 1829.

The term *police*, introduced into England from France, is derived from the Greek word *polis* meaning "city." The principles of Peelian reform stated,

- Police must be stable, efficient and organized militarily.
- Police must be under governmental control.
- The deployment of police strength by both time and area is essential.
- The securing and training of proper persons is at the root of efficiency.
- Public security demands that every police officer be given a number.
- Police headquarters should be centrally located and easily accessible.
- Policemen should be hired on a probationary basis.
- The duty of police is to prevent crime and disorder.
- The test of police efficiency is the absence of crime and disorder, not the visible evidence of police action in dealing with these problems.
- The power of the police to fulfill their duties depends on public approval and on their ability to secure and maintain public respect.
- The police should strive to maintain a relationship with the public that gives reality to the tradition that *the police are the public and the public are the police.*

Peel's principles became the basis of police reform in many large cities in America. In addition, one of Peel's first steps was to introduce reform that abolished the death penalty for more than 100 offenses.

London Metropolitan Police (1829)

British police historian Critchley (1967, p.52) states, "From the start, the police was to be a homogeneous and democratic body in tune with the people, and drawing itself from the people." The London Metropolitan Police, called "bobbies" or "Peelers" after Sir "Bobbie" Peel, were uniformed for easy identification—top hats, three-quarter-length royal blue coats and white trousers—and were armed only with truncheons. Their primary function was crime prevention through patrol.

Unfortunately the London Metropolitan Police were not popular. Soon after the force went on street duty in 1829, a London mob assembled to march on Parliament. A police sergeant and two constables asked the mob leaders to send their people home. Rather than dispersing, the mob attacked the sergeant and constables, killing the sergeant and critically injuring the constables. A jury of London citizens, after hearing evidence clearly indicative of murder, returned a verdict of justifiable homicide. In time, however, police officers discharging their duties with professional integrity created a respect for the law.

City and Borough Police Forces (1835)

Broad public use of the steam engine and railways and better roads helped move many criminals from London to provincial cities, such as Birmingham, Liverpool and Manchester. Soon the citizens of these cities demanded some police organization similar to London's. In 1835 Parliament enacted legislation allowing (but not requiring) every city or borough (unincorporated township) of more than 20,000 people to form a police force.

Women Enter Law Enforcement

In 1883 the London Metropolitan Police appointed two women to supervise women convicts. Their numbers and functions later expanded.

In 1905 a woman was attached to the London Metropolitan Police force to conduct inquiries in cases involving women and children. Each year several more police matrons were hired.

EARLY LAW ENFORCEMENT IN THE UNITED STATES

When the English colonists came to America, they brought with them many traditions, including traditions in law enforcement. From the beginning they were concerned with avoiding anarchy:

> As the *Mayflower* rode at anchor off Cape Cod, some of the passengers threatened to go out on their own, without any framework of government. To avoid this threat of anarchy, the *Mayflower Compact* [1620] agreed that: "We . . . doe . . . solemnly and mutually . . . covenant and combine our selves together into a civil body politike for our better ordering and preservation . . . and by vertue hereof to enact . . . such just and equall lawes . . . unto which we promise all due submission and obedience." (Gardner, 1985, p.26)

The early colonial American settlements relied heavily on self-policing to ensure the peace. Communal pressure was the backbone of law enforcement. The colonists were of similar background, most held similar religious beliefs and there was actually little worth stealing. The seeds of vice and crime were present, however, as noted by Perry (1973, p.24), "These colonists were far from the cream of European society; in many cases they represented the legal and religious castoffs. (Persons found guilty of criminal or religious offenses were banished from Europe and exported to the New World.) Their migration served the dual purpose of removing socially undesirable persons from the Mother country and providing manpower for the outposts of imperial expansion."

Many features of British law enforcement were present in early American colonial settlements. In New England, where people depended on commerce and industry, the night watchman or constable served as protector of public order. In the South, where agriculture played a dominant role, the office of **sheriff** was established as the means of area law enforcement. Most watchmen and sheriffs were volunteers, but many were paid to serve in the place of others who were to patrol as a civic duty.

sheriff
The principal law enforcement officer of a county.

New England adopted the night watchman or constable as the chief means of law enforcement; the South adopted the office of sheriff.

Many different types of law enforcement were tried in different parts of the country. Almost all used some kind of night watch system, with little or no protection during the day. The fastest-growing municipalities were the first to organize legal forces.

The First U.S. Police Forces

The first police forces in the United States were developed in Boston, New York and Los Angeles.

Boston In 1631 the Boston court established a six-man force to guard the city from sunset to sunrise, the first night watch in America. In 1636 a town watch was created and stayed in effect for more than 200 years. At first the primary function was to ring a bell in case of fire. In 1702 the police were to patrol the streets in silence. In 1735 they were required to call out the time of day and the weather.

New York The first colonists in New York, then called New Amsterdam, were the Dutch who settled on Manhattan Island's south end. In 1643 a "burgher guard" was formed to protect the colony. Then, in 1653, New Amsterdam became a city (population 800), and the burgher guard was changed to a **rattle watch**, a group of night-patrolling citizens armed with rattles to call for help (Bailey, 1989, p.346).

rattle watch

A group of citizens patrolling at night and armed with rattles to call for help; used in New Amsterdam in the 1650s.

In 1664 the British took over New Amsterdam and renamed it New York. Thirty years later the first uniformed police officers replaced the nighttime rattle watch, and four years after that New York's streets were lighted.

The system of watchmen was very ineffective. Often the watchman was sentenced to patrol as a form of punishment for a misdemeanor. In addition citizens could avoid watch duty by hiring someone to take their places. Wealthy citizens came to rely on hiring others, and the men they hired then hesitated to invoke their authority against their well-to-do employers. By the mid-1700s, New York City's night watch was "a parcel of idle, drinking, vigilant snorers, who never quell'd any nocturnal tumult in their lives; . . . but would, perhaps, be as ready to join in a burglary as any thief in Christendom" (Richardson, 1970, p.10).

Due to a continuing increase in crime during the day, New York City hired an assortment of watchmen, fire marshals and bell ringers to patrol both day and night. In 1844 a paid day watch was established, consisting of 16 officers appointed by the mayor.

In 1844 New York City established the first modern round-the-clock, paid American city police force, modeled after London's Metropolitan Police.

Soon other cities followed suit, including Chicago, Cincinnati, New Orleans, Philadelphia, Boston, Baltimore and San Francisco.

Although patterned after the London Metropolitan Police, New York police officers protested wearing uniforms. Not until 12 years later did the New York police adopt a full police uniform and become the first uniformed law enforcement agency in the country. Likewise, although Fielding established the Bow Street Runners (the first detective unit) in 1750, nearly 100 years passed before American police agencies recognized a need for detective units, as discussed shortly. Other important differences from the London police were that police in the United States were armed and they were under local, not national, control.

Los Angeles In 1850 California became a state, and Los Angeles incorporated as a city with a population of 1,610. During its first year, the city elected a mayor, a city marshal and a sheriff. "The duties assumed by the sheriff and marshal included the collection of local taxes. The sheriff's obligations required him to traverse a vast area on horseback, fighting bands of Indians and marauding desperadoes. Lacking paid assistants, the marshal was permitted to deputize citizens whenever necessary to maintain order" (Bailey, 1989, pp.310–316).

In 1853 the city council established a police force of 100 volunteers, called the Los Angeles Rangers. Four years later they were replaced by the Los Angeles City Guards, who were charged with maintaining the peace. Finally, in 1869, the police force changed from a voluntary organization to a paid department.

Police Investigators and Detectives

At about the same time New York was adopting a full-time police force, Allan Pinkerton was setting the stage for early police investigations in Chicago. Pinkerton, who immigrated from Glasgow, Scotland, to the United States in 1842, played a significant historical role in modern police investigations. He was appointed the first detective in Chicago in 1849 and was a co-founder of the Northwestern police agency that later became the Pinkerton National Detective Agency. Their motto was a watchful eye and the saying, "We never sleep." His agents were the forerunners for the U.S. Secret Service, and his agency was employed at the federal level for many famous cases including protecting Abraham Lincoln in his presidency.

Pinkerton developed several investigative techniques still used today in law enforcement that include stings and undercover work, as well as the surveillance methods of shadowing and following targets or suspects. He was also known for working on a centralized database of criminal identification records that is now maintained by the FBI.

Investigative units began cropping up in other police agencies after Chicago's lead, with Detroit establishing a detective bureau in 1866, followed by New York in 1882 and Cincinnati in 1886.

Slave Patrols

Law enforcement in the South evolved differently. By 1700 most Southern colonies, concerned about the dangers posed by oppressed slaves, established a code of laws to regulate slaves, for example, prohibiting slaves from possessing weapons, congregating in groups, resisting punishment or leaving the plantation without permission.

Not surprisingly, many slaves resisted their bondage, attempting to escape or lashing out through criminal acts or revolts. The threat of harm by slaves was compounded by their growing number; in some southern states, blacks outnumbered whites by more than two to one. The white colonists' fear of this large and potentially dangerous slave population led to the creation of special enforcement officers—**slave patrols** (Reichel, 1999, p.82). By the mid-1700s, every southern colony had a slave patrol, most of whom were allowed to enter any plantation and break into slaves' dwellings, search slaves' persons and possessions at will and beat and even kill any slaves found violating the slave code. Asirvatham (2000, p.2) states, "Twentieth-century southern law enforcement was essentially a direct outgrowth of the 19th-century slave patrols employed to enforce curfews, catch runaways and suppress rebellion. Even later on, in northern and southern cities alike, 'free men of color' were hired as cops only to keep other African Americans in line [enforcing Jim Crow laws supporting segregation]. Until the 1960s black cops, by law or by custom, weren't given powers of arrest over white citizens, no matter how criminal."

slave patrols

Special enforcement officers during the mid-1790s who were allowed to enter any plantation and break into slaves' dwellings, search slaves' persons and possessions at will and beat and even kill any slaves found violating the slave code.

Evolution of the City Police

When city police were first established, their only contact with their departments was face-to-face meetings or messengers. One early means of communication was a telephone-pole light system to notify police of a call awaiting response. During the 1850s, however, telegraph networks linked police headquarters directly with their districts. Several decades later a modified telegraph system linked the patrol officers directly to the station. A fire alarm system, first introduced in Boston, was adopted for police use. Call boxes placed on city street corners were equipped with a simple lever that signaled the station that the officers were at their posts. A bell system was added that allowed the patrol officers to use a few simple signals to call an ambulance, a "slow wagon" for routine duties or a "fast wagon" for emergencies. The introduction of a special "Gamewell" telephone into the call box in 1880 made this a two-way communication system, greatly improving contact between patrol officers and their station houses.

The Civil War brought new social control problems. As centers of population became increasingly urbanized, fringe areas became incorporated suburbs of the hub city. These newly developed fringe cities had their own police forces, which fostered complex, uncoordinated relationships, compartmentalization and inefficiency.

Although cities developed police departments and maintained a certain level of law and order, this was not the case in many areas, especially the frontiers. In such areas Americans came to rely upon vigilante groups for law and order.

The Vigilante Movement

In response to the absence of effective law and order in frontier regions, as many as 500 vigilante movements were organized between 1767 and 1900 (Klockars, 1985, p.30).

vigilante

A person who takes the law into his or her own hands, usually in the absence of effective policing.

The **vigilante** movement refers to settlers taking the law into their own hands in the absence of effective policing.

The first American vigilante movement occurred from 1767 to 1769 in South Carolina:

> The disorder in the South Carolina back country of the 1760s was typical of later American frontier areas. . . . Outlaws, runaway slaves, and mulattoes formed their own communities where they enjoyed their booty. . . . By 1766 and 1767 the back country was in the grip of a "crime wave," and the outlaws were almost supreme. (Brown, 1991, p.61)

regulators

Respectable settlers of average or affluent means who joined others as vigilantes to attack and break up outlaw gangs and restore order in the 1760s.

Because there was no sheriff or court, "respectable settlers of average or affluent means" organized as **regulators** in 1767 to attack and break up the outlaw gangs and restore order. As noted by Brown (1991, p.60), "An American tradition had begun, for, as the pioneers moved across the Appalachian Mountains, the regulator-vigilanted impulse followed the sweep of settlement toward the Pacific."

A characteristic of the vigilante movement was that the leader was usually one of the most powerful men in the community, thus making the movement highly respectable: "Two presidents (Andrew Jackson and Theodore Roosevelt), eight state governors (including Leland Stanford, Sr., founder of Stanford University),

Judge Roy Bean dispensed frontier justice and cold beer in the Texas territory west of the Pecos River.

and four U.S. senators had either been vigilantes or expressed strong support for vigilante movements" (Klockars, 1985, p.31).

An uneven judicial system and a lack of jails added to the strength of the vigilante tradition. The movement was evidence of the value Americans placed on law and order and the desire to be rid of those who broke the law. It was also evidence of a basic paradox in the illegal means used to the desired end: "Perhaps the most important result of vigilantism has not been its social-stabilizing effect but the subtle way in which it persistently undermined our respect for law by its repeated insistence that there are times when we may choose to obey the law or not" (Brown, 1991, p.72).

As the country grew and its society became more complex, federal and state agencies were established to meet needs that could not be met at the local level.

ESTABLISHMENT OF FEDERAL AGENCIES

Congress created several federal law enforcement agencies to meet demands created by the nation's changing conditions. The oldest federal agency is the U.S. Marshals Office, created in 1789. Figure 1.2 illustrates the most common federal agencies before the reorganization that followed the September 11, 2001 (9/11) attacks on the United States.

Among the earliest federal law enforcement agencies were the U.S. Marshals Office, created in 1789, the Immigration and Naturalization Service, the Secret Service and the Internal Revenue Service.

The Department of Justice

The Department of Justice is the largest law firm in the country, representing U.S. citizens in enforcing the law.

The attorney general is head of the Department of Justice and the chief law officer of the federal government.

The Department of Justice's law enforcement agencies include the Federal Bureau of Investigation, the Federal Drug Enforcement Administration, the U.S.

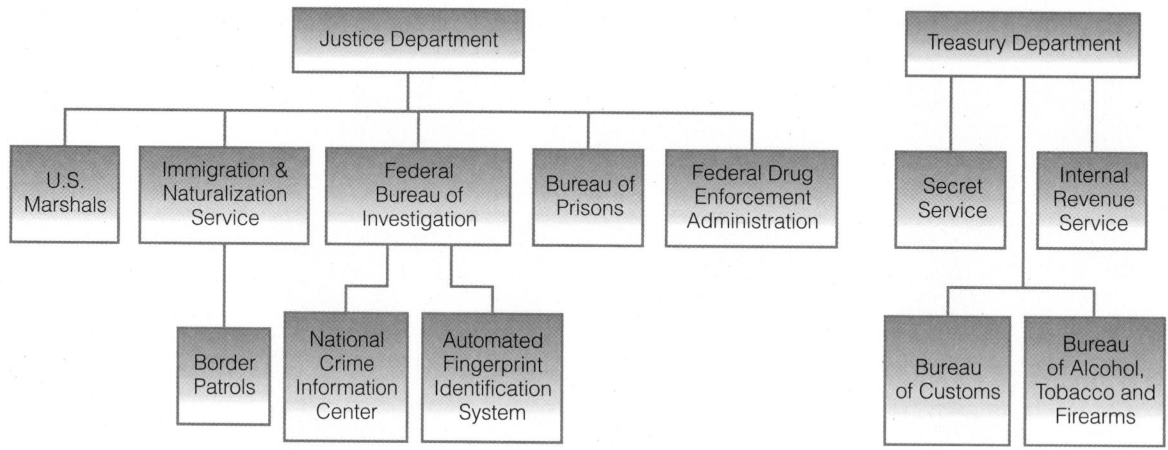

FIGURE 1.2 Federal Agencies, Original Organization

Marshals, the Immigration and Naturalization Service (pre-9/11) and the Bureau of Prisons. Figure 1.3 shows the current organization of the Department of Justice.

The Federal Bureau of Investigation (FBI) Created as the Bureau of Investigation and renamed the Federal Bureau of Investigation in 1935, this is the primary investigative agency of the federal government. The first director of the FBI was J. Edgar Hoover, and early agents were transferred from the Secret Service, most having little or no actual law enforcement experience but, instead, white-collar backgrounds.

Today, FBI special agents have jurisdiction over more than 200 federal crimes. Their responsibilities include investigating espionage, interstate transportation of stolen property and kidnapping; unlawful flight to avoid prosecution, confinement or giving testimony; sabotage, piracy of aircraft and other crimes aboard aircraft; bank robbery and embezzlement; and enforcement of the Civil Rights Acts. The FBI also provides valuable services to law enforcement agencies throughout the country:

- The *Identification Division* is a central repository for fingerprint information, including its automated fingerprint identification system (AFIS), which greatly streamlines the matching of fingerprints with suspects.
- The *National Crime Information Center (NCIC)* is a computerized database network containing records of wanted persons, stolen vehicles, vehicles used in the commission of felonies, stolen or missing license plates, stolen guns and other stolen items serially identifiable, such as television sets and boat motors.
- The *FBI Laboratory*, the largest criminal laboratory in the world, is available without cost to any city, county, state or federal law enforcement agency in the country.
- *Uniform Crime Reports (UCR)* are periodical publications provided by the FBI, which, since 1930, has served as a national clearinghouse for U.S. crime statistics. States report their monthly crime statistics to the FBI, which in turn releases information semiannually and annually regarding all crimes reported to it.

The Drug Enforcement Administration (DEA) DEA agents seek to stop the flow of drugs at their source, both domestic and foreign, and to assist state and local police in preventing illegal drugs from reaching local communities. They become

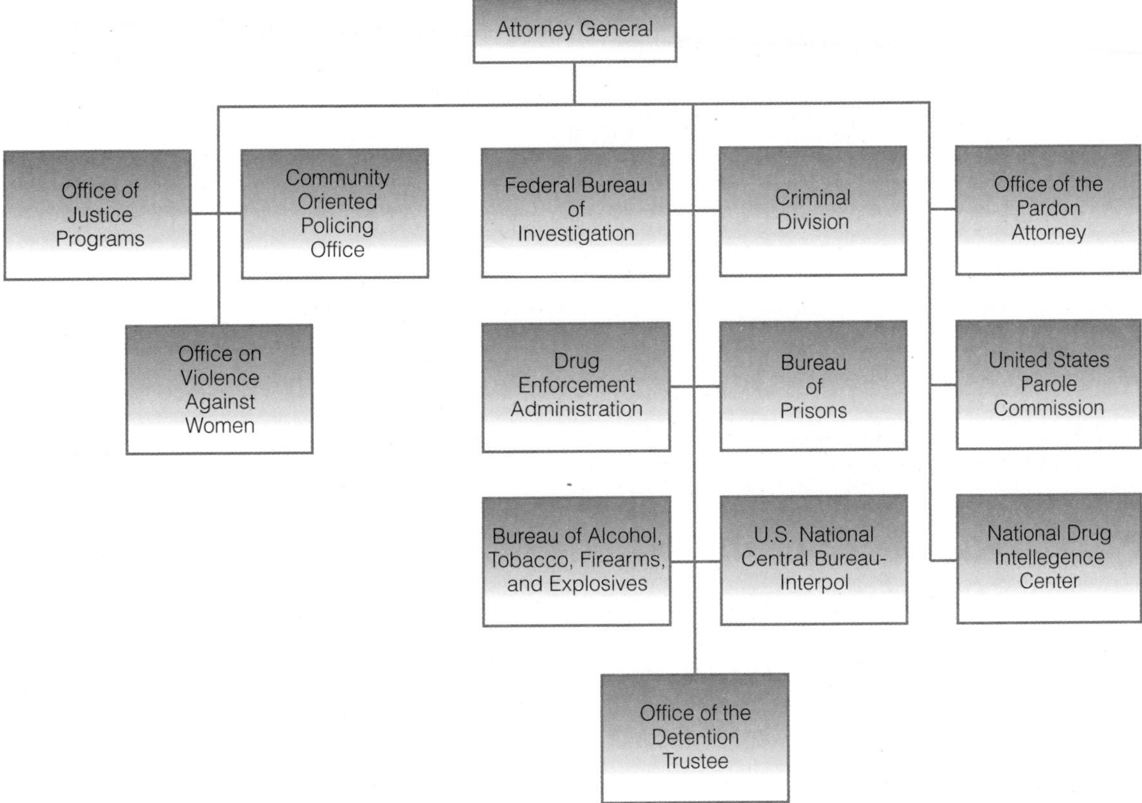

FIGURE 1.3 Current Organization of the Department of Justice

involved in surveillance, raids, interviewing witnesses and suspects, searching for evidence and seizure of contraband.

The DEA is charged with the full responsibility for prosecuting suspected violators of federal drug laws. It has liaison with law enforcement officials of foreign governments and highly trained agents stationed in all major U.S. cities and in 30 countries.

The U.S. Marshals Marshals are appointed by the president and are responsible for (1) seizing property in both criminal and civil matters to satisfy judgments issued by a federal court, (2) providing physical security for U.S. courtrooms, (3) transporting federal prisoners and (4) protecting government witnesses whose testimony might jeopardize their safety.

The Immigration and Naturalization Service (INS) The INS originally had border patrol agents who served throughout the United States, Canada, Mexico, Bermuda, Nassau, Puerto Rico, the Philippines and Europe. They investigated violations of immigration and nationality laws and determined whether aliens could enter or remain in the United States.

When the Department of Homeland Security (DHS) was organized in 2002, the INS was moved from the Justice Department to the DHS as two separate agencies: Citizenship and Immigration Service Ombudsman and the Bureau of Citizenship and Immigration Services, effective March 1, 2003. The DHS is discussed more fully in Chapter 10.

CAREER PROFILE

John Adie (Retired Special Agent with the Federal Bureau of Investigation [FBI])

My interest in the FBI started in college; my major was in education, and I was studying to be a teacher. However, a good friend of mine wanted, in the worst way, to become an FBI special agent when he graduated from college. He even convinced me to take a criminal justice course as an elective. After graduating, I went with my friend to talk to an FBI recruiter about the prospects of a career in the FBI, but the recruiter told both of us that we needed to get a few years of professional work experience before we could apply. As a result, both of us began our careers as teachers, but I always kept the idea of becoming an agent in the back of my mind.

After working for a few years as a teacher, and having achieved the position of school principal, I came across an article stating how the FBI was currently hiring special agents. Because I still held an interest in the FBI and was ready for a new challenge, I applied. The process took over a year, but I made it through the written test, interview, physical exam and background investigation and entered the FBI Academy as a member of New Agent's Class 84-6. During the 16 weeks at the Academy, new agents are trained and tested in investigations, criminal law, firearms, defensive tactics and physical fitness. Halfway through the training, new agents receive orders for their first office. Mine were to Milwaukee, Wisconsin, to work on a white-collar crime squad. So after Academy training was complete, my wife and I moved to Milwaukee.

As a first office agent, you are on probation and assigned to a training agent, who sees that you get a variety of investigative experiences during your probationary year. During that first year I was assigned to work background investigations and white-collar crime cases, but I also had opportunities to assist with bank robbery, kidnapping, foreign counterintelligence, organized crime and drug investigations. I was even able to take one of my fraud cases to trial, and I won.

After three years in Milwaukee, I received orders to New York City, the FBI's largest field office. In New York I was initially assigned to a foreign counterintelligence squad and later a counterterrorism squad. Working counterintelligence, I had the opportunity to recruit a foreign intelligence officer and work an undercover assignment with the CIA. I was in New York during the first World Trade Center Bombing in 1993 and assisted with the evidence collection of that crime scene. In New York I also became a firearms instructor and police trainer. After 8 years in New York, I had the opportunity to take an "office of preference" transfer to Minneapolis, Minnesota.

When I arrived in Minneapolis, they were looking for an agent to run the office's firearms program. I applied and was selected to the position of principal firearms instructor. Within three years, I also became the office's police training coordinator and was responsible for all training provided by the Minneapolis Division. I enjoyed both jobs because I could use my teaching background and the skills that I had learned as an agent to train other law enforcement officers. During my time as training coordinator, I had the opportunity to train local, state and federal law enforcement officers on a variety of topics in locations around the country and at the FBI Academy. In 2002, I received the FBI's Master Police Instructor Award for the amount and quality of training that I had provided during my career.

I retired from the FBI after 22 years but only because I had reached the mandatory retirement age of 57. I have since started another career as an instructor of criminal justice at a community college. While my college friend never did pursue a career in the FBI, I am grateful that he started me down the path of a career that was rewarding and provided me with many unique experiences. Most of all, it gave me the opportunity to work with many talented law enforcement officers from around the country.

The Bureau of Prisons (BOP) The BOP is responsible for the care and custody of persons convicted of federal crimes and sentenced to federal penal institutions. The bureau operates a nationwide system of maximum-, medium- and minimum-security prisons, halfway houses and community program offices.

The Department of the Treasury

The Department of the Treasury also had several agencies directly involved in law enforcement activities, including the Bureau of Customs, the Internal Revenue Service, the Secret Service and the Bureau of Alcohol, Tobacco and Firearms. They too were affected by the reorganization following the 9/11 attacks. In addition, a new bureau may be added to the department to track monies flowing to terrorist groups.

The Bureau of Customs The Bureau of Customs originally had agents stationed primarily at ports of entry to the United States, where people and goods enter and leave. Customs agents investigated frauds on customs revenue and the smuggling of merchandise and contraband into or out of the United States. Since the reorganization of federal agencies, the Bureau of Customs is now within the DHS under the Border and Transportation Security directorate and has shifted its priority to fighting terrorism.

The Internal Revenue Service (IRS) The IRS, established in 1862, is the largest bureau of the Department of the Treasury. Its mission is to encourage the highest degree of voluntary compliance with the tax laws and regulations. IRS agents investigate willful tax evasion, tax fraud and the activities of gamblers and drug peddlers.

The Secret Service The Secret Service was established in 1865 to fight currency counterfeiters. In 1901 it was given the responsibility of protecting the president of the United States, the president's family, the president-elect and the vice president. The Secret Service has also been transferred to the DHS.

The Bureau of Alcohol, Tobacco and Firearms (ATF) The ATF is primarily a licensing and investigative agency involved in federal tax violations. The Firearms Division enforces the Gun Control Act of 1968. Under the post-9/11 reorganization, this bureau has been transferred to the Justice Department and renamed the Bureau of Alcohol, Tobacco, Firearms and Explosives.

Other Federal Law Enforcement Agencies

Although most federal law enforcement agencies are within either the Department of Justice or the Department of the Treasury, other federal agencies are also directly involved in law enforcement activities, such as U.S. Postal Inspectors, the Coast Guard and the armed forces military police, as well as investigators, intelligence agents and security officers for other federal agencies.

Current Organization

The major changes occurring as a result of the attacks on the United States on September 11, 2001, were the creation of the Department of Homeland Security, established November 25, 2002, and activated January 24, 2003, and the transfer of several agencies from the Department of Justice and the Department of the Treasury to this new agency.

The Department of Homeland Security (DHS) The DHS is the third-largest cabinet department in the federal government after the Department of Defense and the Department of Veterans Affairs. Its budget in 2004 was $36.5 billion, and it employed 184,000 in 2005.

The DHS oversees the U.S. Secret Service, the Bureau of Customs and Border Protection, the Bureau of Citizenship and Immigration Services (formerly the Immigration and Naturalization Service, or INS) and the U.S. Coast Guard. Other DHS agencies with investigative and law enforcement roles include the Transportation Security Administration (TSA), the Office of Inspector General and the Federal Computer Incident Response Center.

The creation of the DHS is the most significant transformation of the U.S. government since 1947, when Harry S. Truman merged the various branches of the U.S. Armed Forces into the Department of Defense to better coordinate the nation's defense against military threats. DHS represents a similar consolidation, both in style and substance. In the aftermath of the 9/11 terrorist attacks against the United States, President George W. Bush decided 22 previously disparate domestic agencies needed to be coordinated into one department to protect the nation against threats to the homeland (see the DHS Web site, http://www.dhs.gov). Chapter 10 discusses the DHS and its organization in greater detail.

ESTABLISHMENT OF STATE AGENCIES

Many federal agencies have state counterparts, including state bureaus of investigation and apprehension and state fire marshal divisions, as well as departments of natural resources, driver and vehicle services divisions and departments of human rights.

In 1835 the republic of Texas's provisional government established the Texas Rangers, a military unit responsible for border patrol. The apprehension of Mexican cattle rustlers was a primary task (Folley, 1980, p.88). In 1874 the Texas Rangers were commissioned as Texas police officers, with duties that included tracking down murderers, robbers, smugglers and mine bandits.

The Texas Rangers were the first agency similar to our present state police; they were commissioned in 1874.

Massachusetts was next to establish a state law enforcement agency by appointing a small force of state officers in 1865 to control vice. The state also granted them general police powers; therefore, Massachusetts is usually credited with establishing the first law enforcement agency with general police authority throughout the state.

Most state police agencies established before the 20th century were created in response to a limited need. This was not the case in Pennsylvania, which established the Pennsylvania Constabulary in 1905 to meet several needs: (1) to provide the governor an executive arm for help in fulfilling his responsibilities, (2) to provide a means to quell riots occurring during labor disputes in the coal regions and (3) to improve law enforcement services in the rural portions of the state (Folley, 1980, p.66). The Pennsylvania state police served as a model for other states and heralded the advent of modern state policing.

Today the most visible forms of state law enforcement are the *state police*, who often have general police powers and enforce all state laws but do not usually work within municipalities that have their own forces unless requested; and *state highway patrols*, who focus their attention on the operation of motor vehicles on public highways and freeways, enforcing state traffic laws and all laws governing the operation of vehicles on a state's public highways. The highway patrols usually operate in uniform and drive distinctively marked patrol cars and motorcycles.

DEVELOPMENT OF COUNTY AGENCIES

The three main county agencies are the county sheriff, the county police and the coroner or medical examiner.

The County Sheriff

Many state constitutions have designated the sheriff as the chief county law enforcement officer. The sheriff is usually elected locally for a two- or four-year term, an obvious mixing of police and politics.

State law establishes the sheriff's powers and duties. Each sheriff is authorized to appoint deputies to assume responsibility for providing police protection, as well as a variety of other functions, including (1) keeping the public peace, (2) executing civil and criminal process (such as serving civil legal papers and criminal warrants), (3) keeping the county jail, (4) preserving the court's dignity and (5) enforcing court orders.

The hundreds of sheriff's departments vary greatly in organization and function. In some states the sheriff is primarily a court officer; criminal investigation and traffic enforcement are delegated to state or local agencies. In other states, notably in the South and West, the sheriff and deputies perform both traffic and criminal duties, including correctional functions, prison transport and court duties.

The sheriff's staff ranges from one (the sheriff only) to several hundred, including sworn deputies as well as civilian personnel. One major difference between sheriffs' offices and municipal police departments is that sheriffs often place greater emphasis on civil functions and operating corrections facilities.

The County Police

County police departments are often found in areas where city and county governments have merged and are led by a chief of police, usually appointed from within the department.

The Coroner or Medical Examiner

The office of coroner has a history similar to that of the sheriff and comes to modern law enforcement from ancient times (Adams, 1980, p.150). The coroner's principal task is to determine the cause of death and to take care of the remains and personal effects of deceased persons. The coroner need not be a medical doctor or have any legal background to be elected. In some jurisdictions, however, the coroner has been replaced by the medical examiner—a physician, usually a pathologist, who has studied forensic science.

DEVELOPMENT OF LOCAL AGENCIES

In addition to federal and state agencies, much power is vested in local agencies.

Township and Special District Police

The United States has approximately 19,000 townships, which vary widely in scope of governmental powers and operations. Most townships provide a limited range of services for predominantly rural areas. Some townships, often those in well-developed fringe areas surrounding a metropolitan complex, perform functions similar to municipal police.

The Constable

Several states have established the office of constable, usually an elected official who serves a township, preserving the peace and serving processes for the local justice court. The constable may also serve as the tax collector, enforce city codes, be in charge of the pound, or be authorized to execute arrest warrants or transport prisoners.

The Marshal

In some parts of the United States, a marshal serves as a court officer, serving writs, subpoenas and other papers issued by the court and escorting prisoners from jail or holding cells in the courthouse to and from trials and hearings. The marshal also serves as the bailiff and protects the municipal judge and people in the court. In some jurisdictions the marshal is elected; in others the marshal is appointed. In many areas, the sheriff's department has these responsibilities.

Municipal Police

The United States has more than 40,000 police jurisdictions and approximately 450,000 police officers, all with similar responsibilities but with limited geographical jurisdictions. The least uniformity and greatest organizational complexity are found at the municipal level due to local autonomy. Most of these police forces consist of fewer than 10 officers. This level of law enforcement is the primary focus of this text.

TRIBAL LAW ENFORCEMENT

More than 200 police departments operate in Indian Country, serving an even larger number of tribal communities. These departments range in size from only 2 or 3 officers to more than 200 officers. They serve communities as small as the Grand Canyon–based Havasupai Tribe (population about 600) and as large as the Navajo Nation (population more than 250,000 and a land area larger than Connecticut). These agencies are overseen by the Bureau of Indian Affairs (BIA), which is responsible for 55.7 million acres of land held in trust by the United States for American Indians, Indian tribes and Alaskan natives.

Tribally operated agencies provide a broad range of public safety services and functions. Nearly all such agencies respond to calls for service, and a substantial majority engage in crime prevention activities, execute arrest warrants, perform traffic law enforcement and serve court papers. Most of these tribal law enforcement agencies provide court security and search and rescue operations. Many operate one or more jails. Some have a mounted patrol unit, known as *lighthorsemen*.

OVERLAP

U.S. police forces may be classified according to the level of government each serves. However, no uniform pattern of police administration exists at any level of government, and no mechanism exists to coordinate the agencies' activities and goals.

The five levels of government authorized to have law enforcement agencies are (1) township and special district police, (2) municipal police, (3) county police, (4) state police and (5) federal police. In addition, tribal law enforcement agencies operate throughout the country.

The preceding discussion makes evident how law enforcement in the United States did not evolve in a consistent, regulated or sequential manner, resulting in considerable duplication and overlap in providing services. Overlapping jurisdictions and potential competition when two (and often many more) forces find themselves investigating the same offense pose serious problems for law enforcement and highlight the need for education and professionalism.

The evolution of policing is much more than a history of agencies that have emerged to meet society's needs. Policing itself has evolved in how it views itself, its responsibilities and the most effective means to meet those responsibilities.

THE TRADITIONAL THREE ERAS OF POLICING

Kelling and Moore (1991, pp.3–25) and others have traditionally described three eras of policing: the political era, the reform era and the community era.

The Political Era (1840–1930)

One basic difference between England's first police and those in the United States was that in England, bobbies could be fired. In the United States, this was not the case:

> In New York, for example, the first chief of police could not dismiss officers under his command. The tenure of the chief was limited to one year. Consequently, any early New York cop who was solidly supported by his alderman and assistant alderman could disobey a police superior with virtual impunity. So while the British were firing bobbies left and right for things like showing up late to work, wearing disorderly uniforms and behaving discourteously to citizens, American police were assaulting superior officers, refusing to go on patrol, extorting money from prisoners and releasing prisoners from the custody of other officers. . . .
>
> Perhaps the only good thing about the corrupt, inefficient, ineffective and disobedient early American police is that as an institution it could not be well controlled by anyone—not even the local politicians. (Klockars, 1985, p.42)

In the **political era**, police forces were characterized by a broad social service function, a decentralized organization, an intimate relationship with the community and extensive use of foot patrol.

During the political era, police got their authority from politicians and the law. This close tie to politics often caused problems.

Police Corruption As in other countries, corruption became a problem in U.S. law enforcement. One primary factor underlying this corruption was the prevalent **spoils system**, whose motto, "To the victor go the spoils," resulted in gross

political era
(1840–1930) The first era of policing; characterized by authority coming from politicians and the law, a broad social service function, decentralized organization, an intimate relationship with the community and extensive use of foot patrol.

spoils system
A political system whereby "friends" of politicians were rewarded with key positions in the police department.

political interference with policing. The winning party felt its members should be immune from arrest, given special privileges in naming favorites for promotion and assisted in carrying out vendettas against their political opponents. This system led politicians to staff many of the nation's police forces with incompetent people as rewards for support, "fixing" arrests or assuring that arrests were not made, and securing immunity from supervision for certain establishments or people.

 The spoils system encouraged politicians to reward their friends by giving them key positions in police departments.

Organizational Modifications Reform movements began early but moved slowly against the solidly entrenched political "untouchables." Cities sought to break political control through a variety of organizational modifications, including electing police officers and chiefs, administering forces through bipartisan lay boards, asking states to assume local policing and instituting mayor–council or council–city manager municipal government.

Electing the municipal chief of police was common with the establishment of local departments. Remembering the corrupt officials who served as long as they pleased the king, the people elected police officials to serve short terms, so they would not have time to become too powerful or corrupt. However, this system had several drawbacks. Not only were the officials not in office long enough to become corrupt, but also they were not in office long enough to become proficient in their jobs. Officials would just get to know their own officers and have enough experience to run the police department when their terms would expire. The police chief position had also become a popularity contest. Furthermore, since terms were so short, officials often kept their civilian jobs and generally devoted most of their time to them, giving only spare time to running the police force. Therefore, most municipalities decided that having a permanent police chief, with experience and ability, was the best way to achieve effective law enforcement. Today the elected police chief system remains in only a few cities.

In the mid-1800s administrative police boards or commissions were established. Comprised of judges, mayors and private citizens, the board served as the head of the police department, with the police chief following its orders. The rationale was that though the chief of police should be a professional and hold the job continuously, civilian control was necessary to maintain responsibility to community needs. This system lasted many years but had serious weaknesses; board members often proved more of a hindrance than a help, and the system fostered political corruption.

In an attempt to control corrupt police agencies and the incompetent local boards behind them, some areas adopted state control of local agencies, believing such a system would ensure citizens adequate and uniform law enforcement. However, most cities and states found this was not the answer because laws were not equally enforced and the system lacked responsiveness to local needs. Therefore, control was returned to local government in most instances.

The next system to be tried was the commission government charter. Commissioners were elected and charged with various branches of city government. This system, also on the decline, was as inadequate as the administrative police board.

The most prevalent current local system is the mayor–council or council–city manager government. The former is very efficient when the mayor is a full-time, capable administrator. The latter ensures more continuity in the business administration and executive control of the overall operations because a professional, nonpolitical administrator manages the community's affairs. In either system the police chief is selected on merit.

The Pendleton Act In 1883 a major step toward reducing police corruption occurred when Congress passed the Pendleton Act. Before this act, most government positions were filled by political appointment, with those appointed commonly incapable of performing their tasks well. One government worker whom President Garfield was going to replace shot and killed him. This incident caused a public outcry and resulted in passage of the Pendleton Act.

The Pendleton Act created the civil service system for government employees and made it illegal to fire or demote a worker for political reasons.

The act established a Civil Service Commission to enforce its provisions. The new laws called for a test open to all citizens and for new workers to be hired on the basis of who had the highest scores. The act also relieved government workers from any obligation to give political service or payments.

The Social Service Function During the political era, police served a broad social service function: "Police ran soup lines; district or precinct stations were designed to provide brief lodging for immigrant workers when they arrived in cities; police assisted ward leaders in finding work for immigrants, both in police and other forms of work; and police provided a wide variety of other services" (Kelling and Moore, 1991, p.7).

The department organization during the political era was decentralized, primarily because of lack of effective communication. Toward the end of this era, the call box made communication easier and helped to centralize the police organization.

During this era, police were usually close to their community. Foot patrol was the most common strategy used, bringing the beat officer into contact with the people. Most police officers lived in the area they policed and were of the same ethnic background.

Minorities Little has been published about minority police officers in the early history of the United States. According to Sullivan (1989, p.331), African Americans first served as police officers as early as 1861 in Washington, DC. Most were hired in large cities, and by around 1900 they made up 2.7 percent of all watchmen, police officers and firefighters. That number declined until about 1910 when less than 1 percent of police officers were African American.

During this era many African American police officers rode in cars marked "Colored Police," were often hired exclusively to patrol black areas and were allowed to arrest only other black citizens (Sullivan, 1989, p.331). In addition, few were promoted or given special assignments.

During the political era, African American officers were often segregated and discriminated against.

Women Initially women were restricted to processing female prisoners and to positions as police matrons. Many misconceptions about a woman's ability to perform certain "masculine" tasks were dispelled as a result of changing social attitudes; yet room for improvement remained.

At the end of the 1800s, a movement to employ women as regular police officers gained support. In 1893 Marie Owens became the first woman "police officer" in the United States, although her designation as such is a matter of debate within the law enforcement community. Owens was a widow of a police officer, and the mayor of Chicago at the time of her husband's death decided to appoint her to the position as a way of providing financially for her, keeping her on the payroll as a "patrolman" for 30 years until her retirement on pension. During her tenure, Owens assisted detectives in cases involving women and children and had court duties, functions that were commonly performed by police matrons (Horne, 2010).

On April 1, 1908, Lola Baldwin, age 48, was sworn in as the first female police detective in Portland, Oregon. Although she is now considered to be the first woman to be hired to carry out actual police duties, Baldwin's role at the time was not seen as equivalent to that of uniformed male police officers, as she did not wear a uniform or carry a gun. She was viewed as more of a community resource for woman and children in the community. Then, in September of 1910, Alice Stebbins Wells was hired as a police officer for the Los Angeles Police Department. Stebbins was a 37-year-old social worker and pastor who held two college degrees. Again she worked with woman and juveniles in the community. Before the discovery of Baldwin, police historians long believed Stebbins to be the first actual female police officer in America. Shortly thereafter, in 1912, the first woman chief of police was appointed by the mayor of Milford, Ohio. By the end of World War I, more than 220 cities employed policewomen.

A major reason for this relatively rapid acceptance of female peace officers was a change in the public's view of the police function and the newly accepted emphasis on citizen protection and crime prevention rather than exclusive concentration on enforcing laws and detecting crimes. Women were welcomed into police departments, where they were assigned to handle cases involving children and women. "There is little doubt that early policewomen were assigned to handle children and their problems because of the female nurturing role. This role coincided with societal values that made mothers responsible for insuring that children grew up to be good citizens. Furthermore, the early policewomen's movement (1910–1930) received support from both national women's groups and prestigious civic and social hygiene associations" (Hale, 1992, pp.126–127).

In 1925 August Vollmer opened the Crime Prevention Division in the Berkeley, California, Police Department. This unit was headed by policewoman Elizabeth Lossing, a psychiatric social worker. According to Hale (1992, p.127), "The separate roles of policemen and policewomen were emphasized by the International Association of Chiefs of Police (IACP) at its meeting in 1922 where it was recommended that policewomen meet higher education and training standards than policemen. . . . The IACP stated that policewomen were essential to police work and recommended that police departments establish separate units."

During the political era, the roles of policewomen were clearly separated from those of policemen, with women serving a protective and nurturing role.

A Separately Evolving System for Juveniles Also during this time justice professionals began recognizing a need for a different, more "forgiving" system of handling juveniles who came in contact with law enforcement and criminal justice, either because the youths had caused trouble themselves or because they were victims of other circumstances, such as poverty or neglect. The juvenile justice system, discussed in greater detail in Chapter 13 in the context of courts, was effectively born following Illinois' passage of the Juvenile Court Act in 1899 and since that time has developed along a separate path from that of the adult criminal justice system.

The system for juveniles focused on rehabilitation and giving youths a second chance. The spirit of that treatment-oriented philosophy, as opposed to the generally punitive-oriented approach of the criminal justice system, continues to this day. However, when youths commit violent offenses, society has been increasingly supportive of placing these offenders into the criminal, not the juvenile, justice system. In fact, many youths (some professionals would contend *most* youths) who find themselves ensnared in the criminal justice system have had prior contact with the juvenile justice system. Because of the interrelationship between these two systems, students of criminal justice must also be cognizant of and understand the existence of the separate yet related juvenile justice system.

Prohibition The Prohibition movement (1920–1933) resulted from passage of the Eighteenth Amendment in 1919, which outlawed the manufacture, sale or transportation, including importing and exporting, of intoxicating liquor beverages within the United States and its territories. Manning (1997, p.91) suggests that Prohibition resulted in one of the most important transformations in policing in the United States: "It placed what had been a relatively corrupt and symbiotic form of police organization in large cities in opposition to large segments of the respectable classes in the communities in which they functioned. The enforcement of Prohibition laws not only created hostility and hatred of the police and made contacts between police and public increasingly adversarial, it increased the opportunities for legally created and defined corruption."

Prohibition ended in 1933 with passage of the Twenty-First Amendment repealing the Eighteenth Amendment. The inability of the police to control consumption of alcoholic beverages might be likened to the contemporary challenge of controlling use of illegal drugs.

The Wickersham Commission and Police Professionalism In 1929 President Herbert Hoover appointed the national Commission on Law Observance and Enforcement to study the U.S. criminal justice system. Named after its chairman, George Wickersham, the commission devoted 2 of its 14 reports to the police. Report 11, *Lawlessness in Law Enforcement*, delineated the problem of police brutality, concluding that "the third degree—the inflicting of pain, physical or mental, to extract confessions or statements—is extensively practiced." Report 14, *The Police*, concentrated on police administration and called for expert leadership, centralized administrative control and higher personnel standards—in short, police professionalism.

The Reform or Professional Era (1930–1980)

In reaction to the shortcomings of the political era, the reform strategy developed, taking hold in the 1930s and thriving during the 1950s and 1960s before beginning to erode during the late 1970s (Kelling and Moore, 1991, p.6).

reform era

(1930–1980) The second era of policing; characterized by authority coming from the law and professionalism; crime control as the primary function of law enforcement; a centralized, efficient organization; professional remoteness from the community; and an emphasis on preventive motorized patrol and rapid response to crime.

In the **reform era** or the professional era, police forces were characterized by authority coming from the law and professionalism; crime control as their primary function; a centralized, efficient organization; a professional remoteness from the community; and emphasis on preventive motorized patrol and rapid response to crime.

As early as the 1920s, August Vollmer was calling for reforms in policing. Vollmer was first town marshal and then police chief in Berkeley, California, from 1905 until 1932: "Vollmer is often called the 'Father or Dean of Modern Police Administration.' Some of his important contributions include the early use of motorized patrol and the latest advancements in criminalistics. He suggested the development of a centralized fingerprint system that was established by the FBI; he established the first juvenile unit, was the first to use psychological screening for police applicants, and was the first to emphasize the importance of college-educated police officers" (Roberg and Kuykendall, 1993, p.71).

Vollmer developed the first degree-granting program in law enforcement at San Jose State College. He also advocated that police officers serve as social service workers and act to prevent crime by intervening in the lives of potential criminals, especially juveniles. In addition, "Vollmer's emphasis on the quality of police personnel was tied closely to the idea of the professional officer. . . . Another concern of Vollmer's dealt with the efficient delivery of police services. His department became the first in the nation to use automobiles and the first to hire a full-time forensic scientist to help solve crimes" (Dunham and Alpert, 1989, p.27). In short, Vollmer is credited with beginning the movement to professionalize the police.

Manning (1997, p.92) describes three changes made in the 1930s that were fundamental to altering the police role:

1. Crime statistics were linked to police professionalism through establishment of the Uniform Crime Reports.
2. Police began to tie their fate to changes in crime rates as measured by these published figures.
3. Police began to symbolize their mission in terms of the technological means by which they were said to accomplish it.

Manning (1997, p.92) suggests, "By the mid-1930s the use of the radio, of the automobile for mobile patrol, and the collection and systematization of crime statistics began to characterize large urban departments. . . . The police eagerly espoused, displayed and continued to seek a technologically based, rationalized crime control mandate."

professional model

The style of policing used during the reform era, based on the philosophies of August Vollmer and O. W. Wilson.

One of Vollmer's protégés, O. W. Wilson, became the primary architect of the reform era and the style of policing known as the **professional model**. Wilson accepted a professorship at the University of California, Berkeley, and in 1947 he founded the first professional school of criminology.

Like his mentor, Wilson advocated efficiency within the police bureaucracy through scientific techniques. He became police chief in Wichita, Kansas, and conducted the first systematic study of the effectiveness of using one-officer squad cars. Wilson's classic text, *Police Administration*, set forth specific ways to use one-officer patrol cars, to deploy personnel and to discipline officers.

Wilson (1950, pp.17–18) decried political influence on the police: "When the police department is controlled by the machine, political influence begins with the appointment of the recruit, rallies to save him from discipline, helps him to secure unearned wages or disability benefits, grants him unusual leaves of absence, secures an unwarranted promotion for him, or gives him a soft job. In countless ways the creeping paralysis of political favoritism spreads and fastens itself upon the force to sap its vitality and destroy its morale for the benefit of the party, at the expense of both the public and of the police force itself."

Wilson (1950, p.388) also called for cooperation with the public: "Public cooperation is essential to the successful accomplishment of the police purpose. Public support assists in many ways; it is necessary in the enforcement of major laws as well as of minor regulations, and with it arrests are made and convictions obtained that otherwise would not be possible." The reformers sought to disassociate policing from politics. They were to become professionals whose charge was to enforce the law, fairly and impartially. The social service function became of lesser importance or even nonexistent in some departments as police mounted an all-out war on crime. Two keys to this war were preventive patrol in automobiles and rapid response to calls. This is the style of policing most Americans are familiar with and have come to expect.

Unfortunately, the war on crime was being lost. Crime escalated, and other problems arose as well. In the 1960s violent ghetto riots caused millions of dollars in damages, thousands of injuries and many deaths: "Most of these riots were triggered by incidents in which white officers were policing in black ghetto areas. The National Advisory Commission on Civil Disorder was formed to study the situation. The resulting Kerner Report (1968) was comprehensive and scathing, and placed a large part of the blame for the riots on racism in society and the severe under-representation of blacks in police departments" (Sullivan, 1989, p.333).

As a result of this report and other studies, many cities began to actively recruit minorities for their police departments. The civil rights and anti–Vietnam War demonstrations and riots had other ramifications: "They expanded civil protest beyond the inner city to middle-class colleges, main-street America and television. They brought large numbers of middle-class and minority protestors into open conflict with the police. When the police employed tactics that included the use of force and mass arrests against protestors, they were portrayed as agents of repression who maintained order at the expense of justice. As a result, the rational-legal bureaucratic model of policing began to be questioned by a broader spectrum of the American people" (Fyfe et al., 1997, p.17).

Blue-Ribbon Commissions Kelling (2003, p.14) describes five national commissions that resulted from the turmoil in U.S. cities and controversy surrounding police practices in the 1960s and early 1970s:

- The President's Commission on Law Enforcement and Administration of Justice, which published its reports in 1967 and 1968, was influenced by urban racial turmoil. Among the outgrowths of its work were the Safe Streets Act of 1968 and the Law Enforcement Assistance Administration, which provided significant funding for police-related programs.

- The National Advisory Commission on Civil Disorders (popularly known as the Kerner Commission) was similarly inspired by riots and other disorders in many U.S. cities in the summer of 1967. Its report examined patterns of disorder and prescribed responses by the federal government, the criminal justice system and local governments.
- The National Commission on the Causes and Prevention of Violence was established after the assassinations of Martin Luther King Jr. and Robert Kennedy in 1968. Its report, *To Establish Justice, To Insure Domestic Tranquility*, was published in 1969.
- The President's Commission on Campus Unrest was established following student deaths related to protests at Kent State and Jackson State Universities in 1970.
- The National Advisory Commission on Criminal Justice Standards and Goals issued six reports in 1973 in an attempt to develop standards and recommendations for police crime-control efforts.

The Law Enforcement Education Program (LEEP) Following publication of the Presidential Crime Commission's recommendation that by 1984 all police officers be required to have at least a bachelor's degree, Congress created and funded the Law Enforcement Education Program (LEEP). This program poured thousands of dollars into police education, and by the mid-1970s, more than 1,000 academic institutions offered police-related courses to thousands of students nationwide. Eventually, however, LEEP was phased out of the federal budget.

Another relatively short-lived federal boost to the professionalization of law enforcement was the Law Enforcement Assistance Administration.

The Law Enforcement Assistance Administration (LEAA) In 1968 Congress enacted the Omnibus Crime Control and Safe Streets Act; Title 1 of this act established the Law Enforcement Assistance Administration, which existed through September 1979.

LEAA worked in partnership with state and local governments, historically responsible for crime reduction and law enforcement. Congress affirmed this historical responsibility in the act: "Crime is essentially a local problem that must be dealt with by state and local governments if it is to be controlled effectively." Of even greater significance is the statement of Richard W. Velde, LEAA administrator, foreshadowing the community policing movement: "Crime control is everyone's business. It is not just the business of the criminal justice system—of police, courts and corrections—but of all citizens who want to live in harmony and peace." LEAA awarded more than $9 billion to state and local governments to support tens of thousands of programs and projects.

The National Institute of Justice (NIJ) The Omnibus Crime Control and Safe Streets Act also established the National Institute of Justice as a research and development agency to prevent and reduce crime and to improve the criminal justice system. Among the institute's mandates were that it sponsor special projects and research and development programs to improve and strengthen the criminal justice system, conduct national demonstration projects that used innovative or promising approaches for improving criminal justice, develop new technologies to fight crime and improve criminal justice, evaluate the effectiveness of criminal justice programs and identify those that promised to be successful if continued or repeated and carry out research on criminal behavior.

Advances for Women and Minorities A boost was given to women and minorities when the Supreme Court ruled in *Griggs v. Duke Power Company* (1971) that any tests used for employment must be job-related. Another boost was the passage of the Equal Employment Opportunity Act (EEOA) in 1972.

The Equal Employment Opportunity Act prohibits discrimination on the basis of sex, race, color, religion or national origin in employment of any kind, public or private, local, state or federal.

That same year, women began to seek positions as patrol officers. Tension and conflict resulted. Accepted as assistants to policemen, they were seldom accepted as partners on patrol: "Clearly, policewomen on patrol have faced many obstacles from both their peers and management, who believed that they cannot perform patrol duties because they have neither the physical strength to do the job; the authoritarian presence to handle violent confrontations; nor the ability to serve as backup to their partners in high-pressure situations. Attempts by supervisors to either overprotect policewomen, or keep them from areas with high violence further reinforce the view that women are not capable of performing patrol" (Hale, 1992, p.128).

During the reform or professional era, minorities and women obtained legal equality with white male officers but still often encountered discrimination.

The Kansas City Preventive Patrol Experiment Another event during 1972 had a great impact on eroding the reform strategy; the classic Kansas City Preventive Patrol Experiment called into serious question the effectiveness of preventive patrol or rapidity of response, the basic strategies of the reform era. The Kansas City Experiment showed that "it makes about as much sense to have police patrol routinely in cars to fight crime as it does to have firemen patrol routinely in fire trucks to fight fire" (Klockars, 1983, p.130).

Increasing Challenges to the Professional Model The professional model faced many challenges, including the inability of "traditional" police approaches to decrease crime; the rapidly escalating drug problem; the pressing problems associated with the deinstitutionalization of thousands of mentally ill people, many of whom became homeless; dealing with thousands of immigrants, some legal, some illegal, many speaking no English; and the breakdown of the family unit.

Many began asserting that the police and the criminal justice system could not control crime and violence alone: "All of the major factors influencing how much crime there is or is not are factors over which police have no control whatsoever. Police can do nothing about the age, sex, racial or ethnic distribution of the population. They cannot control economic conditions; poverty; inequality; occupational opportunity; moral, religious, family or secular education; or dramatic social, cultural or political change. These are the 'big ticket' items in determining the amount and distribution of crime. Compared to them what police do or do not do matters very little" (Klockars, 1991, p.250).

Police operating under the professional model, isolated in their patrol cars from the communities to which they had been formerly close, were ill equipped to deal with the overwhelming social changes and challenges of the 1960s, including the exploding crime rates and deep social unrest. Circumstances were right for the third era of policing, the community era.

The Community Era (1980–Present)

Paralleling changes being made in the business world, many police departments became "customer oriented," viewing people within the community as consumers of police services. Just as in business it is important to know what the customer really wants and needs, so in policing it became important to know what the citizens of a community want and need.

community era

(1980–present) The third era of policing; characterized by authority coming from community support, law and professionalism; provision of a broad range of services, including crime control; decentralized organization with more authority given to patrol officers; partnerships with the community; and use of foot patrol and a problem-solving approach.

Police forces in the **community era** are characterized by authority coming from community support, law and professionalism; provision of a broad range of services, including crime control; decentralized organization with more authority given to patrol officers; partnerships with the community; and use of foot patrol and a problem-solving approach.

reactive

Responding to crimes after they have been committed.

proactive

Seeking to find the causes of crime and to rectify those problems, thereby deterring or even preventing crime; acting before the fact rather than reacting to something that has already occurred.

In contrast to policing during the reform era, which was **reactive**, responding to crime after it was committed, policing during the community era is more **proactive**, seeking the causes of crime and trying to rectify those problems, thereby deterring or even preventing crime. The community-oriented approach to policing is discussed in Chapter 7. Largely because of civil service and a grassroots-inspired groundswell of general reform, most police forces have shaken the influence of corrupt politics. In contrast to conditions at the beginning of the 20th century, appointment to the forces and police administration generally is vastly improved. Police recruitment, discipline and promotion have been removed from politics in most cities.

Communications involving police service have also greatly improved. The radio and patrol car transformed the relationship between the police and the public and offered increased protection for everyone. The continuous expansion of the telephone in the 1960s and 1970s made it easier for people to call the police. Police dispatchers were added to tie radio systems directly into telephone networks, and computers greatly increased the efficiency and effectiveness of operations. The use of fingerprint systems and the increased employment of women as police officers, as well as many other advances, occurred at an accelerated pace.

Despite advanced technology, which greatly improved police officers' abilities to respond to requests for aid and increased their mobility, the basic strategy of police has not altered. Crime waves in metropolitan areas prompt cities to improve their street lighting, to increase the number of police officers on the streets and to demand more severe punishment for convicted criminals.

The human factor has assumed greater importance as police agencies cope with the tensions and dislocations of population growth, increasing urbanization, developing technology, the civil rights movement, changing social norms and a breakdown of traditional values. These factors have enormously complicated law enforcement, making more critical the need for truly professional police officers.

Today's local police officers must be law enforcement generalists with a working knowledge of federal, state, county and municipal law; traffic law; criminal law; juvenile law; narcotics; liquor control; and countless other areas. However, this accounts for only approximately 10 percent of what a modern police officer does. Today's officers spend 90 percent of their time providing a variety of services while protecting life, property and personal liberty. They must be aware of human factors and understand the psychological and sociological implications of their work. They must deal with all citizens, rich and poor, young and old, in ways that maintain the community's support and confidence. Policing and partnering with this greatly diverse citizenship is no small challenge or responsibility.

Table 1.1 summarizes the distinguishing characteristics of the three eras of policing that are traditionally identified.

An Emerging Fourth Era of Policing

Law enforcement continues to evolve, shifting paradigms along the way. A **paradigm** is a way of thinking, of viewing the world. Kuhn (1970) defined and popularized the idea of a "paradigm shift" explaining it as one conceptual worldview replacing

paradigm

A way of thinking, of viewing the world.

TABLE 1.1 The Three Eras of Policing

	Political Era 1840–1930	Reform or Professional Era 1930–1980	Community Era 1980–present
Authorization	Politicians and law	Law and professionalism	Community support (political), law and professionalism
Function	Broad social services	Crime control	Broad provision of services
Organizational Design	Decentralized	Centralized, classical	Decentralized, task forces, matrices
Relationship to Community	Intimate	Professional, remote	Intimate
Tactics and Technology	Foot patrol	Preventive patrol and rapid response to calls	Foot patrol, problem solving, public relations
Outcome	Citizen, political satisfaction	Crime control	Quality of life and citizen satisfaction

SOURCE: Linda S. Miller, Kären Matison Hess and Christine Hess Orthmann. *Community Policing: Partnerships for Problem Solving*, 6th ed. New York: Delmar/Cengage Learning, 2008, p.17. Reprinted by permission. (Summarized from George L. Kelling and Mark H. Moore, "From Political to Reform to Community: The Evolving Strategy of Police." In *Community Policing: Rhetoric or Reality*, edited by Jack R. Greene and Stephen D. Mastrofski. New York: Praeger Publishers, 1991, pp.6, 14–15, 22–23.)

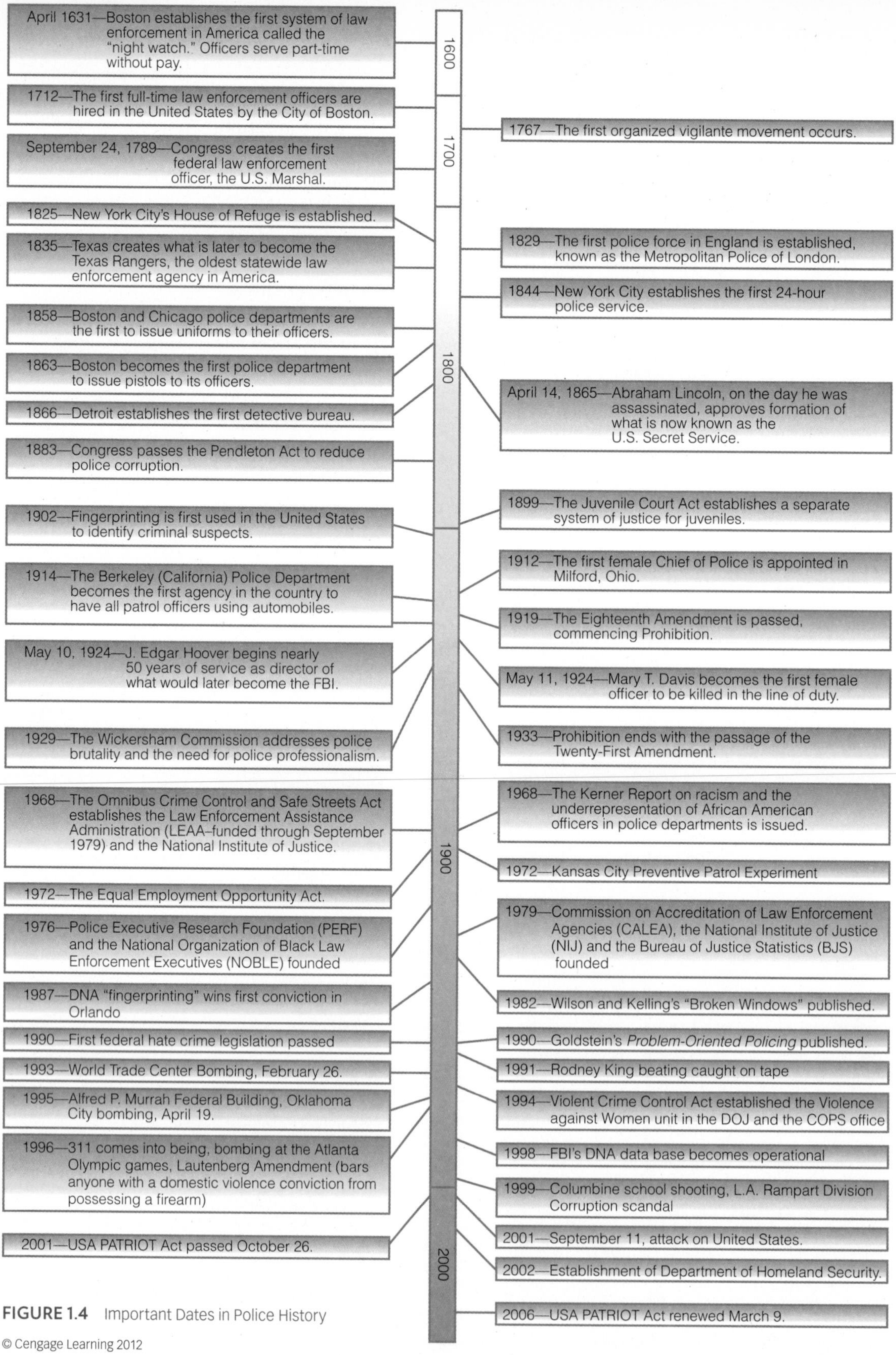

- April 1631—Boston establishes the first system of law enforcement in America called the "night watch." Officers serve part-time without pay.
- 1712—The first full-time law enforcement officers are hired in the United States by the City of Boston.
- 1767—The first organized vigilante movement occurs.
- September 24, 1789—Congress creates the first federal law enforcement officer, the U.S. Marshal.
- 1825—New York City's House of Refuge is established.
- 1829—The first police force in England is established, known as the Metropolitan Police of London.
- 1835—Texas creates what is later to become the Texas Rangers, the oldest statewide law enforcement agency in America.
- 1844—New York City establishes the first 24-hour police service.
- 1858—Boston and Chicago police departments are the first to issue uniforms to their officers.
- 1863—Boston becomes the first police department to issue pistols to its officers.
- April 14, 1865—Abraham Lincoln, on the day he was assassinated, approves formation of what is now known as the U.S. Secret Service.
- 1866—Detroit establishes the first detective bureau.
- 1883—Congress passes the Pendleton Act to reduce police corruption.
- 1899—The Juvenile Court Act establishes a separate system of justice for juveniles.
- 1902—Fingerprinting is first used in the United States to identify criminal suspects.
- 1912—The first female Chief of Police is appointed in Milford, Ohio.
- 1914—The Berkeley (California) Police Department becomes the first agency in the country to have all patrol officers using automobiles.
- 1919—The Eighteenth Amendment is passed, commencing Prohibition.
- May 10, 1924—J. Edgar Hoover begins nearly 50 years of service as director of what would later become the FBI.
- May 11, 1924—Mary T. Davis becomes the first female officer to be killed in the line of duty.
- 1929—The Wickersham Commission addresses police brutality and the need for police professionalism.
- 1933—Prohibition ends with the passage of the Twenty-First Amendment.
- 1968—The Omnibus Crime Control and Safe Streets Act establishes the Law Enforcement Assistance Administration (LEAA–funded through September 1979) and the National Institute of Justice.
- 1968—The Kerner Report on racism and the underrepresentation of African American officers in police departments is issued.
- 1972—The Equal Employment Opportunity Act.
- 1972—Kansas City Preventive Patrol Experiment
- 1976—Police Executive Research Foundation (PERF) and the National Organization of Black Law Enforcement Executives (NOBLE) founded
- 1979—Commission on Accreditation of Law Enforcement Agencies (CALEA), the National Institute of Justice (NIJ) and the Bureau of Justice Statistics (BJS) founded
- 1982—Wilson and Kelling's "Broken Windows" published.
- 1987—DNA "fingerprinting" wins first conviction in Orlando
- 1990—First federal hate crime legislation passed
- 1990—Goldstein's *Problem-Oriented Policing* published.
- 1991—Rodney King beating caught on tape
- 1993—World Trade Center Bombing, February 26.
- 1994—Violent Crime Control Act established the Violence against Women unit in the DOJ and the COPS office
- 1995—Alfred P. Murrah Federal Building, Oklahoma City bombing, April 19.
- 1996—311 comes into being, bombing at the Atlanta Olympic games, Lautenberg Amendment (bars anyone with a domestic violence conviction from possessing a firearm)
- 1998—FBI's DNA data base becomes operational
- 1999—Columbine school shooting, L.A. Rampart Division Corruption scandal
- 2001—USA PATRIOT Act passed October 26.
- 2001—September 11, attack on United States.
- 2002—Establishment of Department of Homeland Security.
- 2006—USA PATRIOT Act renewed March 9.

FIGURE 1.4 Important Dates in Police History

another, for example, the shift from an agricultural society to an industrial one. Such paradigm shifts are seen in the three eras of policing just described. And yet, remnants of the previous worldview often remain. For example, the community era harkens back to Peel's principle that the police are the public and the public are the police. Likewise, the emerging fourth era of policing retains several elements of the professional model and of community policing. This most recent era of policing can be traced to a single event: the 9/11 terrorist attacks on the United States.

A fourth era of policing is emerging as the result of the 9/11 attacks on America, and is termed variously as homeland security, data-driven, intelligence-led, predictive and evidence-based policing, based on risk assessment and risk management.

"Policing changed profoundly with that event in ways that will continue to shape the profession for years" (Beck and McCue, 2009, p.18). This emerging data-driven style of policing and its relationship to traditional and community policing is the focus of Chapter 7.

A BRIEF RECAP OF U.S. POLICING

A fitting conclusion for this chapter is a brief recap of the sequence of events from the beginning of law enforcement in the United States to 2010, presented in Figure 1.4.

Although the community era stresses working with the community, the government has recognized that to effectively combat terrorism, law enforcement officers need additional tools. On October 26, 2001, the Uniting and Strengthening America by Providing Appropriate Tools Required to Intercept and Obstruct Terrorism Act (USA PATRIOT Act) was signed into law (renewed in 2006). This act is discussed in depth in Chapter 10.

Summary

Our current laws and the means by which they are enforced have their origins in the distant past, perhaps as far back as the cave dwellers. A system of law and law enforcement began earlier than 2000 BC as a means of controlling human conduct and enforcing society's rules. Keeping the peace was the responsibility of the group. Many features of our present system of law enforcement are borrowed from the Greeks, Romans and particularly the English.

The English tithing system (groups of 10 families) established the principle of collective responsibility for maintaining local law and order. If a law was broken, the hue and cry sounded, the origin of the general alarm and the citizen's arrest.

The constable was the first English police officer, and he had charge of the weapons and horses of the community. In response to a need for more regional law enforcement, the office of shire-reeve was established. The shire-reeve, the forerunner of today's sheriff, was the law enforcement agent for an entire county.

In 1066 William the Conqueror invaded England and changed the tithing system to the Frankpledge system, requiring loyalty to the king's law and mutual local responsibility for maintaining the peace. William's son, Henry I, became known as Henry the Lawmaker. His

Leges Henrici made law enforcement a public matter and separated offenses into felonies and misdemeanors. Henry II established the jury system.

The next significant development was the Magna Carta, a precedent for democratic government and individual rights. The Magna Carta laid the foundation for

- Requiring rulers to uphold the law
- Forbidding taxation without representation
- Requiring due process of law, including trial by jury
- Providing safeguards against unfair imprisonment

During the 14th century, the shire-reeve was replaced by the justice of the peace. Later, during the Middle Ages, the parish constable system was used for rural law enforcement; the Watch and Ward system was used for urban law enforcement.

Of importance to English law enforcement were the contributions of Sir Robert (Bobbie) Peel. Peel's principles for reform called for local responsibility for law and order; appointed, paid civilians to assume this responsibility; and standards for these individuals' conduct and organization. His proposals resulted in the organization of the first police force in England, the Metropolitan Police of London, established in 1829. In 1883 the London Metropolitan Police appointed two women to supervise female convicts. Their numbers and functions later expanded.

The early American settlers brought with them several features of English law and law enforcement. New England adopted the night watchman or constable as the chief means of law enforcement; the South adopted the office of sheriff. The first modern American police force, modeled after London's Metropolitan Police, was the New York City Police Department, established in 1844.

Although cities began having organized police forces, the vast frontier region remained relatively lawless. In response to the absence of effective law and order in frontier areas, as many as 500 vigilante movements were organized between 1767 and 1900. The vigilante movement refers to taking the law into one's own hands in the absence of effective policing.

Although law enforcement was generally considered a local responsibility, Congress created several federal law enforcement agencies, under the jurisdiction of the Departments of Justice and the Treasury, to meet demands created by the nation's changing conditions. Among the earliest federal law enforcement agencies were the U.S. Marshals Office, created in 1789, the Immigration and Naturalization Service, the Secret Service and the Internal Revenue Service. The U.S. Attorney General, as head of the Department of Justice, is the chief federal law enforcement officer. The beginning of state law enforcement agencies occurred with the establishment of the Texas Rangers in 1874.

Law enforcement in the United States is a cooperative effort among local, county, state, federal and specialized law enforcement officers. The five levels of government authorized to have law enforcement agencies are (1) township and special district police, (2) municipal police, (3) county police, (4) state police and (5) federal police. In addition, tribal law enforcement agencies operate throughout the country.

The three eras of policing traditionally identified are the political era, the reform or professional era and the community era. In the political era, police forces were characterized by authority derived from politicians and the law, a broad social service function, a decentralized organization, an intimate relationship with the community and extensive use of foot patrol.

During the political era, the spoils system encouraged politicians to reward their friends by giving them key positions in police departments. In 1883 the Pendleton Act created the civil service system for government employees and made it unlawful to fire or demote a worker for political reasons. During the political era, African American officers were often segregated and discriminated against. The roles of policewomen during this era were clearly separated from those of policemen, with women serving a protective, nurturing role.

Police forces in the reform or professional era were characterized by authority derived from law and professionalism; crime control as their primary function; a centralized, efficient organization; a professional remoteness from the community; and emphasis on preventive motorized patrol and rapid response to crime. During this era, in 1972, the Equal Employment Opportunity Act was passed. This act prohibits discrimination on the basis of sex, race, color, religion or national origin in employment of any kind, public or private, local, state or federal. This gave minorities and women legal equality with white male officers and prompted many women to seek patrol assignments. Despite the passage of the Equal Employment Opportunity Act, many minorities and women still often encountered discrimination.

Community era police forces are characterized by authority derived from community support, law and professionalism; the provision of a broad range of services, including crime control; a decentralized organization with more authority given to patrol officers; partnerships with the community; and the increased use of foot patrols and a problem-solving approach.

A fourth era of policing is emerging as the result of the 9/11 attacks on America, and is termed variously homeland security, data-driven, intelligence-led, predictive and evidence-based policing, based on risk assessment and risk management.

Discussion Questions

1. What common problems have existed throughout the centuries for people in law enforcement?
2. Why was there no law enforcement during the daytime for many centuries?
3. Why did it take so long to develop a police force in England? In the United States?
4. In today's society, how has the power of the *posse comitatus* assisted and how has it worked against law enforcement?
5. At present, how does the government respond to increased crime in the United States in comparison with the responses in the 17th century?
6. Should police chiefs be appointed or elected?
7. What demands that were not present 20 or 30 years ago are made on the modern police officer?
8. Do you think a position in law enforcement should require a college degree? Is a law enforcement officer better equipped to do their job if they are more educated?
9. What are some of the challenges law enforcement will face with intelligence-led policing as it emerges in the new era of policing?
10. What makes American law enforcement differ from law enforcement agencies around the world?

Gale Emergency Services Database Assignments

- Use the Gale Emergency Services Database to help answer the Discussion Questions as appropriate.
- Using the Gale Emergency Services Database, find the article "Once Upon a Time on Patrol": http://find.galegroup.com/gps/retrieve.do?contentSet=IAC-Documents&resultListType=RESULT_LIST&qrySerId=Locale%28en%2C%2C%29%3AFQE%3D%28KE%2CNone%2C23%29law+enforcement+history%24&sgHitCountType=None&inPS=true&sort=DateDescend&searchType=BasicSearchForm&tabID=T003&prodId=IPS&searchId=R14¤tPosition=1&userGroupName=cpg3&docId=A216989757&docType=IAC&contentSet=IAC-Documents

  Assignment: Read the article, choose the era of American Policing that interests you most and outline the key features and highlights of that era. Be prepared to discuss with the class why you chose that specific era and what interests you about it.
- Using the Gale Emergency Services Database, find the article "General History of Policing": http://find.galegroup.com/gps/retrieve.do?contentSet=EBKS&resultListType=RESULT_LIST&qrySerId=Locale%28en%2C%2C%29%3AFQE%3D%28KE%2CNone%2C18%29bow+street+runners%24&sgHitCountType=None&inPS=true&sort=Relevance&searchType=BasicSearchForm&tabID=T001&prodId=IPS&searchId=R16¤tPosition=1&userGroupName=cpg3&docId=CX3448200013&docType=EBKS&contentSet=EBKS

  Assignment: Read, outline and be prepared to discuss your outline in class.
- Using the Gale Emergency Services Database, find the article "Prohibited Discrimination Under the Americans with Disabilities Act": http://find.galegroup.com/gps/retrieve.do?contentSet=IAC-Documents&resultListType=RESULT_LIST&qrySerId=Locale%28en%2C%2C%29%3AFQE%3D%28K0%2CNone%2C21%29equal+opportunity+act%24&sgHitCountType=None&inPS=true&sort=DateDescend&searchType=BasicSearchForm&tabID=T003&prodId=IPS&searchId=R28¤tPosition=2&userGroupName=cpg3&docId=A69441916&docType=IAC&contentSet=IAC-Documents

  Assignment: Read and be prepared to discuss in class how this act is related to the Equal Opportunity Act and how it affects law enforcement.

Internet Assignments

- Go to the Web site of the Pendleton Act and focus on "Background on the Pendleton Act." Note the new special skills required with the introduction of typewriters. As you read the document, write down what strike you as the most important areas covered by the act.
- Go to the Web site of the Central Intelligence Agency (http://www.odci.gov/) and take their "virtual tour" of CIA headquarters in Langley, Virginia.

References

Adams, T. F. *Introduction to the Administration of Criminal Justice*, 2nd ed. Englewood Cliffs, NJ: Prentice-Hall, 1980.

Asirvatham, Sandy. "Good Cop, Bad Cop." *Baltimore City Paper*, May 2000, p.2.

Bailey, W. G. (ed.). *The Encyclopedia of Police Science*. New York: Garland Publishing, 1989.

Beck, Charlie, and McCue, Colleen. "Predictive Policing: What Can We Learn from Wal-Mart and Amazon about Fighting Crime in a Recession?" *The Police Chief*, November 2009, pp.18–24.

Brown, R. "The American Vigilante Tradition." In *Thinking about Police: Contemporary Readings*, 2nd ed., edited by C. B. Klockars and S. D. Mastrofski. New York: McGraw-Hill, 1991.

Critchley, T. A. *A History of Police in England and Wales*. Montclair, NJ: Patterson Smith, 1967.

Dunham, R. G., and Alpert, G. P. *Critical Issues in Policing: Contemporary Issues*. Prospect Heights, IL: Waveland Press, 1989.

"Employment and Expenditure." Washington, DC: Bureau of Justice Statistics, Updated January 28, 2010. http://bjs.ojp.usdoj.gov/index.cfm?ty=tp&tid=5

Folley, V. L. *American Law Enforcement*. Boston: Allyn & Bacon, 1980.

Fyfe, James J.; Green, Jack R.; Walsh, William F.; Wilson, O.W.; and McLaren, Roy Clinton. *Police Administration*, 5th ed. New York: McGraw-Hill, 1997.

Gardner, T. J. *Basic Concepts of Criminal Law, Principles and Cases*, 3rd ed. St. Paul, MN: West Publishing Company, 1985.

Hale, Donna C. "Women in Policing." In *What Works in Policing*, edited by G. W. Gardner and D. C. Hale. Cincinnati, OH: Anderson Publishing Company, 1992.

Horne, Peter. "Policewomen: Their First Century and the New Era." *The Police Chief*, January 2010.

Kelling, George L. "The Evolution of Contemporary Policing." In *Local Government Police Management*, 4th ed., edited by William A. Geller and Darrell W. Stephens. Washington, DC: International City/County Management Association, 2003, pp.3–25.

Kelling, George L., and Moore, Mark H. "From Political to Reform to Community: The Evolving Strategy of Police." In *Community Policing: Rhetoric or Reality*, edited by J. R. Greene and S. D. Mastrofski. New York: Praeger, 1991.

Klockars, Carl B. *Thinking about Police: Contemporary Readings*. New York: McGraw-Hill, 1983.

Klockars, Carl B. *The Idea of Police*. Newbury Park, CA: Sage Publications, 1985.

Klockars, Carl B. "The Rhetoric of Community Policing." In *Community Policing: Rhetoric or Reality*, edited by J. R. Greene and S. D. Mastrofski. New York: Praeger, 1991.

Kuhn, Thomas S. *The Structure of Scientific Revolutions*, 2nd ed. Chicago: University of Chicago Press, 1970.

Lunt, W. E. *History of England*. New York: Harper & Brothers, 1938.

Manning, Peter K. *Police Work: The Social Organization of Policing*, 2nd ed. Prospect Heights, IL: Waveland Press, 1997.

Perry, D. C. *Police in the Metropolis*. Columbus, OH: Charles E. Merrill, 1973.

Reichel, Philip L. "Southern Slave Patrols as a Transitional Police Type." In *Policing Perspectives: An Anthology*, edited by Larry K. Gaines and Gary W. Cordner. Los Angeles: Roxbury Publishing Company, 1999, pp.79–92.

Richardson, J. F. *The New York Police*. New York: Oxford University Press, 1970.

Roberg, R. R., and Kuykendall, J. *Police & Society*. Belmont, CA: Wadsworth Publishing Company, 1993.

Sullivan, P. S. "Minority Officers, Current Issues." In *Critical Issues in Policing: Contemporary Readings*, edited by R. D. Dunham and G. P. Alpert. Prospect Heights, IL: Waveland Press, 1989.

Wilson, O.W. *Police Administration*. New York: McGraw-Hill, 1950.

Case Cited

Griggs v. Duke Power Company, 401 U.S. 424 (1971)

Federal Agencies on the Web

Finding information about federal programs can be difficult as no central phone or address directory exists for the layers upon layers of special offices. Fortunately, most federal agencies have Web sites providing almost everything a person would want to know, including career opportunities. You may need to include "http://www" at the beginning.

Bureau of Alcohol, Tobacco, and Firearms and Explosives—atf.treas.gov

Central Intelligence Agency—odci.gov

Department of Homeland Security—dhs.gov

Drug Enforcement Administration—usdoj/gov/dea

Federal Bureau of Investigation—fbi.gov

Federal Bureau of Prisons—bop.gov

National Criminal Justice Reference Service—ncjrs.org

U.S. Department of Justice—usdoj.gov

U.S. Secret Service—ustreas.gov/usss

CHAPTER 2

The American Quest for Freedom and Justice: Our Laws

> We hold these truths to be self-evident: that all men are endowed by their creator with certain unalienable rights; that among these are life, liberty, and the pursuit of happiness.
>
> —Thomas Jefferson

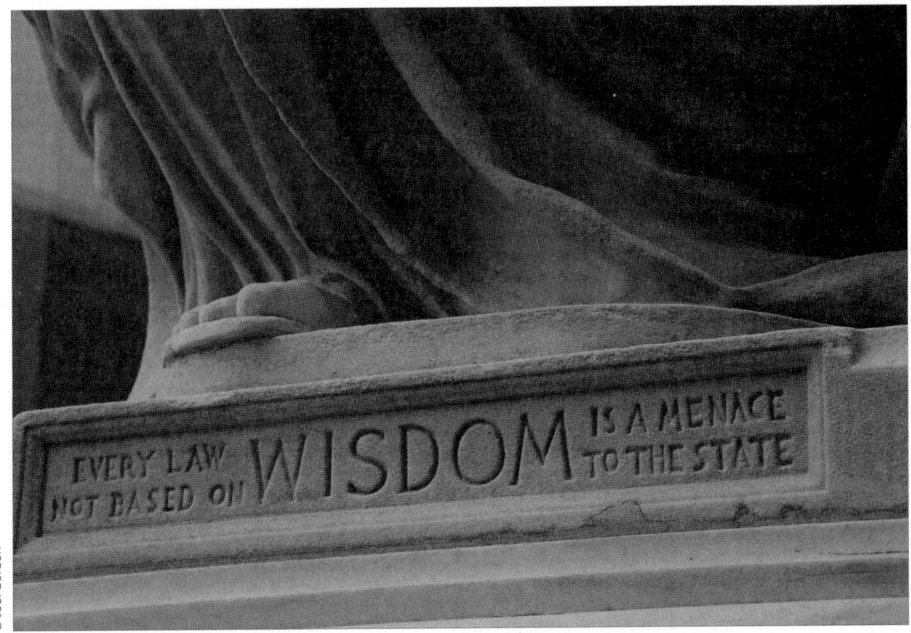

© Joel Gordon

"Every Law Not Based On WISDOM Is A Menace To The State"—the phrase carved on the base of a statue outside the New York State Supreme Court Appellate Division Courthouse—is symbolic of the rule of law.

Do You Know . . .

- What the Declaration of Independence says about civil rights and civil liberties?
- What document is the basic instrument of government and the supreme law of the land?
- What document established the foundation for the criminal justice system?
- How federalism affected development of the criminal justice system?
- What law takes precedence if two laws conflict?
- What the Bill of Rights is?
- What specific rights are guaranteed by the First, Second, Fourth, Fifth, Sixth, Eighth and Fourteenth Amendments?
- What criminal law does?
- What is usually necessary to prove that a crime has been committed?
- What civil law refers to?
- What the basic differences between a crime and a tort are?
- What Section 1983 of the U.S. Code, Title 42, stipulates?
- Where police get their power and authority and what restrictions are placed on this power and authority?
- What the scales of justice symbolize?
- What two conflicting models of criminal justice need to be balanced?
- How the conservative camp differs from the liberal camp in crime control efforts?
- Who exercises discretion within the system?
- What two views of justice conflict?

Can You Define?

actus reus
American creed
Bill of Rights
case law
civil law
civil liberties
civil rights
common law
conflict theory
consensus theory
constitution
corpus delicti
crime control
criminal intent
criminal law
double jeopardy
due process of law
ecclesiastical (church) law
elements of the crime
equity
federalism
felony
incorporation doctrine
indicted
landmark decision
mala in se
mala prohibita
mens rea
misdemeanor
motive
ordinances
police power
procedural criminal law
procedural due process
restorative justice
retributive justice
scienter
selective incorporation
statutory law
strict liability
substantive criminal law
substantive due process
symbolic speech
tort

INTRODUCTION

To ensure each U.S. citizen the right to "life, liberty, and the pursuit of happiness," those who settled here established laws that all are expected to obey. The supreme law of the land is embodied in the U.S. Constitution and its Bill of Rights as discussed later in this chapter. Our system of laws is extremely complex and may be classified according to:

- *Form*—written or unwritten common law
- *Source*—constitutional, statutory, case

- *Parties involved*—public, private
- *Offense*—criminal, civil

This chapter explores each of these overlapping classifications.

THE CHAPTER AT A GLANCE

The chapter begins with a discussion of the types of law that can be operating simultaneously within the country, followed by a discussion of the Declaration of Independence and the law that operated in the newly created nation. Next is a description of the law found in the U.S. Constitution and the Bill of Rights—the first 10 amendments, which guarantee all American citizens' civil rights and civil liberties—as well as the Fourteenth Amendment, which made the Constitution and portions of the Bill of Rights applicable to the states. Following the discussion of constitutional law is an explanation of criminal and civil law. The chapter next describes police power in the United States—where it comes from and how it is restricted—and the needs of society balanced with individual rights and how this conflict has influenced development of the criminal justice system. Next is a discussion of whether law and policy or discretion should be the most important guide for criminal justice professionals and for the conflicting views of justice. The chapter concludes with discussions of retributive versus restorative justice and the criminal justice pendulum.

TYPES OF LAW

In addition to the classification of law provided in the introduction, several types of law must be understood to appreciate their complexities and effect on criminal justice. Recall that law is a body of rules for human conduct enforced by imposing penalties for their violation. Laws define social obligations and determine the individuals' relation to society and to each other. The purpose of law is to regulate individuals' actions to conform to the way of life the community or the people's elected representatives consider essential.

Social or Moral Law

Obedience to law often is obtained through social pressure—ridicule, contempt, scorn or ostracism. Moral or social law refers to laws made by society and enforced solely by social pressure. Moral or social laws include laws of etiquette, "honor" and morality. When moral laws break down and social sanctions fail to obtain conformity, other laws may be enacted and enforced.

Precedents: Common Law and Case Law

The beginnings of law are found in social custom. Custom is simply precedent—doing what has been done before. In early times custom, religion, morals and the law were intermingled. Some early customs have, over the centuries, become law. Precedent explains why many good ideas in criminal justice are so slow to materialize.

Some customs were enforced physically rather than morally, and the violator was expelled from the community, sacrificed to the gods or hanged. Other violations of custom not felt to be harmful to the whole community were punished by the injured group or the injured individual with the aid of the family (self-help, vengeance, feud). As long as such vengeance might lead to retaliation, the sanctions behind the rules of custom were still purely moral. When the community began to protect those who had taken *rightful* vengeance, however, these persons became agents of the community. This kind of self-help met early society's needs when the right to take vengeance or redress was clear. It did not provide a way to settle controversies. Therefore, courts were established to interpret customs and settle controversies. Custom was replaced by judicial precedent.

common law

In England, the customary law set by judges as disputes arose; the law in force before and independent of legislation.

ecclesiastical law

Law of the church.

case law

A collection of summaries of how statutes have been applied by judges in various situations; the precedents established by the courts.

In England, **common law** referred to the precedents set by the judges in the royal courts as disputes rose. This was in contrast to local custom or **ecclesiastical (church) law**. When Parliament supplemented and modified the existing legal principles, the term *common law* described the law in force before, and independent of, any acts of the legislature.

The common law brought to the United States by the early settlers forms the basis of modern American law in all states except Louisiana, which established and kept the system of French civil law. In essence, common law describes the precedent generally followed in the absence of a specific law, known in the United States as case law. **Case law** refers to judicial precedents; no specific law exists, but a similar case serves as a model. When cases not covered by the law come before the courts, the judges' rulings on previous similar cases will, for all practical purposes, be treated as law.

Statutory Law

statutory law

Law passed by a legislature.

The United States has largely replaced common law (unwritten law) with **statutory law**, that is, legislated and written law. Statutory law may be passed at the federal or state level and includes constitutional, criminal and civil law as discussed shortly.

Federal constitutional law is based on the U.S. Constitution, its amendments and interpretations by the federal courts. Ordinary federal law consists of acts of Congress, treaties with foreign states, executive orders and regulations, and interpretation of the preceding by federal courts. State constitutional law is based on the state's constitution, its amendments and interpretations of them by the state's courts. State ordinary law consists of acts of the state legislatures, decisions of the federal courts in interpreting or developing the common law, executive orders and regulations, and municipal ordinances.

ordinances

Local laws or regulations.

In addition, in most states, each county and city is given the right to pass laws for its local jurisdiction, providing the law does not conflict with the state's laws. Local **ordinances** (laws) are primarily enacted to protect the community. Local ordinances can apply to the same violations addressed in state or federal statutes, but can add additional stipulations and punishments. This is also true for state statutes, which may be harsher than federal law. In other words, local ordinances can impose stricter penalties than state laws, which can, in turn, impose harsher sanctions than federal laws. However, this order cannot be reversed—local ordinances cannot be more lenient than either state or federal law. Although the states and the federal government have the right to pass laws, these laws must reflect the needs of society.

Equity

The need for laws to change as society changes has long been recognized, as illustrated in a letter written by Thomas Jefferson in the nineteenth century, "Laws and institutions must go hand in hand with the progress of the human mind, as that becomes more developed, as more discoveries are made, new truths disclosed, and manners and opinions change with the changing circumstances, institutions must advance also, and keep pace with the times. We might as well require a man to wear still the coat which fitted him as a boy as civilized society to remain ever under the regiment of their barbarous ancestors." Indeed, laws that once made good sense now appear ridiculous. For example, an old law in Truro, Massachusetts, stated that a young man may not marry until he has killed either six blackbirds or three crows; and in Gary, Indiana, it was illegal to go into a theater within four hours of eating garlic.

Equity demands that laws change as society changes, resorting to general principles of fairness and justice whenever existing law is inadequate. It requires the "spirit of the law" to take precedence over the "letter of the law." Equity describes a system of rules and doctrines supplementing common and statutory law and superseding laws inadequate to fairly settle a case. Closely related to equity are the principles embodied in the Declaration of Independence.

equity

A concept requiring that the "spirit of the law" takes precedence over the "letter of the law."

THE DECLARATION OF INDEPENDENCE

The Europeans' original immigration to the New World was heavily motivated by a desire to escape the religious, economic, political and social repressions of traditional European society. North America was seen as a land where people could get a new start, free to make of themselves what they chose.

Sometimes, however, reality did not fully coincide with the **American creed** of individual freedom, as seen in the treatment of Native Americans, the importation of slaves, the establishment of state churches and the repressiveness involved in such episodes as the Salem witchcraft trials. Nevertheless, the spirit of liberty and justice remained strong. As noted by Myrdal (1944), "The American creed is the national conscience; a body of beliefs about equality, liberty and justice which most Americans believe in, in spite of the fact that America has, and always has had, multiple wrongs."

American creed

The belief in individual freedom.

In the 1760s the British began taking away rights Americans felt were naturally theirs, and the American Revolution resulted. In effect, the United States was born out of a desire—indeed, a demand—for civil rights and civil liberties. **Civil rights** are those claims that citizens have to the affirmative assistance of government. **Civil liberties** are an individual's immunity from governmental oppression.

civil rights

Claims that citizens have to the affirmative assistance of government.

civil liberties

An individual's immunity from governmental oppression.

Civil rights and civil liberties are recurring themes in America's development and reflect values forcefully stated in the Declaration of Independence. The Declaration is not only a statement of grievances against England but also a statement of alternative basic premises underlying human freedom. As Thomas Jefferson phrased it in the Declaration, the United States was demanding "the separate and equal station to which the laws of nature and of nature's God entitle them."

The Declaration of Independence asserts that all individuals are created equal and are entitled to the unalienable rights of life, liberty and the pursuit of happiness. It further asserts that governments are instituted by and derive their power from the governed, that is, the people.

The Declaration of Independence was an idealistic statement of philosophy. It broke our ties with England but did not establish how the United States should be structured or governed. Each colony developed its own means of policing and protecting itself. However, if every locality and state were left alone, our legal system would be chaos. Fortunately, our Founding Fathers foresaw this danger and wrote the Constitution of the United States, a carefully drafted document that established the workings of our democracy.

The colonists cherished the freedom from tyranny they had fought for and wanted to ensure that when they set up their new government no single entity would have absolute power. They also, however, wanted to ensure that law and order were a part of this new country. The importance of a system of checks and balances and of establishing entities that could ensure law and order is seen in the first three articles of the Constitution.

THE U.S. CONSTITUTION

constitution

A system of fundamental laws and principles that prescribe the nature, functions and limits of a government or other body; the basic instrument of government and the supreme law of the United States; the written instrument defining the power, limitations and functions of the U.S. government and of each state.

A **constitution** is a system of fundamental laws and principles that prescribe the nature, functions and limits of a government or other body. The U.S. Constitution was drafted by the Constitutional Convention of 1787 and became effective in 1789.

The U.S. Constitution, ratified in 1789, is the basic instrument of government and the supreme law of the land. The U.S. Constitution laid the foundation for the criminal justice system by establishing

- The legislative branch to make laws (Article 1).
- The executive branch to enforce the laws (Article 2).
- The judicial branch to judge when the law has been broken (Article 3).

The three branches of government served as a system of checks and balances on each other, providing a *lateral* balance of power. In addition, because the states feared an all-powerful government, even with its system of checks and balances, the Tenth Amendment to the Constitution established the principle of **federalism**, whereby power is shared by the national government and the states.

federalism

A principle whereby power is shared by the national government and the states.

Federalism allowed the criminal justice system to develop at both the state and federal level and established a vertical balance of power.

The states, in turn, allowed local jurisdictions to establish their own law enforcement agencies. This intentionally fragmented system with both vertical and

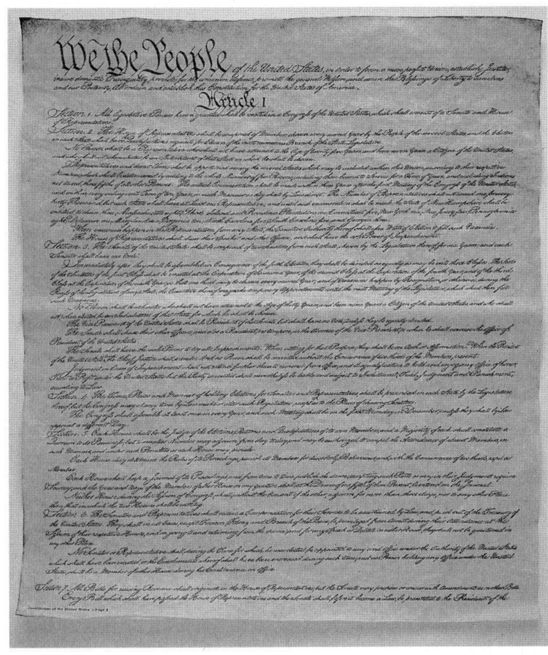
We the People

Article I

The opening paragraph of the U.S. Constitution clearly states its purpose: "We the People of the United States, in Order to form a more perfect Union, establish Justice, insure domestic Tranquility, provide for the common defense, promote the general Welfare, and secure the Blessings of Liberty to ourselves and our Posterity, do ordain and establish this Constitution for the United States of America."

horizontal checks and balances ensures that no one entity will become too powerful, but it also poses challenges to coordination when joint efforts, such as homeland security, are needed.

Order of Authority of Law

If two laws conflict, a set order of authority has been established.

The order of authority of law is the federal Constitution, treaties with foreign powers, acts of Congress, the state constitutions, state statutes and, finally, common law or case law.

Before they would accept the Constitution, the states demanded additional amendments guaranteeing them certain rights with which the government could not interfere. The first 10 amendments guaranteeing these rights are called the Bill of Rights.

THE BILL OF RIGHTS

The Constitution organized the government of the new nation but contained few personal guarantees. Ten amendments, with personal guarantees, came into effect in 1791. They became known as the **Bill of Rights**, a fundamental document protecting a person's right to "life, liberty, and the pursuit of happiness."

Bill of Rights
The first 10 amendments to the U.S. Constitution.

The Bill of Rights refers to the first 10 amendments to the Constitution, which protect the peoples' liberties and forbid the government to violate these rights.

Individual constitutional rights are clearly specified in each amendment. Of special importance to criminal justice professionals are the First, Second, Fourth, Fifth, Sixth, Eighth, Ninth, Tenth and Fourteenth Amendments.

The First Amendment

The First Amendment guarantees freedom of religion, freedom of speech, freedom of the press, freedom of peaceable assembly and freedom of petition.

Freedom of Religion The First Amendment clearly separates church and state and requires the government to be neutral on religious matters, favoring no religion over another.

Freedom of Speech The Supreme Court has ruled that the First Amendment does not protect all forms of expression. Highly inflammatory remarks that advocate violence and clearly threaten the peace and safety of the community spoken to a crowd are not protected.

Courts have recognized that **symbolic speech**, involving tangible forms of expression such as wearing buttons or clothing with political slogans or displaying a sign or a flag, is protected by the First Amendment. The Supreme Court has also held that burning the American flag is protected by the First Amendment, as is cross burning.

symbolic speech

Tangible forms of expression such as wearing buttons or clothing with political slogans or displaying a sign or flag; protected by the First Amendment.

Freedom of the Press The Founding Fathers recognized the importance of a free interplay of ideas in a democratic society and sought to guarantee the right of all citizens to speak or publish their views, even if contrary to those of the government or society. As with freedom of speech, the right to publish is not absolute; for example, the sale of obscene or libelous printed materials is not protected.

The police and the press often come into conflict because of the Sixth Amendment guarantee of the right to a fair trial and protection of the defendant's rights. The guarantees of the First and Sixth Amendments must be carefully balanced. The public's right to know cannot impinge upon others' right to privacy or to a fair trial.

Freedom of Peaceable Assembly Americans have the right to assemble peaceably for any political, religious or social activity. Public authorities cannot impose unreasonable restrictions on such assemblies, but they can impose limitations reasonably designed to prevent fire, health hazards or traffic obstructions.

Freedom of Petition The right of petition is designed to allow citizens to communicate with their government without obstruction. When citizens exercise their First Amendment freedom to write or speak to their senators or representatives, they participate in the democratic process.

The Second Amendment

The Second Amendment guarantees the right to keep and bear arms as necessary for a well-regulated militia.

Gun rights have been a topic of controversy for decades, with many jurisdictions enacting bans in an effort to curtail violence. In 2008 the U.S. Supreme Court ruled that the District of Columbia's ban on handguns was unconstitutional, a decision heralded by many citizens such as Dick Heller (pictured), who argued that if he was allowed to have a handgun at his job as a security guard, he also had a constitutional right to have one at home. The Court agreed, holding that the Second Amendment protected an individual's right to keep and bear arms for lawful purposes and that the DC ban was unconstitutional.

The Supreme Court has ruled that state and federal governments may pass laws that prohibit carrying concealed weapons, require registering firearms and limit the sale of firearms for other than military use. All federal court decisions involving the amendment have used a collective militia interpretation and/or held that firearms control laws are constitutional.

Dozens of federal and state court decisions have held that the Second Amendment limits only the federal government, not the states, and that the right to keep and bear arms is a collective rather than an individual right. On June 26, 2008, in *District of Columbia v. Heller*, the Supreme Court held in a 5–4 vote that the Second Amendment protects an individual's right to possess firearms for traditional lawful purposes and that "the District's ban on handgun possession in the home violates the Second Amendment, as does its prohibition against rendering any lawful firearm in the home operable for the purpose of immediate self defense." Spector (2009, p.25) notes, "At the heart of the court's opinion is the right to self-defense. Banning handguns, the weapon of choice for self-defense, and/or requiring that guns be kept inoperable at all times, would make it impossible for citizens to use such guns for the purpose of self-defense. The basis of the court's decision is not clear, unequivocal or obvious by any stretch of the imagination. The narrow 5–4 vote and vehement dissent is indicative as to how fragile the ruling may be."

Heller is likely to send right-to-carry laws in an entirely new direction: "With respect to right-to-carry considerations, *Heller* was not dispositive. To the contrary. It is the opening of the door to years of future litigation and legislation before this matter will be resolved conclusively" (Neil and Neil, 2009, p.118).

The Fourth Amendment

The Fourth Amendment requires probable cause and forbids unreasonable searches and seizures.

The Fourth Amendment has the most impact on law enforcement of any of the amendments, dictating how officers carry out their responsibilities without violating anyone's civil rights or civil liberties. Chapter 8 discusses the restrictions placed on law enforcement by this amendment, such as the exclusionary rule and stop-and-frisk limitations.

The Fifth Amendment

The Fifth Amendment *guarantees* due process—notice of a hearing, full information regarding the charges, the opportunity to present evidence in one's own behalf before an impartial judge or jury and the right to be presumed innocent until proven guilty by legally obtained evidence. The Fifth Amendment *prohibits* double jeopardy and self-incrimination.

Grand Jury The Fifth Amendment requires that before individuals are tried in federal court for an "infamous" crime, they must first be **indicted**, that is, formally accused of a crime by a grand jury. The grand jury's duty is to prevent people from being subjected to a trial when insufficient proof exists that they have committed a crime.

indicted

Formally charged with a specific crime by a grand jury, based on probable cause.

Due Process The words **due process of law** express the fundamental ideas of American justice. A due process clause occurs in the Fifth and Fourteenth Amendments as a restraint on the federal and state governments, respectively, and protects against arbitrary, unfair procedures in judicial or administrative proceedings that could affect a citizen's personal and property rights.

due process of law

Not explicitly defined but embodies the fundamental ideas of American justice expressed in the Fifth and Fourteenth Amendments.

Due process requires that during judicial proceedings, fundamental principles of fairness and justice must prevail, including both substantive and procedural due process. **Substantive due process** protects individuals against unreasonable, arbitrary or capricious laws and limits arbitrary government actions. **Procedural due process** deals with notices, hearings and gathering of evidence. The vast majority of due process cases are in the area of procedural due process.

substantive due process

Protects individuals against unreasonable, arbitrary or capricious laws and limits arbitrary government actions.

procedural due process

Deals with notices, hearings and gathering evidence in criminal matters.

Double Jeopardy The Fifth Amendment also guarantees that citizens will not be placed in **double jeopardy**; that is, they will not be tried before a federal or state court more than once for the same crime. A second trial can occur, however, when the first trial results in a mistrial, when the jury cannot agree on a verdict or when a second trial is ordered by an appellate court.

double jeopardy

Unconstitutionally being tried for the same crime more than once.

Double jeopardy does not arise when a single act violates both federal and state laws and the defendant is prosecuted in both federal and state courts, nor does a criminal prosecution in either a state or federal court exempt the defendant from being sued for damages in civil court by anyone harmed by the criminal act. This occurred in the O. J. Simpson case in which Simpson was found not guilty in criminal court but later was found responsible for wrongful death in civil court and ordered to pay restitution.

Further, a defendant may be prosecuted more than once for the same conduct if it involves the commission of more than one crime. For instance, if a person kills three victims at the same time and place, he or she can be tried separately for each slaying.

Self-Incrimination In any criminal case, every person has the right not to be a witness against him- or herself; that is, individuals are not required to provide answers to questions that might convict them of a crime. To ensure against self-incrimination, the Court ruled in the landmark case *Miranda v. Arizona* (1966) that citizens must be warned *before* custodial interrogation of their right to remain silent, that what they say may be used against them in court and that they have a right to counsel, which will be furnished to them. (A **landmark decision** is a judicial ruling that significantly alters or affects existing law and guides future decisions on the same issue.) If these *Miranda* warnings are not given, any statements obtained by the questioning are inadmissible in later criminal proceedings.

landmark decision

A judicial ruling that significantly alters or affects existing law and guides future decisions on the same issue.

The Sixth Amendment

The Sixth Amendment establishes requirements for criminal trials. It guarantees the individual's right to have a speedy public trial by an impartial jury, to be informed of the nature and cause of the accusation, to be confronted with witnesses against him or her, to subpoena witnesses for defense and to have counsel for defense.

The Sixth Amendment requires that accused persons be told how it is claimed they have broken the law so they can prepare their defense. The crime must be clearly established by statute beforehand. In general accused persons are entitled to have all witnesses against them present their evidence orally in court. Accused persons are entitled to the court's aid in obtaining their witnesses, usually by subpoena, which orders them into court as witnesses.

In *Melendez-Diaz v. Massachusetts* (2009), the Supreme Court ruled 5–4 that the prosecution's submission of a chemical drug test report, in the absence of testimony from the scientist who performed the test, was a violation of the Sixth Amendment right to confront witnesses. The four dissenting justices in *Melendez-Diaz* cautioned that the decision could place a tremendous burden on the nation's criminal justice system by requiring analysts to attend trials rather than focusing on forensic responsibilities (Liptak, 2010). Nonetheless, in January 2010, the Supreme Court dismissed a pending challenge to this ruling by issuing a one-line order sending the case back to a Virginia state court for another hearing. This leaves intact the ruling that gives defendants the right to demand live testimony from experts who prepare reports for the prosecution (Savage, 2010).

The Sixth Amendment also provides a right to be represented by counsel. For many years this was interpreted to mean that defendants had a right to be represented by a lawyer if they could afford one. *Gideon v. Wainwright* (1963) changed that. Writing for the majority, Justice Hugo Lafayette Black stated,

> In our adversary system of criminal justice, any person hauled into court, who is too poor to hire a lawyer cannot be assured a fair trial unless counsel is provided for him. . . .

> This seems to us to be an obvious truth .... That government hires lawyers to prosecute and defendants who have money to hire lawyers to defend are the strongest indications of the widespread belief that lawyers in criminal courts are necessities, not luxuries. The right of one charged with a crime to counsel may not be deemed fundamental and essential to fair trials in some countries, but it is in ours.

The court ruled 9–0 that the due process clause of the Fourteenth Amendment requires states to provide free counsel to indigent (destitute or poverty-stricken) defendants in all felony cases.

The Eighth Amendment

The Eighth Amendment forbids excessive bail, excessive fines and cruel and unusual punishments.

Bail Bail has traditionally meant payment by the accused of a sum of money, specified by the court based on the nature of the offense, to ensure the accused's presence at trial. A defendant released from custody who fails to appear for trial forfeits bail to the court. The Eighth Amendment does not specifically provide the right to bail, only that bail will not be excessive.

The leading Supreme Court decision on excessive bail is *Stack v. Boyle* (1951) in which 12 community leaders were indicted for conspiracy, and bail was set at $50,000 per defendant. The defendants moved to reduce this amount on the grounds it was excessive, and the Supreme Court agreed, "This traditional right to freedom before conviction permits the unhampered preparation of a defense, and serves to prevent the infliction of punishment prior to conviction. . . . Unless this right to bail before trial is preserved, the presumption of innocence, secured only after centuries of struggle, would lose its meaning."

Cruel and Unusual Punishment Whether fines or confinement are cruel and unusual must be determined by the facts of each case. Such excessive practices as torture would be invalid. The Supreme Court has heard numerous cases concerning cruel and unusual punishment and has held the death penalty itself to be cruel and unusual in certain circumstances if it is not universally applied.

The Ninth Amendment

The Ninth Amendment emphasizes the Founding Fathers' view that government powers are limited by the rights of the people and that it was *not* intended, by expressly guaranteeing in the Constitution certain rights of the people, to recognize that government has unlimited power to invade other rights of the people.

Griswold v. Connecticut (1965) addressed the issue of whether the right to privacy is a constitutional right and, if so, whether the right is reserved to the people under the Ninth Amendment or is derived only from other rights specifically mentioned in the Constitution. The Court in *Griswold* ruled that the Third and Fifth Amendments, in addition to the First and Fourth, created zones of privacy safe from governmental intrusion and, without resting its decision on any one amendment or on the Ninth Amendment itself, simply held that the right of privacy is guaranteed by the Constitution.

The Tenth Amendment

The Tenth Amendment embodies the principle of federalism, which reserves for the states the residue of powers not granted to the federal government or withheld from the states. However, through the Fourteenth Amendment, many civil rights and civil liberties ensured by the Bill of Rights were made applicable to the states.

The Fourteenth Amendment

The Fourteenth Amendment requires each state to abide by the Constitution and the incorporation doctrine of the Bill of Rights. It guarantees due process and equal protection under the law.

The Incorporation Doctrine Harr and Hess (2008, p.115) explain, "Considering the Constitution was aimed primarily at limiting the power of *federal* government, it seemed unthinkable that the federal government would be kept in line only to have state authority left unbridled. The **incorporation doctrine**, also known as **selective incorporation**, prevents the unthinkable."

The Supreme Court has held that there were rights "so rooted in the traditions and conscience of our people as to be ranked as fundamental," meaning "essential to justice and the American system of political liberty" (*Palko v. Connecticut*, 1937). The selective incorporation doctrine holds that only those provisions of the Bill of Rights fundamental to the American legal process are made applicable to the states through the due process clause. For example, if a state law were to abridge freedom of religion, it would be violating the First Amendment as applied to it through the Fourteenth Amendment.

incorporation doctrine

Holds that only those provisions of the Bill of Rights fundamental to the American legal process are made applicable to the states through the due process clause; also called *selective incorporation*.

selective incorporation

Holds that only those provisions of the Bill of Rights fundamental to the American legal process are made applicable to the states through the due process clause; also called the *incorporation doctrine*.

Due Process The Bill of Rights applies only to actions by the federal government. Thus state and local officers could proceed with an arrest without any concern for the accused's rights. The Fourteenth Amendment duplicates the Fifth Amendment, except it specifically orders state and local officers to provide the legal protections of due process. *In re Gault* (1967) extended the due process clause of the Fourteenth Amendment to apply to proceedings in state juvenile courts, giving juveniles many of the same rights and protections afforded to adult criminal defendants.

Equal Protection The Fourteenth Amendment also prohibits denial of equal protection of the laws. A state cannot make unreasonable, arbitrary distinctions between different people's rights and privileges. Because "all people are created equal," no law can deny red-haired men the right to drive an automobile, although it can deny minors the right to drive. The state can make reasonable classifications, but classifications based on race, religion, gender and national origin have been held unreasonable.

The Constitution and the Bill of Rights are at the heart of constitutional law. In addition to the great body of constitutional law, criminal and civil law also are important to the criminal justice professional.

CRIMINAL LAW

Criminal law includes rules and procedures for investigating crimes and prosecuting criminals, regulations governing the constitution of courts, the conduct of trials and the administration of penal institutions. American criminal law has

criminal law
The body of law that defines crimes and assigns punishments for them.

substantive criminal law
Statutes specifying crimes and their punishments.

felony
A major crime
for example, murder, rape, arson; the penalty is usually death or imprisonment for more than one year in a state prison or penitentiary.

misdemeanor
A minor offense—for example, breaking a municipal ordinance, speeding; the penalty is typically a fine or a short imprisonment, usually less than one year, in a local jail or workhouse.

mala in se
"Bad in itself," a crime such as murder or rape so offensive that it is obviously criminal.

mala prohibita
"Bad because it is forbidden," a crime that violates a specific regulatory statute and would not usually be considered a crime if no law prohibited it, for example, certain traffic violations.

procedural criminal law
Laws specifying how law enforcement officers are to carry out their responsibilities.

actus reus
A guilty, measurable act, including planning and conspiring.

mens rea
Guilty intent; literally "a guilty mind."

a number of unique features. In establishing criminal law, the federal government and each state government are sovereign within the limits of their authority as defined by the Constitution. Therefore, criminal law varies from state to state. Despite the many differences, most states have a tradition derived from English common law.

Criminal law defines crimes and fixes punishments for them.

The Bureau of Justice Statistics defines *crime* as "all behaviors and acts for which a society provides formally sanctioned punishment." Crimes are made so by law. State and federal statutes define each crime, the elements involved and the penalty attached to each. The statutes that define what acts constitute social harm are called **substantive criminal law**, for example, a statute defining homicide. A substantive criminal law not only defines the offense but also states the punishment. Omission of the punishment invalidates the law.

In most countries, crimes and punishments are expressed in statutes, with punishments including removal from public office, fines, exile, imprisonment and death. Unless the act for which a defendant is accused is expressly defined by statute as a crime, no indictment or conviction for committing the act is legal. This establishes the difference between government by law and arbitrary dictatorial government.

Like English law, American criminal law classifies crimes with respect to their gravity as felonies and misdemeanors. A **felony** is a serious crime, generally punishable by death or by imprisonment for more than one year in a state prison or penitentiary. A **misdemeanor** is any minor offense, generally punishable by a fine or a short term, usually not to exceed one year, in a jail or workhouse.

Misdemeanors are typically categorized into various levels, ranging from petty to more severe. State criminal codes vary in their classification of offenses considered misdemeanors. Crimes usually defined as misdemeanors include libel, assault and battery, malicious mischief and petty theft. In some states the distinction between felonies and misdemeanors is practically discarded, with the punishment for each particular crime prescribed by statute.

Crimes have also been classified as ***mala in se*** (bad in itself) and ***mala prohibita*** (bad because it is forbidden). A *mala in se* crime is one so offensive it is obviously criminal, for example, murder or rape. A *mala prohibita* crime is one that violates a specific regulatory statute, for example, certain traffic violations. These would not usually be considered crimes if no law prohibited them.

Proving That a Crime Has Been Committed

In addition to establishing what specifically constitutes a crime and the punishment for it, **procedural criminal law** specifies what must be proved and how, that is, legally within the constraints of the Constitution and the Bill of Rights.

To prove that a crime has been committed, it is usually necessary to prove the following:

- The act itself (***actus reus***)—the material elements of the crime.
- The criminal mental state (***mens rea***)—intent to do wrong.

Material Elements—The Criminal Act Basic to the commission of a crime is the concept of *actus reus*—literally the "guilty act." The *actus reus* must be a measurable act, including planning and conspiring. What constitutes this forbidden act is usually spelled out very specifically in state statutes and is called the *corpus delicti*.

Contrary to popular belief, the ***corpus delicti*** of a crime is not the body in a murder case. It is, quite literally, the body of the crime itself—the distinctive elements that must exist for a particular crime to be proved. These **elements of the crime** make up the *corpus delicti*. Law enforcement officers are most responsible for proving the actual act occurred—establishing the elements of a specific crime. Much more difficult to establish is the defendant's mental state.

corpus delecti

Literally, the body of the crime itself—the distinctive elements that must exist for a particular crime to be proven.

elements of the crime

The distinctive acts making up a specific crime; the elements make up the *corpus delicti* of the crime.

Criminal Intent—the *Mens Rea* The second key requirement of a crime is **criminal intent** or *mens rea*, literally the "guilty mind." The standard test for criminal liability is expressed in the Latin phrase *actus nonfacit reum nisi mens sit rea*, which translates as "the act does not make a person guilty unless the mind is also guilty."

To convict someone of a crime, it must be proven the defendant intentionally, knowingly or willingly committed the act. *Mens rea* refers to evil intent, criminal purpose and knowledge of the wrongfulness of conduct. Before the 1960s, *mens rea* was a vague, confusing concept. However, since that time the formulation of *mens rea* set forth in the American Law Institute Model Penal Code has clarified the different levels of *mens rea* into four general classes: (1) intentionally, (2) knowingly, (3) recklessly and (4) negligently.

criminal intent

A resolve, design or mutual determination to commit a crime, with full knowledge of the consequences and exercise of free will; the *mens rea* or, literally, the "guilty mind."

1. *Intentionally* is where a person has a clear foresight of the consequences of an action and wants those consequences to occur.
2. *Knowingly* is where a person knows or should know that the results of his or her conduct are reasonably certain to occur.
3. *Recklessly* is where a person foresees that particular consequences may occur and proceeds with the given conduct, not caring whether those consequences actually occur or not.
4. *Negligently* occurs when a person does not actually foresee particular consequences of his or her actions, but a reasonable person in the same circumstances would foresee the consequences.

To differentiate among the four types of *mens rea*, consider Charley, who walks into a room that is in total darkness and contains valuable china objects:

1. Knowing the room is full of valuable objects, Charley's objective is to cause a maximum amount of damage.
2. Knowing the room is full of valuable objects, Charley simply blunders about rather than finding the light switch.
3. Knowing the room is full of valuable objects, Charley hopes to walk quickly to the center of the room where the light switch is located.
4. Without being aware of anything valuable in the room and not knowing where the light switch is located, Charley simply wants to find someplace quiet to sit.

In each of the preceding instances, if Charley damaged some of the valuable objects, the *mens rea* is present if a reasonable person would have taken more care when entering an unfamiliar room.

Mens Rea in Statutes An example of *mens rea* in the Model Penal Code is, "A person commits murder if he (1) *purposely* or *knowingly* (2) causes the death of a human." This is similar to the *mens rea* in common law: "It shall be unlawful for a person to cause the death of a human with *malice aforethought*."

Ignorance of the Law and *Mens Rea* The general rule under U.S. law is that ignorance of the law or a mistake of law is not a defense in a criminal prosecution. In some crimes intent is not an element. These are known as **strict liability** crimes.

strict liability

Intent is not required; the defendant is liable regardless of his or her state of mind when the act was committed.

Strict Liability Crimes Strict liability crimes generally involve traffic violations, liquor violations and hunting violations. In strict liability crimes, defendants are liable regardless of their state of mind when committing the act. For example, a liquor-store owner cannot use the excuse that a minor who bought beer from the store looked at least 30 years old. A man who has consensual sex with a minor female cannot use the excuse that she said she was 21, nor can a speeder claim ignorance of the posted speed limit or claim a faulty speedometer. Intent is not at issue—only the speed.

motive

Reason for doing something.

Intent versus Motive Intent is *not* to be confused with **motive**, which is a *reason* for doing something. Motive is not an element of any crime, but it can help to establish intent. If police officers can show why a suspect would benefit from committing a certain act, this greatly strengthens the case. A classic example is Robin Hood, who allegedly stole from the rich to give to the poor. He intended to steal, and although his motives were "righteous," he was still committing a crime. A more contemporary example would be the actions of Dr. Jack Kevorkian, who helped terminally ill people commit suicide. Although motive is not relevant to the issue of guilt or innocence, it can affect sentencing.

scienter

A degree of knowledge that makes an individual legally responsible for the consequences of his or her acts.

Another element of a crime that must sometimes be proven is ***scienter***, guilty knowledge making individuals legally responsible for their acts. In other words the person committing the act knew it was a crime. For example, to be guilty of harboring a felon, the person harboring the felon has to know the person is a felon, or the person who buys stolen property has to know the property is indeed stolen. This is closely related to *mens rea*. Figure 2.1 illustrates the elements that may be essential to the proof of the crime.

Crimes can be categorized in many ways. You have already seen one such classification: A criminal act can be either a misdemeanor or a felony. Another common classification differentiates between violent crimes (formerly crimes against persons) and property crimes. Violent crimes against persons include homicide, rape, assault and robbery—actions that involve force or the threat of force against a person. In contrast, property crimes do not involve force and include larceny, burglary, motor vehicle theft and arson. Chapter 3 discusses these crimes. Consider next the third major type of law—civil law.

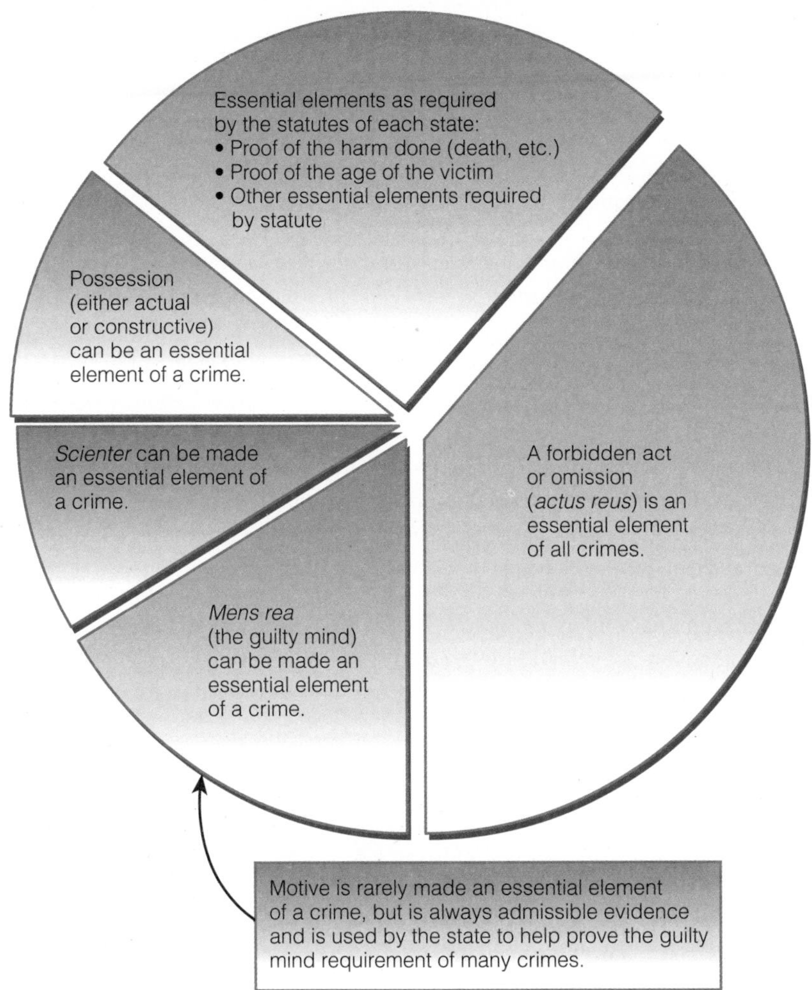
Essential elements as required by the statutes of each state:
• Proof of the harm done (death, etc.)
• Proof of the age of the victim
• Other essential elements required by statute
Possession (either actual or constructive) can be an essential element of a crime.
Scienter can be made an essential element of a crime.
Mens rea (the guilty mind) can be made an essential element of a crime.
A forbidden act or omission (*actus reus*) is an essential element of all crimes.
Motive is rarely made an essential element of a crime, but is always admissible evidence and is used by the state to help prove the guilty mind requirement of many crimes.

FIGURE 2.1 Elements That May Be Essential to the Proof of a Crime

SOURCE: Thomas J. Gardner and Terry M. Anderson. *Criminal Law*, 9th ed. Belmont, CA: Wadsworth, 2006, p.51. Reprinted by permission.

CIVIL LAW AND TORTS

The criminal/civil distinction is of interest to law enforcement officers because they must deal with those who break criminal laws and at the same time not violate the "criminal's" civil rights. Officers who do not deal legally with criminal matters may find themselves the target of a civil lawsuit. In addition, law enforcement officers must be able to tell the difference between a criminal and a civil offense because they are responsible for investigating only criminal matters. Civil offenses are not within their jurisdiction.

Although laws vary from state to state, generally such actions as trespassing, desertion of family, slander, failure to make good on a contract or similar actions against an individual would be covered under civil law. Officers may also respond to civil disputes that have the potential to escalate to a criminal matter. Common examples of civil issues that police officers may encounter include custody exchanges of children between separated parents, disputes between neighbors, issues between renters and landlords and some civil court violations.

civil law

All restrictions placed upon individuals that are noncriminal in nature; seeks restitution rather than punishment.

tort

A civil wrong for which the court seeks remedy in the form of damages to be paid.

Civil law refers to all noncriminal restrictions placed on individuals. It seeks not punishment but restitution. The offense is called a **tort**.

> A tort is not the same thing as a crime, although the two sometimes have many features in common. The distinction between them lies in the interests affected and the remedy afforded by the law. A crime is an offense against the public at large, for which the state, as the representative of the public, will bring proceedings in the form of criminal prosecution. . . . A criminal prosecution is not concerned in any way with compensation of the injured individual against whom the crime is committed. . . . The civil action for a tort, on the other hand, is commenced and maintained by the injured person himself, and its purpose is to compensate him for the damage he has suffered, at the expense of the wrongdoer. (Prosser, 1955, p.7)

Law enforcement officers recognize when a matter is covered by criminal law and when it is covered by civil law (noncriminal matters). An act can be both a crime and a tort.

The distinctions between crimes and torts are as follows:

Crime	Tort
Public wrong	Private wrong
State prosecutes	Individual prosecutes
Seeks to punish	Seeks redress for injury
Criminal intent is required	Intent not necessary

The Law Enforcement Officer and Civil Liability

The threat of a lawsuit comes with being a law enforcement officer. Citizens can bring action against the police and have been doing so with increasing frequency, and the settlements are often large.

The threat of civil liability can affect police officer responses, including arrest decisions, by creating a "lawsuit paranoia" that can permeate and undermine the effective operation of law enforcement agencies and can affect every law enforcement officer, both professionally and personally. In one case an officer reported that he and his partner did not fire on an offender pointing two pistols at them because they were afraid of liability if the pistols were not real. The offender shot and killed one of the officers. These officers were more afraid of a lawsuit than of being killed. Incidents such as this have led to new focus in how officers are trained in deadly force situations.

Grossi (2009, p.24) notes, "Although most street cops and use-of-force experts would rather see outrageous and/or frivolous lawsuits go to trial, the fact is that many settle out of court. Settlements bother cops because they never get their 'day in court.' In addition, the 'bad guys' often walk away with a lot of money."

Policing within the law is the focus of Chapter 8. One way to avoid being sued is to know the law, and one of the most important laws officers should be familiar with is the Civil Rights Act, often referred to as Section 1983.

The Civil Rights Act (Section 1983) The U.S. Code, Title 42, Section 1983, passed after the Civil War in 1871 states, "Every person who, under color of any statute, ordinance, regulation, custom, or usage, of any State or Territory, subjects, or causes to be subjected any citizen of the United States or other person within the jurisdiction thereof to the deprivation of any rights, privileges, or immunities secured by the Constitution and laws, shall be liable to the party injured in an action at law, suit in equity, or other proper proceeding for redress."

Section 1983 of the U.S. Code, Title 42, stipulates that anyone acting under the authority of local or state law who violates another person's constitutional rights—even though he or she is upholding a law—can be sued.

The two basic requirements for a Section 1983 action are that (1) the plaintiff must be deprived of a constitutional right and (2) the defendant must deprive the plaintiff of this right while acting under the "color of the law" (*Adickes v. Kress and Co.*, 1970). Like criminal law, civil law has levels of "intent":

- Strict liability—the wrongdoer is liable even if no harm was intended (for example keeping wild animals).
- Intentional wrong—the person knows the act was unlawful but did it anyway.
- Negligence—the person did not set out to do harm but acted carelessly.

Intentional wrong and negligence are the two categories with which law enforcement officers are most frequently involved. Intentional wrongs that may affect law enforcement include assault, battery, excessive force, false imprisonment, false arrest, malicious prosecution, intentional infliction of emotional distress, trespass, illegal electronic surveillance, invasion of privacy, defamation and wrongful death. Later chapters introduce procedures to minimize the likelihood of a civil lawsuit for an intentional wrong.

The second category of civil charges frequently filed against law enforcement officers and their agencies is *negligence*, the failure to use due care to prevent foreseeable injury. Routine police duties that most often lead to negligence lawsuits are care of incapacitated persons, duty to render emergency aid, caring for arrestees, aiding private citizens, investigating unusual circumstances and operating emergency vehicles carelessly, for example during high-speed chases. Officers deal with intense circumstances and are often under great time pressure to make rapid decisions based on very little information. Given the inherently dangerous nature of police work, such as the carrying of lethal weapons and the authority to drive at high speeds, officers are unquestionably vulnerable to lawsuits when mistakes or errors in judgment occur that lead to unnecessary injury of a private party. The results of such lawsuits, even when judgments are in favor of the police, can have far-reaching, long-lasting adverse effects on the officers involved and their agencies, as well as on the police profession and the community as a whole.

Much of the civil action taken against police officers and their agencies results from the tremendous power officers have and, indeed, require.

CAREER PROFILE

Floyd T. Stokes (Retired Police Chief, Retired Lieutenant and Retired Navy Officer)

I believe I am somewhat of an anomaly as far as a law enforcement career is concerned. I wanted to be a police officer since I was a little boy, but I set aside that goal until many years later. I started my adult life in the military, dropping out of high school and entering the service at 17 years as an enlisted airman. During the Vietnam years I obtained an officer's commission in the U.S. Navy and flew off aircraft carriers as a navigator/electronic warfare evaluator. After three combat tours, I transferred to Naval Intelligence—and eventually to the Naval Investigative Service as a reserve officer agent after 15 years of active duty.

In the mid-1970s I started my law enforcement career as a reserve deputy sheriff, attending the San Joaquin County Sheriff's Academy in California. From there I was hired as a full-time criminal investigator with the Humboldt County District Attorney's Office, working on homicides and other major crimes for 10 years. During that time, I completed two college degrees—an Associate's Degree and a Bachelor's Degree—fulfilling an educational quest I had started in the Navy. I left my District Attorney Investigator position in the late '80s to write and publish law enforcement textbooks and to return to uniformed law enforcement as a police sergeant for a small department in Northern California.

After completing a second police academy (which was required by the California Commission on Peace Officer Standards and Training [POST] in the late '80s because my basic street officer certification had lapsed while I was an investigator), I was hired as a deputy sheriff with the Humboldt County (California) Sheriff's Department, working in a remote resident post until I retired in 1993 to become a small-town chief of police. During this time I also retired from the Naval Reserve as a senior officer (Captain) after 28 years of combined regular and reserve duty. During the next 10 years, I worked as a police administrator for three police departments, including serving as a tribal police chief with the Hoopa Valley Tribe on the largest Indian reservation in California.

Because of a developed love for police canines while a resident sheriff's deputy, I trained and worked with a number of K-9s over the years, including dual-trained drug and explosives detection dogs. That love continues today. After retiring as police chief with my last agency, the Trinidad (California) Police Department, I agreed with the City Council to stay on as a Lieutenant to assist my replacement. Because of my love for law enforcement and the community I serve, and also because of my love for police canines, I continue today as a police lieutenant, working at the regional airport with my dual-trained explosives detection German Shepherd K-9, Ingo. I also manage investigations and training with the department, and I teach part-time at the local college and police academy. In addition to these activities, I run a law enforcement consulting and investigations firm under my private investigator's license, which I acquired in the late '80s.

My only explanation for such a long-lasting and varied career in law enforcement is this: During my years as a law enforcement administrator, I developed a reputation for problem solving. This reputation apparently resulted in my being hired to rebuild two additional police departments after retiring from the first.

My greatest challenge regarding police administration centered on navigating through the minefield of public opinion. Small departments provide no insulators, such as a bureaucratic chain of command, to keep the people, including detractors, at bay. You walk or drive the streets daily with your officers, and you are always in the forefront and exposed if something bad happens, such as a use-of-force incident.

As far as training and education are concerned, during my career I ended up with a four-year college education and dual California POST certification (Management General Law Enforcement Certificate and Advanced Specialized Investigator Certificate). The POST certification process goes from Basic, Intermediate and Advanced to Management and Executive certification for administrators. Police chiefs must have a management certificate within one year of employment. Although most smaller police departments do not require a four-year college diploma for their administrators, having one is of great value when competing with other experienced administrators for the job.

My advice to those wishing to pursue a career in law enforcement: Always be ethical and true to yourself—and what you know to be right. Establish your life goals—then work toward them . . . and don't give up. Be a leader and not a follower.

POLICE POWER

Without means of enforcement, the great body of federal, state, municipal and common law would be empty and meaningless. Recall that *law* implies not only the rule but also enforcement of that rule. All forms of society rely on authority and power. *Authority* is the right to direct and command. *Power* is the force by which others can be made to obey.

Police power describes the ability of federal, state or municipal governments to enforce the laws they pass by granting government agents at each level the authority to use force against those who fail to comply with the laws.

police power
The power of the federal, state or municipal governments to pass laws to regulate private interests, to protect the health and safety of the people, to prevent fraud and oppression and to promote public convenience, prosperity and welfare.

Police power is derived from the U.S. Constitution, U.S. Supreme Court decisions, federal statutes, state constitutions, state statutes, state court decisions and various municipal charters and ordinances.

Police power was defined by the Supreme Court in 1887 as "embracing no more than the power to promote public health, morals, and safety" (*Mugler v. Kansas*). For example, traffic laws are passed to preserve the general safety and to make the highways safe for the motoring public. States' police powers are delegated to them by the Bill of Rights in the Tenth Amendment, giving the states those powers not delegated to the federal government. In other words, the will of the people (law) gives authority and power to other people (police) to enforce the law whatever it happens to be at the time.

Police power ultimately rests with the people because their elected representatives create the laws that the police enforce.

Figure 2.2 illustrates the sources of police authority.

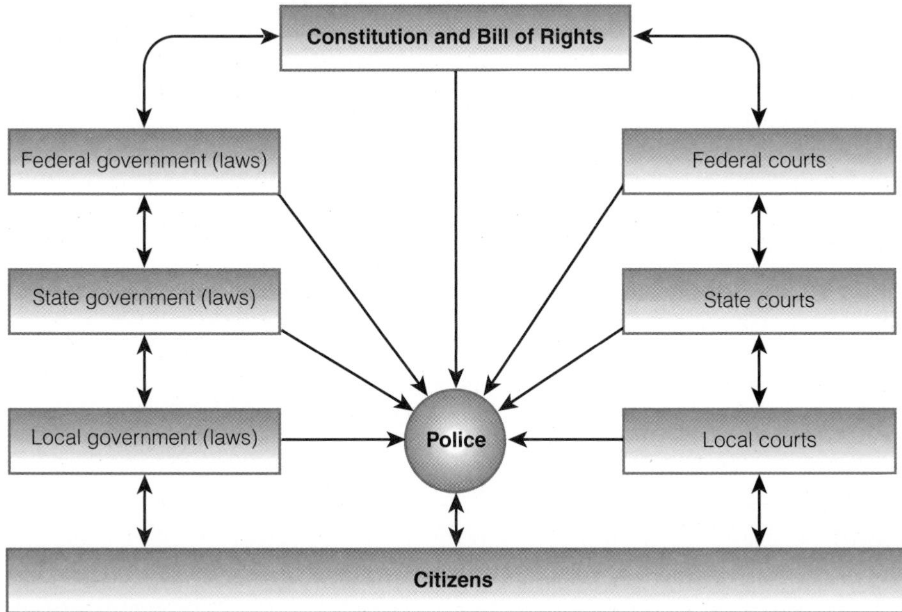

FIGURE 2.2 Sources of Police Authority

Note in Figure 2.2 that the arrows between the citizens, governments and courts go two ways—citizens are not only governed by laws passed by the legislation, interpreted by the courts and enforced by the police, but they also play a role in establishing laws by electing the representatives whose actions and decisions ultimately influence policing. Because each state is responsible for its citizens' health, safety and general well-being, they usually assign these functions to municipal police departments in the cities and to sheriffs and constables in rural areas. State legislatures may define the powers and duties of police officers; however, police officers' authority and powers cannot conflict with the Constitution.

Although state legislatures pass laws, the courts decide the purpose and character of the statutes, as well as whether these statutes conflict with the Constitution or are contrary to proper public policy. Acceptable police power requires the regulations to be (1) reasonable, (2) within the power given to the states by the Constitution and (3) in accord with due process of law.

Police power is restricted by the Constitution, the Fourteenth Amendment and the courts.

Many have noted the irony and inherent conflict present in our system of law enforcement—the designation of a police entity authorized to use coercive force to eradicate violence and effect a peaceful society. This paradoxical scheme often places officers, whose defining characteristic is the right to use force, in an awkward relationship with the citizens they are sworn to serve and protect. In addition law enforcement is faced with balancing the needs of society with the needs of the individuals within that society.

THE NEEDS OF SOCIETY AND THE RIGHTS OF THE INDIVIDUAL

America was founded on the desire for liberty and freedom from England's tyranny. Although the Founding Fathers crafted our government to ensure it would not impinge on individual liberties, the desire for law and order was also strong. They had brought with them the common law of England, and it was expected that these laws would be obeyed.

The scales of justice symbolize the desire to balance the needs of society with individual rights.

This tension between society's needs and individual liberty has its roots in two conflicting views of social control: conflict theory and consensus theory.

Conflict Theory

conflict theory

Contends that certain behaviors are criminalized to keep the dominant class in power.

Conflict theory contends that certain behaviors are criminalized to keep the dominant class in power. The roots of this theory are found in Marx and Engels' *Manifesto of the Communist Party* (1848, p.419): "The history of all hitherto existing society is the history of class struggles. Freeman and slave, patrician and plebeian, lord and serf, guild-master and journeyman, in a word, oppressor and oppressed stood in constant opposition to one another, carried on an interrupted, now hidden, now open fight, a fight that each time ended in either a revolutionary reconstruction of society at large, or in the common ruin of the contending classes."

Marx referred to the lower class as a "slum proletariat" made up of vagrants, prostitutes and criminals. The law was intended to maintain the power of the upper class and control this "slum proletariat."

Consensus Theory

Consensus theory holds that individuals within a society agree on basic values, on what is inherently right and wrong. Acts that are wrong are considered crimes. This theory goes back in history at least as far as Plato and Aristotle. Deviant acts are unlawful because society in general feels they are unacceptable behavior. French sociologist Émile Durkheim (1858–1917), in explaining the criminal law, suggests that crime is conduct "universally disapproved of by members of each society." An act is criminal when it offends strong and defined states of the collective conscience.

consensus theory
Holds that individuals within a society agree on basic values, on what is inherently right and wrong.

These two opposing views of social control parallel the two competing models within the criminal justice system: crime control and due process.

Crime Control versus Due Process

A major function of our criminal justice system is **crime control**. However, the Fifth Amendment of the Bill of Rights and the Fourteenth Amendment both guarantee citizens due process of law. *Due process of law* was defined in the Magna Carta as the "law of the land." And while the different state supreme courts have given varying definitions, the basic meaning of *due process* is that all legal proceedings will be fair and just. In other words, due process is a constitutional guarantee that no law or legal proceeding shall be unreasonable, arbitrary or capricious.

crime control
Emphasizes collective needs of society and the idea that all offenders should receive the harshest penalty allowed by law.

Two conflicting models of the criminal justice system are crime control and due process of law.

The crime control and due process models of justice are described as "two separate value systems that compete for priority in the operation of the criminal process" (Packer, 1968, p.153). The *crime control model* is seen as assembly-line justice, which is more administrative than adversarial, focuses on the law enforcement component of the system and pretrial activities, and relies on discretion, efficiency of operations, facts and repression of crime. Crime control emphasizes collective needs and the idea that all offenders should receive the harshest penalty allowed by law.

The *due process model*, in contrast, views the process as obstacle-course justice that focuses on the judicial component of the system, relying on laws, emphasizing reliability and seeking to preserve individual liberties. Due process contends that offenders should receive the least severe penalty and that the state must justify more severe penalties. According to Packer, the due process model incorporates the public's idealistic values, whereas the crime control model incorporates the reality of criminal justice in America. Closely paralleling this conflict is the conflict between conservative crime control policies and liberal crime control policies.

Conservative versus Liberal Crime Control Policies

Messner and Rosenfeld (2007, p.104) suggest, "*Conservative crime control* policies are draped explicitly in the metaphors of war. We have declared war on crime and on drugs, which are presumed to promote crime. Criminals, according to this view, have taken the streets, blocks and sometimes entire neighborhoods from law-abiding citizens. The function of crime control policy is to recapture the streets from criminals to make them safe for the rest of us." In contrast: "The *liberal crime control* approach emphasizes correctional policies and broader social reforms intended to expand opportunities for those 'locked out' of the American Dream" (Messner and Rosenfeld, p.107). From a correctional standpoint, the conservative camp emphasizes punishment for criminal behavior, whereas the liberal camp supports rehabilitation.

The conservative camp traditionally wages war on crime and drugs; the liberal camp wages war on poverty and on inequality of opportunity.

Another duality within the justice system is whether the actions of those operating within the criminal justice system should be guided by law and policy or by discretion. If the latter, who should exercise it and within what limits?

LAW AND POLICY VERSUS DISCRETION

Discretion is the freedom to make judgments, judgments that affect not only individuals but also the entire criminal justice system. For example, passage of the Eighteenth Amendment (1919) establishing prohibition led to severe prison overcrowding in the 1920s much as the drug laws are doing today. Discretion may be found throughout the criminal justice system, as illustrated in Table 2.1.

Discretion is exercised by legislators, police, prosecutors, judges, correctional officials and paroling authority.

Some feel there should be one set of rules for law enforcement, courts and corrections that would permit little, if any, discretion. Justice should be exercised with swiftness and certainty. The main purpose of criminal justice should be to restrain and suppress criminal activity. If the criminal does not want to abide by society's rules, why should the criminal have the rights of society? The weaker the enforcement of the law, the greater the likelihood of citizens being victimized.

Others point out that because no case is identical to another, allowances must be made for wide degrees of discretion for law enforcement, courts and corrections. Constraints and guarantees in the criminal justice process should protect the innocent from being found guilty. Individual rights are paramount to the rights of society. The process of determining guilt or innocence should be founded on information and hard evidence. Guilt "beyond a reasonable doubt" should be the

TABLE 2.1 Opportunities for Discretion

These Criminal Justice Officials	Must Often Decide Whether or Not or How to
Police	Enforce specific laws
	Investigate specific crimes
	Search people, vicinities, buildings
	Arrest or detain people
Prosecutors	File charges or petitions for adjudication
	Seek indictments
	Drop cases
	Reduce charges

SOURCE: *Report to the Nation on Crime and Justice*. U.S. Department of Justice, Bureau of Justice Statistics, March 1988, pp.56–60.

cornerstone of criminal justice. It is better to set 10 criminals free than to convict 1 innocent person.

If an individual is found guilty of a crime, what then? Should the criminal be punished or helped?

RETRIBUTIVE VERSUS RESTORATIVE JUSTICE

The evolution of our criminal justice system involved a shift from the community taking care of itself and of those who broke its rules to a system whereby the king or ruler took on that responsibility. Under this new system, a person who broke the rules (or the law) must pay—an eye for an eye (*lex talionis*) or **retributive justice**. In the United States, crime is still most often viewed as an offense against the state rather than against an individual.

retributive justice

System where a person who breaks the rules must pay; an eye for an eye.

Criminal justice is defined by the Federal Crime Control Act of 1973 as any "activity pertaining to crime prevention, control or reduction, or the enforcement of the criminal law." In this definition, the emphasis is on the crime, the criminal and the punishment. Many academicians and practitioners feel this emphasis is misplaced and partially responsible for some of the system's failure. They have called for a new approach to justice: restorative justice.

Restorative justice is a philosophical framework that focuses on crime as an act against another individual rather than against the state and focuses on the harm done and how that harm might be repaired. The goal of restorative justice is to reconcile the needs of victims and offenders with the community's needs. Unlike retributive justice, which is primarily concerned with punishing crime, restorative justice focuses on repairing the injury that crime inflicts.

restorative justice

Philosophical framework that focuses on crime as an act against another individual rather than against the state and focuses on the harm done and how that harm might be repaired; goal is to reconcile the needs of victims and offenders with the community's needs.

Retributive justice and restorative justice offer two competing ways to view justice, with retributive justice stressing punishment and restorative justice emphasizing involving the victim and the community to assist in correcting the wrong that has been done.

TABLE 2.2 Retributive versus Restorative Justice

Retributive Justice	Restorative Justice
Crime is an act against the state, a violation of a law, an abstract idea.	Crime is an act against another person or the community.
The criminal justice system controls crime.	Crime control lies primarily in the community.
Offender accountability defined as taking punishment.	Accountability defined as assuming responsibility and taking action to repair harm.
Crime is an individual act with individual responsibility.	Crime has both individual and social dimensions of responsibility.
Punishment is effective. A. Threat of punishment deters crime. B. Punishment changes behavior.	Punishment alone is not effective in changing behavior and is disruptive to community harmony and good relationships.
Victims are peripheral to the process.	Victims are central to the process of resolving a crime.
The offender is defined by deficits.	The offender is defined by capacity to make reparation.
Focus on establishing blame, on guilt, on past (did he/she do it?).	Focus on problem solving, on liabilities/obligations, on future (what should be done?).
Emphasis on adversarial relationship.	Emphasis on dialog and negotiation.
Imposition of pain to punish and deter/prevent.	Restitution as a means of restoring both parties; goal of reconciliation/restoration.
Community on sideline, represented abstractly by state.	Community as facilitator in restorative process.
Response focused on offender's past behavior.	Response focused on harmful consequences of offender's behavior, emphasis on the future.
Dependence upon proxy professionals.	Direct involvement by participants.

SOURCE: *The Balanced and Restorative Justice Project: Program Summary*. Washington, DC: Office of Juvenile Justice and Delinquency Prevention, October 1994. (NCJ 149727)

Table 2.2 illustrates the important differences between these two ways of viewing justice.

Which view of justice a community believes in will have a major effect on the courts and on corrections. Likewise, a community's tendency toward one of the other dualities will directly affect how law enforcement officers operate.

THE CRIMINAL JUSTICE PENDULUM

The dual responsibility of seeking out and punishing the guilty while simultaneously protecting the innocent is one of law enforcement's greatest challenges. The dualities within the system might be viewed as existing on the arc of a pendulum, with crime control, rigid adherence to policy, conservative crime control policies and a view of justice as retribution at the right end of the pendulum's arc. At the left end of the arc are due process, use of discretion, liberal crime control policies

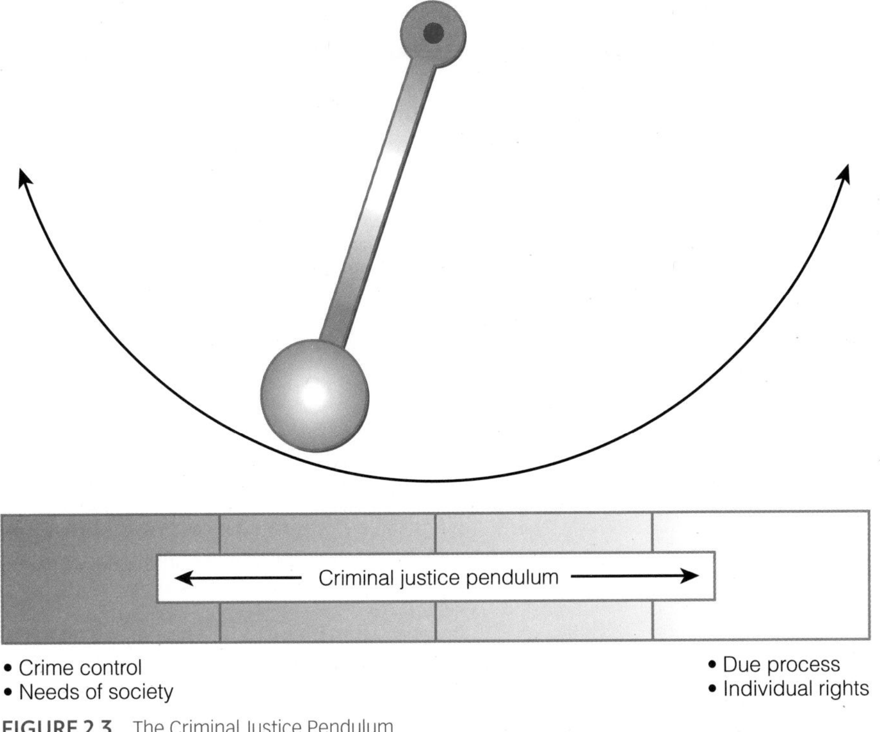

FIGURE 2.3 The Criminal Justice Pendulum

and a view of justice as restorative. Sometimes the pendulum slows and is near the middle, but at other times it swings more heavily to one side or the other, as shown in Figure 2.3.

Summary

If the fundamental values of our society are to be preserved and extended, citizens must understand and support those institutions and statutes that, in practice, reflect the principles set forth in the Declaration of Independence, the Constitution and the Bill of Rights.

The Declaration of Independence asserts that all individuals are created equal and are entitled to the unalienable rights of life, liberty and the pursuit of happiness. It further asserts that governments are instituted by and derive their power from the governed, that is, the people.

To achieve the goals set forth in the Declaration of Independence, the U.S. Constitution was drafted as the basic instrument of government and the supreme law of the United States. The U.S. Constitution, ratified in 1789, laid the foundation for the criminal justice system by establishing the legislative branch to make laws (Article 1), the executive branch to enforce the laws (Article 2) and the judicial branch to judge when the law has been broken (Article 3). Federalism allowed the criminal justice system to develop at both the state and federal level and established a vertical balance of power. The order of authority of law is the federal U.S. Constitution, treaties with foreign powers, acts of Congress, the state constitutions, state statutes and, finally, common law or case law.

Some states, however, refused to ratify the Constitution if it did not contain personal guarantees. As a result the Bill of Rights was drafted, containing the first 10 amendments to the Constitution, which protect the peoples' liberties and forbid the government to violate these rights:

- The First Amendment guarantees freedom of religion, freedom of speech, freedom of the press, freedom of peaceable assembly and freedom of petition.
- The Second Amendment guarantees the right to keep and bear arms as necessary for a well-regulated militia.
- The Fourth Amendment requires probable cause and forbids unreasonable searches and seizures.
- The Fifth Amendment guarantees due process—notice of a hearing, full information regarding the charges, the opportunity to present evidence in one's own behalf before an impartial judge or jury and the right to be presumed innocent until proven guilty by legally obtained evidence. The Fifth Amendment prohibits double jeopardy and self-incrimination.
- The Sixth Amendment establishes requirements for criminal trials. It guarantees the individual's right to have a speedy public trial by an impartial jury, to be informed of the nature and cause of the accusation, to be confronted with witnesses against him or her, to subpoena witnesses for defense and to have counsel for defense.
- The Eighth Amendment forbids excessive bail, excessive fines and cruel and unusual punishments.
- The Fourteenth Amendment requires each state to abide by the Constitution and the incorporation doctrine of the Bill of Rights. It guarantees due process and equal protection under the law.

In addition to constitutional law, the criminal justice professional must also be familiar with criminal and civil law. Criminal law defines crimes and fixes punishments for them. Crimes may be classified as felonies or misdemeanors. A felony refers to a serious crime, generally one punishable by death or by imprisonment for more than one year in a state prison or penitentiary. A misdemeanor refers to any minor offense, generally punishable by a fine or a short term, usually not to exceed one year, in a jail or workhouse. To prove a crime has been committed, it is usually necessary to prove the act itself (*actus reus*)—the elements of the crime—and prove the criminal mental state (*mens rea*)—intent to do wrong. In strict liability crimes, however, such as traffic violations, the defendant is liable regardless of intent.

Civil law refers to all noncriminal restrictions placed on individuals. It seeks not punishment but restitution. The offense is called a tort. The distinctions between crimes and torts are as follows:

Crime	Tort
Public wrong	Private wrong
State prosecutes	Individual prosecutes
Seeks to punish	Seeks redress for injury
Criminal intent is required	Intent not necessary

Section 1983 of the U.S. Code, Title 42, stipulates that anyone acting under the authority of local or state law who violates another person's constitutional rights—even though he or she is upholding a law—can be sued.

Without means of enforcement, the great body of federal, state and municipal law would be meaningless. To ensure enforcement, police have been given power and authority from local, state and federal sources. Police power is derived from the U.S. Constitution, U.S. Supreme Court decisions, federal statutes, state constitutions, state statutes, state court decisions and various municipal charters and ordinances. Police power ultimately rests with the people because their elected representatives create the laws that the police enforce. Police power is also restricted by the Constitution, the Fourteenth Amendment and the courts. Police have the power to enforce the laws so long as they do not violate the civil rights and liberties of any individual. The scales of justice symbolize the need to balance the needs of society with individual rights. A similar balance is needed between the two models of criminal justice: crime control and due process of law.

Paralleling these two models are the crime control policies of conservatives and liberals. The conservative camp traditionally wages war on crime and drugs; the liberal camp wages war on poverty and on inequality of opportunity. Conflict between following the letter of the law and using discretion also exists. Discretion is exercised by legislators, police, prosecutors, judges, correctional officials and paroling authority. Retributive justice and restorative justice offer two competing ways to view justice with retributive justice stressing punishment and restorative justice emphasizing involving the victim and the community to assist in correcting the wrong that has been done.

Discussion Questions

1. What specific restrictions are placed on police officers by the Bill of Rights?
2. Why has the Supreme Court said that state and federal governments can pass laws against carrying weapons when the Second Amendment specifically guarantees the right to bear arms?
3. How can law enforcement officers get past their fear of litigation? How can those who employ police officers help in this effort?
4. What is the basic difference between civil rights and civil liberties?
5. In what well-known cases has the Fifth Amendment been repeatedly used?
6. What do police power and authority consist of?
7. The Declaration of Independence states that all people are created equal. Does this mean all people have the same opportunities?
8. If a person's reckless driving of a car injures another person who dies two weeks later as a result of the injuries, could the reckless driver be charged with a crime, sued for a tort, or both? How would the type of charge affect the possible consequences faced by the reckless driver?
9. Should law enforcement officers be immune from tort action?
10. Should Fourth Amendment rights be extended to include general searches?

 Gale Emergency Services Database Assignments

- Use the Gale Emergency Services Database to help answer the Discussion Questions as appropriate.

- Using the Gale Emergency Services Database, find the article "Law Enforcement Physical Fitness Standards and Title VII": http://find.galegroup.com/gps/infomark.do?&contentSet=IAC-Documents&type=retrieve&tabID=T003&prodId=IPS&docId=A76880862&source=gale&srcprod=SP02&userGroupName=cpg3&version=1.0

  Assignment: How does this standard not violate the Civil Rights Act of 1964? Do you agree with certain exceptions or do you think it defeats the purpose of this Act? Be prepared to explain your position in class.
- Using the Gale Emergency Services Database, find the article "Criminal Procedure in Perspective": http://find.galegroup.com/gps/infomark.do?&contentSet=IAC-Documents&type=retrieve&tabID=T002&prodId=IPS&docId=A179455605&source=gale&srcprod=SP02&userGroupName=cpg3&version=1.0

  Assignment: Read and choose two or three cases to outline and discuss in depth in class.
- Using the Gale Emergency Services Database, find the article "Un-Incorporating the Bill of Rights: The Tension between the Fourteenth Amendment and the Federalism Concerns that Underlie Modern Criminal Procedure Reforms": http://find.galegroup.com/gps/infomark.do?&contentSet=IAC-Documents&type=retrieve&tabID=T002&prodId=IPS&docId=A194192402&source=gale&srcprod=SP02&userGroupName=cpg3&version=1.0

  Assignment: Identify the conflicts between Federalism and the Fourteenth Amendment in regard to modern criminal procedure. Be prepared to discuss your findings with the class.

Internet Assignment

- Use the key words *actus reus* to review what is called the "guilty mind" in criminal law. Write your own definition for *actus reus*, and compare your definition with others in your class.

References

Grossi, Dave. "Civil Suits & Settlements." *Law Officer Magazine*, July 2009, pp.24–27.

Harr, J. Scott, and Hess, Kären M. *Constitutional Law and the Criminal Justice System*, 4th ed. Belmont, CA: Wadsworth Thomson Learning, 2008.

Liptak, Adam. "With New Member, Supreme Court Takes New Look at Crime Lab Ruling." *The New York Times*, January 12, 2010. Retrieved from http://www.nytimes.com/2010/01/12/us/12scotus.html?ref=us&pagewanted=print

Marx, Karl, and Engels, Friedrich. *Manifesto of the Communist Party*. The Great Books Chicago: Encyclopedia Britannica, Inc., 1984, p.419.

Messner, Steven F., and Rosenfeld, Richard. *Crime and the American Dream*, 4th ed. Belmont, CA: Wadsworth Thomson Learning, 2007.

Myrdal, G. *The American Dilemma*. New York: Harper & Brothers, 1944.

Neil, Benjamin A., and Neil, Brian A. "The *Heller* Decision and Its Possible Implications for Right-to-Carry Laws

Nationally." *Journal of Contemporary Criminal Justice*, February 2009, pp.113–118.

Packer, Herbert L. *The Limits of the Criminal Sanction*. Stanford, CA: Stanford University Press, 1968.

Prosser, W. L. *Handbook of the Law of Torts*, 2nd ed. St. Paul, MN: West, 1955.

Savage, David G. "Supreme Court Dismisses Challenge to Ruling on Forensic Experts." *LA Times*, January 26, 2010. Retrieved from http://articles.latimes.com/2010/jan/26/nation/la-na-court-forensics26-2010jan26

Spector, Elliot. "*District of Columbia v. Heller* and the 2nd Amendment." *Law and Order*, February 2009, pp.25–28.

Cases Cited

Adickes v. Kress and Co., 398 U.S. 144 (1970)
District of Columbia v. Heller, 128 S.Ct. 2783 (2008)
Gideon v. Wainwright, 372 U.S. 355 (1963)
Griswold v. Connecticut, 381 U.S. 479 (1965)
In re Gault, 387 U.S. 1 (1967)
Melendez-Diaz v. Massachusetts, 129 S.Ct. 2527 (2009)
Miranda v. Arizona, 384 U.S. 436 (1966)
Mugler v. Kansas, 123 U.S. 623 (1887)
Palko v. Connecticut, 302 U.S. 319 (1937)
Stack v. Boyle, 342 U.S. 1 (1951)

CHAPTER 3

Crime in the United States: Offenses, Offenders, Victims

> Something insidious has happened in America: crime has made victims of us all. Awareness of its danger affects the way we think, where we live, where we go, what we buy, how we raise our children, and the quality of our lives as we age. The specter of violent crime and the knowledge that, without warning, any person can be attacked or crippled, robbed, or killed, lurks at the fringes of consciousness.
>
> —Statement of the Chairman, President's Task Force on Victims of Crime

Dwayne Dail hugs the victim in the William J. Neal rape case after Neal was sentenced to life in prison Wednesday, April 28, 2010, in Wayne County (North Carolina) Superior Court. Dail spent 18 years in prison for the 1987 rape of a 12-year-old girl before DNA evidence exonerated him and indicated Neal as the perpetrator.

Do You Know . . .

- What the three major sources of information about who commits crime are?
- What serious crimes are reported in the Uniform Crime Reports?
- What other serious crimes present a challenge to law enforcement?
- What the most common types of white-collar crime are?
- What four key characteristics of computer-related crime are?
- What two characteristics of organized crime set it apart from other crimes committed by a group of individuals?
- What types of bias may be involved in hate crimes?
- What the classical and the positivist theories of crime causation state?
- What some causes of crime are?
- When violent offending is most likely to begin and with what group of offenders?
- What groups of people are most likely and least likely to become victims of crime?
- How crime affects its victims?
- What second victimization may occur?
- What victims' rights may involve them in the criminal justice system?

Can You Define?

arson
assault
battery
burglary
carjacking
classical theory
criminal sexual conduct
dark figure of crime
delinquency
determinism
direct victims
8% problem
first-degree murder
homicide
identity theft
indirect victims
justifiable homicide
larceny-theft
manslaughter
motor vehicle theft
murder
negligent homicide
organized crime
phishing
positivist theory
primary victims
rape
recidivist
ritualistic crime
robbery
secondary victims
second-degree murder
skimming
spoofing
status offenses
victim impact statement (VIS)
victim statement of opinion (VSO)
white-collar crime
xenophobia

INTRODUCTION

Crime is more than laws and cases. Crime involves hurtful acts committed by individuals against other individuals or their property. Until recently, however, crimes have been examined as acts against the state and prosecuted as such. This is changing. Whether it is called restorative justice, balanced justice or community justice, the system is beginning to view criminals, victims and society as all equally affected by criminal acts.

THE CHAPTER AT A GLANCE

This chapter begins with a description of the major sources of information on crime and offers cautions on interpreting crime statistics. This is followed by classification and definition of major crimes including homicide, assault, rape and robbery; crimes against property, including burglary, larceny-theft, motor vehicle theft and arson; and crimes that are less serious in either their use of violence or the value of the property involved. Next those who commit crimes are briefly described, including a discussion of why people commit crime. The final major discussion is about those affected by crime—the victims. The chapter concludes with a discussion of police officers as victims themselves.

SOURCES OF INFORMATION ON CRIME

Several sources of information about crime are available.

The most frequently used sources of information about crime are *official government statistics*, self-report surveys and the media.

For criminal justice professionals, the most authoritative sources of information about crime in the United States are official sources, and even these sources are not without problems.

Official Sources

Two of the most frequently consulted official sources of crime data are those compiled by the Federal Bureau of Investigation (FBI) and the Bureau of Justice Statistics (BJS).

The FBI's Uniform Crime Reports and National Incident-Based Reporting System (NIBRS) Information about crime comes from statistics gathered from around the country. In 1930 Congress assigned the FBI to serve as a national clearinghouse for crime statistics. The FBI's National Crime Information Center (NCIC) instituted a program called the Uniform Crime Reports (UCR) to collect offense information for the Part I offenses of murder and nonnegligent manslaughter, forcible rape, robbery, aggravated assault, burglary, larceny-theft and motor vehicle theft. In 1978 arson was added to the list as a Part I reportable offense.

The FBI's Uniform Crime Reports contain statistics on violent crimes (murder, aggravated assault causing serious bodily harm, forcible rape, robbery) and property crimes (burglary, larceny-theft, motor vehicle theft and arson).

The UCR Program also collects arrest data on Part I offenses and 21 other crimes that comprise the Part II offenses, such as driving under the influence. The annual publication of this program, *Crime in the United States*, reports that in 2009 more than 17,000 law enforcement agencies serving 295 million inhabitants, or 96.3 percent of U.S. citizens, contributed data to the FBI either directly or through state UCR programs.

The UCR holds the unique position of being the "sole national source of official law enforcement statistics" (Barnett-Ryan and Swanson, 2008, p.18). Over the years the UCR has developed into a broad utility for summary-based reporting of crime. The Part I crimes were considered by experts of the time to be the most serious and most commonly reported crimes occurring in the United States, as well as the most likely to occur with sufficient frequency to provide an adequate basis for comparison. As such, from 1960 to 2004, the eight Part I crimes served as a collective Crime Index, a general snapshot of offenses occurring throughout the country used to gauge fluctuations in the volume and rate of crime reported to law enforcement.

However, by the late 1970s the law enforcement community saw a need for a more-detailed crime-reporting program to meet the needs of law enforcement in the 21st century. One of the primary criticisms of the UCR Index program was that it used a *hierarchy system* in which only the most serious offense in an incident was recorded. For example, if an individual was beaten and robbed, UCR would record only one offense—the assault; the robbery would go unrecorded. Also, in recent years, the Crime Index has not been a true indicator of the degree of criminality of a locality. For example, larceny-thefts currently account for almost 60 percent of the total crimes reported. Consequently the volume of larcenies overshadows more serious but less frequently committed crimes.

Because of these numerous shortcomings, in June 2004 the FBI's Criminal Justice Information Services (CJIS) Division, Advisory Policy Board (APB), approved discontinuing the use of the Crime Index in the UCR Program and its publications. The CJIS APB recommended that the FBI publish a violent crime total and a property crime total until a more viable index is developed.

A summary of the figures for these crimes committed in 2008 is depicted in the Crime Clock (Figure 3.1). The Crime Clock should be viewed with care. Being

2008 Crime Clock

Every 22.8 seconds	**One violent crime**
Every 32.3 minutes	One murder
Every 5.9 minutes	One forcible rape
Every 1.2 minutes	One robbery
Every 37.8 seconds	One aggravated assault
Every 3.2 seconds	**One property crime**
Every 14.2 seconds	One burglary
Every 4.8 seconds	One larceny-theft
Every 33.0 seconds	One motor vehicle theft

FIGURE 3.1 The Crime Clock 2008. The Crime Clock should be viewed with care. The most aggregate representation of UCR data, it conveys the annual reported crime experience by showing a relative frequency of occurrence of Part I offenses. It should not be taken to imply a regularity in the commission of crime. The Crime Clock represents the annual ratio of crime to fixed time intervals.

SOURCE: Department of Justice, Federal Bureau of Investigation. Retrieved from http://ovc.ncjrs.gov/ncvrw2008/pdf/crime_clock_hr.pdf

the most aggregate representation of UCR data, it is designed to convey the annual reported crime experience by showing the relative frequency of occurrence of the Index crimes. This graphic does not imply a regularity in the commission of offenses; rather it represents the annual ratio of crime to fixed time intervals. The most recent UCR figures are available online at http://www.fbi.gov/ucr/ucr.htm.

Efforts to redesign and modernize the UCR program resulted in development of the NIBRS in 1988. Intended to supplement or replace the summary data of the UCR and enhance crime analysis capabilities, the NIBRS collects detailed incident information on 46 offenses representing 22 categories of crimes (see Table 3.1), including offenses related to domestic violence, use of guns, hate crimes and terrorism. A special issue of *Justice and Research Policy* (Fall 2007) focused on research using the NIBRS and concluded the new system "provides significant potential for the study of crime" (Faggiani, 2007, p.2).

TABLE 3.1 The National Incident-Based Reporting System Group A Offenses

- Arson
- Assault offenses
  - Aggravated assault
  - Simple assault
  - Intimidation
- Bribery
- Burglary/breaking and entering
- Counterfeiting/forgery
- Destruction/damage/vandalism of property
- Drug/narcotic offenses
  - Drug/narcotic violations
  - Drug equipment violations
- Embezzlement
- Extortion/blackmail
- Fraud offenses
  - False pretenses/swindle/confidence game
  - Credit card/ATM fraud
  - Impersonation
  - Welfare fraud
  - Wire fraud
- Gambling offenses
  - Betting/wagering
  - Operating/promoting/assisting gambling
  - Gambling equipment violations
  - Sports tampering
- Homicide offenses
  - Murder/nonnegligent manslaughter
  - Negligent manslaughter
  - Justifiable homicide
- Kidnapping/abduction
- Larceny/theft offenses
  - Pocket picking
  - Purse snatching
  - Shoplifting
  - Theft from building
  - Theft from coin-operated machines
  - Theft from motor vehicle
  - Theft of motor vehicle parts/accessories
  - All other larceny
- Motor vehicle theft
- Pornography/obscene material
- Prostitution offenses
  - Prostitution
  - Assisting or promoting prostitution
- Robbery
- Sex offenses, forcible
  - Forcible rape
  - Forcible sodomy
  - Sexual assault with an object
  - Forcible fondling
- Sex offenses, nonforcible
- Stolen property offenses
- Weapon law violations

SOURCE: Brian A. Reaves. *Using NIBRS Data to Analyze Violent Crime.* Washington, DC: Bureau of Justice Statistics Technical Report, October 1993, p.1.

Despite the NIBRS expanded analysis capabilities, it has been slow to be accepted at the state and local levels, with cost cited as a major factor. In 2009 more than 7,900 agencies submitted NIBRS data, representing 28 percent of the U.S. population and 44 percent of crime statistics collected by the FBI (*Crime in the United States, 2009*).

As agencies change from the summary reporting system to NIBRS, they have called on many vendors to develop a system that complies with the UCR Program standards yet accommodates their agency's unique requirements. To assist in these efforts the FBI periodically publishes *State Program Bulletins*, which are updated as needed ("Developments in the National Incident-Based Reporting System," June 2009).

One reason departments may be reluctant to switch to NIBRS is that they will doubtless see a significant increase in crime statistics, even though actual crime may, in fact, be decreasing.

The Bureau of Justice Statistics National Crime Victimization Survey The BJS National Crime Victimization Survey (NCVS) began in 1973 and gathers information on personal crime experience through interviews with approximately 160,000 people age 12 years and older in 86,000 households nationwide. The survey collects data on crimes against individuals and households, regardless of whether the offenses were reported to law enforcement. The data from this representative sample is then extrapolated to estimate the proportion of each crime type reported to law enforcement and details reasons given for reporting or not reporting.

The NCVS collects detailed information on the frequency and nature of the crimes of rape, personal robbery, aggravated and simple assault, household burglary, personal and household theft, and motor vehicle theft. The survey provides information about victims' age, sex, race, ethnicity, marital status, income and educational level; their offenders' sex, race, approximate age and victim–offender relationship; and the crimes—time and place of occurrence, use of weapons, nature of injury and economic consequences. Questions also cover the victims' experiences with the criminal justice system, self-protective measures used and possible substance abuse by offenders.

The UCR and NCVS Compared The UCR and NCVS differ significantly. As noted, the NCVS projects crime levels from a selected source of information and reports a substantially higher number of crimes than those reported in the UCR. Some analysts believe that neither report is accurate and that true crime is two to five times higher than either source reports.

The UCR captures crimes reported to law enforcement but excludes simple assaults. The NCVS includes crimes both reported and not reported to law enforcement but excludes homicide, arson, commercial crimes and crimes against children under age 12 (all included in the UCR program). Even when the same crimes are included in the UCR and NCVS, the definitions vary.

Another difference is how rate measures are presented. The UCR crime rates are largely per capita (number of crimes per 100,000 persons), whereas the NCVS rates are per household (number of crimes per 1,000 households). Because the number of households may not grow at the same rate as the total population, trend data for rates measured by the two programs may not be compatible. Table 3.2 compares UCR and NCVS data gathering.

TABLE 3.2 A Comparison of the UCR and the NCVS

	Uniform Crime Reports	National Crime Victimization Survey
Offenses measured:	Homicide Rape Robbery (personal and commercial) Assault (aggravated) Burglary (commercial and household) Larceny (commercial and household) Motor vehicle theft Arson	Rape Robbery (personal) Assault (aggravated and simple) Household burglary Larceny (personal and household) Motor vehicle theft
Scope:	Crimes reported to the police in most jurisdictions; considerable flexibility in developing small-area data	Crimes both reported and not reported to police; all data are available for a few large geographic areas
Collection method:	Police department reports to FBI or to centralized state agencies that then report to FBI	Survey interviews; periodically measures the total number of crimes committed by asking a national sample of 49,000 households encompassing 101,000 persons age 12 and over about their experiences as victims of crime during a specified period
Kinds of information:	In addition to offense counts, provides information on crime clearances, persons arrested, persons charged, law enforcement officers killed and assaulted and characteristics of homicide victims	Provides details about victims (such as age, race, sex, education, income and whether the victim and offender were related to each other) and about crimes (such as time and place of occurrence, whether or not reported to police, use of weapons, occurrence of injury and economic consequences)
Sponsor:	Department of Justice Federal Bureau of Investigation	Department of Justice Bureau of Justice Statistics

SOURCE: Bureau of Justice Statistics. *Report to the Nation on Crime and Justice*, 2nd ed. Washington, DC: U.S. Department of Justice, 1988, p.11.

A Caution Be mindful of several limitations present when interpreting crime data. Official statistics reflect only reported crimes, and these reports are voluntary and vary in accuracy and completeness. In addition, not all police departments submit crime reports, and federal crimes are not included. Furthermore, it is estimated that less than half the crimes committed are reported to the police. The true number of crimes, called the **dark figure of crime**, is unknown.

dark figure of crime

The actual, unknown number of crimes being committed.

Another caution: Any large-scale data collection program has many possible sources of error, and many variables can affect the accuracy and outcome of crime reports. For example in the UCR program, a police officer may classify a crime incorrectly; and in the NCVS, a Census Bureau interviewer may incorrectly record a victim's response. Crime data is also affected by how victims perceive and recall events. In addition clerical errors may occur at any stage. Both programs have extensive accuracy checks to minimize errors. Despite these difficulties police departments make frequent use of the information from the UCR program. Another source of information is self-report surveys.

Self-Report Surveys

Self-report studies are used by sociologists and criminologists to determine the extent of crime and deviance. Self-report studies were introduced into criminology in the 1940s and 1950s to balance the FBI data, which focused primarily on street crimes to the exclusion of white-collar crime and minor forms of delinquency. Most self-report studies involve confidential questionnaires with respondents voluntarily recording whether or not they have committed any of the listed offenses and, if so, when and how often.

Most self-report studies show that criminal acts are much more common than official statistics indicate, sometimes twice as prevalent. For example, the Rape, Abuse and Incest National Network (RAINN) estimates that 60 percent of sexual assaults are not reported to police. Self-report studies also show that crimes are spread throughout the population, with official differences between male and female or working and middle class rates far smaller than official statistics would suggest.

Self-report surveys are typically conducted with school-age youths. For example, the *Sourcebook of Criminal Justice Statistics* includes such information as high school seniors reporting involvement in selected delinquent activities in the past 12 months, involvement with drugs and alcohol, and involvement in traffic violations.

Comparing self-report surveys with court data sometimes yields different conclusions from comparing them with research based on official records. Self-reports usually produce a much higher incidence of criminal offending than official (court) records, as shown in Table 3.3.

Self-report surveys are not without their problems. Answers may be unreliable because respondents may lie or exaggerate, be embarrassed, forget about incidents, or be fearful that the survey is not truly anonymous and they will be caught if they report involvement in crime. The selection of offenses may be biased, revealing trivial or uncommon offenses, or ignoring middle class crime. The selection of interviewees may also be biased, with researchers unable to access certain categories of offenses. Many self-report studies involve "captive audiences" such as school age students or prisoners. Despite these shortcomings, self-report data appears acceptably valid and reliable for most research purposes (Thornberry and Krohn, 2000, p.34).

A third source of information about crime and delinquency is the media.

The Media

Much of what the public knows about crime comes from the media, which may overdramatize and distort the true extent and seriousness of the problem. Study after study shows that the media focuses on crime and violence to the neglect of other aspects of law enforcement. As the adage states, "If it bleeds, it leads."

Moore (2007, p.106) observes, "Over the past few years the growing antipathy between law enforcement and the media has turned into the 800-pound gorilla in the room. . . . Reporters bring their biases and political agendas to their jobs, just like everyone else. And many media outlets are dominated by factions that look upon police and the military with suspicion and, sometimes, outright hostility."

A political reporter and television news anchor, Putney, suggests, "I think that you in policing and those of us in the media are doing this strange dance together, and each of us believes that we are leading, and that makes for some awkward

TABLE 3.3 Prevalence and Frequency of Offending: Court Records versus Self-Report

	Prevalence		Frequency	
	Court	**Self-Report**	**Court**	**Self-Report**
Age				
11	1.7	28.4	1.1	2.9
12	2.1	27.9	2.1	4.6
13	8.0	41.5	2.8	11.6
14	10.6	46.4	2.8	13.5
15	13.1	47.6	3.1	16.8
16	13.6	51.3	2.2	18.3
17	12.7	61.1	2.4	21.8
Total	34.0	85.9	4.6	49.2
Offense Type				
Burglary	4.7	22.3	1.6	3.2
Vehicle theft	23.8	33.1	1.8	5.9
Larceny	25.6	66.1	2.0	11.6
Robbery	3.3	8.6	1.2	5.6
Assault	12.7	61.3	2.4	11.4
Vandalism	8.4	47.9	1.9	8.2
Marijuana use	1.8	49.1	1.2	29.9
Drug selling	3.9	21.7	1.6	28.8
Property	27.5	71.8	3.6	14.3
Aggressive	17.4	70.4	2.9	16.1
Drug	4.5	50.8	1.8	41.1

Notes: Prevalence = % offending; Frequency = Average offenses per offender.

SOURCE: David P. Farrington, Darrick Jolliffe, J. David Hawkins, Richard F. Catalano, Karl G. Hill, and Rick Kosterman. "Comparing Delinquency Careers in Court Records and Self-Reports." *Criminology*, August 2003, p.941. Reprinted by permission.

moments" ("Reporters Offer PERF Chiefs Hard-Boiled View," 2008, p.5). The basic, unavoidable conflict is that the First Amendment protects the media in reporting—protecting the public's "right to know." Law enforcement, on the other hand, must protect the Sixth Amendment and the defendant's right to a fair trial, which includes maintaining investigative integrity by not giving out certain vital information that might jeopardize the case. Despite this inherent constitutionally based conflict, a police-media partnership benefits the common goal of public safety.

> In reality, police and reporters have a lot in common. Both law enforcement agencies and the media are highly visible, powerful institutions. Both professions attract ambitious, strong-minded employees who possess a strong sense of justice and a desire to help others. Both professions are frequently criticized by the public they serve and are highly sensitive to that criticism. The professionals of both can be highly defensive and feel that they are poorly understood by their critics. Both

> professions are sometimes secretive about their operations and their methods for gathering information. Professionals in both endeavors see themselves as vital to the public welfare.
>
> As successful leaders in both law enforcement and journalism can relate, both sides can win in the police-media relationship. Getting along is much more rewarding than fighting. Each field of work has a lot to offer the other. (Garner, 2009, p.52)

Law enforcement agencies are the best source of crime news and of the news the public is interested in. The media can help law enforcement educate residents to protect themselves and can warn them of imminent dangers, as well as report on the good work being done by law enforcement.

Research conducted by Montana State University in 2006 reveals numerous misperceptions on the part of the law enforcement community and indicated overwhelming support for police officers and their efforts to reduce crime and keep neighborhoods safe (Tooley et al., 2009, p.63). On the street, however, it is easy for officers to believe that the opposite is true, because they generally do not come into contact with the supportive segment of the population. The same research indicates that many police officers do, in fact, feel distrusted and unappreciated by the public. In this study, 77 percent of respondents said media coverage of law enforcement agencies did not change their opinion of police officers one way or another (Tooley et al., p.65). Of the remainder, more people gained a more positive view of law enforcement through the media than a negative view, numbers that "run totally counter to the perceptions of many law enforcement officers."

Regardless of the format used to obtain information on crime, the crimes must be defined and classified.

CLASSIFICATION AND DEFINITIONS OF MAJOR CRIMES

The FBI classifies the major crimes as violent crimes (formerly crimes against persons) and property crimes.

Violent Crime

A surge in violent crime began in 2005 and continued in 2006, ending the historic drop in the U.S. crime rate and marking the first significant increase in violent crime since the early 1990s. Reasons given for this "crime wave" included a rise in gang activity, violent offenders who returned from prison, youths with easy access to guns as well as an overall decrease in funding for police, whose resources were stretched thin by increased mandates to protect against terrorism and other national security threats.

In August 2006 the Police Executive Research Forum (PERF) held a National Violent Crime Summit to discuss the "gathering storm" of violence in the United States. At this summit, Wexler contended that crime was at a "tipping point" in this country, and, as Chief Esserman of Providence, Rhode Island, stated, "We are turning the country over to our young people, and they are killing each other"

(*A Gathering Storm—Violent Crime in America*, 2006). Throughout the conference, participants referred to what Chief Flynn of Springfield, Massachusetts, termed "the monster that ate criminal justice—homeland security," which in his view jeopardized hometown security (p.12). However, in 2007 the violent crime rate dropped 1.8 percent; in 2008 it dropped 3.5 percent; and in 2009 it dropped an estimated 5.3 percent. These decreases occurred in all four of the violent crimes the FBI collects data on: murder (homicide), assault, rape and robbery (*Crime in the United States, 2009*).

murder
The willful killing of a human by another human; also called *homicide*.

homicide
The willful killing of a human by another human; also called *murder*.

first-degree murder
Willful, deliberate and premeditated (planned) taking of another person's life.

second-degree murder
The unpremeditated but intentional killing of another person.

manslaughter
Accidentally causing the death of another person; no malice or intent is involved.

negligent homicide
An accidental death that results from the reckless operation of a motor vehicle, boat, plane or firearm.

justifiable homicide
Includes killing in self-defense or in the defense of another person if the victim's actions and capability present imminent danger of serious injury or death.

assault
An unlawful attack by one person upon another for the purpose of inflicting severe bodily injury.

battery
Physical assault.

rape
Carnal knowledge of a woman or man through the use of force or the threat of force; also called *sexual assault*.

Murder (Homicide) **Murder** or **homicide** is defined in the UCR program as the willful (nonnegligent) killing of one human by another. The generally recognized levels of homicide are (1) first-degree, (2) second-degree, (3) manslaughter (or nonnegligent manslaughter) and (4) negligent homicide. The first three categories are classified as felonies.

First-degree murder is the willful, deliberate and premeditated (planned) taking of another person's life. **Second-degree murder** is *not* premeditated, but the intent to kill is present. In **manslaughter** the element of malice is absent; the death was accidental with no original intent, hatred, ill will or disregard for the lives of others. **Negligent homicide** refers to an accidental death resulting from the reckless operation of a motor vehicle, boat, plane or firearm. **Justifiable homicide** includes killing in self-defense or in the defense of another person. This classification includes killing an enemy during war, capital punishment, death caused by a public officer while carrying out a court order and deaths caused by police officers or citizens as a course of self-defense.

Assault **Assault** is the unlawful attack by one person on another for the purpose of inflicting severe bodily injury. Assaults are frequently committed in conjunction with rape and robbery. Some states have two distinct crimes, assault and battery. Where two crimes exist, assault refers to the threats made, whereas **battery** refers to any physical contact that occurs. If a state recognizes only one crime, it is usually assault, and battery is included within that crime. Assault may be aggravated or simple.

Rape **Rape** is having sexual intercourse through force or threat of force. Rape may be aggravated (the more violent offense), simple or statutory. *Statutory rape* involves sexual intercourse with a minor, with or without consent. Age of consent differs from state to state. The severity of this crime is often considered to be less if the offender and victim are close to the same age, with severity increasing as the age difference expands. Other factors, such as a position of authority, also contribute to the level of severity of this crime. **Criminal sexual conduct** (CSC) encompasses all sex crimes regulated by law, including rape and other minor sexually deviant related behaviors.

Robbery **Robbery** is taking anything of value from the care, custody or control of a person by force or threat of force. Many states divide robbery into degrees.

This violent crime often results in injury to the victim. Robbers may shoot, assault or torture their victims to find where valuables are located. Many victims who have refused to cooperate, and even some who have, have been ruthlessly killed.

The preferred weapon of most robbers is the handgun. Other weapons used include knives, baseball bats, acids and explosives. Armed robbers frequently attack drugstores (often for narcotics), supermarkets, liquor stores, jewelry stores, gas stations, banks, residential homes, cab drivers and pedestrians.

One form of robbery appeared late in 1990—**carjacking**, which is taking a motor vehicle by force or threat of force. Congress enacted the Carjacking Corrections Act of 1996 to establish strict penalties for people convicted of carjacking, with sentences up to 25 years in prison for cases involving "serious bodily injury" to a victim.

Crimes against Property

Like violent crime, property crimes have also decreased. Property crime decreased by 1.7 percent in 2007, by 4.1 percent in 2008, and by 6.1 percent (preliminary figures) in 2009, with a decrease in each of the four major crimes against property: burglary, larceny-theft, motor vehicle theft and arson. Although these crimes do not usually involve violence, they can leave their victims feeling violated and fearful.

Burglary **Burglary** is unlawful entrance into a building to commit theft or another felony. Burglary has three subclassifications: forcible entry, unlawful entry where no force is used and attempted forcible entry.

Larceny-Theft **Larceny-theft** is unlawfully taking and removing another's personal property with the intent of permanently depriving the owner of the property. It includes shoplifting, pocket picking, purse snatching, thefts from motor vehicles, thefts of motor vehicle parts and accessories, and bicycle thefts. The category does not include embezzlement, "con" games, forgery, passing worthless checks or motor vehicle theft.

Larceny-theft may be classified as either a misdemeanor or a felony. It differs from robbery in that it does not involve force, threats of force or violence. The severity of punishment usually depends on the value and type of property taken, whether it was taken from a building or a person and the specific circumstances of the case.

Some states categorize larceny into degrees. *Grand* and *petty larceny* are common identifications for the value of property taken and punishment imposed. First-, second- and third-degree larceny also indicate a certain minimum value of the property taken and various degrees of punishment. The most common type of theft is the theft of items from motor vehicles and motor vehicle parts and accessories, such as cell phones, stereos and CD/tape players, pagers, CB radios, clothing and photography equipment.

Other forms of larceny are thefts from underground garages where maintenance equipment, such as lawnmowers, snow blowers, lawn hoses and fertilizers, is the target. Bicycles are also targets for thieves. Thefts from coin-operated vending machines, pocket picking, purse snatching and shoplifting are other forms of larceny-theft.

Theft can refer to several different crimes, depending upon state statutes. It can describe a type of larceny, a theft from the person, a theft by force or a burglary. Table 3.4 summarizes the most commonly referred to forms of theft.

One of the country's fastest-growing crimes is **identity theft**, an offense involving misappropriation of names, social security numbers, credit card numbers or other pieces of personal information for fraudulent purposes. Identity theft became

---

criminal sexual conduct (CSC)
Encompasses all sex crimes regulated by law, including rape and other minor sexually deviant related behaviors.

robbery
Stealing anything of value from the care, custody or control of a person in his or her presence, by force or by the threat of force.

carjacking
Stealing a car from the driver by force.

burglary
An unlawful entry into a building to commit a theft or felony.

larceny-theft
The unlawful taking and removing of the property of another with the intent of permanently depriving the legal holder of the property.

identity theft
A crime involving misappropriation of names, social security numbers, credit card numbers or other pieces of personal information for fraudulent purposes.

TABLE 3.4 Forms of Taking and Types of Theft

Shoplifting (retail theft) or price altering
- Shoplifting—the most common form of theft in retail stores—is the taking by concealment to avoid payment for goods.
- Price altering avoids payment of the full price of an object by lowering the amount on the price tag.

Taking by employee, bailee or trustee
- Employee theft of money and other objects causes large losses in business places.
- Embezzlement of funds or negotiable securities that are in the custody of employees, bailees or trustees.

Snatch and run
- The taking is observed, and the offender flees to avoid apprehension.

Till tap
- Thief opens cash register unobserved and takes cash and coins.
- While store employee has cash drawer open, money is grabbed and the thief flees (snatch and run).

Taking by trick, deception or fraud (stings, scams or swindles)
- Con games and operations.
- Deceptions and tricks to obtain property illegally.
- Obtaining property by false pretense.

Taking by force, or the threat of the use of force (robbery)

Taking during a burglary (trespass with intent to steal or commit a felony)

Taking by extortion (threats of future violence or threats to reveal embarrassing information—blackmail)

Taking from a person
- Purse snatching (a form of snatch and run).
- Pickpocketing.
- Rolling a drunk (taking from person incapacitated by alcohol, drugs or other means).
- Taking from a corpse.

Taking of lost or mislaid goods or money

Taking of objects or money delivered by mistake
- Example: a check for too much money is mailed to a person by mistake.

Looting
- Taking property from or near a building damaged, destroyed or left unoccupied by tornado, fire, physical disaster, riot, bombing, earthquake and so on.

Taking by failure to return a leased or rented object
- Example: failure to return a rented car or videotape within the time specified by state statutes or city ordinance.

Taking by illegal entry into locked coin box
- Vending machine, pay telephone, parking meter and so on.

Smash and run
- A store or other window is broken, and after snatching objects, the thief runs to avoid apprehension.
- Women drivers waiting at stoplights are sometimes subjected to this tactic. The thief breaks the car window, takes the woman's purse from the front seat and runs.[1]

Taking by illegally obtaining or using information
- Such as in the "insider trading" scandals. See the 1987 U.S. Supreme Court case of *Carpenter v. United States*, 108 S.Ct. 316. One of the defendants in the case was the coauthor of a *Wall Street Journal* column.

Taking by illegal use of a credit card or credit card number

Taking from a person with a superior right of possession
- People may acquire a superior right of possession over the owner of property because of a bailment, pledge or contract. State criminal codes may make taking from a person with a superior right of possession a crime.

Theft by possession of stolen property
- See 832 P.2d 337 (Idaho, 1992), 473 N.W.2d 84 (Nebraska, 1991) and 419 S.E.2d 759 (Georgia, 1992).

Ordinary theft
- Taking occurs observed or unobserved by owner or other people.

[1] The "bump" technique is also used. An expensive car with only a driver occupant is usually picked as the victim. While the victim is waiting at a stoplight, the victim's car is bumped intentionally. When the victim gets out of the car to view damages, one of the thieves distracts him or her while the other thief sneaks around to get into the victim's car. Because the victim generally leaves the keys in the ignition, the thief drives off in the victim's car. The other thief jumps in his or her car and also speeds away, leaving the victim stranded.

SOURCE: Thomas J. Gardner and Terry M. Anderson. *Criminal Law*, 9th ed. Belmont, CA: Wadsworth Publishing Company, 2006, p.305. Reprinted by permission.

a federal crime in the United States in 1998 with passage of the Identity Theft Assumption and Deterrence Act: "Identity theft was the number one consumer complaint made to the Federal Trade Commission [in 2006]. It affected more than eight million Americans and cost nearly $50 billion" (Spadanuta, 2007, p.18). In 2008 9.9 million Americans were identity theft victims, an increase of 22 percent over 2007 (Kanable, 2009, p.28). It is estimated that one in four people in the United States will become victims of this crime (Barton and Higgins, 2008, p.14).

Identity theft is both a high-tech and low-tech crime. Offenders can intercept mail with personal identifying information on it, such as social security numbers, bank account numbers and the like. Waiters, retail clerks, gas station attendants and other service personnel can steal credit and debit card numbers either manually or by **skimming**, using a small, portable device that copies and stores data from such cards' magnetic strips. At ATM machines, a skimmer can be inserted into the slot where customers insert their cards; the device is virtually undetectable and can allow the offender to drain the victim's account after the victim has completed their transaction and left the scene.

skimming

Using a small, portable device that copies and stores data from debit and credit cards' magnetic strips.

Identity theft can have a devastating impact on individuals, with victims suffering not only financial loss but also severe and long-lasting damage to their credit scores and personal reputations, and possibly being arrested for crimes they did not commit (Keenan and O'Neal, 2007, p.32). The average time it takes to restore an identity once it has been compromised is 264 hours (Kanable, 2009).

Motor Vehicle Theft **Motor vehicle theft** is the unlawful taking or stealing of a motor vehicle without the owner's authority or permission. Motor vehicles include automobiles, trucks, buses, motorcycles, motorized boats and aircraft. The economic impact of motor vehicle theft can be great, with drivers absorbing such losses through higher insurance premiums.

motor vehicle theft

The unlawful taking or stealing of a motor vehicle without the authority or permission of the owner; includes automobiles, trucks, buses, motorcycles, motorized boats and aircraft.

One motive for auto theft is joyriding—the car is stolen for entertainment, taken for a ride and then abandoned. Autos are also stolen for revenge, for transportation, for commercial use and for use in committing other crimes, such as kidnapping, burglary and bank robbery. Autos are stolen and stripped for parts such as transmissions, engines, rims and seats. Automobiles are also stolen, modified, given altered serial numbers and fraudulent titles, and sold to an unsuspecting public.

Arson **Arson** is intentionally damaging or destroying, or attempting to damage or destroy, by means of fire or explosion the property of another without the consent of the owner or one's own property, with or without the intent to defraud: "Arson is a crime punishable in a court of law, regardless of the motive behind it, be it revenge, peer-pressured vandalism, criminal concealment, insurance fraud, extreme activists or simple boredom" (Manley, 2008). It is a felony in all 50 states. Arson has increased more than 400 percent in the past 10 years. FEMA reports an estimated 30,500 intentionally set structure fires occurred in 2008, resulting in 315 civilian deaths and $866,000,000 in property loss. In addition, 17,500 intentionally set vehicle fires occurred, causing $139,000,000 in property damage ("Intentionally Set Structure Fires," 2010).

arson

Intentionally damaging or destroying, or attempting to damage or destroy, by means of fire or explosion the property of another without the consent of the owner or one's own property, with or without the intent to defraud.

One of the most serious problems often encountered in arson investigations is the joint jurisdiction of firefighters and law enforcement officers. All too frequently this results in duplication of effort and inefficiency.

Crimes Excluded from the UCR

Several other crimes can be either misdemeanors or felonies. They include counterfeiting, curfew violations (juveniles), disorderly conduct, driving under the influence (DUI), drug abuse violations, drunkenness, embezzlement, forgery, fraud (confidence games, etc.), gambling, liquor law violations (bootlegging, etc.), loitering (juveniles), offenses against the family and children (child abuse, neglect, nonsupport), other assaults (intimidation, coercion, hazing, etc.), prostitution and commercialized vice, runaways (juveniles), sex offenses (except forcible rape, prostitution and commercialized vice), stolen property (buying, receiving, possessing), vagrancy, vandalism, weapons violations (carrying, possessing, etc.) and many other offenses (bigamy, contempt of court; the list goes on and on).

Other serious crimes include white-collar crime, computer-related crime, organized crime, bias or hate crime and ritualistic crime.

white-collar crime

Occupational or business-related crime; also called *economic crime*.

White-Collar Crime **White-collar crime** is occupational or business-related crime. The term *white-collar* crime was reportedly coined in 1939 by Sutherland and has become synonymous with the full range of frauds committed by business and government professionals ("White-Collar Crime," n.d.). In the "age of Bernie Madoff" and the economic crisis, the FBI has revived its priority on white-collar crime, with pending FBI investigations of mortgage fraud increasing 71 percent from fiscal year (FY) 2008 to FY 2009 and the collection of $199 million in fines from corporate criminals in FY 2008 ("Financial Crimes Report to the Public," 2009).

In the wake of the recent wave of corporate wrongdoing, research has focused on whether the public is concerned about controlling crime in the business world. One study found that a sizeable majority of Americans (77.7 percent) strongly support getting tough on corporate illegality, including stricter penalties, longer prison terms and higher fines for corporate executives who conceal their company's true financial condition (Unnever et al., 2008, p.177). The analysis also found group differences in public support for punitive corporate crime policies: "Although liberals and conservatives equally support punishing corporate criminals more harshly, African Americans are more likely than Whites to endorse more restrictive and more punitive policies toward corporate criminals" (Unnever et al., 2008, p.163).

A study of the perceived seriousness of white-collar versus street (the UCR) crimes found that, in four of six comparisons, white-collar crimes were perceived to be more serious than street crimes, with the remaining two comparisons perceiving white-collar crimes to be equally serious as street crimes (Piquero et al., 2008, pp.305–306). Almost two-thirds of the sample (65 percent) thought that the resources allocated to dealing with white-collar crime should be at least—if not more than—that which is spent on street crime.

In addition to corporate crime, larceny-theft and some of the other offenses can also be classified as white-collar crimes. These crimes often involve billions of dollars and pose an extremely difficult challenge to law enforcement officers. In recent years several agencies, including the FBI, U.S. Secret Service and American Society for Industrial Security (ASIS), have renamed this category of crime to reflect a change in scope, now referring to it as *economic crime*. To help fight white-collar crime the National White Collar Crime Center (NW3C) bridges the gap between local and state criminal justice agencies and links criminal justice agencies across international borders.

White-collar crime includes (1) credit card and check fraud including identity theft; (2) securities theft and fraud; (3) insurance fraud; (4) consumer fraud, illegal competition and deceptive practices; (5) bankruptcy fraud; (6) embezzlement and pilferage; (7) bribes, kickbacks and payoffs; (8) money laundering; and (9) receiving stolen property.

The FBI's Financial Crimes Section (FCS) investigates matters related to fraud, theft or embezzlement occurring within or against the national or international financial community. It concentrates on such crimes as corporate fraud; health care fraud; mortgage fraud; identity theft; insurance, telemarketing and investment fraud; bankruptcy fraud; hedge fund fraud; and money laundering. Identity theft is included in the FBI's economic crime priorities, illustrating the overlap in many offenses and the difficulty in cleanly classifying some offenses.

One valuable resource for local law enforcement is the NW3C. This center has served law enforcement for a quarter century, providing nationwide support for state and local enforcement agencies involved in preventing, investigating and prosecuting high-tech and economic crimes. The NW3C has partnered with the FBI to establish the Internet Crime Complaint Center (IC3) to investigate computer-related crime. Its 2008 Annual Report stated a record high of 275,284 complaints, a 33.1 percent increase over 2007, with a total dollar loss linked to online fraud of $265 million ("Complaints of Online Crime," 2009). Its 2009 annual report cited another record high of 327,251 online complaints (*NW3C Annual Report July 2008–June 2009*, p.8).

Computer-Related Crime Most big corporations have been victims of computer-related crime, from employees' snooping through confidential files to criminals stealing trade secrets. The most common crimes are credit card fraud, telecommunications fraud, employee use of computers for personal reasons, unauthorized access to confidential files and unlawful copying of copyrighted or licensed software. Although a large portion of cybercrime is committed internally by employees, companies and private users are finding themselves increasingly vulnerable to outside hackers.

Computer fraud may involve the input data, the output data, computer time or the program itself. *Input data* may be altered; for example, fictitious suppliers may be entered, figures may be changed or data may be removed. Some schools have experienced difficulties with student grades being illegally changed. *Output data* may be obtained by unauthorized persons through such means as wiretapping, electromagnetic pickup or theft of data sheets. *Computer time* may be taken for personal use, an example of pilferage. Some employees have even used their employer's hardware and company time to set up their own computer services for personal profit. The *computer program* itself might be tampered with to add costs to purchased items or to establish a double set of records. Compounding the challenge is the fact that most computer crime is not reported.

Through technology, computers allow offenders to gain access to victims and can be used to violate restraining orders, harassment orders and other orders for protection in which contact between offender and victim is legally prohibited. One area of computer crime that is becoming more publicized is sex-related computer crimes, including child pornography and contact leading to harassment, molestation and other variants of victimization. The Internet has generated an explosion in the prevalence of child pornography and the pursuit of children by online predators. The privacy and anonymity of the Internet makes it ideal for offenders seeking children for sex.

Several entities have been created to address the emerging threat to children and challenge to law enforcement presented by online victimization. The National

Center for Missing and Exploited Children (NCMEC), with support from the Office of Juvenile Justice and Delinquency Prevention (OJJDP), serves as the nation's resource center for child protection and operates both the Cyber Tipline and the Child Pornography Tipline. The Cyber Tipline, a reporting mechanism for child sexual exploitation, has handled more than 440,000 leads, with a staggering 1,452 percent increase in tips from 1998 to 2005 (Collins, 2007, p.40).

In 1998 the NCMEC initiated the Internet Crimes Against Children (ICAC) task force program to help state and local law enforcement agencies acquire the skills, equipment and personnel resources necessary to respond to online offenses against children. Since then, 46 federally funded task forces on Internet crimes against children have formed, with 7,328 arrests made as a result of task force investigations over seven years (Collins, 2007).

The FBI's Innocent Images National Initiative (IINI), founded in 1995 as part of their Cyber Crimes Program, is an intelligence-driven, proactive, multiagency investigative operation to combat the proliferation of child pornography/sexual exploitation facilitated by online computers. According to their Web site, "Innocent Images grew exponentially between fiscal years 1996 and 2007, with a 2,062 percent increase in cases opened; 1,003 percent increase in information and indictments; a 2,501 percent increase in arrests, locates and summons; and a 1,404 percent increase in convictions and pretrial diversions" ("Innocent Images National Initiative," 2007).

The FBI has also established a Computer Analysis and Response Team (CART) that provides assistance to FBI field offices in searching and seizing computer evidence as well as forensic examinations and technical support for FBI investigation ("Computer Analysis and Response Team," 2000). The FBI has published *Electronic Crime Scene Investigations: A Guide for First Responders*, second edition (2008) to assist local and state law enforcement agencies.

In addition to efforts by the FBI, the Department of Homeland Security is also involved in curbing cybercrime and has developed a *National Strategy to Secure Cyberspace* (2003):

> Our nation's critical infrastructures are composed of public and private institutions in the sectors of agriculture, food, water, public health, emergency services, government, defense industrial base, information and telecommunications, energy, transportation, banking and finance, chemicals and hazardous materials, and postal and shipping, Cyberspace is their nervous system—the control system of our country. Cyberspace is composed of hundreds of thousands of interconnected computers, servers, routers, switches, and fiber optic cables that allow our critical infrastructures to work. Thus, the healthy functioning of cyberspace is essential to our economy and our national security. . . . Securing cyberspace is a difficult strategic challenge that requires coordinated and focused effort from our entire society—the federal government, state and local governments, the private sector, and the American people.

Another major consideration in discussing computer crimes is that it often crosses jurisdictional, even national, boundaries. On the World Wide Web, criminals can commit crimes from any location in the world, with the victim and offender located in entirely different countries. Thus it is necessary to work with foreign law enforcement agencies to fight this crime and find a resolution.

No matter what type of computer crime is involved, some common characteristics are usually found.

Characteristics of computer-related crime include
- They are relatively easy to commit.
- They are relatively difficult to detect.
- They are most often committed by insiders.
- They are most often not prosecuted.

Other sites and services allow computer-crime victims themselves to get more directly involved in the war on cybercrime. One example is the Internet Fraud Complaint Center (IFCC), created by the FBI and the NW3C.

Another resource is the Cyber Incident Detection Data Analysis Center (CIDDAC), a cyber-threat reporting system centralizing information from participating organizations in response to the 9/11 attack on the United States. This nonprofit, private sector organization connects those who join CIDDAC to "Real-time Cyber Attack Detection Sensors" (RCADSs) on their computer networks. If these networks are attacked, the sensors instantly send valuable forensic data to the CIDDAC operations center for analysis. CIDDAC personnel monitor the situation, analyze the data and immediately send information to their cyber investigators and to the Department of Homeland Security. This organization recognizes that cyber criminals can, and have, attacked major infrastructures—hospitals, water systems, power grids, banks, 911 services, universities, transportation systems and the like. Given that eighty-five percent of these infrastructures are owned by private industry, it is critical to have real-time attack data from these agencies and organizations.

The National Crime Prevention Council has also entered the fight against computer crime with its "Take a Bite Out of Cyber Crime" campaign. McGruff, the well-known crime dog, will be "Guarding the Home Net," training thousands of Junior Cyber Guards to spot and report cyber crime in homes and businesses across America (*"Take a Bite Out of Cyber Crime" Campaign*, 2006).

Adding to the importance of computer crime is that information vital to solving other cases and obtaining convictions is turning up in computer systems, on the Internet and in portable, digital computing devices. For example, information found on computers has been highly valuable in investigations of organized crime.

Organized Crime Organized crime goes by many names—the mob, the syndicate, the rackets, the Mafia and La Cosa Nostra. A basic definition of **organized crime** is a continuing criminal conspiracy seeking high profits with an organized structure that uses fear and corruption.

organized crime
A continuing criminal conspiracy seeking high profits with an organized structure that uses fear and corruption.

Organized crime is distinct from other forms of crime in that it is characterized by corruption and enforcement powers.

These features make organized crime especially threatening, not only to the police but also to our entire democratic process.

The FBI's Organized Crime Program's mission is to eliminate criminal enterprises that pose the greatest threat to American society. To accomplish the mission the FBI has the following units: the La Cosa Nostra/Italian Organized Crime/Labor Racketeering Unit, the Eurasian Organized Crime Unit and the Asian/African Criminal Enterprise Unit (*Organized Crime*, n.d.).

Organized crime is particularly challenging to law enforcement because of the numerous types of groups involved. The President's Commission on Organized Crime has identified 11 different groups: La Cosa Nostra (Italian); outlaw motorcycle gangs; prison gangs; Triads and Tongs (Chinese); Vietnamese gangs; Yakuza (Japanese); Marielitos (Cuban); Colombian cocaine rings; and Irish, Russian and Canadian cartels. Despite the various and distinct origins of organized crime groups, many of them participate in the same activities, including heavy involvement in gambling, drugs, prostitution, pornography, loan sharking and infiltration of legitimate businesses—anything that offers the potential for high profits. For example, La Cosa Nostra (LCN), the most well-known organized crime faction currently operating in the United States, is involved in drug trafficking, extortion, illegal gambling, money laundering, murder, obstruction of justice and a variety of financial fraud schemes.

Russian organized crime (ROC) is a growing threat in the United States and may present law enforcement with its toughest challenge yet. ROC engages in money-laundering facilities and trafficking in humans (women and children sold as sex slaves and indentured household servants). ROC is also extensively involved in a variety of frauds and scams, including health care fraud, insurance scams, antiquities swindles, forgery and tax evasion schemes. Threatening and using violence are defining characteristics of Russian organized crime. Contract murders, kidnappings and arson are also commonly used.

Most organized crime groups have their hands in the drug trade. For many such organizations, drug trafficking is their economic mainstay. Another challenge for law enforcement is found in the partnering of different organizations for profit in illegal narcotics. In addition, Internet fraud, called **phishing** or **spoofing**, is rising and is often linked to organized crime groups. In phishing or spoofing, criminals use technology to misrepresent themselves and mask their true identity from others, in an attempt to acquire personal or financial gain. Spoofing is a crime. Eastern European crime gangs are increasingly involved in phishing scams, most frequently some form of identity theft.

phishing
A form of Internet fraud; also called *spoofing*.

spoofing
Uses technology to misrepresent a criminal and mask his or her true identity from others, in an attempt to acquire personal or financial gain; also called *phishing*.

Many contend that the public and government play active roles in perpetuating organized crime and are sometimes directly responsible for creating opportunities that allow such enterprises to thrive. Politicians and the citizens they serve must take an active stance against organized crime by discontinuing their associations with these entities. Yet another area of concern for law enforcement is the dramatic increase in bias or hate crimes.

Hate Crimes The FBI defines a *bias* or *hate crime* as a criminal offense committed against a person, property or society motivated, in whole or in part, by the offender's bias against a race, religion, disability, sexual orientation or ethnic/national origin. Hate is divided into two general categories: rational and irrational. Unjust acts may cause rational hate. Hate based on a person's race, religion, sexual orientation, ethnicity or national origin constitutes irrational hate. Hate crimes may also be seen as a form of **xenophobia**, the fear and hatred of strangers or foreigners.

xenophobia
Fear or hatred of strangers or foreigners.

Hate crimes may be motivated by bias against a person's race, religion, disability, sexual orientation or ethnicity.

FBI statistics report 7,783 criminal incidents involving 9,168 offenses resulting from bias or hate in 2008. Race was the most frequent motivation of hate crime offenses (51.3 percent), followed by religion (19.5 percent), sexual orientation (16.7 percent) and ethnicity/national origin (11.5 percent). Of the hate crime offenses, 5,542 were classified as crimes against persons, with intimidation accounting for 48.8 percent of these crimes. Of the hate crimes classified as crimes against property, 82.3 percent were acts of destruction/damage/vandalism (*Hate Crime Statistics*, 2008).

In October 2009 President Obama signed major civil rights legislation, the Matthew Shepard & James Byrd Jr. Hate Crimes Prevention Act, named jointly after Matthew Shepard, a gay college student kidnapped, tortured and killed in 1998, and James Byrd Jr., a black man who was chained by three white supremacists to a pickup truck and dragged to his death that same year (Weiner, 2009). The Act expands current hate crimes law by making it a federal hate crime to assault people based on sexual orientation, gender and gender identity.

Hate crimes differ from other attacks on people or property in some important ways, especially their viciousness, as shown in Table 3.5. Hate crimes carry

TABLE 3.5 Hate-Based Crimes and Non–Hate-Based Crimes Compared

Characteristic	Non–Hate-Based Incidents	Hate-Based Incidents
Relationship of victim to perpetrator	Most assaults involve two people who know each other	Assaults tend to be "stranger" crimes
Number of perpetrators	Most assaults have one perpetrator and one victim	Involve an average of four assailants for each victim
Nature of the conflict	Tends to be even	Tends to be uneven—hate crime perpetrators often attack younger or weaker victims, or arm themselves and attack unarmed victims
Amount of physical damage inflicted	Not typically "excessive"	Extremely violent, with victims being three times more likely to require hospitalization than "normal" assault victims
Treatment of property	In most property crimes, something of value is taken	More likely that valuable property will be damaged or destroyed
Perpetrator's personal gain	Attacker settles a score or profits from the crime	In most, no personal score is settled and no profit is made
Location of crime	No place with any symbolic significance	Frequently occur in churches, synagogues, mosques, cemeteries, monuments, schools, camps and in or around the victim's home

SOURCE: Adapted from Christina Bodinger-deUriarte. *Hate Crime: The Rise of Hate Crime on School Campuses.* Research Bulletin No. 10 of Phi Delta Kappa, Center for Evaluation, Development, and Research, December 1991, p.2.

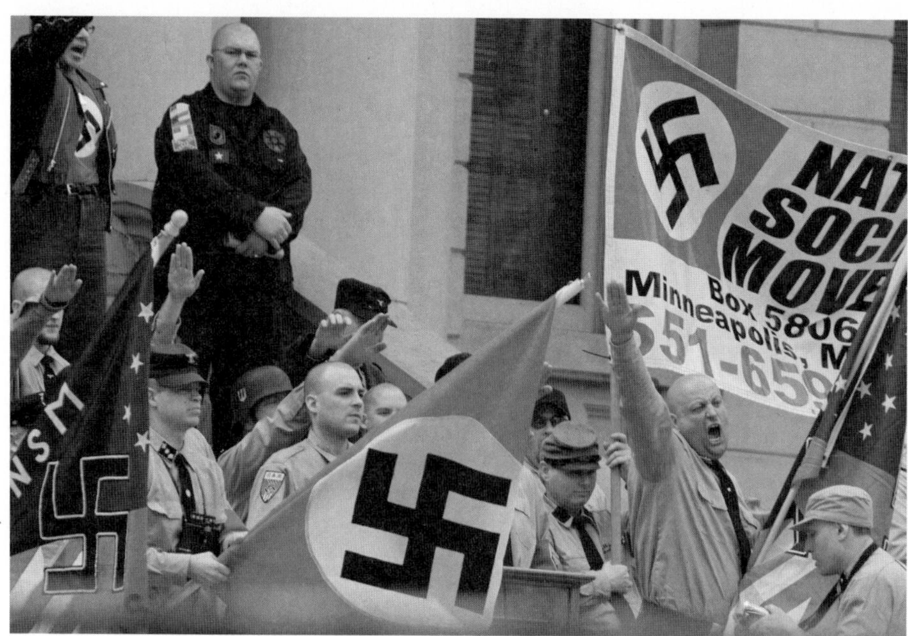

Members of the National Socialist Movement, a neo-Nazi group, rally at the Michigan state capitol building in Lansing. State police erected chain link fences and deployed hundreds of police officers to prevent clashes with anti-Nazi protesters.

more serious penalties if they are proved in court to be motivated by bias. Offenses frequently involved in bias crimes include cross burning, swastika painting, bombing, hanging in effigy, disturbing a public meeting, graffiti, obscene letters or phone calls, or face-to-face oral abuse. As with other types of crimes, the Internet is being used by hate groups to build a sense of community through encrypted messages, chat rooms, e-mail communication and Web sites.

The Southern Poverty Law Center ("Hate Map," 2010) counted 932 active hate groups in the United States in 2009. Figure 3.2 shows the distribution of these groups throughout the United States.

Passage of the Hate Crime Statistics Act of 1990 directed the U.S. Justice Department (DOJ) to collect bias-crime data nationwide. The program is voluntary, however, and no budgetary provisions were made.

Many states have also passed legislation mandating the collection of bias crime statistics. In addition, hate crime laws have resulted in legislation providing additional sentencing options and penalty enhancements for convicted perpetrators. Currently all states have some form of hate crime legislation. Trends in hate crime legislation include (1) expanding the number of "protected groups," in particular adding gender, sexual orientation and disability; (2) providing penalty enhancement for hate- and bias-motivated crime; and (3) requiring data collection and statistical reporting. Appendix A summarizes the statutory provisions of hate crime legislation state by state.

Many states allow victims to bring civil suits against perpetrators. In most of these states, victims can sue for actual and punitive damages and obtain an injunction. Suits can be brought regardless of criminal proceedings, with the burden of proof being a preponderance of evidence (a lesser standard than in criminal

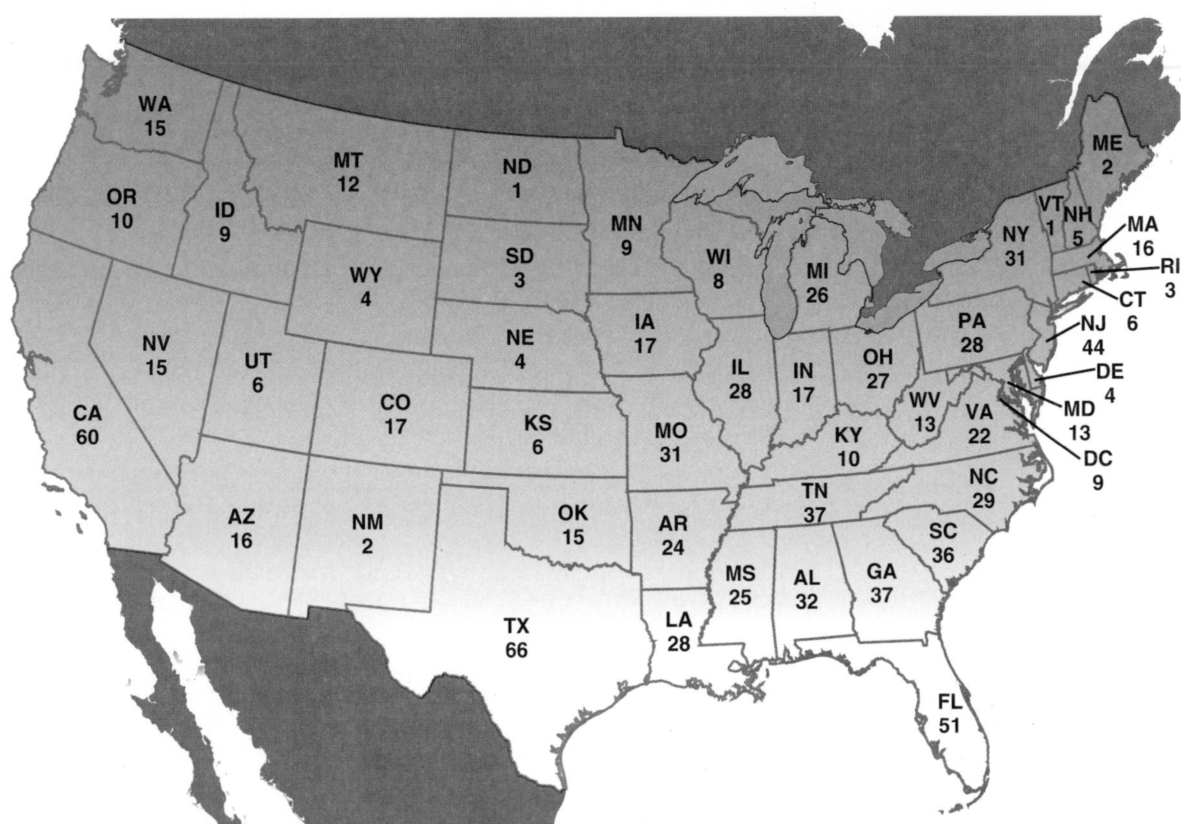

FIGURE 3.2 Hate Map

SOURCE: Courtesy of Southern Poverty Law Center, 2010, http://www.splcenter.org/get-informed/hatemap

proceedings). In some states if the offense is committed by a juvenile, the parents are liable up to $5,000.

Closely related to, and sometimes classified as, hate crimes are crimes against the homeless. The most recent official estimate reports about 675,000 people on any given night. In any given year, 2.5 million to 3.5 million people will experience at least one night of homelessness ("About Homelessness: FAQs," 2010). People living on the streets may become easy targets for assault and other forms of criminal victimization.

Ritualistic Crime A *ritual* is a system of rites, a ceremonial act. Rituals are heavily linked to a belief system and may include symbols, artifacts, words, gestures, costumes and music. Whether this belief system is a formal religion or not, it is protected by the First Amendment right to worship as one wishes.

Rituals have a rich heritage. The Egyptians used amulets as good-luck charms to ward off evil or to bring about good fortune. The Greeks practiced several forms of ritual, including hydromancy, similar to our wishing wells. They also put much faith in astrology and the signs of the zodiac. The Romans, too, practiced rituals, primarily fertility rites. Later in Europe and in the United States, witchcraft became a focus. In Europe more than 200,000 witches were killed for their beliefs.

All recognized religions have rituals meaningful to their members. Cults also use rituals to draw their members together. Satanic cults have one strong leader to whom all members give allegiance. Often the leader is worshipped as an anti-God—the embodiment of Satan and evil. Members are often youths who do not fit in with their peers and have no self-identity. In the cult they are accepted and given a feeling of belonging, worth and power. They are often influenced by heavy metal music and may dress in a punk style. Members of satanic cults frequently wear pentagrams and inverted crosses. Dark clothing is common, as is self-mutilation, such as sticking safety pins through nipples. Satanic rituals commonly include robes (red or black), daggers, candles, altars and pentagrams. They often involve chanting, occur at night and are conducted in strict secrecy. None of this ritualistic activity is illegal, and the majority of cults stay within the boundaries of the law. Some, however, do not.

When the rituals of a group involve crimes, such as desecration of cemeteries, grave robbing, cruelty to animals, child sexual abuse and even murder, they become a problem for law enforcement. As noted by Los Angeles Police Department Investigator Patrick Metoyer, "We don't investigate warlocks, satanists, vampires, Jews, Catholics, or Protestants. We investigate *crime*." A **ritualistic crime** is an unlawful act committed during a ceremony related to a belief system. The crime, *not* the belief system, must be investigated.

ritualistic crime

An unlawful act committed during a ceremony related to a belief system; the crime, not the belief system, must be investigated.

Indicators of satanic or ritualistic involvement in a crime include inverted crosses, candles, altars, animal parts, colored salt, incense, such symbolism as 666 (referring to an anti-Christ), swastikas or books on the occult. Normal investigative techniques are not effective with ritualistic crime. Usually multiple victims and multiple suspects are involved, and often logic will not work.

A cult of the late 1900s was the People's Temple, lead by Jim Jones. Hundreds of his followers moved into a rural community called Jonestown in Guyana, South America. When the commune came under investigation, Jones ordered his followers to commit suicide, resulting in 900 deaths. Another notorious cult was the Branch Davidians, led by David Koresh. In 1993 a 51-day confrontation between the cult and federal forces near Waco, Texas, ended with the apparent mass suicide of over 80 cult members, including Koresh.

Having examined the various classifications and types of crime law enforcement must handle, consider next the types of people involved in such crimes and the factors contributing to their involvement.

OFFENDERS—WHAT LEADS PEOPLE TO COMMIT CRIME?

Why people commit crime has been debated since crime was first defined. Some blame crime on the failings of the criminal justice system—understaffed police forces, lenient judges, overcrowded jails and prisons, and overworked, burned-out probation and parole officers. Others blame society and the overwhelming absence of personal and community responsibility and accountability—abusive or permissive parents, inadequate schools and incompetent teachers, the decline of religion, media violence, drugs and high rates of unemployment. A detailed discussion of the causes of crime is beyond the scope of this text. Only the major theories are briefly discussed.

Theories of Criminality and Causes of Crime

The **classical theory**, developed by Italian criminologist Cesare Beccaria (1738–1794), holds that people are rational and responsible for their acts.

The classical theory sees people as free agents with free will: People commit crimes because they want to.

classical theory
Theory developed by eighteenth-century Italian criminologist Cesare Beccaria that sees people as free agents with free will; people commit crimes because they want to.

A refinement of the classical theory is the *routine activity theory* developed by Lawrence Cohen and Marcus Felson, which states that the volume and distribution of predatory crime (where an offender tries to steal an object directly) correlates highly with three variables found in everyday American life:

1. The availability of suitable targets (homes/stores containing easily sold goods)
2. The absence of watchful guardians (homeowners, neighbors, friends, relatives, guards, security systems, etc.)
3. The presence of motivated offenders (unemployed individuals, drug abusers, etc.)

The intersection of these three variables increases the chances of a predatory crime occurring. This theory gives equal weight to the role of victim and offender. It also suggests that the opportunity for criminal action depends on the victim's lifestyle and behavior.

The classical theory of crime causation was called into question toward the end of the 19th century. Among the leading opponents was Cesare Lombroso (1835–1909), an Italian criminologist who developed the **positivist theory**. Lombroso's studies (1911) supported a biological causation for deviant behavior, suggesting that individuals who did not conform to society's laws and regulations were biologically inferior. *Biological theorists* hold that how a person acts is basically a result of heredity.

positivist theory
Theory developed at the turn of the century by Italian criminologist Cesare Lombroso that sees criminals as "victims of society" and of their own biological, sociological, cultural and physical environments.

The positivist theory sees criminals as "victims of society" and of their own biological, sociological, cultural and physical environments.

Lombroso maintained that criminals are born with a predisposition to crime and need exceptionally favorable conditions in life to avoid criminal behavior. Building on Lombroso's idea that environmental influences affect criminal behavior, some scholars developed the positivist view based on the concept of **determinism**. Determinism regards crime as a consequence of many factors, including population density, economic status and the legal definition of crime. This multiple-factor causation theory brought the positivist view into direct conflict with the notion of free will.

determinism
Maintains that human behavior is the product of a multitude of environmental and cultural influences.

The Influence of Biology

A medieval law states, "If two persons fall under suspicion of crime, the uglier or more deformed is to be regarded as more probably guilty." Such a law is based on a belief that criminals are born, not made. While we have come a long way in our understanding of the causes of crime since the Middle Ages, a person's biological makeup continues to be among those factors many believe are correlated with criminality. Biological functions and conditions that have been related to criminal behavior include such variables as brain tumors, disorders of the limbic system, endocrine abnormalities, chromosomal abnormalities and neurological dysfunction produced by the prenatal and postnatal experience of infants.

Adoption studies have lent support to the biological theory of criminal behavior. A fairly powerful argument can be made for a biological basis of criminality when it can be shown that the adopted-away children of criminal biological parents grow up to display criminal behavior, especially when the adoptive (nonbiological) parents are not themselves criminal.

A counterposition to the biological theory is the *behavioral/environmental theory*, which suggests that criminals are made, not born.

The Influence of the Environment

Many environmental factors have been identified as contributing to criminality, including poverty, unemployment, the disintegrating family, and drug and alcohol abuse.

Poverty is a pervasive, persistent, devastating threat to many of our nation's families, particularly to youths. Poverty encompasses a host of problems, including overcrowded and unhealthy living conditions in unsafe, crime-ridden neighborhoods; inadequate schools; limited access to health care; and single and/or teen parenthood. Poverty was identified by the Census Bureau as one of six parameters that indicate a risk to children's welfare, the other parameters being absent parents, single-parent families, unwed mothers, parents who have not completed high school and welfare dependence.

Unemployment is intimately linked to poverty. Numerous studies suggest that a booming economy leads to decreased levels of unemployment, alleviating poverty and translating into a drop in crime.

The *family* is another strong environmental influence on criminal activity. As mentioned, the Census Bureau has identified unwed mothers and single-parent families as two risks to children's welfare. Sadly, many families serve as the training ground for violent behavior, perpetuating what has been termed the "cycle of violence." Studies show, "Being abused or neglected as a child increased the likelihood of arrest as a juvenile by 59 percent, as an adult by 28 percent, and for a violent crime by 30 percent" (Widom and Maxfield, 2001, p.1). In many violent homes, drug and alcohol abuse is a continual presence.

The role *drugs and alcohol* play in crime can be viewed two ways: (1) drug and alcohol use physically alters individuals, lowering inhibitions and increasing confidence, which can then lead them to commit criminal acts (domestic abuse, rape, assault, drunk driving, etc.) or (2) a dependence on drugs and/or alcohol may lead a person to commit crime to support the addiction (robbery, burglary, etc.).

The Combination of Biology and Environment Comparisons of groups of criminals with groups of noncriminals have failed to produce any single characteristic that absolutely distinguishes the two groups. However, a growing body of evidence suggests that the forces operating to stimulate criminal behavior may be a complex interaction between predisposing biological/genetic factors and certain environmental agents that trigger criminal tendencies.

 Criminal behavior is likely the result of both heredity and life experiences.

Table 3.6 summarizes the major theories on the causes of crime.

TABLE 3.6 Review of the Major Theories of the Causes of Crime

Theory	Major Premise
Choice Theory	People commit crimes when they perceive that the benefits of law violation outweigh the threat and pain of punishment.
Biosocial Theories	
Biochemical	Crime, especially violence, is a function of diet, vitamin intake, hormonal imbalance or food allergies.
Neurological	Criminals and delinquents often suffer brain impairment. Attention deficit disorder and minimum brain dysfunction are related to antisocial behavior.
Genetic	Delinquent traits and predispositions are inherited. The criminality of parents can predict the delinquency of children.
Psychological Theories	
Psychoanalytic	The development of personality early in childhood influences behavior for the rest of a person's life. Criminals have weak egos and damaged personalities.
Social Learning	People commit crimes when they model their behavior after others they see being rewarded for the same acts. Behavior is enforced by rewards and extinguished by punishment.
Cognitive	Individual reasoning processes influence behavior. Reasoning is influenced by the way people perceive their environment and by their moral and intellectual development.
Social Structure Theories	
Social Disorganization	The conflicts and problems of urban social life and communities control the crime rate. Crime is a product of transitional neighborhoods that manifest social disorganization and value conflict.
Strain	People who adopt society's goals but lack the means to attain them seek alternatives, such as crime.
Social Process Theories	
Learning	People learn to commit crimes from exposure to antisocial behaviors. Criminal behavior depends on the person's experiences with rewards for conventional behaviors and punishments for deviant ones. Being rewarded for deviance leads to crime.
Social Control	A person's bond to society prevents him or her from violating social rules. If the bond weakens, the person is free to commit crimes.
Conflict Theories	
Conflict	People commit crimes when the law, controlled by the rich and powerful, defines their behavior as illegal. The immoral actions of the powerful go unpunished.
Left Realism	Crime is a function of relative deprivation; criminals prey on the poor.
Radical Feminism	The capital system creates patriarchy, which oppresses women. Male dominance explains gender bias, violence against women and repression.
Peacemaking	Peace and humanism can reduce crime; conflict resolution strategies can work.
Integrated Theories	
Latent Trait: General Theory of Crime	Crime and criminality are separate concepts. People choose to commit crime when they lack self-control. People lacking in self-control will seize criminal opportunities.
Developmental	Criminals go through lifestyle changes during their offending career. As people mature, the factors that influence their propensity to commit crime change. In childhood, family factors are critical; in adulthood, marital and job factors are key.
Victimization Theories	
Victim Precipitation	Victims trigger criminal acts by their provocative behavior. Active precipitation involves fighting words or gestures. Passive precipitation occurs when victims unknowingly threaten their attackers.
Lifestyle	Victimization risk is increased when people have a high-risk lifestyle. Placing oneself at risk by going out to dangerous places results in increased victimization.
Routine Activities	Crime rates can be explained by the availability of suitable targets, the absence of capable guardians and the presence of motivated offenders.

SOURCE: Joseph J. Senna and Larry J. Siegel. *Introduction to Criminal Justice*, 9th ed. Belmont, CA: Wadsworth Publishing Company, 2002, pp.102–103. Reprinted by permission.

Messner and Rosenfeld (2007, p.7) contend, "The American Dream itself and the normal social conditions engendered by it are deeply implicated in the problem of crime. [The American Dream is] a broad cultural ethos that entails a commitment to the goal of material success, to be pursued by everyone in society, under conditions of open, individual competition." The exaggerated emphasis placed by society on monetary achievement, to the near exclusion of other alternative criteria of success, promotes an "ends over means" preoccupation with financial wealth and possession of property and erodes the social structures required to restrain criminogenic cultural pressures (Messner and Rosenfeld, p.10).

A turning point in addressing crime can be found in the works of James Q. Wilson, whose 1975 book *Thinking about Crime* focused on the role of the criminal justice system as an influence on the individual decision making of offenders. Wilson, in collaboration with George Kelling, developed the idea of "broken windows" and redirected attention to concepts such as physical and social disorder and their role in not only generating crime, but fear of crime, which in turn can generate more crime and affect quality of life, especially in urban communities.

Two theories on the causation of crime prevalent in the 21st century are lack of self-control and strain theory. The oft-cited self-control theory of Gottfredson and Hirschi (1990) posit that individuals low in self-control have a greater propensity to commit deviant acts, harkening back to classical theory. In testing this theory, Beaver et al. (2009, p.710) report three major findings: "First, low self-control was consistently related to criminal justice system involvement as measured by police contacts, arrests, age at first police contact and arrest contact. . . . Second, the effects of low self-control on arrest withstood controls for early police contacts and total number of police contacts. . . . Third, the effects of low self-control on conviction remained significant with controls for arrest onset and arrest for a violent crime."

The second theory being actively researched is general strain theory (GTS), harkening back to the positivist view of crime. A leading researcher in this theory, Agnew (2005, p.3) explains, "A general theory must describe the relationship between those individual traits, family factors, school experiences, peer factors, and work experiences that cause crime. . . . Researchers have increasingly come to argue that the causes of crime have reciprocal effects on one another (e.g., individual traits, influence family experiences, and family experiences influence individual traits." Research by Kaufman (2009) finds strong support for GTS. Thus the debate about and research into the causation of crime continues at a theoretical level.

On a more practical level, *Crime in the United States* points out that their annual statistics can lead to simplistic and/or incomplete analysis that often create misleading perceptions and that to assess criminality from jurisdiction to jurisdiction, one must consider many variables, some of which, while significantly affecting crime, are not readily measurable or applicable among all locales. It stresses that valid assessments are possible only with careful study and analysis of the many unique conditions affecting each local jurisdiction. It lists several factors known to affect the volume and type of crime occurring from place to place, including,

- Population density and degree of urbanization.
- Variations in composition of the population, particularly youth concentration.
- Stability of the population with respect to residents' mobility, commuting patterns, and transient factors.

- Modes of transportation and highway system.
- Economic conditions, including median income, poverty level, and job availability.
- Cultural factors and educational, recreational, and religious characteristics.
- Family conditions with respect to divorce and family cohesiveness.
- Climate.
- Effective strength of law enforcement agencies.
- Administrative and investigative emphases of law enforcement.
- Policies of other components of the criminal justice system (i.e., prosecutorial, judicial, correctional, and probational).
- Citizens' attitudes toward crime.
- Crime reporting practices of the citizenry.

A study of whether suburbanization was a cause or a consequence of crime in U.S. metropolitan areas found reciprocating evidence that it was, in fact, both:

> Inner-city crime is a motivating factor for middle-class flight. Therefore, crime is a cause of suburbanization. Movement of the middle and upper classes to the suburbs, in turn, isolates the poor in central-city ghettos and barrios. Sociologists and criminologists have argued that the concentration of poverty creates an environment within which criminal behavior becomes normative, leading impressionable youth to adopt criminal lifestyles. Moreover, from the perspective of routine activity theory, the deterioration of social capital in high-poverty areas reduces the capacity for guardianship. Therefore, suburbanization may also cause crime. UCR data and census data shows a positive relationship between suburbanization and metropolitan crime. (Jargowsky, 2009, p.28)

Because the concepts of crime, delinquency and deviancy apply to such a wide range of behaviors, having in common only the fact that they have been declared illegal, no single causal explanation is possible. The complex interplay of factors leading to the commission of a crime is illustrated in Figure 3.3.

Characteristics of Known (Arrested) Offenders

According to the FBI (*Crime in the United States, 2009*), the majority of those arrested in 2009 were for drug-related offenses, including alcohol. Males accounted for 74.7 percent of those arrested; 69.1 percent or those arrested were white; 28.3 percent were black and the remaining 2.6 percent were of other races.

Career Criminals or Recidivists

Of major concern are the chronic or career criminals—a small group of offenders arrested five or more times as juveniles. Such an offender is also called a **recidivist**. Although most offenders "age out," chronic offenders continue a life of crime. Traditional programs aimed at rehabilitation have little effect on such criminals.

recidivist

One who habitually or repeatedly breaks the law.

Some refer to our criminal justice system as a revolving door, with criminals getting out of prison faster than the authorities can convict and incarcerate others. Often those who were released are involved in more crime and are right back in

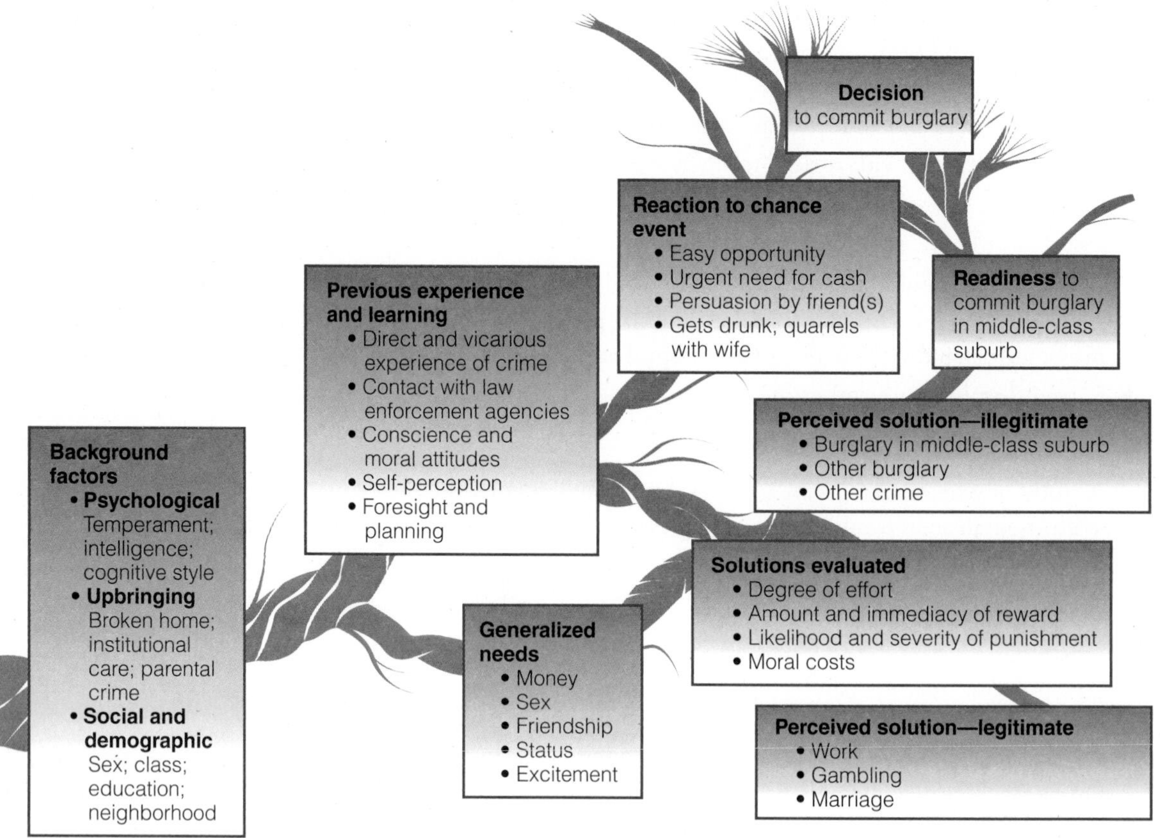

FIGURE 3.3 Criminal Involvement: The Decision to Get Involved in Crime

SOURCE: From ***Criminal Justice***, 3rd ed. by Joel Samaha. Used by permission of Wadsworth Publishing Company.

prison. The Violent Crime Control and Law Enforcement Act of 1994 reflects the desire to deal with recidivism and the perpetual revolving door, calling for "mandatory life imprisonment without possibility of parole for federal offenders with three or more convictions for serious violent felonies or drug-trafficking crimes." Some states, such as California, have enacted similar "three strikes and you're out" legislation.

Juvenile Offenders

In addition to targeting career criminals, the criminal justice system must focus attention on youths, especially juvenile delinquents, because delinquency is often the beginning for the career criminal. In addition: "Official data consistently show that crime rates rise rapidly in the teenage years, peak in late adolescence, then decline through the life course" (Bosick, 2009, p.472).

State specifications as to the age of a juvenile vary, but most state statutes define a juvenile as an individual under the age of 16 or 18. Juvenile delinquency, therefore, is considered behavior by a person not of legal age that violates a local, state or federal law. **Delinquency** refers to actions or conduct by a juvenile in

delinquency

Actions or conduct by a juvenile in violation of criminal law or constituting a status offense; an error or failure by a child or adolescent to conform to society's expectations of social order.

violation of criminal law or constituting a status offense—an error or failure by a child or adolescent to conform to society's expectations of social order. The term *delinquent* has fallen into disfavor, being replaced by *juvenile offender*, referring to a child adjudicated to have violated a federal, state or local law; a minor who has done an illegal act; or a minor who has been proved in court to have misbehaved seriously. A child may be found delinquent for a variety of behaviors not criminal for adults (status offenses).

Juvenile delinquency presents a serious challenge with an enormous number of youths involved. Delinquents are no longer just boys from the wrong side of the tracks, as an increasing percentage of juvenile offending is committed by females and youth from wealthier families (Moore, 2009, p.16). Self-report studies indicate approximately 90 percent of all young people have committed at least one act for which they could be brought to juvenile court. However, many of these offenses are minor (for example, fighting and truancy), and state statutes often define juvenile delinquency so broadly that virtually all youngsters could be classified as delinquent.

Status Offenders A special category of offenses has been established for juveniles, designating certain actions as illegal for any person under the state's defined juvenile age. These are **status offenses**, violations of the law applying to only those under legal age. They include absenting from home, truancy, drinking alcoholic beverages, smoking, violating curfew and incorrigibility. Youths and their families brought before the court for status offenses occupy a great share of the court's workload and may try the court's patience because such youths often are considered as simply being in need of better supervision.

status offenses

Crimes restricted to persons under the legal age—for example, smoking, drinking, breaking curfew, absenting from home, truancy, incorrigibility.

Serious and Violent Offenders Murder statistics, often used as a barometer for the overall level of serious and violent crime, indicate that violent juvenile offending peaked in 1993 and then began a steady decline,

Most often violent offending begins among juveniles who have themselves been victimized.

The Orange County (California) Probation Department tracked a small group of first-time offenders for three years and found that a small percentage (8 percent) of the juveniles were arrested repeatedly (a minimum of four times within a three-year period) and were responsible for 55 percent of repeat cases. According to the report (*The 8% Solution*, 2001, p.1):

> The characteristics of this group of repeat offenders (referred to as "the **8% problem**") were dramatically different from those who were arrested only once. These differences did not develop after exposure to the juvenile justice system, as some might expect; they were evident at first arrest and referral to juvenile court, and they worsened if nothing was done to alleviate the youth's problems. Unfortunately, in wanting to "give a break" to first-time offenders, the juvenile justice system often pays scant attention to those at greatest risk of becoming chronic offenders until they have established a record of repeated serious offending. [emphasis added]

8% problem

A group of repeat offenders dramatically different from those who are arrested only once; account for a disproportionate amount of youth crime.

CAREER PROFILE

Hon. Michael A. Corriero (ret.) (Judge of the Court of Claims, former presiding Judge of Manhattan's Youth Part)

As a teenager growing up in Manhattan's Little Italy in the 1950s, I saw how easily a careless choice could draw one into a situation that carried "the appearance of a culpability not necessarily justified by the true facts." To be sure, as children we encountered many crossroads, pinpoints in time where a step to the right could lead to accomplishment and honor, a step to the left to trouble and tragedy. But I also remember Mulberry Street as a place where America's promise could become a reality, a place where with hard work, diligence and the support of family a child could fully realize his or her potential.

My parents and I lived across the street from the "Tombs," as the Manhattan House of Detention was known. The Tombs was connected to and a part of the Manhattan Criminal Court building. We lived in a three-room apartment on the top floor of a five-story walkup at the corner of Baxter and White Streets. My father was a longshoreman at the Brooklyn Army Terminal; my mother was a seamstress in a factory on lower Broadway. How I went from playing stickball against the walls of the Criminal Court building to presiding over cases as a judge in that very same building is a story more aptly reserved for a memoir; suffice it to say that my parents prepared me as best they could for those inevitable pinpoints in time when as a teenager I would be confronted with choices. Although they did not have a formal education, my parents saw the value of education as the only way to change the circumstances of life.

When the legendary Manhattan District Attorney Frank Hogan gave me an opportunity to work in his office, his policy toward young offenders was especially significant to me. He believed that courts and prosecutors had a special obligation to make sure that young people were treated fairly and effectively, recognizing that young offenders were malleable and could be positively influenced. As a judge, I was able to weave that sensitivity into my work, but I soon realized the limitations of laws that inhibited a constructive response to juvenile offending.

In 1984, I was assigned to the Criminal Term of the Kings County Supreme Court. Shortly thereafter, I presided over my first "juvenile-offender" murder case. A 13-year-old boy was accused of brutally murdering an elderly neighbor by stabbing her repeatedly with a screwdriver and then setting her body on fire. The boy was convicted and sentenced pursuant to the Juvenile Offender Law to an indeterminate term of nine years to life imprisonment. The case highlighted the special problems of trying children as young as 13 in adult courts—the impact of their immaturity on the admissibility of incriminating statements, on their interaction with counsel and ultimately on their understanding of the consequences of their behavior.

In 1990 my concern for the issues presented to judges dealing with juvenile-offender cases led me to synthesize my thoughts in an article I wrote for the *New York Law Journal* entitled "Youth Parts: A Constructive Response to the Challenge of Youth Crime." The article traced the history of New York's special treatment of young offenders, describing the operation of the special Youth Parts that had existed in the adult courts and arguing that reestablishment of Youth Parts was even more crucial than ever, as the jurisdiction of the adult criminal courts was expanded in 1978 to include children as young as 13. I suggested that several advantages could be realized in reestablishing such Parts: uniform treatment of teenage defendants; the concentration and integration of court and private agencies dealing with youths; and a greater diversion of teenage offenders to private agencies for supervision and counseling, thereby supplementing an already overworked and overburdened Probation Department. The article set in motion a series of events that culminated in the creation of Manhattan's Youth Part in 1992, a Part that I have presided over since its inception.

The Youth Part is a special court in New York City with the responsibility of resolving cases of children as young as 13 who are tried as adults pursuant to New York's "Juvenile Offender Law." The Youth Part is designed to facilitate the identification of those youths who can demonstrate they are capable of overcoming their problems without compromising public safety. The process of identifying the malleable child is essential to the fair and effective operation of any juvenile justice system. Once such a child is identified, we can begin the process of "rehabilitation."

When I use the term *rehabilitate*, I do not mean in the sense of "curing" an illness or "changing" character. I view rehabilitation as engaging children in a process that assists them to "develop" character. Judges can play a significant role in that process, interacting with the children who come before them in such a way as to enable them to act as catalysts for change in a child's life. That is essentially what we try to do in the Youth Part. That is the challenge, as I see it, with respect to each child.

Each generation must recognize the imperative for justice and must summon the passion to maintain a commitment to its principles. It is passion that converts good intention into commitment, commitment into perseverance and perseverance into accomplishment.

> The good news is that most of the small group of potentially serious, chronic offenders can be identified reliably at first contact with the juvenile justice system. The "8%" offenders enter the system with a complex set of problems or risk factors, which the study identified as (1) involvement in crime at an early age and (2) a multiproblem profile including significant family problems (abuse, neglect, criminal family members and/or a lack of parental supervision and control), problems at school (truancy, failing more than one course or a recent suspension or expulsion), drug and alcohol abuse, and behaviors such as gang involvement, running away and stealing.

As noted, frequently those who have been victimized often become victims themselves.

VICTIMS OF CRIME AND VIOLENCE

Everyone expects law enforcement officers to know how to deal with criminals. Of equal importance, however, is officers' ability to deal with crime victims. This not only enhances the image of police officers as professionals but also enhances communications that likely will result in officers' ability to obtain more crime-related information. Crime victims are often said to be the overlooked element of the criminal process, invisible and forgotten.

Criminal Victimization, 2008 reports that the violent crime rate in 2008—19.3 victimizations per 1,000 persons age 12 or older—was statistically unchanged from the previous year's estimate of 20.7 per 1,000 persons (Rand, 2009, p.1). The property crime rate of 135 victimizations per 1,000 households in 2008 was lower than the rate of 147 per 1,000 households in 2007.

Unfortunately, as noted, victims of violence too often evolve into perpetrators of such harm. Studies have shown that virtually "all violent juvenile delinquents have been abused children," that "all criminals at San Quentin prison . . . studied had violent upbringings as children" and that "all assassins . . . in the United States during the past 20 years had been victims of child abuse." (ten Bensel, n.d., p.41). The *2009 OVC Report to the Nation* (p.ix) states, "To be a victim of crime is to be invaded at the deepest level. As a victim, one's sense of personal safety and autonomy is shattered. A crime inflicted on one person affects dozens, even hundreds more: from emergency responders to victim service providers, from court personnel to the victim's friends and family, from the media to the public. Even a single incident ripples throughout the community and changes the environment."

Types of Victims

Direct or primary victims of crime are those initially harmed by injury, death or loss of property as a result of criminal actions. When a violent crime occurs, the impact often goes further than the victim. Often the entire community suffers. **Indirect or secondary victims** of crime are all other community members who may be threatened or fearful as a result of the commission of crime. This can include family, relatives, friends, neighborhoods, the entire community and even police officers who must deal with the aftermath of violent crimes, such as battered children and grisly deaths.

direct victims
Those who are initially harmed by injury, death or loss of property as a result of crimes committed; also called *primary victims*.

primary victims
Individuals directly affected by an incident, such as the person who is robbed, burglarized or raped.

indirect victims
Family members and friends of victims who also feel pain and suffering along with the victim; also called *secondary victims*.

secondary victims
Family members and friends of victims who also feel pain and suffering along with the victim; also called *indirect victims*.

If a small-town youth murders his entire family or opens fire in the neighborhood school, the community may go into shock. Everyone feels vulnerable. Fear sets in. Morale drops. Trust plummets. In addition convicted criminals sentenced to prison are financially supported by society while incarcerated. In short everyone pays the price as a victim of crime.

Victimization Factors—Who Is at Risk?

Distinct demographic and individual characteristics, called *risk factors*, influence the chance of being victimized. The degree of risk people face is affected by household factors related to how and where they live as well as by individual factors.

Household Factors Data from the NCVS reveals some general trends related to household size and income level, with property crime victimization rates increasing as household income decreases and as the number of household members increases (Rand, 2009, p.4). Additional household risk factors the increase the chances of victimization include households headed by single parents, those in which parents are abusive, and those in which parental education is low.

Individual Risk Factors Data from the NCVS indicate certain individuals are at greater risk than others (Rand, 2009, p.4):

- *Gender*: Males experienced higher rates of victimization than females in all violent crimes except rape or sexual assault.
- *Age*: Generally, for every crime measured by the NCVS, persons age 12 to 24 had the highest rates of victimization and then decreased by age. Persons age 50 or older had the lowest rates.
- *Race*: Blacks experienced higher rates than whites for every violent crime measured except simple assault.

Young (age 12–24), black males from low-income, large households are at greatest risk of victimization. For adults, in general, as income rises and age increases, the victimization rate decreases.

Other Factors in Victimization

Beyond statistics, several other factors enter into understanding victimization, including the relationship between the victim and offender, the use of weapons and how victims protect themselves—or attempt to do so.

The Victim–Offender Relationship When people worry about crime, they are most often worried about being attacked by strangers. This fear is often justified. With the exception of murder and rape, most violent crimes are committed by strangers. Males, African Americans and young people face the greatest risk of violent crime by strangers and are victimized by violent strangers at an annual rate almost triple that of women. African Americans are more than twice as likely as whites to be robbed by strangers.

Women are more vulnerable than men to assaults by acquaintances and relatives, with two-thirds of all assaults on divorced and separated women committed by acquaintances and relatives. Spouses or former spouses committed only 5 percent of the assaults by single offenders. In almost three-fourths of spouse-versus-spouse assaults, the victim was divorced or separated at the time of the incident.

More than half of all homicides are committed by someone known to the victim. Further, victims and offenders are usually of the same race.

How Victims Protect Themselves Victims of violent crime can protect themselves by returning physical force, by verbal response, by attracting attention, by nonviolent evasion or by brandishing a weapon. Rape victims are more likely to use force, try a verbal response or attract attention and are less likely than others to do nothing to protect themselves. In contrast robbery victims are least likely to try to talk themselves out of being victimized and most likely to do nothing.

Effects of Victimization

Victims of violent crimes often suffer from the effects of the victimization for the rest of their lives. Shootings, knifings, acid throwings or beatings are traumatic, with long-lasting physical, emotional and psychological damage to victims and their families. Victims may also suffer financially through the loss or destruction of property (including irreplaceable property with only sentimental value), time lost from work, medical costs and the introduction of security measures to prevent future victimization. The greatest effect of victimization, however, is often psychological.

Victims may suffer physical, economic and psychological harm that lasts their entire lives.

Fear of Victimization

Public opinion polls show that while people do fear crime in general, they usually feel their own neighborhoods are relatively safe. If someone in the neighborhood is victimized, however, the entire neighborhood may feel much more vulnerable.

The people with the highest risk of being victimized, young males, do not express the greatest fear of victimization. Those who express the greatest fear of being victimized are women and the elderly, even though they are at lower risk than other groups. Whether they are at lower risk because they take measures to reduce their chances of being victimized is not known. If the elderly, for example, restrict their activities because they are afraid of becoming crime victims, this fear is in itself a sort of victimization.

The "Second Wound": Further Victimization by the Criminal Justice System

While feeling the impact of being victimized, many victims are subjected to a second victimization.

A second victimization may occur as a result of insensitivity shown by those in the criminal justice system.

Police are trained extensively in dealing with criminals, and police academies have begun devoting greater time and attention to training officers in how to communicate with victims, with the realization that victims are often the only ones who can identify the offender and the property stolen in the crime. The victim's property may be held for months until introduced as evidence in the trial. The victim is often called to testify in a trial and subjected to severe cross-examination, more than the person charged with the crime, since the defendant is not required to take the witness stand.

The investigative and prosecution process may require a number of trips to the court or county attorney's office, which not only is an expense but also requires time off from employment. Victims often complain that once they make their initial contribution to the investigation, they are not kept informed of the case's progress. They often are not notified when the offender is released from custody or incarceration, preventing them from taking safety precautions.

Victims may also be victimized again by lack of release data and notification and by intimidation.

In one case a woman was brutally murdered by her former boyfriend, who had earlier been arrested and charged with her rape. However, he unexpectedly made bail, and two days after his release the man ambushed her as she left work and shot her six times in the head at close range. She died instantly. No one had notified her, the police or the prosecutors that the offender was out of jail.

One solution to this problem is the Victim Information and Notification Everyday (VINE) system spreading across the country, having expanded to include 2,600 communities in 40 states (Halladay, 2009). The system is activated by calling a toll-free number and providing a prisoner's name or ID number. The user receives computerized information about where the prisoner is being held, the date of upcoming parole hearings and when the sentence expires. It also provides the phone number and address of the facility holding the prisoner.

An increasing number of states have passed statutes allowing victims to be notified, if they so request, of certain status changes regarding the offenders. Offender information provided usually includes details related to release, transfer, escape, apprehension or death. Some states now have statutes requiring law enforcement to notify victims of domestic violence of the offenders' status as their cases are processed; thus improvement is occurring on some fronts in an effort to keep victims better informed.

Victims and witnesses are often further victimized by overt or covert intimidation, most commonly in gang and drug cases, as well as in domestic violence cases. Intimidation may occur in the courtroom in the form of threatening looks or gestures or by packing the courtroom with the defendant's friends. Such intimidation seriously hampers the efforts of law enforcement, prosecutors and the entire criminal justice system. One approach to countering such intimidation is to take a class of police cadets into courtrooms where intimidation is suspected.

Assisting Victims—A Brief Historical Overview

In 1965 California established the first crime-victim compensation program. Since then, most states have established similar programs. In 1975 the first "Victim's Rights Week" was organized by the Philadelphia district attorney. In 1979 Frank

G. Carrington, considered by many to be the father of the victims' rights movement, founded the Crime Victims' Legal Advocacy Institute Inc.

Many support groups for victims of crime exist in each state and numerous municipalities or counties—rape crisis centers, family shelters, victims of crime groups, domestic violence groups, Mothers Against Drunk Drivers (MADD), the National Organization for Victim Assistance (NOVA) and other groups. Significant legislation has also been passed to assist crime victims.

The Crime Victims' Reparations Act passed in 1974 gives victims the right to be compensated for the cost of crimes, including medical and funeral costs, loss of income, counseling services and other expenses.

The Victim and Witness Protection Act of 1982 was passed to help victims cope with the labyrinth of police, courts and corrections, mandating that the U.S. Attorney General develop procedures to assist victims and witnesses through this legal process. The act provides for victim impact statements (VIS) at sentencing and parole hearings, discussed in detail shortly.

The Crime Victims' Bill of Rights was passed in 1983, recognizing for the first time the rights of victims to participate in criminal prosecutions. Until then prosecutors were not obligated to inform victims about crucial decisions such as plea bargain arrangements. Victims have acquired even more rights since then, including the opportunity to make a statement at the time of sentencing.

The Victims of Crime Act (VOCA) of 1984 established the Crime Victims' Fund, made up of federal criminal fines, penalties and bond forfeitures to support state victim compensation and local victim service programs. The fund provides grants to states for compensation to crime victims, crisis intervention, salaries of crime-victim service personnel, child abuse and prevention, and victim assistance programs.

The Victim and Witness Protection Act of 1994 provides for compensation and other victim assistance from fines, penalties and forfeited bail bonds paid by convicted federal offenders. Courts often make restitution part of the sentence, depending on the circumstances and merits of each case.

Crime Victims' Rights

At present, while criminal defendants have almost two-dozen separate constitutional rights—15 provided by amendments to the U.S. Constitution—not one word in the Constitution protects crime victims' rights. Although the majority of states have victims' bills of rights, the push for amending the U.S. Constitution to include a federal victims' bill of rights has been defeated several times, first in 1997 and again in 2003. Thus the states have retained individual control over which rights victims of crime may be granted.

Victims' rights may include the right to appear at sentencing, the right to appear at plea bargaining, the use of victim impact statements before sentencing, the right to be informed of their case's status, the right to be informed of an offender's release from prison and the right to receive restitution.

Victim Statements Since the late 1980s, victim impact statements have been included in the federal presentence investigation report to the court, as well as in many state court proceedings. The **victim impact statement (VIS)** includes

victim impact statement (VIS)

A written or spoken statement detailing the medical, financial and emotional injuries resulting from a crime; the information is usually provided to a probation officer who writes a summary to be included in the defendant's presenting packet.

information concerning the effect of the crime on the victim and the community. The victim impact statement itemizes economic losses directly related to and resulting from the offense, describes the necessity of any psychological services needed as a result of the offense, describes changes in family relationship as a result of the offense and identifies physical injuries, their severity and whether the injuries are temporary or permanent—factors that relate to the medical, financial, psychological and social impact on the victim. These impact statements provide victims an opportunity to participate in the judicial process in those cases that go to trial or a sentencing hearing. The **victim statement of opinion (VSO)**, in contrast, is more subjective, allowing victims to tell the court their opinions as to what sentence a defendant should receive. The opinion may be presented verbally in court by the victim or delivered in a written statement to the judge.

victim statement of opinion (VSO)

A spoken or written statement to the judge in which victims tell the court their opinions on what sentence the defendant should receive; more subjective than the victim impact statement.

Victim Restitution Victim restitution may be part of a sentence or may be a condition of probation that requires offenders to compensate their victims for damages or loss incurred as a result of their crime. Restitution has widespread use in cases of larceny, burglary and other property crimes, as well as some crimes of violence.

Restitution may take several forms such as monetary payment equal to the loss incurred or other arrangements that do not directly benefit the victim but may compensate the state or community for prosecution costs. Orders to pay are adjusted to the ability to pay. Many payments are made in monthly installments. The judge may order the defendant to work in a community program. In addition to making payments to the victim, working and making these payments forces offenders to accept responsibility for their crimes. Figure 3.4 illustrates how few offenders actually make restitution to their victims.

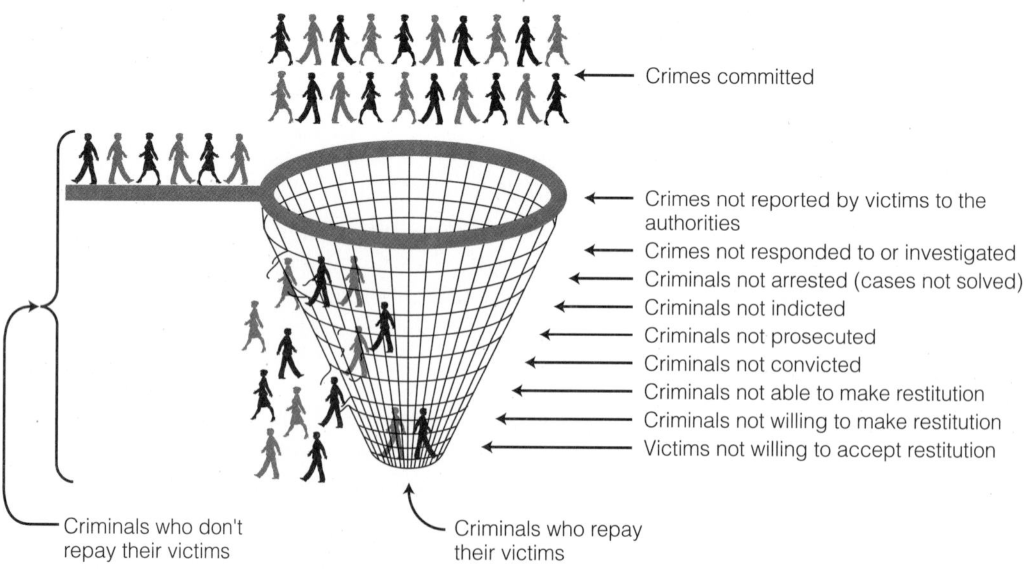

FIGURE 3.4 Funneling or Shrinkage: The Leaky Net

SOURCE: Adapted from KARMEN. *Crime Victims* 6E. © 2007 (p.316) Wadsworth, a part of Cengage Learning, Inc. Reproduced by permission. Www.cengage.com/permissions.

Programs and Services for Crime Victims

Progress continues to be made in the development of programs and services provided to victims. The Office of Victims of Crime (OVC) has developed four technical assistance guides for agencies working with crime victims: Guide to Performance Measurement and Program Evaluation; Guide to Conducting a Needs Assessment; Guide to Hiring a Local Evaluator and Guide to Protecting Human Subjects ("OVC Technical Assistance Guides," 2010). In 1988 through an amendment to the Victims of Crime Act, Congress established the Crime Victims Fund. According to the *2009 OVC Report to the Nation* (p.11), the fund is a mechanism for supporting millions of crime victims annually. Since FY 1996 deposits into the Fund have totaled $7.8 billion. However, over 40 percent was paid by less than 1 percent of criminal defendants' fines.

Appendix B identifies various victim and witness services that may be provided during eight stages of the criminal justice process. Not all services may be provided in every state.

A Parallel Justice System for Victims?

The National Center for Victims of Crime (NCVC) has launched a Parallel Justice Project in an effort to provide a second, parallel set of responses to victims as their cases proceed through the justice system. The NCVC contends that with Parallel Justice, there would be a focused effort to help ensure the victim's safety, to help the victim recover from the trauma of crime and to provide resources to help victims get their lives back on track.

The NCVC also suggests that, unlike most victims' bills of rights, Parallel Justice would be available to *all* victims of crime, not just victims of violent crime. Parallel Justice is undergoing pilot testing in three sites: Burlington, Vermont; Redlands, California; and Winston-Salem, North Carolina. According to the Vermont Center for Crime Victim Services ("Parallel Justice," 2010):

> The concept of Parallel Justice changes the paradigm [of supporting victims of crime]. Instead of asking victims to seek justice solely through the criminal justice process, we instead ask victims to define the problems they face. Then government, partnering with the community, does its best to address those problems. In this new world, there would be a victim-oriented justice process that would kick in with the occurrence of a crime and attend to the needs of victims of all crime, violent and non-violent. Offenders, communities and society at large would be asked to help victims rebuild their lives—to help reintegrate victims back into productive community life.

The goals of Parallel Justice in Vermont are:

- To fill gaps in services for victims and their families.
- To coordinate existing resources that can help victims of crime rebuild their lives and create additional resources.
- To make victim safety a priority among all criminal justice and social service agencies.
- To provide opportunities for victims to explain what happened to them and what they need to rebuild their lives.

For parallel justice to become a reality, all members of a community, including the police, need to be involved. This may begin with the initial contact with law enforcement.

The Police Role

The first and all-important contact between the police and a victim is made during the preliminary investigation. Police officers must be realistic with victims. If a police agency has an "early case closure system," victims should be told that nothing further can be done unless additional information comes to light. Victims should be given the case number and a phone number to call if they should obtain more information about the crime.

Victims should be told of any assistance available and, if applicable, be reminded to call their insurance companies. If victims need legal advice, police officers should advise them about the legal aid office. If a case continues under investigation or will go to court, police should maintain contact with victims (and witnesses). If property is recovered, it should be returned to victims as soon as possible. If a case goes to court, victims should be briefed as to their roles and kept updated. In large departments or those with heavy case loads, maintaining timely contact with victims and witnesses as their cases progress may become a monumental task. Many officers are already overloaded dealing with day-to-day calls and may find little available time to do follow-ups with victims and witnesses. This is one reason online and automated notification systems are gaining in popularity.

Truthfulness and embellishment are problems for the police and prosecution, and indeed some complaints are false, motivated by revenge, jealousy, monetary gain or other reasons. The victim's reluctance to follow through with prosecution is also a problem for police and prosecuting attorneys, especially in cases where the victim knows the offender. The victim may wish to cooperate but may be a poor witness due to mental or emotional instability, fear of reprisal, passage of time or reluctance to testify in court.

POLICE OFFICERS AS VICTIMS

Police officers are not immune from being victimized. Officers are assaulted, robbed, burglarized and victimized in all the ways civilians are, including being killed. The FBI reports that 41 officers were feloniously killed in the line of duty in 19 states in 2008 (*Law Enforcement Officers Killed and Assaulted*, 2009), a significant decline from 2007 and, according to Johnson (2009), the lowest level of all officer fatalities since 1975 in nearly 50 years, despite the fact that there are three times more officers on the streets than in the 1970s. Of the officers feloniously killed in 2008, 35 were killed with firearms, 29 of whom were wearing body armor when fatally shot. Accidental deaths claimed 68 officers in 25 states, 39 of whom died as a result of auto accidents. The number of officers killed by gunfire increased by 24 percent in 2009 (Long, 2009).

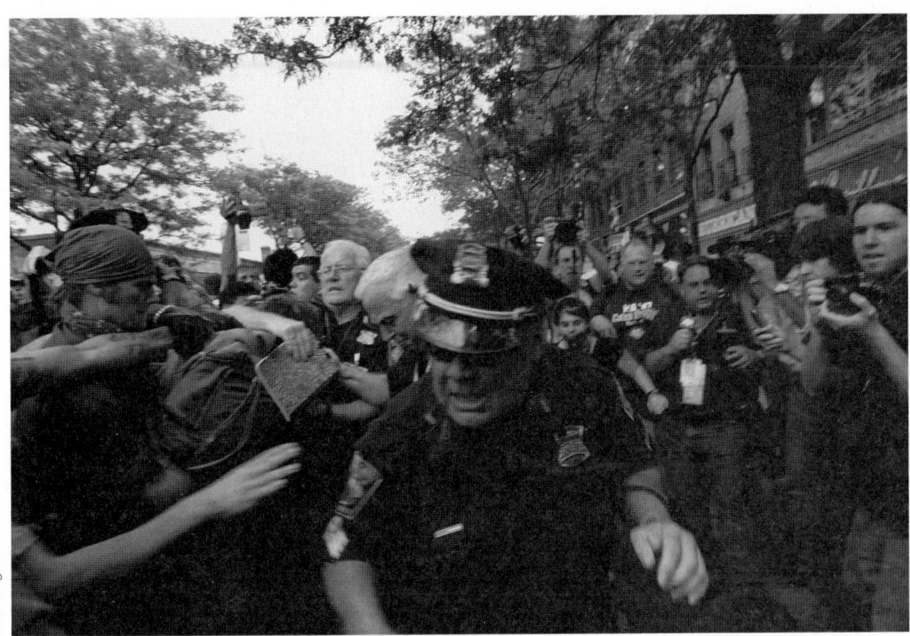

An undeniable risk officers face is becoming victims of the very chaos and violence they are striving to prevent. Here, demonstrators clash with police outside the Democratic Convention in Boston, Massachusetts, in 2004.

Among the officers feloniously killed, the average age was 39 years, with an average 10 years in law enforcement service. Thirty-seven were male; 30 were white, 9 were black, and 1 was American Indian/Alaskan native. The race of one officer was not reported. Of the slain officers, 9 died handling arrest situations, 8 were handling traffic pursuits or traffic stops; 7 died while investigating suspicious persons/circumstances, 7 died during tactical situations (barricaded offender, hostage taking, etc.), 2 died during investigative activity (surveillance, search, etc.), 1 died while handling, transporting or maintaining custody of a prisoner, and 1 died answering a disturbance calls.

The National Law Enforcement Officers Memorial Fund reports that line-of-duty deaths rose nearly 43 percent during the first half of 2009 ("Law Enforcement Officer Deaths," 2010). What is alarming is that nine officers were gunned down for no apparent reason in three separate instances in the spring of 2009. And the ambushes continued into 2010 when a Georgia police lieutenant was killed by a high-powered weapon while he was patrolling an "idyllic countryside rural dirt road" southwest of Atlanta (Raley, 2010). In March 2010, FBI raids in three states netted nine members of a militia group plotting to kill a police officer and then bomb the funeral in the hopes of sparking a war against the government.

The most common way police officers become victims, however, is as secondary victims, dealing with the pain of victims and with the distress of seeing the "bad guys" get off easy or out of prison early. Thus, information about and an understanding of crime, offenders and victims are essential for everyone involved in law enforcement.

Summary

The most frequently used sources of information about crime are the media, official government statistics and self-reporting surveys. The crimes most frequently reported to police, the most serious crimes in the nation, are reported in the FBI's Uniform Crime Reports, which contains data on murder, aggravated assault causing serious bodily harm, forcible rape, robbery, burglary, larceny-theft, motor vehicle theft and arson. Other serious crimes include white-collar crime, computer-related crime, organized crime, bias or hate crime and ritualistic crime.

White-collar crime—occupational or business-related crime—includes (1) credit card and check fraud including identity theft; (2) securities theft and fraud; (3) insurance fraud; (4) consumer fraud, illegal competition and deceptive practices; (5) bankruptcy fraud; (6) embezzlement and pilferage; (7) bribes, kickbacks and payoffs; (8) money laundering; and (9) receiving stolen property.

Of growing concern is white-collar, computer-related crime. Computer crimes are relatively easy to commit and difficult to detect. Most are committed by insiders, and most are not prosecuted. A white-collar crime distinct from other types of crimes is organized crime, which is characterized by corruption and enforcement powers.

Hate crimes may be motivated by bias against a person's race, religion, disability, sexual orientation or ethnicity.

Crimes are committed by youths and adults. Why? Two fundamental philosophies exist. The classical theory sees people as free agents with free will: People commit crimes because they want to. The positivist theory, in contrast, sees criminals as "victims of society" and of their own biological, sociological, cultural and physical environments. Criminal behavior is likely the result of both heredity and life experiences. Most often, violent offending begins among juveniles who have themselves been victimized.

Young (age 12–24) black males from low-income, large households are at greatest risk of victimization. For adults, in general, as income rises and as age increases, the victimization rate decreases. Victims may suffer physical, economic and psychological harm that lasts their entire lives. A second victimization may occur as a result of insensitivity shown by those in the criminal justice system. Victims may also be victimized again by lack of release data and notification and by intimidation. Victims' rights may include the right to appear at sentencing, the right to appear at plea bargaining, the use of victim impact statements before sentencing, the right to be informed of their case's status, the right to be informed of an offender's release from prison and the right to receive restitution.

Discussion Questions

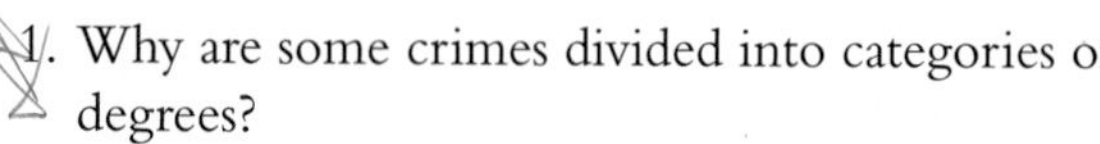

1. Why are some crimes divided into categories or degrees?
2. Would a law that made reporting all crimes to the police mandatory be a good deterrent to future criminal activity?
3. Should additional penalties be imposed on people found guilty of committing bias crimes?
4. Why is it imperative that police officers are skilled at communicating with victims?
5. Do you think a police officer can be considered a "victim of crime" when carrying out their duties, having acknowledged and accepted the dangers ever-present in such a career?

6. Does your state have victim compensation laws? If so how do they compare with those provided in other states?
7. Have you ever been victimized? Has a member of your family? A friend or neighbor? What were the effects?
8. Do you feel that in most cases the police in your area are sensitive to crime victims' needs?
9. Outline the current differences between the rights of criminals and those of victims. Should there be changes in these rights?
10. Should the U.S. Constitution be amended to include victims' rights?

Gale Emergency Services Database Assignments

- Use the Gale Emergency Services Database to help answer the Discussion Questions as appropriate.
- Using the Gale Emergency Services Database, find the article "Swindles, Cons and Rip-Offs: As White Collar Crime Scams Escalate, Law Enforcement's Challenges Mount": http://find.galegroup.com/gps/infomark.do?&contentSet=IAC-Documents&type=retrieve&tabID=T003&prodId=IPS&docId=A138705974&source=gale&srcprod=SP02&userGroupName=cpg3&version=1.0

  Assignment: Read and outline the article, and be prepared to discuss your outline in class.
- Using the Gale Emergency Services Database, find the article "Overcoming obstacles: preparing for computer-related crime": http://find.galegroup.com/gps/infomark.do?&contentSet=IAC-Documents&type=retrieve&tabID=T003&prodId=IPS&docId=A18701405&source=gale&srcprod=SP02&userGroupName=cpg3&version=1.0

  Assignment: Identify some of the challenges law enforcement faces, according to this article, in preparation for this emerging trend in crime. Be prepared to discuss your list with the class.
- Using the Gale Emergency Services Database, find the article "Best Practices of a Hate/Bias Crime Investigation": http://find.galegroup.com/gps/infomark.do?&contentSet=IAC-Documents&type=retrieve&tabID=T003&prodId=IPS&docId=A99696475&source=gale&srcprod=SP02&userGroupName=cpg3&version=1.0

  Assignment: Explain how hate/bias crime is defined by the FBI, and how it is identified. List some of the major challenges of such investigations. Be prepared to discuss your findings with the class.
- Using the Gale Emergency Services Database, find the article "Victims" (Bulletin Reports)(Brief article): http://find.galegroup.com/gps/infomark.do?&contentSet=IAC-Documents&type=retrieve&tabID=T003&prodId=IPS&docId=A143342214&source=gale&srcprod=SP02&userGroupName=cpg3&version=1.0

  Assignment: Find the link within the article and read the pamphlet. Then list what steps you can take if you are a victim of a crime. Again, be prepared to discuss your list in class.

Internet Assignments

- Use the key words *crime news* to search for current articles on crime in the United States.
- Go to the FBI's Web site and then to the Uniform Crime Reports for the latest statistics on serious crime in the United States.
- Select one topic covered in this chapter and research it using the Web.

References

"About Homelessness: FAQs." Washington, DC: National Alliance to End Homelessness, 2010. Retrieved from http://www.endhomelessness.org/section/about_homelessness/faqs

Agnew, Robert. *Why Do Criminals Offend? A General Theory of Crime and Delinquency.* Los Angeles, CA: Roxbury Publishing Company, 2005.

Barnett-Ryan, Cynthia, and Swanson, Gregory. "The Role of State Programs in NIBRS Data Quality." *Journal of Contemporary Criminal Justice*, February 2008, pp.18–31.

Barton, Liz, and Higgins, Dana. "Tips to Help Prevent Identity Theft during Tax Season." *The Police Chief*, March 2008, pp.14–15.

Beaver, Kevin M.; DeLisi, Matt; Mears, Daniel P.; and Stewart, Eric. "Low Self-Control and Contact with the Criminal Justice System in a Nationally Representative Sample of Males." *Justice Quarterly*, December 2009, pp.696–715.

Bosick, Stacey J. "Operationalizing Crime over the Life Course." *Crime & Delinquency*, July 2009, pp.472–496.

Collins, Michelle K. "Child Pornography: A Closer Look." *The Police Chief*, March 2007, pp.40–47.

"Complaints of Online Crimes Hit Record High." Press Release. Washington, DC: Internet Crime Complaint Center, March 30, 2009. Retrieved from http://nw3c.org

"Computer Analysis and Response Team." Washington, DC: FBI Laboratory, 2000. Retrieved from http://www.fbi.gov/hq/lab/org/cart.htm

Crime in the United States, 2009. Washington, DC: United States Department of Justice, Federal Bureau of Investigation, September 2010. Retrieved from http://www.fbi.gov/ucr/09cius.htm

"Developments in the National Incident-Based Reporting System (NIBRS)." Washington, DC: Federal Bureau of Investigation, updated June 2009. Retrieved from http://www.fbi.gov/ucr/nibrs/index.html

The 8% Solution. Washington, DC: OJJDP Fact Sheet #39, November 2001. (FS 200139)

Electronic Crime Scene Investigation: A Guide for First Responders, 2nd ed. Washington, DC: National Institute of Justice, April 2008. (NCJ 219941)

Faggiani, Donald. "Introduction: Special Issue on Research Using the National Incident-Based Reporting System." *Justice Research and Policy*, Fall 2007, Vol.9, No.2, pp.1–7.

"Financial Crimes Report to the Public, Fiscal Year 2008." Washington, DC: Federal Bureau of Investigation, 2009. Retrieved from http://www.fbi.gov/publications/financial/fcs_report2008/financial_crime_2008.htm#corporate

Garner, Gerald W. "Surviving the Circus: How Effective Leaders Work Well with the Media." *The Police Chief*, March 2009, pp.52–57.

A Gathering Storm: Violent Crime in America. Washington, DC: Police Executive Research Forum, October 2006.

Gottfredson, M. R., and Hirschi, T. *A General Theory of Crime.* Stanford, CA: Stanford University Press, 1990.

Halladay, Jessie. "Victim-Notification System Marks 15 Years." *USA Today*, 2009. Retrieved from http://www.usatoday.com/news/nation/2009-12-10-victim-notification-system_N.htm

Hate Crime Statistics 2008. Washington, DC: Federal Bureau of Investigation, November 2009. Retrieved from http://www.fbi.gov/ucr/hc2008/incidents.html

"Hate Map." Montgomery, AL: Southern Poverty Law Center. 2010. Retrieved from http://www.splcenter.org/get-informed/hatemap

"Innocent Images National Initiative." Washington, DC: Federal Bureau of Investigation, revised December 11, 2007. Retrieved from http://www.fbi.gov/publications/innocent.htm

"Intentionally Set Structure Fires." Washington, DC: USFA Arson Fire Statistics, FEMA, 2010. Retrieved from http://www.usfa.dhs.gov/statistics/arson

Jargowsky, Paul A. "Cause or Consequence? Suburbanization and Crime in U.S. Metropolitan Areas." *Crime & Delinquency*, January 2009, pp.28–50.

Johnson, Kevin. "Officer Deaths Up in First Half of '09." *PoliceOne.com News*, July 13, 2009. Retrieved from http://www.policeone.com/police-heroes/articles/1855213-Officer-deaths-up-in-first-half-of-09

Kanable, Rebecca. "The Face of Identity Theft." *Law Enforcement Technology*, April 2009, pp.28–33.

Kaufman, Joanne M. "Gendered Responses to Serious Strain: The Argument for a General Strain Theory of Deviance." *Justice Quarterly*, September 2009, pp.410–444.

Keenan, Vernon M., and O'Neal, Marsha. "Identity Theft File." *The Police Chief*, May 2007, pp.32–34.

"Law Enforcement Officer Deaths: Mid-Year 2010 Report. After 50-Year Low, Law Enforcement Fatalities Surge 43% in First Half of 2010." Washington, DC: National Law Enforcement Officers Memorial Fund (NLEOMF), July 2010. Retrieved from http://www.nleomf.org/assets/pdfs/reports/2010_MidYear_Report.pdf

Law Enforcement Officers Killed and Assaulted 2008. Washington, DC: Federal Bureau of Investigation, October 2009. Retrieved from http://www.fbi.gov/ucr/killed/2008

Lombroso, Cesare. *Crime: Its Causes and Remedies.* Montclair, NJ: Patterson Smith, 1968. Originally published in 1911.

Long, Colleen. "Number of Officers Killed by Gunfire Increased 24 Percent in '09." *PoliceOne.com News*, December 14, 2009. Retrieved from http://www.policeone.com/pc_print.asp?vid=1978133

Manley, John. "Arson Statistics: Who Is Setting the Fires and How Often Does Arson Occur?" SearchWarp.com. April 8, 2008. Retrieved from http://searchwarp.com/swa318089.htm

Messner, Steven F., and Rosenfeld, Richard. *Crime and the American Dream*, 4th ed. Belmont, CA: Wadsworth, 2007.

Moore, Carole. "Making Friends with the Media." *Law Enforcement Technology*, January 2007, p.106.

Moore, Carole. "Not Just from the Other Side of the Tracks Anymore." *Law Enforcement Technology*, June 2009, pp.16–21.

National Strategy to Secure Cyberspace. Washington, DC: Department of Homeland Security. February 2003, reviews and modified July 21, 2009. Retrieved from http://www.dhs.gov/files/publications/editorial_0329.shtm

NW3C Annual Report July 2008–June 2009. Glen Allen, VA: National White Collar Crime Center.

Organized Crime. Washington, DC: Federal Bureau of Investigation (no date).

"OVC Technical Assistance Guides." Washington, DC: Office of Victims of Crime, January 2010. Retrieved from http://www.ovcttac.gov/taResources/OVCTAGuides/welcome.html

"Parallel Justice." Vermont Center for Crime Victim Services, 2010. Retrieved from http://www.ccvs.state.vt.us/joomla/index.php?option=com_content&task=category§ionid=9&id=28&Itemid=103

Piquero, Nicole Leeper; Carmichael, Stephanie; and Piquero, Alex R. "Assessing the Perceived Seriousness of White-Collar and Street Crimes." *Crime & Delinquency*, April 2008, pp.291–312.

Raley, Dan. "Ga. Cop Ambushed, Killed with High Powered Weapon." *PoliceOne.com News*, February 16, 2010. Retrieved from http://www.policeone.com/active-shooter/articles/2004892-Ga-cop-ambushed-killed-with-high-powered-weapon

Rand, Michael R. *Criminal Victimization, 2005* (National Crime Victimization Survey). Washington, DC: Bureau of Justice Statistics Bulletin, September 2009. (NCJ 227777)

"Reporters Offer PERF Chiefs Hard-Boiled View of Media Relations." *Subject to Debate*, May 2008, pp.1, 4–5.

Spadanuta, Laura. "Identity Theft Task Force." *Security Management*, August 2007, pp.18–20.

"Take a Bite Out of Cyber Crime" Campaign. Washington, DC: National Crime Prevention Council, 2006.

ten Bensel, R. Testimony. Quoted in *Child at Risk*, 41. Office of Juvenile Justice and Delinquency Prevention, U.S. Department of Justice. Washington, DC: U.S. Government Printing Office (no date).

Thornberry, Terence P., and Krohn, Marvin D. "The Self-Report Method for Measuring Delinquency and Crime." *Measurement and Analysis of Crime and Justice*, April 2000, pp.33–43.

Tooley, Michael; Linkenbach, Jeff; and Lande, Brian J. "The Media, the Public, and the Law Enforcement Community: Correcting Misperceptions." *The Police Chief*, June 2009, pp.62–67.

2009 OVC Report to the Nation Fiscal Years 2007–2008: Putting Victims First. Washington, DC: Office for Victims of Crime, 2009. (NCJ 226030)

Unnever, James D.; Benson, Michael L.; and Cullen, Francis T. "Public Support for Getting Tough on Corporate

Crime: Racial and Political Divides." *Journal of Research in Crime and Delinquency*, May 2008, pp.163–190.

Weiner, Rachel. "Hate Crimes Signed into Law 11 Years after Matthew Shepard's Death." *The Huffington Post*, October 28, 2009. Retrieved from http://www.huffingtonpost.com/2009/10/28/hate-crimes-bill-to-be-si_n_336883.html

"White-Collar Crime." Washington, DC: Federal Bureau of Investigation, no date. Retrieved from http://www.fbi.gov/whitecollarcrime.htm

Widom, Cathy S., and Maxfield, Michael G. *An Update on the "Cycle of Violence."* Washington, DC: National Institute of Justice Research in Brief, February 2001. (NCJ 184894)

SECTION II

CONTEMPORARY LAW ENFORCEMENT

Section I described the evolution of law enforcement from its historical roots to its development in the United States. Wuestewald (2004, pp.22–23), in addressing the graduation ceremony of the Oklahoma Council of Law Enforcement Education and Training, describes the differences new officers of today will face compared with what they faced 30 years ago as rookies:

> Of all differences between my day and theirs, technology represents the greatest contrast and the supreme challenge. Consider this: when I began my career as an officer, technology was a 1977 Plymouth Fury with a 400-cubic inch, 4 bbi V-8, an old hickory nightstick and a .357 revolver. Now, compare that with the fact that these officers will drive a police car with more sophisticated electronics than the first Apollo moon shot—cars fully equipped with state-of-the-art mobile data computers, digital video cameras and 800 megahertz radios. They will wear lightweight ballistic vests made of space-age material that provide incredible new levels of protection. They will carry high-capacity, 40-caliber semiautomatic pistols, pepper spray and electronic impulse Tasers capable of stopping even the meanest and most determined attacker. They will have access to infrared and thermal-imaging devices to help them see into the darkness. They will use lasers to catch speeding motorists, and they will swipe a digital driver's license to produce an electronic ticket. They will use DNA to identify violent offenders and GPS tracking devices to follow drug dealers, and crime mapping will help them predict where the next burglary will occur.

This section looks at technology and more, beginning with an overview of contemporary policing (Chapter 4) followed by a look at patrol, the backbone of policing, as well as traffic, often a major responsibility of patrol (Chapter 5). Next is a description of specialized roles of police, including investigation, profilers, intelligence officers, juvenile officers, vice officers, special weapons and tactics (SWAT) officers, K-9 assisted officers and reserve officer (Chapter 6). The section concludes with an in-depth discussion of the various strategies being used in policing in the 21st century, including community policing and its emphasis on partnership and problem solving as well as data-driven, intelligence-led and evidence-based policing (Chapter 7).

CHAPTER 4

Contemporary Policing: An Overview

As a law enforcement officer, my fundamental duty is to serve the community; to safeguard lives and property; to protect the innocent against deception, the weak against oppression or intimidation and the peaceful against violence or disorder; and to respect the constitutional rights of all to liberty, equality and justice.

—Law Enforcement Code of Ethics

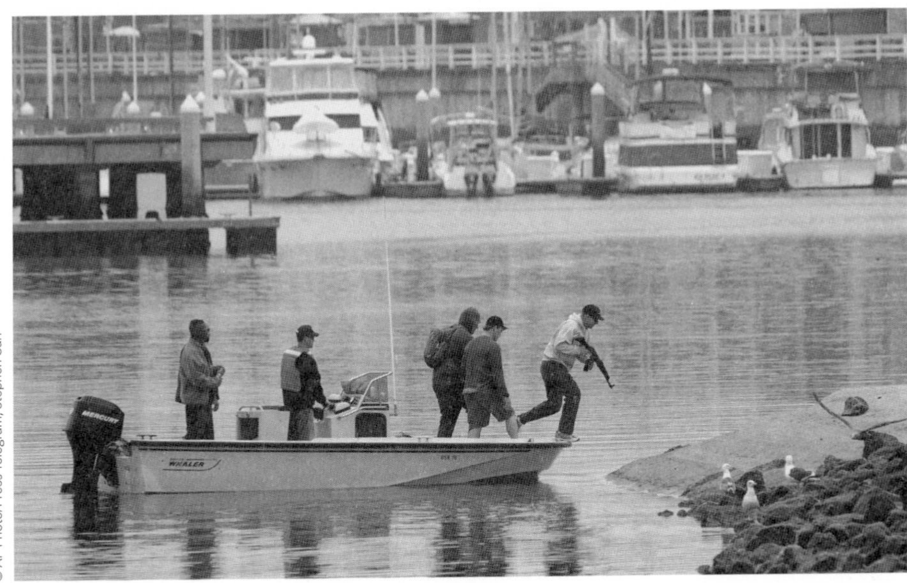
© AP Photo/Press Telegram, Stephen Carr

Policing is always evolving. Here, law enforcement officers portraying terrorists land on the shores at Rainbow Harbor, California, as part of the largest port security full-scale exercise to test the state's readiness for and response to terrorist attacks. More than 3,000 emergency responders from approximately 70 local, state and federal agencies participated in the "Golden Guardian" exercise, which also simulated a terrorist takeover of a passenger ferry near the Port of Long Beach and an active shooter in Shoreline Aquatic Park.

Do You Know . . .

- Why we have police?
- How police agencies relate to the people?
- What five traditional goals most law enforcement agencies set?
- What a principal challenge for law enforcement is?
- What additional goals are established by community policing?
- What two basic units exist in most police departments?
- What functions are handled in administration?
- How officers receive their information?
- What types of records are typically used in law enforcement?
- Why centralization of records is encouraged?
- What is required by a data privacy act?
- What functions are handled in field service?
- What basic styles of policing have been identified?
- How the police image arises?

Can You Define?

administrative services
community policing
discretion
E911
field services
image
interoperability
police authority
organizational culture
reverse 911
roll call
span of control
typologies

INTRODUCTION

A police funeral symbolizes six themes that illuminate the meanings of police in our contemporary society:

> First, the police, to many audiences, represent the presence of the civil body politic in everyday life—they symbolize the capacity of the state to intervene and the concern of the state for the affairs of its citizenry. To many they symbolize as well the continuity and integrity of the society by their visibility and attachment to traditional values of patriotism, honor, duty, and commitment. . . .
>
> Second, the mobilization in uniform of a large body of officers transmits messages about their mutual identification with the corporate body of police—it speaks to the reality of the occupation as formal social control. . . .
>
> Third, the police role conveys a sense of *sacredness* or awesome power that lies at the root of political order, and authority, the claims a state makes upon its people for deference to rules, laws, and norms. . . .
>
> Fourth, the police, and by inversion the death of a police officer, represent also the means by which the political authorities maintain the status quo. They act in the interests of the powerful and the authoritative against those without power and without access to the means to power. . . .
>
> Fifth, the police represent the capacity to deter citizens from committing acts that threaten the order they are believed to symbolize. The police are expected to deter crime, to deter immorality, to deter evil thoughts, or conspiracies to commit crimes. The loss of a police life can be seen as an indication of the vulnerability of

Police officers line the road from the Salem Baptist Church in McDonnough, Georgia, as other officers march alongside the funeral procession carrying the remains of Forest Park Police Officer Richard Cash. Representatives from more than 100 law enforcement agencies from around the state attended the funeral service for Cash, who was shot during a traffic stop in Forest Park.

the society, of the weakness of the sacred moral binding of the society, and of the reduced capacity to deter such acts. . . .

Finally, this drama with its associate public media coverage indicates and reaffirms the centrality of formal social control in everyday life, and it provides a legitimate occasion for the dramatization of the palpable police presence. (Manning, 1997, pp.20–23)

THE CHAPTER AT A GLANCE

This chapter begins with a look at why we have police and what police do. Next is a discussion of how policing relates to the people, followed by a look at the basic goals of policing and the organization of law enforcement agencies, including the division into administrative and field services. Then rural policing is examined, followed by the police culture and styles of policing. The chapter concludes with a discussion of the police image and the public's satisfaction with and confidence in the police.

WHY WE HAVE POLICE

Why does a modern society such as ours need police? Think about that. Why might you call the police? What if a neighbor's barking dog kept you awake night after night and the owner ignored your complaints? You might sue him, but that would involve time and expense. You might consider shooting the dog, but that could get you sued. Society offers you another option: Call the police. Police sociologist Egon Bittner (1974, p.30) says we have this option because situations occur in which "something-ought-not-to-be-happening-and-about-which-something-ought-to-be-done-NOW!"

In our society the police have the authority to do something and to do it now. That something may involve coercive force. Bittner (1980) suggests that this capacity to use force is the core of the police role: "In sum, the role of the police is to address all sorts of human problems when and insofar as their solutions do or may possibly require the use of force at the point of their occurrence. This lends homogeneity to such diverse procedures as catching a criminal, driving the mayor to the airport, evicting a drunk person from a bar, directing traffic, crowd control, taking care of lost children, administering medical first aid, and separating fighting relatives." The police can demand conformity to society's laws and expectations.

 Police are necessary when coercion is required to enforce the laws.

The widespread stereotyped image of the police, however, commonly overemphasizes their role as "crime fighters," often to the exclusion of all other roles.

WHAT POLICE DO

What is it that makes the general public think of the law enforcement aspect of police work more often than the social service aspect, when approximately 90 percent of a police officer's time is spent in the social service function?

> The cover of a major city's annual police report dramatically shows two police officers reaching for their guns as they burst through the doors of a massive black and white police car which is screeching to a halt . . . the flashing red lights and screaming siren complete the illustration. A less dramatic scene on an inside page of the report shows a police officer talking to a grateful mother whose lost child was returned. Which one of these illustrations most accurately describes the police role? . . . The *New York Times* reports that policemen like to think of themselves as uniformed soldiers in an extremely dangerous war against crime . . . in fact the police are more social workers and administrators than crime fighters. (Webster, n.d., p.94)

Most people have ideas about what the police do. According to Manning (1997, p.27), "'To police' means in the most general sense to control by political means the behavior and morality of the members of a politically organized unit. This sense of the word was derived early from the Greek word *polis*, meaning *city*, later roughly translated as *politics*. Policing in this sense means controlling, monitoring (in terms of correcting misguided behavior), tracking and altering, if required, public conduct. Policing also refers . . . to the tasks that people expect the police individually and in the aggregate to perform for them."

So are the police primarily crime fighters or preservers of the peace? The answer varies by department, but in most departments the police serve both functions. Where the emphasis is placed is increasingly influenced by the citizens within the jurisdiction. The police derive their power from the citizens and are accountable to them.

POLICING AND THE PEOPLE

Police authority comes from the people—their laws and institutions. Although the Tenth Amendment reserves police power for state and local governments, these governments must adhere to the principles of the Constitution and the Bill of Rights as well as to federal and state statutes. Police agencies are not only part of their local community but they are also part of state and federal government, which, through legislation, provides their formal base of authority. Police are also part of the state and federal criminal justice system, which, through the court, determines society's course in deterring lawbreakers and rehabilitating offenders, as was illustrated in Figure 2.1.

police authority
The right to direct and command.

The goals and priorities of a police agency are largely established by what the community wants. For example, a community might want more patrols at night, stricter enforcement of traffic regulations during rush hour or reduced enforcement for certain violations such as speeding. The police response to a community's request for specialized enforcement can occur either by direct communication from the community to the police chief or through the local government council, to whom the chief answers.

Priorities are often more influenced by the desires of the policed than by any other consideration. Because the success of policing depends heavily on public support, the citizens' wishes must be listened to and considered.

The people largely determine the goals of policing and give law enforcement agencies their authority to meet these goals. Citizen support is vital.

Because law enforcement is a highly visible representative of local government whose officers are on duty 24/7, people often call upon police for services that they are not specifically required to perform. Other agencies might provide these services, but people do not know of them. For example, if a woman seeks help in dealing with a drunken husband (he is not abusing her—he is just drunk), a drug counselor, minister or social worker might be the appropriate person to call. The woman, however, often does not know this. Because the police agency's reactions to requests for help affect the amount of respect they receive and promote a cooperative relationship with the public, they usually respond as helpfully as possible, even when the matter is technically civil and outside their responsibility.

TRADITIONAL GOALS OF POLICING

Because citizens have such a great influence on the goals of policing within the community, the goals of different police agencies vary. Traditionally, however, five basic goals have been established.

Historically, the basic goals of most police agencies are to

1. Enforce laws.
2. Preserve the peace.
3. Prevent crimes.
4. Protect civil rights and civil liberties.
5. Provide services.

These goals often overlap. For example, officers intervening in a fight may not only enforce a law by arresting a suspect for assault but they may also maintain order; prevent others from becoming involved in the fight; protect the civil rights and civil liberties of the suspect, the victim and the bystanders; and provide emergency service to an injured victim.

Success or failure in meeting each goal directly affects the success or failure of fulfilling the other goals. Although five goals normally established by police are listed, in reality policing is a single role composed of numerous responsibilities. Any discussion of goals in law enforcement must also consider the vast differences between small and large agencies, as well as between rural, suburban and urban departments. Small agencies, often located in rural or suburban areas, tend to have much less specialization, a closer relationship to the citizens being served and less diversity among those citizens and personnel within the agency. Large agencies, often located in urban areas, are likely to have more specialization, a more-distant relationship to the citizens being served and much greater diversity among those citizens.

Enforcing Laws

The designation *law enforcement agency* underscores the central importance of this long-accepted goal. Historically, enforcing laws has been a prime goal of policing. However this goal has become increasingly complex.

Unfortunately, because police are in the closest contact with the public, they are often blamed for failures in the criminal justice system. For example, an assault victim whose attacker is found not guilty in court may feel resentment toward not only the court but also the police department. Right or wrong, the release of a suspect from custody for lack of sufficient evidence, the failure of a prosecutor to take a case to trial or the failure of the corrections system to reform a convict prior to parole or release all directly affect the public image of policing. The public image of policing is critical, considering a large percentage of police work is in direct response to citizen complaints or reports. Public support may be the single most important factor in the total law enforcement effort. Furthermore, public confidence is eroded by the failures of the criminal justice system, as is the confidence of the police, which contributes to them becoming cynical over time about the efficacy of the system.

discretion

The freedom of an agency or individual officer to make choices as to whether to act; freedom to act or judge on one's own.

Because each community and each state has numerous statutes and limited resources, full enforcement of all laws is never possible. Even if it were, it is questionable whether full enforcement would be in keeping with legislative intent or the people's wishes. **Discretion**, that is, judgment, must be exercised as to which laws to enforce. Both the department and the public must accept that not all laws can be enforced at all times. Each department must decide which reported crimes to actively investigate and to what degree, and which unreported crimes to seek out and to what degree. The law does not set priorities; it simply defines crimes, classifies them as felonies or misdemeanors and assesses penalties for them. The department sets its own priorities based on the community's needs.

Usually departments concentrate law enforcement activities on serious crimes—those that pose the greatest threat to public safety and/or cause the greatest economic losses. From that point on, priorities are usually determined by past department experience, citizen wishes and expectations, and available resources.

Preserving the Peace

Preserving the peace has also long been accepted by police as an important goal. They have the legal authority to arrest individuals for disturbing the peace or for disorderly conduct.

Police are often called to intervene in noncriminal conduct such as that which occurs at public events (crowd control), in social relations (domestic disputes) and in traffic control (parking, pedestrians) to maintain law and order. They often help people solve problems that they cannot cope with alone. Frequently such problems, if unresolved, could escalate into a crime. For example, a dispute between business partners or a landlord and tenant might result in bodily harm—assault.

This potential for disputes and disturbances exists in a variety of situations—from parties to traffic crashes, from young people blasting stereos to other incidents where hostility may arise. When alcohol is involved, the potential for violence increases. The fine line between obnoxious behavior that infringes on other people's peace and harmless antics that merely defy standards of "good behavior" is easily crossed. Neighborhood residents may be annoyed when teenagers hang out on the streets, and people walking down a city sidewalk may be disturbed by activists passing out political or religious fliers, yet the teenagers and activists each have a legal right to be doing what they are doing.

Civil disturbances and riots present another challenge to police in preserving community peace and safety. The civil disturbances on campuses throughout the country in the 1960s highlighted the role of the police in controlling such disturbances. Although civil disturbances are not as prevalent today, demonstrations continue throughout the country—for example, antiwar protests, demonstrations against legislative decisions, demonstrations for or against abortion and protests against industries engaged in manufacturing war materials.

In dealing with civil disturbances, the primary responsibilities of police officers are to maintain order and to protect lives and assets. In the event of sit-in demonstrations, it may be necessary to forcibly remove participants. However, police must also be aware of citizens' constitutionally protected right to peacefully assemble. Only when the assembly is no longer peaceful do officers have the responsibility to intervene. Determining what constitutes peaceful assembly places a large amount of discretionary power in the hands of police officers.

Labor–management disputes and strikes may also threaten community peace and safety. Strikes are legal, but as with the right to assemble, the strike must be peaceful. If strikers physically restrict others from crossing the picket line, they are acting illegally, and the police may be called to intervene. In such instances police officers must remain neutral. Their only responsibility is to prevent violence and property damage or loss.

A department's effectiveness in actually preserving the peace is largely determined by public acceptance of this role. Often if police officers simply ask a landlord to allow an evicted tenant access to his or her apartment to retrieve personal possessions or ask the host of a loud party to turn down the stereo, this is enough. Mere police presence may reduce the possibility of a crime—at least temporarily. Here, as in enforcing laws, public support is vital.

Preventing Crime

Crime prevention is closely related to law enforcement and peace preservation. If the peace has been kept, crime has, in effect, been prevented. Crime prevention differs from peacekeeping and law enforcing in that it attempts to eliminate potentially dangerous or criminal situations. It is proactive.

If police are highly visible in a community, crimes may be prevented. For example, a routine patrol might not only discover a crime in progress but also prevent crimes from being committed. This connection is extremely difficult to prove, however, because it is not known what crimes might have been committed if the police were not present.

Crime prevention activities often undertaken by police departments include working with juveniles, cooperating with probation and parole personnel, educating the public, instigating operation identification programs and providing visible evidence of police authority. A crime prevention partnership between the public and the police together is the "Neighborhood Watch." In addition many community services often provided by police departments aid in crime prevention.

Just as police officers cannot be expected to enforce all the laws at all times, they cannot be expected to prevent all crimes from occurring. Klockars (1991, p.244) suggests, "The 'war on crime' is a war police not only cannot win, but cannot in any real sense fight. They cannot win it because it is simply not within their power to change those things—such as unemployment, the age distribution of the population, moral education, freedom, civil liberties, ambitions, and the social and economic opportunities to realize them—that influence the amount of crime in any society."

Protecting Constitutional Rights

Not only are departments charged with enforcing laws, preserving the peace and preventing crime but they are also expected to do so as specified by the U.S. Constitution and Bill of Rights.

The first paragraph of the *Law Enforcement Code of Ethics* concludes with the statement that law enforcement officers have a fundamental duty "to respect the constitutional rights of all to liberty, equality and justice." As noted by the National Advisory Commission on Criminal Justice Standards and Goals (1973, p.9) more than a quarter century ago: "Any definition of the police role must acknowledge that the Constitution imposes restrictions on the power of the legislatures to prohibit protected conduct, and to some extent defines the limits of police authority in the enforcement of established laws."

The commission, however, goes on to state (1973, p.9), "Concern for the constitutional rights of accused persons processed by the police has tended to obscure the fact that the police have an affirmative obligation to protect all persons in the free exercise of their rights. The police must provide safety for persons exercising their constitutional right to assemble, to speak freely, and to petition for redress of their grievances."

Police officers are independent decision makers and have both personal and positional power. One of the most powerful tools officers have is discretion. Right or wrong, officers are often guided by the seriousness of the law violation; who committed it; and the person's age, race and social class. Because of the potential for discretion to appear, instead, as discrimination, or, worse, to actually constitute discrimination, it is imperative that departments hire recruits with high levels of integrity and common sense and to provide ongoing training as to the appropriate application of their discretionary power.

Many citizens are angered when a suspect's rights prevent prosecuting a case. They begin to doubt the criminal justice system. However, should these same people find themselves suspected of a crime, they would expect their rights to be fully protected. As Sir John Fortescue said, "Indeed, one would rather twenty guilty persons should escape the punishment of death than one innocent person should be executed." The United States must guarantee all citizens, even those perceived as unworthy of such protection, their constitutional rights, or there is danger of a police state.

The authority, goals and methods of the police must promote individual liberty, public safety and social justice. Protecting civil rights and civil liberties is perceived by some as the single most important goal of policing. As a case in point, the National Advisory Commission on Criminal Justice Standards and Goals states (1973, p.9), "If the overall purposes of the police service in today's society were narrowed to a single objective, that objective would be to preserve the peace in a manner consistent with the freedoms secured by the Constitution."

These civil rights and civil liberties also extend to juveniles. Juveniles are subjected to a conglomeration of laws and restraints that do not apply to adults, called status offenses. For example, juveniles are often arrested for liquor law violations, curfew violations, absenting from home, truancy, smoking and incorrigibility. Usually the police deal directly with status offenses, warning the youths or returning them to their parents unless the youths have been habitual offenders.

Concern for crime control must be balanced by concern for due process—a principal challenge for law enforcement.

Providing Services

In addition to enforcing laws, preserving the peace, preventing crime and protecting civil rights and liberties, the police are often called on to provide additional services to their community. This role is acknowledged in the first sentence of the *Law Enforcement Code of Ethics*: "As a law enforcement officer, my fundamental duty is to serve the community." Many police departments have as their motto: "To Serve and Protect."

The types of service requested of and delivered by the police include giving information, directions and advice; counseling and referring; licensing and registering vehicles; intervening in domestic arguments; working with neglected children; rendering emergency medical or rescue services; dealing with alcoholics and the mentally ill; finding lost children; dealing with stray animals; and controlling traffic and crowds. In addition many police departments provide community education programs regarding crime, drugs, safety and the like.

Police departments may or may not provide several other services, depending on local policy and available resources, including helping to locate missing persons; investigating damage-to-property incidents; providing a lost and found; dealing with missing and stray animals; providing escort services; assisting people who have locked themselves out of their vehicles or homes; transporting civilians on official business; licensing handguns, parade permits and the like; inspecting buildings for adherence to fire codes, health codes and building codes; inspecting trucks' weights; and answering alarms, which can be a tremendous drain on a police department given the false-alarm problem.

Patrol officers are often the first on the scene of a situation requiring emergency services. For example, at the scene of a traffic crash, police are responsible for providing first aid to any injured persons. They may also be called to help people who have been injured in other ways or who become seriously ill. Police officers need to be thoroughly trained and certified in cardiopulmonary resuscitation (CPR) and advanced first aid, including measures to stop bleeding and to deal with fractures, shock, burns and epileptic seizures. In some states police officers are required to have a minimum license of a first responder.

Police officers may be required to transport accident victims or gravely ill or injured people to the nearest medical facility. In some communities, the police department is the sole ambulance service, and patrol cars are specially equipped to serve as ambulances. This policy of providing ambulance service tends to make the public more appreciative of the police department and may foster citizen cooperation. A benefit of such a policy is that it can be very cost effective in providing, essentially, two professional services for the price of one. Several drawbacks exist, however, including the fact that an officer who wears the "hat" of paramedic, once they have entered an incident as such, must follow through and remain as a medical service provider until the situation is resolved, which leaves the jurisdiction short one police officer until they are cleared from their medical commitment.

Natural disasters, such as floods, tornadoes, hurricanes, fires and earthquakes, can produce emergency conditions requiring police action. Many departments are also actively involved in search-and-rescue operations that may or may not be necessitated by natural disasters.

In some departments police and fire fighting are combined into a public safety department. In such instances police officers must be trained in fire suppression techniques. In departments where the police are not primarily responsible for fire-suppression activities, they may still be the first to arrive at the scene of a fire and can lend valuable assistance to the firefighters.

Many departments are involved in implementing and providing community programs, the most common being programs for youths and educational programs to promote safety and prevent crime. Programs for youths may include Police

Activities League (PAL) programs, school resource officers, McGruff, Explorer posts, the Drug Abuse Resistance Education (DARE) program and bike-safety programs. Safety enhancement and crime prevention programs include neighborhood or block watch programs; Operation Identification programs; and programs aimed at improving home security, store security and automobile security.

Considerable disagreement exists regarding what type and amount of services the police should provide. They are often inappropriately asked to perform functions that might better be performed by another government agency—usually because they are the only government representatives available around the clock and because they have the authority to use force if necessary. However, in many small cities and towns, the police services provided (even though considered by some as inappropriate "social services") could not be provided by any other agency.

Many police departments offer referral services to direct people in need to the proper agency. For example in Washington, DC, the department uses a *Referral Handbook of Social Services* that indexes available governmental and private services by problem and agency. Police in Milwaukee, Wisconsin, have a comprehensive directory of almost 500 community agencies and organizations.

Of primary importance is that people who need help receive it; *who* provides the help is secondary. Because many people are likely to turn first to the police for help, however, the department must be prepared either to provide the help or to refer the person to an agency that can provide it.

CONTEMPORARY GOALS RESULTING FROM COMMUNITY POLICING

Police departments that have implemented the **community policing** philosophy still place importance on the traditional goals of law enforcement. However, most departments have also established two new important goals.

community policing

A philosophy that emphasizes a problem-solving partnership between the police and the citizens in working toward a healthy, crime-free environment; also called *neighborhood policing*.

Goals resulting from implementing community policing usually include forming partnerships with the community and a proactive, problem-solving approach to crime, fear of crime and crime prevention.

Chapter 7 discusses community policing.

ORGANIZATION OF THE DEPARTMENT

The nation's police departments vary greatly, from small, informally organized departments with few employees to highly organized metropolitan police departments with many subdivisions and thousands of employees. The specific organization of a police department is influenced by the department's size, location and the extent and type of crime with which it must deal. For example, small police departments often combine patrol, traffic, community services and investigative tasks in a single division; large police departments usually have separate divisions for each. A community with a major freeway running through its business section faces different problems than a community located on a coast or on a border

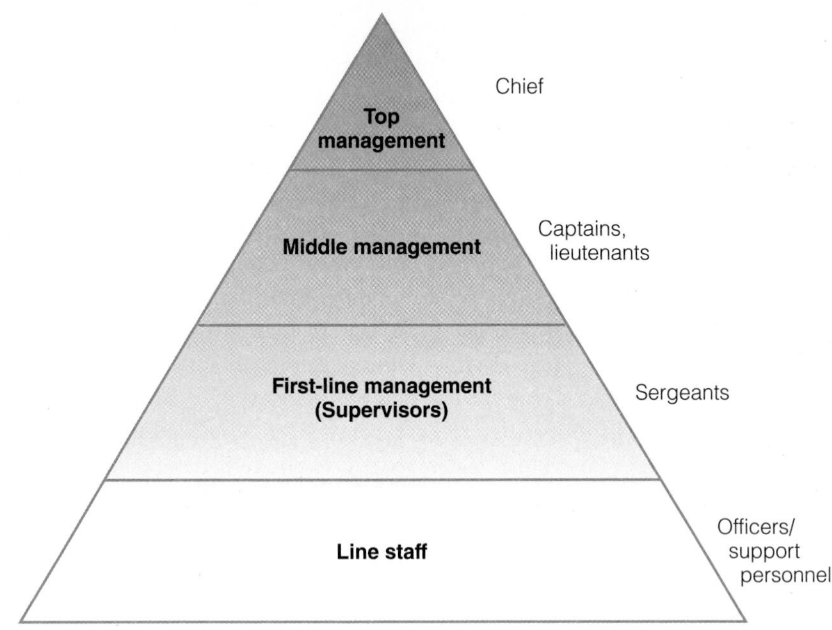

FIGURE 4.1 Typical Police Department Management Structure

between the United States and Canada or Mexico. Communities with large groups of minorities face different problems than those that are homogeneous. For some communities traffic control is a major problem; for others gambling, smuggling or racial unrest may be priorities.

Whatever an agency's size, the police organization seeks "strict accountability through a clear rank structure, military symbols and procedures, a rigid communicational hierarchy, and close supervision" (Manning, 1997, p.96). The chief of police oversees the operation of the entire department. Under the chief, depending on the size of the department, are captains, lieutenants, sergeants and police officers. Traditionally most departments have been structured along a paramilitary model, with a pyramid-shaped hierarchy and the chief at the top, as depicted in Figure 4.1.

Span of Control

span of control
The number of individuals or resources one supervisor can manage effectively during emergency response incidents or special events.

Span of control describes the number of individuals or resources one supervisor can manage effectively during emergency response incidents or special events.

The two main schools of thought in organizational management theory regarding span of control are classical and contemporary. Classical (pre-1950) experts believe supervisors need to control their subordinates and often specify the proper ratio as no more than six subordinates per supervisor. Contemporary management theory contends that such classical command-and-control organizations are inefficient and advocate higher spans of control and flatter organizational structures.

Many departments are moving away from a tall hierarchy to a more-flattened structure with fewer officers in supervisory positions, more officers in the patrol division and an emphasis on teamwork rather than on strict obedience to higher authority. The following factors enable an increased span of control (Lane, 2006, p.76):

1. Efficient use of information technology
2. Higher quality in skills and capabilities of subordinates
3. Enhanced skills and capabilities of the supervisor
4. Improved quality of the department's training program
5. Increased harmony of the workforce

Lane (2006, p.78) also cites factors narrowing the span of control:

1. Change taking place in the work environment
2. Dispersed workforce, either temporally or geographically
3. New and inexperienced workforce
4. Fluctuating administrative requirements
5. Diminished extent of coordination
6. Change in employees' expectations

The primary trend in business and government is to increase the span of control ratios, which create the following advantages (Lane, 2006, p.80):

- Improvement of communications by eliminating multiple levels of management
- More harmonious pay and compensation by eliminating various pay grades and job duplications
- Reduction in operating costs by eliminating multiple layers of management
- Reduction in operating costs by eliminating support staff and space needed for management positions
- Elimination of the confusion of accountability that may exist with multiple layers of management

Whatever the span of control, law enforcement administrators have two sets of obligations:

- *Internal obligations*—concerned with running the organization: organizing, staffing, directing and controlling.
- *External obligations*—concerned with the organization's "environment": dealing with important outside forces that affect the agency, such as politicians, the community, the media, judges, prosecutors and the like.

To meet these obligations the police chief must coordinate the efforts of two primary groups—administrative and field services.

Most police departments are organized into two basic units: administrative services and field services. Tasks and personnel are assigned to one or the other.

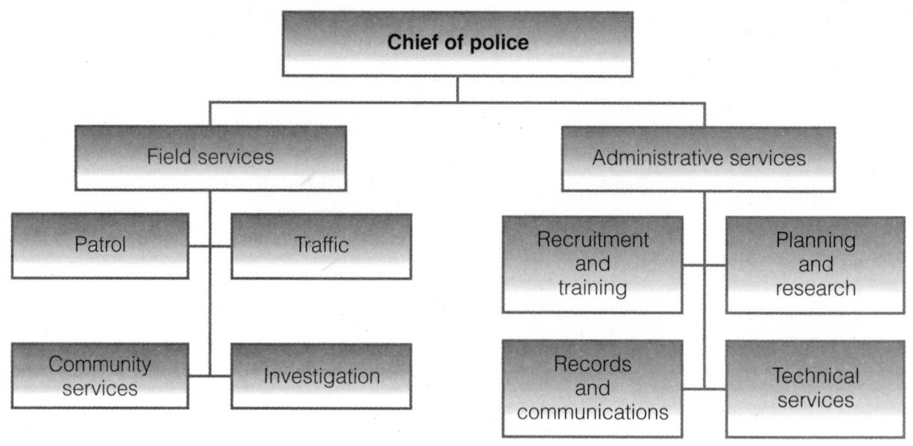

FIGURE 4.2 Typical Department Organization of Services

administrative services
Those services such as recruiting, training, planning and research, records, communications, crime laboratories and facilities, including the police headquarters and jail.

field services
The operations or line divisions of a law enforcement agency, such as patrol, traffic control, community service, and investigation.

Administrative services (also called staff or support services) include recruiting and training, planning and research, records and communications, and crime laboratories and facilities, including police headquarters and jail. Teamwork is essential within and between field services and administrative services. **Field services** (also called operations or line services) include patrol, traffic control, community service and investigation. Whatever the size or configuration of the department, basic administrative and field services are expected. The clear lines depicted in Figure 4.2 may become blurred as departments move to community policing and a team approach.

ADMINISTRATIVE SERVICES

Administrative services provide support for field services and include communications and records, recruitment and training and provision of special facilities and services.

Administrative services are those functions that occur "behind the scenes," away from the front line of the officer in the field. These services include clerical and technical efforts to support and manage the information needed and generated by those in field services. Administrative services' two areas that most directly affect the efficient provision of field services are communications and records.

Communications

Moore (2009, p.10) contends, "The communications center is the heart and soul of an agency's operations." Although some agencies maintain their own in-house communication service, or dispatch center, and smaller agencies often contract with larger agencies for such services, the current trend is for a shared, centralized communication service that dispatches to numerous local jurisdictions. Critic of this trend are concerned that the quality of service to specific communities may suffer as a result of a shared dispatch center; however, proponents argue that communication effectiveness and resource efficiency is maximized when dispatch services are shared.

To properly serve the community, police officers must be kept currently and completely informed. They must know where and how much of each type of crime occurs. They also have to know what services are needed.

 Current information is usually provided at roll call or by radio, phone and computer.

Roll Call One of the most important functions of the administrative division in its support of the other units is keeping members informed of daily police operations and providing administrative instructions, special assignments and tasks to be performed. This is usually done at **roll call**, a briefing at the beginning of a shift, before officers "hit the streets," where information is passed on from the previous shifts, officers' concerns are discussed, training can occur, and awards and reprimands may be made.

roll call
The briefing of officers before their tour of duty to update them on criminal activity and calls for service.

Up-to-date information is usually provided in a daily bulletin, which contains brief summaries of what has transpired in the previous 24 hours. Officers are given a synopsis of each complaint received and acted on, as well as descriptions of missing or wanted persons, stolen personal property and stolen autos.

Radio and Phone Communications The information provided at roll call is continuously updated by radio or cell phone. Data are available to officers in patrol cars or carrying portable radios or cell phones. The introduction of the small hand-carried police radio, cell phone and beeper have extended the communications system so that officers on foot may be reached to assist mobile patrol units and vice versa. This immediate communication has improved law enforcement officers' safety and provided better allocation of resources. Radio transmission dependability has improved steadily over the years and has resulted in a great reduction in response time to calls for service or reported criminal activity.

In January 2010 public safety leaders from across the country met with the Federal Communications Commission (FCC) Chair and the chief of the FCC's Public Safety and Homeland Security Bureau to discuss broadband communications for first responders. The commission announced that it would partner with public safety to bring more robust broadband communications to first responders ("Public Safety Leaders Meet with FCC," 2010).

Computers Computers have revolutionized law enforcement operations, including various administrative functions and communication avenues. Computers have also brought tremendous benefits to the communication efforts of law enforcement, whether occurring within a department, between agencies and departments or with the community. Going online allows officers to access vital data and share information with other officers and managers, locally, nationally and even globally. One network, called the Criminal Justice Information Integration Network (CJIIN), provides e-briefings, which can be accessed online, anytime, by authorized users, as well as e-forms, which contain a repository of necessary documents used by law enforcement that can be completed online and uploaded to the appropriate department, enhancing operational efficiency considerably.

Furthermore, the Internet provides a forum in which a department can communicate with the community, not only to give the public information about police activities and events but also to get information by soliciting leads from citizens to help in crime prevention and detection efforts. Some larger departments use e-reporting, a tool that allows the public to file reports online. Such reports are typically restricted to incidents of low urgency and priority, such as theft or fraud.

interoperability

The capacity of various telecommunications and computing devices to "talk" to each other.

Interoperability The National Institute of Justice defines **interoperability** as "the ability of field units and agencies to talk and share data in real time, when needed and as authorized" (*Communications Interoperability*, 2006). The capacity of various telecommunications and computing devices to "talk" to each other has become an important issue because of the many companies independently producing personal computers (PCs), mobile phones, pagers, printers, display monitors and other devices. In the absence of interoperability, these devices remain virtually isolated from each other, able to communicate only through the use of multiple-proprietary or product-specific cables. Reliance on cable connections greatly limits a user's range of movement and decreases the portability of attached devices.

On September 11, 2001 (9/11) as many as 1,000 firefighters, rather than the usual 10 or 20, were attempting to communicate with each other on one congested channel. In addition, fire, police and EMS could not communicate with each other. Hurricane Katrina, which devastated the north-central Gulf coast of the United States in August 2005, revealed much that still needs to be accomplished. This disaster highlighted the common disadvantage shared by land-based communications systems—outages can occur when transmission facilities are damaged by water, wind, physical destruction or disruptions in power.

Interoperability is also at the center of the controversy surrounding replacing the traditions 10-codes used in law enforcement with plain language.

10-Codes: To Keep or Not to Keep? 10-codes are numbers commonly used to represent common phrases in voice communication. They were designed to allow for brevity and standardization of messages and to keep the "bad guys" from knowing what law enforcement officers were saying. Developed in 1937, the codes expanded in 1974 and were used by agencies throughout the country. Probably the best known 10-code is 10-4, meaning *O.K.* or *message understood*. The 10 precedes each code because, as experienced radio operators know, the first part of a radio message is often not understood. Further, it took older radios a fraction of a second to warm up, and officers frequently forgot to allow this time for the radio transmitter time to come up to full power.

The "10-codes" used for more than 70 years by police and other first responders to communicate in shorthand over the radio are, however, now being questioned. As part of its National Incident Management System (NIMS) protocol, the Department of Homeland Security (DHS) is calling for first responders to replace 10-codes with "plain English," which can be especially important when multiple agencies are responding to the same scene.

Different agencies often use different codes, and some agencies have as many as 100 different codes, leaving ample room for confusion when officers from different agencies are trying to communicate with each other. Opponents of 10-code elimination argue that the 10-codes are more efficient in communicating

TABLE 4.1 Arguments for and against Using 10-Codes

	10-Code Position	Plain Language Position
Officer Safety	10-codes protect officers	There are no "safe" codes. They provide a false sense of security. The codes are often available on the Internet.
Transmitting Sensitive Information	Some information is "sensitive" to the victim or officer and should not be broadcast over a radio.	Those listening in using scanners know every code in the book. Codes offer no additional privacy. Hospital staffs rarely know the codes.
Compatibility with CAD Systems	Plain language requires changes to CAD systems and procedures.	CAD systems should meet department needs and expedite service delivery. CAD systems are routinely updated.
Training and Funding	Transitioning to plain language will be expensive. Who pays for it?	Transitioning is not costly. Write the protocol internally during roll call and implement training.

SOURCE: *Plain Language Guide: Making the Transition from Ten-Codes to Plain Language.* Washington, DC: Department of Homeland Security, no date.

information with less radio time. Some suggest a universal 10-code rather than plain talk ("The End of 10-Codes?," 2009, p.1). Table 4.1 presents both sides of this controversy between using 10-codes and plain language.

One of the key administrative functions is dispatching calls that come into the agency to officers in the field.

Dispatchers "Being a dispatcher is not an easy job and sometimes not a very rewarding one. Every day brings new things. The simplest of tasks becomes a life-saving adventure. The hardest of tasks become routine. And most of the time, good things go unnoticed. Being a dispatcher presents opportunities—to help others, to make a difference, and to feel good because you have just saved another life" (Vigor, 2009, p.35). As Brennan (2009, p.30) notes, "The dispatcher is the gatekeeper during a critical incident."

The police dispatcher receives most citizens' requests for police service. In some instances the calls come directly to the dispatcher, who must act on them and determine their priority. Some agencies have telephone operators screen the calls before giving them to the dispatcher to segregate informational calls from service calls.

Dispatchers are trained to diffuse elevated emotions while enhancing the caller's functionality and ability to answer questions or receive instructions. Dispatchers are responsible for knowing what patrol vehicles are ready for assignment and dispatching them to requests for service. They may also have some records responsibility, for example, making out the original incident complaint report containing the time the call was received, the time the patrol was dispatched, the time it arrived, the time it cleared and the disposition of the call. In addition, dispatchers handle walk-in complaints. Some may also monitor jails through a closed-circuit television hookup. Such a system exists in many smaller and medium-sized departments.

In larger agencies several dispatchers handle incoming calls and assign priority according to seriousness and availability of officers to respond. Larger agencies may also have direct and complete integration of police radio with regular telephone service. In this system any call to the police emergency number is automatically channeled to the dispatcher, who controls squad cars assigned to the area from which the caller is telephoning.

In addition to implementing computer-aided dispatch (CAD), many cities have also implemented a 911 system.

911 Systems According to the National Emergency Number Association (NENA), about 200 million 911 calls are made in the United States every year (McDonagh, 2007, p.52). In a 911 system, a person needing emergency police, fire or rescue service dials 911, and a central dispatching office receives the call directly. The eventual goal is to have 911 as the emergency number for police service in all U.S. cities.

E911 (enhanced 911)

Requires wireless carriers to identify the location of the caller to within 125 meters at least two thirds of the time.

In 1996 in response to the proliferation of cell phones and the public's increasing reliance on them to reach out for help, the FCC issued a mandate for all wireless service providers to implement **E911 (enhanced 911)** technology, which uses geolocation capabilities to quickly trace a caller's location. When fully implemented, E911 service will require wireless carriers to identify the location of the caller within 125 meters at least two thirds of the time. Thus if a victim armed with a cell phone is carjacked and left on the street in an unfamiliar part of town or is locked in the car's trunk and driven to unknown parts, he or she might be able to call 911 and have authorities pinpoint the victim's, and possibly the suspect's, location. The current E911 system allows a call-taker to receive the caller's address and phone number as well as high-level responsible agency information. Depending on a jurisdiction's technical sophistication, additional information may be stored in the communication center's computer-aided dispatch and associated systems.

reverse 911 (R911)

As the name implies, allows agencies to alert the public in emergencies.

Sometimes confused with E911 is **reverse 911 (R911)**, which, as the name implies, allows agencies to alert the public in emergencies.

Since the first 911 call was made over 40 years ago, emergency response communication has undergone numerous transformations, including an accelerated advancement of technological developments and, with the wide use of cell phones, a massive increase in the number of calls for service: "From a telephone, radio, and a notepad in 1968, we have evolved into sophisticated command and control centers equipped with digital phones, trunked radios, and computer-aided dispatch (CAD) systems with map displays and real-time unit tracking" (Pendleton, 2008, p.36). And the changes continue with Next Generation 911 or NG911, which will allow dispatchers for police, fire, and EMS, typically in separate areas, to consolidate these operations (Smith, 2009, p.60).

However, improved public safety through technological advances depends on the ability of departments to effectively use these new tools: "The promise of improved public safety in this NG911 environment is only achieved through a balanced marriage of technology and operations. . . . Will NG911 be defined by those who manage it, or those who use the information it provides to get assistance to people in emergencies?" ("Improved Public Safety with Next Generation 9-1-1,"

2009, p.12). The massive amount of data that will be received by public service answering points (PSAPs) from a wide variety of sources "actually offers little or no improvement to public safety without the related operational and technical modifications required to maximize its utilization." ("Improved Public Safety . . . ," 2009, p.13). Table 4.2 compares today's 911 system with the next generation of 911 systems.

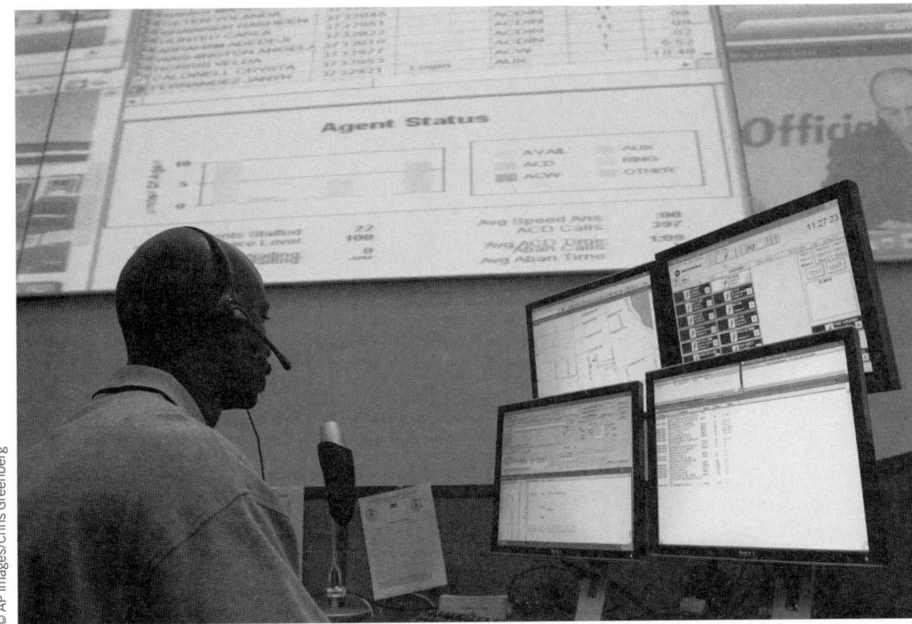

A dispatcher takes fire and 911 emergency calls at a regional communications center. Many jurisdictions have gone to shared regional dispatch services as a way to stretch resources and obtain more of the state-of-the-art technology now available for emergency communication.

TABLE 4.2 Current 911 Systems vs. Next Generation 911 systems

Today's 911	Future 911
Primarily voice calls via telephones, teletype "calls" (mostly by hearing impaired citizens) and an increasing number of voice calls via the "Internet"	**Voice, text or video** emergency calling from any communications device via Internet-like networks
Minimal data with call—at best, Caller ID and location	**Advanced data** from personal safety devices, such as ACN or medical alert systems
No "long distance" 911 access	"**Long distance**" access and transfer and improved interoperability
Reverse 911 practical only for residential landline phones	**Location-specific emergency alerts** possible for any communications device

SOURCE: U.S. Department of Transportation Study, 2006

With the enormous amount of information police departments must receive, transmit and be able to retrieve, an effective, efficient records system is imperative.

Records

The quality of records kept is directly related to the quality of communications and field services provided. To give proper direction, police agencies must have sound records systems as well as efficient communications systems. Police departments throughout the country vary in their reporting systems and their needs in management control and effective operational control. Their activities require keeping records not only of criminal activity but of all vital department activities.

Types of Records

Police records may be categorized as (1) administrative records, (2) arrest records, (3) identification records, (4) evidence records and (5) complaint records.

Administrative records include inventories of police equipment, personnel records, evaluation reports, department memorandums and all general information that reflects correspondence or services rendered. *Arrest records* contain information obtained from arrested persons when booked and information about the control or release of prisoners and court procedures. *Identification records* contain fingerprints, photographs and other descriptive data obtained from arrested persons.

All agencies have their own evidence rooms, and record keeping is imperative for proper prosecution of crimes, efficient case processing, and protection against liability. Evidence can be anything from a weapon used in a crime, to drugs seized at a scene, to audio or video recordings of an incident, and *evidence records* document what has been collected by officers during the course of an investigation or in handling a case.

Complaint records contain information related to complaints and reports received from citizens or other agencies, as well as any actions initiated by the police. Because police work is public business, it requires accurate documentation of complaints received and the action taken by officers. Complaints may be criminal or noncriminal; they may involve lost or damaged property, traffic crashes, medical emergencies or missing persons. Requests for police assistance may also involve robberies, murders, burglaries, vandalism, children playing in the streets or cats up trees.

Most police agencies have a procedure for recording complaint information on either forms or data-processing cards. Initial complaint records are filled out on all complaints or requests for service received by the dispatcher or a police officer. Information on the initial complaint record normally shows the complainant, victim, address of each, type of complaint, time of day, day of week, the officer handling the complaint or request, the area of the community where it occurred, the disposition, whether there was an arrest and whether follow-up reports or further investigation is justified.

Benefits of Efficient Records Management Systems (RMS) An efficient records system is a vital management tool that aids in assessing department accomplishments, developing budget justifications, determining additional workforce needs, evaluating the performance of officers and assessing whether objectives and goals have been met. Perera (2007, p.55) suggests, "When used effectively, an RMS can link information across a broad spectrum, helping officers solve crimes. Additionally, a fully integrated RMS can pass that information across jurisdictional lines, enabling cities, counties, states and even the feds to share information and fight crime on new levels."

Evaluation of carefully kept records will generally reflect needs in training, recruitment, public relations and allocation of resources, as well as general effectiveness. Management's continual or periodic evaluation of records for planning and research has allowed police agencies to provide better service to the public, and in turn they have gained greater public support.

Centralized, integrated, accurate systems of communication and records increase the effectiveness and efficiency of field services.

Privacy of Records The most sensitive aspect of records on persons arrested is the possibility of including in the file unsubstantiated information that might be derogatory, incomplete or incorrect—information that disseminated to the wrong person could prove damaging and provide cause for a civil action against the police agency. In addition, police agencies often tend to retain information longer than necessary.

The Department of Justice has issued regulations to assure that criminal history record information is collected, stored and disseminated in a way that ensures its completeness, integrity, accuracy and security while protecting individual privacy. The regulations apply to all state and local agencies and individuals collecting, storing or disseminating criminal history information either manually or by computer.

A data privacy act regulates the use of confidential and private information on individuals in the records, files and processes of a state and its political subdivisions.

Administrative services are vital to the efficient functioning of any police department, but they are a *support* for the field services.

FIELD SERVICES

Sometimes field services are performed by one division, sometimes by separate divisions. They may be further specialized by the type of individual involved: juveniles, gamblers, prostitutes, burglars, drug dealers and so on; by specific geographic areas (beats); by specific times when demand for service is highest, for example, holiday traffic; or by abnormal conditions, such as strikes and protests.

Field services include patrol, traffic, investigation and community services.

Traditionally police departments have been generalists. That is, most of their personnel are assigned to patrol, and each officer is responsible for providing basic law enforcement services of all types to a specified geographic area or beat. General patrol is the backbone of police work in smaller departments. Larger departments tend to be more specialist-oriented because they typically have more resources and a greater need for specialization.

Patrol

Usually 60 to 70 percent of a department's police officers are assigned to patrol operations, providing continuous police service and high visibility of law enforcement. Tasks include crime prevention, response to calls for service, self-initiated activity and completing administrative functions. Although other divisions may have more prestige, patrol officers are the primary contact between the public and the criminal justice system. They not only initiate the criminal justice system but they also strongly influence the public's perception of this system. Chapter 5 discusses the patrol function in detail.

Traffic

Traffic may be a responsibility of patrol, or it may be a separate function. A well-rounded traffic program involves many activities designed to maintain order and safety on streets and highways. Traffic officers enforce traffic laws, direct and control traffic, provide directions and assistance to motorists, investigate motor vehicle crashes, provide emergency assistance at the scenes of crashes, gather information related to traffic and write reports.

The most frequent contact between the police and the noncriminal public is through traffic encounters. Consequently the opportunity for improving community relations through the handling of traffic violations must be considered. Although the traffic responsibilities of a police officer may not have the glamour of a criminal investigation, they are critical not only to the safety of the citizens but also to the police image. In addition many criminal arrests result from traffic stops, for example, wanted persons and discovery of contraband. Chapter 5 discusses the traffic function in detail.

Investigation

Although some investigations are carried out by patrol officers, the investigation services division (also known as the detective bureau) has the responsibility for follow-up investigation. The success of any criminal investigation relies on the cooperative and coordinated efforts of both the patrol and the investigative functions.

The primary responsibilities of the investigator are to secure the crime scene, write and execute search warrants and subpoenas, conduct surveillance operations, interview witnesses and interrogate suspects, photograph and sketch the crime scene, obtain and identify evidence, record all facts related to the case for future reference and work with county attorneys and the courts to process cases. Chapter 6 discusses investigation in detail.

Community Service/Community Relations

In essence every action of police officers affects community relations—either positively or negatively. Many larger departments have separate community relations divisions or community service divisions to strengthen communication channels between the public and its police department and/or to stress public education programs and crime prevention programs. The importance of community relations and community service is emphasized throughout this text.

Specialized Officers

In addition to the basic divisions within police departments, larger departments frequently train officers to perform highly specialized tasks. Specialized officers may include evidence technicians, identification officers, intelligence officers, juvenile officers, vice officers, K-9 assisted officers and tactical forces officers, to name a few. Chapter 6 discusses specialized officers.

The vast array of required general and specialized functions performed by police presents a special challenge in rural areas.

RURAL POLICING

Novesky (2009), recalling America's frontier and the lone officer riding horseback from town to town to keep the peace, notes, "If you work in a rural area you probably feel the same way at times. It can be no fun being out there alone." He suggests, "For the lone officer, several obstacles make things interesting when conducting the 'routine' traffic stop. Things like terrible radio communications and being outnumbered most of the time."

In addition, rural officers often have to wait a long time for backup to arrive, if it is even available. Many rural departments have only one officer on duty, who may be backed up by an off-duty officer, an on-call officer or a neighboring department, and this backup may be more than 30 minutes away, making rural policing potentially more dangerous. In addition, uniformed patrol officers in rural environments must be better prepared than their counterparts in urban environments, who can defer to specialists when needed.

In some areas of the country, rural policing is performed by a sheriff responsible for a given county. Often the county sheriff is an elected office, making it accountable to the local community. In the majority of states, it is a constitutional office rather than an agency created by state statute, so it can be abolished only through constitutional amendment, and none of its powers or responsibilities may be changed by a county board.

The office of county sheriff has existed for hundreds of years, with roots in 9th-century England. The sheriff's office has evolved into a multipurpose agency with more diverse legal responsibilities than most local police departments, including providing correctional services (transporting prisoners and administering the county jail), providing court security through the assignment of bailiffs, processing judicial writs and court orders, seizing property claimed by the county, collecting county fees and taxes, and selling licenses and permits.

Not all county agencies are rural. Many urban counties also have sheriffs' departments. For example, San Diego County includes the city of San Diego and ranks 17th in population of all U.S. metropolitan areas. The San Diego County Sheriff's Department has more than 3,000 members and 31 facilities located throughout the county.

Within larger departments, urban, suburban or rural, an organizational culture is likely to exist.

THE POLICE ORGANIZATIONAL CULTURE

organizational culture

Any group demonstrating specific patterns of behavior that distinguish it from others within a society; policing has been referred to as "The Blue Brotherhood."

An **organizational culture** refers to any group demonstrating specific patterns of behavior that distinguish it from others within a society: "Organizational culture is derived from customs, rituals and values of the organization, the organization's history and how an organization's members interact with one another and with those outside of the organization" (Vernon, 2008, p.76). Policing has been identified as an organizational culture commonly referred to as "The Blue Brotherhood." Police officers work nights and weekends; deal with highly confidential material that cannot be shared with friends; must enforce the law impartially, even when a friend or relative violates a law; and frequently face public hostility, abuse, name calling and biased reporting in the media. An additional bonding feature not commonly found in other professions is the willingness and readiness of officers to risk their lives for each other. A combination of these factors largely accounts for the existence of a "police culture."

Individuals who become police officers commonly lose their non-police friends within a few years. In addition to working different hours, they may make some of their friends uneasy, especially those who drink and drive, who habitually speed or who engage in other unorthodox behavior. Police officers' friends often do not understand some of the actions police are forced to take in fulfilling their responsibilities.

In addition to losing their non-police friends, officers may also come to realize they are now a part of a group isolated from the rest of society—a fellowship united by risk, hardship and fear. Although officers are highly visible, they are set apart. They may be feared, disliked, hated or even assaulted by citizens. Thus they keep close ranks for protection and security. The closer they become, the more citizens fear and distrust them, leading to even tighter ranks, and so the cycle goes. The police become the "in group," and everyone else is an "outsider." To a police officer the world consists of cops and civilians, perhaps better phrased as cops *versus* civilians.

This "us vs. them" attitude, common in some departments, leads to defensiveness exhibited in such ways as reluctance to give up traditional police responsibilities (e.g., traffic control on state highways) or reluctance to explain their actions to citizens. Official police silence is sometimes necessary to protect the rights of others or to safeguard an investigation, but sometimes it is, in reality, a defensive response. The "us vs. them" mentality may also foster an unofficial "blue wall of silence," which is discussed in Chapter 11.

In addition, as portrayed by the media, the police culture is "an aberrant closed-minded society that revolves around badge-heavy brutes who look forward each day to beating suspects, taking bribes and generally acting like hoodlums" (Oldham, 2006, p.18). Oldham takes exception to this, calling the police culture "a wonderful thing" embodying concepts of duty, honor, dedication and self-sacrifice: "Our culture is about all of the things that are good in life. We are the ones who

CAREER PROFILE

Dennis Conroy (Police Psychologist)

Shortly after a tour in Vietnam sponsored by the U.S. Marine Corps, I was approached by the chief of police in a small town. He said that he needed to hire a police officer and wondered if I would be interested in the job. I thought I could enjoy police work and thereby launched a career that has lasted over 30 years.

When you're a beat cop, one moment you're directing traffic at an intersection where a teenager has been maimed in a head-on collision. Another moment you're comforting a toddler who has been abandoned by his mother. Still another moment you're gathering facts about an elderly man who has been savagely beaten.

When you're a cop, you keep your emotions bottled up. Even when criminals get off scot-free and even when passing motorists shower you with insults, you keep your professional cool. But then you wonder, "Why am I feeling so much stress?" I was becoming much less of a husband and father and was becoming more and more a police officer. It was becoming more of an identity than a career.

I saw many of my fellow officers also stressed and changing. I knew cops who committed suicide, got divorced or became drunks, and I wondered what might be happening to me. We become so involved in being cops, saying we can handle things, that we deny we're affected by what we run across. And we don't take it home with us because we don't want to inflict pain on our spouses and families, so we keep it bottled up tight inside. That's how we become victims. It's like cancer; it doesn't necessarily show up on the outside, but it's eating away at our insides.

After my time as a beat cop, I was a supervisor, an undercover officer and an administrative officer. But one question that kept going through my mind, long before I got into my current position, was, "Who is there to help the cops?" Certainly we all need help sometimes. I wanted to be the one who is able to help the cops, and that is what I do most of the time now.

To prepare for this position I completed an undergraduate degree in Human Services, a master's degree in human development and a doctorate in clinical psychology. I did my dissertation on what price police officers said they had lost by becoming a cop. The overwhelming majority said "loss of innocence." I also heard that many of the officers saw themselves as victims—of the system, of the public's sometimes contradictory expectations, but mostly of their routine exposure to badness, unhappiness, ugliness and loss. I also found that the liars, cheats and thugs of the world did a number on many of the officers' personalities, transforming them into paranoids and cynics. One officer said, "I lost my family. I lost my old friends. And I lost who I was. I lost my humanity."

My dissertation was not heavy on statistics. A lot of people have done quantitative research on the "stressors" that affect police officers' behavior. But statistics don't matter in this case. It's the tears that matter. After completing my doctorate, finally, I became licensed as a psychologist.

In my most recent position as a departmental psychologist, I am responsible for the Employee Assistance Program. I counsel cops and their families, in addition to whatever other "psychological" things came along. I work with the SWAT team to assess situations involving barricaded suspects and make recommendations regarding a potential course of action. I also monitor the pre-employment psychological evaluations for the department.

I've been in this position for about 15 years and find it to be both challenging and fulfilling. Cops are difficult clients for any mental health professional because most of the time they don't want to talk about problems until it is bordering on "too late." Yet there is nothing more fulfilling or satisfying than to hear a cop say, "Thanks for saving my life." It is a statement not made easily, and one that comes from the heart.

people call when they need help, we are the ones who run toward problems and we are the ones who keep our domestic enemies at bay" (Oldham, p.21).

The organizational culture of a department or agency can directly affect the styles of police work within it.

STYLES OF POLICING

Varieties of Police Behavior, a classic study published over 30 years ago by James Q. Wilson, described three distinctive styles of policing: the legalistic, the watchman and the service style. Many studies since then have looked at styles of policing and

typologies

Systematic classifications, as in styles of policing.

have classified these styles into clusters called **typologies**. Few police officers fall completely into a single typology.

 Basic styles of policing include the following:

- Enforcer
- Crime fighter/zealot
- Social service agent
- Watchdog

The *enforcer* focuses on social order and keeping society safe. Enforcers are less concerned with individual rights and due process. Such officers are often critical of the Supreme Court, politicians, police administrators and minority interest groups. Enforcers have little time for minor violations of the law or for the social services aspect, seeing them as a waste of police time and resources. Officers of this typology are most likely to use excessive force.

The *crime fighter/zealot* is like an enforcer in that a primary goal is to keep society safe. These officers tend to deal with all laws and all offenders equally. The crime fighter/zealot is often relatively new, inexperienced or unable to see the gray areas associated with policing. Zealots are less critical of the social service aspects of policing than are enforcers.

The *social service agent* is more accepting of the social service roles and more attuned to due process. Such officers are often young, well educated and idealistic. Like the enforcer and the crime fighter, social service agents are also interested in protecting society but are more flexible in how this is approached.

The *watchdog* is on the opposite end of the spectrum from the enforcer. The watchdog is interested in maintaining the status quo, in not making "waves." Watchdogs may ignore common violations, such as traffic offenses, and tolerate a certain amount of vice and gambling. They use the law more to maintain order than to regulate conduct. They also tend to judge the requirements of order differently depending on the group in which the infraction occurs. Table 4.3 summarizes these typologies as described by three sources.

No officer is purely one type or another, and an officer may change from one style to another depending on the situation. In any given department, it is likely that a variety of policing styles with some combination of the preceding typologies can be found. Policing style is greatly influenced by an officer's personality.

TABLE 4.3 The Typologies of Policing Styles

James Q. Wilson (1968)	Robert Pursley (1987)	Joseph Senna and Larry Siegel (1993)
Legalistic	Enforcer	Law enforcer
	Zealot	Crime fighter
Service style	Social service agent	Social agent
Watchdog	Watchdog	Watchdog

Although Wilson's typology is dated, it continues to capture the major policing styles used in the United States (Hawdon, 2008, p.192). Research that examined the connections between neighborhood levels of social capital, policing styles, resident perceptions of the legitimacy of the policing institution, and resident perceptions of trust in specific officers suggests that neighborhood levels of social capital influence resident perceptions of the police (Hawdon, p.197). These connections can be coupled with insight as to what is known about policing styles to predict which style of policing would be most effective in generating perceptions of trust and legitimacy in specific neighborhoods.

According to Hawdon (2008, p.189), social capital exists in two forms: bonding and bridging capital. *Bonding capital* refers to the trust of specific others such as friends and co-workers and holds people together in groups. *Bridging capital* extends beyond one's immediate social circles to others with whom one has no direct ties or personal connections and connects people across diverse groups. Neighborhoods can be high or low in both types of social capital, or they may be high in one form and low in the other. As shown in Table 4.4, greater understanding of these connections can help predict how important procedural justice (officers treating everyone fairly and with respect) and policing outcomes (reduction in crime) will be in specific settings: "By understanding which policing style generates positive resident views of police in various types of neighborhoods, officers will be freed from a 'one-size-fits-all' model of policing. Instead, they can tailor their policing to the neighborhoods they patrol" (Hawdon, p.198).

Stereotypes

The police deal daily with criminals, complainants and citizens who may be cursing, yelling, lying, spitting, fighting, drunk, high, angry, irrational, demanding, manipulative or cruel. Some officers' reactions to these daily encounters and the negative personality traits displayed may result in *all* officers being stereotyped as suspicious, cynical, indifferent, authoritarian, bigoted and brutal.

TABLE 4.4 Predicted Relationships Within Specific Neighborhood Settings

Levels of Bridging Capital	Levels of Bonding Capital	Perceived Legitimacy of Police Institution	Initial Perceptions of Officer Trustworthiness	Importance of Procedural Justice	Importance of Outcome	Most Effective Style of Policing
High	High	High	High, but dependent on officer behavior	Very high	Relatively unimportant	Legalistic
High	Low	High	High, less dependent on officer behavior	Relatively low	Very high	Any style. Visibility of officers is critical
Low	Low	Low	Low, but can be earned	Relatively low	Very high	Order maintenance
Low	High	Very Low	Low, difficult to earn	Extremely high	Relatively unimportant	Community-oriented (service)

SOURCE: James Hawdon. "Legitimacy, Trust, Social Capital, and Policing Styles." *Police Quarterly,* June 2008, p.196. Reprinted by Permission of SAGE Publications.

Suspicious Police work requires an officer to be wary of people and situations out of the ordinary, for example, a person with an umbrella on a sunny day or a person wearing sunglasses at midnight. Not only is keen observation critical to effective investigation and crime prevention, but it is also critical to self-defense. Danger is possible in any situation. Police officers develop a perceptual shorthand to identify certain kinds of people as potential assailants; that is, officers come to recognize certain gestures, language and attire as a prelude to violence.

Cynical Because police officers deal with criminals, they are constantly on guard against human faults. Officers see people at their worst. They know that people lie, cheat, steal, torture and kill. They deal with people who do not like police, who even hate them, and they feel the hatred. In addition they may see people they firmly believe to be guilty of a heinous crime freed by a legal technicality. This cynicism may also lead to paranoia.

Indifferent When police officers are called to the scene of a homicide, they are expected to conduct a thorough, impartial investigation. Their objectivity may be perceived by grieving relatives of the victim as indifference or coldness. Officers must remain detached, however; one of the grieving relatives might well be the murderer. Further, a certain amount of distancing is required to work with difficult situations.

Authoritarian Effective law enforcement requires authority; authoritarianism comes with the job. Without authority and respect, an officer cannot effectively compel citizens of the community to obey the law. As noted by the French philosopher Pascal: "Justice without force is powerless; force without justice is tyrannical." The physical appearance of the police officer adds to this authoritarian image. The uniform, gun, baton and handcuffs project an image to which many people respond with uneasiness or even fear. However, this image projects the right of the police to exercise the lawful force of the state in serving and protecting as well as in enforcing laws. The difficulty arises when the power that comes with the position is transferred to "personal power."

Bigoted Police are frequently victims of problems they have nothing to do with and over which they have no control. They are not to blame for the injustices suffered by minority groups: housing, educational and employment discrimination. Often, however, members of minority groups perceive the police as a symbol of the society that has denied them its privileges and benefits. Tension between minority groups and any representatives of "authority" has become almost a way of life in many parts of large cities. The minority group members vent their anger and frustration on the police, and some police come to feel anger and dislike for them.

Brutal Sometimes force is required to subdue suspects. Unfortunately the crime-related aspects of a police officer's job are what frequently draw public attention. When police officers have to physically subdue a suspect, people notice. When they help people get into their locked cars, few notice.

Sometimes, however, officers use more force than is required, crossing the line from justifiable force to police brutality. This too is easier to understand if one considers the other traits that often become part of the police "personality," particularly

TABLE 4.5 Police Actions Seen Negatively and Positively

Action by Officer	Negative Person	Positive Person
Steps in to stop a fight in a bar	Interference	Preserving the peace
Questions a rape victim	Indifferent, cold	Objective
Uses a baton to break up a violent mob	Brutal	Commanding respect
Steadily watches three youths on a corner	Suspicious	Observant

cynicism and authoritarianism. Police officers may use excessive force with a rapist if they believe the probability is great that the rapist will never be brought to trial because of the prosecutor's policies on rape cases. Such an officer response is known as *vigilante justice*. They may also erroneously believe violence is necessary to obtain respect from individuals who seem to respect nothing but force and power.

A person who dislikes police officers will probably perceive a specific behavior negatively, whereas the same behavior might be perceived positively by one who has a high regard for police officers. Consider, for example, the actions listed in Table 4.5 and the way each is described by a person who feels negatively about the police and one who feels positively about the police.

Two conflicting views exist today as to why these traits might occur more often among police officers than in the general population. One view, the *unique traits viewpoint,* suggests policing attracts individuals who already possess these traits. The opposing view, the socialization viewpoint, suggests the traits are developed by the experiences the officers have as they become socialized into their departments.

Despite the contention that the police personality may include negative traits, the public image of the police remains high.

THE POLICE IMAGE

Each police officer is an individual. Police officers are fathers, mothers, sons, daughters, uncles, aunts, coaches of Little League teams, church members and neighbors. As people they like to be liked, but often their profession requires that they take negative actions against those who break the law. As a result they are often criticized and berated for simply doing their jobs. Although police officers are individuals just like those in the community they have sworn to "serve and protect," their behavior is very public. It may simply be that they are extraordinarily visible ordinary people.

The public's **image** of the police varies greatly. Some see police officers as protectors; others see them as militaristic harassers. The sight of a police officer arouses feelings of respect, confidence and security in some citizens; fear, hostility and hatred in others; and indifference in yet others.

image

How one is viewed; the concept of someone or something held by the public. Police image results from the media's portrayal of police and from everyday contacts between individual police officers and citizens.

The image of the police officer often portrayed on television has not been helpful. The "Dirty Harry" tactics, with excessive, unjustified violence and disregard for civil rights, are often presented as the way police officers behave. The effects of television on both the police image and the fight against crime cannot be accurately measured. Certainly it has an impact. Hardly an hour passes without an illegal search, a coerced confession, police brutality and general violence dealt out by television police officers. Many modern police "heroes" are shown blatantly indulging in illegal and unconstitutional behavior, which in effect instills in the public the opinion that police misconduct is acceptable and sometimes the only way to apprehend criminals. The same criticisms may be applied to our movies.

The police image results from the media portrayal of police officers and from everyday contacts between individual police officers and citizens.

Despite what is written in books or portrayed on television and in movies, the abstraction called the "police image" is primarily the result of day-to-day contacts between police and citizens.

The behavior of police officers at the patrol level rather than at the command level is of greatest importance in establishing the police image. In turn the individual behavior of the police officer who creates the police image is the result of several factors, including length of service, the community served (ghetto or exclusive suburb), training and experience. Basich (2008, p.54) points out, "Whether the recipient of a speeding ticket, a suspect, or a victim of a crime, seeing that blue uniform usually means something is wrong. Even those who respect police officers might feel uneasy around them." Thus it may seem surprising that, according to a recent Harris poll, most people have a positive view of law enforcement, with the majority of Americans ranking policing among the top 10 most prestigious professions (Basich).

Factors Influencing Police Image

In addition to easily identifiable and predictable factors, such as experience, training and locality served, many subtle factors influence police behavior and image, including the nature of police work itself, the police officer's unique relation to the criminal justice system and the individual officer's appearance.

The Nature of Police Work Many demands are placed on police officers—they are under constant pressure and faced with rapidly changing conditions, sometimes life-threatening situations, with few guidelines, little supervision and little time and information needed to make split-second, potentially life-altering decisions. They often must think on their feet and "play it by ear."

Police officers must interact with people from all walks of life who are involved in criminal and noncriminal activities and must use broad discretion in a wide variety of situations. They deal with crimes already committed and with people who are hurt, confused, angry and upset. Yet officers must remain neutral, calm and objective. They may appear indifferent or unsympathetic, but much like physicians, they cannot become personally involved and still do a professional job.

The image resulting from the nature of police work might easily be compared to the image of a football referee. It is readily accepted that referees are necessary to the game. Without them chaos would reign. Despite their importance, however, their image is often negative. No matter what call they make, a great many people are unhappy with them. They are usually perceived as being on the opponent's side. Defeats are often blamed on referees, but seldom is a referee given credit for a team's victory. It is often a thankless, sometimes dangerous job. Fans have tried to physically assault referees. They call them abusive names. It often makes one wonder what kind of person could work under such pressures.

Unique Relationship to the System Another factor influencing the police image is the officers' relationship to the law. Although police officers are many people's first contacts with the criminal justice system, they often feel like outsiders in the judicial system. They may feel that their investigation and apprehension of criminals is hampered by legal restrictions and that suspects have more rights than victims.

Although police officers are frequently blamed for unacceptable crime rates, their participation in the legal system is often minimized. They may be made to feel as if they were on trial during the court proceedings as the defense attorney cross-examines them. They are seldom included in any plea bargaining, and many defendants are found not guilty because of loopholes or legal technicalities. When a confessed robber is acquitted on a technicality or a known rapist is not brought to trial by the prosecutor, police officers may take this as a personal affront, as a criticism of their investigative expertise. Citizens of the community may also blame the police for the unsuccessful prosecution of a suspect. Legal technicalities may even result in the police officer being sued for false arrest.

SATISFACTION WITH AND CONFIDENCE IN THE POLICE

Five studies funded by the NIJ explored factors that influence public satisfaction with the police and revealed that while satisfaction levels were generally high, they were unevenly distributed (Horowitz, 2007). Satisfaction was found to be shaped by demographic variables, neighborhood crime condition and experiences with the police, whether first hand or indirect. Race was *not* found to directly determine satisfaction level. Rather, race correlated with other demographic variables, neighborhood crime rates and experiences with police (Horowitz).

Another study of the relationship between confidence in the police and concern about crime looked at two models of this relationship based on the factors of accountability and reassurance (Skogan, 2009). The *accountability model* contends that police are responsible for neighborhood conditions and local crime, disorder and fear. This is in contrast to the *reassurance* model, which holds that perceptions of crime are influenced by confidence in police: "Reductions in concern about crime flow from increasing confidence in the police, while an accountability link from concern about crime to confidence in the police was much weaker and not statistically significant" (Skogan, p.301).

The *Sourcebook of Criminal Justice Statistics Online* reports that in 2009 59 percent of Americans reported a "great deal" or "quite a lot of" confidence in the police. Males and females were equally confident; whites had more confidence in police (63 percent) than did nonwhites (51 percent), among whom the least confident were blacks (38 percent). Confidence increased as age, education and income increased ("Reported Confidence in the Police, Table 2.12. 2009").

Summary

Police are necessary when coercion is required to enforce the laws. The people largely determine the goals of policing and give law enforcement agencies their authority to meet these goals. Citizen support is vital.

Historically, the basic goals of most police agencies are to enforce laws, preserve the peace, prevent crimes, protect civil rights and civil liberties and provide services.

Concern for crime control must be balanced by concern for due process—a principal challenge for law enforcement. Goals resulting from implementing community policing usually include forming partnerships with the community and a proactive, problem-solving approach to crime, fear of crime and crime prevention.

Most police departments are organized into two basic units: field services and administrative services. Tasks and personnel are assigned to one or the other. Administrative services provide support for field services and include communications and records, recruitment and training and provision of special facilities and services. Current information is usually provided at roll call or by radio, phone and computer.

In addition to direct communication, police officers also rely upon information contained in various records depositories. Among the types of records the police officer may use are administrative, arrest, identification, evidence and complaint records. Centralized, integrated, accurate systems of communication and records increase the effectiveness and efficiency of field services. Access to information is not always unlimited, however. A data privacy act regulates the use of confidential and private information on individuals in the records, files and processes of a state and its political subdivisions. Among the field services provided in a police department are patrol, traffic, investigation and community services.

Four basic styles of policing are the enforcer, the crime fighter/zealot, the social service agent and the watchdog. The police image results from the media portrayal of police officers and from everyday contacts between individual police officers and citizens.

Discussion Questions

1. How has communications and technology changed the relationship between the police officer out in the field and their administrative staff?
2. What are some specialized police units that have emerged from contemporary policing?
3. What services should police officers provide? Which are provided in your community?
4. What style of policing will you probably lean toward? Why?
5. Have you witnessed police discretion firsthand? Explain.
6. Do you feel police agencies and officers have too little, too much or just the right amount of discretion?
7. What is your image of the police? What do you believe your community thinks of the police?
8. Have you seen examples of unethical behavior in police work? Of actual corruption?
9. What do you see as the greatest challenge for police officers in the 21st century?
10. Do you think that the current trend of the police image is improving or worsening?

Gale Emergency Services Database Assignments

- Use the Gale Emergency Services Database to help answer the Discussion Questions as appropriate.
- Using the Gale Emergency Services Database, locate articles on *interoperability* Outline how communities are dealing with this problem. Be prepared to share your outline with the class.
- Using the Gale Emergency Services Database, find the National Crime Information Center (NCIC) and outline what it has to offer. Select one area of interest to explore and write a brief recap of what you learned. Be prepared to share your outline and recap with the class.
- Using the Gale Emergency Services Database, find the article "Management Roundtable: Two Cents on 2009: Law Enforcement Supervisors Weigh In on the Challenges of 2009, Technology That's Changed Their Jobs and How Policing Continues to Evolve" (Discussion): http://find.galegroup.com/gps/retrieve.do?contentSet=IAC-Documents&resultListType=RESULT_LIST&qrySerId=Locale%28en%2C%2C%29%3AFQE%3D%28KE%2CNone%2C8%29policing%24&sgHitCountType=None&inPS=true&sort=DateDescend&searchType=BasicSearchForm&tabID=T003&prodId=IPS&searchId=R11¤tPosition=5&userGroupName=cpg3&docId=A216989744&docType=IAC&contentSet=IAC-Documents

  Assignment: Use information in the article to answer these questions, and be prepared to discuss your findings with the class:

  a. What are some of the challenges that are discussed in this article by police administrators?

  b. What are some new and emerging technologies effecting policing?

  c. How does policing continue to evolve according to this round table discussion?
- Using the Gale Emergency Services Database, find the article "Use of Force and Community Awareness" (Notable Speech)(Speech): http://find.galegroup.com/gps/retrieve.do?contentSet=IAC-Documents&resultListType=RESULT_LIST&qrySerId=Locale%28en%2C%2C%29%3AFQE%3D%28KE%2CNone%2C8%29policing%24&sgHitCountType=None&inPS=true&sort=DateDescend&searchType=BasicSearchForm&tabID=T003&prodId=IPS&searchId=R11¤tPosition=7&userGroupName=cpg3&docId=A212217831&docType=IAC&contentSet=IAC-Documents

  Assignment: Summarize this article into a paragraph and be ready to discuss it in class.
- Using the Gale Emergency Services Database, find the article "Contemporary Components of Community Policing" (Notable Speech) (Speech): http://find.galegroup.com/gps/retrieve.do?contentSet=IAC-Documents&resultListType=RESULT_LIST&qrySerId=Locale%28en%2C%2C%29%3AFQE%3D%28KE%2CNone%2C8%29policing%24&sgHit

CountType=None&inPS=true&sort=DateDescend&searchType=BasicSearchForm&tabID=T003&prodId=IPS&searchId=R11¤tPosition=13&userGroupName=cpg3&docId=A203929614&docType=IAC&contentSet=IAC-Documents

Assignment: Identify some contemporary components in community policing. Be prepared to discuss your findings with the class.

- Using the Gale Emergency Services Database, find the article "Culture, Mission, and Goal Attainment" (police training techniques): http://find.galegroup.com/gps/retrieve.do?contentSet=IAC-Documents&resultListType=RESULT_LIST&qrySerId=Locale%28en%2C%2C%29%3AFQE%3D%28ke%2CNone%2C14%29police+culture%3AAnd%3AFQE%3D%28pu%2CNone%2C30%29%22FBI+Law+Enforcement+Bulletin%22%24&sgHitCountType=None&inPS=true&sort=DateDescend&searchType=AdvancedSearchForm&tabID=T003&prodId=IPS&searchId=R12¤tPosition=2&userGroupName=cpg3&docId=A13794859&docType=IAC&contentSet=IAC-Documents

  Assignment: Outline this article and be prepared to discuss it in class.
- Using the Gale Emergency Services Database, find the article "Interoperability in Action (Communications Spotlight): http://find.galegroup.com/gps/retrieve.do?contentSet=IAC-Documents&resultListType=RESULT_LIST&qrySerId=Locale%28en%2C%2C%29%3AFQE%3D%28KE%2CNone%2C7%29sheriff%24&sgHitCountType=None&inPS=true&sort=DateDescend&searchType=BasicSearchForm&tabID=T003&prodId=IPS&searchId=R17¤tPosition=8&userGroupName=cpg3&docId=A209188274&docType=IAC&contentSet=IAC-Documents

  Assignment: Read and identify the highlighted benefits in this article. Be prepared to discuss your findings with class.

Internet Assignment

- Use the Internet to search for *police culture*. Select a document that indicates how the police culture changes in or is affected by a multicultural society. Briefly outline the major changes, and be prepared to share your findings with the class.

References

Basich, Melanie. "A Love-Hate Relationship." *Police*, April 2008, pp.54–57.

Bittner, Egon. "Florence Nightingale in Pursuit of Willie Sutton: A Theory of Police." In *The Potential for Reform of Criminal* Justice, edited by H. Jacob. Beverly Hills, CA: Sage Publications, 1974, pp.17–44.

Bittner, Egon. *The Functions of Police in Modern Society*. Cambridge, MA: Oelseschlager, Gunn and Hain, 1980.

Brennan, Jason. "The Dispatcher Is the Gatekeeper during a Critical Incident." *9-1-1 Magazine*, August-September-October 2009, pp.30–31.

Communications Interoperability: Basics for Practitioners. Washington, DC: National Institute of Justice, March 2006. (NCJ 212978)

"The End of 10 Codes?" *ILEETA Digest*, October/November/December 2009, p.1.

Hawdon, James. "Legitimacy, Trust, Social Capital and Policing Styles: A Theoretical Statement." *Police Quarterly*, June 2008, pp.182–201.

Horowitz, Jake. "Making Every Encounter Count: Building Trust and Confidence in the Police." *NIJ Journal*, January 2007, pp.8–11.

"Improved Public Safety with Next Generation 9-1-1." *9-1-1 Magazine*, June/July 2009, pp.12–14.

Klockars, Carl B. "The Rhetoric of Community Policing." In *Community Policing: Rhetoric or Reality*, edited by J. R. Greene and S. D. Mastrofski. New York: Praeger Publishers, 1991.

Lane, Troy. "Span of Control for Law Enforcement Agencies." *The Police Chief*, October 2006, pp.74–84.

Manning, Peter K. *Police Work: The Social Organization of Policing*, 2nd ed. Prospect Heights, IL: Waveland Press, 1997.

McDonagh, Mariann. "Seconds Save Lives: Improving 9-1-1 Call Center Response." *9-1-1 Magazine*, August 2007, pp.52–54.

Moore, Carole. "Telling Your Officers Where to Go—and How to Get There." *Law Enforcement Technology*, May 2009, pp.10–16.

National Advisory Commission on Criminal Justice Standards and Goals. *The Police*. Washington, DC: U.S. Government Printing Office (LEAA Grant Number 72-DF-99-0002, and NI-72-0200), 1973.

Novesky, Pat. "Policing Rural America: Lone Officer Vehicle Contacts." *PoliceOne.com News*, May 22, 2009. Retrieved from http://www.policeone.com/traffic-patrol/articles/1834986-Policing-rural-America-Lone-officer-vehicle-contacts.

Oldham, Scott. "Proud of the Police Culture." *Law and Order*, May 2006, pp.18–21.

Pendleton, Steve. "Information Overload and the 9-1-1 Dispatcher." *9-1-1 Magazine*, April 2008, pp.36–40.

Perera, George. "Record Management Systems." *Law Officer Magazine*, January 2007, pp.52–55.

"Public Safety Leaders Meet with FCC." Washington, DC: Federal Communications Commission (FCC), 2010. Retrieved from http://www.fcc.gov/pshs/bb-meeting.html.

"Reported Confidence in the Police, Table 2.12.2009." Washington, DC: Bureau of Justice Statistics, *Sourcebook of Criminal Justice Statistics Online,* 2009. Retrieved from http://www.albany.edu/sourcebook/pdf/t2122009.pdf

Skogan, Wesley G. "Concern about Crime and Confidence in the Police: Reassurance or Accountability?" *Police Quarterly*, September 2009, pp.301–318.

Smith, Michael. "Next Generation 9-1-1: Interoperability Is the Key." *9-1-1 Magazine*, November/December 2009, pp.60–64.

Vernon, Bob. "Organizational Culture." *Law Officer Magazine*, August 2008, p.76.

Vigor, Laura. "Being a Dispatcher." *9-1-1 Magazine*, April/May 2009, p.35.

Webster, J. A. "Police Task and Time Study." *Journal of Criminal Law, Criminology, and Police Science,* vol. 61 (no date).

Wuestewald, Todd. "The X-Factor in Policing." *FBI Law Enforcement Bulletin*, June 2004, pp.22–23.

CHAPTER 5

Patrol: The Backbone of Policing

> The police officer working the beat makes more decisions, and exercises broader discretion affecting the daily lives of people every day, and to a greater extent, than a judge will exercise in a week.
>
> —Chief Justice Warren Burger

© Johnny Crawford / The Image Works

Patrol is the backbone of policing. The officer on the street has the greatest potential to affect citizens' safety, detect criminal activity and influence the community's perception of law enforcement. Here, Officer Jeffrey Postell of the Murphy (North Carolina) Police Department patrols in his squad. Postell was the young officer who captured Eric Robert Rudolph, also known as the Olympic Park Bomber.

Do You Know . . .

- What three major spheres of activity must be coordinated in the patrol function?
- What type of shift and beat staffing has traditionally been used and what effect it might have on preventive patrol?
- What the traditional patrol response has been?
- What directed patrol does?
- How hot spots or specific problems might be identified?
- What activities officers typically engage in while on patrol?
- How the patrol response might be made more effective?
- What methods of patrol may be used? Which methods are most effective?
- What the NCIC is and how it assists patrol?
- What the responsibilities of the traffic officer are?
- What the primary goal of traffic law enforcement is?
- Why all uniformed officers should enforce traffic laws?
- What the most common violations of traffic law are?
- What implied consent laws are?
- How driving impairment can be detected?
- What the most basic causes of motor vehicle crashes are?

Can You Define?

aggressive patrol
differential response strategies
diffusion of benefits
directed patrol
dual motive stop
environmental anomalies
extra patrol
foot patrol
hot spots
implied consent laws
incident-driven policing
pretext stop
racial profiling
random patrol
residual deterrence effect
road rage
saturation patrols
selective enforcement

INTRODUCTION

The idea of uniformed officers patrolling the streets goes back at least to the Roman states in 400 BC. A reliance on a visible, roaming presence of law enforcement officers has carried into present-day policing, largely unchanged in many jurisdictions. And in all jurisdictions, patrol is the most vital component of police work. All other units are supplemental to this basic unit: "There is no resource more valuable to an agency than its patrol officers. . . . [It] is the core task of any police department" (Griffith, 2008, p.10). As is frequently stated, "The patrol officer is the backbone of American policing" (Scoville, 2008, p.38). He (p.44) points out, "Certainly, the patrol officer and his iconography—badge, helmet, and baton—are the most emblematic of the profession."

Patrol can contribute to each of the common goals of police departments, including preserving the peace, protecting civil rights and civil liberties, enforcing the law, preventing crime, providing services and solving problems. Unfortunately in many departments, patrol officers have the position with the least prestige and they are the lowest paid, the least consulted and the most taken for granted. Many patrol officers strive to move "up" or to seek an area of specialization that offers enhanced pay and greater prestige.

THE CHAPTER AT A GLANCE

This chapter begins with a discussion of the responsibilities of the patrol officer, the structure and management of patrol and the types of patrol most frequently used. This is followed by a description of activities commonly engaged in while on patrol and common methods of patrol. Next, an important subset of patrol is described—the responsibilities of the traffic officer, including the tasks of directing and controlling traffic, enforcing traffic laws, and assisting at and investigating traffic crashes. The chapter concludes with a discussion educating the public as a function of the traffic program.

PATROL OFFICER RESPONSIBILITIES

Traditionally patrol has been responsible for providing continuous police service and high-visibility law enforcement to deter crime and maintain order. Progressive departments also emphasize partnering with the community to solve problems related to crime and disorder. In addition patrol officers must understand the federal, state and local laws they are sworn to uphold and use good judgment in enforcing them.

In recent years, our society has become more diverse, many informal social controls have broken down and information technology has proliferated, making the patrol function increasingly complex and critical to accomplishing the police department's mission. Most officers in a department are assigned to the patrol function, and most of a department's budget is usually spent here. Patrol may cost an average jurisdiction half a million dollars a year in salary and benefits. Patrol officers have the closest contact with the public and have the most influence on how the public perceives the police in general. To those departments instituting community policing, patrol is critical:

> For patrol cops to do their jobs effectively, they must adopt a constructive territoriality about their patrol areas, sometimes known as owning the beat. By becoming increasingly familiar with the geography, economy, personality, and sociology of their beats, patrol officers come to know intuitively what's normal or what's out of place for their respective neighborhoods.
>
> Additionally, by adopting the optimal blend of professional detachment and emotional involvement in their neighborhoods, patrol officers develop what the business world calls buy-in, a personal stake in the welfare of their patrol community, a situation in which it is important to them to keep the peace and provide the highest quality of service: "This is my territory, and I'm going to do everything I can to make sure that it stays safe." (Miller, 2008)

"Not on my watch" is a phrase often used by such officers.

The patrol function is the most visible form of police activity, and individual patrol officers represent the entire police department. The tasks they are expected to accomplish are almost overwhelming. Patrol officers' specific responsibilities in most police departments are to enforce laws, investigate crimes, prevent criminal activity and provide day-to-day police services to the community. The specific duties involved in fulfilling these responsibilities are varied and complex. The size of the department often dictates what functions are assigned to patrol.

As protectors, patrol officers promote and preserve order, respond to requests for services and try to resolve conflicts between individuals and groups. As law enforcers, a key duty of patrol officers is to protect constitutional guarantees (as described in Chapter 8); a second duty is to enforce federal, state and local statutes. Patrol officers encourage voluntary compliance with the law and seek to reduce the opportunity for crimes to be committed.

Patrol officers also serve important traffic control functions, described later in this chapter, and important investigative functions, described in Chapter 6. Patrol officers in any community are the most visible government representatives and are responsible for the safety and direction of thousands of people each day. Table 5.1 summarizes the basic patrol officer functions.

TABLE 5.1 Patrol Officer Functions

Function	Situations
Noncrime calls for service (80–90 percent of calls for service)	Noise and party calls Domestic disturbances Landlord/tenant disputes Nuisance complaints Animal calls Medicals
Traffic control	Traffic delays Pedestrian problems Crashes Traffic violations Drunken drivers
Crime calls	Assaults, rapes, robberies, homicides, thefts, burglaries, motor vehicle thefts, arson cases, vandalism, other property damage, etc.
Preliminary investigations	Scene security Emergency first aid Gathering information Evidence procurement Victim/witness statements
Arrests	Warrants Suspect processing, fingerprinting, booking, etc. Suspect transport Court testimony
Public gatherings	Sporting events Political rallies Rock concerts Parades Special events
Community service	Speeches and presentations Auto and home lockouts Babies delivered Blood transported Home/business security checks Problem solving

MANAGEMENT OF PATROL OPERATIONS

Management of patrol involves overseeing three major spheres of activity, which often occur simultaneously.

The three major spheres of patrol activity are (1) responding to emergencies and calls for service—they are the first responders, (2) undertaking activities to apprehend perpetrators of crime and (3) engaging in strategic problem-solving partnerships with the community to address longstanding or emerging problems of crime and disorder.

Traditionally, rapid response to calls for service has driven most departments, as discussed shortly. The law-enforcing, criminal-apprehending aspect of policing has also been a traditional focus. The action taken by the patrol officer arriving at a crime scene is the single most important factor in the success of a criminal investigation, as discussed in the next chapter.

The third sphere of activity, partnering with the community to solve crime and disorder problems, goes full circle back to Peel's principles that the people are the police and the police are the people and to an emphasis on crime *prevention*. Citizens are often more concerned about disorder and quality-of-life issues than they are about crime.

In addition to overseeing these three spheres of activity, middle management and first-line supervisors must balance structure and authority with discretion and creativity. Management must also attend to infrastructure requirements such as training, performance evaluations, needed equipment and resources, and information support. Furthermore, management must determine how to deploy patrol officers.

Traditionally patrol officers have been assigned a specific time and a specific geographic location, or beat, of equal geographic size, and these assignments have been rotated.

Beats set up to be of equal geographic size pose obvious problems because the workload is not the same at all hours of the day or in all areas. Several attempts have been made to overcome the problems inherent in equal-shift and beat-size staffing. Some departments, usually larger ones, assign officers according to the demand for services, concentrating the officers' time where it is most needed, although union contracts sometimes make this impossible. Software programs are available to help with deployment of patrol. Sometimes beat lines are redrawn to match "natural" neighborhoods identified through profiling adjoining beats. Another important decision is what type of patrol to employ.

TYPES OF PATROL

Patrol is often categorized as either general or specialized. Both general and specialized patrols seek to deter crime and apprehend criminals, as well as to provide community satisfaction with the services provided by the police department. General patrol does so by providing rapid response to calls for service. Specialized patrol does so by focusing its efforts on already-identified problems. Whether general or specialized patrol is used depends on the nature of the problem and the tactics required to deal with it most effectively.

General Patrol

General patrol is also referred to as preventive patrol, random patrol and routine patrol. The term *routine patrol* should not really be used, however, because there is nothing routine about it. The challenges of general patrol change constantly. The patrol officer may be pursuing an armed bank robber in the morning and giving a talk at an elementary school in the afternoon.

Traditionally patrol has been random, reactive, incident driven and focused on rapid response to calls.

These characteristics can be seen in the main activities officers engage in during a typical patrol shift: random/preventive patrol, calls for service, directed patrol, self-initiated activities and administrative duties.

Random/Preventive Patrol

Traditionally patrol officers begin their shifts on **random patrol** in squad cars in hopes of detecting (intercepting) crimes in progress, deterring crime by creating an illusion of police omnipresence or being in the area and able to respond to crime-in-progress calls rapidly.

random patrol
Having no set pattern; by chance; haphazard.

Preventive patrol is generally done by uniformed officers moving at random through an assigned area. Because officers usually decide for themselves what they will do while on preventive patrol, this time is sometimes referred to as "noncommitted" time. It comprises between 30 and 40 percent of patrol time, but it is often broken into small segments because of interruptions by self-initiated activities, service calls, traffic stops, business checks and administrative duties.

Often priorities for preventive patrol are identified or assigned during roll call. For example, patrol officers may be told to drive more often through specific neighborhoods where a rash of car break-ins have been occurring, or through an area of new development where theft of construction material and vandalism of unfinished homes has been reported. This type of effort is also referred to as **extra patrol**, and is typically used when a specific type of crime has occurred several times in a certain area, or if there is a high probability that a crime might occur. Extra patrol, in which officers patrol such identified areas more frequently throughout their shifts, has proved to be effective in finding and arresting suspects.

extra patrol
Typically used when a specific type of crime has occurred several times in a certain area, or if there is a high probability that a crime might occur.

A serious challenge to random patrol came over 30 years ago in the findings of the often-cited Kansas City Experiment. Funded by a grant from the Police Foundation, the Kansas City Preventive Patrol Experiment of 1972 is often deemed the most comprehensive study of routine preventive patrol ever undertaken. The basic design divided 15 beats in Kansas City into three different groups:

- Group 1 Reactive Beats—five beats in which no routine preventive patrol was used. Officers responded only to calls for service.
- Group 2 Control Beats—five beats that maintained their normal level of routine preventive patrol.
- Group 3 Proactive Beats—five beats that doubled or tripled the level of routine preventive patrol.

The study found that decreasing or increasing routine preventive patrol as done in this experiment had no effect on crime, citizen fear of crime, community attitudes toward the police on delivering services, police response time or traffic crashes. Klockars (1983, p.130) asserted that the results of the Kansas City Patrol Experiment indicated, "It makes about as much sense to have police patrol routinely in cars to fight crime as it does to have firemen patrol routinely in fire trucks to fight fire."

This landmark research provided powerful evidence that the traditional goals of random patrol were ineffective. The goal of *interception* was seldom accomplished, probably because two-thirds of Index Crimes are committed indoors, out of view of patrolling officers. The goal of *deterrence* was not reached, probably because deterrence depends on the certainty and swiftness of punishment. The goal of *rapid response* to crimes in progress was also not reached. This may be because fewer than 25 percent of dispatched calls involve crimes in progress (involvement crimes), 75 percent of calls regarding serious crimes are discovery crimes (discovered after the perpetrator left the scene) and that half of victims and witnesses wait five or more minutes before calling the police. The time elapsed between the commission of the crime and the call to dispatch is the most important factor in apprehending perpetrators at the scene.

Furthermore, there may be a delay between when dispatch receives the call and when the dispatcher forwards that information to an officer because some dispatch agencies use call takers to filter calls, separating or triaging incoming calls based on the seriousness of the incident and need for an immediate response. This is, in effect, another person that the reporting party speaks with before getting through to an actual dispatcher, which necessarily adds time to the process. During "in progress" calls such as driving complaints, there may be a time delay of several minutes, which can make a big difference when officers are looking for a moving object.

Although the Kansas City study found no significant differences in the incidence of crime resulting from varying the *level* of patrol, the results might have been different if they had varied the *form* of the patrol. For example, would the outcome differ if patrol officers more aggressively probed individuals, places and circumstances, being *proactive* rather than *reactive*, directed rather than random? Studies conducted in Syracuse, New York; San Diego, California; and Houston, Texas, found that patrol officers could expect to intercept fewer than 1 percent of street crimes, giving credence to the saying: "Random patrol produces random results."

Given that streetwise criminals study police patrol methods and select targets not likely to be detected; given that many crimes are committed on the spur of the moment, particularly crimes of opportunity involving property theft; given that many crimes occur rather spontaneously in the "heat of passion," particularly violent crimes such as murder and assault; and given that much crime is committed inside buildings, out of the patrols' sight, Goldstein (1990, p.35), the father of problem-oriented policing, suggests a different approach: "Focusing on the substantive, community problems that the police must handle . . . requires the police to go beyond taking satisfaction in the smooth operation of their organization; it requires that they extend their concern to dealing effectively with the problems that justify creating a police agency in the first instance." This approach is used in directed patrol.

directed patrol

Uses crime statistics to plan shift and beat staffing, providing more coverage during times of peak criminal activity and in high-crime areas; designed to handle problems and situations requiring coordinated efforts; also called *specialized patrol* or *aggressive patrol.*

Directed Patrol

Directed or aggressive patrol meshes well with problem-oriented policing and with community policing and focuses on high-crime areas or specific offense types.

Directed patrol uses crime statistics to plan shift and beat staffing, providing more coverage during times of peak criminal activity and in high-crime areas.

Aggressive patrol includes saturation, crackdowns, field interrogation, aggressive traffic enforcement and detection of **environmental anomalies**, that is, unusual activities that warrant further investigation. Crackdowns might use stakeouts (the simplest form), plainclothes officers, decoys and surveillance. The positive effects of crackdowns sometimes include a **residual deterrence effect** in that they continue after the crackdowns end. In addition, crackdowns can reduce crime and disorder outside the target area or reduce offenses not targeted in the crackdowns, commonly refer to as a **diffusion of benefits**. Crackdowns are most effective when used in combination with other responses that address the underlying conditions contributing to the problem.

A method that enhances the effectiveness of aggressive patrol is geographic permanence; that is, officers are regularly assigned the same beat. With a permanent assignment, officers get to know the normal activities of the beat, enhancing their ability to recognize what is unusual and thus requires investigation. Geographic permanence also fosters rapport between police and citizens, helping with the overall department mission.

A key to directed patrol is identifying the **hot spots** on the beat, the estimated 10 percent of locations that account for 60 to 65 percent of calls for service. The intent is to break the incident-call-response cycle illustrated in Figure 5.1.

aggressive patrol

Designed to handle problems and situations requiring coordinated efforts; also called *specialized patrol* or *directed patrol*.

environmental anomalies

Unusual activities that warrant further investigation.

residual deterrence effect

The positive effects of crackdowns that continue after a crackdown ends.

diffusion of benefits

Crackdowns can reduce crime and disorder outside the target area or reduce offenses not targeted in the crackdowns.

hot spots

Specific locations with high crime rates.

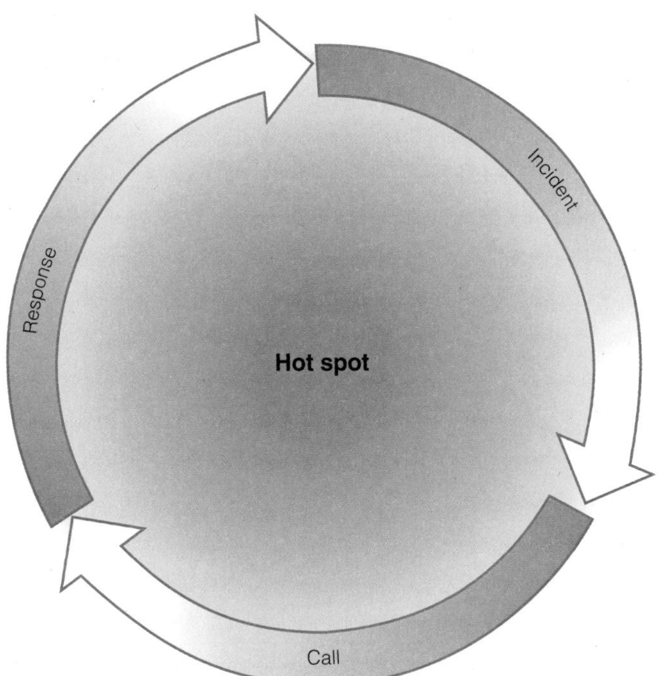

FIGURE 5.1 The Incident-Call-Response Cycle of Hot Spots

Crime analysis using mapping, geographic information systems (GIS) and CompStat can identify hot spots or specific problems to target through directed patrol.

Data-Driven Approaches to Crime and Traffic Safety (DDACTS) is an emerging law enforcement operational model that integrates location-based crime data with traffic data to produce a community hotspot map, thereby allowing a more effective, efficient deployment of law enforcement personnel and other resources (Kanable and Dewey-Kollen, 2009, p.24).

Crime Mapping/Geographic Information Systems (GIS) GIS plays a vital role in data-driven decision making by enabling law enforcement to better use crime information and statistics to help guide policy and practice. Mapping can identify correlations between crime, demographics, societal issues and more and can help departments deploy their resources more effectively. Crime mapping can be used

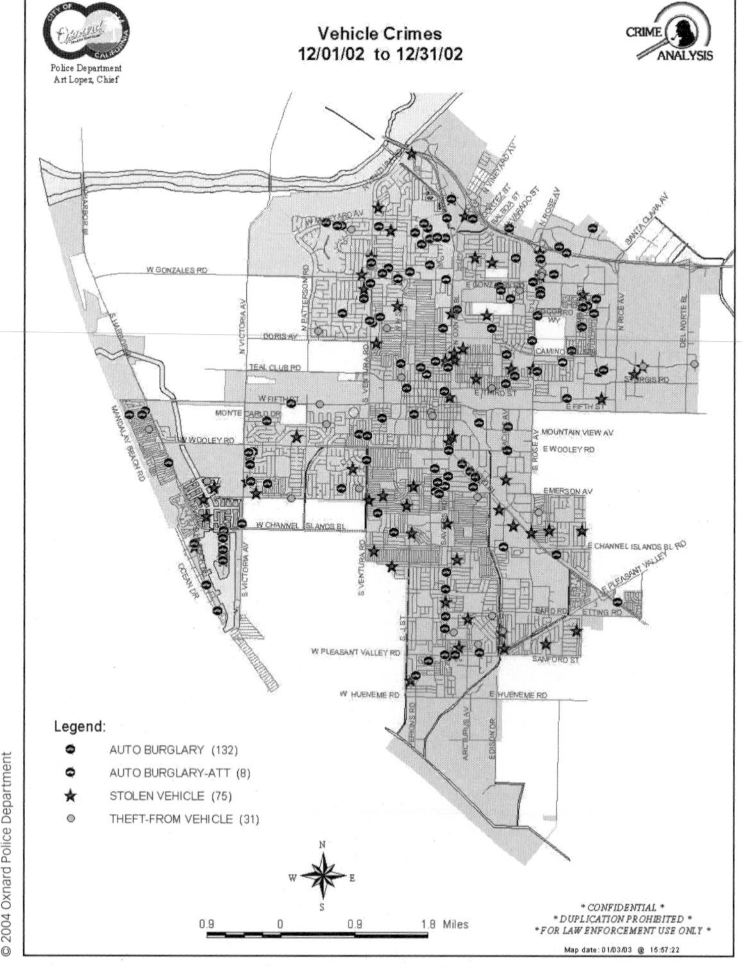

Crime mapping is becoming more popular with law enforcement agencies and can be used to determine where patrol is needed most. This map from the Oxnard (CA) Police Department shows vehicle crimes from December 1 to December 31, 2002.

to determine where patrol is most needed. Individual crimes show up as colored dots, and high-crime areas emerge as large, colored blobs.

The ability to share information across jurisdictional lines can be invaluable, not only in fighting crime locally but also in providing information vital for homeland security.

Closely related to mapping and geographic information systems is CompStat, another crime analysis tool that has been referred to as "high-tech pin mapping" (Grossi, 2008, p.26).

CompStat CompStat, short for computer statistics or comparison statistics, was developed by the New York City Police Department in 1994 and was credited with bringing crime down by 80 percent in the years following its adoption. In essence, CompStat targets police resources to fight crime strategically, revolutionizing the police patrol function (Grossi, 2008). CompStat is based on four crime-reduction principles: (1) accurate, timely intelligence, (2) rapid deployment of personnel and resources, (3) effective tactics and (4) ongoing follow-up and assessment.

Departments across the country have adopted the CompStat model partially because it combines elements of tradition, reactive policing and community-based approaches using a proactive approach. By melding the reactive and proactive approaches of policing, it first focuses on a problem, reacts to it and ultimately uses its resources to address it. Chapter 7 discusses CompStat policing.

ACTIVITIES WHILE ON PATROL

While on patrol, officers respond to calls for service and emergencies, undertake self-initiated tasks and perform administrative duties.

First Responders

First responders need important information to fight crime and save lives, and yet information often fails to make it past the dispatcher or Public Safety Answering Point (PSAP) Next generation 911 (NG911), introduced in the last chapter, is a positive move in this direction.

Calls for Service

The two-way radio has made the service call an extremely important element of patrol. It has also made it necessary to prioritize calls. A radio dispatch almost always takes precedence over other patrol activities. For example, if an officer has stopped a traffic violator (a self-initiated activity) and receives a call of an armed robbery in progress, most department policies require the officer to discontinue the contact with the motorist and answer the service call.

In most departments calls for service drive the department, a response known as **incident-driven policing**. Because 40 to 60 percent of patrol officers' time is spent responding to calls for service, the way police respond to such calls significantly affects every aspect of their function. The response has traditionally been reactive, incident-driven and as rapid as possible. Many departments have found

incident-driven policing
Where calls for service drive the department; a reactive approach with emphasis on rapidity of response.

differential response strategies
Suiting the response to the call.

that **differential response strategies**, suiting the response to the call, are much more effective.

Call-related factors to consider include the type of incident and when it happened, that is, how much time has elapsed since it occurred. An in-progress major personal injury incident would be viewed differently from a minor noncrime incident that occurred several hours ago.

Calls management usually involves call stacking, a process performed by a computer-aided dispatch system in which nonemergency, lower priority calls are ranked and held or "stacked" so the higher priorities are continually dispatched first. The response time and nature of the response may vary considerably, from an immediate on-site response, to an on-site response within an hour, to a response when time permits. The caller may need to arrange an appointment for an officer to respond, or the officer may simply telephone a response without ever meeting the caller face-to-face. If it is determined the call for service does not require the dispatch of an officer, either sworn or nonsworn, the complainant may be told to come to the department to file a complaint, asked to mail in a complaint or be referred to another agency altogether, as illustrated in Figure 5.2. Although police response time is often a cause of citizen complaints, if citizens know what to expect, complaints can be reduced.

Patrol might be more effective if it were proactive, directed and problem-oriented and if it used differential response strategies.

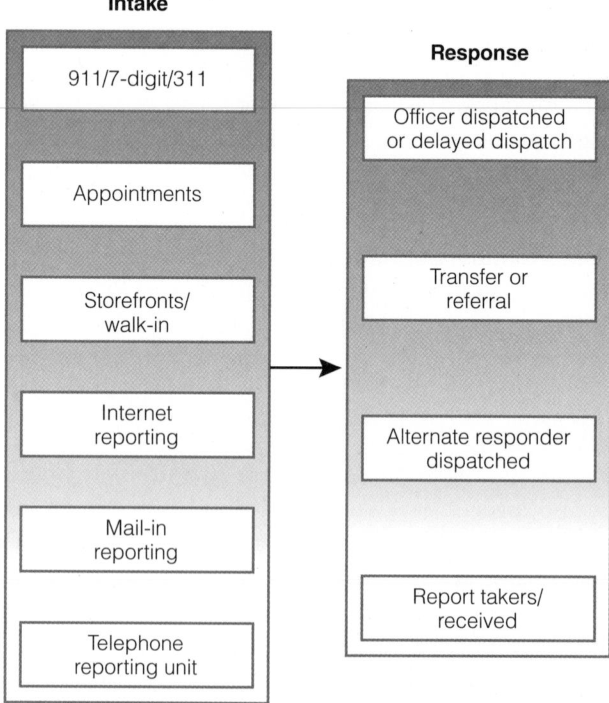

FIGURE 5.2 Call Management: Intake and Response

SOURCE: Tom McEwen, Deborah Spencer, Russell Wolff, Julie Wartell and Barbara Webster. *Call Management in Community Policing: A Guidebook for Law Enforcement.* U.S. Department of Justice, Office of Community Oriented Policing Services, February 2003, p.12.

The problem-oriented approach is often criticized as being unrealistic because it demands so much patrol officer time. However as Goldstein (1990, p.152) suggests,

> The time now wasted between calls for help and in the limited number of self-initiated activities of officers can be put to better use. The value of many of the specialized and permanent jobs (other than patrol) to which officers are currently assigned can be challenged, with reassignment to more useful work. Many hours can be saved by using different responses to problems. Alternatives to arrest, when feasible, can greatly reduce the inordinate amount of time commonly consumed in processing an arrest. Calls to the police can be screened more effectively and, where appropriate, handled by telephone or diverted to another unit of the department or to another agency.

Whether general or specialized, the demands made on patrol officers are many. Patrol officers who are "swamped" responding to calls for service on a first-come, first-served basis have little or no time to perform in the other major spheres of activity or to perform required administrative duties.

Self-Initiated Tasks

Officer-initiated activities usually result from officers' observations while on preventive or directed patrol; that is, they encounter situations that require their intervention. For example, an officer may see a crime in progress and arrest the suspect. Usually, however, officer-initiated activities involve community relations or crime prevention activities such as citizen contacts or automobile and building checks. Officers may see a large crowd gathered and decide to break it up, thereby preventing a possible disturbance or even a riot. Or they may see a break in a store's security, take steps to correct it and thus prevent a later possible burglary.

Officers are sometimes hesitant to get involved in community services and preventive activities because such duties make them unavailable for radio dispatches and interfere with their ability to respond rapidly to service calls. Handheld radios and cell phones have allowed patrol officers more freedom of movement and have allowed them to initiate more activity.

Too often little attention is paid to the officer's use of noncommitted time, which is commonly regarded as having no function other than to ensure that officers are available to quickly respond to service calls. Frequently noncrime service calls interrupt a patrol officer's self-initiated activity that could prevent or deter crime. Emphasis on rapid response to all service calls has sometimes retarded the development of productive patrol services. Obviously not all service calls require a rapid response.

Research by Famega et al. (2005) found that police have large amounts of discretionary time but engage in relatively few proactive policing activities. In the Baltimore Police Department, an average of three-quarters of the shift is unassigned. Officers spend the majority of unassigned time engaged in self-initiated routine patrol or offering backup. Only 6 percent of unassigned time activities are directed by supervising officers or closely connected individuals such as dispatchers. This research suggests that detailed directives based on valid crime analyses can improve patrol officer performance and reduce crime.

CAREER PROFILE

Linda S. Miller (Retired Patrol Officer/Sergeant)

I like to joke that I became a police officer because the police department had free parking. That's not really the reason, but there's a grain of truth there. I was working downtown at the time and paying what I thought was an outrageous amount for parking. My brother called me one day and said there was a job opening for a "civilian" dispatcher at the police department. The department, which had been using police officers as dispatchers, had decided they could save money by hiring nonofficers and freeing up some of the police dispatchers for patrol. The dispatcher position paid more than I was making, it was closer to home—and it came with free parking. I was pretty motivated by money because I was divorced and raising my young son alone. Making ends meet on what was known back then as "women's wages" wasn't working very well for me. So I decided to apply for the dispatcher job and, happily, was one of five people hired.

Everything about the police department was new to me, including the work the officers did day in and day out. Civilian dispatchers were required to ride with an officer for a shift every month, so the dispatchers would have a better idea of what went on when they were dispatching radio calls. While I'll admit I was surprised to find police work a lot less dangerous than I thought would be, it was also interesting and challenging work. No two shifts were ever the same. I found myself thinking a lot about some of the calls I dispatched and how the officers handled them. I read many of their incident reports and began to imagine how I might have handled things if I were an officer. You can probably guess where this was going.

I had never thought about a career in law enforcement, nor had any woman I'd ever known, because there were almost no women in the field. This was 1973, and there were "women's jobs" and "men's jobs." Back then, "Help Wanted" ads in the newspaper were split into categories; jobs for women were listed separately from jobs for men. It was not okay to apply for jobs in the category reserved for the opposite sex, and I had never heard of anyone doing that. My jobs up until that point had always been very traditional, and so had I. I had been a flight attendant, an administrative assistant and a fashion model. I was working for a judge when I applied for the dispatcher position. Despite my traditional female-oriented employment track record, I had started thinking about becoming an officer. The police department, however, was not thinking like that at all.

Nontraditional job opportunities for women and "equal pay for equal work" were controversial ideas in the mid-1970s, and actual progress was still so insignificant that it seemed every woman hired to do "a man's job" got news coverage. Across the board, men made more money than women, even for the exact same job. Most people didn't find that odd.

Although it took court intervention, I did eventually become a police officer and spent over 20 years at the department. I worked in the patrol division for more than 8 years and also worked in crime prevention, community resources, community policing, investigations and research/development. I was promoted to sergeant and spent the last 3 years "on loan" to a federally funded community policing training organization.

The biggest change I saw in policing over the years was the emergence of ideas that have helped change policing from a completely reactive system to one that can anticipate problems and help solve them. Steeped in tradition and resistant to change, police departments were content to respond repeatedly to the same problems in the same way. But as requirements for becoming a police officer began to change, policing began to change. Cops with college degrees weren't content with simply being "911 order-takers." They were more likely to be looking for job satisfaction and meaningful work that mattered in the lives of the community. They wanted to solve problems and to help the communities they served. And so community policing was born.

Along with community policing has come acknowledgement that police officers will not necessarily be successful just because they are 6 feet tall and strong. They need to be smart and to know how to collaborate and solve problems. They need to know how to talk to people and to understand the human condition. In many places they need to speak a second language. These new desirable traits open the door further for diversity among police officers, which of course includes women and minorities, and I think that's good for the community. Of course, my decision to apply for the dispatcher position changed my life in every way. I had an incredibly challenging career, filled with purpose and direction. I took on responsibilities I couldn't have imagined before, met characters I'll never forget, formed great friendships and learned I was capable of far more than I dreamed. Most of all, I was able to support my child and fulfill my parental obligations in a way that makes me proud. I like to think I made a difference for the citizens I had contact with, for my son and for myself. I have never regretted being a police officer.

The emphasis on problem solving in partnership with the community provides an excellent way for officers to use their noncommitted time, which has been estimated at 60 percent of total patrol time. This time could be better used talking with citizens to determine what they perceive as neighborhood problems and possible solutions. In addition, much of an officer's uncommitted time often involves administrative duties.

Famega (2009, p.98) also studied the extent to which traditional patrol officers (identified as "post" officers) engaged in proactive activates and found that overall, 50 percent of post officer time was spent engaged in proactive activities as compared with 29 percent of time engaged in administrative and personal activities and 21 percent of time on reactive activities: "Clearly, post officers have a good deal of time for proactive work, though most of it is spent on patrol." The study also found that post officers spend more time than community officers engaged in proactive patrol and backing up other officers (Famega).

Administrative Duties

Administrative work includes preparing and maintaining the patrol vehicle, transporting prisoners and documents, writing reports and testifying in court. Efforts to make patrol more cost effective have often been aimed at cutting time spent on administrative duties. Some departments have greatly reduced the time officers spend maintaining their vehicles. Other departments have drastically reduced the amount of paperwork required of patrol officers by allowing them to dictate reports, which secretaries then transcribe, or by using computer-generated reports. Nonetheless, the paperwork required of today's officers greatly exceeds that of officers 20 or 30 years ago.

The types of reports police officers frequently use include motor vehicle reports, accident reports, vehicle recovery reports, offense reports, incident reports, driving while intoxicated (DWI) reports, death scene reports, continuation reports, juvenile reports, missing persons reports, evidence reports, arrest/violation reports and record checks.

METHODS OF PATROL

Another factor influencing how patrol officers fulfill their responsibilities is the method of patrol they use. Patrol officers in the United States were originally on foot or horseback. Bicycles were introduced to policing in Detroit in 1897 and automobiles were introduced in 1910. Airplanes were first used by the New York City Police Department in 1930. At that time daredevil pilots were flying all over the city, sometimes crashing in densely populated areas. The New York Airborne police unit was created to control reckless flying over the city. These means of patrol and others can be found in the 21st century.

Patrol can be accomplished by foot, automobile, motorcycle, bicycle, Segway, horseback, aircraft and boat, or via other specialized vehicles such as ATVs, snowmobiles, or Jet Skis. The most commonly used and most effective patrol is usually a combination of automobile and foot patrol.

Foot Patrol

The word *patrol* is derived from the French word *patrouiller*, which roughly means "to travel on foot." **Foot patrol**, the oldest form of patrol, consists of officers walking a "beat" and responding to incidents on foot. It has the advantage of close

foot patrol

Consists of officers walking a "beat" and responding to incidents on foot.

citizen contact and is proactive rather than reactive. Its goal is to address neighborhood problems before they become crimes. Most effective in highly congested areas, foot patrol may help to deter burglary, robbery, purse snatching and muggings. Kelling (n.d., pp.2–3) reports the consistent findings of two foot-patrol experiments:

- When foot patrol is added in neighborhoods, levels of fear decrease significantly.
- When foot patrol is withdrawn from neighborhoods, levels of fear increase significantly.
- Citizen satisfaction with police increases when foot patrol is added in neighborhoods.
- Police who patrol on foot have a greater appreciation for the values of neighborhood residents than do police who patrol the same areas in automobiles.
- Police who patrol on foot have greater job satisfaction, less fear and higher morale than officers who patrol in automobiles.

Miller (2008) notes, "While the actual effect of foot patrol officers on crime statistics is still being debated, surveys clearly show that citizens feel safer and more confident in their local police department when the officers are a living, breathing presence in their daily lives." Ironically, foot patrol is often one of the first items to undergo budget cuts, in part because it is less cost effective or efficient than other forms of patrol, especially for smaller agencies with limited resources, as the majority of police departments across the country are.

The 1980s saw a significant trend back to foot patrol. In the 1990s foot patrol became almost synonymous with community policing. Foot patrol is relatively expensive and does limit the officer's ability to pursue suspects in vehicles and to get from one area to another rapidly. According to the National Neighborhood Foot Patrol Center, Michigan State University School of Criminal Justice (n.d.): "Foot patrol is an exercise in communication—an attempt to develop rapport between the officer on the beat and the citizens he or she serves. Foot patrol officers constantly interact with the community. They instruct citizens in crime prevention techniques and link them to available governmental services. They are catalysts of neighborhood organizations."

In addition to curbing crime, enhancing community partnerships and keeping officers in touch with local activity, foot patrols also are a means for department to lessen the impact of high fuel costs (Craven, 2009).

Most departments who use foot patrol do not intend to replace motorized patrol but rather to provide a combination of foot and motorized patrol, capitalizing on the strengths of each. Used in conjunction with motorized patrol, foot patrol is highly effective. A new trend in combining foot and automobile patrol is called geographic policing, or "geo-policing," in which officers on automobile patrol are assigned beats that they are required to invest time in and to build rapport with area community members, including citizens and local business members. In geo-policing, police supervisors are also assigned areas to work with, to analyze hot spots and crime trends and explore ways to resolve these issues. The goal is to better allocate police resources to the areas within a jurisdiction that need them, making the agency more efficient while at the same time building rapport with the community.

Automobile Patrol

Automobile patrol offers the greatest mobility and flexibility and is usually the most cost-effective method of patrol. It allows wide coverage and rapid response to calls; the vehicle radio provides instant communications with headquarters. The automobile also provides a means of transporting special equipment and prisoners or suspects.

However, while patrolling in a vehicle, officers cannot pay as much attention to details they might see if they were on foot, such as a door ajar, a window broken or a security light out. The physical act of driving may draw attention away from such subtle signs that a crime may be in progress. Furthermore, research on the effectiveness of preventive patrol indicates that a crime prevented by a passing vehicle can be, and usually is, committed as soon as the police are gone. In effect police presence prevents street crime only if the police can be everywhere at once.

Nonetheless, mobile data terminals (MDT) in most patrol vehicles allow officers to access information, not only from headquarters and state databases, but also from the FBI's National Crime Information Center (NCIC), greatly enhancing the officer's effectiveness as well as his or her safety.

The National Crime Information Center One vital source of information for officers in the field is the FBI's online computerized NCIC. In 1967 the FBI implemented this computerized crime-information storage system dedicated to serving law enforcement and criminal justice agencies nationwide. Under this system each state has a number of computer terminals that interface with the FBI's main database in Washington, DC, which contains records of stolen property, such as guns, autos and office machines, and in some cases, records of persons wanted on warrants.

The National Crime Information Center (NCIC) gives all police agencies in the country access to the computerized files of the FBI.

The NCIC computer receives information from other federal law enforcement agencies and from state and local law enforcement agencies. The NCIC makes it possible for a law enforcement officer in Texas who stops a suspicious person or car from California to make an inquiry to the Washington NCIC terminal in a matter of seconds on the status of the individual and/or the car. The officer can be quickly informed if the car has been stolen or if an arrest warrant is outstanding on the person in the car. In addition to MDTs, officers have available many other tools that assist in fulfilling their mission.

The Modern Patrol Car Modern patrol cars are greatly enhanced by technology. MDTs allow officers to access and disseminate information, file reports, pull up mug shots, get directions, communicate more effectively and keep tables on criminal activity (Moore, 2009b). MDTs can also link officers to the Internet, providing access to a variety of databases and other police resources.

Most patrol cars are also equipped with global positioning systems (GPS), a satellite-based navigation system. GPS uses a network of 24 satellites that circle the earth twice a day in a very precise orbit, transmitting signal information to users on the ground. GPS receivers process this information using triangulation to calculate the user's exact location. GPS can be used to track suspects, more efficiently monitor fleets and determine the whereabouts of undercover surveillance officers. GPS also enhances officer safety by providing real-time information about an officer's vehicle location, in case an officer has an emergency and is unable to respond verbally as to their location. Furthermore, GPS is invaluable in search-and-rescue missions, with searchers able to download each specific search area onto a map.

Another type of technology finding its way into patrol cars is the visual surveillance and imaging systems similar to those used by the military, as well as thermal imaging and night vision. A third type of technology commonly used in patrol cars is the dashboard-mounted video camera. Although many officers were skeptical about in-car videos when first introduced, they now rely on it: "In-car video increases convictions and eliminates false claims" (McCallion, 2009, p.34). A survey found "a resounding 93 percent of respondents whose agencies have in-car video now approve of the practice" (Basich, 2009, p.18). Respondents cited evidence and liability protection as the respective top benefits to law enforcement, each with just over 37 percent. Only 16.2 credited in-car video systems with improving officer safety above all other benefits.

Finally, automated license plate recognition (ALPR) technology is greatly enhancing enforcement efforts. ALPR systems use cameras (fixed or mobile) to automatically capture passing vehicle license plates and check the plates against a preloaded database of plates linked with criminal activity. When a plate match occurs, the system sends an alert to the operator indicating a "hit" (Altman et al., 2009). ALPR systems can run thousands of plates per shift, locate America's Missing: Broadcast Emergency Response (AMBER)–alert vehicles, locate wanted and stolen vehicles, and help solve crimes (Morgan, 2009). After only a few months of operation, the Georgetown (South Carolina) Police Department's ALPR system had read more than a million license plates and lead to 20 arrests (Altman et al., p.44). Advocates of this technology assert that is can make communities safer and increase departments' investigative and policing capabilities. Critics of ALPR contend it is still extremely expensive and not cost effective, particularly in this down economy. Also, as with many technology-driven innovations, the issue of privacy concerns arise with ALPR units and their capacity to serve as a Big Brother–like surveillance. Agencies should have policies and procedures in place to ensure that data is managed to meet public safety needs while protecting individuals' privacy interests.

Since almost all departments use squad cars to patrol, several decisions related to use of vehicle patrol must be considered, including how many officers to assign to a squad and whether a department should institute a take-home program.

One-Officer versus Two-Officer Squads One factor of importance when using automobile patrol is whether to have one or two officers assigned per squad. Circumstances should determine whether a one-officer or a two-officer unit is more appropriate. The single-officer unit is the rule rather than the exception, and one officer can handle most incidents. If two or more officers are required, multiple one-officer units can be dispatched to the scene. Two-officer units should be restricted to those areas, shifts and types of activities most likely to threaten the officers' safety, for example, during the evening or in high-crime areas.

The one-officer unit offers several advantages, including cost effectiveness in that the same number of officers can patrol twice the area, with twice the mobility and with twice the power of observation. Officers working alone are generally more cautious in dangerous situations, recognizing that they have no backup. Officers working alone also are generally more attentive to patrol duties because they do not have a conversational partner. The expense of two cars compared to one, however, is a factor.

Police unions usually support two-officer patrol units and may include provisions for two-officer units in their contracts, jeopardizing management's ability to best use available resources and to make rational decisions about personnel deployment and scheduling.

Another consideration in using automobile patrol is whether the department has a take-home patrol car program.

Take-Home Patrol Car Program Many agencies have found that when officers are assigned their own take-home patrol cars, they tend to be more responsible with them, resulting in lower maintenance and repair costs. Such a program also increases visibility of police officers in the community and can be a good recruiting tool. Downsides of take-home programs include increased officer liability and concern about the security of the car and its contents, including uniforms and guns. Nonetheless, such program have gained acceptance in many departments.

Motorcycle Patrol

Motorcycle police officers have been used in America for more than half a century. In fact, motorcycle officers have patrolled our streets since their introduction in Pittsburgh, Pennsylvania, almost 100 years ago. Motorcycles are used for traffic enforcement, escort and parade duty. Motorcycles and automobiles have dominated traffic enforcement for the past seven or eight decades. They can also enhance community relations. A further advantage is that an officer can use it as a barricade because motorcycles are typically large enough to offer some cover (Kozlowski, 2010a, p.16).

Among the disadvantages of motorcycles are their relatively high cost to operate, their limited use in adverse weather and the hazards associated with riding them.

Bicycle Patrol

Bicycle patrols were introduced in Detroit in 1897 and enjoyed great popularity until around 1910, when the introduction of the automobile and the emphasis on rapid response to calls made them impractical. However, they are making a comeback as increasing numbers of departments worldwide are adding bicycles to their arsenal of tools. In fact, nearly every major police department in the country now has a bicycle unit (Moore, 2007, p.58). Bicycle patrols are good community-policing tools and are relatively inexpensive compared to maintaining cars and motorcycles.

Bicycle patrol is sometimes used in parks and on beaches or in conjunction with stakeouts. Bike units are ideal for patrolling small areas and for performing directed patrol assignments. They may even be used to cover small areas some distance apart, with departments mounting bike racks on patrol cars to be transported to various patrol sites. In addition to mobility, bicycles provide a stealth factor, an element of surprise because they are quiet and do not attract attention. In addition, bike officers can smell and hear things officers in cruisers cannot.

Bicycle patrols have been extremely successful on college campuses and in searches for missing children and joggers. Bike-based enforcement can include gaining intelligence to area-specific problems, vehicle stops, pedestrian stops, driving under the influence (DUI) enforcement, narcotics suppression, special events and routine calls for service. Bicycle patrols are also used in search and rescue, private security and airport security.

A study in which bicycle and motor patrols were observed under similar conditions in five cities found that a higher amount of contact with the public was experienced by bike patrols; the rate of serious contacts including arrests, vehicle impoundments and the like were comparatively similar; and in some cases, response time and response capability was clearly superior for bicycle patrols (Menton, 2007, p.78).

Bicycle patrol remains very appealing to agencies, officers and the community, but it does require special training and conditioning. Officers can be injured or killed without proper training and well-maintained equipment. Comprehensive training programs such as the International Police Motor Bike Association (IPMBA) Police Cyclist™ Course, are available and proven (Beck, 2009). Some departments have gone to electronic bicycles or e-bikes. Other departments have gone to another method of patrol offering a combination of the advantages of foot patrol and bicycle patrol—the Segway.

Segways

A relatively new method of patrol is the Segway Personal Transporter, more commonly known as a Segway PT or simply a Segway. Segways were introduced in December 2001 and have been found to be ideal not only for transportation but also for interacting with citizens. Segway technology uses gyroscopes and tilt sensors that monitor a rider's center of gravity, moving forward when a rider leans forward and backward when a rider leans back. Turns are made by twisting the handlebar; the harder the twist of the handlebar, the harder and tighter the turn.

A distinct advantage of the Segway PT is that it puts officers 8 inches above a crowd, the elevated position increasing visibility for both the officer and for the crowd (Bradley, 2008). In addition, the Segway allows officers to connect with the public without giving up a set of wheels (Basich, 2008). The most common uses for agencies have been airport patrols, shopping malls, university campuses, emergency medical response, community street patrol and events, and bomb and hazardous materials (hazmat) response.

Mounted Patrol

Mounted patrol evolved from military antecedents and comprises some of the oldest and most varied police units in the United States. In 1871 the New York City Police Department was one of the first agencies in the country to establish a mounted patrol unit. Mounted patrol offers the opportunity to raise visibility and encourage public interaction in a positive way, as "few things produce commonality like animals do" (Moore, 2009a, p.78). Nonetheless, an officer on horseback commands authority in an unruly crowd in a way an officer on foot could not.

Mounted patrols function in a variety of capacities, from community relations, to park and traffic patrol, to crowd and riot control, to crime prevention. Mounted patrols have also been used to assist in evidence searches at crime scenes, round up straying livestock, search for lost children in tall corn or grass and apprehend trespassers. It has been estimated that one mounted officer is equal to 10 foot patrol officers in crowd-control situations.

Air Patrol

Air patrol is another highly effective form of patrol, especially when large geographic areas are involved, such as with a widespread search for a lost person, a downed plane or an escaped convict. In 2007 about one in five large law enforcement agencies had a specialized aviation unit operating at least one fixed-wing plane or helicopter (Langton, 2009, p.1). These units perform both emergency and nonemergency functions, from general operations (pursuit, speed enforcement, surveillance, responding to calls for service, prisoner transport) to more specialized operations such as homeland security, drug interdiction, emergency medical services, special weapons and tactics (SWAT) and firefighting missions (Solosky, 2009b). The U.S. Customs and Border Protection (CBP) operates a half dozen Predator B unmanned air vehicles (UAVs) over our borders and along our costal waters (Solosky, 2009a). In addition, many state and federal agencies use single-engine airplanes for surveillance work because of their quietness and lower fuel costs. Other advantages of using airplanes include dramatically lower operating costs as well as the fact that initial purchase price, daily operating costs and maintenance sots can be half the cost of a helicopter.

Helicopters have many disadvantages: a relatively short range, significantly slower speed and inability to carry a large amount of equipment compared to a fixed-wing aircraft. Helicopter trips are time-consuming and require several fueling stops. Nonetheless, they remain popular with larger agencies and are often seen as force multipliers (Kozlowski, 2010b). A helicopter 500 feet in the air has 30 times the visual range of a unit on the ground, providing a patrol capacity equal to 15 squad cars. Police helicopters are usually equipped with tools such as thermal imaging units, which provide a distinct advantage in tracking suspects or locating individuals. Furthermore a helicopter can arrive at a crime scene 5 to 10 times faster than street-level units.

Agencies that use helicopters should commit to using them as close to continuously as possible (Kozlowski, 2010b, p.14). Helicopters, even when donated to an agency, are extremely expensive to maintain. Furthermore, many jurisdictions require that the pilot of such aircraft also be a licensed police officer, which can add expense not only from a salary perspective but also from a training perspective.

A cost-effective alternative aircraft for law enforcement is the gyroplane, which carries a much-lower operating cost, requires less training to fly and is generally safer in flight than a helicopter. Even less expensive, yet still in the experimental stage, are *personal* vertical takeoff and landing (VTOL) aircraft.

Water Patrol

Water patrol is used extensively on our coasts to apprehend weapons and narcotics smugglers. Inland, water patrols are used to control river and lake traffic. Water patrol units are highly specialized and are used in relatively few cities in the United States. In those cities with extensive coasts and other waterways, however, they are a vital part of patrol: "Under normal circumstances, marine units keep waterways safe and educate the public about RBS [recreational boating safety, including BUI, aka boating under the influence]. During natural disasters, marine patrol officers prove invaluable to preserving life" (Perin, 2009, p.33). Police dive teams also work closely with water patrol, for obvious reasons, and sometimes share responsibilities.

Watercraft range in size from personal watercraft, such as wave runners, to fully equipped 30-foot cruisers. Cost-effective inflatable equipment is also being used by some departments. Water patrols are used for routine enforcement of such circumstances as vessels exceeding "no-wake" speed limits, intoxicated operators and safety inspections, as well as search-and-rescue operations, emergency transportation in flooded areas, general surveillance and anti-smuggling operations. Water patrol officers need to know how to shoot when their vessels are pitching and rolling, which requires specialized training (Rayburn, 2009).

Special-Terrain Patrol

Some police departments may require special-purpose vehicles for patrol. For example, areas that receive a lot of snow may have snowmobiles as part of their patrol fleet. These vehicles may be especially useful in rescue missions as well as on routine patrol. Police departments with miles of beaches or desert to patrol may use jeeps and dune buggies. Police departments in remote, rugged or mountainous parts of the country may use four-wheel-drive all-terrain vehicles (ATVs). Department of Natural Resources (DNR) or conservation officers frequently use this type of vehicle for patrol. ATVs are also beneficial for crowd control and parking enforcement and are easy to maintain.

Combination Patrol

Combination patrol provides the most versatile approach to preventing or deterring crime and apprehending criminals. The combination used will depend on the size of the police department and on the circumstances that arise. One of the most common combinations is vehicle and foot patrol.

Dye (2009, p.30) cautions, "Over reliance on technology can keep officers in their cars, and administrators must be aware of technology that isolates officers." Under the geo-policing format, officers are directed to connect with the public by getting out of their cars and speaking with people, allowing more rapid identification of community problems and the development of stronger community partnerships (Dye, p.28). Stockton (2008, p.8) suggests that patrol officers practice "random acts of policing," showing up when and where they are not expected, such as at local power plants, shopping malls, and water treatment facilities. If allowed to walk the grounds, they should do so, not only providing a visible deterrent but also being in a position to spot anything out of place and to open lines of communication with people who know when something is not quite right.

Kasper (2009, p.71) also recommends the "park and walk" strategy, targeting high crime areas, business districts, parks, highly residential neighborhoods and schools. Among the advantages of this approach are savings in fuel and vehicle wear and tear, as parking a squad car for two hours during a regular eight-hour shift can lead to a 25 percent decrease in fuel use (Kasper, p.74). "Park and walk" can help strengthen community relations, facilitate the development of informants and assist in recruitment efforts. Another advantage is crime deterrence, perhaps deterring criminal activity and contributing to a greater sense of safety and security within the community. Finally, this approach can provide health benefits to officers: "Breaking up an eight-hour shift with a few 20- to 30-minute walks can do wonders to improve an individual's health" (Kasper, p.75). Table 5.2 summarizes the most common methods of patrol, their uses, advantages and disadvantages.

High Visibility versus Low Visibility

High-visibility patrol is often used in high-risk crime areas in hopes of deterring criminal activity. In addition high-visibility patrol gives citizens a sense of safety, justified or not. Methods of high-visibility patrol include foot patrol, especially

TABLE 5.2 Summary of Patrol Methods

Method	Uses	Advantages	Disadvantages
Foot	Highly congested areas Burglary, robbery, theft, purse snatching, mugging	Close citizen contact High visibility Develop informants	Relatively expensive Limited mobility
Automobile	Respond to service calls Provide traffic control Transport individuals, documents and equipment	Most economical Greatest mobility and flexibility Offers means of communication Provides means of transporting people, documents and equipment	Limited access to certain areas Limited citizen contact
Motorcycle	Same as automobile, except that it can't be used for transporting individuals and has limited equipment	Maneuverability in congested areas and areas restricted to automobiles	Inability to transport much equipment Not used during bad weather Hazardous to operator
Bicycle	Stakeouts Parks and beaches Congested areas	Quiet and unobtrusive	Limited speed Not used during bad weather Vulnerability of officer Physical exertion required
Mounted	Parks and bridle paths Crowd control Traffic control	Size and maneuverability of horse Build rapport with citizens	Expensive Limited carrying capacity Street litter
Air	Surveillance Traffic control Searches and rescues	Covers large areas easily	Expensive Noisy
Water	Deter smuggling Water traffic control Rescues	Access to activities occurring on water	Expensive
Special-terrain	Patrol unique areas inaccessible to other forms Rescue operations	Access to normally inaccessible areas	Limited use in some instances

with a canine partner; mounted patrol; marked police car and motorcycle patrol; and helicopter patrol.

Low-visibility patrol is often used to apprehend criminals engaged in targeted crimes. Many of the specialized patrol operations would fall into this category. Methods of low-visibility patrol include unmarked police cars and bicycles.

The relative effectiveness of high-visibility and low-visibility patrol has not been determined. A combination of both high- and low-visibility patrol is often needed and most effective.

In addition to focusing efforts on crime hot spots and using creative problem-solving partnerships, another basic function of patrol officers is enforcing traffic laws. This duty is often met with mixed reaction from the community—favorably when the police stop neighborhood speeders and other "dangerous drivers," negatively when citizens themselves are the subjects of traffic stops.

THE TRAFFIC DIVISION: AN OVERVIEW

Traffic law enforcement, the most frequent contact between police and otherwise law-abiding citizens, is a critical responsibility of officers. In the United States, the regulation of traffic and enforcement of related laws have existed for more than a century. In 1901 Connecticut established the world's first speed statute limiting horseless carriage speeds to 12 mph in cities and 15 mph in rural areas.

The principal objectives of the traffic division are to obtain, through voluntary citizen compliance, the smoothest possible movement of vehicles and pedestrians consistent with safety and to reduce losses from crashes. Furthermore, because officers are on the streets so much of the time, they often are among the first to know of problems in the transportation system and can provide information as well as advice on overall system planning.

Traffic officers may be responsible for directing and controlling traffic, enforcing traffic laws, assisting at and investigating traffic crashes, and educating the public.

DIRECTING AND CONTROLLING TRAFFIC

Police officers frequently are called on to direct traffic flow, control parking, provide escorts and remove abandoned vehicles. They often are asked to assist in crowd control at major sporting events. They also are responsible for planning traffic routing, removing traffic hazards and assuring that emergency vehicles can move quickly through traffic.

In many jurisdictions officers and other responders, such as ambulances or fire trucks, en route to an emergency can control traffic lights to their favor, eliminating the need to slow or stop at a red light and preventing crashes that may occur when a squad car or other emergency vehicle passes through an intersection against the light. In these systems a frequency-coded signal is emitted from the approaching vehicle to a signal controller device on the traffic light, providing a green light to the emergency vehicle.

ENFORCING TRAFFIC LAWS

Violating traffic laws does not carry the social stigma attached to the violation of other laws, such as laws against murder and rape. Running a stoplight or speeding is not considered a crime, and people regularly and unconsciously violate laws designed to ensure safe use of the streets and highways. Recall the distinction between crimes that are *mala in se* (bad in themselves) and *mala prohibita* (bad because they are forbidden). Traffic laws are excellent examples of *mala prohibita* crimes.

The primary goal of traffic law enforcement is to produce voluntary compliance with traffic laws while keeping traffic moving safely and smoothly.

A properly administered and executed police traffic law enforcement procedure is probably the most important component of the overall traffic program. If people obey the traffic laws, traffic is likely to flow more smoothly and safely, with fewer tie-ups and crashes. Effective traffic law enforcement usually consists of at least five major actions: (1) on-the-spot instructions to drivers and pedestrians, (2) verbal warnings, (3) written warnings with proper follow-up, (4) citations or summonses and (5) arrests. Traffic officers consider the circumstances of each incident and apply their discretion in determining which action is most appropriate.

The question inevitably arises as to how much enforcement is needed to control traffic and reduce crashes. This local issue must be determined for each jurisdiction: "Unfortunately, in too many agencies, traffic law enforcement is approached as a laborious task rather than a golden opportunity. There's nothing a law enforcement agency can do that has as much potential to save lives and personal injury" (Bolton, 2009, p.90).

Traffic Enforcement and the Apprehension of Criminals

A substantial number of crimes are stopped or discovered by police enforcing traffic in a proactive way: "Traffic enforcement is one of the best crime-fighting tools in the police arsenal. . . . The annals of law enforcement are filled with serious crimes that have been solved and criminals apprehended as the result of simple traffic stops and identifications made through the basic traffic stop" (Sweeney, 2009, p.1). Alert traffic officers have helped catch some of America's worst criminals, including terrorists. A case in point: Oklahoma state trooper Charles Hanger stopped Timothy McVeigh's car because it did not have license plates. During the stop, Trooper Hanger discovered that McVeigh had a concealed gun. While McVeigh was sitting in a jail cell being processed, investigators handling the immediate aftermath of the bombing of the Alfred P. Murrah Building were searching for suspects, including McVeigh. Their database search turned up a "hit," and the trooper was credited for apprehending, albeit unwittingly, a terrorist. McVeigh was later convicted and executed for his involvement in the bombing.

All uniformed officers should enforce traffic laws because of the potential for apprehending a felon.

Although being assigned to traffic duty may not be considered "real" police work by many officers, "Study after study has shown that more arrests are made as a result of traffic stops than any undercover operation. Additionally, numerous studies have shown that traffic-related issues continue to be citizen's number one complaint to police" (Casstevens, 2008, p.45). Criminals are five times more likely to be involved in a traffic crash (of any severity) than the general public; therefore: "Aggressive traffic enforcement is a win-win. It reduces crime and increases safety" (Sanow, 2009, p.6). For example, Oklahoma County, Oklahoma, has documented a 90 percent reduction in both crashes and criminal activity after implementing aggressive traffic enforcement: "Traffic enforcement equals crime reduction" (Sanow, p.6).

Selective Traffic Enforcement

Because traffic violations occur every hour of every day, police departments cannot enforce all traffic regulations at all times. It is impossible to achieve 100 percent enforcement, and it is almost always unwise to try to do so. Based on thorough investigations of crashes, summarization and careful analysis of the records, **selective enforcement** targets specific crashes or high-crash areas, such as excessive speed around a schoolyard or playground where young children are present. Because of this, accurate records are essential to the overall effectiveness of the selective enforcement program.

selective enforcement

Targets specific crashes or high-crash areas.

Selective enforcement is not only logical but also practical because most police departments' limited workforces require them to spend time on violations that contribute to crashes. Enforcement personnel, such as officers on motorcycles or officers assigned to a radar unit, are usually the officers assigned to selective traffic enforcement. The officers' activity is directed to certain high-crash areas during certain days of the week and certain hours of the day or night. This is comparable to the data-driven crime reduction and traffic safety approach discussed earlier in the chapter.

Studies in city after city have proved a definite relationship between crashes and enforcement. In analyzing crash reports, one finds at the top of the list year after year the same traffic violations contributing to crashes and the same group of drivers being involved. Crashes are discussed later in the chapter.

Almost everyone has heard in exhaustive detail a friend's version of getting an "unfair" speeding ticket. The person will tell several people about it. In quality and selective enforcement, this has the effect of informing the general public that the police are doing their job. High-quality enforcement not only is supported by the public but it also has an important effect on the would-be traffic violator when the public is informed of the police department's enforcement program and that program is understood and believed to be reasonable.

Among the most common violations of traffic laws are speeding, red-light running, nonuse of seatbelts, aggressive driving and road rage, and driving under the influence of drugs or alcohol. Distracted drivers often also violate traffic laws.

Speeding

Speeding—most everyone does it at one time or another, if not all the time, and many justify it as "just going with the flow of traffic." However, speeding has become an increasing problem for law enforcement, as more cars travel the streets and people seem to be more in a hurry than ever before. Some do not even realize they are speeding until they see the flashing lights of the police in their rearview mirror.

Data from the National Highway Traffic Safety Administration (NHTSA) indicates that in 2008 speeding was a contributing factor in 31 percent of all fatal crashes, with 11,674 lives lost and a cost to society of $40.4 billion per year (*Traffic Safety Facts*, 2009, p.7). Furthermore, public opinion surveys typically identify speed enforcement in residential areas as the number-one problem for the local police.

To combat the problem of lead-footed drivers, some agencies are using portable Speed Monitoring Awareness Radar Trailers (SMARTs) parked alongside the road. These trailers clock and digitally display motorists' speeds beneath a posted speed-limit sign in an effort to gain voluntary compliance with speed laws and reduce crashes.

A new tool for capturing speed data of traffic violators is light detection and ranging (LIDAR), which, unlike radar, allows very specific target acquisition when determining the speed of a particular vehicle on a crowded road. LIDAR can provide a complete sequence of video-recorded speeding events, as well as create a high-resolution image identifying vehicle make, model, license plate number and facial characteristics of the driver (Galvin, 2009a, p.60).

In addition, a Distance between Cars (DBC) Mode can be used to record distance between two vehicles to document tailgating, an offense that has long frustrated law enforcement due to lack of proof: "For years traffic officers have struggled to bring tailgating violators to justice in courts, but without definitive proof, their efforts have been stymied" (Galvin, 2009b, p.70). But now LIDAR can detect, with pinpoint accuracy, vehicles driving too closely.

If a vehicle driver is stopped and ticketed for tailgating or speeding, e-ticketing is rapidly replacing the traditional handwritten ticket: "With a mobile computer equipped with electronic traffic citation software, officers can clear a traffic stop three to five times faster, thereby reducing the risk on the roadside" (Hillard, 2008, p.58). E-ticketing not only increases officer safety but also increases revenue and makes for safer roadways and less paperwork (Griffin, 2009, p.30).

Many motorists use radar detectors to avoid getting a speeding ticket. Although such devices do work, they only respond after they have been targeted by a police radar, making them relatively ineffective in avoiding detection in most instances. Such detectors are legal in all states except Virginia; Washington, DC; and U.S. military bases. Radar detectors are not legal in commercial vehicles, having been banned in all states by a directive of the U.S. Department of Transportation in February 1995.

Red-Light Running

A problem related to speeding is red-light running. Many people think they simply do not have a spare minute to spend sitting at an intersection. Furthermore, traveling at 5 or 10 miles per hour, or more, over the posted speed limit makes stopping for red lights that much more difficult. The Insurance Institute for Highway Safety's Highway Loss Data Institute estimates more than 800 people die each year in crashes that involve red-light running, and more than 200,000 people are injured in such crashes (Highway Loss Data Institute, n.d.).

Some jurisdictions are installing red-light cameras to help enforce traffic laws. These cameras photograph red-light runners, take a picture of the vehicle's driver and license plate for identification, and typically stamp the date, time of day, time elapsed since the light turned red and the vehicle's speed. Many different photo enforcement camera systems are available, some using Doppler radar with others using laser pulse technology, automatic number plate recognition, pressure-sensitive embedded strips or a combination of technologies (Moore, 2008, p.115). The Highway Loss Data Institute estimates that as of March 2010, 439 communities were using red-light cameras.

Several U.S. manufacturers sell photo traffic enforcement systems, working on a contingency basis, collecting fees paid for citations issued. However, some jurisdictions consider this a conflict from an ethical standpoint: "The biggest outcry over photo enforcement lies with whether private corporations should enforce traffic laws" (Garrett, 2009, p.12). Because of this concern, some states prohibit use of automated enforcement, while others restrict the use or regulate how money generated by citations is spent.

Others have questioned whether these cameras are an appropriate enforcement tool or an excessive government intrusion (Wasilewski and Olson, 2009). Civil liberties groups have expressed concern that the cameras could be used to spy on people, and some critics dislike the fact that owners of cars could be penalized for infractions committed by others driving their vehicles.

Traffic Enforcement in Construction Zones

Even though construction zones are announced in advance with flashing barricades, reduced speed zones and flaggers, statistics from the Federal Highway Administration (FHWA) indicate that in 2008 there were 720 work zone fatalities in addition to over 40,000 injuries in work zones ("Work Zone Safety Fact Sheet," n.d.). In an effort to reduce this hazard, the Work Zone Safety Act was passed in 2005, doubling fines for speeding in a work zone and making convictions of two or more speeding violations in a work zone result in a suspended driver's license (Salmon, 2009, p.146).

Use of Seat Belts

Another initiative aimed at saving lives on our highways is promoting use of seat belts. According to NHTSA, ejection from the vehicle accounted for 27 percent of all passenger vehicle occupant fatalities in 2008. More than half of the passenger vehicle occupants killed in traffic crashes in 2008 were unrestrained (*Traffic Safety Facts*, 2009, p.10). According to NHTSA studies, safety belts are 45 percent effective in preventing fatalities, 50 percent effective in preventing moderate-to-critical injuries and 10 percent effective in preventing minor injuries. When safety belts are combined with air bags, injuries are reduced by 68 percent. Beginning in 1998 all new cars were required to have driver and passenger air bags along with seat belts.

Seven years and 13 waves of seat belt mobilization after the first national mobilization in 1997, 50 million more Americans are now buckled up. In 2008, seat belt use stood at 83 percent, a gain from 82 percent in 2007, a statistically insignificant increase from the previous year, yet an increase nonetheless ("Seat Belt Use in 2008," 2008). NHTSA estimates that 13,250 lives were saved in 2008 by the use of seat belts (*Traffic Safety Facts*, 2009, p.3).

Several possible reasons use of safety belts has increased include enhanced laws at the state level, a better educated and more safety conscious consumer, and targeted marketing.

More and more states are turning from secondary to primary seat belt laws, which means a motorist can be stopped and cited for a seat belt violation alone, instead of being stopped for another primary reason and being cited for the secondary seat belt violation. New Hampshire is the only state without a seat belt law for adults.

According to the NHTSA survey, too many children are still riding in the front seat of passenger vehicles. Despite public education campaigns to teach parents that children are safer in the back seat, 15 percent of infants under age 1, 10 percent of children ages 1 to 3 and 29 percent of children ages 4 to 7 are still riding in the front seat.

Interestingly, among those killed in crashes, at least 40 percent of the 64 police officers killed between 2004 and 2008 were not wearing seat belts (Mendoza, 2010). Complacency is one reason. Some officers worry that belts would slow them down if they needed to get out of their vehicle quickly. In addition to increasing officer safety, it becomes a question of obeying the law when they buckle up themselves.

Aggressive Driving and Road Rage

A tailgater on the freeway veers into the next lane, speeds up to pass and then cuts back in front of the car it was once behind. The car now tailing speeds up so the two cars' bumpers nearly touch. Tempers flare, words fly, fingers flip. Both drivers wish they had a gun. Is this a case of aggressive driving or road rage? They are not the same. The NHTSA makes the distinction that aggressive driving is a traffic violation and **road rage** is a criminal offense, with aggressive driving often precipitating road rage incidents.

road rage
An angry, frequently violent response to an aggressive-driving incident; not the same as aggressive driving.

According to the NHTSA, aggressive driving has emerged as one of the leading safety hazards on U.S. highways and, according to several recent studies, is considered by many American drivers to be more dangerous than drunk driving or driving without seat belts. Common behaviors of aggressive drivers include tailgating, changing lanes unsafely, weaving in and out of traffic, exceeding speed limits, driving too fast for road conditions and ignoring traffic control devices such as stoplights and yield signs. A study by the American Automobile Association (AAA) found the most common reasons given for driving aggressively were lateness, slow traffic in the high-speed lane and frustration at traffic congestion. In many instances alcohol or drugs were also involved.

Driving under the Influence of Alcohol or Drugs

In the early 1970s, law enforcement gave contacts with drunk drivers a low priority, preferring to avoid such encounters. But the situation has changed considerably, and reducing impaired driving has become a top priority of the NHTSA and police.

This offense goes by several names: *driving under the influence* (DUI), *driving while intoxicated* (DWI) or *driving while impaired* (also DWI). The terms are used interchangeably throughout this discussion. Regardless of which acronym is used, all are based on a vehicle driver's level of blood-alcohol concentration (BAC). In the fall of 2000 President Clinton signed into law a measure that established a national 0.08 percent BAC standard for drunken driving. States failing to comply with the national standard risked losing increasing percentages of their federal highway grants with each passing year. Currently, all 50 states and the District of Columbia have per se DWI laws defining it as a crime to drive with a BAC at or above the proscribed 0.08 level.

Impaired driving is one of the most frequently committed crimes in the United States and one of the deadliest. In fact, alcohol-related crashes claim an average of one life every half hour. The Centers for Disease Control and Prevention (CDC) reports that every day 36 people in the United States die and approximately 700 more are injured in motor vehicle crashes that involve an alcohol-impaired driver. The annual cost of alcohol-related crashes totals more than $51 billion ("Impaired Driving," 2009). According to the NHTSA, in 2008 there were 11,773 alcohol-impaired-driving fatalities, a decrease of 10 percent compared with 2007 (*Traffic Safety Facts*, 2009, p.4). Young people are especially affected by drunk driving, with motor vehicle crashes representing the leading cause of death for 15- to 20-year-olds. In addition, two-thirds of children killed in alcohol-related crashes were riding in the vehicle with the drinking driver.

Detecting Impairment One of the indicators officers use to detect impaired driving is a vehicle that is swerving on the roadway, providing probable cause for a stop. But sometimes officers receive an anonymous tip reporting a drunken driver. The question arises as to whether officers can act on this tip or whether after locating the vehicle they have to wait to observe the driver swerving before making the stop.

Ideally the officer should continue to observe the vehicle and witness their own probable cause (PC) for a stop; however, there are times when this is not possible, such as when an officer arrives behind the vehicle just as that vehicle is about to pull into a garage in either the driver's own or someone else's residence. Also, if an impaired driver is aware that they are being followed by an officer, they may attempt to quickly pull into a local business' parking lot and enter a building with the hope of avoiding a stop. From inside, the driver can call to find another means of transportation. In incidents like these, it is important to get the reporting party's information and a witness statement, if possible. Other factors can be considered in building probable cause without direct observation, such as time of day, if the person is a known repeat offender, and if there are multiple reports from several different witnesses regarding the same driver.

Courts vary in the way they treat anonymous calls reporting drunk drivers: "Some courts approve of police officers stopping a car based only on the anonymous caller's information. Other courts require the police themselves to observe a traffic infraction before initiating the stop" (Means and McDonald, 2010, p.10). In October 2009 the Virginia Supreme Court sought a review of a case involving such a situation, but the court denied the petition, leaving the lower courts to decide.

Most courts examining investigative stops of allegedly drunk or erratic drivers, even when the police did not personally witness any traffic violations before the stops, have upheld the stop, highlighting the imminent danger of having a drunk driver on the highway (Means and McDonald, 2010, p.12). Once a stop is made, officers need to determine whether the driver is legally drunk, usually relying upon implied consent laws. In 1953 New York enacted the first implied consent statute.

Implied consent laws state that any person driving a motor vehicle is deemed to have consented to a chemical blood test of the alcohol content of his or her blood if arrested while intoxicated; refusal to take such a test can be introduced in court as evidence.

implied consent laws

Laws stating that any person driving a motor vehicle is deemed to have consented to a chemical test of the alcohol content of his or her blood if arrested while intoxicated; refusal to take such a test can be introduced in court as evidence.

The police, as agents of the state, are authorized to conduct such tests because driving is not a constitutional right; driving is a *privilege* authorized through licensure from the state.

Many factors influence an individual's BAC, including genetically based physiological differences, food consumption, the amount of alcohol ingested and the time elapsed between drinking and testing. In the field, officers commonly use a breath analyzer as a preliminary test of the BAC. A preliminary breath test (PBT) used on the roadside is not part of an official standardized field sobriety test (SFST), although it can help build probable cause. Furthermore, the PBT is not, in itself, sustainable alone in court as an Intoxilyzer result is. PBTs are calibrated frequently, usually monthly, with strict records kept for court.

In addition to a preliminary breath test, officers can detect impairment through standardized field sobriety tests (SFSTs) and with the help of drug recognition experts (DREs).

The SFST battery commonly consists of three separate tests: the one-leg stand test, the walk-and-turn test and the horizontal-gaze nystagmus (HGN) test. HGN refers to an involuntary bouncing or jerking of the eyeball when a person looks to the side, keeping their face forward and moving only their eyes. Some states require attending an additional class to be certified in administering HGN because of its status as a scientifically validated test.

The actual BAC can be determined through breath, urine or blood tests. The courts have held that this is not a violation of a person's Fifth Amendment privilege against self-incrimination. One of the first cases to test the constitutionality of forcibly taking blood from an arrested person was *Breithaupt v. Abram* (1957) in which the conviction was upheld. Then in 1966 in the landmark case of *Schmerber v. California*, the issue was greatly clarified. The Supreme Court upheld the conviction and stressed that taking a blood sample was not a violation of the privilege against self-incrimination: "We hold that the privilege protects an accused only from being compelled to testify against himself, or otherwise provide the state with evidence of a testimonial or communicative nature, and that the withdrawal of blood and use of analysis in question in this case did not involve compulsion to these ends."

The Court did caution that the blood sample should be taken by medical personnel in a medical environment. The Court also ruled that the blood test did not violate the Fourth Amendment even though there was no warrant. The Court reasoned that the blood-alcohol content might have dissipated if the officer had been required to obtain a warrant before ordering the test.

saturation patrol

Involves an increased enforcement effort targeting a specific geographic area to identify and arrest impaired drivers.

Efforts to Reduce Impaired Driving Getting impaired drivers off the road can be improved by using saturation patrols or periodic "safe and sober" enforcement campaigns. **Saturation patrols** involve an increased enforcement effort targeting a specific geographic area, often during targeted times such as New Year's Eve or the Fourth of July, to identify and arrest impaired drivers. Saturation patrols concentrate their enforcement on impaired driving behaviors, such as driving left of center, following too closely, reckless driving, aggressive driving and speeding.

Many states use sobriety checkpoints to deter driving while under the influence of alcohol. Sobriety checkpoints have become profitable operations that are more likely to seize cars from unlicensed, and often illegal immigrant, motorists than to catch drunken drivers (Gabrielson, 2010). Nonetheless, sobriety checkpoints are shown by research to be the most immediate method to drive down deaths and injuries from DWI. Such checkpoints have been used for the past 25 years in the United States and have withstood numerous legal challenges. In *Michigan Department of State Police v. Sitz* (1990) the Supreme Court ruled, "Sobriety checkpoints are constitutional" because the states have a "substantial interest" in keeping intoxicated drivers off the roads and because the "measure of intrusion on motorists stopped at sobriety checkpoints is slight." Although 10 states (Idaho, Iowa, Michigan, Minnesota, Oregon, Rhode Island, Texas, Washington, Wisconsin and Wyoming) have banned such checkpoints, the states that use them contend they are a proven deterrent to DWI.

Safety for motorists and officers at any checkpoint must be a primary consideration, including proper lighting, warning signs and clearly identifiable official vehicles and personnel. A neutral formula must be used to decide whom to stop, for example, every third car. Finally, each motorist should be detained only long enough for officers to briefly question the driver and to look for signs of intoxication, such as the odor of an alcoholic beverage on the breath, slurred speech and glassy or bloodshot eyes. Officers must always be aware of the possibility that an impaired driver might be experiencing a life-threatening medical crisis. For example, one officer encountered a belligerent, apparently drunken driver who had driven his car through a service station and into a wall. However, the man had not felt right, smelled right, or acted right for a drunk: He was cold, clammy and smelled sweet. Fortunately the officer found a medical alert tag around the driver's neck; he was a diabetic and he was in serious trouble. The paramedics were called and took over (Smith, 2010, p.84).

New Technologies Among existing technologies to help law enforcement officers identify drunk drivers and separate them from their vehicles are ignition interlocks, passive alcohol sensors and Secure Continuous Remote Alcohol Monitor (SCRAM) devices. Emerging technologies include infrared sensing models that enforcement officers can use to help determine an offender's alcohol content level, subdural blood-alcohol concentration sensing through the steering wheel and algorithms to detect weaving, so a vehicle would be able to determine whether the driver was impaired. If all police officers used passive alcohol-sensing technology on every traffic stop and at all checkpoints, it is possible that anywhere from 140,000 to 700,000 more drunk drivers would be detected and arrested every year (Dewey-Kollen, 2007).

Another technology being developed is touch-based alcohol testing using optical technology. Two types of this technology are available: near infrared (NIR) spectroscopy and multispectral imaging to look beneath the fingerprint. Touch-based alcohol testing is noninvasive, rapid (done in 30 seconds or less), accurate and requires only passive contact with the individual being tested.

Alcohol is not the only substance that may impair drivers. Drugs, whether legal over-the-counter (OTC) prescription medications or illegal substances, can adversely affect a person's driving competency. Fatigue or tiredness can also impair a driver's ability to operate a vehicle safely. Another way drivers may be "impaired" is being distracted, especially by using cell phones while driving.

The Distracted Driver

According to the National Safety Council (NSC), "Talking on cell phones while driving is estimated to increase crash risk fourfold. Over 50 research studies have shown that using phones while driving is risky. Each year it results in about 1.6 million crashes, hundreds of thousands of injuries and thousands of deaths" ("Distracted Driving," 2010). According to the NSC's recent study, the vast majority of those crashes (1.4 million annually) are caused by cell phone conversations, and 200,000 are blamed on text messaging. Research from the Virginia Tech Transportation Institute provides a picture of driver distraction and cell phone use under real-world driving conditions from continuously observing drivers for more than 6 million miles of driving. They found that text messaging on a cell phone was associated with highest risk of all cell phone-related tasks, increasing the risk of a crash or near-crash even 23.2 times as high as non-distracted driving (Box, 2009). The Institute's recommendation: "Texting should be banned in moving vehicles for all drivers. As shown in the findings overview, this cell phone task has the potential to create a true crash epidemic if texting-type tasks continue to grow in popularity and as the generation of frequent text message senders reach driving age in large numbers" (Box, 2009).

Many people seem "addicted" to their cell phones, and even banning altogether their use while driving is difficult to enforce if hands-free phones are used. More than 120 studies of cell phone use suggest that hands-free devices do not eliminate the distraction (Halsey, 2010).

Once an officer has probable cause, whether it is having clocked a driver exceeding the posted speed limit, witnessing a red-light runner or an impaired driver, or some other traffic violation, a traffic stop can be made.

The Traffic Stop

Officers assigned to a traffic unit often feel they are not doing real police work. And when citizens are stopped, they often complain that the officers should be concentrating on real criminals, not on them. However, traffic stops are one of the most dangerous duties performed by officers. When an officer stops a motorist, the driver could be a law-abiding citizen, a sociopath high on an illegal substance, a gang banger, a bank robber on the run or a serial killer with a body in the trunk. Traffic stops are not to be taken lightly.

An important issue related to the traffic stop is the charge of using the stop as an excuse to stop the vehicle for an unrelated reason. This is often associated with racial profiling, discussed shortly. Police are sometimes accused of making a **pretext stop**, also called a **dual motive stop**—using the traffic stop as an excuse to execute another agenda, such as searching a vehicle or driver for drugs.

pretext stop

When an officer stops a vehicle for ulterior motives; also called a *dual motive stop*.

dual motive stop

When the officer has an ulterior motive for the stop; also called a *pretext stop*.

The question arises: Is the temporary detention of a motorist whom the police believe has committed a civil traffic violation constitutional under the Fourth Amendment if the officer, in fact, had some other law enforcement objective? The Supreme Court's decision, through its ruling in *Whren v. United States* (1996), is yes: "The temporary detention of a motorist upon probable cause to believe he has violated the traffic laws does not violate the Fourth Amendment's prohibition against unreasonable seizures, even if a reasonable officer would not have stopped the motorist absent some additional law enforcement objective."

In other words, the test for the validity and constitutionality of a stop is not whether police officers "would have" made the stop but rather whether the officers "could have" made the stop. In *Whren*, the officers could have made and did make a valid stop because the driver committed a traffic violation, even if the actual purpose for making the stop was to search for drugs. Consequently the real purpose of a stop, even if ulterior, does not render the stop and subsequent search invalid if there was in fact a valid reason for the stop.

An issue often associated with traffic stops is that of racial profiling. **Racial profiling** is the use of discretionary authority by law enforcement officers in encounters with minority motorists, typically within the context of a traffic stop, that result in the disparate treatment of minorities. Racial profiling is discussed in Chapter 11 as an important issue facing police officers.

racial profiling

Any police-initiated action that relies on the race, ethnicity or national origin rather than on the behavior of an individual for the police to believe a particular individual is engaged in criminal activity.

ASSISTING AT AND INVESTIGATING TRAFFIC CRASHES

Billions of dollars are lost annually through motor vehicle crashes, and the cost in human suffering and loss is impossible to estimate. In 2008 there were an estimated 5,811,000 police-reported traffic crashes, in which 37,261 people were killed and 2,346 people were injured; 4,146 crashes involved property damage only (*Traffic Safety Facts*, 2009, p.1). An average of 102 people died each day in motor vehicle crashes in 2008—one every 14 minutes (*Traffic Safety Facts*, p.2). Most crashes involve factors relating to the driver, the vehicle and the road. The interaction of these factors often sets up a series of events that culminate in the mishap.

The basic causes of motor vehicle crashes are human faults, errors, violations and attitudes; road defects; and vehicle defects.

Good driving attitudes are more important than driving skills or knowledge, a fact frequently overlooked in driver education programs. Drivers who jump lanes, try to beat out others as they merge from cloverleaves, race, follow too closely or become angry and aggressive account for many of our serious motor vehicle crashes. Negative driver behavior, such as illegal and unsafe speed, failure to yield the right of way, crossing over the center line, driving in the wrong lane, driving while under the influence of alcohol or drugs and road rage, increases the number of crashes and causes traffic statistics to rise year after year.

Responsibilities of the Officer Called to a Crash Scene

Frequently police officers who are equipped, trained and legally responsible for providing services—perhaps lifesaving services if they act quickly and effectively—are the first to arrive on the scene of a traffic crash. In addition to rendering first aid to crash victims, police officers have several other duties to perform, such as protecting victims from further harm; reducing to the greatest extent possible the involvement of other cars as they arrive on the scene; summoning emergency services for victims and, if needed, towing services for the vehicles involved; coordinating traffic control with emergency medical services; protecting the victims' personal property; locating witnesses and suspects; transmitting information to dispatch and other officers in hit-and-run cases; securing evidence; performing SFSTs if DWI is suspected, and making an arrest if necessary; writing accident reports; and in other ways investigating the crash and keeping traffic moving as though no crash had occurred.

Crash reports by police officers provide a guide for many other department activities. In addition a host of other agencies involved in traffic make use of the information in crash reports. Public information agencies, such as newspapers, television and radio, disseminate information about traffic, traffic conditions, road conditions and crashes. Attorneys and the courts use crash reports to determine the facts about the crashes that result in lawsuits. The state motor vehicle department or state department of public safety, which has the power to suspend or revoke driver's licenses, also uses information contained in these reports. Legislative bodies in each state may rely on crash reports when they plan for providing funds, equipment and personnel to effectively enforce traffic safety programs and when they determine what laws must be passed to control traffic.

Traffic crash reports may be used by engineers, both federal and state, who research ways to improve highway systems and by the National Safety Council and state safety councils that compile statistics related to crashes: Who is having them? Where? When? How? The reports may be used by insurance companies that base their automobile insurance rates on the crash record of the community.

Crash reports serve as the basis of traffic law enforcement policy, crash prevention programs, traffic education, legislative reform of traffic laws, traffic engineering decisions and motor vehicle administrative decisions.

Crash Reconstruction

Crash reconstruction using videotape can establish the facts of crashes and help in lawsuits, insurance cases and vehicular criminal cases. In video reconstruction, scale models of the vehicles are used, often with a photo or video of the crash scene itself as the background. Speed calculations are made from the reporting officer's diagrams and notes.

Many computer software programs are also available to help crash investigators re-create the scene and determine some of the "unknowns," such as how fast the vehicles were traveling, if and how environmental elements factored into the crash and how stationary objects may have affected vehicle trajectory. Most departments use some sort of survey equipment to diagram a collisions scene, including scanners that can measure a scene with a flip of a switch and output a three-dimensional diagram that looks like a photo (Brown, 2008, p.45). Because collision investigators are involved in potential murder cases as often, if not more often, than homicide investigators, it is crucial that such personnel receive proper training and use appropriate equipment (Brown, p.47).

EDUCATING THE PUBLIC

The police also strive to educate the public in traffic safety. Although education is not their primary responsibility, they often participate in local school programs, private safety organizations, local service clubs and state safety councils. The police know that these programs are important and that they can contribute to the community good.

A department's traffic safety education program can benefit from specific applications of intelligence-led policing: "Driver behavior research is important to targeting educational messages, whether delivered in speeches to community groups as media public service announcements or through other communication avenues" (Bolton, 2008, p.86).

Traffic safety education, including wearing seat belts, also has high public relations value. An officer on school grounds supervising the school crossing guards (patrols) or teaching children bicycle safety contributes much to the police officers' image by reflecting their concern for the safety and welfare of the community's youths. Safety education, however, is a community responsibility.

Summary

Of all the operations performed by the police, patrol is the most vital. The three major spheres of activity of patrol are (1) responding to emergencies and calls for service, (2) undertaking activities to apprehend perpetrators of crime and (3) engaging in strategic problem-solving partnerships with the community to address longstanding or emerging problems of crime and disorder.

Traditionally patrol officers have been assigned a specific time and a specific geographic location, or beat, of equal geographic size to patrol, and these assignments have been rotated. In addition, patrol has traditionally been random, reactive, incident driven and focused on rapid response to calls.

Directed patrol uses crime statistics to plan shift and beat staffing, providing more coverage during times of peak criminal activity and in high-crime areas. Crime analysis using mapping, geographic information systems (GIS) and CompStat can identify hot spots or specific problems to target through directed patrol.

While on patrol, officers respond to calls for service and emergencies, undertake self-initiated tasks and perform administrative duties. The patrol response might be more effective if it were proactive, directed and problem oriented and if it used differential response strategies. Patrol can be accomplished by foot, automobile, motorcycle, bicycle, Segway, horseback, aircraft and boat, or via other specialized vehicles such as ATVs, snowmobiles, or Jet Skis. The most commonly used and most effective patrol is usually a combination of automobile and foot patrol.

The National Crime Information Center (NCIC) gives all police agencies in the country access to the computerized files of the FBI, which can be of tremendous assistance to patrol officers.

Traffic officers have many responsibilities and specific tasks to perform. Traffic officers may be responsible for directing and controlling traffic, enforcing traffic laws, assisting at and investigating traffic crashes, and educating the public. The primary goal of traffic law enforcement is to produce voluntary compliance with traffic laws while keeping traffic moving safely and smoothly. All uniformed officers should enforce traffic laws because of the potential for apprehending a felon. Among the most common violations of traffic laws are speeding, red-light running, nonuse of seat belts, aggressive driving and road rage, and driving under the influence of drugs or alcohol. Distracted drivers often also violate traffic laws.

Alcohol is often involved in traffic crashes. In an effort to determine if a driver is intoxicated, legislatures have enacted implied consent laws, which state that any person driving a motor vehicle is deemed to have consented to a chemical test of the alcohol content of his or her blood if arrested while intoxicated; refusal to take such a test can be introduced in court as evidence. In addition to a preliminary breath test, officers can detect impairment through standardized field sobriety tests (SFSTs) and with the help of drug recognition experts (DREs).

However effective a traffic program may be, motor vehicle crashes will occur. The three basic causes of crashes are (1) human faults, errors, violations and attitudes; (2) road defects; and (3) vehicle defects.

Discussion Questions

1. What type of patrol is used in your community?
2. Compare and contrast the positive and negative aspects between patrol and investigation. Which role do you prefer?
3. Why is patrol considered a hazardous assignment by some and a boring assignment by others?
4. Which do you support, a one-officer or two-officer patrol unit? Why?
5. If you had your choice of patrol, what method would you select? Why?
6. What kind of traditional patrol do you feel is effective? Which of the suggested changes do you support?
7. Have you ever been involved in a traffic crash? How would you evaluate the performance of the officer(s) responding to the call?
8. How can the public truly improve traffic safety? Do you think police effort makes the primary difference?
9. Does your state have a seat belt law? If so, when was it passed, and what kind of penalty does it impose?
10. When do you think police officers should issue warning tickets rather than citations for people who are speeding?

Gale Emergency Services Database Assignments

- Use the Gale Emergency Services Database to help answer the Discussion Questions as appropriate.
- Using the Gale Emergency Services Database, find articles on *police patrol* and locate those that discuss the Supreme Court case *Atwater v. City of Lago Vista* (arrest for minor traffic offenses). This case covers arrest, discretion and police punishment. It is historical and could be used as a guideline. Outline important points of the case, and be prepared to share and discuss your notes with the class.
- Using the Gale Emergency Services Database, find the article "Contemporary Components of Community Policing" (Speech): http://find.galegroup.com/gps/retrieve.do?contentSet=IAC-Documents&resultListType=RESULT_LIST&qrySerId=Locale%28en%2C%2C%29%3AFQE%3D%28ke%2CNone%2C6%29patrol%24&sgHitCountType=None&inPS=true&sort=DateDescend&searchType=BasicSearchForm&tabID=T003&prodId=IPS&searchId=R6¤tPosition=26&userGroupName=cpg3&docId=A203929614&docType=IAC&contentSet=IAC-Documents

  Assignment: Identify and define the three components to Contemporary Community Policing. Be prepared to share your definitions with the class.
- Using the Gale Emergency Services Database, find the article "Going Mobile: How Mobile Devices, Surveillance Tools and Apps. Have Changed the Beat of Community Patrol": http://find.galegroup.com/gps/retrieve.do?contentSet=IAC-Documents&resultListType=RESULT_LIST&qrySerId=Locale%28en%2C%2C%29%3AFQE%3D%28ke%2CNone%2C6%29patrol%24&sgHitCountType=None&inPS=true&sort=DateDescend&searchType=BasicSearchForm&tabID=T003&prodId=IPS&searchId=R6¤tPosition=4&userGroupName=cpg3&docId=A219013153&docType=IAC&contentSet=IAC-Documents

  Assignment: Read the article and pick one of the ways going mobile has changed today's police patrol. Prepare to discuss this method in class.
- Using the Gale Emergency Services Database, find the article "Carbon Motors E7: A Cop's Car" (Technology on Patrol): http://find.galegroup.com/gps/retrieve.do?contentSet=IAC-Documents&resultListType=RESULT_LIST&qrySerId=Locale%28en%2C%2C%29%3AFQE%3D%28ke%2CNone%2C6%29patrol%24&sgHitCountType=None&inPS=true&sort=DateDescend&searchType=BasicSearchForm&tabID=T003&prodId=IPS&searchId=R6¤tPosition=44&userGroupName=cpg3&docId=A198888626&docType=IAC&contentSet=IAC-Documents

  Assignment: After reading this article, write your opinion as to whether there should be a police specific patrol car. How would this vehicle benefit police departments and the officers who would use them? What cutting-edge technology does it offer? Be prepared to discuss your opinion with the class.
- Using the Gale Emergency Services Database, find the article "Professional Police Stops: Law Enforcement Response to Racial Profiling": http://find.galegroup.com/gps/retrieve.do?contentSet=IAC-Documents&result

ListType=RESULT_LIST&qrySerId=Locale%28en%2C%2C%29%3AFQE%3D%28ke%2CNone%2C23%29police+racial+profiling%24&sgHitCountType=None&inPS=true&sort=DateDescend&searchType=BasicSearchForm&tabID=T003&prodId=IPS&searchId=R8¤tPosition=3&userGroupName=cpg3&docId=A68660194&docType=IAC&contentSet=IAC-Documents

Assignment: Read and summarize the article. Be prepared to discuss your summary in class.

- Using the Gale Emergency Services Database, find the article "Community Policing: Implementation Issues" (Perspective): http://find.galegroup.com/gps/retrieve.do?contentSet=IAC-Documents&resultListType=RESULT_LIST&qrySerId=Locale%28en%2C%2C%29%3AFQE%3D%28ke%2CNone%2C13%29police+patrol%24&sgHitCountType=None&inPS=true&sort=DateDescend&searchType=BasicSearchForm&tabID=T003&prodId=IPS&searchId=R10¤tPosition=12&userGroupName=cpg3&docId=A145015100&docType=IAC&contentSet=IAC-Documents

  Assignment: What are some issues and challenges that the author identifies in this article? Be prepared to discuss your findings with the class.

Internet Assignments

- Go to http://www.ih2000.net/ira/copbook.htm and read through the patrol scenarios listed. This book presents discretionary problems patrol officers have encountered. Be prepared to discuss some of these problems with the class.
- Use the Internet to search for *directed patrol.* Select a jurisdiction that has implemented this type of patrol and outline the points they stress about this strategy (advantages, disadvantages). Be prepared to share your findings with the class.
- Select one topic covered in this chapter and research it using the Web.

References

Altman, David; Heater, Daniel; and Besco, Michael. "Advanced Surveillance." *Law Officer,* 2009, pp.41–44.

Basich, Melanie. "Rapid Transit." *Police,* May 2008, p.22.

Basich, Melanie. "Officers Overwhelmingly Approve of In-Car Video." *Police,* February 2009, p.18.

Beck, Kirby. "Why Bike Training for Police?" *Law and Order,* April 2009, pp.44–49.

Bradley, Jennifer. "Mission Creep." *Law Officer Magazine,* April 2008, pp.48–52.

Bolton, Joel. "Intelligence-Led Traffic Safety." *The Police Chief,* July 2008, p.86.

Bolton, Joel. "Why Are Traffic Laws Enforced?" *The Police Chief,* February 2009, p.90.

Box, Sherri. "New Data from Virginia Tech Transportation Institute Provides Insight into Cell Phone Use and Driving Distraction." *Virginia Tech News Press Release,* July 27, 2009. Retrieved from http://www.vtti.vt.edu/PDF/7-22-09-VTTI-Press_Release_Cell_phones_and_Driver_Distraction.pdf.

Brown, Weston. "Collision Investigation: Know and Use the Tech behind Vehicle Crashes." *Law Officer Magazine,* February 2008, pp.44–47.

Casstevens, Steven. "Traffic Enforcement Is Real Police Work." *Law and Order,* August 2008, pp.44-46.

Craven, Kym. "Foot Patrols: Crime Analysis and Community Engagement to Further the Commitment to Community Policing." *Community Policing dispatch,* February 2009.

Dewey-Kollen, Janet. "DUI Tech." *Law Officer Magazine,* April 2007, pp.42–45.

"Distracted Driving." Itasca, IL: The National Safety Council. 2010. Retrieved from http://www.nsc.org/safety_road/Distracted_Driving/Pages/distracted_driving.aspx.

Dye, Steve. "Policing in Local Law Enforcement: A Commitment to Getting Out-of-the-Car." *The Police Chief*, October 2009, pp.28–34.

Famega, Christine N. "Proactive Policing by Post and Community Officers." *Crime & Delinquency*, January 2009, pp.78–104.

Famega, Christine N.; Frank, James; and Mazerolle, Lorraine. "Managing Police Patrol Time: The Role of Supervisor Directives." *Justice Quarterly*, 2005, pp.540–559.

Gabrielson, Ryan. "Sobriety Checkpoints Catch Unlicensed Drivers." *The New York Times*, February 14, 2010. Retrieved from http://www.nytimes.com/2010/02/14/us/14sfcheck.html?pagewanted=print.

Galvin, Bob. "Gaining on Speeders." *Law Enforcement Technology*, October 2009a, pp.60–67.

Galvin, Bob. "Laser Device Takes on Tailgating." *Law Enforcement Technology*, January 2009b, pp.70–73.

Garrett, Ronnie. "Red Light/Green Light." *Law Enforcement Technology*, October 2009, pp.10–17.

Goldstein, Herman. *Problem-Oriented Policing*. New York: McGraw-Hill, 1990.

Griffin, Michelle. "Going Mobile: Building a Case for e-Ticketing." *Law Officer Magazine*, February 2009, pp.30–32.

Griffith, David. "In Praise of the Patrol Officer." *Police*, January 2008, p.10.

Grossi, Dave. "Patrol Tactics: What Works Best?" *Law Officer Magazine*, September 2008, pp.26–29.

Halsey, Ashley, III. "28 Percent of Accidents Involve Talking, Texting on Cell Phones." *Washington Post*, January 13, 2010, p.A06.

Highway Loss Data Institute, Insurance Institute for Highway Safety, no date. Retrieved from http://www.hwysafety.org.

Hillard, Terry. "Deploying an e-Ticketing Solution." *Law and Order*, January 2008, pp.58–61.

"Impaired Driving." Atlanta: GA: Center for Disease Control, January 2009. Retrieved from http://www.cdc.gov/MotorVehicleSafety/Impaired_Driving/impaired-drv_factsheet.html.

Kanable, Rebecca, and Dewey-Kollen, Janet. "Data-Driven Crime Reduction and Traffic Safety." *Law and Order*, September 2009, pp.24–27.

Kasper, Jody. "Park and Walk, an Old Strategy Revisited." *Law and Order*, June 2009, pp.71–76.

Kelling, George L. *Foot Patrol*. Washington, DC: National Institute of Justice, no date.

Klockars, Carl B. *Thinking about Police: Contemporary Readings*. New York: McGraw-Hill, 1983.

Kozlowski, Jonathan. "Behind the Handlebars." *Law Enforcement Technology*, January 2010a, pp.16–20.

Kozlowski, Jonathan. "The High Price of a Bird's Eye View." *Law Enforcement Technology*, February 2010b, pp.8–14.

Langton, Lynn. *Aviation Units in Large Law Enforcement Agencies, 2007*. Washington, DC: Bureau of Justice Statistics Special Report, July 2009. (NCJ 226672)

McCallion, Teresa. "In-Car Video Increases Convictions and Eliminates False Claims." *Law Officer Magazine*, April 2009, pp.34–39.

Means, Randy, and McDonald, Pam. "Wait for the Drunk Driver to Swerve?" *Law and Order*, January 2010, pp.10–14.

Mendoza, Moises. "Despite Fatal Crashes, Seat Belts Don't Click with All Officers." *PoliceOne.com News*, March 2, 2010. Retrieved from http://www.policeone.com/pc_print.asp?vid=2012638.

Menton, Chris. "Bicycle Patrols versus Car Patrols." *Law and Order*, June 2007, pp.78–81.

Miller, Laurence. "Patrol Psychology 101: Communication and Conflict Resolution." *PoliceOne.com News*. April 18, 2008. Retrieved from http://www.policeone.com/health-fitness/articles/1685390-Patrol-psychology-101.

Moore, Carole. "Hit the Pavement: Where the Past Meets the Future in Police Bike Patrols." *Law Enforcement Technology*, April 2007, pp.56–65.

Moore, Carole. "Caught on Camera." *Law Enforcement Technology*, October 2008, pp.112–120.

Moore, Carole. "Horses and Public Relations." *Law Enforcement Technology*, August 2009a, p.78.

Moore, Carole. "Not Just for Driving Anymore: Today's Modern Patrol Cars House More Gadgets than Kitchens." *Law Enforcement Technology*, April 2009b, pp.18–25.

Morgan, Christopher. "Search the Data and Solve the Crime." *Law Officer Magazine*, June 2009, pp.30–33.

National Neighborhood Foot Patrol Center (pamphlet). East Lansing: Michigan State University, no date.

Perin, Michelle. "On the Water: The Many Faces of Law Enforcement Marine Patrol." *Law Enforcement Technology*, September 2009, pp.26–33.

Rayburn, Mike. "Shooting from a Boat." *Police*, May 2009, pp.56–59.

Salmon, David A. "New York's Traffic Incident Management and Targeted Traffic Enforcement Efforts." *The Police Chief*, August 2009, p.146.

Sanow, Ed. "Traffic Enforcement Equals Crime Reduction." *Law and Order*, March 2009, p.6.

Scoville, Dean. "Working on the Front Line." *Police*, July 2008, pp.38–48.

"Seat Belt Use in 2008—Overall Results." Washington, DC: Department of Transportation Traffic Safety Notes, September 2008. Retrieved from http://www.nrd.nhtsa.dot.gov/Pubs/811036.PDF

Smith, Dave. "Not Your Average Drunk." *Police*, January 2010, p.84.

Solosky, Kenneth J. "Airplanes Are Still a Vital Tool in Law Enforcement." *PoliceOne.com News*. December 14, 2009a. Retrieved from http://www.policeone.com/airborne-maritime/articles/1978321-Airplanes-are-still-a-vital-tool-in-law-enforcement.

Solosky, Kenneth J. "Your Eye in the Sky." *Law Officer Magazine*, February 2009b, pp.38–43.

Stockton, Dale. "Intervene and Prevent." *Law Officer Magazine*, February 2008, p.8.

Sweeney, Earl M. "The Value of Traffic Enforcement." *Big Ideas for Smaller Police Departments*. Spring 2009, pp.1–5.

Traffic Safety Facts, 2008 Data. Washington, DC: NHTSA's National Center for Statistics and Analysis, 2009. (DOT HS 811 162)

Wasilewski, Mike, and Olson, Althea. "Effective Law Enforcement or Big Brother?" *LawOfficer.com*, June 1, 2009. Retrieved from http://www.lawofficer.com/article/technology-and-communications/cop-box.

"Work Zone Safety Fact Sheet." Washington, DC: Federal Highway Administration, no date. Retrieved from http://safety.fhwa.dot.gov/wz/facts_stats.

Cases Cited

Breithaupt v. Abram, 352 U.S. 432 (1957)
Michigan Department of State Police v. Sitz, 496 U.S. 444 (1990)
Schmerber v. California, 384 U.S. 757 (1966)
Whren v. United States, 517 U.S. 806 (1996)

Useful Web Site

http://www.nhtsa.dot.gov/people/outreach/state_laws-belts04/safeylaws-states.htm

CHAPTER 6

Specialized Roles of Police

> Knowledge is of two kinds. We know a subject ourselves, or we know where we can find information upon it.
>
> —Samuel Johnson

© AP Images/Brattleboro Reformer, Zachary P. Stephens

An investigator from the Vermont State Police Crime Lab studies evidence at the scene of a stabbing death in Brattleboro, Vermont. Brattleboro police say a 26-year-old man was stabbed to death following an early morning fight near the town's parking garage.

Do You Know . . .

- What the primary characteristic of an effective investigator is?
- What the primary responsibilities of the investigator are?
- What questions investigators seek answers to?
- Why both sketches and photographs of a crime scene are usually needed?
- How investigators must deal with evidence?
- What DNA profiling is?
- What issues related to DNA testing are?
- What the three basic types of identification are?
- What changes in lineup identification protocol research supports?
- In what two areas intelligence units work?
- Why all officers are juvenile officers much of the time?
- In what areas vice officers become involved?
- What characterizes SWAT team officers and what they seek to accomplish?
- How K-9s are used? In what categories they may be specifically trained?

Can You Define?

ballistics
chain of custody
complainant
contamination
crime scene investigation
criminalistics
discovery crimes
DNA profiling
field identification
forensic science
informant
interrogate
interview
involvement crimes
modus operandi (MO)
solvability factors
suppressible crimes
totality of circumstances
vetted

INTRODUCTION

In addition to the general function of patrol, including traffic assignments, a number of specialized functions are also required of law enforcement personnel. Sometimes all the functions are performed by a single person—a formidable challenge. In large departments, however, separate divisions may exist for each specialized function. Some patrol officers receive special training to deal with specific problems, such as hostage and sniper situations, VIP protection, riot or crowd control, rescue operations and control of suppressible crimes.

Suppressible crimes are crimes that commonly occur in locations and under circumstances that give police officers a reasonable opportunity to deter or apprehend offenders. Included among suppressible crimes are robbery, burglary, car theft, assault and sex crimes. Such problems often involve a need for covert surveillance and decoys, tactics that cannot be used by uniformed patrol officers.

suppressible crimes
Crimes that commonly occur in locations and under circumstances that provide police officers a reasonable opportunity to deter or apprehend offenders; includes robbery, burglary, car theft, assault and sex crimes.

Specialized operations are often used to saturate particular areas or to stake out suspects and possible crime locations. Countermeasures to combat street crimes have included stings and police decoys to catch criminals—one of the most cost-effective and productive apprehension methods available. Officers have posed as cab drivers, old women, truck drivers, money couriers, nuns and priests. They have infiltrated drug circles as undercover agents. Usually operating in high-crime areas, decoy officers are vulnerable to violence and injury. The results are considered worth the risk because an attack on a decoy almost always results in the attacker's conviction.

THE CHAPTER AT A GLANCE

This chapter begins with a brief discussion of the pros and cons of specialization. It then looks at what is often considered the most glamorous aspect of policing—investigation, specifically crime scene investigation, and its reliance on forensics. Next the specialized functions of profilers, psychics and intelligence officers are explored. This is followed by a discussion of juvenile officers, vice officers and SWAT officers. The chapter concludes with a discussion of K-9 assisted officers, reserve officers and other types of specialized policing.

THE ADVANTAGES AND DISADVANTAGES OF SPECIALIZATION

Vernon, a 40-year veteran of law enforcement, has worked both as a generalist and specialist and sees positives and negatives with each approach. The positive aspects of specialization are that (2007, p.58)

- Attention is narrowly focused.
- Officers develop expertise.
- Efficiency is improved.
- Officers become very effective in accomplishing their mission.
- It is fairly simple to measure effectiveness.

The downside of specialization includes less flexibility, a tendency to miss the big picture, the failure to coordinate with other units and the need for supervision. Departments must function as a unit, whether with specialization or not: "In law enforcement, no one should miss the primary mission of protecting and serving the public. Specialization should never be an excuse for failing to be flexible when needed, neglecting to coordinate activities with the rest of the organization, developing an elitist attitude or creating a difficult supervisory problem" (Vernon, 2007, p.59). In other words, specialists must be able to see the big picture, the forest, and not just the trees.

Specialization may result from the method of patrol an officer is assigned: bike, motorcycle, air and water in larger departments, as discussed as part of patrol. And all officers at times are community officers, traffic officers and investigators, depending on the circumstances in which they find themselves. Nonetheless, the division between generalist and specialist is widening. Inducements to work specialized units include "cool tools, flexible schedules, prestige, and the ability to work at something one is truly interested in" (Scoville, 2008, p.44). Officers need to be flexible and versatile: "Those who can readily adapt to their changing environment and who are willing to wear as many hats are thrown at them will continue to thrive" (Scoville, p.44).

However, the attraction of specialty work for experienced officers may seriously affect the quality of patrol officers on the street, as well-qualified, skilled generalist officers are also critical to the department (Scoville, 2008, p.47). A balance is imperative. "Specialization is often necessary to develop expertise, focus and effectiveness. But officers working those units or agencies must remember that we all work in unison to bring about a stable society. The more specialized we become, the more teamwork is required. We are all law officers" (Vernon, 2008, p.55). In no other specialized area is this more critical than in investigation.

INVESTIGATION/THE DETECTIVE UNIT

To the general public, the term *criminal investigation* often brings to mind the detective as portrayed in novels, on the radio, in magazines and on television. The detective or investigator single-handedly digs out evidence, collects tips from informants, identifies criminals, tracks them down and brings them to justice. While investigation is a prestigious assignment, it is important to note that an investigator with a background in and experience with patrol has a distinct advantage in understanding the full spectrum of an investigation, from the initial call to the submission of a case to the Attorney General's Office.

Forensic Science

Investigation is often highly dependent on forensics. **Forensic science** deals with examining physical evidence to answer legal questions. Forensic experts can be found in a wide array of occupations, including forensic accountants, anthropologists, artists, chemists, dentists, entomologists, nurses, geologists, pathologists, psycholinguists, psychologists and toxicologists. **Criminalistics** is a branch of forensic science that deals with physical evidence related to a crime. This may include fingerprints, firearms, tool marks, blood, hairs, documents and other types of physical evidence. Often the two terms are used interchangeably. *Forensic science* is the more general term, a part of science answering legal questions related to examining, evaluating and explaining physical evidence related to crime. Other branches of forensic science include pathology (study of tissue to determine the cause of death), toxicology (detection of poisons or other chemicals in the body), physical anthropology (identification of a victim's skeletal remains), odontology (examination and evaluation of dental evidence, including bite marks), psychiatry, questioned documents, ballistics, tool-work comparisons (examination of pry marks or other evidence from tools) and serology (study of blood serum to link a perpetrator to a crime, for example, a rapist being matched to semen found on a victim's clothing).

forensic science
The study of evidence.

criminalistics
A branch of forensic science that deals with physical evidence related to a crime, including fingerprints, firearms, tool marks, blood, hair, documents and other types of physical evidence.

A Congress-ordered report released by the National Academy of Sciences (NAS), *Strengthening Forensic Science in the United States: A Path Forward*, has called into question the entire basis of forensic science, stating that with the exception of nuclear deoxyribonucleic acid (DNA) analysis "no forensic method has been rigorously shown to have the capacity to consistently, and with a high degree of certainty, demonstrate a connection between evidence and a specific individual or source" (2009, p.7). The report also states,

> Existing data suggest that forensic laboratories are underresourced and understaffed, which contributes to case backlogs and likely makes it difficult for laboratories to do as much as they could to (1) inform investigations, (2) provide strong evidence for prosecutions, and (3) avoid errors that could lead to imperfect justice.

> What is needed to support and oversee the forensic science community is a new, strong, and independent entity that could take on the tasks that would be assigned to it in a manner that is as objective and free of bias as possible—one with no ties to the past and with the authority and resources to implement a fresh agenda. (p.18)

The NAS calls on Congress to establish and fund an independent federal entity, dubbed by the NAS as the National Institute of Forensic Science (NIFS), to "focus on establishing standards for the mandatory accreditation of forensic science laboratories and the mandatory certification of forensic scientists and medical examiners/forensic pathologists—and identifying the entity/entities that will develop and implement accreditation and certification" (*Strengthening Forensic Science in the United States*, 2009, p.19). The report proposed the following: "Recommendation 4: To improve the scientific basis of forensic science examinations and to maximize independence from or autonomy within the law enforcement community, Congress should authorize and appropriate incentive funds to the NIFS for allocation to state and local jurisdictions for the purpose of removing all public forensic laboratories and facilities from the administrative control of law enforcement agencies or prosecutors offices" (*Strengthening Forensic Science in the United States*, p.24).

Wethal (2009, p.28) summarizes the NAS report like this: "Being called infirm, disparate, fragmented, inconsistent and faulty is not exactly a raving review. But that's what a special committee under the National Academy of Sciences, assigned to review the forensic disciplines and report to U.S. Congress, came back with earlier this year." Noting the high degree of respect the NAS commands as a research institution, Feigin (2009, p.3) cautions that the report "could be used to significant effect in court by defense lawyers, to cast doubt on virtually the entire range of forensic evidence produced by prosecutors."

These are not the only negative reactions to the NAS report. The International Association of Chiefs of Police (IACP) has expressed considerable concern over the NAS report and the fact the report was developed without input from law enforcement practitioners (Polski, 2009, p.25). While agreeing with the NAS report's stated need for accreditation and certification of forensic science providers, the IACP strongly opposes the idea of removing forensic crime laboratory services from the administrative control of law enforcement (Polski, 2009, p.25). How Congress will balance these views remains to be seen, and the outcome will affect every one of the approximately 18,000 police departments in the United States.

However, it has long been recognized that criminal investigation is a union of art and science. Criminal investigators rely on both as they seek to answer two primary questions: (1) Has a crime been committed, and (2) who did it?

The Investigator

Throughout this chapter when the term *investigator* is used, it may refer either to a patrol officer performing investigative duties, to a detective or to a forensic specialist. In many departments across the country, the detective is a patrol officer—no special detective or investigative division exists. In other departments a crime scene investigation unit is available to assist in processing crime scenes, as discussed shortly. Investigators do not determine the suspects to be guilty; they remain objective in their investigation.

The primary characteristic of an effective investigator is objectivity.

The investigator seeks the truth, not simply proof of the suspect's guilt. Article 10 of the *Canons of Police Ethics* (International Association of Chiefs of Police, 1957) states,

> The law enforcement officer shall be concerned equally in the prosecution of the wrongdoer and the defense of the innocent. He shall ascertain what constitutes evidence and shall present such evidence impartially and without malice. In so doing, he will ignore social, political and all other distinctions among the persons involved, strengthening the tradition of the reliability and integrity of an officer's word.
>
> The law enforcement officer shall take special pains to increase his perception and skill of observation, mindful that in many situations his is the sole impartial testimony to the facts of a case.

The Preliminary Investigation

The *preliminary investigation* consists of actions performed immediately upon receiving a call to respond to a crime scene and is usually conducted by patrol officers, because they are most likely the first responders. The actions patrol officers take as first responders can determine the value of crime scene evidence for investigators and prosecutors. In cases where the investigation is likely to either be very complex or to carry a high probability of attention or liability, first responding officers will often secure the crime scene area and set a perimeter until an investigations team can arrive to take the investigation over. Figure 6.1 provides a crime scene management checklist to help officers be effective first responders at a crime scene.

The importance of response time has been debated. Traditionally, rapid response has been stressed, but this has been called into question. Some studies have found that arrests are seldom attributed to fast police response to reported serious crimes because about 75 percent of all serious crimes are **discovery crimes**, crimes uncovered after they have been committed. Only the remaining 25 percent, the **involvement crimes**, require rapid response.

discovery crimes
Illegal acts brought to the attention of the victim and law enforcement after the act has been committed—a burglary, for example.

involvement crimes
Illegal acts discovered while being committed.

The first responders arriving at a crime scene should approach and enter the scene cautiously, observing any people or vehicles present, potential evidence and environmental conditions. The officers' safety and that of others in and around the crime scene are the responding officer(s') first priority. After controlling any dangerous situations or persons, the officer(s') next responsibility is to ensure that medical attention is provided to injured persons while minimizing contamination of the scene. Although securing the integrity of the crime scene and any possible evidence until it can be processed is a high priority of responding officers, some variables and situations are unavoidable. For example, if a victim requires medical attention at the crime scene, the presence and actions of firefighters or paramedics can contaminate a scene as they tend to the victim.

Because there's so much to do as a crime scene first responder, a checklist can help you ensure that all necessary steps have been taken. The following checklist is presented as a guideline only. Each agency should develop a list that's geared to its specific requirements.

Arrival and Assessment
- Establish perimeter and secure area.
- Render aid to victim and ensure scene is safe for medical personnel.
- Coordinate arriving units.
- Record names and unit numbers of fire/rescue, medical personnel and LEOs [law enforcement officers] on scene.
- Remove unnecessary personnel from scene as soon as possible.
- Assign officer to escort or ride with victim to hospital.
  - Secure clothing and evidence.
  - Obtain tape-recorded statement, if possible.
- Initial assessment. Does this appear to be a crime? If so, what type of crime.
- Assign officer to suspect.
  - Assess need for immediate suspect arrest.
  - Does probable cause exist?
  - Is evidence present on the suspect?
  - Collect perishable evidence from suspect if exigency exists.
  - Is it necessary to bag hands, etc.?

Establishing Command
- Designate command. Who's in charge?
- Designate common radio channel for all arriving personnel.

Stabilize and Secure Scene
- Clear crime scene and establish clearly delineated perimeter with crime scene tape.
  - Record time.
  - Make scene bigger than it needs to be.
  - Create one entry/exit point in scene to reduce contamination.
- Assign crime scene security personnel and start detailed crime scene access log.
- Begin initial areas canvass. Assign officers to locate witnesses, separate witnesses and obtain initial statements from witnesses.
- If required, assign personnel to search immediate area for additional evidence or crime scenes.
- Establish a command post and staging area.
  - Incident command vehicle available?
  - Building or home nearby?
  - Secure area for equipment and evidence?
  - Bathroom facilities?
- Obtain case number. Have number broadcast by communications/dispatch.

Notifications
- Detective supervisor paged.
- Coroner paged.
- Public information officer/media relations paged.
- Management staff paged.
- Victim Services paged.

Maintenance
- Key witnesses separated, officer assigned, witnesses secured or transported to police department.
- Obtain voluntary written statements.
- Suspect/s secured, transported.
- Given Miranda warning?
- Record any spontaneous statements/utterances made by suspect. Tape record if possible.
- Perishable evidence protected from elements or tampering.
- Photograph overall area of scene.
- Create staging and briefing area for media.

Transfer of Command
- Meet and brief detective supervisor and other personnel.
- Help determine need for warrant.
- Help prepare initial statement for press release.
- Direct all patrol personnel to complete detailed reports as soon as possible.
- Logistics covered.
  - Do you need more equipment, personnel, etc., to respond?
- Meet with crime scene investigators to discuss scene and evidence.
- Transfer command to detective supervisor.

FIGURE 6.1 Patrol Crime Scene Management Checklist

SOURCE: David Spraggs. "Crime Scene Response for the Patrol Officer." *Police*, January 2006, p.42.

An example of an *avoidable* contamination is when other officers, administrators or politicians arrive on scene to view the area before it has been processed. It is imperative that the security of the scene remains intact, as the more people who enter the scene, the higher likelihood that evidence may be lost or contaminated. Officers who enter a crime scene are required to write a report stating what their business at the scene entailed. This requirement is often a great deterrent for curious law enforcement personnel who just want to view the scene but who have no justifiable reason to be there.

The preliminary investigation results are written in an incident report containing the basic facts about the crime, the crime scene and any suspects. Some cases are solved during this phase. For those that are not, the decision must be made as to whether to pursue the case. Usually this decision is based on **solvability factors**, factors affecting the probability of successfully concluding the case, such as whether there are witnesses, physical evidence or leads with the potential to provide credible information relevant to the investigation. If the solvability factors indicate the case might be successfully resolved, a follow-up investigation is conducted. If not, the case will remain open and inactive pending further information, at which time it may become active again.

solvability factors

Factors affecting the probability of successfully concluding a case.

The Follow-Up Investigation

The *follow-up investigation* may be conducted by the investigative services division, sometimes known as the detective bureau. Therefore, successful investigation relies on cooperative, coordinated efforts of both the patrol and the investigative functions. In most small departments, the same officer handles both the preliminary and the follow-up investigations.

Investigative Responsibilities

The responsibilities of investigators are many and varied.

Investigative responsibilities often include

- Securing crime scenes, although this most often falls to patrol officers.
- Recording all facts related to cases.
- Photographing, video recording, measuring and sketching crime scenes.
- Obtaining and identifying evidence, thus starting the chain of custody.
- Protecting and storing evidence.
- Processing evidence, if the investigator is also an evidence technician.
- Interviewing victims, witnesses and possible suspects.
- Interrogating likely suspects.
- Assisting in identifying suspects.
- Identifying missing persons and human remains.

Securing the Crime Scene "The success of many a criminal prosecution can be traced back to how the first officers who responded handled the crime scene" (Scoville, 2010, p.34). However, "The crime scene can become a study in conflicting agendas. EMS services may have a shot at saving a life. Officers may have to clear adjacent rooms. Panicked or distraught witnesses may disrupt your evidence by taking flight. The haphazard clearing of an area and the assumption that suspects have vacated have proven problematic" (Scoville, p.34).

contamination

The introduction of something foreign into the scene, moving items at the scene or removing evidence from it.

Any area that contains evidence of criminal activity is considered a crime scene and must be secured to eliminate **contamination**, that is, the introduction of something foreign into the scene, moving items at the scene or removing evidence from it. Galvin (2009, p.68) likens the crime scene to a kaleidoscope: "Similar to twisting the end, with the kaleidoscope's array of mirrors and colored shapes, the slightest alteration to a fresh crime scene can give an entirely different look and reality to it." It is important to realize that crime scenes can be mobile as well as stationary, and may extend to distances of several blocks or even many miles, presenting a formidable challenge for the preservation of evidence. The first officer on the scene must protect it from any change. This single responsibility may have far-reaching effects on solving the crime. Physical evidence must be properly protected to have legal and scientific validity.

Recording Relevant Information Investigators record all necessary information by taking photographs and video recordings, making sketches and taking notes to be used later in a written report and testifying in court.

The investigator must obtain answers to the questions: Who? What? Where? When? How? and Why?

Answers to these questions are obtained by observation, through evidence and by talking to victims, witnesses, complainants and suspects, as discussed shortly. They are recorded in notes, photographs and sketches or are in the form of physical evidence.

Photographing, Videoing, Measuring and Sketching the Crime Scene The scene is usually photographed, video recorded, measured and sketched. The photographs show the scene as it was found, taken in a series to tell a story. Close-up photographs of evidence, such as footprints, tire tracks and tool marks, are also taken, using scaling or comparative measurements to indicate size. In addition to traditional photography, other types of photography such as ultraviolet, infrared and aerial are used. Video recording has become increasingly common in recording crime scenes.

The digital camera has made photography much more efficient and cost effective. Benefits of digital photography are that digital pictures are immediately available for viewing and printing, that they are easy to store, and the investigator is less restricted in the number of images that can be taken (versus using film). Many agencies use high-end digital single-lens reflex (SLR) cameras with respectively high-end lenses to photograph crime scenes, as high megapixels matter in details such as blood spatter, etc. Digital imaging may include photography, video recording, photogrammetry, three-dimensional (3-D) scanning and panoramas (Galvin, 2009, p.68). Many high-end digital SLR cameras now have high-definition video recording capabilities as well. A panoramic camera can record high-resolution photographs and record measurements with photogrammetry software. A 3-D laser scan can create both a panoramic photograph and then automatically record millions of highly accurate measurements.

Both photographs and sketches are usually needed. The photographs include all details and can show items close up. Sketches can be selective and can show much larger areas.

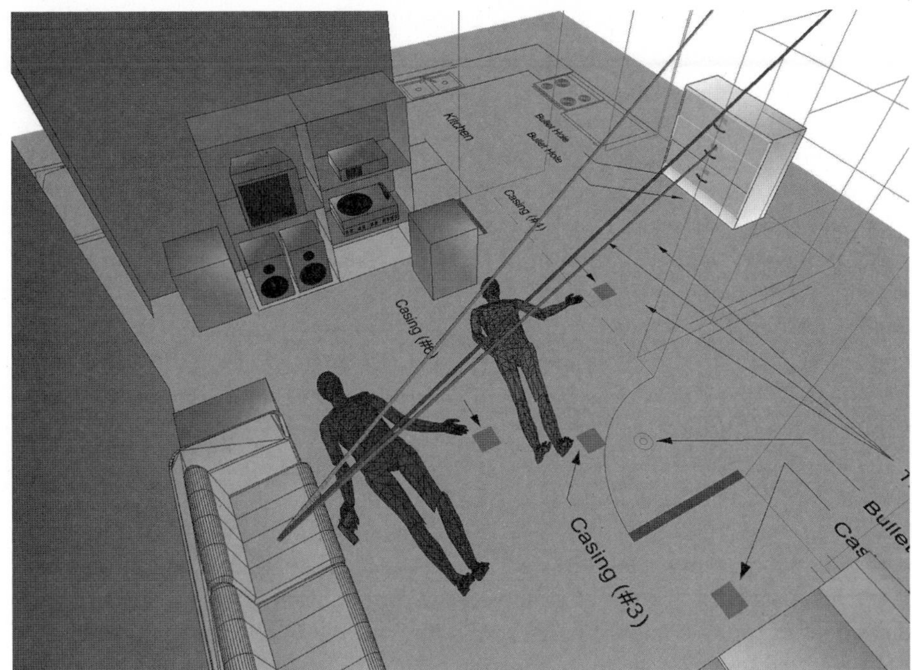

FIGURE 6.2 SmartDraw or CAD Zone's Crime Zone

SOURCE: This is a 3-D recreation of a homicide shooting, showing in detail the bullet trajectories and the final resting positions of the fatalities. The diagram contains both solid and "see-through" walls to display a more correct perspective. The diagram was created with the Crime Zone diagramming software, available from the CAD Zone, Inc. Image created by CAD Zone, Inc.

This level of crime scene investigation, where sketches are completed along with digital photos, usually occurs for severe crimes against persons.

Computer programs based mostly on computer-aided design (CAD) have made crime scene sketching much easier. New software is continuously being developed for use by law enforcement agencies in investigations, courtroom proceedings and other applications (see Figure 6.2).

Obtaining and Identifying Physical Evidence A large part of an investigator's role centers around obtaining information and evidence—proof that a crime has been committed, as well as proof that a particular person (the suspect) committed the crime. Locard's Exchange Principle, developed in 1928, states that when any two objects come into contact, a transfer of material from each object to the other always occurs. Investigators use such material to build connections between objects, people and locations. All important decisions will revolve around the available evidence and how it was obtained.

Some agencies have established the position of *evidence technician*. The evidence technician is usually a patrol officer who has received extensive classroom and laboratory training in crime scene investigation. In departments that have small detective bureaus and relatively inexperienced officers, this position fills a notable void. The officer is not relieved of regular patrol duties but may be called on to conduct crime scene investigations. Larger departments may have crime scene investigative units. **Crime scene investigation (CSI)**, as a noun, is a specialized unit that focuses on the discovery, investigation, and collection of

crime scene investigation (CSI)

As a noun, is a specialized unit that focuses on the discovery, investigation, and collection of evidence of a crime; CSI as a verb is a highly methodological way of evidence collection that leads to information about a crime, including the identification and conviction of suspects.

evidence of a crime. CSI as a verb is a highly methodological way of evidence collection that leads to information about a crime, including the identification and conviction of suspects.

A CSI must have both a general knowledge of lab analysis and a deep understanding in evidence recognition, documentation and recovery. According to the International Crime Scene Investigators Association (ICSIA), the crime scene investigator must successfully complete a minimum of 720 hours training in crime scene processing with a minimum of 80 hours training in latent fingerprint processing and 40 hours in each of the following: major death investigation, advanced death investigations, photography, blood spatter interpretation and other training courses in arson investigation and forensic pathology. In addition, the crime scene investigator must be certified by the International Association for Identification, Crime Scene Certification.

Public interest in this field has been heightened by popular television shows such as *CSI, Crime Scene Investigation*, which first aired in October 2000 and has spawned several spin-off series. On these shows, the forensic evidence is almost always convincing and able to be developed very quickly (in under an hour, which is the length of most shows), and the investigator is never wrong. However, such depictions of forensic science have skewed the viewing public's perception of reality in a phenomenon called the "CSI Effect," which "refers to the real-life consequences of exposure to Hollywood's version of law and order," affecting criminal investigations and driving jury verdicts across America (*Strengthening Forensic Science*, 2009, p.48). Consequently, people who find themselves on jury duty often think they know a great deal about forensic science and the kind of science necessary to solve crimes.

Prosecutors say juries expect scientific evidence in every case, even though most criminal cases do not call for such evidence. A National Institute of Justice (NIJ) survey found that out of 1,000 prospective jurors, 46 percent expected to see some kind of scientific evidence in *every* criminal case; 22 percent expected to see DNA evidence in *every* criminal case; 36 percent expected to see fingerprint evidence in *every* criminal case; and 32 expected to see ballistics or other firearms laboratory evidence in *every* criminal case (Shelton, 2008, p.3). Despite such expectations, "There was scant evidence in our survey results that *CSI* viewers were either more or less likely to acquit defendants without scientific evidence" (Shelton, p.5).

Investigators recognize, collect, mark, preserve and transport physical evidence in sufficient quantity for analysis, without contamination, while generating and maintaining the chain of custody.

All evidence collected is marked to identify who collected it. To have validity and integrity in court, should the case go to trial, evidence must be lawfully collected and documented in a chain of custody, also called a chain of evidence. The **chain of custody** is generated as evidence is collected and provides written documentation of who has had possession of the evidence from the time it was discovered and taken into custody until the present time.

chain of custody

Documenting who has had possession of evidence from the time it was discovered and taken into custody until the present time.

The kind of evidence to be anticipated is often directly related to the type of crime committed. Scenes of violent crimes frequently contain such evidence as blood, hair, fibers, fingerprints, footprints and weapons. Scenes of property crimes are commonly characterized by forcible entry with tools leaving marks on doors, windows, safes, money chests, cash registers and desk drawers. Among the most common types of evidence found at the crime scene are fingerprints, blood, hair, fibers, documents, footprints or tire prints, tool fragments, tool marks, broken glass, paint, insulation from safes, bite marks, firearms and explosives.

An in-depth discussion of evidence is beyond the scope of this text. The following discussion is limited to fingerprints, recognized by the courts; DNA, found to be scientifically valid by the NAS; and firearms, since most murders in the United States are committed with handguns (*Crime in the United States 2008*).

Fingerprints One of the first uses of computers in law enforcement was to assist in identifying fingerprints. By the 1980s automated fingerprint identification systems (AFIS) were developed, allowing a computer to automatically search its files and identify a list of likely matches that could then be visually examined by a fingerprint technician.

The Federal Bureau of Investigation (FBI) and the Department of Homeland Security (DHS) have merged their databases of fingerprints of millions of criminals and illegal immigrants. The resulting system, the Integrated Automated Fingerprint Identification System (IAFIS), is the world's largest biometric database, enabling law enforcement officials to search the fingerprints and criminal history information of more than 47 million people.

The current IAFIS expands the science of fingerprints out to the officer in the field. Portable, digital, wireless technology allows police to scan a subject's finger with a handheld device that creates a digital image of the fingerprints, quickly packages the data and sends it over a wireless data server to the IAFIS database, which then processes the results immediately and reports back to the officer in the field. The availability of real-time identification technology can mitigate potentially dangerous situations and greatly enhance officer safety, as an estimated 40 percent of people questioned during a police encounter lack proper identification (Geoghegan, 2008, p.46). Consider, for example, the situation in Huntington Park, California, in January 2009, when officers stopped an individual who gave a false name and date of birth. Using a fingerprint reader to positively identify the individual, officers determined he had a felony domestic violence warrant and had fled the country after the warrant was issued, having returned several years later with a different name and address to avoid arrest: "With the ability to strip away the cloak of anonymity that criminals have used against the community and law enforcement agencies for ages, mobile fingerprint readers have enhanced officer safety as well as the safety of the country's many communities" (Norton, 2009, p.39).

And the future holds even greater promise: "Biometric technology continues to evolve, as is evidenced by the FBI's $1 billion project to build the world's largest database of physical characteristics. In addition to fingerprints, digital images of palm patterns and faces are currently being added to the database" (Geoghegan, 2008, p.48).

DNA DNA is the basic building block comprising each person's genetic code. DNA is found in virtually every cell in a person's body, including blood, semen, hair and skin cells, and it provides a blueprint for the various characteristics that make each person unique. A person's distinctive DNA composition remains the same throughout life, making it a powerful investigative tool.

DNA profiling

Uses the material from which chromosomes are made to positively identify individuals; no two individuals except identical twins have the same DNA structure.

DNA profiling uses the material from which chromosomes are made to positively identify individuals. No two individuals, except identical twins, have the same DNA structure.

DNA fingerprinting, first used in the early 1980s, has "revolutionized forensic science, providing law enforcement with the ability to connect offenders with crime scenes. . . . Since the National Research Council recognized the reliability of DNA testing in the early 1990s, the technology has become mainstream in our court system" (Geoghegan, 2009, p.49).

To enhance DNA's evidentiary value to criminal investigations, the FBI has developed a database similar in concept to IAFIS, known as the Combined Offender DNA Index System (CODIS). CODIS is an electronic national database and searching mechanism containing 6.7 million DNA profiles obtained from evidence samples from unsolved crimes and from known offenders. The FBI expects to accelerate CODIS's growth rate from 80,000 new entries a year to 1.2 million by 2012, a 17-fold increase (Moore, 2009a).

A "revolutionary" new DNA test can provide information on the subject's ethnicity, pinpointing hair, eye and skin color (Garrett, 2009, p.51). This advanced technology was put to use in Florida, where a forensics lab studied the DNA from the crime scenes of the Baton Rouge killer and concluded the suspect was likely 80 percent African American and 15 percent Native American. This information broke the case that had frustrated investigators for four months and helped police arrest the killer just four days later (Garrett).

Another advance in DNA testing is "touch DNA," which refers to microscopic amounts of cellular material, assumed to be from epithelial or skin cells, that are sloughed off or transferred from an individual onto another item. In some cases, as few as three-dozen cells—fewer than that contained in a pinpoint of blood or a flake of skin—are all that is needed to perform the test. Laboratory technicians can liberate these cells from evidence and test them for DNA using standard procedures (Spraggs, 2008, p.26) "Touch DNA" has expanded the types of items that can contain physical evidence from gun and knife handles to steering wheels, including any physical object the suspect has touched (Spraggs, p.28).

"Touch DNA" has also raised the question whether officers processing the scene might contaminate it by inadvertently touching something and should have their DNA on file. To counter this problem, police officers and crime scene investigators should be DNA-profiled and entered into the Police Elimination database to avoid them unintentionally contaminating crime scenes (Hope, 2008). Many officers, however, feel this is an invasion of their privacy.

Dwyer (2010), a critic of such DNA collection, cautions, "There are so many issues which jump out here, including privacy rights, employment considerations, constitutional safeguards, disciplinary concerns, and informational security. . . . DNA is not simply a more sophisticated fingerprint. . . . DNA is a Pandora's Box of information which the government can store and potentially use."

Issues related to DNA testing include the Police Elimination database, which crimes to include for testing, preconviction collection, prisoners' rights to testing, familial DNA testing and whether the analyst who performed the test must testify in court.

An issue related to collecting DNA is which crimes should make use of the technology due to its expense and the huge backlog of samples waiting to be collected. Should cold cases, some decades old, be candidates now that technological advances make the DNA evidence from such cases valuable? What of the further laboratory backlog this would create? Technology has improved to the point where DNA can be used with very small and very old samples. The potential for DNA to solve cold cases is increasing "exponentially," and the NIJ and some states have initiated comprehensive investigative assistance programs to assist DNA collection and analysis supporting cold cases investigation (Wallentine, 2010, p.13).

Although murders and sexual assaults currently receive top priority for DNA analysis, many practitioners and researchers suggest it might be more productive to collect DNA for property crimes as well. A NIJ study that examined New York City's first 1,000 CODIS hits found the majority of criminal suspects had been linked to prior lesser crimes such as burglary or drug involvement. Similar results were obtained from data analysis of Florida records.

A study by the Urban Institute, in which five agencies tracked evidence from nonviolent crimes (residential and commercial burglaries and theft from automobiles) from crime scene to prosecution, compared the outcomes of traditional investigations using only fingerprint evidence and investigations in which DNA evidence was added (Johns and Rushing, 2009). In the study, a DNA profile was identified in more than half (55 percent) of the cases, of which 41 percent yielded a hit that helped identify a suspect—2½ times more frequently than when traditional methods only were used. Arrest and prosecution rates were also doubled when DNA was added. In addition, DNA databases are demonstrating that a significant number of hits for violent offenses are linked to offenders who were first put into the database for nonviolent offenses.

A closely related issue is when DNA samples should be taken and entered into the database. As of January 1, 2009, per the DNA Fingerprint Act of 2005, any adult arrested for a federal crime is required to provide a DNA sample (Berson, 2009, p.10). Before passage of this act, about 20 states had enacted legislation that required the gathering of DNA samples from people who were arrested but not yet convicted, with some states limiting preconviction DNA collection to violent offenders and sex crimes and other states including all felonies (Berson). Several studies have demonstrated that the collection of DNA upon arrest can prevent further violent crimes, including homicide and rape, as many offenders are recidivists: "Proponents argue that DNA sampling upon arrest catches repeat offenders before they continued a protracted pattern of violent crime" (Wallentine, 2010, p.12). Opponents claim it raises serious Fourth Amendment issues and that health insurers or employers' might illicitly access an individual's DNA profile and discriminate on the basis of potential future medical costs. Thus the debate becomes one of public safety versus individual privacy rights and potential discrimination. As a safety measure, however, all states with laws allowing preconviction DNA sampling also require a way to expunge a suspects' DNA profile if they are not convicted (Berson, p.11).

Another issue is whether those convicted of crime have a right to DNA testing to prove their innocence. According to the Innocence Project (*2009 Innocence Project Annual Report*), there have been 252 post-conviction exonerations in the United States based on DNA testing. Seventeen of these people were on death row at the time of their exoneration. DNA exonerees had spent, on average, 13 years behind bars for crimes they didn't commit. Thus, although DNA analysis is a powerful tool for helping wrongfully convicted prisoners prove their innocence, the Supreme Court ruled 5–4 in *District Attorney's Office for the Third Judicial District et al. v. Osborne* (2009) that inmates have no such right, with the majority emphasizing that 46 states already have laws allowing some prisoners to gain access to DNA evidence (Liptak, 2009a). Assenting, Chief Justice John Roberts stated, "To suddenly constitutionalize this area would short-circuit what looks to be a prompt and considered legislative response."

Yet another issue is whether potential suspects can, or should, be identified by testing the DNA of the suspect's family members, in an effort to narrow the search for the perpetrator. The technique, known as a "familial DNA" search, looks for a near-match in a close male relative of the perpetrator to gain information that helps investigators zero in on the perpetrator. Because the technology relies on the Y chromosome, this method cannot trace female suspects (Banda, 2010). Civil rights advocates and some legal experts claim this is the equivalent of "guilt by association" and is, therefore, unconstitutional. Nonetheless, many law enforcement agencies are considering adopting this promising technique. According to a Harvard medical professor, familial DNA searches could solve as many as 40 percent more crimes in which DNA evidence is present (Banda).

A controversial new DNA technology available to investigators is DNAWitness, a predictive forensic analysis tool that uses data from the Human Genome Project and advanced statistical algorithms to determine the most likely population affiliation of a suspect, based on genetic markers commonly shared among certain racial groups (Spraggs, 2005). Much the same way blood evidence can include or exclude persons as suspects, DNAWitness can include or exclude certain individuals based on their ancestry. It is helping to identify previously unidentified bodies, is finding application in cold case investigations and is helping investigators narrow their search for suspects. Critics, however, say the technology can lead to racial profiling.

Depending on how each of these issues is resolved, the result may be thousands, perhaps millions, more requests for testing of DNA samples. According to the FBI, DNA processing backlogs, now standing at more than 500,000 cases, is expected to increase (Moore, 2009a). In addition to adding convicted felon DNA profiles to their database, the FBI aims to add genetic profiles for arrested but not convicted felons as well as immigrant detainees—an estimated 1.2 more profiles—by 2012 (Moore, 2009b). The current crime laboratory backlog already causes "significant delays in evidence being analyzed, resulting in investigative and court proceeding delays" (*Increasing Efficiency in Crime Laboratories*, 2008).

Adding to the burden of overloaded crime laboratories is the Supreme Court ruling in *District Attorney's Office for the Third Judicial District v. Osborne* (2009) that laboratory analysts must testify in court on the results stated in their reports: "The ruling was as an extension of a 2004 decision that breathed new life into the Sixth Amendment's confrontation clause, which gives a criminal defendant the right 'to be confronted with the witnesses against him'" (Liptak, 2009b).

In dissent, Justice Anthony Kennedy, noting that the 500 employees of the FBI's laboratory conduct more than a million tests a year, wrote, "The court's decision means that before any of those million tests reaches a jury, at least one of the laboratory's analysts must board a plane, find his or her way to an unfamiliar courthouse and sit there waiting to read aloud a note made months ago." The practical effects of this ruling on law enforcement are obvious.

Firearms Another type of evidence often found at crime scenes is a *firearm*. A firearm left at a crime scene may be traced to its owner through the serial number, the manufacturer's identification or the dealer who sold it. The firearm might also contain the suspect's fingerprints or other marks that could lead to identification.

The make of the weapon is usually determined by the riflings, spiral grooves cut into the gun's barrel during its manufacture. The riflings vary considerably from manufacturer to manufacturer. **Ballistics** deals with the motion and effects of projectiles, including bullets, and can refer to projectile characteristics inside a weapon or outside a weapon after leaving the muzzle but before impact; to terminal effects and behavior, such as when the bullet impacts an object and comes to rest; and to forensic qualities such as those involved in comparing bullets, casings and the firearm from which they were shot. As with fingerprints and DNA, a communications network to link crimes through ballistic evidence has been developed by the Bureau of Alcohol, Tobacco, Firearms and Explosives (ATF): The National Integrated Ballistic Information Network (NIBIN).

ballistics

A science dealing with the motion and effects of projectiles such as bullets and bombs.

A high-tech police tool that can pinpoint where a gun is fired from is called *gunshot detection technology*. Sixteen cities across the country have installed Shot Spotter, a system of rooftop listening devices that triangulate the origin of gunshots and pinpoint the location on a map in seconds (Arnoldy, 2007). The system can gather forensic evidence such as when the shots were fired, how many shots were fired and from what angle, and, in some drive-bys, the direction the vehicle was moving. Again civil libertarians are critical, noting that this technology, although initially installed for one legitimate purpose, could be exploited later for another purpose such as eavesdropping on private conversations. And as Garrett (2007, p.8) stresses, "In the United States, privacy is a right not a preference." The company insists, however, that the sensors do not pick up voices.

Protecting and Storing Evidence After evidence is collected, it is packaged, labeled and placed in the evidence room until needed. If it is removed from the evidence room for any reason, strict check-out and check-in procedures are followed to maintain the chain of custody. The importance of maintaining the chain of custody of evidence cannot be overstated. If chain of evidence cannot be accounted for, evidence that may lead to the conviction of a suspect can be thrown out, as the defense can simply call into doubt the integrity of the evidence or claim it was tampered with. A case can be lost from a mishandled chain of custody, a police agency can be held legally liable, and whoever the last person was to have custody of the evidence could face possible criminal charges. In addition, such chain of custody mishandling is typically a violation of departmental policy, leaving the last person in custody open to internal discipline that may lead to loss of employment.

Computerized evidence tracking systems (ETS) can prevent countless problems. Many such systems are available. Often they incorporate barcodes.

Processing Evidence In many smaller departments, an investigator or patrol officer is also trained and certified as an evidence technician. Larger departments generally staff dedicated evidence technicians or contract with a separate forensic laboratory to perform the necessary tests for their investigations. The details of this responsibility and the myriad forensic tests such technicians may be called on to perform is beyond the scope of this discussion. However, suffice it to say that in many jurisdictions, the investigator who collects the evidence is also the person who processes it.

Interviewing and Interrogating A large part of any investigation is talking with people to obtain information. Investigators **interview** those with information about a crime. They talk with victims, witnesses and friends, coworkers, neighbors or immediate members of victims' potential suspects and suspects' families: "Interviewing is your most important investigative tool. . . . With even the exponential growth of technology, the face-to-face interview remains a critical and indispensable police skill" (Nyberg, 2009, p.65). Entire texts and courses are devoted to interview and interrogation techniques, including the cognitive interview. Such a discussion is beyond the scope of this text, but students must be aware that this aspect of law enforcement is extremely crucial and heavily structured by state and federal law.

interview

To question a witness or person with information relating to an incident.

A *witness* is a person other than a suspect who has helpful information about a specific incident or a suspect. A witness may be a **complainant** (the person reporting the offense), an accuser, a victim, an observer of the incident, an eyewitness, an expert or a scientific examiner of physical evidence.

complainant

A person who makes a charge against another person.

Victims are especially important to police officers as often they are the sole source of information about crimes. The Office for Victims of Crime (OVC) has supported a collaborative, multidisciplinary approach to supporting victim-centered care throughout the criminal justice process. In such cases as robbery, assault or rape, eyewitness testimony of the victim or a witness may be all that is necessary for a conviction. It is always ideal, however, to have physical evidence to corroborate the eyewitness testimony, that is, to support or confirm the testimony.

Too often, a victim or witness will make a statement during an interview, only to recant weeks or months later when the case goes to trial and they are on the witness stand. Law enforcement agencies, having tired of unfruitful back-and-forth debates over who said what, have begun requiring that all interviews with witnesses, victims and suspects be recorded (Anand, 2008, p.60). Because the burden of proof in a criminal trial is on the prosecution, such taping helps them disprove any allegations that the interviewer acted inappropriately.

Officers may also use an **informant**, an individual who did not witness the offense but knows something about who committed it. There are different levels of informants, such as credible informants and criminal informants, both often referred to as CIs. A *credible informant* carries more weight than a *criminal informant* when using the information to gain administrative approval to act or getting things

informant

Person who furnishes information concerning accusations against another person or persons.

such as search warrants or other legal documents approved by a judge. Credible sources usually include other law enforcement officers as well as citizen informants: "The citizen informant is not motivated by an expectation of gain, concession, revenge or leniency. So it usually takes a minimal number of steps to verify the person's credibility" (Petrocelli, 2009a, p.16). In contrast, criminal informants might provide information to police for a number of "dubious reasons," such as revenge, a reduction of pending charges or a hope of leniency in sentencing. The most common way to establish a criminal informant's reliability is documenting past use.

One obstacle to obtaining information from witnesses, victims and informants, including criminal informants, is the *Stop Snitching* video produced in Baltimore in 2004, where drug dealers threatened violence against anyone who cooperated with police. This campaign against those who cooperate with police has worsened as rap staffs spread their message instantly through the Internet ("Lesson from PERF Conference," 2008, p.1).

Investigators must determine the credibility of a source before acting on any information they receive (Petrocelli, 2009a, p.16). Some information comes from tips, and it is recommended that all tips, especially anonymous tips, be **vetted**, that is verified. Verifying the reliability of a tip is a two-step process: detail development and independent verification (Petrocelli, p.18).

vetted

Thoroughly checked out; verified.

In addition to receiving information from witnesses and informants, investigators also talk with suspects. When investigators talk with suspects, they technically **interrogate** them, although the questioning may also be called an interview. Any *custodial* interrogation requires a reading of the suspect's *Miranda* rights before any questioning. FBI statistics show that the national clearance rate for violent crimes plunged 28 percent after the *Miranda* decision and has never recovered (Rutledge, 2009, p.62). These findings suggest officers are not well-advised to give unnecessary *Miranda* warnings and that, when possible, interrogations should be conducted in noncustodial settings such as the suspect's home, a public place or on the street, thus avoiding the need to Mirandize the suspect. Interrogations may take place in a police setting without *Miranda* warnings if several factors indicate lack of arrest or restraint (Rutledge, p.65):

interrogate

To question a suspect.

- The suspect agrees to talk and comes in voluntarily.
- No restraints or threats of detention or arrest are used.
- The suspect is questioned for an hour or two, with breaks offered.
- The suspect is allowed to leave and is arrested sometime later.
- A "Beheler admonition" is given.

A Beheler admonition such as the following would allow questioning without Mirandizing: "You are not under arrest and are free to leave anytime you want, OK?" This admonition establishing the noncustodial nature of the interrogation came out of the Supreme Court's decision in *California v. Beheler* (1983), where the Supreme Court held that no reasonable person would have felt himself to be under arrest having been told that he was not and having come voluntarily and left without police restraints (Rutledge, 2009, p.64).

As a protection against liability, many departments require video recording interviews and interrogations. Some states have passed laws requiring law enforcement officers who are conducting a suspect interview or interrogation to digitally record, either via audio or video, the procedure. In Minnesota, this is known as the "Scales" law. Other states that mandate the recoding of suspect interviews and interrogation are Massachusetts, New Jersey and Wisconsin. However, some investigators are concerned that recording might deter confessions and cause some people to refuse to speak freely with officers. Others oppose such recording believing jurors may be offended by their interrogation techniques—for example, shouting, using foul language and street talk, suggesting leniency, expressing sympathy for the suspect, blaming victims, falsely asserting that incriminating evidence has been obtained and the like.

Nonetheless, videotaping reduces the need for copious note taking and provides greater accuracy in documenting suspects' statements. In addition, the tapes can be reviewed by detectives and can be used in training.

Identifying Suspects If officers do not witness a crime, eyewitness identification plays an important part in the arrest, as well as in the trial proceedings. Very specific questions and use of an identification diagram may aid witnesses in identifying suspects. Other information related to the suspect is also obtained: for example, how the suspect left the scene—running, walking, in a vehicle—and in what direction. Occasionally a lead is called in or otherwise provided to the police that implicates a specific subject as the suspect in a crime. Departments often use forms such as that shown in Figure 6.3 to record such leads and track the investigative progress of the lead.

If the witness knows the suspect, the investigator asks about the suspect's personal associates, habits and where he or she is likely to be found. Usually, however, the witness does not know the suspect. In such cases investigators must obtain identification in other ways.

The three basic types of identification are,

- Field identification.
- Photographic identification.
- Lineup identification.

Each type of identification is used in specific circumstances, and each must meet certain legal requirements to be admissible in court, as the Fourteenth Amendment's due process clause protects suspects from "impermissibly suggestive" identification procedures (Schuck, 2009). Sometimes more than one type of identification is used. In *Neil v. Biggers* (1972) the Supreme Court held five factors to be considered in determining a witnesses' reliability: (1) the *opportunity* of the witness to view the defendant during the crime (distance, lighting), (2) the witness' *level of attention*, (3) the *accuracy* of any descriptions of the defendant before the identification, (4) the witness' *level of certainty*, and (5) the *time* between the crime and confrontation.

field identification

At-the-scene identification, made within a reasonable time after a crime has been committed.

Field identification is at-the-scene identification, made within a short time after a crime has been committed. Generally the suspect is returned to the crime scene for possible identification, or the witness may be taken to where the suspect is being held. Field identification is used when a suspect matches the description given by a witness and is apprehended close to the crime scene. The critical element in a field identification is time.

SAMPLE

Case number: Lead number:

Priority level: ☐ **Low** ☐ **Medium** ☐ **High**

SUBJECT	INFORMANT
Name:	Name:
Address:	Address:
Race: DOB: Sex:	
Hgt: Wgt: Eyes: Hair:	Home telephone:
Identifying features:	Other telephone:
Employed: Occupation:	How informant knows subject:
Telephone numbers: Home: Work:	

Vehicle make: Yr: Model: Color: Condition: Tag:

Associates:

ID confirmed: ☐ Yes ☐ No How?

Details of lead:

Lead received by: Date/time:

Lead # assigned:

Lead status: ☐ Good lead ☐ Questionable lead ☐ Suspicious informant ☐ Insufficient information

Lead assigned to: Date/time:

Findings:

______Open lead: ☐ Additional investigation required ☐ Could not locate subject ☐ Subject has weak alibi ☐ Other:

______Closed lead: ☐ Unfounded ☐ Subject has alibi ☐ Cleared by evidence ☐ Other:

Other lead number references:

Report completed: Y/N Report #:

Investigative supervisor: Date:

Lead-room supervisor: Date:

FIGURE 6.3 Investigative Lead Sheet

totality of circumstances

Considering all factors involved in a given situation.

Field identification is based on a **totality of circumstances**, considering the witness's concentration on the suspect when the crime was committed, the accuracy of the description, the certainty at the time of the confrontation and the length of time between crime commission and the field identification. A reasonable basis for believing that immediate identification is needed must exist because the suspect does not have the right to have counsel present (*United States v. Ash, Jr.*, 1973).

Photographic identification is another option. Most people are familiar with the procedure of having victims and witnesses go through mug shot books in hopes of finding a picture of the person they saw commit a particular crime. This type of identification is time consuming and is profitable only if the suspect has a record.

Mug shots are not the only types of photographs used in suspect identification. Frequently officers know or have a strong suspicion about who committed a given crime. If the suspect is not in custody or if it is not possible to conduct a fair lineup, officers may present photographs of people of similar general descriptions to victims or witnesses, who may identify the suspect from among the photographs.

A third option is a *lineup*, allowing witnesses to observe several individuals, one of whom is the suspect, to see if the witnesses can identify the suspect. A suspect may be asked to speak, walk, turn, assume a stance or make a gesture. If for any reason a suspect refuses to cooperate in a lineup, photographic identification may be used. The suspect's refusal to participate may be used against him or her in court.

The police lineup is a time-honored staple of police departments and crime shows. However, recently many cities and states have changed their lineup procedures because of wrongful convictions, three-quarters resulting from bad eyewitness identification.

Controversy exists over simultaneous versus sequential lineups. The traditional "six-pack" lineup has serious problems. According to researchers, when witnesses are shown all the people in a lineup at once (simultaneously), asked to compare faces and then judge which looks most like the person they saw, the witnesses use a process of elimination rather than selecting the person most like who they saw. In a sequential lineup, witnesses look at possible suspects one at a time, deciding in each case whether that person is the offender before moving on to the next. Another suggested change in procedure is that the person conducting the lineup not know who the suspect is, called a "blind" lineup. More than a quarter century of scientific study has led to support for these two aspects of lineup reform—that lineups be "blind" and sequential (Gaertner and Harrington, 2009, p.130).

Research tends to support a change from the traditional simultaneous lineup to a blind, sequential lineup protocol.

modus operandi (MO)

A method of criminal attack specific to an individual offender.

Another way to identify a suspect may be the **modus operandi or MO**. Computer software is useful for managing large volumes of data in MO files.

Identifying Missing Persons and Human Remains

The FBI's National Crime Information Center has more than 100,000 active missing persons cases on any given day, as well as some 5,800 sets of unidentified remains. The challenge posed to law enforcement by missing and unidentified person cases can be formidable: "Investigating these cases can demand extensive time and effort, and there are often few leads to follow. An estimated 4,400 new unidentified human remains cases are generated each year, and approximately 1,000 of these remain unidentified after one year" (Evans, 2009, p.104). A new centralized system for finding missing persons and identifying unknown remains is the National Missing and Unidentified Persons System, or NamUs. NamUs provides a bridge via the Internet between all the work being done independently by law enforcement, medical examiners, coroners, families and anyone who is involved and touched by a missing persons case (Pearsall and Weiss, 2009, p.4).

CAREER PROFILE

Richard Gautsch (Retired Criminal Investigator)

Cops weren't the most popular people on the University of Minnesota campus in the 1970s, and my friends thought it peculiar that I wanted to become a one. My dad worried that police work was too dangerous. (This from a guy who lost part of his foot to a hunk of flack over Nazi Germany as a lead bombardier in a B-17.) Honestly, I just thought it would be cool to be a detective some day. My senior year was rapidly coming to a close, and the athletic department would soon stop footing my bills. The job market for middleweight wrestlers was limited. Armed with degrees in sociology and criminal justice studies, I headed off to make my mark in law enforcement.

I was fortunate to receive job offers from several police organizations. I selected a department with plenty of activity and a progressive chief who allowed new officers to substitute years of college for years of experience. This meant I could test for detective after one year on the street as a patrol officer. That first year was a serious adjustment from the sheltered life of a college jock. My college studies were helpful in a theoretical way, but the street is seldom theoretical. I learned the job by being kicked in the face by a kid I failed to handcuff, performing CPR on a man who hung himself in a jail cell and helping collect skull fragments at a shotgun suicide. I thought Christmas Eve would be a peaceful shift, but before Santa had slid down the chimney, I had already responded to a fight with multiple stabbings and arrested an intoxicated father who had thrown his kids' gifts and Christmas tree out the front door. "Welcome to the real world," I was told. I did some serious growing up that first year.

I'm not certain if it was luck and timing or if the administration was just tired of my low ticket production, but I made detective at age 24. It was an awesome feeling, clipping that detective badge on my duty belt next to my gun each morning. I sometimes lingered in front of the mirror to make sure I had that cool detective look. Two weeks later I was standing over the body of a 15-year-old murder victim with little regard for how cool I looked.

A week earlier the boy was reported missing from his job at a gas station. I assured his parents that he probably ran away like so many other teens. Now I was on my way to tell them we'd found his bound and bullet-ridden body discarded in a wooded area. My voice cracked and my eyes welled up as I shared the bad news. The kid's mother broke down, hugged me and asked if I was okay. As we left their home, a seasoned detective put his arm around me and told me something every cop learns: "Kid, you can't grieve everyone's tragedies in this business. You've got to save some emotion for your own life." During my career, I guess I've seen about every brutal thing one human being can do to another. I lost one of my best police friends to some delusional nut with a gun. I tried but wasn't always able to follow that old detective's wise advice.

I was fortunate to work a wide variety of assignments as a detective, including numerous drug and other undercover operations. Much of a detective's job is tedious and mundane, but there are exciting and fun times too. The job can be dangerous but so is driving a truck or working on a farm. I never experienced anything close to the terror those young B-17 bomber crews must have felt. The real dangers in police work are less physical than psychological.

There were times I wanted to quit the crazy police world, but more often than not, I would have worked for free. There is nothing more exhilarating than slapping the cuffs on a couple of creeps like the two who murdered that young boy or the coward who killed my buddy. I'd be lying if I told you some of the gratification wasn't retribution, but there is a deeper satisfaction in knowing that you've made the world a slightly better place to live.

I retired as a captain after 27 years of service. At the time I was managing an investigation unit and a multi-jurisdictional drug task force. I currently write and teach classes in communications. During a recent presentation at a high school, a student asked me to list the attributes of a good detective. I told her knowledge, common sense, compassion, a sense of humor and the ability to communicate. Another student piped up and said that could be true of any profession, to which I answered, "Indeed."

PROFILERS

Since the first police investigation, detectives have focused on relatively superficial characteristics to identify suspects, such as height, weight, race, gender, age, accent, type of car driven, MO and so on. Although these descriptors remain valid and are still considered when searching for suspects, profilers have begun delving deeper into suspects' personalities, psyches, pathologies and resultant behaviors to develop more complete portraits of serial criminals. Such profiles can and often do exist in the absence of any physical descriptors. Profiling has been popularized through the television series *Criminal Minds*.

Profiling evolved as a discipline during the 1970s with the FBI's increasing understanding of serial murder. Drug courier profiling emerged as part of the war on drugs during the 1980s, began in airports, and was upheld as constitutional in *United States v. Sokolow* (1989). Profiling can be reactive or proactive. In reactive profiling, investigators attempt to solve crimes that have already occurred. Proactive profiling, in contrast, attempts to interdict and foil crime before it happens.

Profiling uses pattern recognition through systematically collecting, organizing and analyzing information gathered through observation or measurement; drawing conclusions in assessing criminal suspicion; and sharing data with others. Although race, sex and religion are among the most controversial elements in profiling, profilers also use such things as travel patterns, socioeconomic status, geographic locations and clothing. It is essential to distinguish between racial profiling and psychological profiling, geographic profiling and criminal profiling. The former is a crime and violation of civil rights already discussed, whereas the latter are accepted tools for investigators.

Crimes suitable for profiling include sadistic torture in sexual assaults, eviscerations, postmortem cases of slashing and cutting, motiveless arson, lust and mutilation murders, rapes, occult crimes, child sexual abuse including pedophilia and bank robberies. According to the FBI, profiling techniques have assisted in 77 percent of cases, provided leads for stakeouts solving cases 45 percent of the time and have actually helped identify the perpetrator or unidentified subject (UNSUB) in 17 percent of cases.

In addition to criminal or psychological profiling, departments may use geographic profiling. Like mapping, geographic profiling uses software to spatially analyze crime sites, allowing investigators to determine the most likely areas where offenders live. Geographic profiling is not likely to become a routine practice because it is very labor-intensive, which is also the case with psychological profiling; however: "When you have a major case and you're out of investigative leads, the effectiveness of these two tools can be the difference between capturing the bad guy and having him continue to prey on the citizens you serve" (Dees, 2008, p.71).

PSYCHICS

In addition to profiling, some departments have turned to using psychics, a highly controversial practice. The use of psychics in investigations has also been popularized by the media, including the television series, *The Mentalist*. According to Lee (2008, p.55), "The interest in psychic detectives isn't restricted to the general public. Their use by police agencies has been well documented for some time. The results, however, are open to endless debate." Many investigators place absolutely no faith in psychics, but other investigators have found them to be helpful, especially in cold cases.

One notable case involved psychic Annette Martin, who assisted Sgt. Fernado Realybasquez of the Pacifica (California) Police Department in cracking the missing person case of Denis Prado, a former paratrooper, 71, who went missing on May 1, 1997. According to the sergeant: "I'm just as skeptical as I was before, but the only reason we found Prado was because of the information Martin provided" (Lee, 2008, p.45).

INTELLIGENCE OFFICERS

Most large departments have an intelligence division whose top officer reports directly to the chief and whose activities are kept from the rest of the department. Intelligence units work in two areas.

Intelligence officers may be undercover officers investigating crime or internal affairs officers investigating complaints against officers within the department.

Undercover Officers

The goal of undercover officers is to identify suspects and gather evidence for prosecution. Undercover (UC) employees often work on cases in cooperation with county, state and federal investigators. Undercover work generally includes ongoing drug investigations; stings, including warrant stings and fencing stings that involve buying and selling stolen goods and other contraband; decoy operations targeting robbery, burglary and assault; antiprostitution operations; and operations involving infiltration and arrest of people involved in organized crime, white-collar crime and corruption. Federal undercover investigations generally seek to detect and arrest people involved in political corruption, insurance fraud, labor racketeering and other types of organized conspiracy crimes. More recently undercover officers have been involved in investigating terrorist sleeper cells, as discussed in Chapter 10.

Given the nature of such assignments and their reliance on anonymity and obscurity, undercover intelligence officers do not wear uniforms or drive marked cars, and they may use assumed names and fictitious identities. UC officers also do not have to comply with traditional uniform standards and appearance policies of their agencies, as they are required to "blend" in among the people they are attempting to target. Often this means wearing torn or gang related clothing, ungroomed hair, facial hair, tattoos, piercings, and the like. To avoid identification problems, some large agencies use officers who have just graduated from rookie school because they are not known on the street.

Two broad categories of undercover work are the light cover and the deep cover. Light undercover officers may have a fake identification (ID) but usually go home to their families and real life, most likely in another city. They may pose as a utility worker or phone company repair person to gain access to a suspect's living quarters or place of work. They might plant listening devices or look for signs of illegal activity.

One approach to light undercover work is the sting operation or ruse, where police deceive criminals into openly committing illegal acts; these operations save months of investigative work and can be just as effective. Such operations, however, carry legal risks for law enforcement. Officers must adhere to department policies and procedures and accurately document their activity, lest the undercover agents and the agency be accused of entrapment.

Deep undercover officers live their roles 24/7, with a false ID and a false personal history. The first name is usually kept so answering to the name comes naturally, and the personal history will be as close to the truth as possible to avoid slip-ups. These officers usually have actual employment, own a house or rent an apartment and establish a role that provides them access inside whatever group or organization they want to infiltrate. Deep undercover operations are usually designed to target big-time drug dealers, gangs or crime bosses.

Although undercover operations are often perceived as mysterious and glamorous assignments, psychological and physical dangers abound. Family and social relationships may suffer from such assignments, as officers are precluded from sharing what they are involved in with those closest to them. In addition, intense, long-term operations may also lead to officer burnout, which may couple with complacency, causing an agent to lose focus, not pay attention to important details or misread a potentially threatening situation. Furthermore many undercover officers find it difficult to return to routine police work once the covert operation is over.

The grueling work of going undercover requires a carefully crafted persona and unrelenting self-discipline: "Nothing is worth compromising your integrity as a police officer. Whether it's sleeping with a snitch or taste-testing the stash, you're committing a crime, destroying your own credibility and damaging your profession—not to mention risking your life" (Grossi, 2009, p.28).

Undercover officers seek to melt into their surroundings, making complicated, often dangerous, decisions about when to back off, to make arrests and to shoot. Even the most cautious undercover officers may find themselves unavoidably immersed in the violence that defines the criminal world and become victims of assault, shootings and worse, sometimes at the hands of other officers who are unaware of their undercover status.

Internal Affairs

The second area of intelligence work involves investigating other officers in the department. Since the 1950s when the first internal affairs units were established, policing the police has been difficult. Both the IACP and the Commission on Accreditation for Law Enforcement Agencies (CALEA) have developed policies and standards addressing the need for effective, efficient methods for receiving and processing all complaints of misconduct involving law enforcement personnel.

In most agencies the internal affairs (IA) bureau or professional standards unit is charged with investigating violations of an agency's policies and procedures, ranging from rudeness or discourtesy toward a citizen to allegations and accusations of theft, corruption and other criminal conduct. These cases require a department to face the unenviable task of investigating itself and its own officers while not appearing biased to the public.

Standards and Guidelines for Internal Affairs (2009) confirms the "vital importance" of Internal Affairs as a critical police agency function: "Internal Affairs serves two communities—law enforcement and the general public—and is essential in building and maintaining mutual trust and respect between the two." The litigious nature of American society, as well as a citizenry that is increasingly intolerant of transgressions by police, has required agencies to assume a more proactive role, often involving the establishment of some sort of early warning system to identify officers who have the potential for unacceptable behavior.

Criminal and IA investigations should always remain separate and be conducted by different investigators, with an IA investigation always subordinate to a criminal investigation. Anything learned in a criminal investigation can be used in the IA investigation, but the reverse is not so simple.

IA officers must be aware of the ruling in *Garrity v. New Jersey* (1967). In *Garrity* the U.S. Supreme Court held that the government violates the Fourteenth Amendment if it uses a police officer's statement in a criminal trial against that officer if the statement resulted from his being told that if he refused to answer the question, it might cost him his job.

JUVENILE OFFICERS

Yet another specialized assignment is that of the juvenile officer. Police officers are often the first contact for youths in legal trouble. Therefore, it is justifiable and logical to have juvenile police specialists. Because most juvenile work is informal and officer discretion plays a critical role, such as determining whether to release, refer or detain, juvenile officers must be chosen from the most qualified officers in the department. The usual flow of how police interact with youths in the juvenile justice system is illustrated in Figure 6.4.

Because juveniles commit a disproportionate number of local crimes, all officers are juvenile officers much of the time. Also, the police usually are youths' initial contact with the juvenile justice system. They have broad discretion and may release juveniles to their parents, refer them to other agencies, place them in detention or refer them to a juvenile court.

Whether a juvenile is actually taken into custody usually depends on a number of factors, the most important of which is the seriousness of the offense. Other considerations include age, attitude, family situation, previous record and the attitudes of the school and the community.

The police may also be responsible for some specific services involving children, such as helping to locate missing or runaway children, conducting fingerprinting programs and investigating reports of neglected or abused children. On October 12, 1982, the Missing Children Act was signed into law, requiring the attorney general to "acquire, collect and preserve any information that would assist in the location of any missing person (including children) and provide confirmation as to any entry (into FBI records) for such a person to the parent, legal guardian

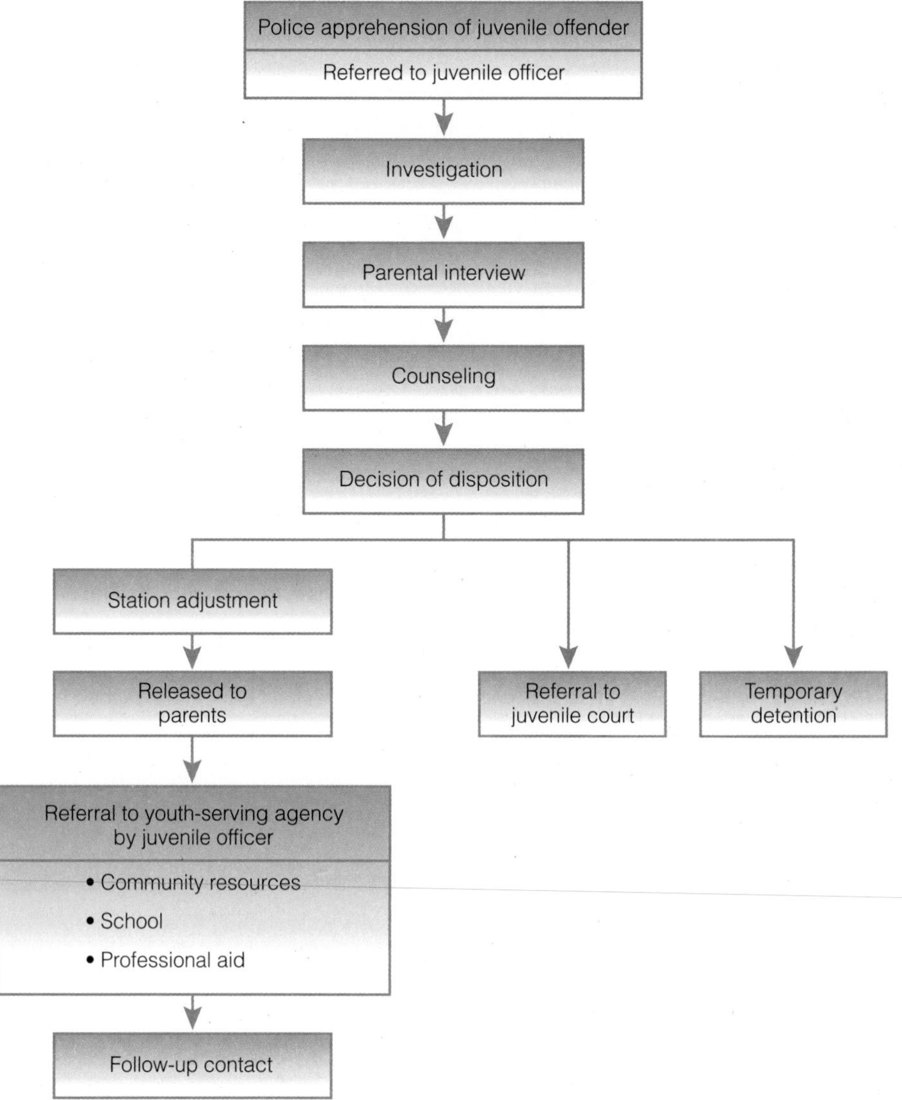

FIGURE 6.4 Police Responsibility for Juveniles

SOURCE: Reprinted by permission. Copyright held by The International Association of Chiefs of Police, Inc. Further reproduction without express written permission is prohibited.

or next of kin." Though this law does not require that the FBI investigate the case, it does give parents, legal guardians or the next of kin access to the information in the FBI National Crime Information Center's (NCIC) Missing Person File.

Because of this law, it is important that children be fingerprinted. Many schools have instituted such a program in conjunction with the local police department. The same procedures used to search for a missing child might be used to locate a runaway child.

Police are also called on to investigate reports of neglected or abused children. In most jurisdictions parental abuse or neglect of children is a crime, but jurisdictions vary in what constitutes abuse or neglect. Usually neglect includes failure to feed and clothe a child or provide adequate shelter.

A special type of juvenile officer is the school resource officer (SRO). Many schools have turned to SROs to help address the problems of gang violence, drug use, property crime, assaults and other crimes committed on school grounds. SROs are enhancing their effectiveness through specialized training in such areas as critical incident response, legal issues for SROs and school administrators, identifying adolescent drug use, and bullying prevention and intervention. Like officers on the streets, officers in schools are now using crime prevention through environmental design (CPTED) to identify, prevent and solve crime problems.

VICE OFFICERS

Vice officers usually concentrate their efforts on illegal gambling, prostitution, pornography, narcotics and liquor violations.

Vice problems vary from community to community. Sometimes the work is coordinated with that of intelligence officers.

Illegal and Legal Gambling

Some people view gambling as a vice; others view it as a harmless form of entertainment. Within the gambling industry, the term *gambling* has fallen into disfavor and has been replaced with the term *gaming*, perhaps to make it more socially acceptable. The most significant forms of illegal gambling in the United States are numbers betting with bookmakers or bookies and sports pools or sports cards. The Internet is a rapidly growing source of gambling with an estimated 300 gambling-related sites, some set up offshore. Charitable gaming, pari-mutuel betting, casino gaming and lotteries are legal in most states.

The current view is that the presence of casinos increases crime and changes the nature of the community in several ways, both positively (e.g., stimulating the economy and adding employment and entertainment options) and negatively (e.g., adding traffic congestion, altering traditional patterns of interaction and introducing large numbers of nonresidents into a community). Crime does not appear to be an inevitable or necessary product of casino presence.

However, research by the National Institute of Justice (*Gambling and Crime among Arrestees*, 2004) using the Arrestee Drug Abuse Monitoring (ADAM) Program as a survey vehicle found that arrestees had significantly more problem gambling behaviors than did the general population. The percentage of problem or pathological gamblers among the arrestees was three to five times higher than in the general population.

Prostitution and Pornography

"Prostitution has flourished in every stratum of society in every part of the world. Prostitution takes many different forms from high-priced call girls who meet clients in hotel rooms to street prostitutes who ply their trade in public" (Petrocelli, 2009b, p.20). Some areas of the country legally allow prostitution, but most do not.

For areas where prostitution is illegal, it often seems to law enforcement as if they are fighting a losing battle.

Street prostitution is the type of prostitution citizens complain most about. The traditional police response to street prostitution has been to arrest them, often as a result of expensive, personnel-intensive street sweeps (Petrocelli, 2009b, p.20). Street sweeps, however, are expensive and they are ineffective at reducing prostitution. Often such sweeps merely move the problem from one area to another: "Arresting prostitutes only addresses half of the problem—officers who are interested in combating street-level crime must also investigate and arrest the johns who solicit the prostitutes. One effective way to do so is to plan and conduct a sting operation in which a female police officer wears a recording device and poses as a streetwalker" (Jetmore, 2008, p.92). Some jurisdictions publish the names of people arrested for soliciting prostitutes in hopes of deterring the activity. For agencies that post their john lists on the Web and can track the number of "hits," such pages are proving to be very popular sites.

In addition to complaints from citizens, other reasons police should be concerned about prostitution include moral concerns, public health concerns, personal safety concerns, economic concerns, civil rights concerns and spillover effect concerns. Other concerns include the fact that street prostitution and street drug markets are often linked. Prostitutes create parking and traffic problems where they congregate, and prostitution attracts strangers and criminals to a neighborhood.

Studies have found that many women enter prostitution as minors and use the income to support a drug habit or to stave off homelessness. Many suffered abuse as children and have extremely high rates of job victimization. For most this is not a chosen career but a means of survival. A better solution to a prostitution problem than arrest might be to consider the prostitutes as victims and provide rehabilitative services to them.

Vice officers usually work covertly behind the scenes. In contrast, much more visible and often the center of media attention are tactical forces or special weapons and tactics (SWAT) officers.

SWAT OFFICERS

SWAT teams began in 1967 when the Los Angeles Police Department organized such a unit to respond to critical incidents: "The concept of a police tactical unit inspired by military special forces units makes some people uncomfortable. Newspaper and magazine columnists use SWAT as an example of how American law enforcement has become too violent, too paramilitary in nature. Activists like to paint SWAT as storm troopers. And in TV programs and movies, SWAT is portrayed as a group of cowboys who shoot first and ask questions later or ninjas who kill without mercy" (Griffith, 2008, p.50).

A SWAT team is a unit of law enforcement officers specifically trained and equipped to work as a team to respond to critical incidents including but not limited to hostage taking, barricaded suspects, snipers, terrorist acts and other high-risk incidents. Sometimes the teams are full time, as with most large departments in major metropolitan cities, but more typically the teams are drawn from officers on the force who, for the most part, perform more traditional assignments. Often, teams can be formed by officers from several neighboring law enforcement agencies.

SWAT team officers are immediately available, flexible, mobile officers used to deploy against critical incidents. They seek to contain and neutralize dangerous situations.

SWAT team members are highly trained in marksmanship, guerrilla tactics, night operations, camouflage and concealment, and use of chemical agents. They often participate in field exercises to develop discipline and teamwork. In 2008 the National Tactical Officers Association (NTOA) established the first national SWAT standards, prompted partly by the realization that in the case of a large-scale terror attack, multiple SWAT teams will need to work together: "Having all American SWAT teams on the same page could make a difference in a major incident, and NTOA's recommended SWAT standards are a huge step in the right direction" (O'Brien, 2009, p.60).

One of the specialists on a SWAT team is the sniper, an expert sharpshooter. Snipers are most often used in hostage or barricaded suspect situations. They are also used in situations involving suicidal individuals.

Some have criticized the overemphasis on physical assault and combat techniques by tactical teams, yet such aggressive measures are becoming more necessary as today's street gangs and drug traffickers become better armed, stocking arsenals of semiautomatic and assault weapons that would make many law enforcement agencies envious. Most studies of SWAT activity show that such teams are rarely deployed in an offensive situation; rather, they are almost always called out for defensive purposes.

The question has also been raised as to how SWAT teams can coexist with officers operating with a community policing mind-set. SWAT team officers are by definition reactive; community policing officers seek to be proactive. The challenge is to teach officers to function in either mode, depending on the circumstances.

Some SWAT teams are combining and training with other specialized units such as the hazardous materials (hazmat) unit, emergency medical service (EMS) providers or K-9 units for tactical operations: "As first responders, tactical operators enter volatile situations and need to function in a certain way to meet their mission. The inclusion of a hazardous material changes both the scenario and response. To meet these challenges, several Florida agencies incorporate hazardous material training into their tactical operations" (Perin, 2009, p.22). SWAT officers are trained in the Occupational Safety and Health Administration (OSHA) requirements regarding SWAT operations in hazardous environments and provided with personal protective equipment.

In a similar vein: "Like army medics, SWAT paramedic teams combine fire, EMS and police training to provide tactical defense can first aid care in situations civilian teams can't touch. . . . Agencies who have designed their own Tactical Emergency Medical Service (TEMS) units within the last decade or so can't imagine not having these highly skilled, highly versatile men and women onboard" (Schreiber, 2009, p.28).

Miami Beach SWAT team members move into position in front of a houseboat on the Intracoastal Waterway where an armed suspect had been discovered. SWAT team members are trained to contain and neutralize high-risk situations.

If a SWAT deployment involves a search, many departments find that K-9s can greatly enhance the safety of their officers as well as enhance the search itself. K-9s can be invaluable assets to a department.

K-9 UNITS

The first organized K-9 unit in the United States began in 1907 in New York City. Police dogs are often used in place of a second officer on automobile and foot patrols. Service K-9s can run down a suspect, jump barricades and maneuver through confined spaces more readily than a human officer, thereby significantly decreasing the risks to their two-legged counterparts. Accelerant-sniffing dogs can assist in investigating cases of suspected arson. Detector dogs can be used in airports and on planes, in schools, in the workplace and at border checkpoints. In addition to functioning in active crime fighting and prevention duties, K-9 units have helped in search and rescue (SAR) efforts to locate victims of bombings and plane crashes and are also used to enhance community relations as well as to enhance SWAT efforts, as discussed previously. Some overlap and cross-training of K-9s does occur, although rarely is one dog trained or expected to perform in all capacities.

K-9s are used to detect concealed suspects, drugs, weapons and explosives; find evidence discarded by fleeing suspects; control crowds and break up fights; recover lost articles; locate distressed persons and dead bodies; and help apprehend suspects.

According to a *Police* magazine survey, almost 50 percent of agencies routinely use K-9s. Of those using K-9 units, 90 percent use the dogs for drug detection, 71 percent for tracking, 48 percent for overall enforcement and 39 percent for bomb/ballistic/substance detection, 31 percent for search and rescue, and 11 percent for cadaver search. Various breeds of dogs are used, but the most popular is the German shepherd, used by 74 percent of departments, followed by the Belgian Malinois, used by 44 percent ("Almost 50 Percent," 2008, p.14).

Today's police dog has intensive schooling with one officer—the dog's partner. Both spend many weeks under a special trainer and receive instruction specific to one of five general categories.

K-9s may be specifically trained in search, apprehension, drug, bomb and cadaver detection, and crime deterrence.

The cost of training such dogs can be a major deterrent to small departments. Some agencies are fortunate enough to receive donated dogs, but many must

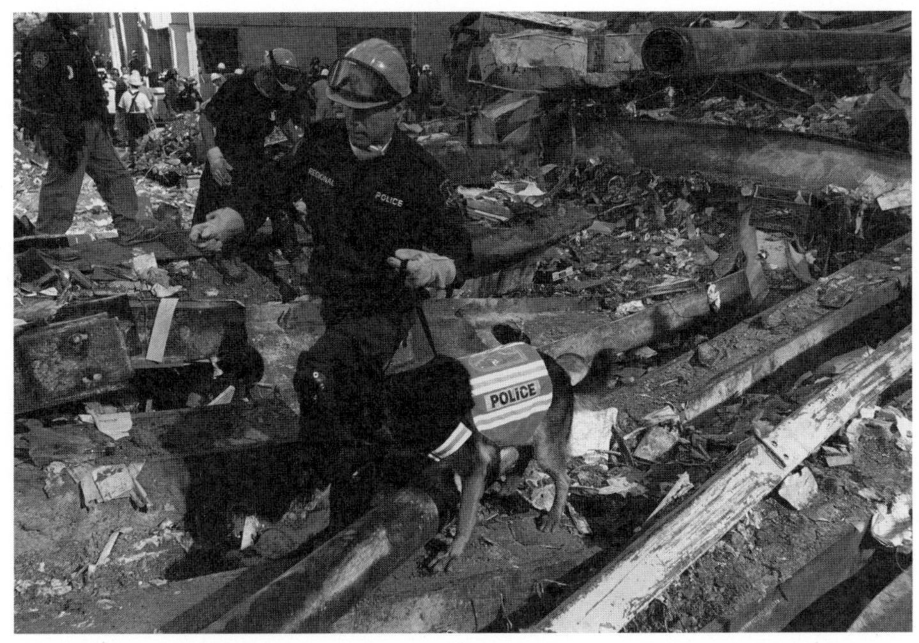

Officer James Symington and his German shepherd, Trakr, search through rubble at the World Trade Center tower collapse site in New York, on September 13, 2001. Symington and Trakr were among the first search and rescue teams to arrive at Ground Zero following the terrorist attacks. Years later, Symington wrote an essay for a contest to find the world's most "cloneworthy dog," and Trakr's selection was announced June 30, 2008.

purchase their canines, which can be quite costly. Whatever the cost, the benefits of K-9 units are numerous.

Although ballistic vests have been developed for K-9s, they are used sparingly because they are heavy, hot and cumbersome (Basich, 2009, p.32). In addition, K-9s can now be fitted with video cameras, some of which are so complex the officer partner can give the dog commands from the camera and see what he sees, giving the officer a tactical edge.

Police dogs are being held to a higher standard than ever before, just like their human counterparts in law enforcement. Dogs are still dogs, though officers must answer to any complaint lodged regarding the actions of their canine partners. Officers should also be familiar with legal issues when using K-9s.

K-9 Case Law

Because K-9 deployment falls within the realm of use of force, police administrators and trainers must be familiar with the case law pertaining to the specialty of police canines. Most issues revolve around the Fourth Amendment's right to be free from unreasonable search and seizure. In *United States v. Place* (1983) the U.S. Supreme Court ruled that the exposure of luggage to a canine sniff did not constitute a search.

K-9s can be used as a "force multiplier" and provide a psychological advantage over other use-of-force options. Many suspects are not afraid of getting shot, but most fear police dogs and will give up quickly once they see that a K-9 is about to be deployed. The courts have also usually sided with law enforcement on use-of-force issues, ruling several times that dogs are considered reasonable, not deadly force.

RESERVE OFFICERS

Some departments have reserve units to help achieve departmental goals. Reserve officers, also called auxiliary police, patrol in uniform and are visible symbols of law enforcement. Although reserve officers usually cannot write citations, some jurisdictions do permit such activity under city ordinance. Reserve officers provide additional uniformed personnel in times of need such as riots, natural disasters, major exhibitions, fairs or festivals; they convert a one-officer car into a two-officer unit, freeing other one-officer cars to respond to calls for service; and they can perform tasks not requiring advanced or technical law enforcement skills, such as prisoner transport, hospital guarding details, delivery of documents and the like (Ferguson, 2008, p.87).

Reserve officers also help in education programs, informing the public about such things as drugs, bike safety and Operation Identification, in which valuables are marked for identification in case of theft. When a crime does occur, reserves can guard the crime scene while the officers continue with their routine or specialized patrol. Like K-9s, police reserves are considered "force multipliers." They can also greatly contribute to homeland security efforts.

Besides performing traditional street patrol, reserves may be found on bicycles, in the water and in the air. Volunteer aviators may extend the resources of law enforcement agencies. Although departments of all sizes across the country supplement their policing efforts with reserve officers, the sheriff of Union County, North Carolina, acknowledges that volunteers engaged in search-and-rescue missions and other reserve activities are really an extension of community policing. Reserve officers are not always welcomed with open arms, however, and controversy often accompanies their use.

OTHER SPECIALIZED POLICE

There are many other specialized details developed by various law enforcement agencies, however space does not permit an in depth review on all of them. Some of these units include senior service officers, family liaison officers, the Mint Police, community service officers, transit police, airport police, campus police, and so on.

Summary

The primary characteristic of an effective investigator is objectivity. Investigative responsibilities often include securing the crime scene; recording all facts related to the case; photographing, video recording, measuring and sketching the crime scene; obtaining and identifying evidence, thus starting the chain of custody; protecting and storing evidence; processing evidence; interviewing victims, witnesses and possible suspects; interrogating likely suspects; assisting in identifying suspects; and identifying missing persons and human remains.

Investigators must obtain answers to the questions: Who? What? Where? When? How? and Why? Usually they must obtain both photographs and sketches because although photographs include all details and can show items close up, sketches can be selective and can show much larger areas.

A primary responsibility of investigators is to recognize, collect, mark, preserve and transport physical evidence in sufficient quantity for analysis and without contamination, while generating and maintaining the chain of custody. DNA profiling uses the material from which chromosomes are made to positively identify individuals. No two individuals, except identical twins, have the same DNA structure. Issues related to DNA testing include the Police Elimination database, which crimes to include for testing, preconviction collection, prisoners' rights to testing, familial DNA testing and whether the analyst who performed the test must testify in court.

If officers do not witness a crime, eyewitness identification plays an important part in the arrest, as well as in the trial proceedings. The three basic types of identification are field identification, photographic identification and lineup identification. Research tends to support a change from the traditional simultaneous lineup to a blind, sequential lineup protocol.

Most large departments have an intelligence division whose top officer reports directly to the chief and whose activities are kept secret from the rest of the department. Intelligence officers may be undercover officers investigating crime or internal affairs officers investigating other officers within the department.

Because juveniles commit a disproportionate number of local crimes, all officers are juvenile officers much of the time. Also, the police usually are youths' initial contact with the juvenile justice system. They have broad discretion and may release juveniles to their parents, refer them to other agencies, place them in detention or refer them to a juvenile court.

Larger departments often have several types of specialized officers. Vice officers usually concentrate their efforts on illegal gambling, prostitution, pornography, narcotics and liquor violations. SWAT officers are immediately available, flexible, mobile officers used to deploy against critical incidents. They seek to contain and neutralize dangerous situations.. K-9s have been used to detect concealed suspects, drugs, weapons and explosives; find evidence discarded by fleeing suspects; control crowds and break up fights; recover lost articles; locate distressed persons and dead bodies; and help apprehend suspects. K-9s may be specifically trained in search, apprehension, drug detection, bomb detection and crime deterrence.

Discussion Questions

1. What are the goals of an investigating officer?
2. What does a preliminary investigation consist of?
3. What differences exist between a studio photographer and a crime scene photographer?
4. Why is DNA profiling not more commonly used in criminal investigations?
5. Why and how are computers being used in investigations?
6. What are some of the dangers and challenges undercover officers face that uniformed officers typically do not?
7. What is the difference between an interview and an interrogation?
8. Does your local police department use reserve officers? If so, how many are there and what are their main duties?
9. Does your police department have a SWAT team? If so, when is it used?
10. Does your police department use K-9s? If so, what are they used for?

Gale Emergency Database Services Assignments

- Use the Gale Emergency Services Database to help answer the Discussion Questions as appropriate.
- Using the Gale Emergency Services Database, find the article "Police Investigations of the Use of Deadly Force can Influence Perceptions and Outcomes": http://find.galegroup.com/gps/retrieve.do?contentSet=IAC-Documents&resultListType=RESULT_LIST&qrySerId=Locale%28en%2C%2C%29%3AFQE%3D%28ke%2CNone%2C21%29police+investigations%24&sgHitCountType=None&inPS=true&sort=DateDescend&searchType=BasicSearchForm&tabID=T003&prodId=IPS&searchId=R1¤tPosition=1&userGroupName=cpg3&docId=A217380889&docType=IAC&contentSet=IAC-Documents

  Assignment: Read and outline the article. Be prepared to discuss your outline in class.
- Using the Gale Emergency Services Database, find the article "Investigating the Social Web: New Training Helps Investigators Find Criminals and

Evidence on the Internet": http://find.galegroup.com/gps/retrieve.do?contentSet=IAC-Documents&resultListType=RESULT_LIST&qrySerId=Locale%28en%2C%2C%29%3AFQE%3D%28ke%2CNone%2C21%29police+investigations%24&sgHitCountType=None&inPS=true&sort=DateDescend&searchType=BasicSearchForm&tabID=T003&prodId=IPS&searchId=R1¤tPosition=2&userGroupName=cpg3&docId=A219013176&docType=IAC&contentSet=IAC-Documents

Assignment: Identify some of the emerging trends in social networking and how it relates to the future of law enforcement investigations. Be prepared to discuss your findings with the class.

- Using the Gale Emergency Services Database, find the article "Behavioral Profiling & Risk Assessment Using Written Communication" (Report): http://find.galegroup.com/gps/retrieve.do?contentSet=IAC-Documents&resultListType=RESULT_LIST&qrySerId=Locale%28en%2C%2C%29%3AFQE%3D%28ke%2CNone%2C18%29criminal+profiling%24&sgHitCountType=None&inPS=true&sort=DateDescend&searchType=BasicSearchForm&tabID=T002&prodId=IPS&searchId=R3¤tPosition=7&userGroupName=cpg3&docId=A189957240&docType=IAC&contentSet=IAC-Documents

  Assignment: How does this article relate to criminal profiling? Be prepared to discuss your thoughts with the class.

- Using the Gale Emergency Services Database, find the article "Four Legs, A Tail, and Lots of Heart: Police K-9's Really Are Something Special": http://find.galegroup.com/gps/retrieve.do?contentSet=IAC-Documents&resultListType=RESULT_LIST&qrySerId=Locale%28en%2C%2C%29%3AFQE%3D%28ke%2CNone%2C11%29police+dogs%24&sgHitCountType=None&inPS=true&sort=DateDescend&searchType=BasicSearchForm&tabID=T003&prodId=IPS&searchId=R7¤tPosition=5&userGroupName=cpg3&docId=A155671909&docType=IAC&contentSet=IAC-Documents

  Assignment: Read and outline the process of selecting a police K-9, considering the legal issues. Be prepared to discuss your outline with the class.

Internet Assignment

- Search for the key words "*undercover officer*," "*vice officer*," or "*internal affairs*." Find an article about this specialized area of law enforcement and outline it. Be prepared to discuss your outline with the class.

References

"Almost 50% of Agencies Routinely Use K9s." *Police*, March 2008, p.14.

Anand, Radhika. "Trends in Recording Police Interviews." *Law Enforcement Technology*, February 2008, pp.60–65.

Arnoldy, Ben. "High-Tech Police Tool Pinpoints Where a Gun Is Fired." *The Christian Science Monitor*, January 22, 2007.

Banda, P. Solomon. "Police Debate Use of Family DNA to ID Suspects." *Associated Press*, February 9, 2010.

Retrieved from http://www.msnbc.msn.com/id/35317812/ns/technology_and_science-science/

Basich, Melanie. "Teaching All Dogs New Tricks." *Police*, November 2009, pp.28–33.

Berson, Sarah B. "Debating DNA Collection." *NIJ Journal*, November 2009, pp.9–13.

Canons of Police Ethics. Washington, DC: International Association of Chiefs of Police, 1957.

Crime in the United States 2008. Washington, DC: Federal Bureau of Investigation, Uniform Crime Reports. Retrieved from http://www.fbi.gov/about-us/cjis/ucr/crime-in-the-u.s/2008

Dees, Tim. "Crime Mapping and Geographic Profiling." *Law Officer Magazine*, December 2008, pp.68–71.

Dwyer, Terrence P. "Police Liability and Litigation." *PoliceOne.com News*. February 24, 2010. Retrieved from http://www.policeone.com/legal/articles/2008924-Should-cops-be-required-to-submit-DNA-samples/

Evans, Fred. "NamUs.gov—New Centralized System for Finding the Missing and Identifying the Unknown." *The Police Chief*, December 2009, pp.104–105.

Feigin, Matthew. "Landmark NAS Report Questions Entire Basis of Forensic Sciences in U.S." *Subject to Debate*, April 2009, pp.3–5.

Ferguson, John. "Auxiliary Police . . . Just Add Training." *Law and Order*, April 2008, pp.87–90.

Gaertner, Susan, and Harrington, John. "Successful Eyewitness Identification Reform: Ramsey County's Blind Sequential Lineup Protocol." *The Police Chief*, April 2009, pp.130–141.

Galvin, Bob. "Getting the 'Big Picture.'" *Law Enforcement Technology*, October 2009, pp.68–75.

Gambling and Crime among Arrestees: Exploring the Link. Washington, DC: National Institute of Justice, July 2004. (NCJ 203197)

Garrett, Ronnie. "Data Mining Watch Dogs." *Law Enforcement Technology*, April 2007, p.8.

Garrett, Ronnie. "New DNA Testing Technique Pinpoints Hair, Eye and Skin Color." *Law Enforcement Technology*, July 2009, pp.51–57.

Geoghegan, Susan. "The Latest in Mobile AFIS." *Law and Order*, June 2008, pp.46–49.

Geoghegan, Susan. "Forensic DNA." *Law and Order*, June 2009, pp.49–53.

Griffith, David. "SWAT: Breaking the Mold." *Police*, August 2008, pp.50–57.

Grossi, Dave. "Going Under." *Law Officer Magazine*, April 2009, pp.24–28.

Hope, Christopher. "DNA-Profile Police to Prevent Crime Scene Contamination." Telegraph Media Group, April 11, 2008. Retrieved from http://www.telegraph.co.uk/news/uknews/1584683/DNA-profile-police-to-prevent-crime-scene-contamination.html

Increasing Efficiency in Crime Laboratories. Washington, DC: National Institute of Justice, January 2008.

Jetmore, Larry F. "The Oldest Profession: Investigating Street-Level Prostitution." *Law Officer*, October 2008, pp.92–96.

Johns, Susan, and Rushing, Patricia. "Using DNA to Solve Property Crimes." *Community Policing Dispatch*, December 2009.

Lee, Bob. "Psychic Detectives." *Law Officer Magazine*, August 2008, pp.54–65.

"Lesson from PERF Conference: Don't Just Denounce 'Stop Snitching': Understand It." *Subject to Debate*, March 2008, pp.1, 4.

Liptak, Adam. "Justices Reject Inmate Right to DNA Tests." *The New York Times*, June 18, 2009a. Retrieved from http://www.nytimes.com/2009/06/19/us/19scotus.html

Liptak, Adam. "Justices Rule Lab Analysts Must Testify on Results." *The New York Times*, June 25, 2009b. Retrieved from http://www.nytimes.com/2009/06/26/us/26lab.html

Moore, Solomon. "FBI and States Vastly Expand DNA Database." *The New York Times*, April 18, 2009a. Retrieved from http://www.nytimes.com/2009/04/19/us/19DNA.html

Moore, Solomon. "In a Lab, an Ever-Growing Database of DNA Profiles." *The New York Times*, May 12, 2009b. Retrieved from http://www.nytimes.com/2009/05/12/science/12quan.html

Norton, Leo M. "Who Goes There? Mobile Fingerprint Readers in Los Angeles County." *The Police Chief*, June 2009, pp.32–39.

Nyberg, Ramesh. "Blood from a Turnip." *Police*, October 2009, pp.64–69.

O'Brien, Bob. "Standardizing SWAT." *Police*, March 2009, pp.56–60.

Pearsall, Beth, and Weiss, Danielle. "Solving Missing Persons Cases." *NIJ Journal*, November 2009, pp.4–8.

Perin, Michelle. "HAZSWAT Changed?" *Law Enforcement Technology*, May 2009, pp.20–25.

Petrocelli, Joseph. "Patrol Response to Information and Tips." *Police*, December 2009a, p.16–19.

Petrocelli, Joseph. "Patrol Response to Street Prostitution." *Police*, February 2009b, pp.20–22.

Polski, Joseph. "IACP's Position: Forensic Science: A Critical Concern for Police Chiefs." *The Police Chief*, September 2009, pp.24–25.

Rutledge, Devallis. "Non-Custodial Stationhouse Interrogation." *Police*, January 2009, pp.62–65.

Schreiber, Sara. "Medics with Guns." *Law Enforcement Technology*, October 2009, pp.28–33.

Schuck, Jason. "Eyewitness Identifications: Determining the Admissibility." *LawOfficer.com*. April 25, 2009. Retrieved from http://www.lawofficer.com/article/needs-tags-columns/eyewitness-identifications

Scoville, Dean. "Can the Average Cop Survive in the Age of Specialization?" *Police*, May 2008, pp.44–49.

Scoville, Dean. "To Preserve and Protect." *Police*, February 2010, pp.34–40.

Shelton, Donald E. "The CSI Effect: Does It Really Exist?" *NIJ Journal*, March 2008, pp.1–8.

Spraggs, David. "The Eliminator." *Police*, March 2005, pp.36–40.

Spraggs, David. "Just a Touch." *Police*, December 2008, pp.26–29.

Standards and Guidelines for Internal Affair: Recommendations from a Community of Practice. Washington, DC: Office of Community Oriented Policing Services, August 21, 2009.

Strengthening Forensic Science in the United States: A Path Forward. Washington, DC: National Institute of Justice, August 2009. Retrieved from http://www.ncjrs.gov/pdffiles1/nij/grants/228091.pdf

2009 Innocence Project 2009 Annual Report. The Benjamin N. Cardozo School of Law at Yeshiva University. Retrieved from http://www.innocenceproject.org

Vernon, Bob. "Working Specialized Units: Potential Pitfalls to Avoid." *Law Officer Magazine*, February 2007, pp.58–59.

Vernon, Bob. "The Big Picture." *Law Officer Magazine*, February 2008, pp.54–55.

Wallentine, Ken. "Collection of DNA upon Arrest: Expanding Investigative Frontiers." *The Police Chief*, January 2010, pp.12–13.

Wethal, Tabatha. "Flawed Forensics?" *Law Enforcement Technology*, July 2009, pp.28–34.

Cases Cited

California v. Beheler, 463 U.S. 1121 (1983)

District Attorney's Office for the Third Judicial District v. Osborne, 557 U.S. ___ (2009)

Garrity v. New Jersey, 385 U.S. 493 (1967)

Neil v. Biggers, 409 U.S. 188 (1972)

United States v. Ash, Jr., 413 U.S. 300 (1973)

United States v. Place, 462 U.S. 696 (1983)

United States v. Sokolow, 490 U.S. 1 (1989)

CHAPTER 7

Policing after 9/11: Traditional, Community and Data-Driven Policing

> Data-driven approaches to resource allocation should become a common practice within the law enforcement industry.
>
> —Mike Brown, Former Commissioner of the California Highway Patrol

Graffiti on Kenmore Avenue, just north of Pico Blvd. in the Mid-City area of Los Angeles. It shows the initials of the local gang, PBS, which stands for Playboys Gang, and some of the individual gang members' names.

Do You Know . . .

- What five broad strategic or organizational approaches currently operating in contemporary policing are?
- How U.S. citizens established the "public peace"?
- What the two critical key elements of community policing are?
- How public and private law enforcement differ?
- What the most important consideration in selecting strategies to implement community policing is?
- Which means more during evaluation—failures or successes?
- What problem solving requires of the police?
- What four strategies are involved in the SARA model of problem-solving policing?
- What three data-driven strategies for policing currently being used are?
- What the four principles of CompStat are?
- What the 3-I model of intelligence-led policing consists of?
- Who may be valuable partners in evidence-based policing?
- What role failure plays in evidence-based policing?

Can You Define?

American Dream
bowling-alone phenomenon
broken-window phenomenon
community policing
CompStat policing
demographics
evidence-based policing (EBP)
fusion center
incident
incivilities
integrated patrol
intelligence-led policing (ILP)
medical model
meta-analysis
participatory leadership
problem-solving policing
SARA model
social capital
social contract
symbiotic relationship

INTRODUCTION

Chapter 1 introduced an emerging fourth era of policing—data-driven policing—which not only retains the key elements of traditional, professional policing—random patrol, rapid response, and reactive investigations—but combines them with the essential elements of community policing—partnerships, problem solving and prevention. The emergence of this fourth era of policing can be traced directly to one event: the September 11, 2001 (9/11) terrorist attacks on the United States (Beck and McCue, 2009, p.18). This single event has led to a paradigm shift in policing, dramatically altering the importance placed on information sharing and fostering a variety of data-driven approaches to policing.

In September 2009 the NIJ and the Harvard Kennedy School held an Executive Session on Policing and Public Safety, offering *New Perspectives in Policing* (Sparrow, 2009). This session focused on five broad strategic or organizational approaches currently found in post-9/11 policing.

Five broad strategic or organizational approaches currently operating in contemporary policing are community policing, problem-solving policing, CompStat policing, intelligence-led policing and evidence-based policing.

Sparrow (2009) notes, "Police departments across the United States vary in how many of these approaches they have embraced and which ones. Moreover, implementations of any one of these strategies vary enormously from jurisdiction to jurisdiction and over time. As implementations mature, they tend to become more versatile and better adapted to local circumstances, departing from more standardized models originally imported or copied from other jurisdictions."

The impact of 9/11 on the organizational development of state and local law enforcement agencies resulted in a renewed focus on community policing and problem solving policing as well as on other data-driven models. The overlap and interplay of these approaches is apparent, yet each approach offers its own contribution to policing and challenges to those who manage and lead within their agencies. In addition, the professional model continues to thrive alongside these strategies in most departments, responding to calls and fighting crime.

THE CHAPTER AT A GLANCE

This chapter looks at these five strategies currently operating, most often in some combination, in departments throughout the county. The chapter begins with a discussion of community policing and then turns to problem-solving policing, which may or may not involve the community and may or may not be data driven. The third area of discussion, CompStat-policing, like community policing and problem-solving policing, began before the events of 9/11, but continues to be embraced by many departments and has had a profound effect on the next two strategies discussed and that now dominate the literature: intelligence-led and evidence-based policing. The chapter concludes with a look at two specific initiatives—Target's Safe City Program and Data-Driven Approaches to Crime and Traffic Safety (DDACTS)—that use partnerships between police and citizens to more effectively and efficiently deploy law enforcement resources and create safe communities.

CONTEMPORARY COMMUNITY POLICING

community policing

A philosophy that emphasizes a problem-solving partnership between the police and the citizens in working toward a healthy, crime-free environment; also called *neighborhood policing*.

Since the 1980s, community policing has been a dominant innovation in American policing (Connell et al., 2008). "**Community policing** is an organization-wide philosophy and management approach that promotes community, government, and police partnerships; proactive problem solving; and community engagement to address the causes of crime, fear of crime and other community issues" (Upper Midwest Community Policing Institute, n.d., bold added). Community policing stresses working proactively in partnership with citizens to prevent crime and to solve crime-related problems.

Although community policing is considered innovative, recall from Chapter 1 that its roots can be found in the Anglo-Saxon tithing system establishing the principle of collective responsibility for maintaining local law and order and in the Norman Frankpledge system requiring all freemen to swear loyalty to the king's law and to take responsibility for maintaining the local peace. The importance of citizens in maintaining the peace was also recognized by Sir Robert Peel in 1829, whose central tenets of involvement with and responsiveness to the community were clearly stated when he asserted, "The police are the public and the public are the police."

The opening sentence of the American Creed, adopted by the House of Representatives on April 3, 1918, uses language attributed to Abraham Lincoln in his address at Gettysburg on November 19, 1863: "We here highly resolve that these dead shall not have died in vain; that this nation, under God, shall have a new birth of freedom; and that government of the people, by the people, and for the people, shall not perish from the earth." The philosophy implicit in the American Creed is central to the concept of "community" in the United States. Each community is part of a larger social order.

The U.S. Constitution and Bill of Rights, as well as federal and state statutes and local ordinances, establish the "public peace" in the United States.

Americans established a criminal justice system in an effort to live in "peace," free from fear, crime and violence. To ensure the peace, U.S. citizens have also entered into an unwritten **social contract**, which stipulates that for everyone to receive justice, each person must relinquish some freedom.

social contract
Provides that for everyone to receive justice, each person must relinquish some freedom.

In civilized society, people cannot simply do as they please. They are expected to conform to federal and state laws as well as to local rules and regulations established by and for the community in which they live. Increased mobility and economic factors have weakened the informal social contract that once helped to keep the peace. As a result, the police, as agents of social control, have had to fill the breach, increasing the need for law-abiding citizens to join with the police in making their communities free from fear, drugs, crime and terrorism.

The Importance of Community

Community has many definitions. It can refer to a social group or class having common interests. Community may even refer to society as a whole—the public. This text uses a specific, admittedly simplistic, meaning for community. *Community* refers to the specific geographic area served by a police department or law enforcement agency and the individuals, organizations and agencies within that area.

Police officers must understand and be a part of this defined community if they are to fulfill their mission. The community may cover a small area with a limited number of citizens, organizations and agencies, perhaps policed by a single officer. Or the community may cover a vast area, have thousands of individuals and hundreds of organizations and agencies, and be policed by several hundred officers. And although police jurisdiction and delivery of services are based on geographic boundaries, a community is much more than a group of neighborhoods administered by a local government. The schools, businesses, public and private agencies, churches and social groups are vital elements of the community.

Also of importance are the individual values, concerns and cultural principles of the people living and working in the community and the common interests they share with neighbors. Where integrated communities exist, people share a sense of ownership and pride in their environment. They also have a sense of what is acceptable behavior, which makes policing in such a community much easier. Community also refers to a feeling of belonging—a sense of integration, a sense of shared values and a sense of "we-ness." Research strongly suggests that a sense of community is the "glue" that binds communities to maintain order and provides the foundation for effective community action.

social capital
The bond among family members and their immediate, informal groups as well as the networks tying individuals to broader community institutions, such as schools, civic organizations and churches, and to various levels of government, including the police.

Social Capital Communities might also be looked at in terms of their **social capital**, a concept developed by Coleman (1990, p.302) and defined as "A variety of different entities having two characteristics in common: They all consist of some aspect of a social structure, and they facilitate certain actions of individuals who are within the structure."

Social capital exists at two levels: local and public. *Local social capital* is the bond among family members and their immediate, informal groups. *Public social capital* refers to the networks tying individuals to broader community institutions, such as schools, civic organizations, churches and the like, as well as to networks linking individuals to various levels of government—including the police. The greater the social capital, the greater the sense of community. Unfortunately, many neighborhoods lack this sense of community.

Sociologists have described for decades the loss or breakdown of "community" in modern, technological, industrial, urban societies such as ours. A community is not healthy if unemployment and poverty are widespread, people are hungry, health care is inadequate, prejudice separates people, preschool children lack proper care and nutrition, senior citizens are allowed to atrophy, schools remain isolated and remote, social services are fragmented and disproportionate, and government lacks responsibility and accountability.

A factor that negates a sense of community is the prevalence of violence. We live in a violent society. The United States was born through a violent revolution. The media emphasizes violence, constantly carrying news of murder, rape and assault. Even children's cartoons contain more violence than most adults realize and teach children that violence is acceptable and justified. Citizens expect the police to prevent violence, but the police cannot do it alone. Individuals must come together to help stop violence and in so doing can build a sense of community.

Putnam's 1995 exploration of social capital in America, entitled "Bowling Alone," described a drastic decline in league bowling and proposed that this seemingly minor observation actually reflected a striking drop in social capital and civic engagement—dubbed the **bowling-alone phenomenon**—in the United States that had begun in the 1960s. The article caused fierce academic debate and prompted Putnam to study the issue in depth. Extensive research supported his central thesis that, during the period from the 1960s to 2000, Americans had become increasingly isolated from family, friends and neighbors.

bowling-alone phenomenon

Refers to a striking decline in social capital and civic engagement in the United States.

In *Bowling Alone: The Collapse and Revival of American Community* (2000), Putnam draws on evidence from nearly 60,000 interviews over the past 25 years to show that we sign fewer petitions, belong to fewer organizations that meet, know our neighbors less, meet with friends less frequently and even socialize with our families less often. Several possible reasons for this decline include changes in family structure (more people living alone); electronic entertainment; and, perhaps most important, generational change (Putnam). The "civic" generation born in the first third of the 20th century is being replaced by baby boomers and Generation X-ers, who have been characterized as being much less civic minded.

In a classic article, "The Police and Neighborhood Safety: Broken Windows," Wilson and Kelling (1982, p.31) contend,

> Social psychologists and police officers tend to agree that if a window in a building is broken and is left unrepaired, all the rest of the windows will soon be broken. This is as true in nice neighborhoods as in run-down ones. Window-breaking does not necessarily occur on a large scale because some areas are inhabited by

determined window-breakers whereas others are populated by window-lovers; rather, one unrepaired broken window is a signal that no one cares, and so breaking more windows costs nothing. (It has always been fun.)

The **broken-window phenomenon** suggests that if it appears "no one cares," disorder and crime will thrive. Wilson and Kelling based their broken-window theory partly on research done in 1969 by a Stanford psychologist, Philip Zimbardo. Zimbardo arranged to have a car without license plates parked with its hood up on a street in the Bronx and a comparable car on a street in Palo Alto, California. The car in the Bronx was attacked by vandals within 10 minutes, and within 24 hours it had been totally destroyed and stripped of anything of value. The car in Palo Alto sat untouched. After a week Zimbardo took a sledgehammer to it. People passing by soon joined in, and within a few hours that car was also totally destroyed: "Untended property becomes fair game for people out for fun or plunder, and even for people who ordinarily would not dream of doing such things and who probably consider themselves as law-abiding" (Wilson and Kelling, 1982, p.31).

broken-window phenomenon
Maintains that if a neighborhood is allowed to run down, it will give the impression that no one cares and crime will flourish.

Broken windows and trashed cars are very visible signs of people not caring about their community. Other more subtle signs include unmowed lawns, piles of accumulated trash, litter, graffiti, abandoned buildings, rowdiness, drunkenness, fighting and prostitution, often referred to as **incivilities**. Incivilities and social disorder occur when social control mechanisms have eroded. A rise in incivilities may increase the fear of crime and reduce citizens' sense of safety. They may physically or psychologically withdraw, isolating themselves from their neighbors. Or increased incivilities and disorder may bring people together to "take back the neighborhood."

incivilities
Visible signs of people not caring about their community, for example, broken windows, unmowed lawns, piles of accumulated trash, litter, graffiti, abandoned buildings, rowdiness, drunkenness, fighting and prostitution.

For departments wishing to implement the community policing philosophy, it is critical to understand how our population has changed in recent generations.

Serving and Protecting Our Increasingly Diverse Population

Our society has changed tremendously over the past decades, as have the challenges facing law enforcement. Technology has made the task easier, but the increasing diversity of our population has made it more difficult. **Demographics** refers to the characteristics of the individuals who live in a community and include a population's size, distribution, growth, density, employment rate, ethnic makeup and vital statistics such as average age, education and income.

demographics
Refers to the characteristics of the individuals who live in a community, including a population's size, distribution, growth, density, employment rate, ethnic makeup and vital statistics such as average age, education and income.

Although people generally assume that the smaller the population of a community, the easier policing becomes, this is not necessarily true. Small communities generally have fewer resources. It is also difficult being the sole law enforcement person, in effect on call 24 hours a day. A major advantage of a smaller community is that people know each other. A sense of community is likely to be greater in such communities than in large cities such as Chicago or New York.

When assessing law enforcement's ability to police an area, density of population is an important variable. Studies have shown that as population becomes denser, people become more aggressive. In densely populated areas, people become more territorial and argue more frequently about "turf." Rapid population growth can invigorate a community, or it can drain its limited resources. Without effective planning and foresight, rapid population growth can result in serious problems for a community, especially if the population growth results from an influx of immigrants or members of an ethnic group different from the majority in that area.

The community's makeup is extremely important from a police–community partnership perspective. For example, what is the average age? Are there more young or elderly individuals? How many single-parent families are there? What is the divorce rate? What is the common level of education? How does the education of those in law enforcement compare? What is the school dropout rate? Do gangs operate in the community?

Income and income distribution are also important. Do great economic disparities exist? Would the community be described as affluent, moderately well off or poor? How does the income of those in law enforcement compare to the average income? Closely related to income is the level of employment. What is the ratio of blue-collar to professional workers? How much unemployment exists? How do those who are unemployed exist? Are they on welfare? Do they commit crimes to survive? Are they homeless?

The ethnic makeup of the community is another consideration. Is the community basically homogeneous? A *homogeneous* community is one in which people are all quite similar. A *heterogeneous* community, in contrast, is one in which individuals are quite different from each other. Most communities are heterogeneous. Establishing and maintaining good relations among the various subgroups making up the community is a challenge. Usually one ethnic subgroup will have the most power and control. Consider the consequences if a majority of police officers are also members of this ethnic subgroup.

Our elderly population is increasing rapidly, as is our minority population. In addition, hundreds of thousands of immigrants are pouring into the United States, a great many of whom speak no English. The gap between those who live in poverty and those who are more affluent is widening; the homeless population is growing at an alarming rate; and the number of people with infectious diseases is escalating. Each of these populations presents a challenge to police.

American Dream

Belief that anyone who works hard and is willing to sacrifice for a while can be successful.

In addition, the **American Dream**, that anyone can succeed through hard work and sacrifice, is becoming much more difficult to attain, not only for members of minority groups but also for middle-class people of all ethnic and racial backgrounds. This widening gap and the increase in the number of people surviving below the poverty line translates into potentially more theft and the types of violence that accompany offenses motivated by economic gain. At the same time that many corporate executives are being paid millions of dollars economic criminals such as Bernard Madoff are perpetrating Ponzi schemes involving millions, sometimes billions of dollar, and defraud hard-working, honest American citizens, shattering their dreams of a secure future. In addition, professional sports figures sign million-dollar contracts while many Americans are losing their jobs because of the economic downturn since 2008. The continued decline of the economy and an increasing gap between social classes may result in an increased crime rate as well.

Just as it is important for police to understand the diverse population they serve and protect, it is also is also important for the police to help citizens understand what police do and why they do it.

Involving and Educating Citizens

Community members often have great interest in their local police departments and have been involved in a variety of ways for many years. This involvement, though it accomplishes important contacts, should not be mistaken for community policing. Citizen involvement in the law enforcement community and in understanding policing has taken the form of civilian review boards, citizen patrols, citizen police academies, ride-alongs and similar programs.

Civilian Review Boards Civilian review boards have been used in the United States since the mid-1950s. A civilian review board consists of citizens who meet to review complaints filed against the police department or against individual officers. The movement for citizen review has been a major political struggle for more than 40 years and remains one of the most controversial issues in police work today.

Supporters of civilian review boards believe it is impossible for the police to objectively review actions of their colleagues and emphasize that the police culture demands that police officers support each other, even if they know something illegal has occurred. Opponents of civilian review boards stress that civilians cannot possibly understand the complexities of the policing profession and that it is demeaning to be reviewed by an external source. Many police administrators today still resist such "interference by outsiders," asserting that their jobs are tough enough without having civilian review boards constantly looking over their shoulders. Police leaders insist that only police officers can understand and judge the actions of other officers and that civilian oversight diminishes police morale and impedes officer performance.

An alternative to civilian review boards, a civilian ombudsman, has been used successfully in several jurisdictions. A community ombudsman provides a liaison between police and residents and makes policy recommendations to the police, mayor and city council.

Citizen Patrols Community policing is rooted in law enforcement's dependence on the public's eyes, ears, information and influence to exert social control. Citizen patrols are not new. The sheriffs' posses that handled law enforcement in America's Wild West have evolved to present-day citizen patrols, reserve police programs and neighborhood watch groups. Some citizen patrols have formed as part of partnerships with the local police department, some independent of police partnerships and some in the face of police opposition. It is often difficult for citizen volunteers to win the respect, trust and support of the police. Police frequently have strong opinions about civilian involvement in what they consider police business or see them as critics of department efforts.

Many citizen patrols established throughout the country focus on the drug problem. Some citizen groups have exchange programs to reduce the chance of retribution by local drug retailers. Such exchange programs provide nearby neighborhoods with additional patrols while reducing the danger because local dealers are less likely to recognize a vigil-keeper who lives in another neighborhood.

Citizen Police Academies Another type of community involvement is through citizens' police academies designed to familiarize citizens with law enforcement and to keep the department in touch with the community. Police academies, while popular with police departments and citizens, have the benefits of building community support for law enforcement and of helping citizens understand the police.

The first recorded U.S. citizen police academy began in 1985 in Orlando, Florida, and was modeled after a citizen police academy founded in England in 1977. Such academies help a community's residents become more familiar with their police department's daily operations and understand the procedures, responsibilities and demands placed on their officers.

Citizen police academies are not without limitations. First, even if attendees sign hold-harmless waivers, the agency may still be sued if a participant is injured or killed while attending the academy. Second, officers and administrators may resist an academy, feeling law enforcement activities should not be open to the public. Third, an agency may feel its resources could be better used.

Ride-Along Programs Ride-along programs are a popular yet controversial means to improve police-community relations and get citizens involved in the efforts of the department and its officers. These programs are designed to give local citizens a close-up look at the realities of policing and what police work entails while giving officers a chance to connect with citizens in a positive way.

Many ride-along programs permit any responsible juvenile or adult to participate, but other programs have restrictions and may limit ridership. Participation by officers in a ride-along program is usually voluntary. Whether riders are allowed to use still or video cameras during a ride-along varies by department. Many departments also require their riders to dress appropriately.

Despite the numerous benefits of ride-along programs, some departments do not get involved for legitimate reasons such as insurance costs, liability and concerns about the public's safety. Some departments ask participants to sign a waiver exempting the officer, the department and the city from liability.

Citizen involvement in understanding and helping to police their communities is important, but it in itself is *not* community policing. At the heart of the community policing philosophy is an emphasis on partnerships and on problem solving.

The two critical key elements of community policing are partnerships and problem solving.

Partnerships

Community partnerships are crucial for police agencies serious about community policing. Community policing cannot succeed without them. Collaborations may be with businesses, schools, youths, residents, organizations, the media, private security and other government agencies, depending on the problem and who the stakeholders are.

Traditional policing expected community members to remain in the background. Crime and disorder were viewed as police matters, best left to professionals. That meant most citizen–police interactions were *negative contacts.* After all, people do not call the police when things are going well. Citizens' only opportunity to interact with officers was as a victim of crime, as being involved in some other emergency situation or as the subject of some enforcement action such as receiving a traffic ticket.

Partnerships usually result in a more effective solution to a problem because of the shared responsibilities, resources and goals. They also foster a shared feeling of ownership through having a vested interest in the matter. Police/public partnerships exist on two levels. On a more passive level, the community assumes a compliant role and shows support for law and order by what they *do not* do—they do not interfere with routine police activities and they do not themselves engage in conduct that disrupts the public peace.

On an active level, citizens step beyond their daily law-abiding lives and get directly involved in projects, programs and other specific efforts to enhance their community's safety. Such participation may include neighborhood block watches, citizen crime patrols and youth-oriented educational and recreational programs. Citizens may respond independently or form groups, perhaps collaborating with the local police department.

However, today's heterogeneous communities often foster differing and conflicting interests, which are sometimes represented by competing interest groups. Clashes may result between the elderly and the youths within a community or between various ethnic and cultural groups within a neighborhood.

To be successful, several components of a partnership or collaboration are necessary, as illustrated in Figure 7.1.

The September 11, 2001, terrorist attacks on the United States, while unquestionably horrific and devastating, had a positive effect by bringing even the most

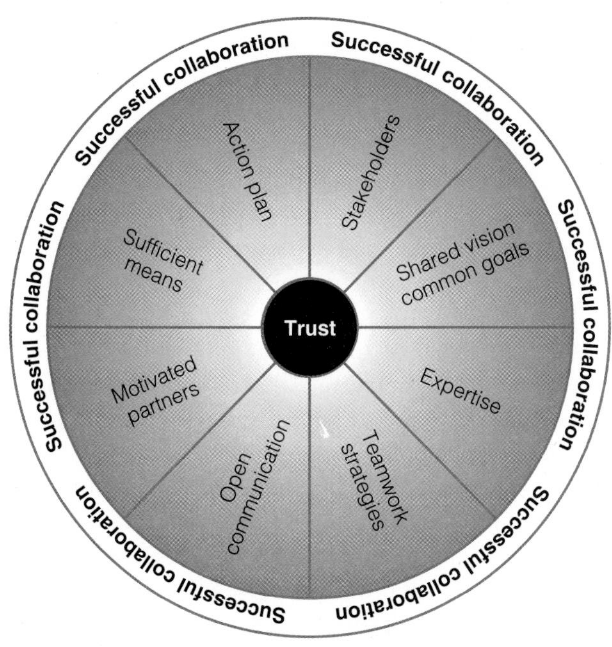

FIGURE 7.1 Core Components of a Successful Collaboration/Partnership

SOURCE: Tammy A. Rinehart, Anna T. Laszlo, and Gwen O. Briscoe. *Collaboration Toolkit: How to Build, Fix and Sustain Productive Partnerships.* Washington, DC: U.S. Department of Justice, Office of Community Oriented Policing Services, 2001, p.7.

diverse, fragmented communities together in ways rarely seen before. The government's appeal to the nation's public to become "soldiers" in the effort to preserve the American way of life and to be increasingly vigilant about activities occurring in their neighborhoods is a direct application of the community policing philosophy. Everyone is made to feel they have a part to play, an implicit responsibility, in keeping themselves, their communities and their country safe from harm.

Law enforcement can also partner with local businesses to help combat community problems. Various partnerships may be formed to tackle specific community crime problems. For example, in the City Heights area of San Diego, a neighborhood challenged by a culturally diverse population, widespread poverty and a violent crime rate more than double the citywide average, local residents identified drug-related crime and juvenile delinquency as their primary concerns. Partnering members of law enforcement with community members was considered a potential solution to these problems.

The community benefits from partnerships by a commitment to crime prevention, public scrutiny of police operations, accountability to the public, customized police service and involvement of community organizations. The police benefit by greater citizen support and increased respect, shared responsibility and greater job satisfaction.

medical model

In corrections, assumes criminals are victims of society and need to be "cured."

Partnerships are also a focal point of the **medical model** sometimes used to explain the relationship between the police and the community. In this model, patients are primarily responsible for their own health, with physicians advising patients on how to be healthy, as well as assisting when health problems arise. So, too, in the community citizens are responsible for public safety and keeping their neighborhoods healthy, and they cannot expect the police to take sole responsibility for it. In this community wellness concept, the police and the public share responsibility for the causes of crime, the fear of crime and actual crime.

Another aspect of the medical model is an emphasis on prevention rather than cure, on being proactive rather than reactive and on treating causes rather than symptoms. The medical profession has found that rather than investing all its resources in curing disease, it is more effective in preventing disease in the first place. Such prevention requires the skill and expertise of the professional, as well as the willing, responsible cooperation of the patient.

Partnerships with Private Security In years past, much competition and animosity existed between public and private police. Public law enforcement officers regarded private security personnel as police "wannabees," and those in the private sector considered public police officers ego-inflated crime fighters who often held themselves to be above the law. Recently, however, these two groups have learned to work together to ensure the common goal of public safety.

Since the attacks of September 11, 2001, law enforcement–private security partnerships have been viewed as critical to preventing terrorism and terror-related acts. The private sector owns and protects 85 percent of the nation's infrastructure; local law enforcement, on the other hand, often possesses threat information regarding these infrastructures. Thus, a law enforcement–private security partnership can put vital information into the hands of the people who need it most. To effectively protect the nation's infrastructure, law enforcement and private security must work together because, alone, neither possesses the necessary resources to do the job adequately. For private security and law enforcement to collaborate effectively, it is critical that they understand each others' authority and responsibilities.

Private security forces include guards, patrols, investigators, armed couriers, central alarm respondents and consultants. Private security agencies and their officers perform many of the same functions as police and other government law enforcement agencies and their officers: They control entrances and exits to facilities; promote safety and security inside government buildings, courthouses and airports; safeguard equipment, valuables and confidential material; prevent and report fires and other property damage; and patrol restricted areas. Businesses and educational, industrial and commercial organizations often hire private security guards to protect their premises and investments. In addition, police agencies commonly subcontract with private companies and labs for evidence testing, fingerprint and handwriting analysis and applicant screening.

There are, however, important differences between private security officers and police officers. Police officers are salaried with public funds, responsible to a chief of police and ultimately accountable to the community's citizens. Technically they are on duty 24 hours a day and have full authority to enforce all laws and protect all people and property, including the authority to make arrests and to carry a concealed weapon. Still police officers cannot be everywhere. Therefore, many businesses and organizations have elected to hire special protection.

Private security officers differ from police officers in that private security officers are salaried with private funds, are responsible to an employer and have limited authority extending to only the premises they are hired to guard. Security officers have no authority to carry concealed weapons, although they can carry unconcealed weapons, and, unless deputized, they have no authority to make arrests except as a citizen's arrest.

Many benefits to law enforcement may be realized through partnerships with private security. While usually complementing law enforcement efforts, private security officers can assist in responding to burglar alarms, investigating internal theft and economic crimes, protecting VIPs and executives, moving hazardous materials, and controlling crowds and traffic for public events. Private policing, or privatization, also has an advantage in that security officers are not bound by many constraints of public police officers, such as having to give the *Miranda* warning to suspects. Furthermore, private-sector development of police stations, sheriffs' stations and jails is being advocated as an option for replacing outdated facilities.

It should be noted however that in dealing with public safety, the likelihood of liability is high. Private sector officers are not afforded the same protections as public officers, and they often times are dealing with high liability incidents with little training or support from their agencies. Furthermore, the private sector answers to private management, who may not understand the dynamics of public safety.

School/Law Enforcement/Community Partnerships Table 7.1 summarizes the differences between traditional policing in the schools and community policing in the schools. One of the oldest and most commonly used partnerships is assigning police officers to schools—the school resource officer (SRO).

TABLE 7.1 Comparison between Traditional and Community Policing in Schools

Traditional Policing in Schools	Community Policing in Schools
Reactive response to 911 calls	Problem oriented
	Ongoing school–law enforcement partnership to address problems of concern to educators, students and parents
Incident driven	
Minimal school–law enforcement interaction, often characterized by an "us vs. them" mentality	Police role extended beyond law enforcement to include prevention and early intervention activities
Police role limited to law enforcement	Educators, students and parents are active partners in developing solutions
Police viewed as source of the solution	Partners value information sharing as an important problem-solving tool
Educators and law enforcement officers reluctant to share information	Consistent responses to incidents is ensured— administrative and criminal, as appropriate
Criminal incidents subject to inadequate response; criminal consequences imposed only when incidents reported to police	Law enforcement presence viewed as taking a positive, proactive step to create orderly, safe and secure schools
Law enforcement presence viewed as indicator of failure	Policing effectiveness measured by the absence of crime and disorder
Police effectiveness measured by arrest rates, response times, calls for service, etc.	

SOURCE: Anne J. Atkinson. *Fostering School-Law Enforcement Partnerships.* Portland, OR: Northwest Regional Educational Laboratory, September 2002, p.7. Reprinted by permission.

© Joel Gordon

School resource officers (SROs) are law enforcement officers assigned to the school "community" to serve in a proactive capacity and to promote a safe, orderly educational environment.

Partnerships with the Media The media can be a powerful ally or a formidable opponent in implementing the community policing philosophy. The press can shape public opinion, and most police agencies are concerned about their public image. Positive publicity can enhance both the image and the efforts of a department. Conversely, negative publicity can be extremely damaging. Therefore, police agencies can and should make every effort to build positive working partnerships with the media.

The police and the media share a **symbiotic relationship**; they are mutually dependent on each other. The police and members of the media share the common goal of serving the public.

symbiotic relationship
Mutually dependent on each other.

Police departments and individual officers rely on the press to disseminate vital public safety information to the community and to reach out to the community for help in solving cases. At the same time, reporters rely on the police for information to provide to their readers and viewers. Administrators know that crime and police activities are covered by the media regardless of whether the police provide reporters with information. Most police departments understand that the level of police cooperation with the media will ultimately affect how the public views the police.

Understanding the relationship between the police and the media starts with being aware of what rights the media have, what their mission is and why law enforcement does not always appear in a positive light in the media. The First Amendment to the U.S. Constitution states: "Congress shall make no law . . . abridging the freedom of speech or of the press." The free flow of information is a fundamental right in our society. The First Amendment to the U.S. Constitution guarantees the public's right to know—that is, freedom of the press.

Our society deems the public's right to know so important that the media operate without censorship but are subject to legal action if they publish untruths. The courts have usually stood behind journalists who act reasonably to get information, but they also have upheld the privacy protections fundamental under the Fourth Amendment.

In addition, the Sixth Amendment to our Constitution establishes that "in all criminal prosecutions, the accused shall enjoy the right to a speedy and public trial, by an impartial jury of the state and district wherein the crime shall have been committed." Police officers, responsible for investigating crimes that suspects are accused of committing, sometimes view reporters as an impediment to fulfilling their duties. Law enforcement officers often try to protect information they deem imperative to keep out of the media and may therefore be at odds with reporters. Such conflicts arise when police try to prevent public disclosure of information that may tip off a criminal of impending arrest, make prosecution of a particular crime impossible or compromise privacy rights or safety of a victim or witness. Reporters are eager to do well on their assignments, whereas officers try to avoid weakening their case and reprimands for being too open with the press. The parties' conflicting interests may result in antagonism.

To improve police–media relations, the press should be informed of a department's policies and procedures regarding the media and crime scenes. Officers should avoid police jargon and technical terminology and respect reporters' deadlines by releasing information in a timely manner so the press has a chance to fully

CAREER PROFILE

Penny A. Parrish (Communications Instructor, FBI Academy)

When students consider a career in law enforcement, they are usually thinking about sworn positions, such as officers, deputies, troopers or agents. But there is another exciting aspect to this profession: the civilian or support employee. I am fortunate to be a part of this group that also serves the public good.

I am currently a member of the Federal Bureau of Investigation (FBI), working as an instructor at the FBI Academy in Quantico, Virginia. Since 1999 I've taught communication skills and media relations to police officers in the National Academy program. That program brings together law enforcement leaders from throughout the United States and from several foreign countries for an intensive 10-week school. We offer four of these sessions each year, with 300 students in each session. The FBI Academy is considered the premiere law enforcement training venue in the world, and I am honored to be an instructor here.

My journey here took a rather circuitous route. I had spent most of my professional career as a television journalist, beginning as a reporter in a small town in Florida and working my way up as a producer, managing editor and finally news director at a station in Minneapolis, Minnesota. For nearly a decade, I ran a newsroom there in the 15th-largest TV market in the country.

During this time I often found myself trying to referee arguments or controversy between my reporters or photographers and local cops. There were issues of access to crime scene areas or getting timely information, and I found myself wanting to know more about the criminal justice process and profession. So I enrolled in the law enforcement program at Normandale Community College (Bloomington, Minnesota), initially intending to take just one or two courses, but I found the field fascinating and kept registering for more classes. Over a period of three years I basically ran my newsroom during the day and attended classes at night. A progressive and forward-thinking police chief even allowed me to serve an internship with his department, which is not something most working journalists get to do. All of this culminated in the receipt of my associate's degree, of which I am very proud.

I knew by this time that I wanted to work *with* law enforcement agencies on media issues. I wanted to help both officers and the media better understand each other and work together for the benefit of the public. With that goal in mind, I left the television station and searched for a position in my new field. I found it with the Minneapolis Police Department in their newly created job of public information officer (PIO). They were looking for a former journalist with some law enforcement background or experience to help the department more effectively get information to citizens through various media outlets. I applied, went through a rigorous test and interview, and was hired in July of 1993.

Coming in to a large metropolitan police department as a female, a civilian and a former member of the media is a daunting task. There were major issues of trust to overcome. I still had a lot to learn about the criminal justice system in general and that department in particular. It was a steep learning curve, very different from classroom preparation. I figure it took me one whole year to earn the respect of the officers so that they would come to me when they needed help with media issues.

Those 6 years in local law enforcement, combined with my time as a journalist, are the reasons I was chosen for my current position. In my unit at the FBI Academy, there are three civilian instructors who regularly teach sworn personnel. We have decades of practical experience in our fields to share, and we are respected for our knowledge and teaching skills. Students who graduate stay in touch and invite us to hold "road schools" in their towns or states. It is a wonderful way to combine teaching and travel opportunities.

The rewards of my job are great, but there are always challenges. Officers and journalists have different goals and serve different purposes in our society, and in times of crisis it can be hard to reconcile those. Furthermore, law enforcement has not kept up with the media profession when it comes to technology. At the Academy we're teaching about streaming video or news-on-demand when we don't even have access to some of these things on our FBI computers. But overall, this position is my dream job. I get to work with the finest law enforcement professionals in the world. Who could ask for a better career?

More and more law enforcement agencies are turning to civilian personnel to augment or supplement duties held by sworn officers. It makes sense: Keep those who are in uniform on the street and bring in civilian subject-matter experts to assist them. Therefore, when you're looking at a career in this fascinating field, consider the role played by support personnel as well.

understand the situation. As police departments adopt the community policing philosophy and implement its strategies, public support is vital. The media can play an important role in obtaining that support—or losing it.

Instead police were to incorporate problem-oriented policing techniques into their approach, they would examine the conditions underlying the problem. This would likely include collecting additional information—perhaps by surveying neighborhood residents and park users, analyzing the time of day when incidents occur and determining who the offenders are.

Changes in Management Style and Organization

Community policing usually requires a different management style. The traditional autocratic style effective during the industrial age will not have the same effect in the 21st century. One viable alternative to the autocratic style of management is participatory leadership. In **participatory leadership** each individual has a voice in decisions, but top management still has the ultimate decision-making authority.

participatory leadership
Each individual has a voice in decisions, but top management retains the ultimate decision-making authority.

The leader must also have a vision for the department and the community. This vision should include the essential elements of the community policing philosophy: problem solving, empowering everyone, forming community partnerships and being proactive—making preventing crime as important as enforcing the law. Changes in the organization usually include the following:

- The bureaucracy is flattened and decentralized.
- Roles of those in management positions change to being leaders and mentors rather than managers and supervisors.
- Patrol officers are given new responsibilities and are empowered to make decisions and problem solve with their community partners.
- Permanent shifts and areas are assigned.
- Despecialization reduces the number of specialized units, channeling more resources toward the direct delivery of police services to the public.
- Teams improve efficiency and effectiveness by pooling officer resources in groups.
- Civilianization replaces sworn personnel with nonsworn personnel to maximize cost effectiveness; reassigning sworn personnel to where they are most needed.

The most important consideration in selecting strategies to implement community policing is to ensure that the strategies fit a community's unique needs and resources.

Table 7.2 provides a sample of common policing strategies that should be linked to organizational change and problem-solving efforts, discussed in greater depth later in the chapter.

If community policing is successfully implemented, several benefits might be anticipated.

Potential Benefits of Community Policing

The benefits of implementing community policing are numerous, both to the department and to the community at large. Community policing brings police closer to the people, building relationships between police and community and

TABLE 7.2 Common Community Policing Strategies

For community policing to work best, these (and other) individual strategies should be linked by a broad organizational commitment to the community policing philosophy.

Community Partnership	Organizational Change	Problem-Solving
Post crime information on police web sites	Assign officers to specific geographic locations for extended periods	Conduct community surveys to identify problems and evaluate performance
Hold regular meetings with local businesses	Build principles into recruitment activities and selection decisions	Systematically identify problems at all levels (block, beat, neighborhood and city)
Attend and present at homeowners association meetings	Incorporate community policing into performance evaluations and reward systems	Use problem analysis/crime analysis to better understand problems/issues
Build working relationships with the media	Develop technology and data systems that make information more accessible to officers and the community	Examine and incorporate best practices from other agencies
Inform citizens about major police initiatives	Train all staff in community policing principles	Seek input from members of the community to identify and prioritize problems
Use citizen volunteers	Increase officer discretion and accountability for solving problems at their level	Encourage and enable officers to think about problem solving when responding to calls for service
Operate a citizen police academy	Encourage officers to propose innovative solutions to long-standing problems	Evaluate the effectiveness of crime and problem reduction efforts
Develop working partnerships with other local government departments	Reduce hierarchical structures	Examine the causes for crime hot spots and develop appropriate responses based on underlying conditions
Get feedback from partners about the nature and priority of community problems	Increase agency transparency for activities and decision making	Analyze factors and characteristics of repeat victims to support targeted interventions
Brainstorm new solutions with stakeholders	Incorporate community policing into field officer training	Gather information about repeat offenders to make future offending more difficult
Involve community partners and service providers in problem-solving process	Give officers latitude in developing innovative responses to problems	Conduct surveys of the physical environment of problem locations to make places less susceptible to crime
Use foot patrol/bike patrol	Develop technology systems that support problem analysis and evaluation	Develop formal response plans
Use partners to help implement responses to problems	Build community policing into mission/vision/strategic plans	Systematically document problem solving efforts in a database

SOURCE: Robert Chapman and Matthew Scheider. *Community Policing for Mayors: A Municipal Model for Policing and Beyond*. Washington, DC: Office of Community Oriented Policing Services, no date, p.5.

among community members themselves. As police interaction with the community becomes more positive, productive partnerships are formed and community and officer leadership skills are developed. Citizens see that problems have solutions, giving them courage to tackle other community issues. As citizens feel more empowered to get involved, prevention and detection of crime increases, leading to reduced fear of crime in the community and improved quality of life. Reduced levels of crime allow more police resources to be allocated to services with the

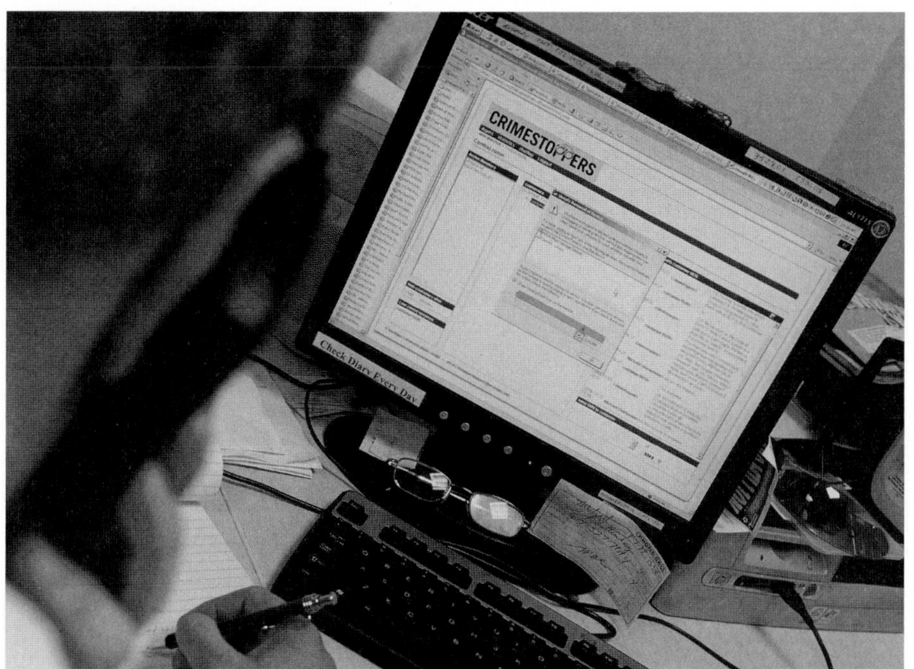

© AP Images/Lisa Poole

A Boston police officer with the department's Crime Stoppers Unit takes down information during a phone call. Police across the country are getting help from text-a-tip programs that allow people to send anonymous messages from their cell phones.

greatest impact on the quality of community life. Making effective use of the talents and resources available within communities further extends severely strained police resources. Community policing also provides real challenges for officers, making them more than "order takers and report writers" and leading to increased job satisfaction.

Despite these numerous benefits, not everyone will be receptive to the change to community policing.

Resistance to Community Policing

Many officers have difficulty accepting or appreciating the community-oriented policing philosophy. Some wonder whether officers will or should readily accept the increased accountability that accompanies greater decision-making responsibilities. Others question the willingness of police administrators to embrace decentralization, to "loosen the reins" and empower officers with greater authority, responsibility and decision-making capabilities. These organizational impediments are some of the chief barriers to implementation.

Other challenges to implementation include community resistance, a concern that community policing is "soft" on crime and structural impediments involved with making the change from a reactive to a proactive policing mission. The impediment of limited resources is also a reality: how to simultaneously respond to calls for service, solve crimes and conduct activities involved with community policing. Another large obstacle is the difficulty of changing the police culture.

The perception that community policing goes against aggressive law enforcement practices is perhaps one of the most difficult impediments to overcome. No agency wishes to be perceived as "soft" on crime, and no community wants to place crime control and safety in the hands of "pushovers." However, the goals of community policing and aggressive enforcement are not mutually exclusive. The combination of these two elements has been termed **integrated patrol**.

integrated patrol

An operational philosophy that combines community-based policing with aggressive enforcement and provides a balanced, comprehensive approach to addressing crime problems throughout an entire jurisdiction rather than merely in targeted areas within a community.

Impediments to community-oriented policing (COP) include

- *Organizational impediments*—resistance from middle management, line officers and unions; confusion about what COP is; problems in line-level accountability; officers' concern that COP is "soft" on crime; and lack of COP training
- *Union impediments*—resistance to change, fear of losing control to community, resistance to increased officer responsibility and accountability, and fear that COP will lead to civilian review boards
- *Community impediments*—community resistance, community's concern that COP is "soft" on crime, civil service rules, pressure to demonstrate COP reduces crime and lack of support from local government
- *Transition impediments*—balancing increased foot-patrol activities while maintaining emergency response time

Common pitfalls in making the transition to community policing include unrealistic expectations and focusing on short-term instead of long-term results, adopting a task-force approach, resisting the move toward community empowerment and misrepresenting an inadequate program as legitimate in order to receive funding.

Evaluating Progress

As the Community Policing Consortium (CPC) warns, without specifying desired outcomes as part of the strategic plan, the community policing initiative could be reduced to another series of community relations exercises rather than the anticipated cultural, organizational and structural change achieved through community policing in partnership and problem solving. The SARA model of problem solving shows there are no failures, only responses that do not provide the desired goal.

Evaluating progress can take many forms. It should be built into the strategic plan in concrete form. Which goals and objectives have been met? Which have not? Why not? The evaluation might also consist of conducting a second needs assessment of both the department and community a year later to determine whether needs are being better met. It can be done through additional surveys and interviews assessing reduced fear of crime and improved confidence in police. Are citizens making fewer complaints regarding police service? Are officers filing fewer grievances?

When evaluating progress, failures should be as important as successes—sometimes more important—because a department learns from what does not work.

Evaluating effectiveness is difficult. Police have long been able to evaluate their efficiency by looking at police activity—what police do rather than what effect it had. It is far easier to look at numbers—crime reports filed, arrests made, tickets issued, drugs seized—than to measure how problems have been solved. Measuring effectiveness requires realistic and meaningful performance indicators. These indicators need to be responsive to community concerns and reflect police capability to adapt, consult, mobilize, diagnose and solve problems.

The second basic component of community policing is problem solving, also referred to as problem-oriented policing. Many law enforcement agencies have now combined the operational strategies of community policing and problem solving to address a broad range of crime problems and the quality-of-life issues associated with them.

PROBLEM-SOLVING POLICING

Problem-solving policing and community policing are sometimes equated. However, **problem-solving policing** is an essential strategy of community policing. Its focus is on determining the underlying causes of problems, including crime, and identifying solutions:

> Where traditionally policing has been reactive, responding to calls for service, community policing is proactive, anticipating problems and seeking solutions to them. The term *proactive* is beginning to take on an expanded definition.
>
> Not only is it taking on the meaning of anticipating problems, but it is also taking on . . . that of accountability and choosing a response rather than reacting the same way each time a similar situation occurs. Police are learning that they do not obtain different results by applying the same methods. In other words, to get different results, different tactics are needed. (Miller et al., 2011, p.17)

problem-solving policing
A departmental-wide strategy aimed at solving persistent community problems; police identify, analyze and respond to the underlying circumstances that create incidents.

Eck and Spelman's classic, *Problem Oriented Policing* (1987), defines *problem-solving policing* as a "departmental-wide strategy aimed at solving persistent community problems. Police identify, analyze and respond to the underlying circumstances that create incidents." Problem-solving policing requires the police mission to be redefined "to help the police become accustomed to fixing broken windows as well as arresting window-breakers" (Wilson and Kelling, 1989, p.49).

Herman Goldstein is credited with originating POP and coining the term. Although he suggests community involvement is a positive development, his problem-oriented policing relies mostly on police participants. In addition, Goldstein's model emphasizes problem solving over partnerships. Table 7.3 summarizes the differences between problem-oriented policing and community policing.

Goldstein (1990, p.20) was among the first to criticize the professional model of policing as being incident driven: "In the vast majority of police departments, the telephone, more than any policy decision by the community or by management, continues to dictate how police resources will be used." The primary work unit in the professional model is the **incident**, that is, an isolated event that requires a police response. The institution of 911 has greatly increased the demand for police services and the public's expectation that the police will respond quickly.

incident
An isolated event that requires a police response.

TABLE 7.3 Selected Comparisons between Problem-Oriented Policing and Community Policing Principles

Principle	Problem-Oriented Policing	Community Policing
Primary emphasis	Substantive social problems within police mandate	Engaging the community in the policing process
When police and community collaborate	Determined on a problem by problem basis	Always or nearly always
Emphasis on problem analysis	Highest priority given to thorough analysis	Encouraged, but less important than community collaboration
Preferences for responses	Storing preference that alternatives to criminal law enforcement be explored	Preference for collaborative response with community
Role for police in organizing and mobilizing community	Advocated only if warranted within the context of the specific problem being addressed	Emphasizes strong role for police
Importance of geographic decentralization of police and continuity of officer assignment to community	Preferred, but not essential	Essential
Degree to which police share decision-making authority with community	Strongly encourages input from community while preserving ultimate decision-making authority to police	Emphasizes sharing decision-making authority with community
Emphasis on officer's skills	Emphasizes intellectual and analytical skills	Emphasizes interpersonal skills
View of the role or mandate of the police	Encourages broad, but not unlimited role for police, stresses limited capacities of police and guards against creating unrealistic expectations of police	Encourages expansive role for police to achieve ambitious social objectives

SOURCE: Michael S. Scott. *Problem-Oriented Policing: Reflections on the First 20 Years*. Washington, DC: U.S. Department of Justice, Office of Community Oriented Policing Services, 2000, p.99.

Goldstein (1990, p.33) asserts, "Most policing is limited to ameliorating the overt, offensive symptoms of a problem." He suggests that police are more productive if they respond to incidents as symptoms of underlying community problems. He (p.66) defines a problem as "a cluster of similar, related, or recurring incidents rather than a single incident, a substantive community concern, and a unit of police business." Once the problems in a community are identified, police efforts can focus on addressing the possible causes of such problems.

Problem solving requires police to group incidents and, thereby, identify underlying causes of problems in the community.

Although problem solving may be the ideal, law enforcement cannot ignore specific incidents. When calls come in, most police departments respond as soon as possible. Problem solving has a dual focus. First, it requires that incidents be linked to problems. Second, time devoted to "preventive" patrol must be spent proactively, determining community problems and their underlying causes.

As noted by Goldstein (1990, p.2): "The dominant perspective of policing is heavily influenced by the primary method of control associated with the work—the authority to enforce the criminal law." He suggests that this view has "disproportionately influenced the operating practices, organization, training, and staffing of police agencies." It is like tunnel vision. Effective problem-oriented policing requires abandoning the "simplistic notion that the criminal law defines the police's role" and accepting that "policing consists of developing the most effective means for dealing with a multitude of troublesome situations." He suggests, "These means will often, but not always, include appropriate use of the criminal law."

Goldstein illustrates this change in perspective with the way the police have approached the drug problem, that is, with a law enforcement approach. Gradually the police and the public are coming to realize that this approach, arresting and prosecuting drug dealers, is ineffective. Goldstein (1990, p.2) contends, "The challenge is to determine what use should be made by the police of the criminal law (given the difficulty of the process and limited resources); what other means are available to the police for dealing with the problem; and what the police (given their first-hand knowledge of the magnitude and complexity of the problem) should be urging others to do in responding to it."

In addition, the following key elements of problem-solving policing should be considered.

The Key Elements of Problem-Solving Policing

- A problem, rather than a crime, a case, calls or incidents, is the basic unit of police work.
- A problem is something that concerns or causes harm to citizens, not just the police. Things that concern only police officers are important, but they are not problems in this sense of the term.
- Addressing problems means more than quick fixes; it means dealing with conditions that create problems.
- Police officers must routinely and systematically analyze problems before trying to solve them, just as they routinely and systematically investigate crimes before making an arrest. Individual officers and the department as a whole must develop routines and systems for analyzing problems.
- The analysis of problems must be thorough, although it may not need to be complicated. This principle is as true for problem analysis as it is for criminal investigation.
- Problems must be described precisely and accurately and broken down into specific aspects. Problems often are not what they first appear to be.
- Problems must be understood in terms of the various interests at stake. Individuals and groups of people are affected in different ways by a problem and have different ideas about what should be done about the problem.

- The way the problem is currently being handled must be understood, and the limits of effectiveness must be openly acknowledged in order to come up with a better response.
- Initially, any and all possible responses to a problem should be considered so as not to cut short potentially effective responses. Suggested responses should follow from what is learned during the analysis. They should not be limited to, nor rule out, the use of arrest.
- The police must proactively try to solve problems rather than just react to the harmful consequences of problems.
- The police department must increase police officers' freedom to make or participate in important decisions. At the same time, officers must be accountable for their decision making.
- The effectiveness of new responses must be evaluated so these results can be shared with other police officers and the department can systematically learn what does and does not work (Goldstein, 1990; Scott, 2000).

The concept of problem-oriented policing can be illustrated by example. Suppose police find themselves responding several times a day to calls about drug dealing and vandalism in a neighborhood park. The common approach of dispatching an officer to the scene and repeatedly arresting offenders may do little to resolve the long-term crime and disorder problem. If, instead, police were to incorporate problem-oriented policing techniques into their approach, they would examine the conditions underlying the problem. This would likely include collecting additional information—perhaps by surveying neighborhood residents and park users, analyzing the time of day when incidents occur, determining who the offenders are and why they favor the park, and examining the particular areas of the park most conducive to the activity and evaluating their environmental design characteristics. The findings could form the basis of a response to the problem behaviors. Although enforcement might be a component of the response, it would unlikely be the sole solution because, in this case, analysis might indicate the need to involve neighborhood residents, parks and recreation officials and others.

Eck and Spelman (1987, p.2) explain that problem-oriented policing is the result of 20 years of research into police operations converging on three main themes:

1. Increased effectiveness by attacking underlying problems that give rise to incidents that consume patrol and detective time.
2. Reliance on the expertise and creativity of line officers to study problems carefully and develop innovative solutions.
3. Closer involvement with the public to make sure the police are addressing the needs of citizens.

The SARA Model of Problem Solving

Eck and Spelman (1987) developed the SARA model of problem-solving policing.

 The four strategies of the **SARA model** of problem-solving policing are

1. *Scanning*—grouping individual incidents into meaningful "problems."
2. *Analyzing*—collecting information from all available sources (not just police data).
3. *Responding*—selecting and implementing solutions.
4. *Assessing*—evaluating the impact of the solution.

SARA model

Four strategies used in problem-oriented policing: scan, analyze, respond, assess.

Miller et al. (2011, p.98) explain,

> Scanning refers to identifying recurring problems and prioritizing them to select one problem to address. The problems should be of concern to the public as well as the police. At this stage broad goals may be set.
>
> Analysis examines the identified problem's causes, scope and effects. It includes determining how often the problem occurs, how long it has been occurring and what conditions appear to create the problem. Analysis also should include potential resources and partners who might assist in understanding and addressing the problem.
>
> Response is acting to alleviate the problem—that is, selecting the alternative solution or solutions to try. This may include finding out what other communities with similar problems have tried and with what success and looking at whether any research on the problem exists. Focus groups might be used to brainstorm possible interventions. Experts might be enlisted. Several alternatives might be ranked and prioritized according to difficulty, expense and the like. At this point goals are usually refined and the interventions are implemented.
>
> Assessment refers to evaluating the effectiveness of the intervention. Was the problem solved? If not, why? Assessment should include both qualitative and quantitative data. Qualitative data examines the excellence (quality) of the response—that is, how satisfied were the officers and the citizens? This is most frequently determined by surveys, focus groups or tracking complaints and compliments. Quantitative data examines the amount of change (quantity) as a result of the response. This is most frequently measured by pre/post data.
>
> The SARA model of problem solving stresses that there are no failures, only responses that do not provide the desired goal. When a response does not give the desired results, the partners involved in problem solving can examine the results and try a different response. Other communities might benefit from what was learned.

Eck (2002, p.10) describes two types of evaluations to conduct: *Process evaluation* determines if the response was implemented as planned, and *impact evaluation* determines if the problem declined. Several nontraditional measures will indicate if a problem has been affected by the interventions (Eck, p.27):

- Reduced instances of repeat victimization.
- Decreases in related crimes or incidents.
- Neighborhood indicators: increased profits for legitimate businesses in target area, increased use of area/increased (or reduced) foot and vehicular traffic, increased property values, improved neighborhood appearance, increased occupancy in problem buildings, less loitering, fewer abandoned cars, less truancy.

- Increased citizen satisfaction regarding the handling of the problem, which can be determined through surveys, interviews, focus groups, electronic bulletin boards and the like.
- Reduced citizen fear related to the problem.

Common Mistakes in Problem Solving

As Bennett and Hess (2007, p.160) note, "Common mistakes in problem solving and decision making include spending too much energy on unimportant details, failing to resolve important issues, being secretive about true feelings, having a closed mind and not expressing ideas. . . . Inability to decide, putting decisions off to the last minute, failing to set deadlines, making decisions under pressure and using unreliable sources of information are other common errors in problem solving and decision making." Other mistakes commonly made during problem solving and decision making include making multiple decisions about the same problem, finding the right decision for the wrong problem (that is, dealing with symptoms rather than causes), failing to consider the costs, delaying a decision and making decisions while angry or excited.

Following is a checklist against which to evaluate decisions (Bennett and Hess, 2007, p.161): Is the decision (1) consistent with the agency's mission, goals and objectives; (2) a long-term solution; (3) cost effective; (3) legal, ethical, practical; and (4) acceptable to those responsible for implementing it?

The goals of problem solving policing and aggressive enforcement are not mutually exclusive. The combination of these two efforts is called integrated patrol. As has been stressed, law enforcement agencies are expected to combat crime but are also being asked to look at causes for problems existing within communities and address them as well. Much of this depends on data-driven approaches to policing. Kanable and Dewey-Kollen (2010, p.12) quote the Nashville Police Department police chief as saying, "It is critical for the community to know that the police department is very focused and specific as to where resources are deployed. It's critical for the community to know that daily decisions are based on data. We cannot afford to be random in our efforts."

Three data-driven strategies to policing are CompStat, intelligence-led policing and evidence-based policing.

COMPSTAT POLICING

CompStat policing

A method of management accountability and a philosophy of crime control.

CompStat policing as "a method of management accountability and a philosophy of crime control" (Godown, 2009, p.36). The essence of CompStat, which is short for "Computer Comparison Statistics," is that police cannot manage what they do not measure: "CompStat is pin-mapping on steroids. It simply helps to draw sharp attention to problem areas. It puts facts in the place of impressions" (Sanow, 2009, p.6). CompStat was first fully operational in 1994 in the New York Police Department and quickly gained in popularity: "This proactive and outcome-oriented approach to organizing and managing police operations has been described as a vastly new approach to managing police operations and, as such, a 'sea change' in law enforcement" (Dabney, 2010, pp.28–29).

CompStat and community policing are not mutually exclusive and, in fact, are rather dependent upon each other for contemporary policing (Peak and Barthe, 2009, p.72). CompStat can be invaluable in the analysis phase of the SARA model and has grown in popularity among law enforcement agencies throughout the United States as well as in other countries: "CompStat is not a quick-fix answer to crime but rather a process of organized problem solving. . . . The CompStat process can be described as a two-pronged examination of police operations. The first prong looks outwardly at crime and its effects in the community, while the second examines the organization internally to identify best practices in managing such police personnel and risk management issues as sick time, use of force, pursuits, complaints, and accompanying municipal liability" (Godown, 2009, p.36). The four principles upon which CompStat rests are (Godown, p.38):

1. Accurate and timely intelligence: know what is happening.
2. Effective tactics: have a plan.
3. Rapid deployment: do it quickly.
4. Relentless follow-up and assessment: if it works, do more, if not, do something else.

Again, as a method of problem solving, the emphasis of CompStat policing is on *strategy*.

The four principles of CompStat involve accurate, timely intelligence; effective tactics; rapid deployment; and relentless follow-up.

The Columbia (South Carolina) Police Department implemented CompStat in an effort to address a series of armed robberies, placing the problem in the department's open forum and enabling a brainstorming and problem-solving session (Crisp and Hines, 2007). The goal was to capture the robbers by saturating the area with officers, pooling all available staffing and resources from other law enforcement agencies. The strategy involved sharing real-time crime reports, field reports, and investigative reports, thus allowing the information to get to patrol officers within hours after an offense, enhancing officer awareness and increasing the possibility of apprehension. Additional strategic efforts involved enlisting the aid of the media to disseminate news of the robberies and informing community leaders, residents and merchants of the problem.

The CompStat process greatly enhanced police effectiveness and efficiency: "The CompStat process has created an air of openness, seamless communication, and enhanced teamwork in the department. It also improved relations with neighboring law enforcement agencies and community organizations. Most importantly, it has drastically reduced the incidences of crime within the city and increased the number of arrests" (Crisp and Hines, 2007, p.48). In short: "There can be little debate that CompStat processes in police agencies across the United States have revolutionized crime fighting and made communities safer" (Serpas and Morley, 2008, p.60).

However, some research has identified potential pitfalls of CompStat, such as a tendency to downplay the core set of management principles and mistakenly focus on the analysis as primarily an auditing function rather than as a tool for precision diagnosis of crime patterns (Dabney, 2010, pp.44–45). Furthermore: "There was ample evidence of breakdowns in the two-way flow of communication within the organization. The goals and strategies formulated at CompStat meetings or follow-up planning sessions were often diluted or diverted as they made their way down to the rank-and-file officers. It appeared that mid-level supervisors took care to forward along these initiatives in intermittent fashion but poor follow-through among low-level supervisors was sufficient to derail the tactical focus" (Danby, p.45).

The connection between CompStat and intelligence-led policing is obvious in that the first principle of the CompStat process is accurate, timely intelligence.

INTELLIGENCE-LED POLICING

When information is gathered and analyzed, it becomes *intelligence*. There was a time in policing when intelligence was considered clandestine, obtained from confidential informants. Secrecy and silo-ing information were common practices. However, the events of September 11, 2001, changed that view considerably. Information sharing is now expected, and competent analysis of this information to provide law enforcement with the intelligence they need to keep our communities safe is what intelligence-led policing is about.

intelligence-led policing (ILP)

A methodical approach to prevent, detect and disrupt crime, including terrorist activities.

Intelligence-led policing (ILP) is a methodical approach to prevent, detect and disrupt crime, including terrorist activities. Two types of intelligence are distinguished in discussions of ILP: tactical and strategic. Tactical intelligence is information that is analyzed and contributes directly to a specific incident. Immediate action is usually taken on tactical intelligence. Strategic intelligence, in contrast, is analyzed information that evolves and develops over time, contributing to broad scope, "big picture" issues, such as planning and resource allocation (Peterson, 2005, p.3).

Early detection of crime trends through ILP allows police to be proactive in preventing continued crime instead of taking the traditional reactive, and less-effective, response to identified crime trends (Brewer, 2009, p.68). "Intelligence-led policing is a business model and managerial philosophy where data analysis and crime intelligence are pivotal to an objective, decision-making framework that facilitates crime and problem reduction, disruption and prevention through both strategic management and effective enforcement strategies that target prolific and serious offenders" (Ratcliffe, 2008, p.89). Figure 7.2 illustrates the intelligence process.

Beck and McCue (2009, pp.18, 24) explain,

> ILP does not replace the community involvement and problem-solving approaches in the community-policing model; it extends them to include research-based approaches, information and communications technology, and increased information sharing and accountability. Moreover, ILP encourages the use of criminal intelligence in support of collaborative, multi-jurisdictional approaches to crime prevention; and it emphasizes the role of analysis in tactical and strategic planning. ILP also includes attention to privacy and civil liberties. As a policing approach, ILP deftly integrates the exploitation of technology embodied in the professional-policing era, and the emphasis on community involvement implicit in community policing....

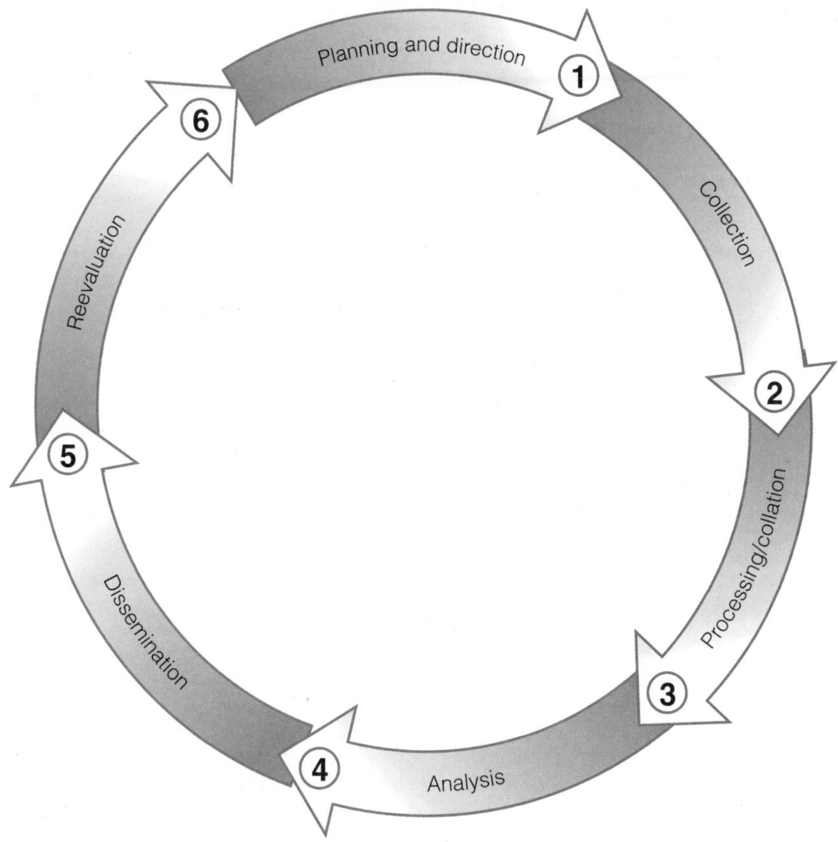

FIGURE 7.2 The Intelligence Process

SOURCE: Marilyn Peterson. *Intelligence-Led Policing: The New Intelligence Architecture.* Washington, DC: U.S. Department of Justice, Bureau of Justice Assistance, September 2005.

> This recession will end, but the predictive-policing model will continue to change public safety outcomes through information-based approaches to tactics, strategy, policy and resource allocation, allowing us to effectively deploy resources in front of crime in order to do more with less and change outcomes.

In March 2002, the International Association of Chiefs of Police (IACP) and the Office of Community Oriented Policing Services (COPS) held a summit on criminal intelligence sharing in the United States, one result of which was development of fusion centers through the United States. A **fusion center**, according to the FBI, does not just *collect* information; it also *integrates* new data into existing information, *evaluates* it to determine its worth, *analyzes* it for links and trends, and *disseminates* its findings to the appropriate agency in the best position to do something about it. Fusion centers pool the resources and personnel of multiple agencies into one central location to facilitate information sharing and intelligence development regarding criminal activities (Johnson and Dorn, 2008). Currently there are 70 fusion centers around the country—50 state and 20 regional—and some have expanded their focus from information on terrorism threats to include public safety matters and major criminal threats ("Fusion Centers," 2009).

fusion center

An effective, efficient mechanism to exchange information and intelligence, maximize resources, streamline operations and improve the ability to fight crime and terrorism by merging data from a variety of sources.

In October 2007 the White House released the *National Strategy for Information Sharing*, intended to ensure that those responsible for combating terrorism and protecting local communities have timely, accurate information. The strategy works by:

- Providing a framework for enhanced information sharing among federal, state, local, and tribal officials; the private sector; and foreign partners to aid their individual missions and to help secure the U.S. homeland.
- Describing the federal government's approach to supporting state and major urban area fusion centers, as well as national efforts to fight crime and make local communities safer.
- Recognizing that as information-sharing capabilities are enhanced, it is imperative that the legal rights of U.S. citizens continue to be protected, especially in the area of privacy and civil liberties. (McNamara, 2008, p.46)

The *National Summit on Intelligence: Gathering, Sharing, Analysis, and Use after 9-11* (2009) reports that since 9/11, law enforcement agencies have made "great strides" in their ability to share intelligence, a capability considered critical to preventing terrorism. The report also concludes, however, that some agencies consider themselves too small or too remote to participate in criminal intelligence sharing: "The participants in the follow-up 2007 IACP Criminal Intelligence Sharing Summit made it clear that many of the nation's law enforcement agencies do not participate in the criminal intelligence sharing plan. . . . Too many state, local, and tribal agencies, it would seem, underestimate their importance to the criminal intelligence sharing process, overestimate the burdens of full participation, and/or remain unaware of how to contribute to the vital work of the plan."

Among the recommendations of the follow-up summit are the following (pp.3–4):

- Every state, local, and tribal law enforcement agency in the United States should strive to develop and maintain a criminal intelligence capability consisting of at least the following requirements: formal criminal intelligence awareness training for at least one sworn officer; training all levels of law enforcement personnel to recognize behavior indicative of criminal activity associated with terrorism; and defined procedures and mechanisms for communication with the nearest fusion center and/or a regional information sharing network.
- A nationwide marketing and training initiative should be designed to convince every law enforcement agency to participate in criminal intelligence sharing and make every law enforcement agency aware of the criminal intelligence resources available to it.
- All law enforcement organizations and agencies should explore potential partnerships to enhance analytical capacity within their agencies.
- The U.S. Department of Homeland Security, the Office of the Director of National Intelligence and the U.S. Department of Justice should work together to simplify and streamline security classifications.
- Law enforcement agencies should develop ways to measure the success of criminal intelligence sharing and recognize those individuals involved in that success.

McGarrell et al. (2007) present a model of intelligence-led policing as a framework for responding to terrorism but caution, "Applying the model only to terrorism would be unfortunate because of terrorists' involvement in such a wide variety of routine and preparatory crimes" (pp.151–152). They suggest that, in addition to taking an all-crimes approach, intelligence-led policing is most likely to be effective if it is focused on particular crime types, criminal organizations and terrorist threats of particular concern to a locality.

Ethical Considerations in Intelligence-Led Policing

Maintaining ethics and integrity is an ever-present concern and obligation of police. A department using ILP should "zealously endorse proactive investigative tactics" while maintaining "an equal vigilance toward protecting the privacy rights of innocent people and suspects alike" (Martinelli and Shaw, 2009, p.141). In this new ILP environment, a key acronym to bear in mind is CAP: common sense, audits and purges.

It is critically important that intelligence unit supervisors rigorously review and amend intelligence data before allowing it to be passed on to other agencies: "In the intelligence field, 'Garbage in, Gospel out' refers to data included in an intelligence file although they have not been properly cross-checked or investigated for their veracity and reliability. The intelligence-led policing mantra must be 'corroborate, substantiate and validate'" (Schafer and Martinelli, 2009, p.144).

ILP is vulnerable to noble cause corruption, which refers to a law enforcement officer breaking the rules (aka, the law), commonly violating the Fourth Amendment, in an effort to contain society's terrorists and criminals (Martinelli, 2009, p.124). This abuse of police power, in which the ends are used to justify the means, is a felony. Such corruption may occur through reliance on suspicious activity reports (SARs), which have no mandatory prerequisite to establish probable cause or a criminal predicate nexus to generate reports. SARs, tips and leads, arrest reports and other sources are used by intelligence analysts to piece together tougher puzzle parts to thwart serious crime threats. They rely on their puzzle pieces being true, putting most faith in law enforcement-generated reports than anonymous tips or leads. If an arrest is made: "Today's street-level supervisors must emphasize the need to specifically articulate the probable cause facts of arrests so warrants may be issued and convictions successfully obtained" (Martinelli, 2009, p.124).

The 3-I Model

Within the context of intelligence-led policing, a 3-I model can be used to illustrate the purpose of crime analysis in the modern policing environment (Ratcliffe, 2008).

The 3-I model of intelligence-led policing consists of *interpreting* the criminal environment, *influencing* decision makers and *impacting* the criminal environment.

Interpreting the criminal environment is the first step in crime analysis, gaining a thorough understanding of the local environment in which criminals' operate. Intelligence must then be actively directed to the decision makers, a step that involves first deciding who the key decision makers are and then deciding on the best way to influence their thinking, keeping in mind that such individuals might be outside the law enforcement environment. Finally, for an organization to be truly intelligence-led, the decision makers must use the intelligence they receive to positively affect the criminal environment. Like CompStat: "Intelligence-led policing requires a fundamental commitment to data collection and analysis. Too many departments react to headlines and political winds, at the expense of cold, hard facts" (Serrao, 2009, p.10). Taking this 3-I model one step further, leads to the final strategy increasingly being advocated: evidence-based policing.

EVIDENCE-BASED POLICING

Although evidence-based policing (EBP) was first advocated by criminologist Lawrence Sherman in 1998, it is only recently being discussed and written about. EBP takes what is known about criminology and applies this "evidence" toward more cost-effective police policies and practices. In the context of EBP, the "evidence" does not pertain to a suspect's guilt or innocence but rather to "statistical and individual assessments of costs, risks and benefits" (Sherman, 2009). **Evidence-based policing (EBP)** takes what has been shown, through scientific research, to be effective and applies it to real-world policing: "EBP is about monitoring and evaluating program outcomes and delivery processes, analyzing whether this is making a difference in people's lives, and making adjustments to improve and enhance outcomes. It is about training, so that services are administered effectively and consistently. It is about innovation, efficiency, fiscal responsibility, and ongoing communication—with partners, stakeholders, and researchers—about what works and what does not. It is about continuing to push for better results" (Rodriguez, 2008, p.1).

evidence-based policing (EBP)

Takes what has been shown, through scientific research, to be effective and applies it to real-world policing.

The assessment phase in the SARA model of problem solving might be considered a form of evidence-based policing, depending on how rigorous the assessment is.

Police Research during the Past 20 Years

Braga and Weisburd (2007) discuss research results focused on eight innovations in American policing during the 1980s and 1990s: community policing, "broken windows" policing, problem-oriented policing, "pulling levers" policing, third-party policing, hot spots policing, CompStat and evidence-based policing. They note that the list of innovations is not exhaustive and that overlap exists. Following is an adaptation of their explanation of the form and character of these innovations (pp.3–8) as well as what research from the past 20 years has shown (pp.11–15):

> *Community policing* broadened the police function to recognize that the community should play a central role in defining the problems police address and that these problems should extend much beyond conventional law enforcement to include order maintenance, provision of services through problem solving and partnerships. As a general strategy, community policing has not been found to be effective in preventing crime. Unfocused community actions such as foot patrol, storefront

officers do not reduce crime and disorder. However, there is strong evidence to suspect that community policing tactics reduce fear of crime.

The *"broken window"* thesis suggested that serious crime developed because the police and citizens did not work together to prevent urban decay and social disorder [as discussed earlier]. The available evidence of broken windows policing is mixed.

Pulling levers policing strategies adopted a problem-oriented approach, but was broader and more comprehensive than traditional problem-solving strategies. The strategy consisted of selecting a particular crime problem, convening an inter-agency working group of law enforcement practitioners, conducting research to identify key offenders, groups and behavior patterns, framing a response to offenders and groups of offenders that used a varied means of sanctions to stop them from continuing their violent behavior. Pulling levers strategies seem to be promising in controlling the violent behavior of groups of chronic offenders.

Third party policing asserts that police cannot successfully deal with many problems on their own, that they have limits to their power. Third party policing uses civil ordinances and civil courts or the resources of private agencies to extend social control over law breakers. Third party policing is effective in dealing with drug problems, violent crime problems and problems involving young people.

Hot spot policing focuses resources on places where crime is clustered based on research showing that only 3 percent of the addresses in a city produce more than half of all the requests for police response as well as other research showing that 10 percent of places are the sites of about 60 percent of crimes (p.11). Researchers have found problem-oriented policing to be effective in controlling a wide range of specific crime and disorder problems.

CompStat policing focuses less on ways in which the police carry out their tasks and more on the nature of the police organization itself, empowering the command structure to do something about crime problems. Simple analyses of crime trend data suggest that cities experience decrease in crime after their police departments adopt CompStat. However, CompStat has yet to be proven as an effective crime control strategy.

Evidence-based policing calls for basing police policies and practices on rigorous, scientific evidence rather than on tradition or random observations. It places more credence in solid evidence than in experience. Evidence-based policing has not been empirically tested as an overall model of policing. However, evidence-based police departments would draw policies and practices from a solid research base of strategies that have proven to be effective in controlling crime.

Braga and Weisburd (2007, pp.2–3) are optimistic about the results, stating, "This period of innovation has demonstrated that police can prevent crime and can improve their relationships with the communities they serve."

The importance of research and the assimilation of empirical findings into organizational practices cannot be overstated: "Researchers have found that what distinguishes high-performance organizations from the rest are significant investments in R&D [research and development] and the integration of R&D principles into the fabric of the organization" (Bond, 2009, p.4). Unfortunately, only a tiny fraction of police budgets (typically less than 1 percent) are dedicated to R&D, despite the fact that police hold some of the most powerful responsibilities in society (Bond, p.5).

Effective Research

The "gold standard" in research is a randomized, controlled experimental design that states a hypothesis for a causal relationship and uses a randomized control group and treatment group. The larger the subject population, the more reliable the results are. However, in the real world it is impossible to control all the variables. Therefore, most of the research being reported on is quasi-experimental, lacking the key element of randomization.

Quasi-experimental research is not a true experiment in the strictest scientific sense but attempts to uncover a causal relationship, even if the researcher cannot control all the factors that might affect the outcome. It might or might not have a control group. The most common form of quasi-experimental design uses a pre- and post-test, looking at behavior before and after some sort of change or program is implemented with one group of subjects and comparing it with another comparable group that does not undergo the change or experiment.

For example, a study conducted by the city of Lowell, Massachusetts, from 2005 to 2009, had researchers and police concentrate on 34 crime hot spots. In half of the hot spots authorities repaired street lights, cleaned up trash, secured abandoned buildings and expanded mental health services and homeless aid referrals. At the end of the experiment, calls to police in the cleaned up areas decreased by 20 percent. The *Boston Globe* called the experiment a "breakthrough" in linking crime with conditions (Schreiber, 2010, p.24). Despite criticism that no good social science or criminological evidence has demonstrated that Broken Windows-type policing actually reduces crime, the results of the Lowell study seem to refute this (Schreiber, p.28).

meta-analysis

Provides a rigorous, objective, and quantitative strategy to make effective use of an existing body of research, even when the results seem inconsistent and inconclusive.

Such conflicting views are often presented in **meta-analysis**, which "provides a rigorous, objective, and quantitative strategy to make effective use of an existing body of research, even when the results seem inconsistent and inconclusive" (Wells, 2009, p.268). Many scientific fields have adopted meta-analysis to synthesize large bodies of research for evidence-based development of practical policies and for empirical resolution of difficult questions. The Braga and Weisburd report (2007) on lessons learned from police research over the past 20 years is a good example of meta-analysis.

In an effort to advance evidence-based policing and provide law enforcement with what seems to be "best practices," the IACP Research Advisory Committee (RAC) has partnered with the National Institute of Justice (NIJ) to create a National Law Enforcement Research Agenda (NLERA). The agenda is a list of priority research topics based on a survey of over 1,000 IACP members from all sizes and types of law enforcement agencies. "The NLERA presents, for the first time in the history of both the NIJ and the IACP, a nation-wide, survey-based, focused research agenda to guide both police leaders and researchers as they undertake research initiatives" (*Improving 21st Century Policing through Priority Research*, 2008). Figure 7.3 shows across the top of the chart the final set of eight research issues that function as the core elements of the NLERA.

From a law enforcement perspective, this change to empirical, evidence-based policy and practice represents a significant paradigm shift for which most agencies are not adequately prepared (Abrahamson and Taylor, 2007, p.3). Few agencies have the training or requisite resources to conduct scientific research during their day-to-day operations and apply it to decision-making about policies and practices. Because of this, many departments are partnering with colleges and

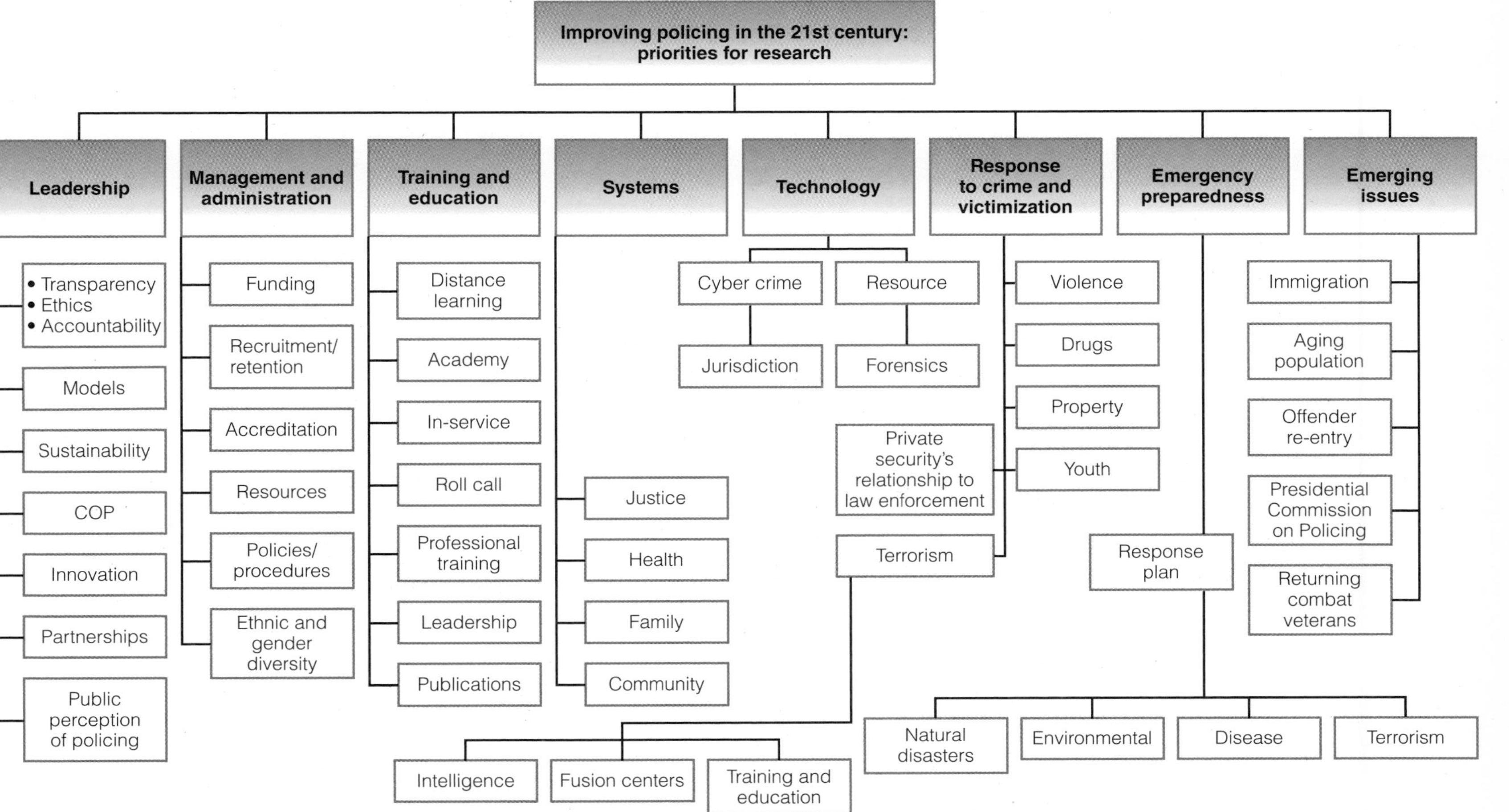

FIGURE 7.3 The Eight Core Research Issue Areas of the National Law Enforcement Research Agenda (NLERA)

SOURCE: *Improving 21st Century Policing through Priority Research: The IACP's National Law Enforcement Research Agenda.* Arlington, VA, International Association of Chiefs of Police, September 2008, p.7.

universities. Such partnerships are embraced by the IACP NLERA and are perceived as essential.

Partnering with Colleges or Universities

Students or staff at local or regional colleges or universities can be valuable partners for agencies wanting to participate in evidence-based policing.

For partnerships between police agencies and researchers to be successful, the participants need to identify and locate each other, specify mutually interesting projects, determine compensation, and set ground rules clarifying expectations for how the project will proceed (Sanders and Fields, 2009, p.58). One important expectation to clarify is data use and attendant confidentiality or anonymity requirements. It is also important to have a clear but flexible timeline for projects, ensuring that researchers are aware of the real-life emergencies that may arise for a law enforcement agency and that may make meeting deadlines difficult. On the other hand, researchers, too, often have deadlines for journal articles or conference presentations and need to have their time and talents respected, especially if the researchers are donating their time.

Such partnerships can have long-term benefits for both groups (Sanders and Fields, 2009, p.61). For researchers the main benefit of a police partnership is access to a data source. In addition colleges and universities can benefit from having contacts at a local police agency for internships and for future job opportunities. Police departments benefit by having researchers who are trained in statistical analysis evaluate the effectiveness of their programs, data gathering processes and the like.

Reporting Failure

Over a century ago Abraham Lincoln observed, "Men are greedy to publish the successes of their efforts, but meanly shy as to publishing the failure of men. Men are ruined by this one-sided practice of concealment of blunders and failures."

Evidence-based policing must report failures as well as successes to reach its full potential.

It has been suggested that, in the criminal justice world, *failure* is a whispered word (Berman et al., 2007, p.7). For evidence-based policing to move forward, failure must be openly discussed to foster an environment promoting new thinking and testing of new ideas. In fact: "The expectation should be that failure is normal. Even with clear-headed designs, savvy implementation strategies, robust training, skilled staff and committed executive leadership, some things are likely to go wrong. . . Even when a program is going relatively well, it is difficult to get anyone interested in writing about failure" (Immarigeon, 2008, p.43).

Throughout the chapters that follow, the preceding strategies will be referred to as currently practiced in *larger* police departments. Schafer et al. (2009, p.263) studied the impact of 9/11 on small municipal agencies and found that, although homeland security has been the focus of "ample rhetoric" since the 9/11 terrorist attacks, empirical research on actual effects has been lacking. They (pp.282–283) studied perceptions of risk, engagement in preparatory measures and perception of response capacities in Illinois and found only modest improvements in homeland security innovation in small departments in the first 6 years after 9/11:

> Small agencies perceived their risk of a terrorist attack to be low. Whether the limited innovation was a function of minimal perception of risk is difficult to disentangle with cross-sectional data. Agencies reported struggling to secure training, equipment, and other resources to enhance homeland security efforts, though open comments suggested variation in whether this was actually a cause for concern for agency representatives. When considered in light of extant literature on small police agencies, the findings suggest little has changed in the policing of Mayberry post-9/11.

A current example combining traditional, community policing and data-driven policing is found in the Safe City projects being conducted throughout the country.

TARGET'S SAFE CITY PROGRAM

Safe City is a program "launched" by Target Corporation in 2004 in Minneapolis, Minnesota, to build partnerships between local police and their communities to reduce crime. Since then Target and local partners have started Safe City projects in more than 20 other cities, achieving significant levels of success. Each program is unique, has different focuses and is at different levels of development (*Target's Safe City Program*, 2010, p.1).

The project developed out of Target's desire to help bridge the gap where risks are going up and resources are going down—the familiar call for police and communities to "do more with less" (*Target's Safe City Program*, 2010, pp.24–25). In 1976 Brad Brekke, currently a vice president with Target, entered a two-year program to become a police officer. In 2009 his son also entered the field of policing, and Brekke was struck by the realization that almost 80 percent of the law enforcement curriculum was the same as what he had taken 30 years earlier. Says Brekke (*Target's Safe City Program*, 2010, p.24), "The World has changed, and I think police need to start understanding that there are so many new skills sets in play."

Target focuses on four areas for police agencies to remain competitive. First is talent: Unless police managers look for a different talent mix in new recruits, they will have a difficult time succeeding in the future. Second is the tremendous amount of information available—intelligence, analytics, and data of all forms and fashion. Third is technology, mobility devices, PDAs, communication links, mapping techniques, high-tech surveillance and the like. Fourth is partnerships—what Brekke calls the "game changer," noting, "Target doesn't want to just be in the community, it wants to be a *part* of the community. And that philosophy has given us a freedom or latitude that not all companies have, to stretch our boundaries and get involved." The conclusion of *Safe Cities* (2010, pp.43–43) reports,

> Safe City programs embody most of the major advances in thinking about policing over the last 40 years.
>
> To begin with, the biggest innovation in policing has been the development of community policing, and Safe City clearly is a community policing program. . . . incorporating a new concept: Community members take the initiative and contact the police in order to propose some type of joint police-community project. . . .

> Second, Safe City incorporates the lessons of problem-oriented policing. In Safe City programs police officials and business leaders and other community members . . . meet to share information about crime patterns and trends, and to develop plans for solving crime problems. . . .
>
> Third, Safe City incorporates the lessons of the "Broken Windows" thesis . . . that seemingly small indications of disorder in a neighborhood, if left unattended, can lead to further deterioration of the neighborhood and more serious crime.
>
> Finally, Safe City programs include the ideas of CompStat. . . . using up-to-the-minute statistics and other information to inform their decision.

The examples of six successful Safe City programs included in the Target report show how innovations are being used along with the tradition strategies commonly used for years by law enforcement.

DATA-DRIVEN APPROACHES TO CRIME AND TRAFFIC SAFETY

A final model to consider in this discussion of data-driven policing is the Data-Driven Approaches to Crime and Traffic Safety (DDACTS) initiative, a model that follows relatively closely with ILP, EBP and community policing. This operational model is supported by a partnership between the National Highway Traffic Safety Administration (NHTSA), the Bureau of Justice Assistance and the National Institute of Justice and uses location-based crime and crash data to more effectively and efficiently deploy law enforcement resources: "The model's focus on collaboration with law enforcement, community members, and organizations reinforces the crucial role that partnerships play in reducing social harm and improving quality of life" (*Data-Driven Approaches to Crime and Traffic Safety*, 2009, p.i).

This model's dynamic approach uses evidence-based policing such as geo-mapping to collect crime and crash information, working with the community members and using strategic intelligence to fight and reduce crime and improve traffic safety. The model collects local intelligence to identify crime and traffic related "hot spots," a technique referred to as *spatial clustering*. The rationale behind this model is, again, presented within the context of "doing more with less": "Because a shortage of law enforcement resources is likely to continue in the foreseeable future, police executives should continue to explore new strategies to further improve quality of life in communities that suffer from the effects of high-crime and crash rates" (*Data-Driven Approaches to Crime and Traffic Safety*, 2009, p.6).

Summary

Five broad strategic or organizational approaches currently operating in contemporary policing are community policing, problem-solving policing, CompStat policing, intelligence-led policing and evidence-based policing. Community policing, a philosophy that stresses working proactively with citizens to prevent crime and to solve crime-related problems, focuses on having citizens assist police in keeping the "public peace." The U.S. Constitution and Bill of Rights, as well as federal and state statutes and local ordinances, establish the "public peace" in the United States. Two critical elements of community policing are partnerships and problem solving.

One key partnership law enforcement can make is with private security forces. Private security officers differ from police officers in that private security officers are salaried with private funds, are responsible to an employer and have limited authority extending only to the premises they are hired to guard. Security officers have no authority to carry concealed weapons, although they can carry unconcealed weapons, and, unless deputized, they have no authority to make arrests except as a citizen's arrest.

The most important consideration in selecting strategies to implement community policing is to ensure that the strategies fit a community's unique needs and resources. When evaluating progress in implementing community policing, failures should be as important as successes—sometimes more important—because a department learns from what does not work.

Problem solving requires police to group incidents and thereby identify underlying causes of problems in the community. The SARA model of problem-solving policing uses four strategies: (1) scanning—grouping individual incidents into meaningful "problems," (2) analyzing—collecting information from all available sources (not just police data), (3) responding—selecting and implementing solutions and (4) assessing—evaluating the impact of the solution. Implementing community policing requires a change in management style, mission statement and departmental organization.

Three data-driven strategies in policing are CompStat policing, intelligence-led policing and evidence-based policing. The four principles of CompStat involve accurate, timely intelligence; effective tactics; rapid deployment; and relentless follow-up.

The 3-I model of intelligence-led policing consists of *interpreting* the criminal environment, *influencing* decision makers and *impacting* the criminal environment. Students or staff at local or regional colleges or universities can be valuable partners for agencies wanting to participate in evidence-based policing. Evidence-based policing must report failures as well as successes to reach its full potential.

Discussion Questions

1. Is there still a need for traditional policing methods in our contemporary society?
2. What do you feel are the greatest strengths of community policing?
3. What is the relationship of problem-solving policing to community policing?
4. Might community policing dilute the power and authority of the police?
5. Why do you think it took the events of 9/11 to begin a paradigms shift in how we police in America?
6. How is policing in America now different that it was pre-9/11?
7. How has CompStat improved law enforcement's ability to fight crime?
8. What other forms of intelligence-based approaches to policing might exist in the future?
9. Is citizen fear of crime more or less important than actual levels of crime? Why do you think this?
10. Are there any aspects of policing where research and scientific evidence offers little potential for improving efficiency or effectiveness?

Gale Emergency Services Database Assignments

- Use the Gale Emergency Services Database to help answer the Discussion Questions as appropriate.
- Using the Gale Emergency Services Database, find articles on *data-driven policing*, *intelligence-led policing*, *evidence-based policing* or *hot spots*. Select an article to outline and be prepared to share and discuss your outline with the class.
- Using the Gale Emergency Services Database, find the article "CompStat Process": http://find.galegroup.com/gps/retrieve.do?contentSet=IAC-Documents&resultListType=RESULT_LIST&qrySerId=Locale%28en%2C%2C%29%3AFQE%3D%28ke%2CNone%2C8%29compstat%24&sgHitCountType=None&inPS=true&sort=DateDescend&searchType=BasicSearchForm&tabID=T003&prodId=IPS&searchId=R1¤tPosition=6&userGroupName=cpg3&docId=A116578444&docType=IAC&contentSet=IAC-Documents

  Assignment: Read the article and identify the principles of CompStat. Be prepared to discuss these principles with the class.
- Using the Gale Emergency Services Database, find the article "CompStat Implementation": http://find.galegroup.com/gps/retrieve.do?contentSet=IAC-Documents&resultListType=RESULT_LIST&qrySerId=Locale%28en%2C%2C%29%3AFQE%3D%28ke%2CNone%2C8%29compstat%24&sgHitCountType=None&inPS=true&sort=DateDescend&searchType=BasicSearchForm&tabID=T003&prodId=IPS&searchId=R1¤tPosition=4&userGroupName=cpg3&docId=A119108753&docType=IAC&contentSet=IAC-Documents

  Assignment: Read this article and outline the major points. Be prepared to discuss your outline in class.
- Using the Gale Emergency Services Database, find the article "Demands on Police Services in a WMD Incident" (Weapons of Mass Destruction): http://find.galegroup.com/gps/retrieve.do?contentSet=IAC-Documents&resultListType=RESULT_LIST&qrySerId=Locale%28en%2C%2C%29%3AFQE%3D%28ke%2CNone%2C25%29Intelligence+Led+Policing%24&sgHitCountType=None&inPS=true&sort=DateDescend&searchType=BasicSearchForm&tabID=T003&prodId=IPS&searchId=R2¤tPosition=2&userGroupName=cpg3&docId=A177274846&docType=IAC&contentSet=IAC-Documents

  Assignment: What is the conclusion of this article based on the concepts of intelligence-led policing (ILP)? Answer this question and be prepared to discuss and defend your answer in class.
- Using the Gale Emergency Services Database, find the article "Coplink CompStat Analyzer Automates Crime Data Analysis" (Software Technology): http://find.galegroup.com/gps/retrieve.do?contentSet=IAC-Documents&resultListType=RESULT_LIST&qrySerId=Locale%28en%2C%2C%29%3AFQE%3D%28K0%2CNone%2C11%29data+police%24&sgHitCountType=None&inPS=true&sort=DateDescend&searchType=BasicSearchForm&tabID=T003&prodId=IPS&searchId=R6¤tPosition=13&

userGroupName=cpg3&docId=A188963954&docType=IAC&contentSet=IAC-Documents

Assignment: How would this software be used in data-driven policing? List some ways and be prepared to discuss your answers in class.

Internet Assignment

- Use the search engine Google.com to find a number of community policing programs that failed. List them and comment on why they failed. Be prepared to share your comments with the class.

References

Abrahamson, Doug, and Taylor, Bruce. "Evidence-Based Policing: Are We Ready, Willing and Able?" *Subject to Debate*, February 2007, pp.3, 5.

Beck, Charlie, and McCue, Colleen. "Predictive Policing: What Can We Learn from Wal-Mart and Amazon about Fighting Crime in a Recession?" *The Police Chief*, November 2009, pp.18–24.

Bennett, Wayne W., and Hess, Karen M. *Management and Supervision in Law Enforcement*, 5th ed. Belmont, CA: Wadsworth Publishing Company, 2007.

Berman, Greg; Bowen, Phillip; and Mansky, Adam. "Trial and Error: Failure and Innovation in Criminal Justice Reform." *Executive Exchange*, Summer 2007, pp.7–11.

Bond, Brenda. "The Application of Private-Sector Best Practices to Strategic Decision-Making: Investing in Police Research and Development." *Subject to Debate*, December 2009, pp.4–5.

Braga, Anthony A., and Weisburd, David L. *Police Innovation and Crime Prevention: Lessons Learned from Police Research over the Past 20 Years.* Washington, DC: National Institute of Justice, May 2007.

Brewer, Brad. "C.R.I.M.E. Fights Crime with Intelligence-Led Policing." *Law and Order*, May 2009, pp.68–74.

Coleman, J. *Foundations of Social Theory*. Cambridge, MA: Harvard University Press, 1990.

Connell, Nadine M; Miggans, Kristen; and McGloin, Jean Marie. "Can a Community Policing Initiative Reduce Serious Crime?" *Police Quarterly*, June 2008, pp.127–150.

Crisp, H. Dean, and Hines, R. J. "The CompStat Process in Columbia." *The Police Chief*, February 2007, pp.46–49.

Dabney, Dean. "Observations Regarding Key Operational Realities in a CompStat Model of Policing." *Justice Quarterly*, February 2010, pp.28–51.

Data-Driven Approaches to Crime and Traffic Safety (DDACTS): Operational Guidelines. Washington, DC: U.S. Department of Transportation, National Highway Transportation Safety Administration, August 2009. (DOT HS 811 185)

Eck, John E. *Assessing Responses to Problems: An Introductory Guide for Police Problem-Solvers.* Washington, DC: Office of Community Oriented Policing Services, 2002.

Eck, John E., and Spelman, William. *Problem-Solving: Problem-Oriented Policing in Newport News.* Washington, DC: The Police Executive Research Forum, 1987.

"Fusion Centers." Washington, DC: Federal Bureau of Investigation Headline Archives, March 12, 2009.

Godown, Jeff. "The CompStat Process: Four Principles for Managing Crime Reduction." *The Police Chief*, August 2009, pp.36–42.

Goldstein, Herman. *Problem-Oriented Policing*. New York: McGraw-Hill, 1990.

Immarigeon, Russ. "What Does Not Work? Lessons from the Center for Court Innovations Failure Roundtable." *Criminal Justice Research Review*, January/February 2008, pp.43–44.

Improving 21st Century Policing through Priority Research: The IACP's National Law Enforcement Research Agenda. Alexandria, VA: The International Association of Chiefs of Police, September 2008.

Johnson, Bart R., and Dorn, Shelagh. "Fusion Centers: New York State Intelligence Strategy Unifies Law Enforcement." *The Police Chief*, February 2008, pp.34–46.

Kanable, Rebecca, and Dewey-Kollen, Janet. "Nashville PD Makes the Data Sing." *Law and Order*, February 2010, pp.10–16.

Martinelli, Thomas J. "Dodging the Pitfalls of Noble Cause Corruption and the Intelligence Unit." *The Police Chief*, October 2009, pp.124–130.

Martinelli, Thomas J., and Shaw, Lawrence E. "ILP Abbreviations for the ISE and NCISP Can Spell Trouble." *The Police Chief*, October 2009, pp.138–141.

McGarrell, Edmund F.; Freilich, Joshua D.; and Chermak, Steven. "Intelligence-Led Policing as a Framework for Responding to Terrorism." *Journal of Contemporary Criminal Justice*, May 2007, pp.142–158.

McNamara, Thomas E. "U.S. National Strategy for Information Sharing Release." *The Police Chief*, April 2008, p.46.

Miller, Linda A.; Hess, Kären Matison; and Orthmann, Christine Hess. *Community Policing: Partnerships for Problem Solving*, 6th ed. Clifton Park, NY: Delmar/Cengage Publishing, 2011.

National Strategy for Information Sharing, Washington, DC: The White House, October 2007.

National Summit on Intelligence: Gathering, Sharing, Analysis, and Use after 9-11. Washington, DC: Office of Community Oriented Policing, July 3, 2009.

Peak, Ken, and Barthe, Emmanuel P. "Community Policing and CompStat: Merged, or Mutually Exclusive?" *The Police Chief*, December 2009, pp.72–84.

Peterson, Marilyn. *Intelligence-Led Policing: The New Intelligence Architecture*. Washington, DC: U.S. Department of Justice, Bureau of Justice Assistance, September 2005. (NCJ 210681)

Putnam, Robert D. *Bowling Alone: The Collapse and Revival of American Community*. New York: Simon & Schuster, 2000.

Ratcliffe, Jerry H. *Intelligence-Led Policing*. Cullompton, Devon, UK: Willan Publishing, 2008.

Rodriguez, Pamela F. "Understanding Evidence-Based Practice." *TASC News and Views* (Treatment Alternatives for Safe Communities), Winter, 2008, p.1.

Sanders, Beth A., and Fields, Marc L. "Partnerships with University-Based Researchers." *The Police Chief*, June 2009, pp.58–61.

Sanow, Ed. "Measure Equals Manage." *Law and Order*, June 2009, p.6.

Schafer, Joseph A.; Burruss, George W., Jr.; and Giblin, Matthew J. "Measuring Homeland Security Innovation in Small Municipal Agencies: Policing in a Post-9/11 World." *Police Quarterly*, September 2009, pp.263–288.

Schafer, Joseph A., and Martinelli, Thomas J. "The Privacy Police: Sense-Enhancing Technology and the Future of Intelligence-Led Policing." *The Police Chief*, October 2009, pp.142–147.

Schreiber, Sara. "Zone Defense: The Hopeful Case for 'Broken Windows' in Disordered Streets." *Law Enforcement Technology*, March 2010, pp.24–28.

Scott, Michael S. *Problem-Oriented Policing: Reflections on the First 20 Years*. Washington, DC: U.S. Department of Justice, Office of Community Oriented Policing Services, 2000.

Serpas, Ronal W., and Morley, Matthew. "The Next Step in Accountability-Driven Leadership: 'CompStating' the CompStat Data." *The Police Chief*, May 2008, pp.60–70.

Serrao, Stephen G. "Intelligence-Led Policing: Beyond the Fusion Center—Strategic Intelligence." *Law Officer Magazine*, July 2009, p.10.

Sherman, Lawrence. "Evidence-Based Policing: What We Know and How We Know It." Preview of an address to be presented at the Scottish Police College, October 1, 2009.

Sparrow, Malcolm K. *One Week in Heron City—A Case Study, Teaching Notes. New Perspectives in Policing*. Washington, DC: National Institute of Justice and the Harvard Kennedy School Program in Criminal Justice Policy and Management, 2009.

Target's Safe City Program: Community Leaders Take the Initiative in Building Partnerships with the Police. Washington, DC: Police Executive Research Forum, January 2010.

Upper Midwest Community Policing Institute. "Community Policing Defined." No date.

Wells, Edward. "Uses of Meta-Analysis in Criminal Justice Research: A Quantitative Review." *Justice Quarterly*, June 2009, pp.268–293.

Wilson, James Q., and Kelling, George L. "The Police and Neighborhood Safety: Broken Windows." *The Atlantic Monthly*, March 1982, pp.29–38.

Wilson, James Q., and Kelling, George L. "Making Neighborhoods Safe." *The Atlantic Monthly*, February 1989, pp.46–52.

SECTION III

CHALLENGES TO THE PROFESSION

Section II presented how contemporary law enforcement fulfills its mission through administrative and field services. The evolving importance of community policing and its influence on patrol and the other specialized roles of police were also explored. This section examines challenges facing law enforcement. A major challenge in everything officers do is policing within the law. Officers must be knowledgeable of and perform within the limits set by our Constitution and by their respective state constitutions and local ordinances (Chapter 8).

Two persistent, often-interlinked challenges are combating gangs and illegal drugs in our country. Billions of dollars and personnel hours are spent in this effort (Chapter 9). A challenge that has always been present but, until September 11, 2001, had not been a priority, is terrorism. The threat of terrorism is now a top priority at the local, county, state and national level (Chapter 10). In addition to these very specific challenges, issues related to officer conduct must be addressed. Such issues include discrimination, use of force, pursuits, civil liability, corruption, ethics and integrity (Chapter 11). The last major series of challenges are found within law enforcement agencies throughout the country: recruiting, selecting, training and retaining the best qualified officers; federal guidelines and regulations related to hiring officers; unionization; moonlighting; accreditation; and professionalization of law enforcement (Chapter 12).

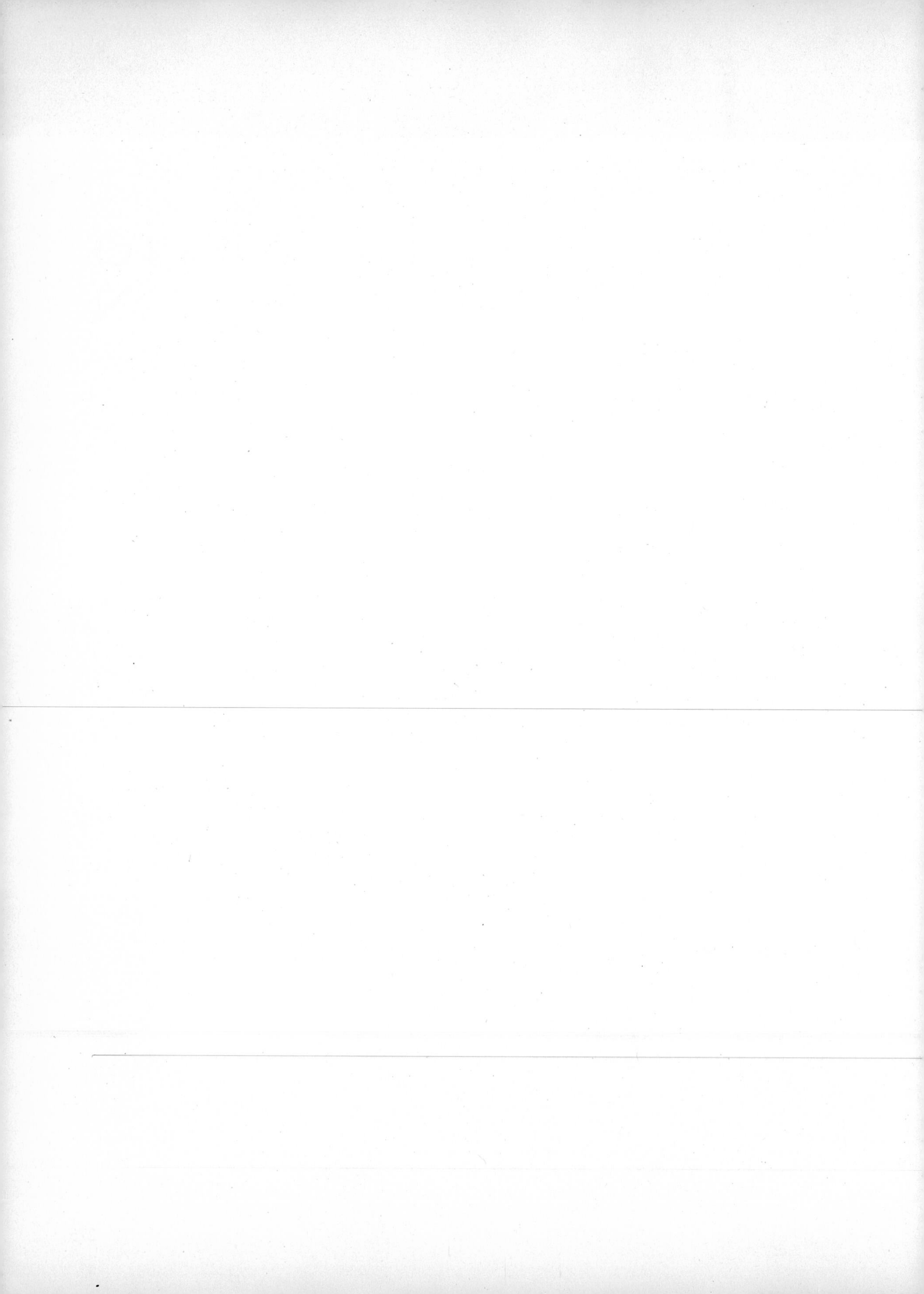

CHAPTER 8

Policing within the Law

The patrol officer is the first interpreter of the law and in effect performs a quasi-judicial function. He makes the first attempt to match the reality of human conflict with the law; he determines whether to take no action, to advise, to warn, or to arrest; he determines whether he must apply physical force, perhaps sufficient to cause death. It is he who must discern the fine distinction between a civil and a criminal conflict, between merely unorthodox behavior and a crime, between a legitimate dissent and disturbance of the peace, between the truth and a lie. As the interpreter of the law, he recognizes that a decision to arrest is only the first step in the determination of guilt or innocence. He is guided by, and guardian of, the Constitution.

—*Task Force Report: The Police*, President's Commission on Law Enforcement and the Administration of Justice, 1967.

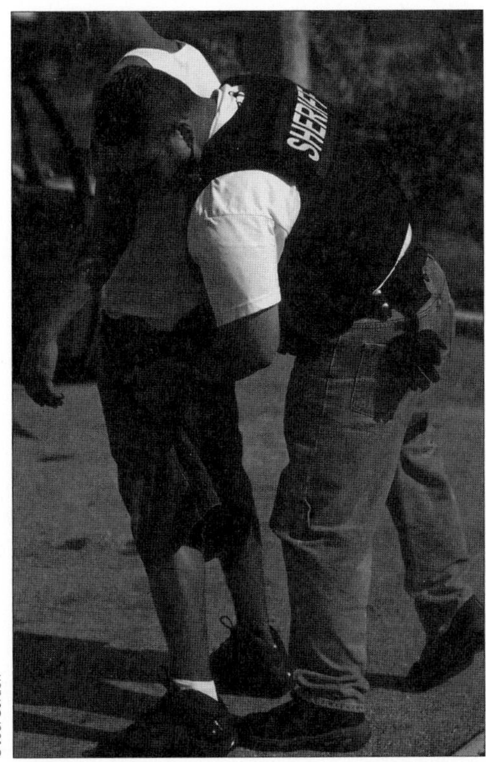

© Joel Gordon

Stop and frisk is a protective search for weapons in which the intrusion must be limited to a scope reasonably designed to discover guns, knives, clubs and other concealed instruments that may be used to assault a police officer or others.

Do You Know . . .

- The major provisions of the Fourth Amendment?
- On what sources probable cause can be based?
- What basic principles underlie stop and frisk and what differences distinguish them?
- What significance the *Terry* case has in relation to the Fourth Amendment?
- When roadblocks and checkpoints are constitutional?
- What principal justifications are set forth by the courts for reasonable searches?
- What a search warrant is and what it must contain? What may be seized?
- What limitations are placed on searches?
- When warrantless searches are justified and the conditions placed on each?
- How a warrantless search can be challenged?
- What authorities and restrictions are provided by the following cases: *Chimel*? *Carroll*? *Chambers*? *Coolidge*? *Maryland v. Wilson*?
- What special conditions apply to searches of vehicles?
- Whether open fields, abandoned property or trash can be searched without a warrant?
- Whether using thermal imaging to view inside a house without a warrant is constitutional?
- When general searches are constitutional?
- What the elements of a criminal arrest are?
- What four rights the *Miranda* warning establishes?
- When the *Miranda* warning must be given?
- What the public safety exception provides?

Can You Define?

administrative warrant
affidavit
arrest
***Buie* sweep**
consent
contraband
curtilage
custody
de facto arrest
detention
entrapment
exclusionary rule
exigent circumstances
field inquiry
forced entry
frisk
immediate control
inevitable discovery doctrine
inspection warrant
instruments of a crime
investigatory stop
magistrate
nightcap warrants
no-knock search warrant
open fields doctrine
pat down
plain feel/touch doctrine
plain view
probable cause
protective sweep
public offense
public safety exception
reasonable
reasonable suspicion
search warrant
seizure
stop
***Terry* stop**
totality of the circumstances
waiver
wingspan

INTRODUCTION

Decency, security and liberty alike demand that governmental officials shall be subjected to the same rules of conduct that are commands to the citizen. In a government of laws, existence of the government will be imperiled if it fails to observe the law scrupulously. Our government is the potent, the omnipresent teacher. For good or ill, it teaches the whole people by its example. Crime is contagious. If the government becomes a lawbreaker, it breeds contempt for the law; it invites every man to become a law unto himself; it invites anarchy. To declare that in the administration of the criminal law the end justifies the means—to declare that the

> government may commit crimes in order to secure the conviction of a private criminal—would bring terrible retribution. Against this pernicious doctrine this court should resolutely set its face.

This synopsis was delivered by Supreme Court Justice Louis Brandeis in *Olmstead v. United States* (1928) and says, in effect, that government agents, including police officers, are subjected to certain restrictions in enforcing the laws. Those entrusted with the responsibility of protecting life and property must understand the principles of the federal and state constitutions and the duties that flow from their application, as well as the many laws and statutes that have been enacted. In short, police officers must know the law without the benefit of having gone to law school. Any violations of the law can result in evidence being disallowed under the exclusionary rule, as discussed in Chapter 2.

This chapter discusses primarily cases from the Supreme Court. However, the mere fact that the Court chooses not to hear a state court ruling does *not* mean the Court "upholds" that ruling, despite media headlines to that effect. For example, after the Court declined to review a case involving a caller's tip, some headlines read "Supreme Court upholds ban on traffic stops based on a caller's tip" (Rutledge, 2010a, p.64). The headlines do not include the fact that it is only for the state in which the case was heard and does not apply to any other states. The Court can review only about one percent of the 8,000+ cases it is asked to review year and has stressed that no position is to be inferred as to its views on the issues raised in the other 99 percent of cases. The Court has repeatedly said that non-review of a case "imports no expression of opinion upon the merits of the case" and no one should assign "any precedential value" to the non-review of a lower court ruling (*Teague v. Lane*, 1989). Officers need to know their own state's laws and precedent cases as well as those emanating from the Supreme Court.

In addition, the law of criminal procedure continues to change over time because this law reflects social norms that are never static. An example, to be discussed in detail in Chapter 11, is the USA PATRIOT Act, which was enacted immediately following and as a direct result of the September 11, 2001, terrorist attacks. This law expanded government authority in ways some say are too little, but others say are too much. The final answers will result from congressional changes to the law and judicial findings regarding those changes.

THE CHAPTER AT A GLANCE

This chapter begins with a brief look at discretion as it pertains to officers' abilities to police within the law and then turns to the Fourth Amendment, which governs searches and seizures. This is followed by an explanation of the police-citizen contact continuum and the objective of voluntary contact. Next, the *Terry* stop is discussed, as well as the constitutionality of road blocks and checkpoints and when a suspect may be lawfully detained. The chapter then examines lawful searches and lawful arrests, including de facto arrests, and discusses the importance of protecting suspects' rights (*Miranda* warning). The chapter concludes with a summary of the key cases presented.

POLICE DISCRETION AND THE LAW

Although our Constitution guarantees to all persons "equal protection of the law," police officers can and do exercise discretion in how they apply the law. They select options on what actions to take under certain circumstances. Chief Justice Warren Burger once stated: "The officer working the beat makes more decisions and exercises broader discretion affecting the daily lives of people every day and to a greater extent than a judge will exercise in a week."

Research by Stroshine et al. (2008) examined the informal "working rules" that govern police behavior and affect their discretionary decision making when determining when to stop, search or arrest a suspect. Among the working rules the researchers identified were the following:

- The importance of time, place, and appearance—officers look for things that do not fit (Stroshine et al., 2008, pp.322–324).
- "Do Unto Others"—being fair. Officers would not take action if they engaged in the same behavior themselves, for example, not wearing seat belts (p.325).
- "Threshold"—stopping only individuals who exceed a particular limit, for example speed limits (pp.327–329).

CAREER PROFILE

Erv Weinkauf (Retired Chief of Police, Concordia University–Saint Paul [Minnesota], Criminal Justice Department Chair)

The Lord often works in mysterious ways—my life has been no exception! During high school and college, I was preparing to become a Lutheran minister. Midway through my first year at Northwestern College I experienced a life-changing event and my life began to go in a different direction. I enlisted in the Army near the end of the Vietnam Conflict and became an airborne military policeman, serving in Germany for eighteen months. It was during that time that I developed an interest in law enforcement.

After returning from oversees, I worked for the Brown County (Minnesota) Sheriff's Office for several years prior to transferring to the New Ulm (Minnesota) Police Department. After being promoted to corporal, I began to develop a desire to teach and realized that in order for that opportunity to become a reality, I first would need to become better educated. Through the years, I earned three degrees in law enforcement and criminal justice leadership and graduated from the National FBI Academy. During that time, I was also privileged to teach for three colleges and two universities as well as for the Minnesota Chiefs' Leadership and CLEO [Chief Law Enforcement Officer] and Command Academies. I was trying to prepare myself to become a competitive candidate for a position in college academia after I retired from the profession I loved. Little did I realize God was grooming me for the next chapter in my life and my law enforcement and teaching experience would serve me well.

My wife and I took a pre-retirement vacation to Mexico three weeks before I retired. I started teaching four online classes that week and realized I was too old to handle two full-time jobs. Ironically, one of those classes was for Concordia University, Saint Paul. I retired as chief of police from the police department in 2009, after 35 years of service. Nine months later, I was a finalist for the Criminal Justice Department Chair position (my alma mater) for the university's online programs. The rest is history!

I assumed my responsibilities at Concordia University on January 1, 2010. I'm convinced that my education combined with the professional training and experience I received enabled me to be a competitive candidate for this position. I encourage working practitioners who have a desire to advance in their career or prepare themselves for another career, to seize as many learning opportunities as possible in order to become the best that they can be.

Make no mistake—working in criminal justice is not for everyone. There are certainly other vocations that offer greater monetary rewards, better hours, and are less dangerous, but there is no other profession that is eminently more gratifying in terms of giving back. Criminal justice is one of the noblest of professions, and I'm honored to have had the opportunity to serve.

- POP—"Pissing off the Police"—suspect demeanor influences officer's response to citizens. "Leniency might be afforded to persons who treat officers with respect, whereas the heavy hand of the law is extended to persons who are disrespectful, ill mannered or rude" (p.329).

In situations where officers use discretion—their professional judgment to choose from alternative courses of action—there is no liability unless evidence indicates the officer was guilty of a willful or malicious wrong. However, when there is no discretion, when officers are faced with a fixed, certain and imperative policy, there is no immunity.

Although officers have broad discretion, they are guided by several constitutional amendments and the holdings of the Supreme Court related to these amendments.

THE FOURTH AMENDMENT

> The right of the people to be secure in their persons, houses, papers, and effects, against unreasonable searches and seizures, shall not be violated, and no warrants shall issue, but upon probable cause, supported by oath or affirmation, and particularly describing the place to be searched, and the persons or things to be seized.

Arbitrary searches and seizures have no place in a democratic society. Colonial grievances against unreasonable searches and seizures partly led to the revolt against English authority. The Fourth Amendment to the Constitution guarantees the right of citizens to be secure from such arbitrary searches and seizures.

The constitutional standards for searches and seizures, including arrests, are contained in the Fourth Amendment, which requires that searches and seizures be reasonable and based on probable cause.

The terms *reasonable* and *probable cause* provide a very fine, but significant, weight to balance the scales of justice, which measure the conduct of all people. Without what is referred to as probable cause, the laws that govern us might easily become unbalanced, that is, too permissive or too restrictive. The second part of the Fourth Amendment, called the "warrant clause," states, "No warrants shall issue but upon probable cause." In other words, all warrants (search and arrest warrants) must be based on probable cause.

Reasonable

The rules for determining what constitutes a reasonable search or reasonable seizure result from interpretation of the first part of the Fourth Amendment, called the "reasonable search and seizure clause," which states, in part: "The right of the people to be secure in their persons, houses, papers, and effects, against unreasonable searches and seizures shall not be violated." ***Reasonable*** means sensible, justifiable and logical. A key determinant in whether an officer's actions are lawful is whether the officer has reasonable suspicion that criminal activity is occurring.

Reasonable suspicion, also referred to as *arguable suspicion*, is a legal standard that was defined in *United States v. Cortez* (1981) as "a particularized and objective basis for suspecting the particular person stopped of criminal activity." Reasonable

reasonable
Sensible, justifiable and logical.

reasonable suspicion
A legal standard defined in *United States v. Cortez* (1981) as "a particularized and objective basis for suspecting the particular person stopped of criminal activity"; also referred to as *arguable suspicion*.

suspicion is the basis for the *Terry* stop or frisk, to be discussed shortly, and requires less evidence than probable cause: "Reasonable suspicion is a lower level of justification than the probable cause required for arrest, and it can be established with evidence that is lower in both reliability and amount than would be needed for PC [probable cause]" (Rutledge, 2010c, pp.70–71).

Reasonable suspicion is used by law enforcement primarily for officer safety and is not to be used to search for illegal drugs, which would require probable cause. However, reasonable suspicion can quickly transition into probable cause.

In a pivotal case, a U.S. border patrol agent stopped a vehicle near Douglas, Arizona, suspecting the operator was smuggling aliens or drugs because it was traveling a usually deserted road and set off a sensor. A search of the vehicle turned up more than100 pounds of marijuana for which Arvizu, the driver, was convicted. However, the U.S. Court of Appeals reversed the district court decision, holding that each factor of reasonable suspicion should be reviewed independently. In *United States v. Arvizu* (2002), the Supreme Court reversed this decision, relying on past Court decisions that reasonable suspicion is based on the **totality of the circumstances**. The facts on which the suspicion is based must be reviewed as a whole. They are not to be examined individually. *Illinois v. Gates* (1983) likewise stated that the test for probable cause should be a totality of the circumstances.

totality of circumstances
Considering all factors involved in a given situation.

Probable Cause

The concept of probable cause is one of the oldest and most important in criminal law, having existed for more than 2,000 years and occurring in both Roman law and the common law of England. In *Draper v. United States* (1959), the Supreme Court stated, "Probable cause exists where the facts and circumstances within their (the arresting officers') knowledge and of which they had reasonable trustworthy information are sufficient in themselves to warrant a man of reasonable caution in the belief that an offense has been or is being committed."

Smith v. United States (1949) defines ***probable cause*** as "The sum total of layers of information and the synthesis of what the police have heard, what they know, and what they observe as trained officers. We [the courts] weigh not individual layers but the laminated total."

probable cause
Reasonable grounds for presuming guilt; facts that lead a person of ordinary care and prudence to believe and conscientiously entertain an honest and strong suspicion that a person is guilty of a crime.

Probable cause may be based on

- Observation by officers.
- Expertise of officers.
- Circumstantial factors.
- Information communicated to officers.

Often more than one source is involved.

Observational Probable Cause Observational probable cause is what officers see, hear or smell, that is, evidence presented directly to the senses. This is similar to eyewitness testimony and is the strongest form of probable cause. The courts have generally recognized certain types of events as being significant in determining probable cause.

Suspicious activities contribute to probable cause. For example, a car being driven slowly can be suspicious when (1) the car has circled a block several times, (2) the people in the car are carefully observing a building, (3) the building is closed and (4) the building is located in a high-crime area. All four factors contribute to probable cause. *Familiar criminal patterns* also contribute to probable cause. A person's conduct can indicate a familiar pattern associated with the sale of stolen property or narcotics or of someone casing a building. Any one fact by itself may not be sufficient, but collectively they provide justification—probable cause.

Expertise and Circumstantial Probable Cause Expertise and circumstantial probable cause are often tied to observational probable cause. Police officers' experience and knowledge of criminal traits and their ability to "put the pieces together" may also contribute. For example, two police officers questioned two men seen driving from an alley at 2:00 A.M. The officers noted the license number and occupants' names and questioned the driver and passenger. The two men were allowed to continue, but a short time later, when the officers learned there had been a burglary in a nearby town, they forwarded the description of the car and its occupants to the local police, who apprehended the suspects. A search of the vehicle revealed burglary tools, as well as the property taken in two burglaries, which led to the men's arrest and conviction.

Informational Probable Cause Informational probable cause covers a wide range of sources. In the case previously described, the information about the two suspects forwarded by the police to the nearby town constituted informational probable cause. The major categories of informational probable cause are official sources, victims of crimes, informants and witnesses.

Official sources include police bulletins, police broadcasts and roll-call information. This information can be relied on because it is received through official police channels. As in any other case, the original source must be reliable. For instance, if police officers make an arrest based on information obtained from other police officers, the original officers may be required to testify about *their* information source. That source must establish probable cause. Complete and otherwise credible information from an eyewitness, based on personal knowledge, is generally sufficient to establish probable cause.

Figure 8.1 illustrates the general factors that influence the formation of police suspicion and the relative frequency with which officers rely on these sources. The "time and place" factor refers to instances when an officer draws on his or her knowledge

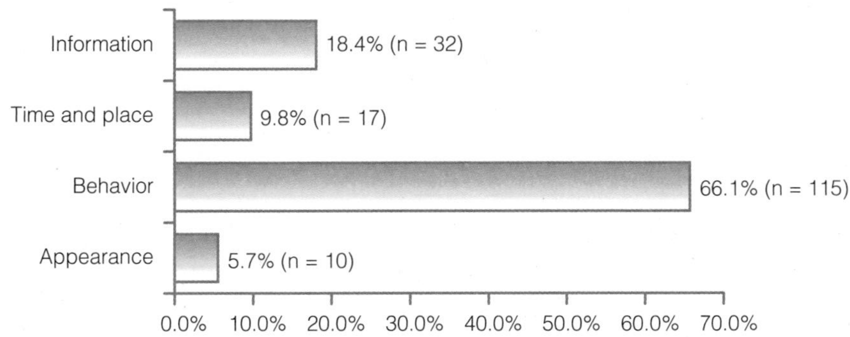

FIGURE 8.1 Main Reasons for Forming Suspicion

SOURCE: Adapted from Roger G. Dunham, Geoffrey P. Alpert, Meghan S. Stroshine and Katherine Bennett. "Transforming Citizens into Suspects: Factors That Influence the Formation of Police Suspicion." *Police Quarterly*, September 2005, p.375. Reprinted by permission of SAGE Publications.

of a particular location (e.g., park, warehouse district) and the types of activities that should or should not be occurring there at a specific time, such as after hours.

THE POLICE–CITIZEN CONTACT CONTINUUM

Police officers interact with citizens on several levels. On the first level, the voluntary contact level, officers ask to talk with a person to gather information about a crime, for example, a door-to-door canvas following a murder. The officers do not suspect the person of involvement in the crime. At the next level is a situation when an officer suspects a person may be involved or is about to be involved in criminal behavior and stops the person to "talk" to him or her. If the person believes he or she is required to comply, this is, in effect, a stop and requires reasonable suspicion. If during the "talk" the officer observes behavior (i.e., has reasonable suspicion) or learns information giving officers probable cause to believe the person is involved in a crime, officers may *briefly* detain the person to investigate further or they may arrest the person on probable cause. This progression is illustrated in Figure 8.2.

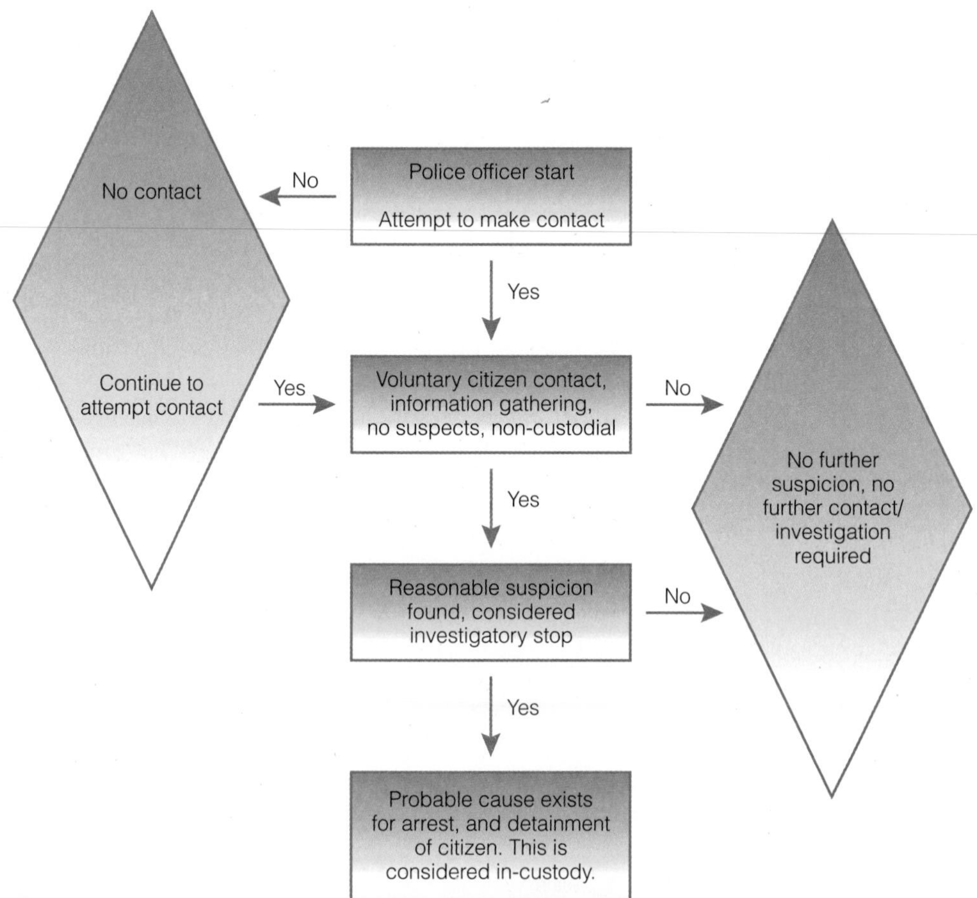

FIGURE 8.2 Progression from Reasonable Suspicion to Probable Cause

VOLUNTARY CONTACT

Voluntary contact is a worthy objective when interacting with citizens: "The key to creating a voluntary contact is to request cooperation in a manner that suggests an option or simply to strike up a normal, noncoercive conversation. The officer's exact words are critical. The officer must request or invite the subject's participation, not order, demand, require, instruct or otherwise coerce it" (Means and McDonald, 2009c, p.27). Advantages of voluntary contacts include a lower probability of causing defensiveness by the subject, a freer flow of information and an increased likelihood that a consent to search may be obtained (Means and McDonald, 2009c). In addition, there is far less risk of complaints, lawsuits and liability, and the federal *Miranda* rule is *not* applicable in this situation. Finally, a few minutes of voluntary contact can heighten rapport and trust and may provide time to acquire needed backup. No suspicion is required.

THE *TERRY* STOP

One basic responsibility of police officers, and one heavily reliant on reasonableness and probable cause, is investigating suspicious behavior. Officers may simply talk to someone acting suspiciously and decide no crime seems to be in progress or about to be committed, or they may confirm their suspicions and investigate further. The simple act of stopping someone based on reasonable suspicion may lead to a **stop**, alternately called an **investigatory stop**, a **field inquiry**, a threshold inquiry or, most commonly, a ***Terry* stop**.

The basic legal considerations in a stop situation were set forth in the landmark Supreme Court decision *Terry v. Ohio* (1968). This case also set forth when a stop might involve a frisk or pat down. Detective McFadden, a veteran police officer with 30 years of investigative experience, saw two men standing near a jewelry store. They seemed to be just talking, but to McFadden, "They just didn't look right." He suspected they were casing the store and were possibly armed. He watched for a while as the men walked around, looked into the store window, walked to the corner and returning to the original spot. A third man joined them, went inside the store for a moment and came back out.

Deciding to act, McFadden approached the three men, identified himself as a police officer, asked for their names and then grabbed one man, John Terry. McFadden made a quick pat down of Terry's outer clothing and felt what might be a gun in Terry's coat pocket. It turned out to be a .38 caliber revolver; another gun was removed from the coat of Chilton. Terry and Chilton were formally charged with carrying concealed weapons and found guilty. Terry and Chilton appealed their conviction to the Supreme Court, but before the Court's decision, Chilton had died, so its review applied only to Terry.

The issue: Is it always unreasonable for a police officer to seize a person and conduct a limited search for weapons unless there is probable cause for arrest? Recognizing McFadden as a man of experience, training and knowledge, the Supreme Court answered "no," upholding the trial court verdict. The Court noted that McFadden, as a man of "ordinary care and prudence," had waited until he had strengthened his suspicions, making his move just before what he believed would be an armed robbery.

stop
Briefly detaining someone who is acting suspiciously; a stop is not an arrest.

investigatory stop
The simple act of stopping someone based on reasonable suspicion, alternately called a *field inquiry*, a *threshold inquiry* or, most commonly, a *Terry stop*.

field inquiry
Briefly detaining or stopping persons to determine who they are or what they are up to.

***Terry* stop**
The simple act of stopping someone based on reasonable suspicion; alternately called an *investigatory stop*, a *field inquiry*, or a *threshold inquiry*.

seizure

A forcible detention or taking of a person or property in an arrest.

pat down

An exploratory search of an individual's clothing; the "search" phase of a stop and frisk.

frisk

A patting down or minimal search of a person to determine the presence of a dangerous weapon.

The Supreme Court (*Terry v. Ohio*) said there is a **seizure** whenever a police officer uses physical force or a show of authority to restrain an individual's freedom to walk away (or to take control of property), and there is a search when an officer explores an individual's clothing even though it is called a "**pat down**" or "**frisk**."

A *stop* is a seizure if physical force or a show of authority is used. A *frisk* is a search.

Although stopping and frisking fall short of an arrest, they are definitely forms of search and seizure. Police officers stop citizens daily, but most encounters cannot be considered "seizure of the person" because the officers do not restrain the individual's liberty. Defining the term *frisk*, however, leaves no other alternative than to consider it a search. As the Supreme Court (*Terry*) cautioned, "It is simply fantastic to urge that such a procedure, performed in public by a police officer, while the citizen stands helpless, perhaps facing a wall with his hands raised, is a 'petty indignity'. . . . It is a serious intrusion upon the sanctity of the person, which may inflict great indignity and arouse strong resentment, and it is not to be undertaken lightly." The Court gave its own definition of *stop and frisk* by calling it a "protective search for weapons."

Stop and frisk is a protective search for weapons in which the intrusion must be limited to a scope reasonably designed to discover guns, knives, clubs and other hidden instruments that may be used to assault a police officer or others. *Terry* established that the authority to stop and frisk is independent of the power to arrest. A stop is *not* an arrest, but it is a seizure within the meaning of the Fourth Amendment and therefore requires reasonableness.

Rutledge (2009a, p.66) cautions, "Although it's common to see the term 'stop and frisk,' it's possible that there might be justification for a stop, but not for a frisk." A frisk is justifiable only if there is a reasonable suspicion the detainee may be armed and dangerous.

A traffic stop is one situation in which this situation may arise. In *Arizona v. Johnson* (2009) officers assigned to the state gang task force in Tucson were patrolling a neighborhood in 2002 known for gang-related activity. They stopped a vehicle after a license plate check showed it had a suspended registration. They did not suspect the occupants were engaging in criminal activity. One officer saw that Johnson, a passenger in the car, was wearing Crips gang colors and had a scanner in his jacket pocket. The officer asked Johnson to step out of the vehicle and, believing he was a gang member, for safety, she patted him down, feeling the butt of a gun at his waist. After a brief struggle Johnson was on the ground, handcuffed and then charged and convicted with unlawful possession of a weapon. The Arizona Court of Appeals reversed suppressing the evidence on the basis that police had no reasonable suspicion that Johnson was engaged in criminal activity as a passenger in a stopped car. The Arizona Supreme Court declined to review, so the state appealed to the U.S. Supreme Court, which unanimously reversed the Arizona suppression ruling. This decision goes back to the *Terry* decision as well as the following three cases upholding the right to frisk (Scarry, 2009b, p.22).

In *Pennsylvania v. Mimms* (1977) the Court held that police officers making a lawful traffic stop may order the driver out of the vehicle and may, without violating the Fourth Amendment, pat down the driver if they believe the driver is armed and dangerous. In this case the Court noted statistics showing that 30 percent of officers shot in the line of duty were fired upon as they approached someone seated in a vehicle (Rutledge, 2009b, p.69). To reduce this risk, officers may routinely order the driver out without a reason given. *Maryland v. Wilson* (1997) extended the rule holding that all passengers in a lawfully stopped vehicle may be ordered out without a reason given (Scarry, 2009b, p.22).

Maryland v. Wilson established that, given the likelihood of a traffic stop leading to either violence or the destruction of evidence when passengers are in the vehicle, officers may order passengers out of the car pending completion of the stop.

Finally, *Brendlin v. California* (2007) held that both drivers and passengers are seized in a traffic stop for purposes of the Fourth Amendment.

Based on *Terry* and these three precedent cases, the Court held in *Arizona v. Johnson*: "In sum, as stated in *Brendlin*, a traffic stop of a car communicates to a reasonable passenger that he or she is not free to terminate the encounter with the police and move about at will. . . . The officer surely was not constitutionally required to give Johnson an opportunity to depart the scene after he exited the vehicle without first ensuring that, in so doing, she was not permitting a dangerous person to get behind her."

In other words: "*Terry* allows officers to take all necessary steps to protect themselves if the circumstances reasonably warrant such measures" (Scarry, 2009a, p.28). In addition to a protective frisk for weapons, some states allow officers to draw their guns, have a reasonable number of backup officers, place individuals in handcuffs or place them in the back seat of a squad car without probable cause. What is allowed varies from state to state.

Several key court cases have clarified when police can and cannot execute a lawful stop and frisk. The decision in *Florida v. J. L.* (2000) established that reasonable suspicion for an investigative stop does not arise from a mere anonymous tip. In this case, police acted solely on a tip describing a man carrying a gun and, with no other reason to suspect the individual of criminal involvement, frisked the man. Although the frisk did yield a firearm and the man was charged with carrying a concealed weapon, in reviewing the case, the Supreme Court upheld lower court rulings that granted the trial court action to suppress the gun as evidence as a result of an unlawful search, noting that reliance solely on an anonymous tip would create a vulnerability to pranks, grudges and other unreliable information.

When police receive an anonymous tip, they must take steps to verify its reliability before taking action. This is easier if the tipster provides predictive information about what the suspect is about to do.

Another case focusing on justification for a stop and frisk is *Illinois v. Wardlow* (2000), in which the Supreme Court ruled that a person's sudden flight upon seeing a police officer can be used to establish reasonable suspicion for a stop. In this case, Wardlow was seen holding an opaque bag in a Chicago neighborhood known for drug activity. When a group of police cars drove past him, he fled. The officers, acting on reasonable suspicion, pursued, stopped and frisked Wardlow, finding a loaded gun.

The trial court convicted Wardlow of possessing a firearm, but the appellate court overturned the conviction, stating the discovery of the gun was the result of an unjustified stop and frisk and thus, that evidence should have been suppressed. The Supreme Court reversed, with Chief Justice William Rehnquist writing, "Headlong flight—wherever it occurs—is the consummate act of evasion; it is not necessarily indicative of wrongdoing, but it is certainly suggestive of such." The Court noted the officers had based their reasonable suspicion on three facts, not just one—the suspect's flight, the location of the incident as a known drug area and the opaque bag in the suspect's hand. Basing reasonable suspicion on only one fact, such as the flight alone, is less likely to hold up if challenged in court.

Requesting Identification

The Supreme Court has ruled states can criminalize a refusal to provide identification to an officer conducting a valid stop. In June 2004, the Supreme Court ruled in *Hiibel v. Sixth Judicial District Court of Nevada, Humboldt County* that police may require persons to identify themselves unless their name would be incriminating. In this case, police stopped Hiibel during an investigative stop involving a reported assault. Nevada's "stop and identify" statute requires a person detained by an officer under suspicious circumstances to identify himself. Hiibel argued that his Fourth Amendment right against unreasonable search and seizure and his Fifth Amendment right against compelled self-incrimination were violated by the Nevada law. Hiibel refused 11 times to identify himself, so he was arrested and charged with the misdemeanor of refusing to identify himself. The Nevada Supreme Court upheld his conviction, as did the Supreme Court.

Plain View and Plain Feel/Touch

plain view

Evidence that is not concealed and is seen by an officer engaged in a lawful activity; what is observed in plain view is not construed within the meaning of the Fourth Amendment as a search.

Plain view refers to evidence that is not concealed and is seen by an officer engaged in a lawful activity. An important distinction exists, however, between an object being in plain view and whether such status implicates the plain view doctrine (Means and McDonald, 2009c, p.26):

> Law enforcement officers commonly use the phrase "it was in plain view" to explain how an officer located an item. Many officers believe that using that phrase in that way is equivalent to saying that the "Plain View Doctrine" applies. In fact, there are two fundamentally different principles involved. . . .
>
> The Plain View Doctrine involves the warrantless seizure of items, not just the visual observation of them. The doctrine only applies to items that are seized from an area that is protected by the Fourth Amendment. The Fourth Amendment protects areas where people have a reasonable expectation of privacy. . . .
>
> The doctrine first requires police to lawfully be present in the physical location from which the item is viewed. Second, the officer must observe the item through his sense of sight without moving or manipulating things to allow the viewing, that is, the items must be in plain view. (*Arizona v. Hicks*, 1987)

Vision can be augmented with binoculars and flashlights, but it is not proper to move or pick up items without probable cause to believe the items are contraband.

Closely related to the plain view doctrine is the **plain feel/touch doctrine** used in several states. A pivotal case in the plain feel/touch doctrine is *Minnesota v. Dickerson* (1993). Two officers saw Dickerson leave a known crack house and, upon seeing their marked squad car, abruptly turn and walk in the opposite direction. This aroused the officers' suspicions, so they followed Dickerson into the alley, ordered him to stop and patted him down. They found a suspicious small lump in Dickerson's jacket. Dickerson was arrested and charged with drug possession. The officer testified in court that during the pat down, he felt a small lump in Dickerson's front pocket and, after manipulating it with his fingers, determined it felt like a lump of crack cocaine but never thought it was a weapon. The trial court found the search to be legal under the Fourth Amendment, stating, "To this Court, there is no distinction as to which sensory perception the officer uses to conclude the material is contraband. An experienced officer may rely upon his sense of smell in DUI [driving under the influence] stops or in recognizing the smell of burning marijuana in an automobile. . . . The sense of touch, grounded in experience and training, is as reliable as perceptions drawn from the other senses. 'Plain feel,' therefore, is no different than 'plain view.' "

plain feel/touch doctrine

Related to the plain view doctrine; an officer who feels/touches something suspicious during the course of lawful activity can investigate further.

The Minnesota Supreme Court, however, overturned the conviction, stating that the sense of touch is less immediate and less reliable than that of sight and is far more intrusive into the personal privacy that is at the core of the Fourth Amendment. A frisk that goes beyond that allowed under *Terry* is not valid. The Supreme Court upheld the ruling of the Minnesota Supreme Court that the cocaine seizure was invalid:

> This goes beyond *Terry*, which authorizes a pat down for only one purpose: officer safety. That was absent here because the officer admitted that what he felt was not a weapon. The Court's decision might have been different, however, had the officer testified that he knew it was not a weapon when he felt the lump, but that he had probable cause to believe—from his experience as a police officer and the circumstances of this case—that the lump was cocaine. If those were the circumstances, the seizure may have been valid, not under stop and frisk, but under probable cause.

This ruling supports limited plain touch/feel during frisks and, if contraband is plainly felt by the officer in good faith, allows any discovered evidence to be admissible in court.

The Court has extended the *Dickerson* logic to luggage searches, ruling that police can visually inspect a bus passenger's luggage but cannot squeeze or otherwise manipulate baggage to determine whether it contains contraband (*Bond v. United States*, 2000). Chief Justice Rehnquist stated, "A bus passenger fully expects that his bag may be handled. He does not expect that other bus passengers or bus employees will feel the bag in an exploratory manner." It is unlikely, particularly in the wake of the September 11, 2001, terrorist attacks, that the ruling will extend to air travel, where the public has a lesser degree of expectation of privacy because of security issues.

In addition to this ruling, in *United States v. Drayton* (2002), the Supreme Court ruled that bus passengers do not need to be advised of their right not to cooperate during an otherwise legitimately structured, consensual, bus interdiction.

- **Plain view**—allow seizure of apparent criminal items seen with lawful access
- **Plain feel**—where an item is felt during lawful touching and is immediately apparent as contraband or a weapon, it can be retrieved
- **Plain smell**—both officers and trained dogs can use the olfactory sense to detect the presence of seizable objects
- **Plain hearing**—conversation carried on in the presence of an officer or informant can be lawfully overheard
- **Plain shape**—containers can be opened where their outward appearance reveals criminal contents

FIGURE 8.3 Plain Sense Cheat Sheet

SOURCE: Devallis Rutledge. "Plain Sense Seizures: Using the Senses to Detect Contraband and Evidence." *Police*, April 2007, p.71.

Figure 8.3 offers a "plain sense cheat sheet" summarizing when officers are lawfully able to apply their senses to detect contraband and evidence.

ROAD BLOCKS AND CHECKPOINTS

Border checkpoints, because they serve a broad social purpose, have been declared constitutional. In *United States v. Martinez-Fuerte* (1976) the Court affirmed that "a vehicle may be stopped at a fixed checkpoint for brief questioning of its occupants even though there is no reason to believe the particular vehicle contains aliens." A similar ruling was handed down in 2004 in *United States v. Flores-Montano*, which involved a search of a vehicle fuel tank at the Mexican border. Speaking for the Court, Chief Justice Rehnquist said,

> Complex balancing tests to determine what is a "routine" search of a vehicle . . . have no place in border searches of vehicles. The government's interest in preventing the entry of unwanted persons and effects is at its zenith at the international border. Time and again, we have stated that searches made at the border, pursuant to the longstanding rights of the sovereign to protect itself by stopping and examining persons and property crossing into this country, are reasonable simply by virtue of the fact that they occur at the border.

Sobriety checkpoints, serving the broad social benefit of protecting motorists from drunk drivers, are another form of stop that have been declared constitutional, provided they are conducted fairly and do not pose a safety hazard (*Michigan Department of State Police v. Sitz*, 1990).

Informational roadblocks have also been declared constitutional. *Illinois v. Lidster* (2004), allowed roadblocks to be used when police are merely seeking witnesses who may have information about crimes.

The Supreme Court has upheld roadblocks at national borders, sobriety checkpoints and informational checkpoints.

Drug checkpoints have been found to violate the Fourth Amendment. In *City of Indianapolis v. Edmond* (2000), the Supreme Court deemed drug interdiction roadblocks an unconstitutional means to a valid law enforcement end, with Justice Sandra Day O'Connor writing for the majority: "We cannot sanction stops justified only by the generalized and ever-present possibility that interrogation and inspection may reveal that any given motorist has committed some crime." This ruling makes *general crime control checkpoints* unconstitutional. In addition, *driver's license checkpoints* are not permitted. Thus, the Fourth Amendment's reasonableness standard keeps officers from randomly stopping vehicles to check driver's licenses and registration.

The Supreme Court has held that drug checkpoints, general crime control checkpoints and driver's license checkpoints are not constitutional.

DETENTION

Rutledge (2010c, p.70) notes, "A **detention** occurs when an officer has said or done something that would cause a reasonable innocent person to believe he is not free to disregard the police presence and go about his business. A detention must be justified by 'reasonable suspicion' of criminal activity on the part of the detainee. Under this standard, it is counterproductive error for officers to speak of 'PC for the stop.' Probable cause is *never* constitutionally required for detentions" (*United States v. Sokolow*).

detention
Occurs when an officer has said or done something that would cause reasonable innocent persons to believe they are not free to disregard the police presence and go about their business; must be justified by reasonable suspicion; the higher standard of probable cause is not constitutionally required for detention.

Length of the Detention

A *Terry* stop generally takes one of two paths: It either progresses to probable cause to arrest or it fails to develop into PC and requires the suspect's release. However: "Reasonable suspicion authorizes the police to detain suspect while they investigate the relevant suspicious circumstances" (Means and McDonald, 2009a, p.22). This stop is a seizure and is governed by the Fourth Amendment: "If a *Terry* stop lasts too long, courts will rule that an arrest has occurred, which of course requires the higher standard of probable cause" (p.22). As such, courts have generally held that investigative detentions are to be resolved within a timeframe measured in minutes, not hours. In *United States v. Place* (1983) the Supreme Court said, "In assessing the effect of the length of the detention, we take into account whether the police diligently pursue their investigation. . . . Although we decline to adopt any outside time limitation for a permissible *Terry* stop, we have never approved a seizure of the person for the prolonged 90-minute period involved here and cannot do so on the facts presented by this case."

Detentions include pedestrian stops, vehicle stops and the restraint of occupants while a search warrant is being served. The latter situation describes a detention that occurred in the case of *Michigan v. Summers* (1981), in which police officers arrived at Summers's home to execute a search warrant. They encountered Summers coming down the steps and asked him to let them in and wait while they conducted their search. They found narcotics in the basement and then searched Summers, finding heroin in his pocket. The court ruled it was legal to require the suspect to reenter his house and remain there until evidence establishing probable cause was found.

In *Illinois v. McArthur* (2001), the Supreme Court ruled that police did not violate the Fourth Amendment when they detained a man outside his trailer home for several hours while officers sought a warrant to search the residence for drugs. McArthur's estranged wife, while moving her belongings out of their home, informed police her husband had "dope" hidden under a couch. When police knocked on the door and asked for consent to search the home, McArthur refused. While one officer left to get a search warrant, McArthur stepped out of the house onto the porch. Suspecting McArthur would destroy the evidence, police told McArthur he could not reenter the residence unless accompanied by an officer until the search warrant was obtained. Two hours later, the search warrant was acquired and police searched the trailer, finding less than 2.5 grams of marijuana.

The trial court suppressed the evidence as a result of an unlawful police seizure, but the Supreme Court, in an 8–1 ruling, reversed:

> The Court determined that this search and seizure was "reasonable" in light of four conditions: (1) the police had "probable cause" to believe contraband was in the home; (2) the police had good reason to believe McArthur would destroy the contraband before they could return with a warrant; (3) the police made "reasonable efforts to reconcile their law enforcement needs with the demands of personal privacy," i.e., they did not search without a warrant, did not immediately arrest him, and did allow him some access to his home in the interim period; and (4) the restraint was for a limited time.

Use of Force during Detention

Courts have generally held that officers may use reasonably minimal force to safely conduct an investigative detention: "And, as a practical matter, if an officer is having to use more than absolutely minimal force in an investigative detention, the subject is almost always doing something at that point for which there would be probable cause to arrest him" (Means and McDonald, 2009b, p.12).

LAWFUL SEARCHES

A search, in the context of the Fourth Amendment, involves governmental invasion of privacy. Searches are intended to obtain incriminating evidence, but must be justifiable.

The principal justifications established by the courts for the right to search are when

- A search warrant has been issued.
- No warrant has been issued but:
  - Consent to search was given.
  - Exigent circumstances exist.

There is no expectation of privacy and thus, no requirement for a search warrant.

These circumstances are the preconditions for a reasonable, legal search.

Searches Conducted with a Warrant

A **search warrant** is an order issued (in writing or over the phone) by a judge, a **magistrate**, with jurisdiction in the area where the search is to be made. The Fourth Amendment states that warrants must particularly describe "the place to be searched and the persons or things to be seized." To get a search warrant, police officers must first prepare an **affidavit**, a written statement about a set of facts establishing probable cause to search. The officer then presents the affidavit to a magistrate and swears under oath that the statement is truthful. If the magistrate determines that probable cause to search exists, a search warrant is issued. The warrant must contain the reasons for requesting the search warrant, the names of the persons presenting affidavits, what specifically is being sought and the signature of the judge issuing it.

search warrant

A judicial order directing a peace officer to search for specific property, seize it and return it to the court; it may be a written order or an order given over the telephone.

magistrate

A judge.

affidavit

A statement reduced to writing and sworn to before a judge or notary having authority to administer an oath.

Technically all searches are to be made under the authority of a search warrant issued by a magistrate. A search warrant is a judicial order, based on probable cause, directing a police officer to search for specific property, seize it and return it to the court. The search must be limited to the specific area and specific items delineated in the warrant.

Anticipatory Search Warrants In *United States v. Grubbs* (2006), the Supreme Court ruled that a search warrant can be procured based on prior knowledge that an illegal product or substance will be delivered. The *Grubbs* decision confirms that anticipatory warrants are valid if it is properly shown that contraband or evidence is likely be found at the target location.

What May Be Seized A search warrant must clearly specify the things to be seized. The prosecution must accept the burden of proof when items not specified in the warrant are seized. Such items can be seized if a reasonable relationship exists between the search and the seizure of materials not described—that is, they are similar to the items described, they are related to the particular crime described or they are contraband. **Contraband** is anything illegal to import, export, produce or possess, such as heroin or a machine gun. The contraband need not be connected to the crime described in the warrant.

contraband

Anything illegal to import, export, produce or possess, such as heroin or a machine gun.

Any evidence illegally seized by police will be considered "tainted" and, thus, inadmissible in court, regardless of how relevant it is to proving the suspect's guilt, through application of the **exclusionary rule**. By extension, any further evidence obtained from the initial illegal search or seizure will also be deemed inadmissible via the *fruit of the poisonous tree doctrine*, a metaphor to explain that a tainted source of evidence (the tree) and anything it bears (the fruit) are unconstitutional. These rules exist to deter police from taking illegal means to achieve a "just" ends.

exclusionary rule

A U.S. Supreme Court ruling that any evidence seized in violation of the Fourth Amendment will not be admissible in a federal or state trial.

Gaining Entrance Police officers are usually required to announce their authority and purpose before entering a home. In *Wilson v. Arkansas* (1995), a unanimous Supreme Court held that, without exigent circumstances, officers are required to "knock and announce" to meet the reasonableness requirements of the Fourth Amendment. Such a requirement protects citizens' right to privacy, reduces the risk of possible violence to both police and occupants and may prevent unnecessary destruction of private property.

Sometimes the suspect will not allow entrance, or there may be no one home. In such cases police officers may forcibly enter the house by breaking an inner or outer door or window. If the dwelling is an apartment, they could get a passkey from a caretaker, but this would still be considered a **forced entry**. Opening a closed but unlocked door or window is also considered a forced entry.

forced entry

An announced or unannounced entry into a dwelling or a building by force for the purpose of executing a search or arrest warrant to avoid the needless destruction of property, to prevent violent and deadly force against the officer and to prevent the escape of a suspect.

In the landmark knock-and-announce case, *United States v. Banks* (2003), the Supreme Court unanimously decided that 15 to 20 seconds is adequate time for officers to wait before forcibly entering a dwelling to execute a search warrant. An audio or video recording of the knock-notice announcement provides evidence of compliance as well as the amount of time elapsed before forcing entry. In *Hudson v. Michigan* (2006) the Court held 5–4 that a violation of the knock-and-announce rule does not automatically invoke the exclusionary rule if deterrence of police misconduct outweighs the social costs. In an opinion clearly supporting law enforcement, Justice Antonin Scalia explained this balance of interests:

> The social costs to be weighed against deterrence are considerable here. In addition to the grave adverse consequence that excluding relevant incriminating evidence always entails—the risk of releasing dangerous criminals—imposing such a massive remedy would generate a constant flood of alleged failures to observe the rule, and claims that any asserted justification for a no-knock entry had inadequate support. Another consequence would be police officers' refraining from timely entry after knocking and announcing, producing preventable violence against the officers in some cases, and the destruction of evidence in others. Next to these social costs are the deterrence benefits. The value of deterrence depends on the strength of the incentive to commit the forbidden act. That incentive is minimal here, where ignoring knock-and-announce can realistically be expected to achieve nothing but the prevention of evidence destruction and avoidance of life-threatening resistance, dangers which suspend the requirement when there is "reasonable suspicion" that they exist. . . . Massive deterrence is hardly necessary. Contrary to Hudson's argument that without suppression there will be no deterrence, many forms of police misconduct are deterred by civil-rights suits, and by the consequences of increasing professionalism of police forces, including a new emphasis on internal police discipline. (*Hudson v. Michigan*, 2006)

Using Restraints in High-Risk Situations In *Muehler v. Mena* (2005), the Supreme Court ruled that the Fourth Amendment permits officers executing high-risk search warrants for dangerous people, weapons or contraband to handcuff and detain occupants of the premises during the duration of the search. Mere police questioning of those detained is not a seizure and does not require Fourth Amendment justification.

Nighttime and No-Knock Search A search warrant is normally to be served during daylight hours and requires officers to knock and announce themselves. As just discussed, however, circumstances sometimes exist where these procedures could render the police less effective. In such instances special warrants may be issued. Two types of search warrants, nighttime and no-knock, must be authorized by a judge as special provisions of a search warrant.

Nighttime search warrants (also called **nightcap warrants**) must state the facts for fearing that unless the search is conducted at night, the objects of the search might be lost, destroyed or removed. Justifications for a nighttime search include the imminent consumption or movement of drugs, knowledge that the drug trafficking occurs only at night, darkness being essential to officer safety or a case where a nighttime search would be less intrusive, for example, in a business open during the day.

nightcap warrants
Nighttime search or arrest warrants.

Unannounced entries to execute search warrants must also receive prior judicial authorization. The **no-knock search warrant** is reserved for situations where the judge recognizes that normal citizen cooperation is unlikely and that an announced entry may result in loss, destruction or removal of the objects of the search. For example, surprise entries are often used in searches for narcotics and gambling equipment. In either instance the court usually acknowledges that evidence can easily be destroyed during the time required to give notice, demand admittance and accept denial of entry.

no-knock search warrant
Authorization by a magistrate upon the issuance of a search warrant to enter a premise by force without notification to avoid the chance that evidence may be destroyed if the officers' presence was announced.

Administrative Warrants An **administrative** or **inspection warrant** is issued by a court to regulate building, fire, plumbing, electrical, health, safety, labor or zoning codes if voluntary compliance cannot be obtained. It does not justify a police entry to make an arrest.

administrative warrant
Official permission to investigate the cause of a fire after the fire has been extinguished.

inspection warrant
Official permission to investigate the cause of a fire after the fire has been extinguished.

Public safety personnel may enter structures that are on fire to extinguish the blaze. After the fire has been extinguished, officials may remain for a reasonable time to investigate the cause of the blaze (*Michigan v. Tyler*, 1978). After this time, if the police want to return to the scene to investigate the cause, they may need an administrative warrant. Such warrants require an affidavit stating the location and legal description of the property; the purpose, area and time of the search; and the use of the building. Searches are limited to items specified in the warrant. Evidence found may be seized, but once officers leave after finding evidence, they must have a criminal warrant to return for a further search.

Searches Conducted without a Warrant

The courts have recognized certain situations and conditions in which officers may conduct a search without first obtaining a warrant. Although laws vary from state to state, three basic exceptions are recognized throughout the country.

Warrantless searches are justified when consent to search is given, when exigent circumstances exist or when no right to privacy exists.

Warrantless Searches with Consent The Supreme Court has ruled that a search conducted following lawfully given consent is an exception to the warrant and probable cause requirements of the Fourth Amendment. In a search where consent is given, the **consent** must not be given in response to a claim of lawful authority by the officer to conduct the search at the moment.

consent
To agree; to give permission; voluntary oral or written permission to search a person's premises or property.

Consent must be free and voluntary, and the search must be limited to the area for which the consent is given.

A recognized exception to this general rule is when undercover operations are involved.

When a court is asked to determine if consent to search was "free and voluntary," it considers the subject's age, background, mental condition and education. Officers must not show weapons when making the request, as the courts have considered such displays coercive. The number of officers involved should not be a factor if no aggressiveness is shown.

The time of day might also be a consideration. Officers should generally avoid seeking voluntary consent to search at night. In *Monroe v. Pape* (1961), Justice Felix Frankfurter said, "Modern totalitarianisms have been a stark reminder, but did not newly teach, that the kicked-in door is the symbol of a rule of fear and violence fatal to institutions founded on respect for the integrity of man. . . . Searches of the dwelling house were the special object of this universal condemnation of official intrusion. Nighttime search was the evil in its most obnoxious form."

Perhaps most important is *how* the request is made. It must not be a command. Furthermore, officers must make known the fact that the consent may be withdrawn at any time, requiring officers to end the search immediately.

One's right to privacy is never greater than when in one's home—a right guaranteed by the Fourth Amendment. The Supreme Court's ruling in *Georgia v. Randolph* (2006) changes the rules governing some consent searches of private premises. When adult co-residents of a dwelling are both present, and one denies consent to enter and search and the other grants consent, the denial of consent by one overrules the consent by the other.

Warrantless Searches under Exigent Circumstances The implicit right to privacy contained within the Fourth Amendment provides the rationale to guide law enforcement in obtaining search warrants whenever possible. However, there are situations when **exigent circumstances**—emergency situations or extenuating circumstances—exist to justify a degree of police infringement on personal privacy to achieve a legitimate, overriding law enforcement objective, such as securing public safety or the safety of the officer. The exigency category includes imminent substantial property damage, imminent destruction of evidence, fresh pursuit of a dangerous offender, preventing escape of someone sought to be detained or arrested in public, public safety/community caretaking, and rescue/emergency aid (Rutledge, 2010b, p.60).

exigent circumstances
The same as emergency situations.

In situations where police officers believe they have established probable cause but have no time to secure a warrant, they can act without a warrant, but a defense lawyer can challenge the search's legality. Although a number of challenges can be raised, two occur most frequently.

When police officers conduct a warrantless search, they may be challenged on the basis that

- Probable cause was not established—given the facts, a magistrate would not have issued a warrant.
- The officers had time to secure a warrant and had no justification to act without one.

In *Brigham City, Utah v. Stuart* (2006) a case where police entered a private home to break up a fight, the Supreme Court ruled that officers may enter a home without a warrant to render emergency assistance to an injured occupant or to protect an occupant from imminent injury. In this case the Court held, "The "emergency aid exception" does not depend on the officers' subjective intent or the seriousness of any crime they are investigating when the emergency arises. It requires only an objectively reasonable basis for believing that a person within the house is in need of immediate aid."

In *Michigan v. Fisher* (2009) officers answered a call from a neighbor that Fisher was "going crazy" in his house. Upon arrival they saw a smashed pickup truck with blood visible on the hood, damaged fencing and broken windows. Through the windows they could see Fisher throwing things and heard him screaming. The officers forced entry and arrested Fisher after he pointed a gun at one of them. He was charged with assault and weapons offenses, but moved to suppress the officers' observations inside the home as products of illegal entry. The motion was granted, upheld by the Michigan Court of Appeals and let stand by the Michigan Supreme Court. The state appealed to the Supreme Court, which reversed the lower courts' decisions, twice applying the emergency aid exception to protect a person *from himself*:

> Officers can enter when it reasonably appears someone inside may need emergency aid, regardless of the officers' actual, subjective motivations for going inside. . . . It would be objectively reasonable to believe that Fisher's projectiles might have a human target (perhaps a spouse or child) or that Fisher would hurt himself in the course of his rage. Officers do not need ironclad proof of a likely serious, life-threatening injury to invoke the emergency aid exception. It does not meet the needs of law enforcement or the demands of public safety to require officers to walk away from a situation like the one they encountered here.

Police are duty bound to prevent violence and restore order: "The police are not required to stand by as if refereeing a fight and wait to intervene only when things are decidedly one-sided; rather, they are required to prevent harm when they are able" (Means and McDonald, 2010, p.20).

Courts have recognized times when exigent circumstances justify reasonable yet warrantless searches and seizures based on police officers' decisions, including (1) searches incidental to a lawful arrest, (2) searches of automobiles and other conveyances and (3) plain view and plain feel/touch situations.

Warrantless Searches Incidental to a Lawful Arrest In a search incidental to a lawful arrest, the search must be made simultaneously with the arrest and must be confined to the immediate vicinity of the arrest (*Chimel v. California*, 1969). In *Chimel*, officers went to the suspect's home with a warrant to arrest Chimel on a charge of burglarizing a coin shop and told him they wanted to "look around."

The officers opened kitchen cabinets, searched through closets, looked behind furniture in every room and even searched the garage. (Before this case, the courts had accepted extensive searches incidental to an arrest.) The officers had Mrs. Chimel open drawers and move contents so they could look for items removed in the burglary. The search took nearly an hour and turned up numerous stolen coins.

Chimel was convicted in a California court but appealed his burglary conviction on the grounds that the coins had been unconstitutionally seized. The Supreme Court determined,

> When an arrest is made, it is reasonable for the arresting officer to search the person arrested in order to remove any weapons that the latter might seek to use in order to resist arrest or affect his escape.
>
> It is entirely reasonable for the arresting officer to search for and seize any evidence on the arrestee's person in order to prevent its concealment or destruction and the area from within which the arrestee might gain possession of a weapon or destructible evidence.

In the *Chimel* case, the Supreme Court specified that the area of search can include only the arrestee's person and the area within his or her immediate control. The Court defined ***immediate control*** as being that area within the person's reach, also called the person's **wingspan**.

immediate control

Within a person's immediate reach; also called *wingspan*.

wingspan

The area within a person's reach; also known as *immediate control*.

Limitations on a search made incidental to an arrest are found in the *Chimel* Rule, which states that the area of the search must be within the suspect's immediate control—that is, it must be within his or her reach.

The Court noted that if an arrest is used as an excuse to conduct a thorough search, such as in the *Chime*l case, the police would have power to conduct "general searches," declared unconstitutional by the Fourth Amendment more than 200 years ago.

In addition to allowing a limited search of suspects and the area within their reach, the Supreme Court has also allowed the **protective sweep**, defined as "a quick and limited *search of premises*, incident to an arrest and conducted to protect police officers and or others" (*Maryland v. Buie*, 1990). A protective sweep, often referred to as a ***Buie* sweep**, might include quick checks of closets or behind doors to see if anyone who may pose a threat is present.

protective sweep

A quick and limited search of premises, incident to an arrest and conducted to protect police officers or others.

Buie sweep

A quick check of closets or behind doors to see if anyone who may pose a threat is present.

Warrantless Searches of Automobiles and Other Conveyances The Supreme Court has "rewritten the rule book on when and what you can search for in an automobile" (Rutledge, 2009b, p.68). The landmark case of *New York v. Belton* (1981) set a "bright-line rule" for searching a vehicle following the arrest of a driver or passenger, with the Court stating unequivocally, "We hold that when a policeman has made a lawful custodial arrest of the occupant of an automobile, he may, as a contemporaneous incident of that arrest, search the passenger compartment of that automobile." *Belton* defined the scope of a search incident to arrest as including the entire passenger compartment and any containers inside.

In *Thornton v. United States* (2004) the Court took a step further, saying that *Belton* applied whenever a "recent occupant" was arrested, even if the person was walking away from the car when arrested. The Court noted that Thornton's argument, that officers should not be allowed to conduct a *Belton* search once the arrestee was secured in the patrol car, would potentially comprise officer safety and place incriminating evidence at risk of concealment or destruction (Rutledge, 2009b, p.68). The Court stated at that time, "The Fourth Amendment does not require such a gamble."

However, five years later, the Court reconsidered and "decided to require just such a gamble" (Rutledge, 2009b, p.68). The court's ruling in *Arizona v. Gant* (2009) "changes the landscape dramatically with regard to an officer's authority to conduct a warrantless search of a vehicle incident to arrest as a matter of routing" (Judge, 2009, p.12). The facts in this case are as follows (Scarry, 2009c, p.20):

> *Arizona v. Gant* involved an arrest of an individual whom officers knew was driving while his license was suspended and had an outstanding warrant for arrest for driving with a suspended license. The driver, Rodney Gant, drove past the officers and parked his car in a driveway. As Gant exited the car, one of the officers called out to him and they met about 10 to 12 feet from Gant's car. Gant was arrested immediately, handcuffed and locked in the rear of a squad car.
>
> The officers then searched Gant's vehicle and located a gun and a bag of cocaine in a jacket pocket. Gant was charged with possession of drugs. His attorney moved to suppress the drugs on the grounds that the warrantless search violated the Fourth Amendment. The officer who arrested Gant testified at the motion-to-suppress hearing. Asked why he conducted the search, the officer truthfully responded, 'Because the law says we can do it.' The court denied Gant's motion to suppress and the case went to trial. A jury found Gant guilty, and he was sentenced to three years.

On appeal the Arizona Supreme Court found the warrantless search of Gant's vehicle was unreasonable because the scene was secure and Gant was in custody, unable to threaten the officers or destroy evidence. The U.S. Supreme Court affirmed the Arizona Court, stating, "We hold that *Belton* does not authorize a vehicle search incident to a recent occupant's arrest after the arrestee has been secured and cannot access the interior of the vehicle. . . . We also conclude that circumstances unique to the automobile context justify a search incident to arrest when it is reasonable to believe that evidence of the offense of arrest might be found in the vehicle." The ramifications of *Gant* are substantial for police (Judge, 2009, p.12):

> The *Gant* decision moves away from the easy-to-understand, bright-line rule of *New York v. Belton*, which was widely interpreted to authorize the routine warrantless search of a vehicle pursuant to the arrest of an occupant of that vehicle. For decades, officers have operated on the presumption and the belief that the law permitted them to search a vehicle whenever a recent occupant of that vehicle was arrested, without regard to whether the arrestee was actually presenting a risk to officer safety or whether there was reason to believe that evidence related to the crime of arrest might be in the vehicle. . . .
>
> The underlying rationale allowing officers to conduct a search incident to arrest is based on two concerns: (1) to search for weapons because the arrestee has a heightened reason to fight and/or flee a custodial arrest and (2) to preserve evidence of the crime for which the person has been arrested. If an arrestee is cuffed and in the back of a patrol car or is being sufficiently guarded, the Court has decided that reason 1 no longer applies. However, reason 2 may still apply and the Court's decision here leaves this option open, as long as it is supported by a belief, based on specific facts, that evidence related to the crime for which the person was arrested may be found in the vehicle.

Before the *Gant* decision was handed down on April 21, 2009, officers would not be subject to civil liability for warrantless searches of vehicles incident to arrest. However: "Because law enforcement training in most U.S. jurisdictions has long led officers to believe they could first secure any arrestee and then search the passenger compartment of his vehicle, it is important for all departments to ensure retraining based on *Gant*" (Rutledge, 2009b, p.71).

Officers who conduct searches without a warrant must prove an emergency or extenuating circumstance existed that did not allow them time to secure a search warrant. Such circumstances often involve vehicles, and the rules of reasonableness are quite different. The courts have long recognized the need for separate exemptions from the requirement of obtaining a search warrant where mobility is at issue.

The precedent for a warrantless search of an automobile resulted from *Carroll v. United States* (1925), a case involving known bootleggers Carroll and Kiro that occurred during Prohibition. Two undercover federal agents recognized Carroll's car and pursued, overtaking it. Having reason to believe the automobile contained bootleg liquor, the agents searched the car and found 68 bottles of whiskey and gin, most behind the seats' upholstery. The contraband was seized, and the two men were arrested.

Carroll and Kiro were charged with transporting intoxicating liquor and convicted in federal court. Carroll's appeal, taken to the Supreme Court, led to a landmark decision defining the rights and limitations for warrantless searches of vehicles. The agents' knowledge of the two men and their operation, combined with the recognition of Carroll's car and the belief it was being used to transport liquor, produced the probable cause necessary to justify a search.

The *Carroll* decision established that the right to search an automobile does not depend on the right to arrest the driver or an occupant. It depends on the officer's probable cause for believing (1) the automobile's contents violated the law and (2) the conveyance would be gone before a search warrant could be obtained.

The requirement of mobility is also present in *Chambers v. Maroney* (1970), which involved the armed robbery of a service station. The station attendant described the two gunmen, and two boys described a car they had seen circling the block before the robbery and later speeding out of the area. Within an hour officers spotted the vehicle and identified the occupants as the men the three witnesses had described. Police stopped the car and arrested the men. Officers took the car to the police station and searched it, finding two revolvers and a glove filled with change stolen from the service station. The evidence was seized and later used to convict Chambers and the other man.

Chambers appealed, with the defense contending the search was illegal because it was not made simultaneously with the arrest. The defense was right; as a search incidental to an arrest, it would have been illegal. However, the Court observed the same set of circumstances in relation to the warrantless search of a vehicle; the seizing officers had probable cause to believe the vehicle's contents violated the law. Therefore, it was the right to search, not the right to arrest, that gave the officers authority for their actions.

The Supreme Court added another opinion to *Chambers* when the Court held that it was not unreasonable under the circumstances to take the vehicle to the police station to be searched. Based on the facts, there was probable cause to search, and because it was a fleeing target, the Chambers vehicle could have been searched on the spot where it stopped. The Court reasoned that probable cause still existed at the police station and so did the car's mobility.

Chambers v. Maroney established that a car may retain its mobility even though it is impounded.

A case that tested mobility requirements was *Coolidge v. New Hampshire* (1971), involving the disappearance of a 14-year-old girl. Her body was found eight days after she disappeared and revealed she had been shot. A neighbor's tip led police to Coolidge, whom officers admitted was fully cooperative. During the next two and a half weeks, evidence against Coolidge began to accumulate, including the murder weapon, which officers had obtained from Mrs. Coolidge.

The arrest and search warrants, however, were drawn up and signed by the man who became chief prosecutor in the case. The search warrant specifically designated Coolidge's car, which was in the driveway in plain view of the house at the time of the arrest. Mrs. Coolidge was told she was not allowed to use the car, and it was impounded before other officers took Mrs. Coolidge to a relative's home. During the next 14 months, the car was searched three times, and vacuum sweepings from the car were introduced as evidence.

Coolidge was convicted, but he appealed, challenging the legality of the evidence seized from the car based on invalid warrants. With the warrants declared void and unable to prove the search of the car was incidental to an arrest, the prosecution was left with only the contention that the seizure of the car should be allowable based on the standards established by *Carroll* and *Chambers*.

Because testimony from witnesses and Coolidge indicated his car was at the murder scene, the Court accepted that probable cause to search had been established. However, was there sufficient cause to fear the automobile might be moved? The Court said no.

Coolidge v. New Hampshire established that the rule of mobility cannot be applied unless there is actually a risk the vehicle will be moved.

Vehicles may also be searched without a warrant when they are used in committing felonies. Such **instruments of a crime** include getaway vehicles as well as automobiles, trailers or similar conveyances used to hide or transport stolen items.

instruments of a crime

The means by which a crime is committed or the suspects or victims transported, for example, gun, knife, burglary tools, car, truck.

United States v. Ross (1982) held that the police may search a car, including containers in the car, without a warrant as long as they have probable cause to believe contraband is somewhere in the car. *Florida v. Jimeno* (1991) extended the *Ross* decision in examining whether a person's consent to a vehicle search allowed the searching officer to open a container in the vehicle. The Supreme Court held, "A criminal suspect's Fourth Amendment right to be free from unreasonable searches is not violated when, after he gives police permission to search his automobile, they open a closed container found within the car that might reasonably hold the object of the search."

Finally, *Colorado v. Bertine* (1987) ruled that police can inventory the contents of an impounded vehicle. Police often routinely inventory the contents of impounded vehicles to accurately record an arrestee's possessions so they may be safely returned. Any contraband or evidence of a crime found during such a routine inventory is admissible in court.

Warrantless Searches Where No Reasonable Expectation of Privacy Exists In some situations, officers may lawfully conduct a warrantless search even in the absence of an arrest or exigent circumstances, simply because the Fourth Amendment protection against unreasonable searches and seizure is not at issue—there is no reasonable expectation of privacy. *Katz v. United States* (1967) established, "The Fourth Amendment protects people, not places. What a person knowingly exposes to the public, even in his own home or office, is not a subject of Fourth Amendment protection. But what he seeks to preserve as private, even in an area accessible to the public, may be constitutionally protected."

In *Katz*, law enforcement officers tape-recorded Katz's conversation with his bookie. They did not have a warrant for the wiretap, which the court found to be illegal as Katz had an expectation of privacy in the phone booth. Following the *Katz* decision, Congress passed the Omnibus Crime Control and Safe Streets Act of 1968. Title III of that act governs interception of wire, electronic and oral communications by the government and private parties. Title III mandates that communications intercepted in violation of Title III may not be received in evidence during any trial, hearing or other proceeding. Recording telephone conversations is not prohibited by Title III when one party consents. Situations involving right-to-privacy concerns also include (1) workplace privacy; (2) open fields, abandoned property and trash; (3) aerial searches; and (4) use of thermal imaging.

Workplace Privacy The issue of workplace privacy and whether public employees have a reasonable expectation of privacy at their jobs is complex. It is generally held that employees' personal effects are subject to full Fourth Amendment protection, even within the workplace, and that searches of items such as purses, wallets, briefcases and personal mail require probable cause and a warrant. However, in *O'Connor v. Ortega* (1987), the Supreme Court, observing that facilities within government and other public agencies are generally shared by and accessible to many, ruled that a public employee's position, by its very nature, allows a degree of intrusion into privacy that would otherwise violate the Fourth Amendment. In *Ortega* the Court held that all an employer needs for a work-related intrusion to qualify as reasonable under the Fourth Amendment is a reasonable suspicion that the investigative search will uncover evidence of an employee's work-related misconduct.

Open Fields, Abandoned Property and Trash The principles governing search and seizure of open fields and trash were established in *Hester v. United States* (1924). In this case, police were investigating bootlegging operations and went to Hester's father's home. As police approached the residence, they saw a man drive up to the house, so they hid. When Hester came out and gave the man a bottle, the police sounded an alarm. Hester ran to a car parked nearby, took out a gallon jug, and he and the man ran across an open field. One officer chased them. Hester dropped his jug, which broke, but about half its contents remained. The other man threw his bottle away. Police found another broken jar containing liquid that appeared to be illegal whiskey. The officers seized the jars, even though they had no search warrant, and arrested Hester, who was convicted of concealing "distilled spirits." On appeal his lawyer contended the officers conducted an illegal search and seizure. The Court disagreed, saying,

> It is obvious that even if there had been a trespass, the above testimony was not obtained by an illegal search and seizure. The defendant's own acts, and those of his associates, disclosed the jug, the jar and the bottle—and there was no seizure in the sense of the law when the officers examined the contents of each after it had been abandoned. . . .
>
> The special protection accorded by the Fourth Amendment to the people in their "persons, houses, papers, and effects," is not extended to the open fields.

The **open fields doctrine** holds that land beyond what is normally associated with use of that land, that is, undeveloped land, can be searched without a warrant. **Curtilage** is the term used to describe the portion of property generally associated with the common use of land, for example, buildings, sheds, fenced-in areas and yards. A warrant is required to search the curtilage. In *Oliver v. United States* (1984) the Supreme Court described the curtilage as "the area to which extends the intimate activity associated with the 'sanctity of a man's home and the privacies of life.'" The courts have generally regarded driveways, walkways to a house's front door and unfenced front yards as areas commonly accessed by neighbors, visitors, postal carriers, delivery drivers, salespeople and other members of the public. As such, these areas receive a lower level of protection in issues of privacy, and courts have upheld police officers' right to enter onto a property's "public access" areas without a warrant.

open fields doctrine

Holds that land beyond what is normally associated with use of that land, that is, undeveloped land, can be searched without a warrant.

curtilage

That portion of property associated with the common use of land—for example, buildings, sheds and fenced-in areas.

If something is open to the public and therefore has no expectation of privacy, it is not protected by the Fourth Amendment. This includes open fields, abandoned property and trash.

In *United States v. Dunn* (1987), the Supreme Court specified four factors to consider in determining if an area is within a home's curtilage:

- The proximity of the area to the home
- Whether the area is within the same enclosure as the home
- The use to which the area is put
- Measures taken by the occupant to protect the area from the view of passersby

Oliver v. United States strengthened the open fields doctrine by ruling that "No Trespassing" signs and locked gates do not constitute a "reasonable expectation of privacy":

> The test of a reasonable expectation of privacy is not whether the individual attempts to conceal criminal activity, but whether the government's intrusion infringes upon the personal and societal values protected by the Fourth Amendment. Because open fields are accessible to the public and because fences or "No Trespassing" signs, etc. are not effective bars to public view of open fields, the expectation of privacy does not exist and police are justified in searching these areas without a warrant.

Once a person throws something away, the expectation of privacy is lost. *California v. Greenwood* (1988) established that garbage left outside the curtilage for regular collection could be inspected: "Here we conclude that respondents exposed their garbage to the public sufficiently to defeat their claim to Fourth Amendment protection. It is common knowledge that plastic garbage bags left on or at the side of a public street are readily accessible to animals, children, scavengers, snoops, and other members of the public."

Some states, however, do not allow such searches. In *State v. Hempele* (1990), a New Jersey Court ruled 5–2 that garbage left on a curb is private property that police officials cannot search through without a warrant:

> Garbage reveals much that is personal. We do not find it unreasonable for people to want their garbage to remain private and to expect that it will remain private from the meddling of the state.
>
> A free and civilized society should comport itself with more decency [than to allow] police to pick and poke their way through garbage bags to peruse without cause the vestiges of a person's most private affairs.

This case illustrates how critical it is that police officers know not only the federal laws but also the laws of their respective states, which often can be more restrictive than federal laws.

Aerial Searches Another area closely related to the plain view doctrine and the open fields doctrine is that of aerial searches. *California v. Ciraola* (1986) expanded the police's ability to "spy" on criminal offenders. In this case, police received a tip that marijuana was being grown in the defendant's backyard. The yard was surrounded by two fences—one 6 feet tall, the other 10 feet tall. Since the height of the fences precluded visual observation from the ground, the officers decided to fly over the curtilage to confirm it contained marijuana plants. Based on this information, a search warrant was obtained and executed, and the evidence was used to convict Ciraola on drug charges. On appeal the Supreme Court found that the defendant's privacy had not been violated because officers traveling in a navigable airspace are not required to avert their eyes when passing over homes or yards.

In *Florida v. Riley* (1989), the Court expanded this ruling when it stated police do not need a search warrant to conduct even low-altitude helicopter searches of private property.

Thermal Imaging The subject of searches has received close scrutiny by the courts and remains, in the public eye, an avenue vulnerable to invasion of privacy by the government. When technology is added to the picture, public concern takes on more of a "Big Brother" uneasiness, especially when the technology is aimed at someone's home. An example of how advancing technology affects Fourth Amendment privacy issues is seen in *Kyllo v. United States* (2001), a case involving thermal imaging.

During a drug investigation, a federal agent used a thermal imager to scan the exterior of the home of a man suspected of growing marijuana. The scan, conducted without a search warrant, revealed abnormally high amounts of heat coming from the home. This data, combined with previously developed information, provided probable cause to secure a search warrant. The search revealed marijuana plants and drug paraphernalia and weapons, and Kyllo was convicted of manufacturing marijuana.

Kyllo appealed, arguing that targeting his home with a thermal imager was an unreasonable Fourth Amendment search. The appeal went to the Supreme Court, which reversed the circuit court's ruling. In a 5–4 decision, the Court asserted that using a thermal imager to surveil a home is a search under the Fourth Amendment and, as such, requires a search warrant based on probable cause.

The Supreme Court has ruled that using thermal imaging to view inside a home without a warrant is unconstitutional.

Limitations on Searches

After establishing the right to search, police officers must determine the limitations on that right—limitations imposed by law and interpreted by the courts.

The most important limitation imposed on any search is that the scope must be narrowed. General searches are unconstitutional.

Often what is found during a search provides the probable cause to make an arrest. As with searches, in an arrest the general rule is that a warrant is required.

LAWFUL ARRESTS

Laws of arrest are generally uniform in all 50 states and in federal criminal proceedings. Statutes throughout the United States generally define ***arrest*** as the taking of a person into custody by the actual restraint of the person or by his or her submission to the custody of the officer so that he or she may be held to answer for a public offense before a judge. For purposes of federal constitutional law, "An arrest is a seizure of a person in which the subject is (1) required to go elsewhere with police, or (2) deprived of his freedom of movement for more than a brief period of time, or (3) subjected to more force than is reasonably part of an investigative detention" (Means and McDonald, 2009b, p.12).

arrest
The taking of a person into custody by the actual restraint of the person or by his or her submission to the custody of the officer so that he or she may be held to answer for a public offense before a judge.

The Fourth Amendment was intended to protect citizens from unjust arrests. The courts must balance this protection against the justice system's charge to protect society against those who violate its laws. Almost every state limits police authority to arrest, especially in the absence of a warrant, even when they have probable cause. However, various jurisdictional limitations for particular crimes are filled with a number of exceptions. The U.S. Supreme Court, in its ruling in *Virginia v. Moore* (2008), did law enforcement a great favor by eliminating many concerns about violation of state statute arrest procedural rules (Spector, 2008, p.12). In this case Moore was stopped by two officers with reasonable suspicion that he was driving with a suspended license. Upon confirming that his license was suspended, the officers made a custodial arrest and conducted a delayed search incident to arrest, which yielded 16 grams of crack cocaine and $516 in cash. Moore was found guilty and sentenced to prison. Under Virginia state law, Moore should have only been issued a summons for driving with a suspended license, not an arrestable offense except for specific circumstances that did not apply. The Supreme Court, however, found that the officers' violation of the state's procedural arrest rule did not make the arrest unreasonable under the Fourth Amendment. In writing the opinion in the 9–0 opinion Justice Scalia said, "The arrest rules that the officers violated were those of state law alone. It is not the province of the Fourth Amendment to enforce state law."

Four elements of a criminal arrest are

1. An *intent* by an officer to make an arrest
2. *Authority* to arrest
3. A *seizure* or restraint
4. An *understanding* by the person that he or she is being arrested

Arrest Warrants

All states have a statute authorizing law enforcement officers to make arrests, but the Constitution stipulates that lawful arrests require an arrest warrant. From a practical point of view, police officers should obtain arrest warrants to protect themselves against civil liability for false imprisonment, in case it is later determined the arrest was unjustified. Like a search warrant, an arrest warrant requires an affidavit stating the facts supporting probable cause and sworn to by the officer presenting the affidavit. The judge determines if probable cause exists and, if so, issues the warrant. The warrant itself must name the person to be arrested, the

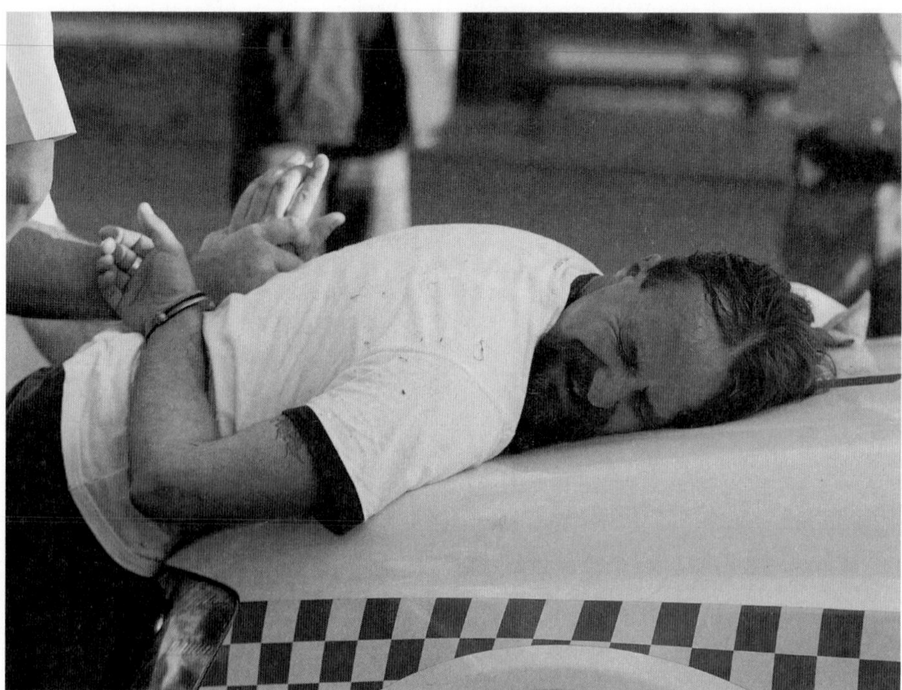

When an arrest is made, the suspect is usually handcuffed for the officer's safety. An arrest is a critical discretionary action, never to be taken lightly because it may change a person's life forever.

offense and the officer(s) directed to make the arrest. The warrant must be signed by an impartial judge.

Arrests without a Warrant

Police officers may make lawful arrests without a warrant for felonies or misdemeanors committed in their presence, called **public offenses**. In *Atwater v. City of Lago Vista* (2001) a police officer arrested a woman driving her pickup truck with her two young children in the front seat, none of them wearing a seat belt. Atwater filed a civil suit against the officer and the city. The case found its way to the Supreme Court, which ruled that the Fourth Amendment does not forbid a warrantless arrest for a minor offense punishable only by a fine.

public offense

Any crime; includes felonies and misdemeanors.

Officers can also make arrests for felonies not committed in their presence if they have probable cause. They may not, however, enter a dwelling to arrest without a warrant. In *Payton v. New York* (1980), the Supreme Court ruled that the Fourth Amendment prohibits warrantless entry into a dwelling to arrest in the absence of sufficient justification for the failure to obtain a warrant. Since then, "dwelling" has been expanded to include temporary residences such as motels and hotels, tents in public campgrounds and migrant farm housing on private property. If, however, an emergency situation exists and officers have probable cause to believe a person has committed a crime, they may make a warrantless arrest. The courts will determine its legality. An arrest is never to be taken lightly. It can change a person's life forever. Officer discretion is critical when arrest decisions are made. It is also vital that officers clearly differentiate between a simple stop-and-frisk situation and an arrest. Sometimes a stop-and-frisk situation leads to an arrest situation. Table 8.1 summarizes the important differences between the two.

Right to Resist Arrest

Sometimes when an arrest is made, the person being arrested resists, and the officer must use force to make the arrest, an issue discussed in Chapter 11. It should be noted here, however, that American courts adopted the common law right to resist arrest until the mid-20th century. The trend during the past 50 years has been to eliminate that right. The decision of whether to continue or eliminate this right rests on the degree to which we value liberty rather than order.

TABLE 8.1 Stop and Arrest

	Stop	Arrest
Justification	Reasonable suspicion	Probable cause
Intent of officer	To resolve an ambiguous situation	To make a formal charge
Search	Possibly a "pat down" or frisk	Complete body search
Record	Minimal	Fingerprints, photographs and booking

DE FACTO ARRESTS

de facto arrest

Occurs when officers who lack probable cause to arrest take a suspect in for questioning; officers' actions have the appearance of an arrest—that is, the suspect is not free to leave.

A **de facto arrest** occurs when officers who lack probable cause to arrest take a suspect in for questioning. If the officers' actions have the appearance of an arrest—that is, the suspect is not free to refuse—it is a detention tantamount to arrest. *Kaupp v. Texas* (2003) involved this issue.

Police suspected Kaupp of involvement in the murder of a 14-year-old girl. Three plainclothes detectives and three uniformed officers went to his house at 3 A.M. His father let them in, and they proceeded to Kaupp's bedroom, awakened him and told him they needed to talk. They handcuffed him and led him shoeless and dressed only in a T-shirt and boxer shorts to their patrol car. At the police station, after 10 or 15 minutes of denying involvement, he admitted he had taken part in the crime. The court ordered the confession suppressed.

PROTECTING A SUSPECT'S RIGHTS—THE *MIRANDA* WARNING

Before interrogating any suspect, police officers must give the *Miranda* warning, as established in *Miranda v. Arizona* (1966). The Supreme Court asserted that suspects must be informed of their rights to remain silent, to have counsel present, to state-appointed counsel if they cannot afford one and to be warned that anything they say might be used against them in a court of law. Many investigators carry a card that contains the *Miranda* warning to be read before interrogating a suspect (see Figure 8.4).

On the evening of March 3, 1963, an 18-year-old female was abducted and raped in Phoenix, Arizona. Ten days after the incident, Ernesto Miranda was arrested by Phoenix police, taken to police headquarters and put in a lineup. The victim identified him, and shortly thereafter he signed a confession. Miranda was convicted and sentenced 20 to 30 years on each count.

Miranda appealed on the grounds he had not been advised of his constitutional rights under the Fifth Amendment. The Arizona Supreme Court ruled in 1965

Miranda Warning

1. You have the right to remain silent.
2. If you give up the right to remain silent, anything you say can and will be used against you in a court of law.
3. You have the right to speak with an attorney and to have the attorney present during questioning.
4. If you so desire and cannot afford one, an attorney will be appointed for you without charge before questioning.

Waiver

1. Do you understand each of these rights I have read to you?
2. Having these rights in mind, do you wish to give up your rights as I have explained them to you and talk to me now?

FIGURE 8.4 *Miranda* Warning Card

that because Miranda had been previously arrested in California and Tennessee, he knowingly waived his rights under the Fifth and Sixth Amendments when he gave his confession to the Phoenix police. In 1966, upon appeal, the Supreme Court reversed the supreme court of Arizona in a 5–4 decision and set up precedent rules for police custodial interrogation. Chief Justice Earl Warren stated, "The mere fact that he signed a statement which contained a typed-in clause stating that he had 'full knowledge of his legal rights' does not approach knowing the intelligent waiver required to relinquish constitutional rights."

The *Miranda* warning contains four specific rights:

1. You have the right to remain silent.
2. If you give up the right to remain silent, anything you say can and will be used against you in a court of law.
3. You have the right to speak with an attorney and to have the attorney present during questioning.
4. If you so desire and cannot afford one, an attorney will be appointed for you without charge before questioning.

After reading these rights, it is important and typical for the officer to follow up with a question to ascertain that the suspect has comprehended the warning, something along the lines of, "Do you understand these rights and, with them in mind, do you wish to speak to me about the incident?"

The Supreme Court has never required a specific wording for the *Miranda* warning. *Florida v. Powell* (2010) addressed the issue of whether a suspect must be expressly advised to his right to counsel during questioning and, if so, whether the failure to provide this express advice vitiates *Miranda*. In this case Powell was convicted of illegally possessing a firearm after telling police he bought the weapon off the street for protection. The Florida Supreme Court overturned the conviction, saying police did not explicitly tell him he had a right to a lawyer during his police interrogation. The Supreme Court, however, writing for the Court's 7–2 majority, reversed and remanded, saying, "Nothing in the words used indicated that counsel's presence would be restricted after the questioning commenced. Instead the warning communicated that the right to counsel carried forward to and through the interrogation." In writing the majority opinion, Justice Ruth Bader Ginsburg praised a different version of the *Miranda* warning, one used by the FBI, which says in part, "You have the right to talk to a lawyer for advice before we ask you any questions. You have the right to have a lawyer with you during questioning" ("Supreme Court Backs," 2010).

The *Miranda* warning must be given to a suspect interrogated in *police* **custody**, that is, when the suspect is not free to leave.

custody
State of being kept or guarded, or being detained.

Two terms are key in this situation: *interrogated* and *in custody*. The circumstances involved in an interrogation and whether it requires a *Miranda* warning were expanded in *Oregon v. Mathiason* (1977) when the Court said,

> Any interview of one suspected of a crime by a police officer will have coercive aspects to it, simply by virtue of the fact that the police officer is part of a law

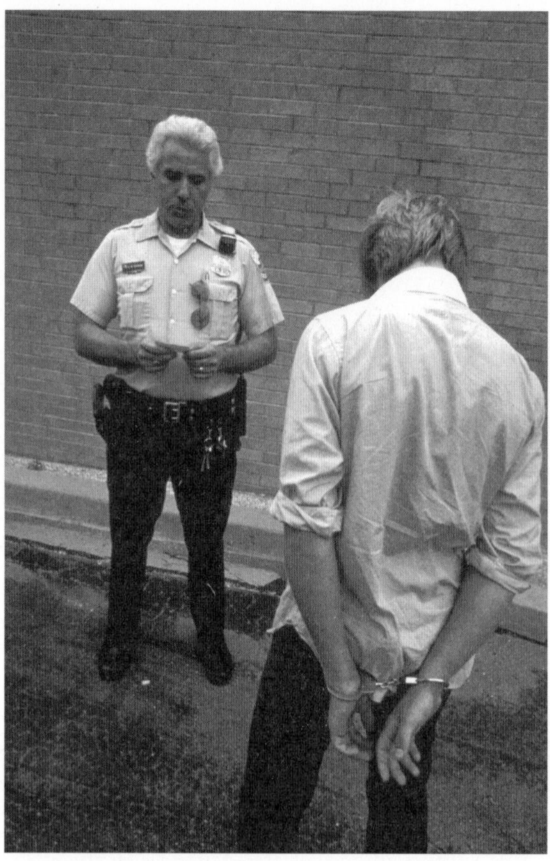
© Paul Conklin/PhotoEdit

An officer reads a suspect's *Miranda* rights from a card. Failure to inform a suspect of these rights can result in important statements or even confessions being inadmissible in court.

> enforcement system which may ultimately cause the suspect to be charged with a crime. But police officers are not required to administer *Miranda* warnings to everyone whom they question. Nor is the requirement of warnings to be imposed simply because the questioning takes place in the station house, or because the questioned person is one whom the police suspect. *Miranda* warnings are required only where there has been such a restriction on a person's freedom as to render him "in custody." It was that sort of coercive environment to which *Miranda* by its terms was made applicable, and to which it is limited.

Related Cases

Custodial interrogation takes place in two situations: (1) when a suspect is under arrest or (2) when a suspect is not under arrest but is deprived of freedom in a significant way. *Miranda* warnings are not required if questioning witnesses, in stop-and-frisk cases, or before fingerprinting or photographing during the arrest or booking process. Police who conduct DUI stops and ask routine questions need not give the *Miranda* warning (*Pennsylvania v. Muniz*, 1990).

Another case significant to the protection of suspects' rights actually resulted in two separate trials with two different prosecutors, yet both trials involved the same defendant, Robert Williams, and the same case, the Christmas Eve disappearance and suspected homicide of a 10-year-old girl. The police developed information leading them to suspect Williams and obtained an arrest warrant. Williams turned himself in to police in a town 160 miles from where the girl disappeared.

All agreed Williams would not be interrogated during the car trip to the case's city of origin. However, during the drive, one officer said the following to Williams, in what has become known as the "Christian Burial Speech":

> I want to give you something to think about while we're traveling down the road.... It's going to be dark early this evening. They are predicting several inches of snow for tonight, and I feel that you yourself are the only person that knows where this little girl's body is, that you yourself have only been there once, and if you get snow on top of it, you yourself may be unable to find it. And since we will be going right past the area on the way [back], I feel that we could stop and locate the body, that the parents of this little girl should be entitled to a Christian burial for the little girl who was snatched away from them on Christmas Eve and murdered.

The detective said he just wanted Williams to think about it. Shortly after, Williams directed the officers to the girl's body. The lower courts admitted Williams' damaging statements into evidence, but the Supreme Court in *Brewer v. Williams* (1977) reversed, holding that any statements made by Williams were inadmissible because the way they were elicited violated his constitutional right to counsel.

The Court granted Williams a second trial with a different prosecutor (*Nix v. Williams*, 1984). Again, Williams' statements were suppressed, but the Court allowed the body to be admitted as evidence, not because of improper questioning by police but because an independent search party would have eventually discovered it. This is the **inevitable discovery doctrine**. Former Chief Justice Burger wrote in the majority opinion, "Exclusion of physical evidence that would inevitably have been discovered adds nothing to either the integrity or fairness of a criminal trial." The point of the inevitable discovery doctrine, he said, was to put the police in the same, not a worse, position than they would have been in if no police error or misconduct occurred.

inevitable discovery doctrine
Holds that illegally obtained evidence may be admitted at trial if the prosecution can prove that the evidence would have been discovered sooner or later (inevitably).

Waiving the Right

Suspects can *waive* their rights against self-incrimination and talk to police officers, but the **waiver** must be voluntary and be preceded by the *Miranda* warning. The suspect must fully understand what rights are being given up and the possible consequences. If after hearing a police officer read the *Miranda* warning, suspects remain silent, this is *not* a waiver. To waive their rights, suspects must state, orally or in writing, that (1) they understand their rights and (2) they will voluntarily answer questions without a lawyer present. Officers are allowed to ask more than once if a suspect would like to waive his or her rights.

waiver
The voluntary giving up of a right.

In *Davis v. United States* (1994) a majority of justices held that officers do *not* have to stop an interrogation if a suspect makes an ambiguous reference to invoking the right to legal counsel, for example, "Maybe I should talk to a lawyer," or "Do you think I need a lawyer?" It is crucial that officers not give any form of legal advice, as this may be used against them in court.

Special care must be taken with individuals who do not speak English well, who are under the influence of drugs or alcohol, who appear to be mentally retarded or who appear to be hampered mentally in any way. It is preferable to get the waiver in writing.

Beachheading or "Question First"

Deliberate "end runs" around *Miranda*—purposely withholding *Miranda* warnings until after a confession is obtained and then giving *Miranda* to re-ask the question—have been found by the Supreme Court to be improper. The Court rejected the prosecution's argument that a confession repeated using a question-first strategy was admissible in *Oregon v. Elstad* (1985), stating that the failure to preliminarily provide the *Miranda* warning was a "good-faith" mistake, not a conscious decision. *Missouri v. Seibert* (2004), in a 5–4 vote, rejected the two-step questioning tactic as a deliberate way to sidestep *Miranda*.

The Public Safety Exception

public safety exception
Allows police officers to question suspects without first giving the *Miranda* warning if the information sought sufficiently affects the officers' or the public's safety.

The **public safety exception** is an important consideration when discussing the *Miranda* decision. On June 12, 1984, in the landmark 5–4 decision in *New York v. Quarles*, the Supreme Court announced that in certain cases police may question suspects in custody without first advising them of their right not to incriminate themselves.

Writing for the Court's majority, Justice Rehnquist cited the Court's decision in *Michigan v. Tucker* (1974) and made the distinction that the *Miranda* warnings are "not themselves rights protected by the Constitution, but are measures to insure that the right against compulsory self-incrimination is protected.... On some facts there is a 'public safety' exception to the requirement that *Miranda* warnings be given before a suspect's answers may be admitted into evidence, and that the availability of that exception does not depend on the motivation of the individual officers." Although the Court set forth the "public safety exception," no attempt was made to determine in what situations this exception might apply.

The public safety exception allows police officers to question suspects without first giving the *Miranda* warning if the information sought sufficiently affects the officer's and the public's safety.

In *Quarles*, a young woman stopped two police officers and said she had been raped. She described her rapist who, she said, had just entered a nearby supermarket armed with a gun. The officers located the suspect, Benjamin Quarles, and ordered him to stop, but Quarles ran, and the officers momentarily lost sight of him. When they apprehended and frisked him, the officers found an empty shoulder holster. When the officers asked Quarles where the gun was, he nodded toward some cartons and said, "The gun is over there." The officers retrieved the gun, arrested Quarles and read him his rights. Quarles waived his rights and answered questions.

At the trial the court ruled that the statement, "The gun is over there," and the subsequent discovery of the gun resulting from that statement were inadmissible. However, the Supreme Court, after reviewing the case, ruled that if *Miranda* warnings had deterred the response to the officer's question, the cost would have been more than just the loss of evidence that might lead to a conviction. As long as the gun remained concealed in the store, it posed a danger to public safety.

The Court ruled that in this case the need to have the suspect talk took precedence over the requirement the defendant be read his rights. The Court ruled that the material factor applying this public safety exception is whether a public threat could possibly be removed by the suspect making a statement. In this case the officer asked the question only to ensure his and the public's safety. He then gave the *Miranda* warning before continuing questioning. Numerous other court decisions have favored public and officer safety over the right of suspects to be immediately read their rights and have recognized that this reasonable precaution should not compromise the admissibility of evidence.

How Long Do *Miranda* Warnings Last?

Edwards v. Arizona (1981) bars police from initiating questioning with criminal suspects who have invoked their right to counsel, but how long does this prohibition last? *Maryland v. Shatzer* (2010) addressed this issue, and in a rare numerical rule, set forth the 14-day clause. The case involved an interrogation that took place nearly three years after the request for an attorney: "In a 9–0 decision in a Maryland child-abuse case, the high court overturned a strict rule set in 1981 that barred police from questioning a suspect once he had asked to remain silent and to speak with a lawyer. Known as the 'Edwards rule,' it was intended to prevent investigators from 'badgering' a suspect who was held in jail after he had invoked his *Miranda* rights" (Savage, 2010). *Maryland v. Shatzer* overturned *Edwards*, holding that if a suspect is freed, the suspect can be questioned over 14 days and any freely given statements can be used against him.

Although every law enforcement officer knows about *Miranda*, many are not familiar with the rights of foreign nationals arrested by federal, state or local law enforcement officers.

Protecting the Rights of Foreign Nationals

Similar to the *Miranda* warning, the U.S. Department of State's *Consular Notification and Access Reference Card* contains consular rights warnings that must be given to arrested or detained foreign nationals. In addition, under some circumstances, law enforcement officers must notify the foreign nationals' consular officials posted in the United States. Most countries, including the United States, are obligated by the *Vienna Convention on Consular Relations and Optional Protocol on Disputes* (VCCR).

Diplomatic immunity is a principle of international law establishing that certain foreign government officials are not subject to the jurisdiction of local courts or other authorities.

Two levels of immunity exist. Diplomatic agents (ambassadors) and their diplomatic staff and family (spouses and children under age 21) are afforded full criminal immunity, meaning they cannot be detained, searched or arrested and cannot be required to provide evidence as a witness. Service staff members have limited criminal immunity. Petrocelli (2005) notes that motor vehicle stops and summons are not considered detentions or arrests and that officers may issue appropriate citations or warnings for any moving violation to drivers having diplomatic immunity.

Involuntary Confessions

Arizona v. Fulminante (1991) established that the "harmless error" doctrine applies to cases involving the admissibility of involuntary confessions. In this case, Fulminante was suspected of murdering his stepdaughter, but evidence was insufficient to charge him. Later he was arrested and jailed on a federal charge of possession of a firearm. While he was in prison, a fellow inmate, Sarivola, a paid FBI informant, told Fulminante the other inmates considered him a child killer and that if he would admit to the crime, Sarivola would protect him from the inmates. Fulminante did confess. When he was released from prison, he also confessed to Sarivola's wife.

Fulminante was charged with the murder, and at the trial his confession was challenged as being coerced and therefore excluded. His confession to the wife was also challenged as "fruit" of the first confession. The confessions were admitted, however, and Fulminante was convicted and sentenced to death. On appeal the Arizona Supreme Court declared that Fulminante's confession was coerced because he feared for his safety and needed Sarivola to protect him.

The question then became, did allowing the confessions to be admitted into evidence harm the defendant's case or was it a "harmless error"? In this case a majority of the court said the error was *not* harmless. If the error is harmful or if the prosecution fails to establish beyond reasonable doubt the error is harmless, the conviction is reversed. Situations in which suspects feel they have been tricked into confessing may also use entrapment as a defense.

Entrapment

entrapment

Occurs when a government agent induces someone to commit a crime that is not normally considered by the person for the purpose of prosecuting that person.

Entrapment is an act of government agents to induce a person to commit a crime that is not normally considered by the person for the purpose of prosecuting that person. Many Supreme Court cases in which entrapment was at issue have led to rulings that help define the boundaries for law enforcement. In *Sorrells v. United States* (1932) the Court stated,

> Society is at war with the criminal classes, and the courts have uniformly held that in waging this warfare the forces of prevention and detection may use traps, decoys and deception to obtain evidence of the commission of a crime. Resort to such means does not render an indictment thereafter found a nullity nor call for the exclusion of evidence so procured. . . . Entrapment is the conception and planning of an offense by an officer, and his procurement of its commission by one who would not have perpetrated it except for the trickery, persuasion or fraud of the officer.

The Alaska Supreme Court's ruling in *Grossman v. State* (1969) helped delineate police conduct constituting entrapment to include appeals to sympathy, guarantees the act is legal and inducements making the crime unusually attractive. The court further defined entrapment in its ruling in *Sherman v. United States* (1958): "Entrapment occurs only when the criminal conduct was 'the product of the creative' activity of law enforcement officials. To determine whether entrapment has been established, a line must be drawn between the trap for the unwary innocent and the trap for the unwary criminal."

This line was clarified in *United States v. Russell* (1973): "There are circumstances when the use of deceit is the only practicable law enforcement technique available. It is only when the government's deception actually implants the criminal design in the mind of the defendant that the defense of entrapment comes into play." The Court elaborated on this ruling in *Jacobson v. United States* (1992) when it held government has the burden of proving "beyond a reasonable doubt" the defendant's predisposition to commit the offense. If the government fails to prove predisposition, the defense wins on the presumption that the defendant is an "unwary innocent" instead of an "unwary criminal."

A RECAP OF THE LANDMARK CASES

The challenge of policing within the law is formidable but critical. Officers must know constitutional restrictions on their powers at both the federal and state levels. Although statutes vary from state to state, holdings of the Supreme Court apply to all states. The most important of these are summarized in Table 8.2.

TABLE 8.2 Summary of Major Court Rulings Regarding the Fourth Amendment (Search and Seizure), Fifth Amendment (Self-Incrimination), Entrapment and Exclusions to These Clauses

Doctrine	Case Decision	Holding
Fourth Amendment		
Probable Cause	*Smith v. United States* (1949)	Probable cause is the sum total of layers of information and the synthesis of what the police have heard, what they know, and what they observe as trained officers. The courts weigh not the individual layers but the laminated total.
	Draper v. United States (1959)	Probable cause exists where the facts and circumstances within the arresting officers' knowledge are sufficient to warrant a person of reasonable caution in the belief that an offense has been or is being committed.
Stop and Frisk	*Terry v. Ohio* (1968)	The authority to stop and frisk is independent of the power to arrest. A stop is not an arrest, but it is a seizure within the meaning of the Fourth Amendment and therefore requires reasonableness.
	Florida v. J. L. (2000)	Reasonable suspicion for an investigative stop does not arise from a mere anonymous tip.
	Illinois v. Wardlow (2000)	A person's sudden flight upon seeing a police officer can be used to establish reasonable suspicion for a *Terry*-type stop.
Sobriety Checkpoints	*Michigan Department of State Police v. Sitz* (1990)	Sobriety checkpoints are a form of stop and are constitutional if they are conducted fairly and do not pose a safety hazard.
Drug Interdiction Roadblocks	*City of Indianapolis v. Edmond* (2000)	Narcotics checkpoints are unconstitutional and violate the Fourth Amendment's protections against unreasonable search and seizure in that their purpose is indistinguishable from the general interest in crime control.
Field Detention	*Michigan v. Summers* (1981)	Police officers may detain suspects with less than probable cause and may legally require suspects to reenter their houses and remain there until evidence establishing probable cause is found.

(continued)

TABLE 8.2 (Continued)

Doctrine	Case Decision	Holding
	Illinois v. McArthur (2001)	Police did not violate the Fourth Amendment when they detained a suspect outside his home for several hours while officers sought a warrant to search the premises for drugs.
Search with a Warrant—Gaining Entrance	*Wilson v. Arkansas* (1995)	Whether police "knock and announce" their presence before executing valid search warrants is part of the Fourth Amendment inquiry into the reasonableness of a search.
	United States v. Espinoza (2001)	A failure to knock and announce does not require suppression of evidence if the target resists.
	District of Columbia v. Mancouso (2001)	Officers who disregard the knock-and-announce rule while serving a search warrant on an empty house, even if the occupants are standing outside the premises "within earshot" of the officers, have violated statutory requirements, thus providing standing for the residents to move to suppress any evidence recovered inside.
Administrative Warrants	*Michigan v. Tyler* (1978)	Public safety personnel may enter structures that are on fire to extinguish the blaze, after which officials may remain a reasonable length of time to investigate the cause of the blaze.
Warrantless Search with Consent	*State v. Barlow, Jr.* (1974)	Consent must be free and voluntary, and the search must be limited to the area for which the consent is given.
Time of Day of Search	*Monroe v. Pape* (1961)	Officers should generally avoid seeking voluntary consent to search at night.
Search Incidental to Lawful Arrest	*Chimel v. California* (1969)	When making an arrest, it is reasonable for an officer to search the person arrested to remove any weapons the latter might use to resist arrest or affect an escape. The search must be made simultaneously with the arrest and must be confined to the area within the immediate control of the suspect—that is, within his or her reach (wingspan).
Protective Sweeps	*Maryland v. Buie* (1989)	A protective sweep is legal and protects the arresting officer from danger posed by unknown third parties. The duration of the sweep is limited and can last no longer than necessary to dispel the suspicion of danger.
Warrantless Searches of Vehicles	*Carroll v. United States* (1925)	The right to search a vehicle is not dependent on the right to arrest the driver or an occupant. It depends on the probable cause the officer has for believing (1) the vehicle's contents violate the law and (2) the conveyance would be gone before a search warrant could be obtained (mobility).
	Chambers v. Maroney (1970)	A car may retain its mobility even though it is impounded.
	Coolidge v. New Hampshire (1971)	The rule of mobility cannot be applied unless there is actually a risk that the vehicle will be moved.
	New York v. Belton (1981)	Officers can search a vehicle's interior and all its contents if an occupant has been lawfully arrested and the vehicle search is subsequent to the arrest.
	United States v. Ross (1982)	Police may search a car, including containers in the car, without a warrant as long as they have probable cause to believe contraband is in the car.
	Colorado v. Bertine (1987)	Police can inventory the contents of an impounded vehicle.
	Florida v. Jimeno (1991)	A criminal suspect's Fourth Amendment right to be free from unreasonable searches is not violated when, after he gives police permission to search his automobile, they open a closed container found within the car that might reasonably hold the object of the search.

(continued)

TABLE 8.2 (Continued)

Doctrine	Case Decision	Holding
Pretext/Dual Motive Traffic Stops	*United States v. Millan* (1994)	If an officer's original intent in stopping a vehicle is to "check it out" and not for a specific violation, any subsequent search will be illegal.
	Whren v. United States (1996)	The real purpose of a stop, even if ulterior, does not render the stop and subsequent search invalid if there was, in fact, a valid reason for the stop, such as a traffic violation.
Danger of Traffic Stops	*Maryland v. Wilson* (1997)	Given the likelihood of traffic stops leading to either violence or destruction of evidence when passengers are in the vehicle, officers making traffic stops may lawfully order all of a vehicle's occupants, including passengers, to get out of the car pending completion of the stop, extending a previous Court decision applicable only to drivers.
Plain Feel/Touch	*Minnesota v. Dickerson* (1993)	Supporting limited "plain touch" or "plain feel" probes in frisk situations, if contraband is plainly felt by the officer in good faith, what he finds will not be suppressed. Under the Plain Feel Doctrine, an officer must determine simultaneously that an item is not a weapon and is, in fact, contraband.
	Bond v. United States (2000)	Extends *Dickerson*, ruling that police can visually inspect passengers' luggage but cannot squeeze or otherwise manipulate baggage to determine whether it contains contraband.
Workplace Privacy	*O'Connor v. Ortega* (1987)	As a general rule, searches of employees' private property (purses, wallets, personal mail) in their workspaces are subject to full Fourth Amendment protection, requiring probable cause and a search warrant. But the nature of a public employee's position allows some intrusion into privacy. All an employer needs for a work-related intrusion to be "reasonable" under the Fourth Amendment is reasonable suspicion the search will reveal evidence of an employee's work-related misconduct or that the search is necessary for a non-investigatory, work-related purpose, such as retrieving a needed file.
Open Fields, Abandoned Property and Trash	*Hester v. United States* (1924)	If something is open to the public and has no expectation of privacy, it is not protected by the Fourth Amendment.
Curtilage	*Oliver v. United States* (1984)	A warrant is required to search the curtilage, the area to which extends the intimate activity associated with the "sanctity of a man's home and the privacies of life." "No Trespassing" signs and locked gates do not constitute a reasonable expectation of privacy.
	United States v. Dunn (1987)	Four factors to consider in determining if an area is within a home's curtilage are (1) the proximity of the area to the home, (2) whether the area is within the same enclosure as the home, (3) the nature of the use to which the area is put and (4) measures taken by the home's occupant to protect the area from the view of passersby.
	California v. Greenwood (1988)	Garbage left outside the curtilage of a home for regular collection may be inspected without a warrant. If no expectation of privacy exists, Fourth Amendment protection does not exist either.
Aerial Searches	*California v. Ciraola* (1986)	A defendant's privacy is not violated when officers traveling in a navigable airspace observe illegal activity or contraband.
	Florida v. Riley (1989)	Expands *California v. Ciraola* by stating police do not need a search warrant to conduct even low-altitude helicopter searches of private property.

(continued)

TABLE 8.2 (Continued)

Doctrine	Case Decision	Holding
Thermal Imaging	*Kyllo v. United States* (2001)	Using a thermal imager to surveil a home is a search under the Fourth Amendment and, as such, requires a search warrant based on probable cause.
Inevitable Discovery Doctrine	*Nix v. Williams* (1984)	Illegally obtained evidence may be admitted at trial if the prosecution can prove the evidence would "inevitably" have been discovered by lawful means.
Arrest without a Warrant	*People v. Ramey* (1976)	The Fourth Amendment prohibits a warrantless entry into a dwelling to arrest in the absence of sufficient justification for the failure to obtain a warrant (California Supreme Court).
	Payton v. New York (1980)	Extended *People v. Ramey* to apply to all states.
Fifth Amendment		
Self-Incrimination	*Miranda v. Arizona* (1966)	Before questioning, police must inform suspects in custody of their rights to remain silent, to have counsel present, to state-appointed counsel if they cannot afford their own attorney and to be warned that anything they say may be used against them in a court of law.
	Oregon v. Mathiason (1977)	Police are not required to give *Miranda* warnings to everyone whom they question, nor is the requirement imposed simply because questioning takes place in the station house or because the questioned person is one whom the police suspect. *Miranda* warnings are required only where there has been such a restriction on a person's freedom as to render him or her "in custody."
Custodial Interrogation	*United States v. Mesa* (1980)	Incriminating statements in a suspect's recorded conversation are not obtained in violation of the suspect's rights if the *Miranda* warning is not first given.
DUI Stops	*Pennsylvania v. Muniz* (1990)	Officers conducting DUI stops who ask routine questions do not need to give the *Miranda* warning.
Right to Counsel	*Brewer v. Williams* (1977)	A suspect's incriminating statements were inadmissible because the way they were elicited violated his constitutional right to counsel.
Public Safety Exception	*Michigan v. Tucker* (1974)	*Miranda* warnings are not themselves rights protected by constitution, but are measures to ensure that the right against compulsory self-incrimination is protected. On some facts there is a "public safety" exception to the requirement that *Miranda* warnings be given before a suspect's answers may be admitted into evidence, and the availability of that exception does not depend upon the motivation of the individual officers.
	New York v. Quarles (1984)	The public safety exception allows police to question suspects without first giving the *Miranda* warning if the information sought sufficiently affects the officer's and the public's safety.
Involuntary Confessions (Harmless Error)	*Arizona v. Fulminante* (1991)	When involuntary confessions are admitted into evidence, the question is, "Did the allowance harm the defendant's case or was it a 'harmless error'"? If the error is harmful or if the prosecution fails to establish beyond reasonable doubt that the error is harmless, the confession is inadmissible and any conviction based on it must be reversed.
Entrapment	*Sorrells v. United States* (1932)	Law enforcement may use traps, decoys and deception to obtain evidence of the commission of a crime. Resort to such means does not render an indictment thereafter found a nullity nor call for the exclusion of evidence so procured.
	Grossman v. State (1969)	Police conduct constituting entrapment includes appeals to sympathy, guarantees that the act is legal and inducements making the crime unusually attractive.

(*continued*)

TABLE 8.2 (Continued)

Doctrine	Case Decision	Holding
	Sherman v. United States (1958)	Entrapment occurs only when the criminal conduct was "the product of the creative" activity of law enforcement officials.
	United States v. Russell (1973)	Only when government deception actually implants the criminal design in the mind of the defendant does the defense of entrapment come into play.
	Jacobson v. United States (1992)	Government has the burden of proving "beyond a reasonable doubt" the defendant's predisposition to commit an offense. Failing to prove such a predisposition, the defense wins on the presumption the defendant is an "unwary innocent" instead of an "unwary criminal."

SOURCE: © Innovative Systems—Publishers Inc., 2001.

Summary

The constitutional standards for searches and seizures, including arrests, are contained in the Fourth Amendment, which requires that searches and seizures be reasonable and be based on probable cause. Probable cause requires more than mere suspicion and may be founded on (1) observation, (2) expertise, (3) circumstantial factors and (4) information conveyed to the officers, including official sources, victims of crimes and informants.

Stop and frisk is a form of search and seizure and, as such, is governed by the intent of the Fourth Amendment. A stop is not an arrest, but it is a seizure if physical force or a show of authority is used. A frisk, however, is a search. Stop and frisk is a protective search for weapons in which the intrusion must be limited to a scope reasonably designed to discover guns, knives, clubs and other hidden instruments that may be used to assault a police officer or others; it is not a search for evidence of a crime. *Terry* established that the authority to stop and frisk is independent of the power to arrest. A stop is *not* an arrest, but it is a seizure within the meaning of the Fourth Amendment and therefore requires reasonableness. *Maryland v. Wilson* established that, given the likelihood of a traffic stop leading to either violence or the destruction of evidence when passengers are in the vehicle, officers may order passengers out of the car pending completion of the stop.

The Supreme Court has upheld roadblocks at national borders, sobriety checkpoints and informational checkpoints. The Supreme Court has held that drug checkpoints, general crime control checkpoints and driver's license checkpoints are not constitutional.

Reasonable searches must also meet the standards set forth in the Fourth Amendment. The principal justifications established by the courts for the right to search are when (1) a search warrant has been issued, (2) no warrant has been issued but consent to search was given, (3) no warrant has been issued but exigent circumstances exist or (4) no warrant has been issued because there is no expectation of privacy and thus no requirement for a search warrant.

Technically all searches are to be made under the authority of a search warrant issued by a magistrate. A search warrant is a judicial order, based on probable cause, directing a police officer to search for specific property, seize it and return it to the court. The search must be limited to the specific area and specific items delineated in the warrant.

Warrantless searches are justified when consent to search is given, when exigent circumstances exist or when no right to privacy exists. The limitations to a search made with consent are that the consent must be free and voluntary, and the scope must be limited to the area for which consent has been given. When police conduct a warrantless search, they may be challenged on the basis that probable cause was not established (i.e., a magistrate would not have issued a warrant) or that the officers had time to secure a warrant and had no justification to act without one. The limitations placed on searches incidental to lawful arrest are found in the *Chimel* Rule, which states that the area of the search must be within the suspect's immediate control—that is, it must be within his or her reach.

Special provisions have been made for warrantless searches of cars and other conveyances because of their mobility. The *Carroll* decision established that the right to search an automobile does not depend on the right to arrest the driver or an occupant. It depends on the officer's probable cause for believing (1) the automobile's contents violate the law and (2) the conveyance would be gone before a search warrant could be obtained. *Chambers v. Maroney* established that a car may retain its mobility even though impounded. *Coolidge v. New Hampshire* established that the rule of mobility cannot be applied unless there is actually a risk the vehicle will be moved. If something is open to the public and therefore has no expectation of privacy, it is not protected by the Fourth Amendment. This includes open fields, abandoned property and trash. The Supreme Court has ruled that using thermal imaging to view inside a home without a warrant is unconstitutional. The most important limitation imposed on any search is that the scope must be narrowed. General searches are unconstitutional.

U.S. citizens are also protected against unreasonable arrest (seizure) by the Fourth Amendment. The four elements of a criminal arrest are *intent* by an officer to make an arrest, *authority* to arrest, a *seizure* or restraint, and an *understanding* by the person that he or she is being arrested.

The *Miranda* warning contains four specific rights:

- You have the right to remain silent.
- If you give up the right to remain silent, anything you say can and will be used against you in a court of law.
- You have the right to speak with an attorney and to have the attorney present during questioning.
- If you so desire and cannot afford one, an attorney will be appointed for you without charge before questioning.

The *Miranda* warning must be given to a suspect who is interrogated in police custody, that is, when the suspect is not free to leave. The public safety exception allows officers to question suspects without first giving the *Miranda* warning if the information sought sufficiently affects the officer's and the public's safety.

Discussion Questions

1. What is the difference between reasonable suspicion and probable cause?
2. Why are the police not given total freedom to help stop crime? Why are they not allowed to use evidence that clearly establishes a person's guilt, no matter how they obtained this evidence?
3. In a state where stop and frisk is legal, can a police officer be sued for stopping and frisking someone?

4. What are the most important factors in determining if and when an arrest occurred?
5. Must all elements of probable cause exist before a lawful arrest can be made?
6. Why is the presence of 10 officers not considered intimidation when a request to search is made?
7. Provide three examples of when a police officer can make a warrantless search or seizure.
8. From what you have learned about search and seizure, do you feel the restrictions placed on police officers are reasonable?
9. Do you support the plain touch/feel doctrine? Why or why not?
10. Is it too easy for criminals to allege entrapment? How can officers protect against this?

Gale Emergency Services Database Assignments

- Use the Gale Emergency Services Database to help answer the Discussion Questions as appropriate.
- Using the Gale Emergency Services Database, search for articles on the *bright-line rule* and zero in on the *Fourth Amendment* and *traffic stops*. Describe the bright-line rules in conjunction with the totality-of-circumstances test. Be prepared to discuss your findings with the class.
- Using the Gale Emergency Services Database, find the article "Protecting Personal Privacy: Drawing the Line Between People and Containers": http://find.galegroup.com/gps/retrieve.do?contentSet=IAC-Documents&resultListType=RESULT_LIST&qrySerId=Locale%28en%2C%2C%29%3AFQE%3D%28K0%2CNone%2C20%294th+amendment+police%24&sgHitCountType=None&inPS=true&sort=DateDescend&searchType=BasicSearchForm&tabID=T003&prodId=IPS&searchId=R1¤tPosition=1&userGroupName=cpg3&docId=A143342217&docType=IAC&contentSet=IAC-Documents

  Assignment: Read and outline the article and be prepared to discuss your notes in class.
- Using the Gale Emergency Services Database, find the article "Drug Detection Dogs Legal Considerations": http://find.galegroup.com/gps/retrieve.do?contentSet=IAC-Documents&resultListType=RESULT_LIST&qrySerId=Locale%28en%2C%2C%29%3AFQE%3D%28K0%2CNone%2C20%294th+amendment+police%24&sgHitCountType=None&inPS=true&sort=DateDescend&searchType=BasicSearchForm&tabID=T003&prodId=IPS&searchId=R1¤tPosition=5&userGroupName=cpg3&docId=A60040494&docType=IAC&contentSet=IAC-Documents

  Assignment: Read article and identify the court's view on cases cited. Cite the results of the cases and why the courts made those decisions. Be prepared to discuss the legal consideration in class.
- Using the Gale Emergency Services Database, find the article "Stop & Frisk: The Power and the Obligation of the Police": http://find.galegroup.com/gps/retrieve.do?contentSet=IAC-Documents&resultListType=RESULT_LIST&qrySerId=Locale%28en%2C%2C%29%3AFQE%3D%28ke%2CNone%2C10%29terry+ohio%24&sgHitCountType=None&inPS=true&sort=

DateDescend&searchType=BasicSearchForm&tabID=T002&prodId=IPS&searchId=R4¤tPosition=1&userGroupName=cpg3&docId=A61487920&docType=IAC&contentSet=IAC-Documents

Assignment: Read the article and explain how the Supreme Court describes "reasonable suspicion" in this case. Be prepared to discuss your explanation in class.

- Using the Gale Emergency Services Database, find the article "Civil Liability for Violations of *Miranda*: The Impact of *Chavez v. Martinez*": http://find.galegroup.com/gps/retrieve.do?contentSet=IAC-Documents&resultListType=RESULT_LIST&qrySerId=Locale%28en%2C%2C%29%3AFQE%3D%28K0%2CNone%2C15%29miranda+warning%24&sgHitCountType=None&inPS=true&sort=DateDescend&searchType=BasicSearchForm&tabID=T003&prodId=IPS&searchId=R5¤tPosition=1&userGroupName=cpg3&docId=A110395579&docType=IAC&contentSet=IAC-Documents

  Assignment: After reading the article list and describe what civil liabilities there are for law enforcement officers who violate the *Miranda* warning. Be prepared to discuss these consequences with the class.
- Using the Gale Emergency Services Database, find the article "Creating Exigent Circumstances" (Warrantless Entry): http://find.galegroup.com/gps/retrieve.do?contentSet=IAC-Documents&resultListType=RESULT_LIST&qrySerId=Locale%28en%2C%2C%29%3AFQE%3D%28ke%2CNone%2C21%29exigent+circumstances%24&sgHitCountType=None&inPS=true&sort=DateDescend&searchType=BasicSearchForm&tabID=T003&prodId=IPS&searchId=R6¤tPosition=1&userGroupName=cpg3&docId=A18826919&docType=IAC&contentSet=IAC-Documents

  Assignment: Read the article and list its main points. Be prepared to discuss these points in class.

Internet Assignment

- Go to *Dickerson v. United States* (http://supct.law.cornell.edu/supct/html/99-5525.ZS.html) and review this Supreme Court case. Note the dissents of Justices Scalia and Clarence Thomas. Outline the arguments on both sides (majority rule versus dissenting opinions), and be prepared to discuss your findings with the class and which position you agree with.

References

Judge, Lisa A. "Bye-Bye Belton? Supreme Court Decision Shifts Authority for Vehicle Searches from Automatic to Manual." *The Police Chief*, June 2009, pp.12–13.

Means, Randy, and McDonald, Pam. "How Long Is Too Long During a Terry Stop?" *Law and Order*, November 2009a, pp.22–24.

Means, Randy, and McDonald, Pam. "The Myth of Investigative Detention vs. Arrest." *Law and Order*, August 2009b, pp.12–14.

Means, Randy, and McDonald, Pam. "Police Law Myths, Part 1." *Law and Order*, May 2009c, pp.26–29.

Means, Randy, and McDonald, Pam. "Warrantless Entry and the Emergency Aid Exception." *Law and Order*, February 2010, pp.17–20.

Petrocelli, Joe. "Diplomatic Immunity." *Law and Order*, May 2005, p.20.

Rutledge, Devallis. "Updating Weapons Frisks." *Police*, April 2009a, pp.66–69.

Rutledge, Devallis. "Vehicle Searches Incident to Arrest." *Police*, June 2009b, pp.68–71.

Rutledge, Devallis. "Beware of False Headlines." *Police*, January 2010a, pp.64–67.

Rutledge, Devallis. "The "Emergency Aid Doctrine." *Police*, February 2010b, pp.60–63.

Rutledge, Devallis. "Justifying Temporary Detentions." *Police*, March 2010c, pp.70–73.

Savage, David G. "Supreme Court Sets Aside Strict Ruling on *Miranda* 'Right to Remain Silent.'" *Los Angeles Times*, February 24, 2010.

Scarry, Laura L. "Less Than Probable Cause: Protective Actions in *Terry* Stops." *Law Officer Magazine*, May 2009a, pp.26–29.

Scarry, Laura L. "Patting Down Passengers: No 4th Amendment Violation." *Law Officer Magazine*, April 2009b, pp.20–24.

Scarry, Laura L. "The Searchers: U.S. Supreme Court Limits Searches Incident to Arrest." *Law Officer Magazine*, June 2009c, pp.20–22.

Spector, Elliot B. "U.S. Supreme Court Diminishes Effect of Arrests That Violate State Procedural Rules." *The Police Chief*, November 2008, pp.12–13.

Stroshine, Meghan; Alpert, Geoffrey; and Dunham, Roger. "The Influence of 'Working Rules' on Police Suspicion and Discretionary Decision Making." *Police Quarterly*, September 2008, pp.315–337.

"Supreme Court Backs Police on Questioning Subjects." *PoliceOne.com News*, February 22, 2010. http://www.policeone.com/pc_print.asp?vid=2008676

Cases Cited

Arizona v. Fulminante, 499 U.S. 279 (1991)
Arizona v. Gant, 556 U.S. ___ (2009)
Arizona v. Hicks, 480 U.S. 321 (1987)
Arizona v. Johnson, 555 U.S. ___ (2009)
Atwater v. City of Lago Vista, 532 U.S. 318 (2001)
Bond v. United States, 529 U.S. 334 (2000)
Brendlin v. California, 551 U.S. 249 (2007)
Brewer v. Williams, 430 U.S. 387 (1977)
Brigham City, Utah v. Stuart, 547 U.S. 398 (2006)
California v. Ciraola, 476 U.S. 207 (1986)
California v. Greenwood, 486 U.S. 35 (1988)
Carroll v. United States, 267 U.S. 132 (1925)
Chambers v. Maroney, 339 U.S. 42 (1970)
Chimel v. California, 395 U.S. 752 (1969)
City of Indianapolis v. Edmond, 531 U.S. 32 (2000)
Colorado v. Bertine, 479 U.S. 367 (1987)
Coolidge v. New Hampshire, 403 U.S. 443 (1971)
Davis v. United States, 512 U.S. 452 (1994)
District of Columbia v. Mancouso, 778 A.2d 270 (D.C.2001)
Draper v. United States, 358 U.S. 307 (1959)
Edwards v. Arizona, 451 U.S. 477 (1981)
Florida v. Jimeno, 500 U.S. 248 (1991)
Florida v. J. L., 529 U.S. 266 (2000)
Florida v. Powell, 559 U.S. ___ (2010)
Florida v. Riley, 488 U.S. 445 (1989)
Georgia v. Randolph, 547 U.S. 103 (2006)
Grossman v. State, 457 P.2d 226 (1969)
Hester v. United States, 265 U.S. 57 (1924)
Hiibel v. Sixth Judicial District Court of Nevada, Humboldt County, 542 U.S. 177 (2004)
Hudson v. Michigan, 547 U.S. 586 (2006)
Illinois v. Gates, 462 U.S. 213 (1983)
Illinois v. Lidster, 540 U.S. 419 (2004)
Illinois v. McArthur, 531 U.S. 326 (2001)
Illinois v. Wardlow, 528 U.S. 119 (2000)
Jacobson v. United States, 503 U.S. 540 (1992)
Katz v. United States, 389 U.S. 347 (1967)
Kaupp v. Texas, 538 U.S. 626 (2003)
Kyllo v. United States, 533 U.S. 27 (2001)
Maryland v. Buie, 494 U.S. 325 (1990)
Maryland v. Shatzer, 559 U.S. ___ (2010)
Maryland v. Wilson, 519 U.S. 408 (1997)
Michigan v. Fisher, 558 U.S. ___ (2009)
Michigan v. Summers, 452 U.S. 692 (1981)
Michigan v. Tucker, 417 U.S. 433 (1974)
Michigan v. Tyler, 436 U.S. 499 (1978)
Michigan Department of State Police v. Sitz, 496 U.S. 444 (1990)
Minnesota v. Dickerson, 508 U.S. 336 (1993)
Miranda v. Arizona, 384 U.S. 436 (1966)
Missouri v. Seibert, 542 U.S. 600 (2004)
Monroe v. Pape, 365 U.S. 167 (1961)
Muehler v. Mena, 544 U.S. 93 (2005)
New York v. Belton, 453 U.S. 454 (1981)
New York v. Quarles, 467 U.S. 649 (1984)
Nix v. Williams, 467 U.S. 431 (1984)
O'Connor v. Ortega, 480 U.S. 709 (1987)

Oliver v. United States, 466 U.S. 170 (1984)
Olmstead v. United States, 277 U.S. 438 (1928)
Oregon v. Elstad, 470 U.S. 298 (1985)
Oregon v. Mathiason, 429 U.S. 492 (1977)
Payton v. New York, 445 U.S. 573 (1980)
Pennsylvania v. Mimms, 434 U.S. 106 (1977)
Pennsylvania v. Muniz, 496 U.S. 582 (1990)
People v. Ramey, 16 Cal.3d 263 (1976)
Sherman v. United States, 356 U.S. 369 (1958)
Smith v. United States, 337 U.S. 137 (1949)
Sorrells v. United States, 287 U.S. 435 (1932)
State v. Barlow, Jr. 320 A.2d 895, 898 (Me. 1974)
State v. Hempele, 576 A.2d 793 (N.J. 1990)
Teague v. Lane, 489 U.S. 288 (1989)
Terry v. Ohio, 392 U.S. 1 (1968)
Thornton v. United States, 541 U.S. 615 (2004)
United States v. Arvizu, 534 U.S. 226 (2002)
United States v. Banks, 540 U.S. 31 (2003)
United States v. Cortez, 449 U.S. 411 (1981)
United States v. Drayton, 536 U.S. 194 (2002)
United States v. Dunn, 480 U.S. 294 (1987)
United States v. Espinoza, 256 F.3d 718, 722 (7th Cir. 2001)
United States v. Flores-Montano, 541 U.S. 149 (2004)
United States v. Grubbs, 547 U.S. 90 (2006)
United States v. Martinez-Fuerte, 428 U.S. 543 (1976)
United States v. Mesa, 638 F.2d 582, 584 (3d Cir. 1980)
United States v. Millan, 36 F.3d 886, (9th Cir.1994) (1994)
United States v. Place, 462 U.S. 696 (1983)
United States v. Ross, 456 U.S. 798 (1982)
United States v. Russell, 411 U.S. 423 (1973)
United States v. Sokolow, 490 U.S. 1 (1989)
Virginia v. Moore, 553 U.S. ___ (2008)
Whren v. United States, 517 U.S. 806 (1996)
Wilson v. Arkansas, 514 U.S. 927 (1995)

CHAPTER 9

Gangs and Drugs: Threats to Our National Security

Gangs are now spreading through our society like a violent plague.

—Jackson and McBride, LAPD

Drug use and the crime it generates are turning the American dream into a national nightmare for millions of Americans.

—Lee P. Brown

Gang members communicate via graffiti and hand signals. They also often wear certain colors, tattoos or items of clothing to identify themselves as members of a particular gang.

Do You Know . . .

- Whether gangs, gang membership and the gang problem are increasing or decreasing?
- What the distinguishing characteristics of gangs are?
- Whether gang membership and violent victimization are linked?
- What the most common reasons for joining gangs are?
- What factors contribute to gang formation?
- What the most important risk factor for becoming a gang member probably is?
- What the most commonly used strategy to combat a gang problem currently is? What other strategies are being used?
- What strategies are reported to be most effective?
- What the dual approach of the Department of Justice to combating gang violence is?
- What the five strategies of the OJJDP's Comprehensive Gang Model are?
- What act made it illegal to sell or use certain narcotics and dangerous drugs?
- What federal law prohibits in relation to narcotics and dangerous drugs?
- What five controlled substances are identified in the *National Drug Threat Assessment?*
- What the most available and abused illegal drug is? What the most frequent drug arrest is for?
- What common effects of the various narcotics and other dangerous drugs are?
- What the three core components of the national drug control policy are?
- What efforts at crime control have been implemented to combat the drug problem?

Can You Define?

Bloods
civil injunction
crack
Crips
drug-defined offenses
drug-related offenses
gang
gateway theory
graffiti
interdiction
methamphetamine
monikers
mules
representing
sinsemilla
stacking
turf
wannabes

INTRODUCTION

Drugs and gangs are often mentioned in the same sentence. The issues of gangs and drugs are both extremely important to today's law enforcement practitioners, and dozens of publications are available addressing each topic individually and in great detail. However, such in-depth coverage of these critical issues is beyond the scope of this introductory text, and the authors encourage students to supplement their learning by seeking additional resources on these subjects, some of which are listed at the end of the chapter.

THE CHAPTER AT A GLANCE

This chapter begins by discussing the threat of gangs. Gangs are defined and the various types of gangs that have developed in the United States are described, including various racial and ethnic gangs and the increasing presence of females in gangs. This is followed by a discussion of specific characteristics of gangs, including the gang subculture and how gang members might be identified. Next, reasons for joining a gang are discussed, followed by a look at the importance of gang intelligence and a discussion of strategies used to address the gang problem. The gang discussion concludes with a discussion of problems in prosecuting gang members.

The link between gangs and drugs provides the transition into the next section—the threat of drugs. Coverage of the drug problem begins with a discussion of drug cartels and an overview of the threat of drugs. Next is a look at the various narcotics and other dangerous drugs under federal regulation regarding their prescription, distribution and possession. This is followed by exploring the various drug-control strategies being used in the war on drugs, ranging from incarceration to legalization. The chapter concludes with a brief examination of the links between crime and illicit drug and alcohol use.

THE THREAT OF GANGS

Gangs have existed in nearly every civilization throughout recorded history. Street gangs probably started in our country in Los Angeles at about the beginning of the 20th century. The *2008 National Youth Gang Survey* (Egley et al., 2010, p.1) reports, "Gang activity remains a widespread problem across the United States, with prevalence rates remaining significantly elevated in 2008 compared with recorded lows in the early 2000s. Approximately one-third of the jurisdictions in the National Youth Gang Survey (NYGS) study population reported gang problems in 2008. This is a significant change over the 2002 estimate, but a statistically negligible one from 2007." The National Gang Center estimates that 32.4 percent of all cities, suburban areas, towns and rural counties experienced gang problems in 2008, a 15 percent increase from 2002 figure (Egley et al., 2010). Among agencies reporting a gang problem, 45 percent characterized their gang problem as "getting worse," whereas fewer than 1 in 10 said their gang problem was "getting better" (Egley et al., p.2).

Obtaining accurate estimates of gang membership is challenging. According to the National Gang Center, about 774,000 gang members and 27,900 gangs are estimated to have been active in the United States in 2008, an increase in membership by 6 percent and in the number of gangs by 28 percent from 2002 to 2008. The *National Gang Threat Assessment 2009* (2009, p.iii) reports, "Approximately one million gang members belonging to more than 20,000 gangs were criminally active in the United States as of September 2008." Although the estimates of these two surveys vary considerably, both highlight the extent of the problem.

Gangs and gang membership increased significantly between 2002 and 2008, and reporting agencies perceive the problem as worsening.

A 2009 survey conducted by the Police Executive Research Forum (PERF) regarding gang activity found that 70 percent of responding jurisdictions had witnessed an increase in gang membership during the past two years, and 60 percent reported an increase in multi-jurisdictional gang-related crimes over that same period. More than 75 percent of the respondents cited "gang activity" as the top factor contributing to violent crime in their communities (*Gang Violence*, 2010, p.iii). During the past two years, increases were also reported in fear of gangs (4 percent of responding agencies), violent disputes between gangs (50 percent), migration of gangs from other states or regions (48 percent), involvement of girls in gangs (47 percent), retaliation shootings (42 percent), presence of illegal immigrants in gangs (42 percent), displacement of gangs geographically (40 percent), drive-by shootings (31 percent) and gang initiations involving a criminal act (29 percent) (*Gang Violence*, p.3).

Trends

Law enforcement respondents to the *National Gang Threat Assessment 2009* (p.iii) acknowledge the following trends:

- Local or neighborhood-based street gangs remain a significant threat because they constitute the largest number of gangs nationwide. Most engage in violence in conjunction with a variety of crimes, including retail-level drug distribution.
- Gang members are migrating from urban to suburban and rural areas, expanding the gangs' influence in most regions. Reasons for migration include expanding drug distribution territories, increasing illicit revenue, recruiting new members, hiding from law enforcement and escaping from other gangs.
- Criminal gangs commit as much as 80 percent of the crime in many communities. Typical gang-related crimes include alien smuggling, armed robbery, assault, auto theft, drug trafficking, extortion, fraud, home invasions, identity theft, murder and weapons trafficking.
- Gang members are the primary retail-level distributors of most illicit drugs. They are also increasingly distributing wholesale-level quantities of marijuana and cocaine in most urban and suburban communities.
- Some gangs are trafficking illicit drugs at the regional and national levels; several are capable of competing with U.S.–based Mexican drug trafficking organizations.
- U.S.–based gang members illegally cross the U.S.–Mexican border for the express purpose of smuggling illicit drugs and illegal aliens from Mexico into the United States.
- Many gangs actively use the Internet to recruit new members and to communicate with members in other areas of the United States and in foreign countries.
- Street gangs and outlaw motorcycle gangs pose a growing threat to law enforcement along the U.S.–Canada border.

DEFINING AND CLASSIFYING GANGS

An important problem in studying gangs is lack of a common definition among local, state and federal agencies, which may result in discrepancy between reported proliferation of gangs. The National Alliance of Gang Investigators Association (NAGIA) defines a **gang** as "A group or association of three or more persons who may have a common identifying sign, symbol or name and who individually or collectively engage in, or have engaged in criminal activity which creates an atmosphere of fear and intimidation."

gang
A group of people who form an allegiance for a common purpose and engage in unlawful or criminal activity.

Many jurisdictions rely on a predetermined list of criteria or descriptors when defining their gang situation. The *National Youth Gang Survey Analysis* (2009) notes, "In general, law enforcement agencies report that group criminality is of greatest importance and the presence of leadership is of least importance in defining a gang. Additionally, law enforcement agencies tend to emphasize the same definitional characteristics in defining a gang irrespective of year of gang onset." These include, in order of frequency of use, having a gang name, displaying colors or other symbols, hanging out together and claiming a turf or territory. In identifying individual gang members, a clear majority of city and suburban agencies emphasize using self-nomination compared with using the criteria for identifying gangs. Rural counties place greater emphasis on display of tattoos, colors or other symbols to designate gang membership.

The *National Gang Threat Assessment 2009* also reports, "Gangs vary extensively regarding membership, structure, age, and ethnicity. However, three basic types of gangs have been identified by gang investigators: street gangs, prison gangs, and outlaw motorcycle gangs (OMGs)."

STREET GANGS

Street gangs exist throughout the country and, because of their sheer numbers and geographical coverage, pose the greatest threat (*National Gang Threat Assessment 2009*). Although most gangs are typically limited to members of the same gender and are ethnically or racially homogeneous—comprising individuals who share the same language, cultural background and, frequently, heritage—more variations to this "norm" are being observed. For example, beginning in the early 1990s some gangs in Southern California were admitting females and persons of other races as members, resulting in hybrid gangs. Therefore, the following discussion, in which the more traditional distinctions among street gangs are discussed, should be read with this caveat in mind.

The major ethnic or racial gang groups operating in the United States are Hispanic or Latin American, African American, Asian and White ethnic gangs, although other smaller groups also exist, such as Native American, Nigerian, Jamaican, Somalian and Russian gangs.

Hispanic or Latin American Gangs

Between 1910 and 1925, a great influx of immigrants arrived from Mexico. These immigrants tended to live with others from their native areas of Mexico, and rivalries developed that eventually resulted in the formation of gangs. These Hispanic gangs lived in barrios that often could trace their heritage back several generations and had a strong system of tradition.

The depression of the 1930s brought Latino families from Arizona, New Mexico and Texas to Los Angeles. They fragmented into groups, each claiming its own territory. In the 1960s freeway displacement drove families from the central city eastward, where they created more new gangs.

Today Hispanic gangs comprise Chicanos, a term reserved for those from Mexico, and Puerto Ricans, Cubans and individuals from various Central and South American countries. Among the most feared gangs is Mara Salvatrucha 13 or MS-13.

Mara Salvatrucha 13 (MS-13) The Mara Salvatrucha 13 is considered by many gang experts to be America's most dangerous gang and is currently spreading from El Salvador to Los Angeles and across the United States. An estimated 1,000 hard-core members of the gang are operating in 33 states, with the largest clusters living in Los Angeles, Washington, DC, and the Mid-Atlantic region. The urgency of dealing with MS-13 is illustrated by the formation of a major national gang task force spearheaded by the Federal Bureau of Investigation (FBI) and described on its Web site:

> The MS-13 National Gang Task Force supports FBI field office investigations of the MS-13 international gang, which has its origins in El Salvador. Started in 2004, the task force coordinates the investigative efforts of federal, state, and local agencies against MS-13 gang targets. MS-13 members and associates have been identified in Central America and in more than 30 states and have a significant presence in Houston, Los Angeles, New York City, and Washington, D.C.

According to the PERF survey (*Gang Violence*, p.5), MS-13 topped the list of gangs in the respondents' areas that have transnational ties.

African American Gangs

African American street gangs also existed in the Los Angeles area for many years. They began as groups of young high school "thugs" who extorted money from students and terrorized teachers. One gang, the **Crips**, had the reputation of being the toughest African American gang in Los Angeles. Another group of African American youths, who began to get together for protection from attacks by Crip sets, applied the term *blood brothers* to their gang name. Thus began the division of African American gangs into the Crips and the non-Crips or **Bloods**, two of the most formidable gangs in the country today.

Crips

Gang with the reputation of being the toughest African American gang in Los Angeles; rivals of the Bloods.

Bloods

Well-known African American gang; rivals of the Crips.

Asian Gangs

The various Asian gangs in the United States consist of members of Chinese, Japanese, Vietnamese, Korean and Filipino ethnicity. In the early 1900s secret Chinese fraternal organizations called the Tongs used boys called Wah Chings as lookouts. As the Tongs became more legitimate and established, they no longer needed the Wah Chings. The Wah Chings, however, refused to disband, taking up where the Tongs left off. Although the Tongs are now primarily benevolent societies, when necessary they will resort to violence through the Wah Chings. Eventually differences developed within the Wah Chings, and they split into two groups, with the older members becoming known as Yu Li and the younger members retaining the name Wah Ching. A member of the Yu Li named Joe Fong became disenchanted and broke off into another gang called the Joe Fong gang or Joe Boys. All three gangs—the Wah Chings, Yu Lis and Joe Boys—exist today.

A newer breed of Asian gang is the home invaders, whose well-armed and well-organized members specialize in home robberies of other Asians. The targeting of Asian victims by Asian gang members is relatively common because of a general unwillingness among the Asian community to report victimization to the police.

Filipino neighborhood street gangs are similar to Hispanic gangs and may gravitate toward Mexican gangs. The most common Filipino gangs are the Santanas, the Tabooes and Temple Street. The Korean community also has active gangs, the most well known being the Korean Killers.

White Ethnic Gangs

White ethnic gangs are composed primarily of European American members. Neo-Nazi skinheads are perhaps the best-known White ethnic gang, with members who are militantly racist and advocate white supremacy. The Aryan Youth Movement (AYM) and White Aryan Resistance (WAR) are groups also aligned by racism. White "stoner" gangs emphasize the occult and satanic rituals.

White ethnic gangs typically engage in hate crimes directed at other ethnic and religious groups and those with "alternative" lifestyles. These gangs may attack African Americans, Hispanics, Jews or homosexuals.

Females and Gangs

Females may be part of an entirely female gang, participants in a coed gang or auxiliary members of a predominantly male gang. A female gang may have a name affiliated with its male counterpart, such as the Vice Ladies (from the Vice Lords). These auxiliaries usually consist of sisters and girlfriends of the male gang members. The females often assist the male gang, serving as decoys for rival gang members, as lookouts during the commission of crimes or as carriers of weapons when a gang war is impending. They may also carry information in and out of prison, harbor or hide gang members from authorities, and provide sexual favors (they are often drug dependent and physically abused). The *National Gang Threat Assessment* reports:

> Female involvement in gangs continues to increase and evolve as females assume greater responsibility in gang activities and grow more independent from their male counterparts. Though gangs are still primarily male-dominated, research indicates that female gang membership is on the rise. . . . The National Council on Crime and Delinquency ranked "young females as the fastest growing offenders in the national juvenile justice population."
>
> Although female gang membership in male-dominated gangs is increasing, the prevalence of predominantly female gangs continues to be a rare phenomenon. In addition, although all-female gangs do exist, they are infrequently the focus of law enforcement. Traditionally, female gangs have received less attention from researchers and law enforcement, and most efforts have focused on intervention programs designed to provide an alternative refuge for girls attempting to escape abusive environments. Furthermore, law enforcement officials are less likely to recognize or stop female gang members, and they have experienced difficulty in identifying female involvement in gang-related activity.

Gangs may also form based not so much on a common ethnicity but on a common setting, lifestyle or criminal enterprise.

Criminal Gangs

As noted earlier, most agencies reported involvement in criminal activities as the most important factor in defining a gang. Table 9.1 summarizes several types of criminal organizations, most of which are gangs, listing their names and the types

TABLE 9.1 Criminal Organizations

Type of Group	Subtype of Group	Specific Groups and Distinct Gangs	Criminal Activity
Asian gangs	Chinese street gangs, Triads, Tongs	Flying Dragons, Fuk Ching, Ghost Shadows, Ping On, Taiwan Brotherhood, United Bamboo, Wah Ching, White Tigers	Extortion of Chinese businesses; gambling; heroin distribution; exploitation of recent immigrants; smuggling of humans
	Japanese gangs (Boryokudan or Yakuza)	Kumlai, Sumiyoshi Rengo, Yamaguchi Gumi	Gambling; prostitution and sex trade; money laundering; trafficking in weapons and drugs
	Korean gangs	AB (American Burger), Flying Dragons, Junior Korean Power, KK (Korean Killers), Korean Power	Prostitution, massage parlors; gambling; loan-sharking; extortion of Korean businesses (particularly produce markets and restaurants)
	Laotian/Cambodian/ Vietnamese gangs	Born to Kill (BTK), Laotian Bloods (LBs), Richtown Crips, Tiny Oriental Crips, Tiny Rascal Gang (TRG[1])	Strong arm and violent crimes related to business extortion; home invasion for theft of gold, jewelry and money, coupled with rape to deter reporting; street crimes; prostitution; drug trafficking; assault; murder
	Hmong gangs	Cobra Gang, Menace of Destruction (MOD), Oriental Ruthless Boys, Totally Gangster Crips, Totally Mafia Crips, True Asian Crips, True Crip Gangster, True Lady Crips (female Hmongs), True Local Crips, Westside Crips, White Tigers	Gang rape; prostitution; burglary; auto theft; vandalism; home invasion; street crimes; strong arm robbery of businesses; drug trafficking; assault; murder
Latin American gangs	Mexican gangs	18th Street Gang, Sureños-Mexican Mafia, Norteños-Nuestra Family, Tijuana Cartel-Arellano Felix Organization, Colima Cartel-Amazcua Contreras Brothers, Juarez Cartel-Amado Carillo Fuentes Group, Sonora Cartel-Miguel Caro Quintero Organization, Sinaloa Cartel-Guzman/Leora Organization, Guadalajara Cartel-Rafael Caro Quintero/Miguel Angel Felix Gallardo, Gulf Cartel	Drug trafficking (cocaine, crack, heroin, marijuana); counterfeiting; pickpocketing; money laundering; murder
	Cuban gangs	Cuban Mafia	Drug trafficking (cocaine, crack, heroin, marijuana); counterfeiting; pickpocketing; money laundering; murder
	Puerto Rican gangs	Latin Kings, Puerto Rican Stones	Street crimes; drug trafficking; burglary; assault; rape; murder
	Columbian gangs and cartels	Cali Cartel, Medellin Cartel, Norte Del Valle Cartel, North Coast Cartel, Bogota Cartel, Santander DeQuilichao Cartel, Black Eagles, United Self-Defense Forces of Columbia (AUC), National Liberation Army (ELN), Revolutionary Armed Forces of Columbia (FARC)	Drug trafficking (cocaine, crack, heroin, marijuana); counterfeiting; pickpocketing; money laundering; murder
	El Salvadoran gangs	Mara Salvatrucha 13 (MS-13)	Street crimes; strong-arming businesses; assault; drug trafficking; rape; murder

(*continued*)

TABLE 9.1 (Continued)

Type of Group	Subtype of Group	Specific Groups and Distinct Gangs	Criminal Activity
Latin American gangs (*continued*)	Peruvian gangs	Shining Path—guerilla organization with a mission for Maoist government	Vandalism and other property damage; assault; rape; murder
Jamaican posses		Shower Posse, Spangler Posse	Drug trafficking (cocaine, crack, marijuana); weapons trafficking; trafficking green cards
Nigerian gangs		Nigerian Criminal Enterprise (NCE)	Heroin smuggling (via mules) and heroin dealing; credit card fraud; infiltration of private security; planned bankruptcy of companies; exploitation of other Africans
Somali gangs		Somali Outlaws, Somalian Hot Boys, Murda Gang, Somali Mafia, Ma Thug Boys, Ruff Tuff Somali Crips[2]	Street crimes; strong-arming businesses; drug trafficking; assault; rape; murder
Russian (or Soviet) gangs		Evangelical Russian Mafia, Malina/Organizatsiya, Odessa Mafia, Gypsy gangs	Theft (diamonds, furs, gold) and fencing stolen goods; export and sale of stolen Russian religious art and gold; extortion; insurance fraud; money laundering; counterfeiting; daisy chain tax evasion schemes; credit card scams and fraud; smuggling illegal immigrants; drug trafficking
Street gangs	African American, Caucasian, Hispanic, and others	Disciples, Latin Kings, Vice Lords, Dog Pound, and many others, including variants of Bloods/Crips (e.g., Westside Crips or Rolling Crips)	Motor vehicle theft; drug sales (especially crack and marijuana); weapons trafficking; assaults; drive-by shootings; robbery; burglary; theft and fencing stolen goods; vandalism; graffiti
Drug-trafficking gangs	Traditional street gangs	Bloods, Crips, Gangster Disciples, Latin Kings and many others	Trafficking of heroin, cocaine, crack and other drugs; violence; arson; indirect prostitution; vandalism, property crime; strong-arm robbery. African American gangs known for crack; Chicano gangs known for heroin and crack.
	International drug cartels	Medellin Cartel, Cali Cartel	Drug trafficking (cocaine, crack, heroin, marijuana)
Graffiti or tagger crews (also tagger posses, mobs, tribes and piecers)		Known by three-letter monikers such as NBT (Nothing But Trouble) or ETC (Elite Tagger Crew)	Graffiti vandalism; tag-banging accompanied by violence
Prison gangs		Aryan Brotherhood, Black Guerilla Family, Consolidated Crip Organization, Mexican Mafia, Nuestra Familia, Texas Syndicate	Drug trafficking; prostitution; extortion; protection, murder for hire
Outlaw motorcycle gangs (OMGs)		Hell's Angels, Outlaws, Pagans, Bandidos	Drug trafficking (methamphetamine/crank, speed, ice, phencyclidine [PCP], lysergic acid diethylamide [LSD], angel dust); weapons trafficking; chop shops; massage parlors; strip bars; prostitution; arson

(continued)

TABLE 9.1 (Continued)

Type of Group	Subtype of Group	Specific Groups and Distinct Gangs	Criminal Activity
Hate groups (including militias and terrorist groups, which also share a focus on ideology)		Aryan Nation, Ku Klux Klan, skinheads (White Aryan Resistance), American Nazi Party, Christian Defense League	Bombings; counterfeiting; loan fraud, armored car and bank robberies; theft rings
La Cosa Nostra (aka the Mafia)		Families such as Bonnano, Columbo, Gambino, Genovese and Lucchese	Gambling; loan-sharking; corruption of public officials/institutions; extortion; money laundering; theft of precious metals, food and clothing; fencing stolen property; labor racketeering; stock manipulation; securities fraud; weapons trafficking; drug trafficking (particularly heroin distribution); systemic use of violence as a tool in business transactions; murder

Note: Although nationality and ethnicity are often unifying characteristics of criminal organizations and used to identify them, this view is overly narrow and promotes ethnic stereotypes. The organization of criminal groups by nationality and ethnicity in this table is not intended to suggest that criminal behavior is characteristics of any group; ethnicity, however, is often a marker to police.

[1] TRGs originated as a Cambodian gang but now allow Laotian members.

[2] Somali gangs often change their name, colors and signs every few months. For example, the Somali Outlaws, Hot Boys and Murda Gang are all one gang that has changed its identity. Somali Mafia and Ma Thugs are break-offs of these gangs.

SOURCE: Adapted from HESS/ORTHMANN/HESS. *Police Operations*, 5e. © 2011 (pp.430–431) Delmar Learning, a part of Cengage Learning, Inc. Reproduced by permission. www.cengage.com/permissions.

of criminal activity in which they engage. The table also includes some previously mentioned gangs, illustrating the difficulty in classifying gang activity.

OUTLAW MOTORCYCLE GANGS

Outlaw motorcycle gangs (OMGs) are among the most dynamic gangs worldwide, influencing the drug trade and using extortion, white slavery and money laundering. Even though the image of the biker gang member remains one of a leather-and-denim rough-and-tough guy, the reality today is that many members of such gangs are well educated, some holding college-level degrees in finance, business and law to improve the gang's profitability. According to the *National Gang Threat Assessment 2009*:

> OMG-related criminal activity poses a threat to public safety in local communities in which these gangs operate because of their wide-ranging criminal activity, propensity to use violence, and ability to counter law enforcement efforts. OMGs are highly structured criminal organizations whose members engage in criminal activities such as violent crime, weapons trafficking, and drug trafficking. OMGs maintain a strong centralized leadership that implements rules regulating membership,

> conduct, and criminal activity. As of June 2008, state and local law enforcement agencies estimate that between 280 and 520 OMGs are operating at the national, regional, and local levels. OMGs range in size from a single chapter to hundreds of chapters worldwide. Current law enforcement intelligence estimates indicate that more than 20,000 validated OMG members, divided among hundreds of OMGs, reside in the United States.

Many of these OMG members end up in prison and continue their gang affiliation within the prison walls.

PRISON GANGS

Many of the country's most violent street gangs have their origins in the U.S. correctional system (Dawe, 2009, p.16). Prison gangs, such as the Mexican Mafia, Nuestra Familia and Aryan Brotherhood, often have close ties to street gangs. Their leaders may serve as "shot callers" for street gangs, coordinating drug trafficking, extortion, intimidation, gambling and other activities from prison. Within the prison walls, gangs engage in drug trafficking, prostitution rings and murder for hire (Dawe, p.16).

Gang experts contend that the proliferation of prison incarcerations for gang members, often as a result of suppression efforts, brings small-time criminals to the big leagues where they learn to be meaner and more dangerous and take what they've learned back to their neighborhoods (Basich, 2009, p.21). Gang membership can often thrive behind bars: "Membership is often the only way for young offenders to survive in an atmosphere where life is ruled by sheer physical power. . . . Harsh reality: cons run the jails and gangs rule the cons" (Fine, 2009, p.17). The *National Gang Threat Assessment 2009* reports:

> Prison gangs are highly structured criminal networks that operate within the federal and state prison systems. Furthermore, these gangs operate in local communities through members who have been released from prison. Released members typically return to their home communities and resume their former street gang affiliations, acting as representatives of their prison gang to recruit street gang members who perform criminal acts on behalf of the prison gang. . . .
>
> Prison gangs are well organized and governed by established sets of rules and codes of conduct that are rigorously enforced by gang leaders. For example, California-based Mexican Mafia (La Eme) uses fear and intimidation to control Hispanic street gangs whose members are in prison and on the street in California. Such control gives La Eme command over 50,000 to 75,000 Sureños gang members and associates.

CHARACTERISTICS OF GANGS

The criteria used by various jurisdictions to define gangs previously discussed are collectively used to distinguish gangs from other groups.

Distinguishing characteristics of gangs include criminal activity, organization, leadership, domain identification, use of symbols and a name.

Criminal Activities

Research indicates that most gang members already were committing crimes before they joined a gang, but their delinquency rates increase dramatically after joining a gang: "Even after controlling for individual level attributes, individuals who join gangs commit more crimes than do nongang members. Furthermore, the offending level of gang members is higher when they report being active members of the gang. Therefore, gang membership clearly facilitates offending above and beyond individual level characteristics" (Tita and Ridgeway, 2007, p.208).

Local law enforcement data shows that as much as 80 percent of the crime in some jurisdictions can be ascribed to gang activity. Although much of the violence is linked to disputes over control of drug territory and enforcement of drug debts, other crimes commonly committed by gang members include auto theft, identity theft, mortgage fraud, insurance fraud, burglary, assault, home invasion robbery, alien smuggling, operation of prostitution rings, extortion, drive-by shootings, homicide, weapons trafficking and other firearms offenses (*National Gang Threat Assessment 2009*).

Gang-related crimes are typically violent and often involve firearms. The PERF survey (*Gang Violence*, 2010, p.3) found that 55 percent of the respondents reported an increase of the use of guns in gang crime, and 60 percent reported an increase in multi-jurisdictional gang-related crimes during the past two years. Violence may be used against members within a gang if it is feared that a member will betray the gang's code of silence by talking to police. Table 9.2 summarizes research findings regarding criminal gang activity.

Organization

Although many gangs are loosely structured, some are quite formally organized. One common organizational element is age, with many gangs typically having two to four age divisions. Another common organizational element is location; two or more gangs may have localized versions of the same gang name, for example, the Southside Warriors and the Tenth Street Warriors.

Perhaps the most prevalent organizational feature is by member investment in or dedication to the gang. If a gang's organization can be visualized as a bull's-eye, at the center are the hard-core members, a relatively small group (5–10 percent of total membership) for whom the gang is their family, their life, their entire world. Hard-core members have been in the gang the longest and frequently are in and out of jail, unemployed and involved with drugs (distribution or usage). The average age is early to mid 20s; however, some hard cores could be older or younger. Hard-core members are very influential in the gang, and the leaders emerge from this group. Leaders are the oldest group members, usually with extensive criminal records. They expect unquestioned obedience from all gang members. Hard-core members in leadership positions pose a threat to the community and the police because they typically possess guns and other weapons, and tend to be aggressively antisocial.

In addition to hard-core members, most gangs have a *marginal membership*, a much larger group of regular members from which hard-core members are recruited. Regular members' average age is 14–17 years old. They have already been

TABLE 9.2 Criminal Activity by Gang Type

Crime	Percent of Police Who Report That Violent Gangs Commit the Offense Very Often or Often (n = 223)	Percent of Police Who Report That Drug-Dealing Gangs Commit the Offense Very Often or Often (n = 148)	Percent of Police Who Report That Entrepreneurial Gangs Commit the Offense Very Often or Often (n = 75)
Motor vehicle theft	25	25	44
Arson	1	1	1
Assault	87	69	57
Burglary	36	25	37
Drive-by shooting	42	49	32
Crack sale	55	80	39
Powder cocaine sale	23	46	29
Marijuana sale	35	54	33
Other drug sale	17	26	25
Graffiti	67	50	38
Home invasion	10	11	27
Intimidation	81	72	74
Rape	7	4	8
Robbery	33	30	36
Shooting	37	41	38
Theft	49	37	52
Vandalism	57	38	37

Note: Reflects aggregation of police estimates of participation in criminal activity by a gang of that type in the jurisdiction.

SOURCE: Deborah Lamm Weisel. "The Evolution of Street Gangs: An Examination of Form and Variation." In *Responding to Gangs: Evaluation and Research.* Washington, DC: National Institute of Justice, July 2002, p.36 (NCJ 190351).

initiated into the gang and tend to back up the hard-core gang members. If they stay in the gang long enough, they could become hard-core.

The outer ring in gang organization consists of claimers, associates or **wannabees**—youths who aspire to become gang members, who dress and talk like gang members and may even write the graffiti of the gang but who have not yet been officially accepted by the gang. The average age of these fringe members is 11 to 13 years old.

wannabees
Youths who dress and act like gang members and hang out on the fringes of the gang, hoping to be invited in some day.

Gangs are also on the lookout for "potentials" or "could be's," youths getting close to an age where they might decide to join a gang. Often these children live in dysfunctional families, are failing in school, are in trouble with the law or live in impoverished environments. Generally, the further into a gang someone is, the harder it is to get out.

A study of gang organization found that even a small, incremental increase in such organizations results in greater congregate behavior among gang members: "When more evidence of gang organization was present, elevated levels of involvement in crime and victimization were observed, a finding consistent with some prior gang research" (Decker et al., 2008, p.169). Important policy implications derive from such research findings: "First, suppression and intervention efforts must pay more attention to the gangs that are the most organized. . . . Second, interventions that reinforce the organizational structure of the gang are likely to produce negative consequences, particularly higher levels of victimization and offending" (Decker et al., p.169).

Respondents at the PERF summit (*Gang Violence*, 2010, p.9) describe a change in the organization of gangs, with many offshoots lacking dedication: "It used to be that if you were a Gangster Disciple, you were a Gangster Disciple. Now there are so many offshoot groups with no allegiance to anything, and they're fighting among themselves." This younger generation of "renegades" is at the forefront of the gang violence. Philadelphia Police Commissioner Ramsey reports having many disjointed, smaller gangs, usually first generation, who "practically shoot each other on sight" (*Gang Violence*, 2010, p.7).

Leadership

In some gangs leadership is quite well defined and may be one of three types: (1) key personality, (2) chain of command or (3) collective. In the key-personality leadership gang, one gang member, often older than the others and from the ranks of the hard-core membership, is a strong, influential leader. He becomes a role model for other gang members. A gang with a chain-of-command form of leadership functions such as a military unit or even a police department, with each group member having a specific rank and with authority going from the top down. A gang with a collective leadership style has several different leaders, each of whom is called to lead in specific circumstances. If the gang is planning a crime, the best criminal mind is the leader. If they are planning an attack on a neighboring gang, the best fighter is the leader.

The PERF summit respondents described a change in leadership occurring in many areas. Chicago Commander Hales (*Gang Violence*, 2010, p.9) reports that an erosion of the gang hierarchy makes law enforcement more difficult: "As in Philadelphia and Milwaukee, there's no real leadership. If we go after the head, then the next biggest, baddest guy will fill in, and the criminal enterprise will continue." The PERF summit respondents (pp.8–9) also indicated that generational gang feuds are occurring as older leaders are released from prison, expecting to be taken back and resume where they left off, but the younger gang leaders have no intention of allowing this. In Chicago returning former gang leaders have been killed when they have attempted to take over.

Domain Identification

turf
The geographic territory claimed by a gang.

Typically gangs stake out a geographic territory, or **turf**, as their domain. This may be a specific facility, such as a school, or it may be an entire neighborhood. If one gang trespasses on another gang's turf, gang violence is likely. Some gangs claim exclusive control over certain activities in an area, such as the right to collect fees from students for using the restrooms or "insurance" payments from local merchants in exchange for protection.

Symbols

Gang *symbols* are common. Clothing, hand signals, graffiti and tattoos are all used as symbolic representations of a person's affiliation with a specific gang.

Clothing can distinguish a particular gang. Sometimes "colors" are used to distinguish a gang. Gang members also use jerseys, T-shirts and jackets with emblems. However, some gangs, such as Asian gangs, seldom have a particular dress code, making identification difficult. **Representing** is visually displaying an allegiance to a gang and commonly encompasses dressing to the "left" or "right" side of the body, depending on the particular gang.

representing

Visually displaying an allegiance to a gang and commonly encompasses dressing to the "left" or "right" side of the body, depending on the particular gang.

Another form of symbolic communication typical of gang members is hand signals. Certain signs are flashed to indicate membership in a specific gang. **Stacking** refers to members demonstrating and representing their own gang by throwing up visual hand signs.

stacking

Gang members demonstrating and representing their own gang by throwing up visual hand signs.

Graffiti is a common form of symbolic communication used by gang members, frequently to stake out a gang's turf. Graffiti is sometimes called the "newspaper of the street," and makes public announcements to gang members and community residents, advertises gang exploits, commemorates fallen gang members and issues challenges to rival gangs (Delaney, 2006). Defacing, erasing or substituting one gang's graffiti by a rival gang constitutes a challenge and usually results in violence and gang warfare. Law enforcement officers can glean important information and develop useful intelligence by "reading" the graffiti in an area. For instance, unchallenged graffiti suggests that a gang holds powerful control of a specific area, and investigators can estimate the "center" and extent of a gang's turf by documenting where cross-outs by rival gangs begin (Delaney, 2006). The farther away from a gang's geographical center of power, the more rival graffiti and cross-outs occur (Delaney, 2006). Petrocelli (2008, p.18) notes, "In a broken-window crime model, graffiti is one of those foothold crimes that leads to a neighborhood's decay. Neighborhoods plagued with graffiti often become breeding grounds for loitering, littering, loud music and public urination." The annual cost of graffiti abatement in the United States is between $10 billion and $12 billion, but such markings can provide valuable intelligence to law enforcement

graffiti

Writing or drawing on buildings and walls; a common form of communication used by gang members to mark their territory; sometimes called the newspaper of the street.

Tattoos are also used by some gangs, particularly outlaw motorcycle gangs and Hispanic gangs. Gang tattoos can illustrate a suspect's history by showing gang affiliation and rank, where he's been, where he did time and for how many years, and how many people he's killed.

Names

Gang names vary from colorful and imaginative to straightforward. They commonly refer to localities (Tenth Streeters), animals (Cobras), royalty (Kings), rebellion (Rebels), leaders (Garcia's Boys), or a combination of these elements (West Side Warlords). Individual gang members also often have colorful street names or **monikers**.

monikers

Street names of gang members.

The Gang Subculture

Taken together, the many characteristics of gangs just described form a gang subculture. These values, norms, lifestyles and beliefs are often found in a gang code of behavior, which may include the requirement to always wear gang colors, to get a tattoo representing the gang and, if arrested, to never reveal anything about the gang, as there is no lower life form than a "snitch." Another part of the gang subculture is that gang members are also sometimes victims of violence as well.

Violent Victimization A review of the literature on youth gang membership and violent victimization reveals, "Gang members' victimization has typically been hidden from public view or at least muted relative to their offending behaviors. Consequently, an entire group of victims have been virtually ignored, diminishing the impact of potentially life-changing experiences among a group of victims who disproportionately come into contact with the juvenile and adult justice systems" (Taylor, 2008, p.125).

 Young gang members are frequently victims of violence as well as offenders.

This violence may exist before joining a gang, while in a gang or after leaving a gang. Noting robust evidence linking delinquency, violence and gang membership, Taylor (2008, p.126) found that 70 percent of gang youths reported being the victim of general violence compared with 46 percent of nongang youths.

Paradoxically, youths frequently report joining a gang for protection from violence. Data from a five-year longitudinal panel study of adolescents in seven U.S. cities found that 28 to 57 percent of self-identified gang youths joined their gangs for protection (Taylor, 2008, p.127). Similar studies have found that girl gang members often join gangs to escape violent homes. However, violent victimization often increases once youths join gangs. Youths may be required to be "beat in" or "jumped in" as part of an initiation ritual or be subjected to harsh discipline for breaking gang rules.

WHY PEOPLE JOIN GANGS

In addition to seeking protection, a variety of other reasons exist for joining a gang, the most frequently cited being the need to "belong." The close ties of gang members are a major motive for membership. Most gang members are underachievers who come from broken homes or homes with no strong male authority figure, and membership provides both psychological and physical security.

 The most common reasons for joining a gang are for belonging, identity or recognition; protection; fellowship and brotherhood; or to make money.

In our society of instant gratification, where happiness and success are often measured by the amount of money one has, it is hard to convince a youth who's making $1,000 a week guarding a crack house that he ought to be getting up at 4 A.M. every day to deliver newspapers.

An estimated 80 percent of gang members are illiterate. Finding it almost impossible to get a job, individuals may turn to gangs as a way to earn a living through drug trafficking, illegal weapons sales, and robbery and theft, and as a way to earn respect.

 Broken families, unemployment, poverty and general despair lead young people to seek economic opportunities frequently available through gang membership.

Criminologists have proposed other theories for why people join gangs, summarized in Table 9.3.

TABLE 9.3 Theories Regarding Why Gangs Exist

Theory	Major Points/Key Factors
1. Social disorganization	Crime stems from certain community or neighborhood characteristics, such as poverty, dilapidated housing, high density, high mobility and high rates of unemployment. Concentric zone theory is a variation that argues that crime increases toward the inner city area.
2. Strain/anomie	Cultural norms of "success" emphasize such goals as money, status and power, while the means to obtain such success are not equally distributed. As a result of blocked opportunities many among the disadvantaged resort to illegal means, which are more readily available.
3. Cultural-deviance	Certain subcultures, including a gang subculture, exist within poor communities, which contain values, attitudes, beliefs, norms and so on that are often counter to the prevailing middle-class culture. An important feature of this culture is the absence of fathers, thus resulting in female-headed households which tend to be poorer. Youths get exposed to this subculture early in life and become embedded in it.
4. Control/social bond	Delinquency persists when a youth's "bonds" or "ties" to society are weak or broken, especially bonds with family, school and other institutions. When this occurs a youth is apt to seek bonds with other groups, including gangs, in order to get his/her needs met.
5. Learning	Delinquency is learned through association with others, especially gang members, over a period of time. This involves a process that includes the acquisition of attitudes and values, the instigation of a criminal act based on certain stimuli and the maintenance or perpetuation of such behavior over time.
6. Labeling	Definitions of delinquency and crime stem from differences in power and status in the larger society, and those without power are the most likely to have their behaviors labeled as "delinquency." Delinquency may be generated, and especially perpetuated, through negative labeling by significant others and by the judicial system. One may associate with others similarly labeled, such as gangs.
7. Rational choice	People freely choose to commit crime based on self-interest because they are goal oriented and want to maximize their pleasure and minimize their pain. A variation is known as *routine activities theory*, which suggests that criminals plan very carefully by selecting specific targets based on such things as vulnerability (e.g., elderly citizens, unguarded premises, lack of police presence) and commit their crimes accordingly. However, choices are often based not on pure reason and rationality.
8. Critical/Marxist	Gangs are inevitable products of social (and racial) inequality brought about by capitalism itself. Power is unequally distributed, and those without power often resort to criminal means to survive.

SOURCE: SHELDON/TRACY/BROWN. *Youth Gangs in American Society*, 3e. © 2004 (p.178) Wadsworth, a part of Cengage Learning, Inc. Reproduced by permission. www.cengage.com/perimssions.

In addition to looking at *why* people join gangs, predisposing or risk factors should be considered.

Risk Factors

Family structure is probably the most important risk factor in the formation of a gang member.

Investigators have found certain common threads running through most families having hard-core gang members. The family is often a racial minority receiving some form of government assistance. It often lacks a male authority figure, or the male figure may be a criminal or drug addict and therefore a negative role model. Children live with minimal adult supervision. When one child first encounters law enforcement authorities, the dominant figure (usually the mother) makes excuses for the child, often accusing society. Thus, children are taught early that they are not responsible for their actions and are shown how to transfer blame to society.

A second common family structure is one with two strong family leaders in a mother and father. Usually graduates from gangs themselves, they see little wrong with their children belonging to gangs. This is known as assembly-line production of gang members.

A third common family structure is one where the parents are non-English speaking immigrants. The children tend to adapt rapidly to the American way of life and, in doing so, lose respect for their parents and the "old ways." They become experts at manipulating their parents, and the parents lose all control. Many of these family structures overlap.

Research examining the early precursors of gang membership found the risk factors most associated with sustained gang membership included early violence, externalizing behaviors, associations with friends who engage in problem behaviors, availability of marijuana and early marijuana use, parental attitudes favoring violence, low household income, having a learning disability, low academic achievement, low school attachment and antisocial beliefs (Hill et al., 2001).

A study of gender and gangs concludes, "Few differences are found between boys and girls in terms of risk factors associated with gang membership and outcomes associated with gang involvement. Instead, the results indicate that parental social control, attachment, and involvement; school safety; peer fighting; age; and race similarly influence boys' and girls' gang involvement" (Bell, 2009, p.363).

GANG INTELLIGENCE

In the war against gangs, information and intelligence are vital. Common sources of information on gangs include internal contacts with patrol officers and detectives, internal departmental records and computerized files, review of offense reports, interviews with gang members, information from other local police agencies, surveillance activities and use of paid or unpaid informants. Information may also be obtained from other criminal justice agencies, other state and federal agencies, schools, surveillance or undercover assignments.

Some states are taking advantage of the ever-expanding network of online computer services to enhance information sharing. For example, a national database called RISSGang™, which is the National Gang Program segment of the Regional Information Sharing System (RISS), is a partnership involving more than 4,500 federal, state and local law enforcement agencies used to track and share gang intelligence. Another computer technology used to track gangs is the Gang Reporting, Evaluation and Tracking (GREAT) system—a combination hot sheet, mug book and file cabinet.

Network analysis, which is very different from mapping, is a useful, cutting-edge technique to obtain information on gang organization that focuses on studying the social relationships (namely rivalries) among groups or individuals (McGloin, n.d.). Through their patterns of relationships, certain gangs may nominate themselves for investigative focus. However, such information is often difficult for law enforcement departments to obtain and thus it is recommended that agencies consider partnering with a university (McGloin).

Social network sites can be a useful source of gang information. In February 2010, in Riverside County, east of Los Angeles, 50 Latino gang members were arrested for drug sales and hate crimes against black residents. Prosecutors said some of the evidence was pulled from MySpace and YouTube, including rap videos taunting police with violent messages and requests among gang members to help in identifying undercover police officers (Watkins, 2010).

GANG CONTROL STRATEGIES

Throughout the country several approaches to addressing the gang problem are being used. These include primary prevention, secondary prevention, intervention, suppression and reentry.

Primary prevention targets the entire population in high-crime, high-risk communities. The key component is a one-stop resource center that makes services accessible and visible to community members. Services include prenatal and infant care, after-school activities, truancy and dropout prevention, and job programs.

Secondary prevention identifies young children (ages 7 to 14) at high risk and, drawing on the resources of schools, community-based organizations and faith-based groups, intervenes with appropriate services before early problem behaviors turn into serious delinquency and gang involvement.

Intervention targets active gang members, close associates and gang members returning from confinement and involves aggressive outreach and recruitment activity. Intervention helps gang members who want to get out of the gang and helps them immediately. They might be referred to a community program and given the chance to finish high school or obtain a GED, have tattoos removed or find employment. Support services for gang-involved youths and their families help youths make positive choices.

Suppression focuses on identifying the most dangerous and influential gang members and removing them from the community.

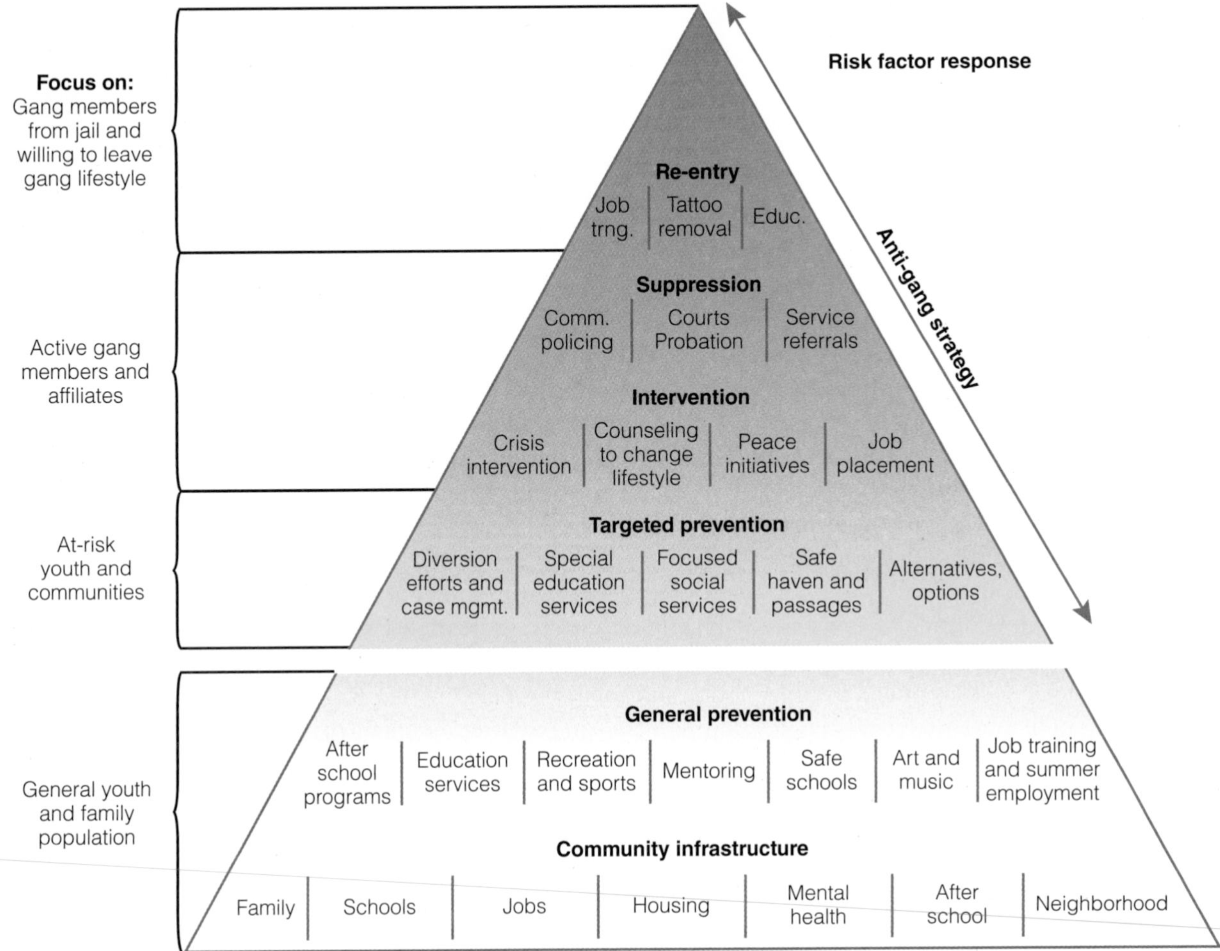

FIGURE 9.1 Healthy Community Pyramid

SOURCE: *Gang Violence: The Police Role in Developing Community-Wide Solutions.* Washington, DC, Police Executive Research Forum, February 2010, p.17.

Reentry targets serious offenders returning to the community after confinement and provides appropriate services and monitoring. Many experts believe this final element is grossly underemphasized and that efforts to combat the gang problem are severely undermined when an agency fails to put resources toward the reentry issue. Gang members who are not effectively educated on how to return and live in the community *without* being in a gang are highly likely to fall back into their old ways. These same components are identified in the Healthy Community Pyramid.

The PERF survey respondents reported that their agency used the following strategies/tactics/activities to combat gang activities (*Gang Violence*, 2010, p.4):

- Targeting gang hot spots (80 percent)
- Targeting known offenders (79 percent)
- Use of informants (79 percent)

- School resource officers (78 percent)
- Saturation patrol of targeted gang areas (79 percent)
- Gang activity tracking (68 percent)
- Graffiti abatement programs (67 percent)
- Task force investigations (66 percent)
- Gang awareness training for teachers (64 percent)
- Community education (63 percent)
- Surveillance operations (63 percent)

Currently the most *commonly used* strategy to combat a gang problem *is* targeting gang hot spots, followed by targeting known offenders, use of informants, school resource officers and saturation patrol of targeted gang areas (*Gang Violence*, 2010, p.5).

The least used strategy to address gang problems reported in the PERF survey was opportunities provision, such as jobs, schooling and the like (Decker, 2010, p.16).

The most *effective* strategies to combat gang violence were saturation patrols and targeting gang hot spots; identifying, tracking and targeting known gang members; zero tolerance initiatives; partnerships and multi-agency initiatives; task forces; and prosecution efforts.

Strategies reported to be less effective included school related programs/activities, parental notification of at-risk youth, community involvement initiatives, temporary saturation of known gang hot spots and injunctions.

In February 2006 Attorney General Alberto Gonzales announced the Department of Justice's twofold strategy to combat gang violence: (1) prioritize prevention programs to provide America's youths and offenders returning to the community with opportunities that help them resist gang involvement and (2) ensure robust enforcement policies when gang-related violence does occur.

The Department of Justice's dual approach to combat gang violence focuses on robust enforcement—suppression—and on prevention programs.

Suppression—The Traditional Response

Suppression tactics include street sweeps, intensified surveillance and policing hot spots. Targeting specific gang crimes, locations, gangs and gang members appears to be the most effective suppression tactic (*Gang Violence*, 2010, p.26).

Gang sweeps, a common form of *suppression*, are highly concentrated law enforcement activities carried out in small areas where gangs are known to be prevalent. Police focus on gang-related crimes of concern to the public, such as drive-by shootings, drug sales, graffiti and assaults. These sweeps, often termed "zero tolerance," incorporate differing enforcement tactics, including traffic enforcement.

Another suppression strategy is the stop and frisk, a common but controversial tactic used by police officers throughout the country when they suspect an individual may be or is about to be involved in criminal activity. According to the New York Civil Liberties Union ("Racial Justice," 2010):

> The NYPD's stop-and-frisk practices raise serious concerns over racial profiling, illegal stops and privacy rights. The Department's own reports on its stop-and-frisk activity confirm what many people in communities of color across the city have long known: The police are stopping hundreds of thousands of law abiding New Yorkers every year, and the vast majority are black and Latino.
>
> An analysis by the NYCLU revealed that more than 2 million innocent New Yorkers were subjected to police stops and street interrogations from 2004 through 2010, and that black and Latino communities continue to be the overwhelming target of these tactics. During the past five years, nearly nine out of 10 stopped-and-frisked New Yorkers have been completely innocent, according to the NYPD's own reports. . . .
>
> During the first three months of 2010, 149,753 New Yorkers were stopped by the police.
>
> - 130,749 were totally innocent (87 percent)
> - 79,853 were black (53 percent)
> - 47,537 were Latino (32 percent)
> - 13,769 were white (9 percent)

Nonetheless, a key responsibility of law enforcement is to prevent crime and to act when their suspicions are aroused. Charges of racial profiling may be minimized and suppression efforts enhanced by using a problem-solving approach to address gang problems. Table 9.4 compares traditional approaches and problem-solving gang-control strategies.

The suppression component may involve collaboration between police, probation and prosecution, targeting the most active gang members and leaders. To enhance suppression efforts, many departments have established gang units or task forces, which are often multi-jurisdictional. A gang unit is a highly specialized group that typically uses criminal informants and often is proactive in creating investigations in enforcing laws on gang members. These units also use many of the same methods of enforcement as do vice or narcotics, such as surveillance and undercover operations.

Department of Justice Gang Targeting, Enforcement and Coordination Center (GangTECC) The multi-agency national Gang Targeting, Enforcement and Coordination Center (GangTECC) was formed in 2006 by the attorney general to serve as a catalyst in leading a unified federal effort to disrupt and dismantle the most significant and violent gangs in the United States. GangTECC investigators come from several federal agencies, including the Federal Bureau of Investigation (FBI); the Drug Enforcement Administration (DEA); the Bureau of Alcohol, Tobacco, Firearms and Explosives (ATF); the Federal Bureau of Prisons (BOP); the U.S. Marshals Service (USMS); and the U.S. Immigration and Customs Enforcement (ICE) at the Department of Homeland Security (DHS). These federal agents collaborate closely with the Gang Squad prosecutors in the Criminal Division of the Department of Justice, as well as with analysts at the National Gang Intelligence Center (NGIC). The goal of this cooperative enterprise is to achieve maximum

TABLE 9.4 Distinctions between Traditional and Problem-Oriented Gang-Control Efforts

	Traditional Gang Enforcement	Problem-Oriented Gang Efforts
Types of responses	Criminal sanctions Harassment	Criminal sanctions Civil remedies Control facilitators Place management Increased guardianship Focus on chronic offenders
Impact measures	Numbers of arrests, field stops; if data available, amount of gang-related crime	Does not focus on arrests; impact reflected by declines in calls, gang-related crime, and citizen concerns. Also monitors quality of case clearances and prosecution
Empirical data	Not used	Calls and FIs [field interviews] used to prioritize places, times, chronic offenders, types of offenses
Community input	General information	May be frequent, depending upon problem
Perceptions of equity and fairness	Not an issue; an end seen as justifying the means	Viewed as important; monitor citizen complaints, use of force; routine polygraph and drug screen of employees
Collaboration within agency and with other agencies	Infrequent	May be frequent, depending on problem; close interaction between patrol and gang unit
Priorities	Arresting large numbers of offenders Reducing visibility of gangs in hot spots	Identifying and reducing patterned groups of offenders, particular problems; facilitators or chronic places

Note: This document is a research report submitted to the U.S. Department of Justice. This report has not been published by the Department. Opinions or points of view expressed are those of the author(s) and do not necessarily reflect the official position or policies of the U.S. Department of Justice.

SOURCE: Deborah Lamm Weisel and Tara O'Connor Shelley. *Specialized Gang Units: Form and Function in Community Policing*. Washington, DC: U.S. Department of Justice, October 2004, Document 207204, p.161. This is an unpublished report, available online at http://www.ncjrs.gov/pdffiles1/nij/grants/207204.pdf; the table appears on p.161.

impact at the regional and national level against the most violent gangs in the country by combining the strengths of each federal agency.

Gang units, however, may seem in conflict with the move to community policing and its emphasis on decentralization and despecialization within law enforcement agencies. Suppression efforts may also include injunctions and legislation.

civil injunction

A court order prohibiting a person or group from engaging in certain activities.

Injunctions and Legislation Sometimes communities pass legislation, such as loitering ordinances, or take other legal measures, including injunctions, to bring gang problems under control. A **civil injunction** is a court order prohibiting a person or group from engaging in certain activities. Figure 9.2 illustrates how the civil injunction process works.

Research has shown a positive short-term effect for disordered areas, including a reduction in gang presence and gang intimidation, with results suggesting that law enforcement can produce modest improvements in community safety and well-being through use of gang injunctions (Maxson et al., 2005). However, injunctions and ordinances may be challenged as unconstitutional violations of the freedom of speech, the right of association and due process rights if they do not clearly delineate how officers may apply such orders.

For example, Chicago passed a gang congregation ordinance to combat the problems created by the city's street gangs. During the three years following passage of the ordinance, Chicago police officers issued more than 89,000 dispersal orders and arrested more than 42,000 people. However, in *Chicago v. Morales* (1999), the Supreme Court struck down the ordinance as unconstitutional because its vague wording failed

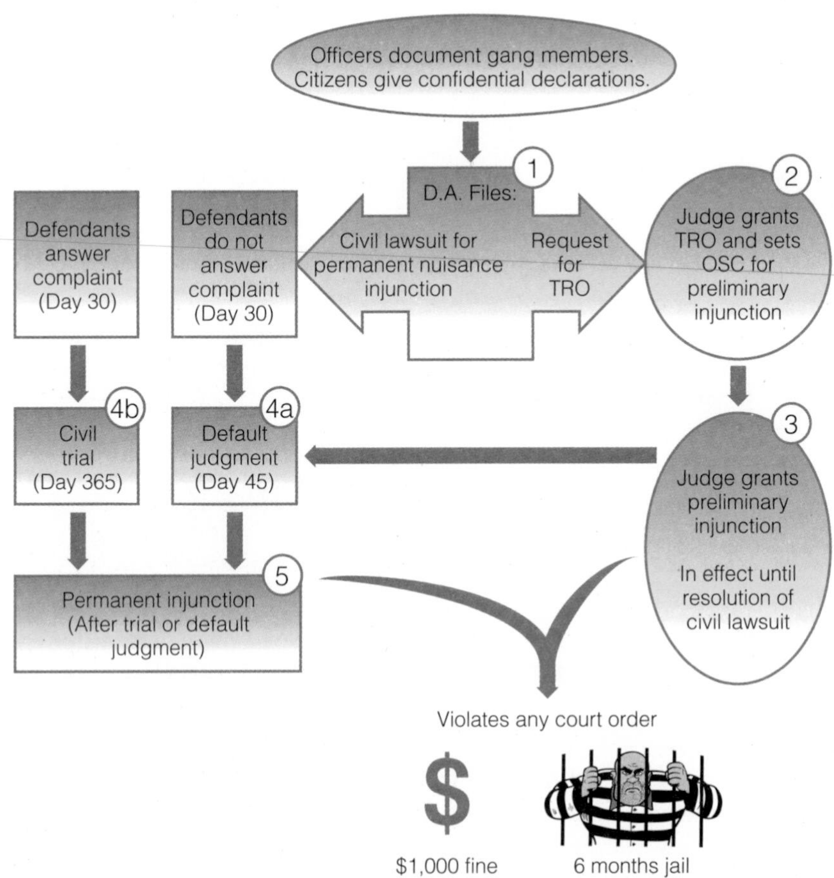

FIGURE 9.2 The Gang Injunction Process

SOURCE: Used by permission of San Diego Deputy District Attorney Bonnie M. Dumanis.

to provide adequate standards to guide police discretion. The lesson here is that any civil injunctions a city passes must be clear in what officers can and cannot do when they observe what they believe to be gang members congregating in public places.

Tougher legislation is also being used as a gang-control approach. Because some gangs use their younger members to commit serious crimes, relying on the more lenient juvenile sentencing laws, some jurisdictions have allowed courts to raise the penalties for teenagers convicted of gang-related offenses. According to the *National Youth Gang Survey Analysis* (2009), 47 states and the District of Columbia have enacted some form of legislation related to gangs. More than half the states have laws providing for enhanced penalties for gang-related criminal acts and against graffiti.

Although injunctions, ordinances and legislation offer ways to help communities handle problems associated with gangs, they also raise serious issues regarding how to balance public safety with individual rights.

Preventing Gang Membership

Common sense suggests that preventing a gang problem in the first place is preferable to finding strategies to deal with such a problem after it surfaces. One well-known program aimed at preventing gang membership is the Gang Resistance Education and Training program.

The G.R.E.A.T. Program The Gang Resistance Education and Training (G.R.E.A.T.) program is a school-based, law enforcement officer-instructed classroom curriculum. With prevention as its primary objective, the program is intended as an immunization against delinquency, youth violence and gang membership. The G.R.E.A.T. program is a proactive approach to deterring violence before it begins. The program builds a foundation focused on teaching children the life skills they need to avoid violence and gang membership.

A study supported by the National Institute of Justice (NIJ) documented the program benefits in a cross-sectional evaluation. The study showed that students who graduated from the G.R.E.A.T. course showed lower levels of delinquency, impulsive behavior, risk-taking behavior and approval of violence. The study also found that students demonstrated higher levels of self-esteem, parental attachment, commitment to positive peers, antigang attitudes, perceived educational opportunities and positive school environments.

Few rigorous evaluations have been conducted on gang prevention programs. Although a careful, five-year longitudinal evaluation of the G.R.E.A.T. program has shown "modest positive effects" on the attitudes held by adolescents regarding gangs, the study also demonstrated no significant effects on actual adolescent involvement in gangs or delinquent behavior (Esbensen, 2004, p.1). Nonetheless, "The G.R.E.A.T. program provides some demonstrable benefits: It educates youths on the consequences of gang involvement, and they develop favorable attitudes toward the police for a relatively small investment of nine hours. In addition, surveys of parents and educators revealed positive attitudes toward the program" (Esbensen, p.4).

A revised curriculum was introduced in 2003 consisting of 13 30- to 40-minute lessons designed to be taught in sequential order by specially trained, uniformed law enforcement officers. The modified G.R.E.A.T. curriculum has three goals: (1) reduce student involvement in gangs and delinquent behavior, (2) teach students the consequences of gang involvement and (3) help them develop positive relations with law enforcement. The program has developed partnerships with nationally recognized organization, such as the Boys & Girls Clubs of America and the National Association of Police Athletic Leagues (G.R.E.A.T. Home Page).

In 2006 the NIJ awarded a five-year grant to the University of Missouri at St. Louis to evaluate the revised program in seven cities across the country. Preliminary analysis has revealed six significant differences between G.R.E.A.T. and non G.R.E.A.T. students: (1) more positive attitudes toward police, (2) fewer positive attitudes about gangs, (3) more use of refusal skills, (4) more resistance to peer pressure, (5) lower rates of gang membership and (6) lower rates of self-reported delinquency (Esbensen, 2008).

A COMPREHENSIVE STRATEGY

The consensus of those attending the PERF summit on gang violence was that a comprehensive strategy is crucial for an effective response to gang crime (*Gang Violence*, 2010, p.15). No one strategy alone will sufficiently address the considerable challenge to social order that gangs present. For example, as important as suppression is, it cannot be successful if used to the exclusion of all other strategies: "As the saying goes, 'We can't arrest our way out of this problem.' There have to be other parts to the solution, such as providing opportunities, jobs, job training, school involvement, social interventions, access to counseling, crisis intervention, and organizational change and development" (Decker, 2010, p.16).

The Office of Juvenile Justice and Delinquency Prevention (OJJDP) has developed just such a strategy, the Comprehensive Gang Model: *Best Practices to Address Community Gang Problems* (2008), based on the work of Spergel and his colleagues in the 1990s. The key distinguishing feature of the model is a strategic planning process empowering communities to assess their unique gang problems and develop a complement of antigang strategies and program activities (p.ix).

The Comprehensive Gang Model holds that two factors largely account for a community's youth gang problem: the lack of social opportunities available to gang members younger than 22 years old and the degree of social disorganization present in a community. The model also suggests other contributing factors, including poverty, institutional racism, deficiencies in social policies and a lack of or misdirected social controls.

The OJJDP Comprehensive Gang Model focuses on five strategies: community mobilization, opportunities provision, social intervention, suppression, and organizational change and development (*Best Practices*, 2008, p.2).

Community mobilization refers to involving local citizens, including former gang-involved youths, community groups and agencies, and coordination of programs and staff functions within and across agencies.

Opportunities provision refers to developing a variety of specific education, training and employment programs targeting gang-involved youths.

Social intervention refers to involving youth-serving agencies, schools, grassroots groups, faith-based organizations, police and other juvenile criminal justice organizations in "reaching out" to gang-involved youths and their families and linking them with the conventional world and needed services.

Suppression refers to formal and informal social control procedures, including close supervision and monitoring of gang-involved youths by agencies of the juvenile criminal justice system and by community-based agencies, schools and grassroots groups.

Organizational change and development refers to developing and implementing policies and procedures that result in the most effective use of available and potential resources, within and across agencies to better address the gang problem.

Whatever approaches are used, a critical element of success is getting the buy-in from the stakeholders in the community. To achieve buy-in, the stakeholders must first be made aware of a gang presence. The second challenge is getting stakeholders to admit that the police do not bear sole responsibility for dealing with gangs. A community that hopes to effectively tackle a gang problem must engage all affected parties in finding a solution—law enforcement, schools, parents, youths, businesses, religious groups and social service organizations.

The National Gang Center

In October 2009, the National Youth Gang Center, which had been funded by the Office of Juvenile Justice and Delinquency Prevention since 1995, merged with the National Gang Center (NGC), which had been funded by the Bureau of Justice Assistance since 2003. This partnership recognizes that street gang activities transcend ages of the members and that a balanced, comprehensive approach is needed to reduce gang crime. Consolidation leverages resources and results in a single, more efficient entity, responsive to the needs of researchers, practitioners and the public.

The National Gang Center's Web site features the latest research about gangs; descriptions of evidence-based antigang programs; and links to tools, databases and other resources to help agencies develop and implement effective community-based gang prevention, intervention and suppression strategies. The site also provides an analysis of nearly 15 years' worth of data collected from 2,500 U.S. law enforcement agencies through the annual NYGS. Furthermore, the site hosts a database of gang-related state legislation and municipal codes; a list of newspaper articles on nationwide gang activity that is updated daily; and GANGINFO, an electronic mailing list for professionals working with gangs.

PROSECUTING GANG MEMBERS

Law enforcement is the first component of the criminal justice system that responds to the gang problem. Officers, along with prosecutors, have great discretionary power when dealing with gang members.

Prosecution of gang-related crimes is often made difficult because victims and witnesses are reluctant to cooperate. One reason for the reluctance is a sense of futility in trying to rid an area of all gang activity; local residents may hesitate to get involved and risk personal harm in an effort to put one gang away when they know another gang is poised to move right into the vacancy. Another reason for victim and witness reluctance is gang intimidation and fear of reprisal.

CAREER PROFILE

Sean Porter (County of Los Angeles Probation Department)

I've always wanted to work with kids. That much I knew. But the probation field wasn't even a consideration for me when I started college. I planned to use my bachelor's degree in physical education for a career as a high school teacher or a coach. But one term, while taking a juvenile delinquency course, a classmate who was working in juvenile hall got me thinking about other options. With his encouragement, I applied to the Los Angeles County Probation Department, and within a few months I was facing a decision: take a job as an assistant park director or one in probation. The rest, as they say, is history.

I was attracted to juvenile justice because I could still apply my interests, strengths and skills as a teacher, coach and counselor but with kids who really needed my help. And I wanted to make a difference working with kids in need. So in 1984 while still in college, I started as a night man, watching kids in probation camp sleep. Shortly after I joined the department, I was promoted to Detention Services Officer, working with minors in juvenile hall. I held that position for almost three years before being promoted to Deputy Probation Officer I at Camp Kilpatrick. During my six years at Camp Kilpatrick, I had the unique opportunity to help develop a competitive high school–level sports program for the minors in camp. These efforts were filmed in 1990 and released in a 1993 documentary called *Gridiron Gang*, later serving as the basis for the motion picture of the same name.

In 1994 a promotion to Deputy Probation Officer II took me out of the camp environment and allowed me to work with juveniles and their families in the community. I found fieldwork very rewarding and enjoyed interacting with kids and their families in their homes, schools and neighborhoods. During this time I worked regular supervision with an emphasis on minors released from camps, school-based intervention programs and investigations. Then in 2001 I became a supervising deputy probation officer and two years later was named director of one of the camps in L.A. County. Both positions brought the tremendously rewarding opportunity to work directly with deputies and influence programming changes.

In 2006 I became a regional director in the Residential Treatment Services Bureau of the L.A. County Probation Department. Here I oversee Camps Headquarters, the Camp Assessment Unit and three camps, each housing over 100 kids. The Camp Assessment Unit evaluates each youth ordered to camp by the Juvenile Courts in L.A. County and identifies an appropriate facility based on the minor's individual criminogenic risk factors, strengths and needs. Los Angeles County has 18 camps and processes more than 4,000 minors through camp programs each year. Camps Headquarters oversees the movement of minors into, out of and between the 18 camps, 3 juvenile halls and 27 courts in L.A. County. The camps themselves are where the kids live while they are receiving services such as education, medical care, mental health counseling and treatment, recreational opportunities and cognitive restructuring through small-group interventions.

Throughout my career, I've worked with young men, and some young women, from almost every gang in Los Angeles. Working with hard-core gang members is both challenging and rewarding. The challenges are many but include overcoming the mind-set that comes with belonging to a gang, a mind-set often as strong as the one most people have for belonging to their own families. Many of these young gang members know no other way of life, nor do they believe they can actually be successful at anything other than gang banging. We can't just *tell* these kids to stopping running with the gang, to stop shooting people and dealing drugs and getting into trouble all the time. We have to *show* them how to live life differently. We need to *teach* them how to make sound decisions and how to develop skills to lead law-abiding lives. And we need to replace the antisocial behavior, attitudes and gang activity with prosocial attitudes, behavior and activities. The strong-arm tactics used 20 years ago with these youths are ineffective and no longer acceptable because we know these methods don't work. Our job in probation has changed from one that relied on forced compliance to one that requires working with our minds, stretching how we think about our clients and finding new ways to get through to them, to meet them on their level and lead them in learning how to become productive members of society as adults. We need to show these kids that they have choices and options other than their current way of life, choices and options that lead to hope for a future without crime, drugs, jail or death. Unfortunately, for too many of the kids I've worked with, these lessons weren't learned. But for many, I think I have made a difference.

When asked, I try to encourage young deputies to remember why they got into the profession and to try not to be disillusioned by the bureaucracy and shortcomings of the system but rather to focus on the successes, no matter how small they seem. What often appear to be little successes to us are actually big successes to our clients. And when I have the opportunity, I tell those considering this career that juvenile probation is special work that requires special people who are able to put the needs of others before their own needs and who are able to work as a team. Most of all, this profession requires people who want to make a difference in the lives of others and in their communities.

Other obstacles to prosecution include uncertain victim and witness credibility, inadequate police reports and a lack of appropriate sanctions for juvenile gang members involved in criminal activities. Some older gang members refer to their younger members as "minutemen" because if they do get "busted," they'll be out in a minute. Adults hire juveniles to run their drugs for them, knowing that if the juveniles get caught, not much will happen to them. Table 9.5 illustrates some of the problems involved in prosecuting gangs.

TABLE 9.5 Problems in Prosecuting Gang Cases—Views of Criminal Justice Officials in Clark and Washoe Counties, Nevada, in Percent

	Gang D.A.s	Track D.A.s	Public Defenders	Judges	Police
Obtaining the Cooperation of Victims/Witnesses					
Not a problem/minor problem	0.0	0.0	27.6	33.3	8.3
Moderate problem	12.5	9.1	44.8	16.7	37.5
Major problem	87.5	90.9	27.6	50.0	54.2
Victim/Witness Credibility					
Not a problem/minor problem	12.5	9.1	10.3	25.0	25.0
Moderate problem	12.5	27.3	41.1	50.0	50.0
Major problem	75.0	63.6	48.3	25.0	25.0
Victim/Witness Intimidation					
Not a problem/minor problem	0.0	0.0	48.2	33.3	13.0
Moderate problem	37.5	45.5	34.5	41.7	39.1
Major problem	62.5	54.5	17.2	25.0	47.8
Heavy Caseloads					
Not a problem/minor problem	47.5	40.0	39.3	25.0	43.5
Moderate problem	62.5	20.0	32.1	41.7	30.4
Major problem	0.0	40.0	28.6	33.3	26.1
Inadequate Police Preparation of Crime Reports					
Not a problem/minor problem	87.5	40.0	51.7	66.6	87.0
Moderate problem	12.5	60.0	37.9	16.7	8.7
Major problem	0.0	0.0	10.3	16.7	4.3
Difficult Proof Requirement to Show That the Offense Was Committed to Further the Gang					
Not a problem/minor problem	25.0	11.1	48.1	25.0	30.4
Moderate problem	62.5	44.4	29.6	50.0	34.8
Major problem	15.5	44.4	22.2	25.0	34.8

SOURCE: Terance D. Miethe and Richard C. McCorkle. "Evaluating Nevada's Antigang Legislation and Gang Prosecution Units." In *Responding to Gangs: Evaluation and Research*, edited by Winifred L. Reed and Scott H. Decker. Washington, DC: National Institute of Justice, July 2002, p.190. (NCJ 190351)

GANGS, DRUGS, CRIME AND VIOLENCE

Closely related to the gang problem is the drug problem because many gang members are involved in the use or sale of illegal drugs. Many gangs can be classified as drug gangs. Table 9.6 summarizes the common differences between street gangs and drug gangs.

Studies have produced conflicting results regarding the relationship between gang membership and drug involvement. Some research suggests that gang membership is weakly associated to drug involvement, including both use and sales, and does not appear to be related to high levels of violent behavior (Bjerregaard, 2010, p.16). Instead, such results suggest that gangs are merely "incidentally involved in these behaviors and that drug use and sales are simply a manifestation of the juvenile's involvement in a variety of delinquent activities" (Bjerregaard, p.16).

Many of the attendees at the PERF gang summit (*Gang Violence*, 2010, p.11), however, would disagree with such findings, arguing that gangs and drugs are "inextricably linked" and that drugs are driving the violence within and between gangs. This link has changed many gangs' priorities and behaviors, with them now caring more about drug trade profits than other kinds of disputes. Chicago Deputy Chief Roti reports that gang violence is directly related to drug activity in Chicago: "Drug activity is the lifeblood or financial engine of almost every gang in Chicago" (*Gang Violence*, p.12).

DRUG CARTELS

Drug cartels, sharing many of the characteristics of gangs, are criminal organizations that promote and control drug trafficking operations. Cartels range from informal agreements among various drug traffickers to formalized commercial

TABLE 9.6 Common Differences between Street Gangs and Drug Gangs

Characteristic	Street Gangs	Drug Gangs
Crime focus	Versatile ("cafeteria-style")	Drug business exclusively
Structure	Larger organizations	Smaller organizations
Level of cohesion	Less cohesive	More cohesive
Leadership	Looser	More centralized
Roles	Ill-defined	Market-defined
Nature of loyalty	Code of loyalty	Requirement of loyalty
Territories	Residential	Sales market
Degree of drug selling	Members may sell	Members do sell
Rivalries	Intergang	Competition controlled
Age of members	Younger on average, but wider age range	Older on average, but narrower age range

SOURCE: *The American Street Gang* by Malcolm Klein © 1995 by Oxford University Press, Inc. Used by permission of Oxford University Press, Inc.

enterprises. Drug cartels operate in many countries throughout Latin America, with some of the more notorious coming from Colombia and Mexico. Afghanistan and some countries in South Asia have also produced drug cartels. Currently the biggest threat is coming from Mexico.

The Mexican Drug War

According to the *National Drug Threat Assessment 2009*, the greatest organized crime threat to the United States currently comes from Mexican drug trafficking organizations (DTOs). Through the seductively corrupt influence of drug money, Mexican drug lords have been able to bribe police and military personnel at the highest levels of the Mexican government and transform areas of Mexico into battlefields, where kidnapping for ransom and gratuitous brutality—the "signature activities" of Mexican DTOs—occur daily (Griffith, 2009a, p.14). In 2008 and 2009, more than 7,200 people were killed through drug-related violence, including police officers, judges, prosecutors, soldiers, journalists, politicians and innocent bystanders (Laine, 2009, p.6).

The violence is not confined to Mexico because states along the southwestern U.S. border and cities throughout the United States have reported increases in crime and violence that can be traced back to Mexican organizations: "Mexican drug cartels are now present in at least 230 U.S. cities compared to about 50 cities in 2005. Mexican drug traffickers affiliated with the Sinaloa, Gulf, Juarez and Tijuana cartels maintain working relationships with at least 20 street gangs, prison gangs and outlaw motorcycle gangs in communities through the country" (Laine, 2009, p.6).

The powerful Sinaloa cartel has established itself as the largest cocaine broker and producer of methamphetamine and marijuana in the Western Hemisphere (Marizco, 2009). This DTO, and its primary rival, the Gulf Cartel, have established their presence in metropolitan area such as Atlanta, Georgia; Chicago, Illinois; St. Louis, Missouri; Seattle, Washington; and Charlotte, North Carolina (O'Neil, 2009).

Phoenix currently leads the nation in kidnappings and home invasions, two crimes frequently committed by drug cartel members (Marizco, 2009). In an interview with ABC News, the Phoenix police chief stated, "We're in the eye of the storm. If it doesn't stop here, if we're not able to fix it here and get it turned around, it will go across the nation" (Stockton, 2009, p.8). In 2008 more than 60 police officers and more than 1,350 civilians were killed in Juarez, Mexico, a city that shares the international border with El Paso, Texas (Stockton, p.8):

> Such horrific violence has occurred along several areas of the border and has included decapitations, bodies hung from overpasses, corpses dissolved in vats of acid and attacks on anyone with the audacity to confront the narco-terrorists. A group of very well organized and equipped Mexican drug trafficking organizations have become increasingly ruthless as they seek to control the lucrative business of exporting drugs into the United States. It would be a serious mistake to underestimate the commitment and capability of these groups. They are extremely well funded and equipped with technology and weaponry on par with sophisticated military operations.

As Stockton (2009, p.8) cautions succinctly, "The war at our border is absolutely a clear and present danger in the United States."

Other U.S. Borders

U.S. law enforcement officials report that more than a third of the cocaine smuggled into the United States from Columbia travels in submersibles (Booth and Farero, 2009). The subs are powered by ordinary diesel engines and are equipped with technologies that make them difficult to intercept, even though U.S. forces use state-of-the-aft submarine warfare strategies against them. U.S. officials and their Columbian counterparts have detected more than 115 submersible voyages since 2006 and have apprehended the crews of more than 22 submersibles since 2007 (Booth and Farero).

Another highly vulnerable border is the vast, often unpopulated Canadian-American border. Canada currently hosts a "sprawling, multibillion-dollar trade" in marijuana, cocaine and MDMA (Ecstasy). For example, British Columbia's marijuana trade smuggles an estimated 30,000 to 80,000 pounds of marijuana per month into the United States, usually by helicopter or light aircraft: "It's a huge business, infusing billions of dollars a year into the province's economy. The province's most prominent gangs—the Hell's, Angels, the United Nations, and the Independent Soldiers—are believed to own most of the smuggled drugs" (Johnson, 2009).

THE HISTORY OF DRUG USE IN THE UNITED STATES

American history is filled with drug use, including alcohol and tobacco. As the early settlers moved west, one of the first buildings in each frontier town was a saloon. Cocaine use was also common by the 1880s. At the beginning of the 20th century, cocaine was the drug of choice, said to cure everything from indigestion to toothaches. It was added to flavor soft drinks such as Coca-Cola.

In 1909 a presidential commission reported to President Theodore Roosevelt that cocaine was a hazard, leading to loss of livelihoods and lives. As the public became increasingly aware of the hazards posed by cocaine and other drugs, it pressed for legislation against use of such drugs.

In 1914 the federal government passed the Harrison Narcotics Act, which made the sale or use of certain drugs illegal.

In 1920 every state required its students to learn about narcotics' effects. In 1937 under President Franklin Delano Roosevelt, marijuana became the last drug to be banned. For a quarter of a century, the drug problem lay dormant.

Then came the 1960s, a time of youthful rebellion, of Haight Ashbury and the flower children, a time to protest the Vietnam War. A whole culture had as its theme: tune in, turn on and drop out—often through marijuana and LSD. By the 1970s marijuana had been tried by an estimated 40 percent of 18- to 21-year-olds and was being used by many soldiers fighting in Vietnam. Many other soldiers turned to heroin. At the same time, an estimated half million Americans began using heroin back in the States.

The United States became the most drug-pervaded nation in the world, with marijuana leading the way. The 1980s saw a turnaround in drug use, with celebrities advocating, "It's not cool to do drugs," and "Just say no to drugs." At the same time, however, other advertisements suggested that alcohol and smoking are where the "fun is."

Today, large or small, urban or rural, communities throughout America confront many of the same threats, with one of the biggest threats being illegal drug abuse. Two national studies of drug use in the United States shed light on the current threat of drugs: the *National Drug Threat Assessment 2009* (2010) and *Monitoring the Future 2010* (Johnston et al., 2010).

National Drug Threat Assessment 2009

The Justice Department's National Drug Intelligence Center (NDIC) provides an annual report describing the availability and distribution of common drugs. According to the Executive Summary of the *National Drug Threat Assessment 2009* (2010, p.1):

> Overall, the availability of illicit drugs in the United States is increasing. In fact, in 2009 the prevalence of four of the five major drugs—heroin, methamphetamine, marijuana, and MDMA (3,4-methylenedioxymethamphetamine)—was widespread and increasing in some areas. Conversely, cocaine shortages first identified in 2007 persisted in many markets. . . .
>
> Although drug use remained relatively stable from 2007 through 2008, more than 25 million individuals 12 years of age and older reported using an illicit drug or using a controlled prescription drug (CPD) nonmedically in 2008. Each year, drug-related deaths number in the thousands, and treatment admissions and emergency department (ED) visits both exceed a million. These and other consequences of drug abuse, including lost productivity associated with abuse, the impact on the criminal justice system, and the environmental impact that results from the production of illicit drugs, are estimated at nearly $215 billion annually.

Monitoring the Future, 2010

Since 1975 the *Monitoring the Future* (MTF) survey has measured drug, alcohol and cigarette use and related attitudes among adolescent students nationwide and is conducted by the University of Michigan's Institute for Social Research. The 35th annual study was conducted during 2009 (Johnston et al., 2010):

> Positive Findings:
>
> - Cigarette smoking is at its lowest point in the history of the survey on all measures among students in grades 8, 10, and 12. These findings are particularly noteworthy since tobacco addiction is one of the leading preventable contributors to many of our Nation's health problems.
> - Between 2004 and 2009, a drop in past-year use of methamphetamine was reported for all grades, and lifetime use dropped significantly among 8th-graders, from 2.3 to 1.6 percent. Among 10th- and 12th-graders, 5-year declines were reported for past-year use of amphetamines and cocaine.

Among 12th-graders, past-year use of cocaine decreased *significantly*, from 4.4 to 3.4 percent.

- From 2004 to 2009, decreases were observed in lifetime, past-year, past-month, and binge use of alcohol across the three grades surveyed.
- In 2009 12th-graders reported declines in use across several survey measures of hallucinogens; past-year use of hallucinogens and LSD fell significantly, from 5.9 to 4.7 percent and from 2.7 to 1.9 percent, respectively; and past-year use of hallucinogens other than LSD decreased from 5.0 to 4.2 percent among 12th-graders.
- Attitudes toward substance abuse, often seen as harbingers of change in use, showed many favorable changes. Among 12th-graders, perceived harmfulness of LSD, amphetamines, sedatives/barbiturates, heroin, and cocaine increased. Across the three grades, perceived availability of several drugs also decreased.

Areas of Concern:

- Marijuana use across the three grades has shown a consistent decline since the mid-1990s. The trend has stalled, however, with prevalence rates remaining steady over the last 5 years. Past-year use was reported by 11.8 percent of 8th-graders, 26.7 percent of 10th-graders, and 32.8 percent of 12th-graders. Also, perceived risk of regular use of marijuana decreased among 8th- and 10th-graders, although perceived availability decreased among 12th-graders.
- From 2008 to 2009, lifetime, past-month, and daily use of smokeless tobacco increased significantly among 10th-graders.
- Past-year nonmedical use of Vicodin and OxyContin increased during the last 5 years among 10th-graders, and remained unchanged among 8th- and 12th-graders. Nearly 1 in 10 high school seniors reported nonmedical use of Vicodin; 1 in 20 reported abuse of OxyContin.
- When asked how prescription narcotics were obtained for nonmedical use, 52 percent of 12th-graders said they were given the drugs or bought them from a friend or relative. Additionally, 30 percent reported receiving a prescription for them, and a negligible number of 12th-graders reported purchasing the narcotics over the Internet.

CONTROLLED SUBSTANCES: AN OVERVIEW

The Controlled Substances Act (CSA) of 1984 placed all federally regulated substances into one of five schedules based on the substance's effects, medical use, potential for abuse and safety or dependence liability. Drugs in Schedule I have the highest potential for abuse, unpredictable effects and no generally accepted medical use. Schedule I drugs include heroin, LSD, gamma hydroxybutyrate (GHB) and marijuana. At the other end of the scale, Schedule V drugs have the lowest potential for abuse, may lead to limited physical or psychological dependence and have many accepted medical uses. Drugs in this category include Lomotil, Robitussin A-C and over-the-counter or prescription drugs containing codeine. Drugs falling between these two extremes include the Schedule II substances of morphine, PCP, cocaine and methamphetamine; Schedule III substances such as anabolic steroids, codeine and some barbiturates; and Schedule IV substances including Valium, Xanax and rohypnol.

In most states narcotics and other dangerous drugs may not be used or sold without a prescription. Federal law prohibits sale or distribution not covered by prescription.

Although drinking alcohol is legal, laws have been established that regulate the age at which it becomes legal to drink, as well as the amount a person can drink and then operate a vehicle. The widespread abuse of alcohol is partly because of its legality but also due to its social acceptance. Many people, although they know it is wrong and illegal, continue to drive after drinking. This problem was addressed in Chapter 5.

According to the *National Drug Threat Assessment 2009,* the five major problem drugs currently are cocaine, heroin, marijuana, methamphetamine and MDMA (Ecstasy).

Cocaine

Cocaine is a central nervous system stimulant narcotic derived from the South American coca bush. Cocaine may be inhaled or injected. Cocaine smuggling is big business, run primarily by Colombians. They often are assisted by tourists and students, called **mules**. Larger quantities are brought in by professional smugglers, often using private planes and boats.

Crack, a form of cocaine, has been called the "equal opportunity drug" because of its low price. Sentencing disparities between conviction of use or sale of cocaine and crack, with much stiffer sentences being imposed for crack, are controversial because most crack users are minorities.

mules

Individuals who smuggle cocaine for professional drug dealers; often tourists or students.

crack

A form of cocaine available at greatly reduced costs.

Heroin

Heroin is a central nervous system depressant that relieves pain and induces sleep. Most heroin originates from opium poppy farms in southwest Asia (the Golden Crescent, primarily Afghanistan and Pakistan), southeast Asia (the Golden Triangle, primarily in Myanmar) and Latin America (primarily Colombia). The opium gum is converted to morphine in labs near the fields and then to heroin in labs within or near the producing country. After importation, drug dealers cut, or dilute, the heroin before selling it to addicts.

Marijuana

Marijuana is the most available and abused illegal drug in the United States. Arrest for possession of marijuana is the most frequent drug arrest.

In addition, marijuana is almost certainly the most socially accepted illegal drug; legislation lessening penalties for its use has frequently been proposed, as discussed shortly. Although it has been known for nearly 5,000 years, it is one of the least understood, yet most versatile, of all natural drugs.

Marijuana, derived from the cannabis plant, is a hardy weed adaptable to most climates. It still grows wild in many parts of the United States. It grows at a phenomenal rate from a seedling to a 20-foot plant in one year. Many domestic marijuana growers are switching from outdoor to indoor cultivation. A highly potent form of marijuana obtained from unpollinated female plants is **sinsemilla**.

sinsemilla

A highly potent form of marijuana obtained from unpollinated female plants.

gateway theory

Contends that marijuana use leads to use of harder drugs.

Marijuana is seen by many as a "gateway" to harder drugs. However, others question the **gateway theory**, which supports a causal relationship between marijuana and other drug use. They contend that most drug users begin using drugs in their teens or young adult years and suggest that most people who try any drugs use marijuana only experimentally or continue use moderately and without ill effects. How many marijuana users proceed to hard drugs is unknown.

Methamphetamine

methamphetamine

A powerful stimulant emerging as a major problem for law enforcement because of its tendency to invoke violence in the user.

Methamphetamine, or "meth," is also known as speed, ice and crystal, and, like cocaine, is a potent central nervous system stimulant. Identified by the DEA as "a dangerous, sometimes lethal and unpredictable drug," meth poses a major problem for law enforcement: "Methamphetamine is second only to alcohol and marijuana as the drug used most frequently in some Western and Midwestern States. More than 50 percent of county law enforcement agencies surveyed in 2006 listed methamphetamine as the No. 1 drug problem in their area" (Page, 2009, p.46). A new technology known as a meth scanner can quickly and reliably detect invisible trace quantities of meth as small as one microgram on almost any surface and without touching the surface (Page).

In 2006 the Combat Methamphetamine Epidemic Act put tough new restrictions on the sale of the precursor chemicals used in manufacturing the drug. This initiative slowed methamphetamine production, as indicated by a sharp 34 percent drop in lab seizures in 2007. In 2008, however, production began increasing but reached nowhere near the levels seen during peak years of 2003 and 2004 ("Domestic 'Meth' Production Rising," 2009, pp.4–5).

Two of the precursor chemicals, ephedrine and pseudoephedrine, are not manufactured in the United States but are usually obtained from over-the-counter cold and allergy medicines. Because meth production requires thousands of these pills, anyone buying bulk amounts of them is suspicious. Other ingredients needed to make meth are lye, rock salt, battery acid and pool acid. Several states have passed legislation requiring individuals purchasing precursor chemicals to provide identification and that the purchase be recorded or that such products be kept in locked display cases and records kept of anyone who buys an excessive amount of these products.

The Bureau of Justice Assistance (BJA) stresses that meth addiction is treatable and that communities can use problem-solving initiatives such as drug courts and innovative reentry programs to stop the cycle of abuse: "The most effective strategies to fight methamphetamine abuse are comprehensive and collaborative ones—those that include prevention, education, treatment and enforcement" (Rose, 2009). Enforcement often focuses on detecting and dismantling clandestine meth labs.

Two basic types of clandestine methamphetamine labs are the super lab and the "Mom and Pop" lab (Petrocelli, 2009). Super labs are highly organized, sophisticated and have highly trained "cooks," specialized assistants and the best equipment available. These labs account for about 10 percent of all labs, but produce more than 80 percent of the meth found on the street. Most are concentrated in Southern California and Mexico. "Mom and Pop" labs, in contrast, are usually run by meth users themselves and produce enough for personal use with a small amount left over to sell: "With their haphazard production techniques, drug-addled cooks and primitive equipment, smaller labs account for the vast majority of explosions, fires and illegal hazardous waste disposal attributable to meth production" (Petrocelli, 2009, p.14).

Many of the chemicals found in meth labs are corrosive, flammable or both. Thus, the presence of meth labs poses a severe hazard to persons and structures surrounding them. Along with the hazards of fire, meth labs threaten the safety of children found in these homes, as exposure to the chemical fumes has been linked to increased risk of toxicological, neurological, respiratory, dermatological and other adverse effects.

MDMA

Perhaps the most prolific club drug currently attracting law enforcement's attention is *MDMA* (3, 4-Methylenedioxymethamphetamine), also called *Ecstasy*. MDMA is a synthetic, psychoactive drug with both stimulant (amphetamine-like) and hallucinogenic (LSD-like) properties that create feelings of emotional closeness to others and break down any personal communication barriers that may exist. MDMA comes in tablet or capsule form and is almost always taken orally, although it can be snorted or dissolved in water and injected.

Other Controlled Substances

Hallucinogens may produce distortion, intensify sensory perception and lessen the ability to discriminate between fact and fantasy. The unpredictable mental effects include illusions, panic, psychotic or antisocial behavior and impulses toward violence and self-destruction. Among the best-known hallucinogens are LSD and PCP. The latter appeared in San Francisco in the 1960s and was called the "Peace Pill." As its use spread across the country, it was called by various other names, including *angel dust*.

Police officers have been injured attempting to subdue a person under the influence of PCP. Overwhelming evidence shows that some users "freaked out" on PCP exhibit superhuman strength while showing aggression. One explanation is that users believe their hallucinations are real. The adrenalin flows, and they fight desperately for survival using any means to escape the terror. The superhuman strength is also directly related to the drug's analgesic qualities under which users feel little or no pain. The use of this drug often times results in suspects suffering excited delirium when police use force.

Rohypnol (flunitrazepam), also called *roofies* or the *date-rape drug*, is not approved for medical use in the United States but is legally prescribed in more than 50 other countries to treat insomnia and as a pre-anesthetic. Rohypnol, when dissolved in a drink, is virtually undetectable because it is colorless and odorless. Because rohypnol causes partial amnesia, users often cannot remember events that occurred while under the influence of the drug. This effect is particularly dangerous when the drug is used to commit a sexual assault because victims may not be able to clearly recall the assault, the assailant or the events surrounding the assault.

Although the various narcotics and other dangerous drugs produce different effects, they have certain common effects.

© AP Images/Denis Poroy

A San Diego County Sheriff's deputy, right, escorts defendant Patrick Hawley, left, into the courtroom during his arraignment in San Diego County Superior Court Tuesday, May 6, 2008. Hawley, who was arrested by officers in Operation Sudden Fall, is charged with the sale of cocaine. Seventy-five San Diego State University students and 21 nonstudents were arrested after an undercover investigation of a college drug ring.

 Common effects of the various controlled substances are

1. They are mind altering.
2. They may become addicting—either physically or psychologically.
3. Overdosage may result in convulsions and death.

Abuse of Prescription Drugs

One source of assistance for law enforcement is RxPatrol, a collaborative effort between the pharmaceutical industry and law enforcement that collects, collates, analyzes and disseminates pharmacy theft information, serving as a clearinghouse of pertinent leads to the law enforcement community.

THE "WAR ON DRUGS" AND THE NATIONAL DRUG CONTROL STRATEGY

In 1973 President Richard Nixon declared "war" on drugs. Since that time, federal spending on this war against drug smugglers, users and sellers has increased 30-fold—from $420 million in 1973 to $12.7 billion in 2004. Drug arrests have nearly tripled since 1980, when the federal drug policy shifted to arresting and incarcerating users.

The White House Office of National Drug Control Policy (ONDCP), a component of the Executive Office of the President, was established by the Anti-Drug Abuse Act of 1988 and has three primary objectives:

1. *Stop drug use before it starts: education and community action.* In homes, schools, places of worship, the workplace and civic and social organizations, Americans must set norms that reaffirm the values of responsibility and good citizenship while dismissing the notion that drug use is consistent with individual freedom.
2. *Heal America's drug users: getting treatment resources where they are needed.* Getting people into treatment will require the creation of a new climate of "compassionate coercion," which begins with family, friends, employers and the community. Compassionate coercion also uses the criminal justice system to get people into treatment.
3. *Disrupt the market: attacking the economic basis of the drug trade.* Domestically, attacking the economic basis of the drug trade involves the cooperative, combined efforts of federal, state and local law enforcement.

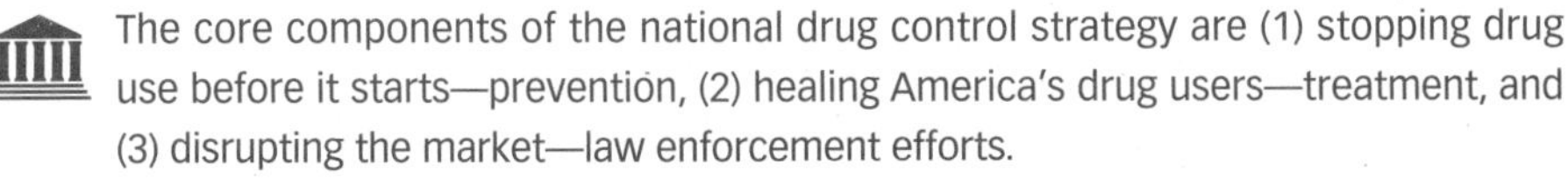

The core components of the national drug control strategy are (1) stopping drug use before it starts—prevention, (2) healing America's drug users—treatment, and (3) disrupting the market—law enforcement efforts.

Prevention: Stopping Drug Use before It Starts

Prevention has been a focus of the National Drug Control Strategy since its inception. One key to stopping drug use is education. Probably the most widely known and evaluated program is D.A.R.E.

The D.A.R.E. Program The Drug Awareness Resistance Education (D.A.R.E.) program was developed in Los Angeles in 1983 and has become one of the most well-known and widespread crime prevention programs in the country. The program has trained hundreds of thousands of police officers and educated millions of children, spreading to 43 different countries.

The D.A.R.E. program came under extreme criticism at the beginning of the 21st century, with many researchers claiming the program simply did not work. According to *Lessons from the Debate over D.A.R.E.* (2009, p.1): "To date there have been more than 30 evaluations of the program that have documented negligible long-term impacts on teen drug use. One intensive six-year study even found that the program increased drug use among suburban teens by a small amount." In addition, many in law enforcement saw the program as a "touchy-feely waste of time and personnel" (Griffith, 2009c, p.8).

Lessons from the Debate (2009, p.2) points out: "To its critics, D.A.R.E. is a cautionary tale of how criminal justice programs can live on despite evidence of failure. To its defenders, D.A.R.E. is a case study of resilience in the face of adversity." The silver lining to the cloud of negative assessments is that the research can provide insight into how the program might be improved if revised (*Lessons from the Debate*).

The new program underwent a massive national research effort in six U.S. cities (Detroit, Houston, Los Angeles, Newark, New Orleans and St. Louis) and involved 9,000 students from 83 high schools and 122 middle schools. The D.A.R.E. Web site notes that the new D.A.R.E. program "is going high-tech, interactive and decision-model-based." Called "Take Charge of Your Life," the program used 25 years of drug-abuse prevention research:

> Gleaming with the latest in prevention science and teaching techniques, D.A.R.E. is reinventing itself as part of a major national research study that promises to help teachers and administrators cope with ever-evolving federal prevention program requirements and the thorny issues of school violence, budget cuts and terrorism.
>
> Gone is the old-style approach to prevention in which an officer stands behind a podium and lectures students in straight rows. Now D.A.R.E. officers are trained as "coaches" to support kids who are using research-based refusal strategies in high-stakes peer-pressure environments. New D.A.R.E. students are getting to see for themselves—via stunning brain imagery—tangible proof of how substances diminish mental activity, emotions, coordination and movement. Mock courtroom exercises are bringing home the social and legal consequences of drug use and violence.

Many acknowledge that the jury is still out on the D.A.R.E. controversy. However, it does accomplish one thing: "It puts cops in the school and in the lives of school children, not in an adversarial way but as mentors and teachers. For some of the kids in the D.A.R.E. program, the D.A.R.E. officer is the only adult they can really talk to" (Griffith, 2009c, p.8). *Lessons from the Debate* (2009, p.6) reports, "Early results, released in late 2002 were encouraging. 'Students who participated in the new Take Back Your Life curriculum showed small but statistically significant improvements in terms of their attitudes toward drugs and their drug refusal skills.' The controversy over the value of programs such as D.A.R.E. teaches an important lesson about the importance of modest expectation when tackling complex social problem (*Lessons from the Debate*, p.8).

When educational and prevention efforts fail, other strategies come into play.

Treatment: Healing America's Drug Users

Critics of the government's approach to the drug war believe the focus should be on funding drug treatment programs rather than spending billions of dollars attacking the drug users and dealers. To address alcohol and drug problems, treatment services should (1) be based on formal theories of drug dependence and abuse, (2) use the best therapeutic tools available and (3) give participants opportunities to build cognitive skills.

Juveniles may be more difficult to diagnose and treat than adults. Many juveniles referred to drug court have no established pattern of abuse or physical addiction. Others have reached serious levels of criminal and drug involvement. Drug courts are discussed in Chapter 13.

A comprehensive approach to the drug problem includes prevention, treatment and efforts aimed at stopping drug sale and use, the third core component of the national drug control strategy.

Crime Control—Disrupting the Market

Crime control includes enforcement at the local level and source control at the national and international level.

Enforcement at the Local Level Strategies to deal with the drug problem include drug raids, surveillance, undercover operations and arresting sellers and buyers.

Drug Raids During the 1980s, drug raids made frequent headlines. Tank-like vehicles, SWAT teams and sophisticated weaponry all have been involved in drug raids, which can be highly successful when used properly.

Surveillance The purpose of surveillance is to gather information about people, their activities and associates that may help solve a crime. Surveillance can be designed to serve several functions including to gather information required for building a criminal complaint, to verify a witness's statement about a crime, to gain information required for obtaining a search or arrest warrant, to identify a suspect's associates, to observe criminal activities in progress, to apprehend a criminal in the act of committing a crime and to make a legal arrest.

A common type of surveillance is the stakeout, a stationary surveillance in which officers set up an observation post and monitor it continuously. Other types of surveillance include aerial surveillance and audio surveillance, or wiretapping. Before a judge will approve an application for electronic surveillance, those requesting it must show why surveillance is necessary—for example, standard techniques have been tried and failed.

Undercover Assignments Undercover assignments, previously discussed in Chapter 6, are most often used to obtain information and evidence about illegal activity when it can be obtained in no other way. *Light cover* involves deception, but the officer is seldom in danger. For example an officer poses as a utility worker or repair person to obtain access to a suspect's home. Or an officer poses as a drug addict to make a drug buy, obtaining evidence to make an arrest. *Deep cover* is much more dangerous but can be very effective. In deep cover an officer lives an assumed identity to infiltrate a group or organization. No identification other than the cover identification is carried. Communication with the police department is carefully planned. Undercover operations now even extend into cyberspace.

Some police departments have used *sting operations* during which undercover police agents sell drugs and then arrest those who buy them. These operations have sometimes been criticized as unethical or even an illegal form of entrapment. Police must exercise extreme care if they use such operations as a strategy to reduce the drug problem.

Arresting Drug Dealers The traditional response to users and sellers has been to arrest them when possible. The current antidrug campaign has increasingly focused on a law enforcement model attacking the supply side (traffickers, smugglers and users). Most law enforcement agencies focus efforts at enforcing laws against dealing drugs and increasing prosecution of drug dealers. The question is sometimes raised whether police attention focused on an illegal drug market causes dealers to simply spatially move their dealing around the corner. However, research using agglomeration economies found that this is not the case because taking the largest and most profitable site from illegal drug deals will make dealing in the surrounding neighborhoods *less* rather than more profitable and lead to a smaller marketplace overall (Taniguchi et al., 2009, p.670).

In addition to being concerned with those who deal in drugs, police officers need to be prepared to manage those who use them.

Recognizing Individuals Using Illegal Drugs Police officers must be able to recognize when a person is probably under the influence of drugs and must be aware of the dangers the person might present. Table 9.7 summarizes the primary physical symptoms, what to look for and the dangers involved in the most commonly used drugs, including alcohol.

Drug recognition experts/evaluators (DREs) are police officers specially trained to identify drug-impaired people. The DRE follows a 12-step procedure to develop and recognize impairment, using different types of field tests. The DRE program originated in 1979 and was developed by the Los Angeles Police Department (LAPD) and National Highway Traffic Safety Administration (NHTSA) into a standardized drug recognition protocol in response to drug-impaired driving. The International Association of Chiefs of Police (IACP), along with the NHTSA and U.S. Department of Transportation coordinates the International Drug Evaluation and Classification Program (DEC). Currently 43 states and thousands of police officers are DRE certified.

When officers recognize a drug user, the question becomes, what happens? Does the user get treatment or get arrested? Figure 9.3 presents an overview of drug-control strategies. Crime control, rehabilitation (including treatment) and prevention fit within the national drug control strategies.

Source Control With the reigning drug lords living and working far from the scenes of their crimes, U.S. law enforcement faces a difficult challenge in controlling these sources of illegal drugs. Some drug sources have the open support of their national governments, with export of drug-related crops bringing substantial revenue to the countries. An example is opium production, the prevention of which would require controlling poppy cultivation and international cooperation (Kaplan, n.d.). It is anticipated that the fall of the Taliban regime in Afghanistan and the de facto end to its national ban on poppy cultivation will return the country to its prior status as one of the world's leading opium producers, providing much-needed economic relief for struggling poppy farmers but adding to the global supply of drugs. Such regionally sanctioned drug sources are very difficult, if not impossible, to control.

International drug rings also pose a significant challenge to U.S. law enforcement. For example, DEA agents have identified a Bangkok heroin cartel that is as powerful as the notorious Medellin and Cali Colombian rings. Difficulties in prosecuting the cartel include Thailand's reluctance to crack down on drug trafficking and the ingenious smuggling used by the cartel. Some narcotics kingpins are virtually ignored by the government of the country in which they reside, whether from intimidation and fear or because the governments have formed clandestine partnerships with such drug lords to profit from the business.

Although the U.S. government cannot dictate how a foreign government should handle its resident drug lords, it can impose legislation aimed at preventing individuals and organizations from conducting illegal narcotics business within

TABLE 9.7 Common Symptoms, What to Look for and Dangers of Commonly Abused Drugs

Drug Used	Physical Symptoms	Look For	Dangers
Alcohol (beer, wine, liquor)	Intoxication, slurred speech, unsteady walk, relaxation, relaxed inhibitions, impaired coordination, slowed reflexes.	Smell of alcohol on clothes or breath, intoxicated behavior, hangover, glazed eyes.	Addiction, accidents as a result of impaired ability and judgment, overdose when mixed with other depressants, heart and liver damage.
Cocaine (coke, rock, crack, base)	Brief intense euphoria, elevated blood pressure and heart rate, restlessness, excitement, feeling of well-being followed by depression.	Glass vials, glass pipe, white crystalline powder, razor blades, syringes, needle marks.	Addiction, heart attack, seizures, lung damage, severe depression, paranoia (see Stimulants).
Marijuana (pot, dope, grass, weed, herb, hash, joint)	Altered perceptions, red eyes, dry mouth, reduced concentration and coordination, euphoria, laughing, hunger.	Rolling papers, pipes, dried plant material, odor of burnt hemp rope, roach clips.	Panic reaction, impaired short-term memory, addiction.
Hallucinogens (acid, LSD, PCP, MDMA/Ecstasy, psilocybin mushrooms, peyote)	Altered mood and perceptions, focus on detail, anxiety, panic, nausea, synaesthesia (e.g., smell colors, see sounds).	Capsules, tablets, "microdots," blotter squares.	Unpredictable behavior, emotional instability, violent behavior (with PCP).
Inhalants (gas, aerosol, glue, nitrites, Rush, White Out)	Nausea, dizziness, headaches, lack of coordination.	Odor of substance on clothing and breath, intoxication, drowsiness, poor muscular control.	Unconsciousness, suffocation, nausea and vomiting, damage to brain and central nervous system, sudden death.
Narcotics Heroin (junk, dope, Black tar, China white), Demerol, Dilaudid (D's), morphine, codeine	Euphoria, drowsiness, insensitivity to pain, nausea, vomiting, watery eyes, runny nose (see Depressants).	Needle marks on arms, needles, syringes, spoons, pinpoint pupils, cold moist skin.	Addiction, lethargy, weight loss, contamination from unsterile needles (hepatitis, AIDS), accidental overdose.
Stimulants (Speed, uppers, crank, Bam, black beauties, crystal, dexies, caffeine, nicotine, cocaine, amphetamines)	Alertness, talkativeness, wakefulness, increased blood pressure, loss of appetite, mood elevation.	Pills and capsules, loss of sleep and appetite, irritability or anxiety, weight loss, hyperactivity.	Fatigue leading to exhaustion, addiction, paranoia, depression, confusion, possibly hallucinations.
Depressants Barbiturates, sedatives, tranquilizers (downers, tranks, ludes, red, Valium, yellow jackets, alcohol)	Depressed breathing and heartbeat, intoxication, drowsiness, uncoordinated movements.	Capsules and pills, confused behavior, longer periods of sleep, slurred speech.	Possible overdose, especially in combination with alcohol; muscle rigidity; addiction, withdrawal and overdose require medical treatment.

SOURCE: Adapted from Drug Education Guide, CBB-600. © 2002/Rev. 10/07 www.positivepromotions.com. Reprinted by permission.

our national borders and prosecuting those who do so or attempt to do so. The Foreign Narcotics Kingpin Designation Act requires federal officials to compile an annual list of suspected drug kingpins and take steps to freeze their U.S. assets and bar them from entering the country. It also subjects anyone who knowingly does business with drug kingpins to criminal penalties.

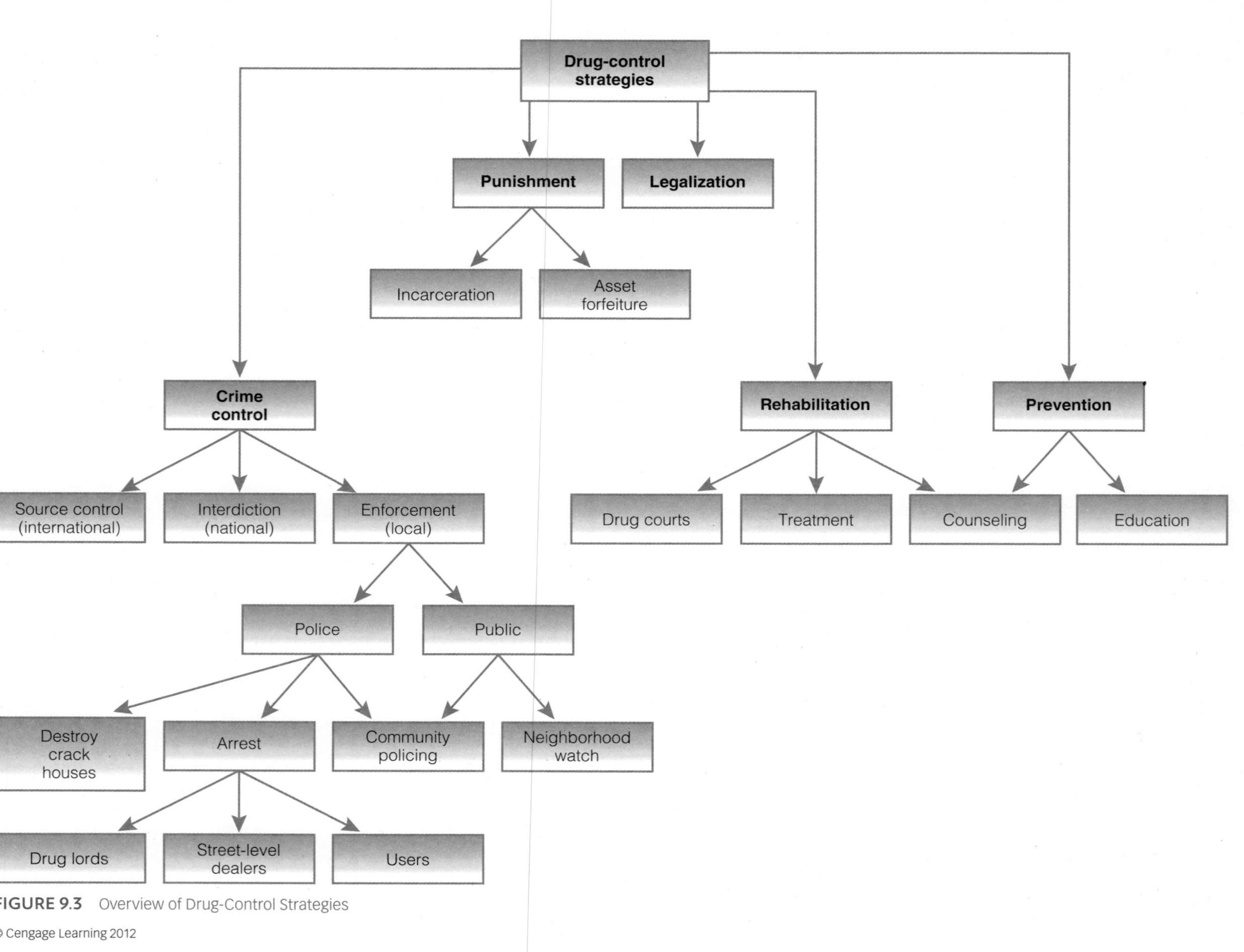

FIGURE 9.3 Overview of Drug-Control Strategies

After international drug sources have been addressed, the focus narrows to ways to keep the drugs that are produced from getting into our country. **Interdiction** is cutting off or destroying a line of communication—in the case of drug control, halting the flow of drugs into the United States. American drug users pay drug traffickers an estimated $140 billion a year. Some dealers hand out free drug samples to hook new buyers. Illegal drugs, from marijuana to cocaine, are readily available. Preventing smuggling is difficult given the more than 12,000 miles of U.S. coastline. Kaplan (n.d.) suggests, for example, that the total heroin requirement of all American addicts for an entire year is probably less than 10 tons, yet 100 million tons of freight come into the United States yearly, and more than 200 million people cross American borders yearly.

interdiction

Cutting off or destroying a line of communication—in the case of drug control, halting the flow of drugs into the United States.

In addition to the three core strategies to deal with the drug problem—prevention, treatment and enforcement—as noted earlier, the controversial strategies of punishment or legalization are frequently suggested.

IS PUNISHMENT AN ANSWER?

One way to handle the drug problem is to punish those involved in selling or using drugs, either through incarceration or asset forfeiture, in hopes such sanctions will deter future criminal behavior.

Incarceration

Spending time behind bars has been a consequence of illegal activity for thousands of years. During the 1970s many citizens and legislators advocated a "get-tough" approach to the growing drug-use crisis, viewing imprisonment of drug offenders as the best solution to the problem. Since the passage of mandatory drug sentencing laws during the 1970s, millions of substance abusers have been incarcerated by the nation's criminal justice system. This nondiscretionary sentencing policy has filled our nation's correctional institutions with drug offenders, leaving less room for what many consider the "real" criminals—murderers, rapists and other violent offenders.

With our correctional facilities overflowing and the increasing number of violent offenders requiring prison space, courts have become more reluctant to incarcerate drug offenders. Adding to this reluctance is the growing body of evidence that tougher sentencing laws have not had much impact on reducing criminality in most drug offenders. Given the many shortcomings of incarceration as an effective punishment for drug offenders, another solution gaining popularity is asset forfeiture.

Asset Forfeiture

Asset forfeiture was introduced in the United States through passage of the Racketeer Influenced and Corrupt Organization (RICO) Act in 1970 and the Continuing Criminal Enterprises Act in 1984. The Asset Forfeiture Program, enacted in 1984, allows the Justice Department to share seized assets with state and local law enforcement agencies that participate in the investigations and arrests. The U.S. Marshals Service administers this program, which has three goals: (1) enforcing the law, (2) improving law enforcement cooperation and (3) enhancing law enforcement through revenue. Under the program's Equitable Sharing Program,

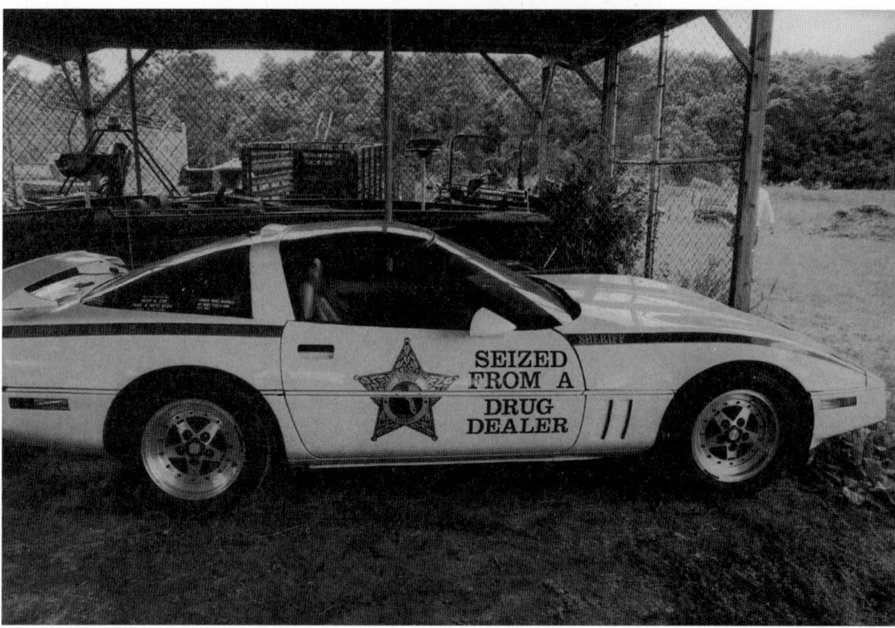
SEIZED
FROM A
DRUG
DEALER

The Asset Forfeiture Program allows the Justice Department to share seized assets with state and local law enforcement agencies that participated in the drug investigations and arrests. Many police departments and sheriffs' departments use seized vehicles to convey a message to drug dealers and the public.

the proceeds from asset sales are often shared with the state and local enforcement agencies that participated in the investigation leading to the asset seizure.

This type of response is intended to deprive drug offenders of ill-gotten gain, material possessions and wealth obtained through the sale or distribution of illegal drugs. Such forfeitures have included a recording studio; a Chevrolet dealership; a one-thousand-acre plantation; a horse farm with 210 Appaloosas, including a stallion worth $1.5 million; luxury homes; cars; boats; and planes. In 2006 the program shared assets totaling more than $6 million with 385 different agencies.

Two key cases in the 1990s set a stronger foundation for issues involving forfeiture. In *United States v. Ursery* (1996), the Court held that civil forfeiture does not constitute double jeopardy, under the rationale that the prohibition against double jeopardy applies only if both proceedings are criminal and not when one is civil. In *United States v. Bajakajian* (1998), the Court held that the Eighth Amendment does apply in civil forfeitures. In this case the offense was failing to make a report to customs agents when taking more than $10,000 out of the country. The Court ruled that the forfeiture of $357,144 was grossly disproportionate to the offense and required Bajakajian to forfeit only $15,000.

IS LEGALIZATION AN ANSWER?

Legalization of drugs has been a topic of debate in the United States since the passage of the Harrison Narcotics Act in 1914. Some advocate making marijuana and other drugs legal, just as alcohol is, claiming this would reduce the cost of maintaining a drug habit and, consequently, reduce the amount of crime committed to obtain money to support the habit.

Legalization proponents say the prohibition on drug use has resulted in enormous profits for drug dealers, jail overcrowding and urban terrorization by gangs. Opponents, however, claim legalization will provide a "green light" for drug use, leading to addiction and, consequently, to increases in crime.

In a survey responded to by 1,775 readers of *Police* magazine regarding legalization of marijuana, only 27 percent of respondents were in favor of decriminalizing marijuana, and only 23 percent supporting legalization of the drug (Griffith, 2009b, p.14). In response to the question "Is it worth law enforcement's time to bust marijuana users?," 65 percent responded "yes." In response to the question, "Would legalization of marijuana have a favorable impact on problems associated with gangs and cartels," only 32 percent responded "yes" (Griffith). Finally, in response to "When it comes to legalizing currently illegal drugs, where would you draw the line?," 68.2 percent would legalize none of them, 19.8 percent would legalize marijuana, 5 percent would legalize prescription pain killers, 2.4 percent would legalize cocaine, 1.1 percent would legalize opiates (heroine, morphine, methadone), 1.1 percent would legalize the stimulants (including meth) and 2.4 percent would legalize them all (Griffith).

Arguments for Legalization

Proponents of drug legalization provide the following arguments:

- *Costs*—Dollars now spent on enforcement could be used for education and treatment.
- *Organized crime*—Legalization would eliminate the drug lords' major source of funds.
- *Revenues*—Taxes on drugs, like taxes on alcohol and tobacco, could be used to finance treatment programs.

The *Police* survey respondents who favored legalizing marijuana gave tax revenue as their main rationale (83.5 percent). Additional arguments included "prohibition has failed" (61.2 percent), "it's no worse than alcohol" (61 percent), "it would allow me to focus on other crimes" (57 percent), "it would reduce prison populations" (54.8 percent), "it would end drug-related violence" (28.4 percent) and other reasons (12.3 percent).

Many believe the way some drug users are currently treated—incarcerated and criminalized for no other reason than that they use drugs—is leading our nation on a downward spiral toward the status of a prison state.

Arguments against Legalization

Those opposed to legalization of drugs give the following reasons for their objection:

- *Increased drug use and addiction*—Inexpensive, widely available drugs would increase addiction.
- *Increased crime*—Because of the proven link between drug use and crime, more drug users/addicts would lead to increased levels of crime.
- *Medical costs*—Health costs of drug abuse would increase.
- *Social values*—Legalizing drugs would make them socially acceptable.

Almost 81 percent of respondents to the *Police* survey opposing legalization felt that marijuana is a gateway drug. Other reasons for opposition included danger of people driving high (79.6 percent), harm to user and society (70.4 percent), cost to government for drug treatment (45.4 percent) and morality (30.2 percent) (Griffith, 2009b).

Where the Debate about Decriminalization of Marijuana Stands

The debate about whether to legalize marijuana continues to be a polarizing concept: "Neither as dangerous or benign as either side would have one believe, marijuana is the most abused narcotic in the country, and, even if its supporters are not winning the war, they have at least made inroads" (Scoville, 2009, p.53). The public appears apathetic to strict enforcement of marijuana laws, as evidenced by the predominant "so what" response to photographs of Olympic swim star Michael Phelps taking a hit off a bong, and the subsequent lack of prosecution (Scoville). In addition, the last three U.S. presidents have admitted "experimenting" with grass, and many police departments no longer consider marijuana "experimentation" as a "hiring deal breaker" (Scoville).

Nearly half of the nation's states and major municipalities have decriminalized nonmedical marijuana, with some penalties such as civil fines or drug treatment imposed in place of criminal prosecution. Federal authorities will no longer raid medical-marijuana dispensaries in the 13 states where voters have made medical marijuana legal, signaling a shift in Washington to address drug use as a matter of public health rather than solely a criminal justice matter, with treatment's role growing relative to incarceration (Fields, 2009).

The movement to legalize marijuana on the West Coast is picking up steam, and a recent poll conducted by SurveyUSA found 56 percent of the 500 respondents in Washington State said legalizing marijuana is a good idea (Wingfield and Scheck, 2010).

On the other side of the debate, former Miami police chief Timoney (2009, p.2) says, "I don't see legalization gaining traction in this country. For one thing, if you legalize drugs, there goes the whole notion of using the criminal justice system as a lever to encourage people to go to a treatment program." He also says that many minorities see enforcing drug laws not as a war on drugs, but as a war on them: "Any talk about legalization should involve mothers and fathers from the minority communities hardest hit by drugs or they will find themselves being accused of genocide."

THE NEXUS BETWEEN ILLICIT-DRUG ABUSE AND CRIME

The relationship between illicit drugs and crime is complex. Four lessons from history and economics provide insight regarding the limitations of criminal law in controlling products or services that a large number of people want (Walker et al., 2007, p.272):

1. If a large number of people want a product or service, someone will try to supply it.

2. Efforts to suppress that supply will result in massive evasion and the creation of criminal syndicates.
3. The enforcement effort itself will generate secondary crime (e.g., turf wars between gangs, corruption of law enforcement), abuse of individual rights (e.g., illegal searches and seizures) and loss of respect for the law.
4. Intensifying the enforcement effort encourages adaptations, either substitution of products (as in the case of some drugs) or transfer of the service to people more willing to take the increased risks.

Some acts involving drugs are illegal and are termed *systemic*, or **drug-defined offenses** in which violent crime occurs as a part of the drug business or culture. Examples of these offenses include marijuana cultivation, methamphetamine production and cocaine distribution. Other acts involve offenses in which the *effect* of the drug or the *need* for the drug is a contributing factor. These are called **drug-related offenses**, examples of which might include a user high on PCP who becomes violent and commits an assault because of the drug's pharmacologic effects, or an addict stealing to get money to buy drugs. Finally the *interaction* of drugs, crime and those involved with the drug culture may come into play, as when drug users and other deviants are exposed to situations that encourage crime, when criminal opportunities arise because of a drug user's contact with illegal markets and other offenders or when offenders exchange criminal knowledge and learn criminal skills from each other.

drug-defined offenses

Illegal acts involving drugs; that is, the crime occurs as a part of the drug business or culture, for example, marijuana cultivation or cocaine distribution. Also called *systemic offenses*.

drug-related offenses

Illegal acts in which the effect of a drug is a contributor, such as when a drug user commits crime because of drug-induced changes in physiological functions, cognitive ability and mood, or in which the need for the drug is a factor, as when a drug user commits crime to obtain money to buy drugs.

The National Institute of Justice (NIJ) has implemented a drug-use forecasting (DUF) system to detect and track drug-use trends among people arrested for serious crimes. In this voluntary program, arrestees in several major cities are interviewed four times a year and asked to provide urine specimens, which are tested for illicit drugs. Initial tests showed a high level of drug use among the arrestees, with 50 to 80 percent of those arrested for serious crimes testing positive. The research also showed that criminals commit four to six times as many crimes when they are actively using drugs as they do when they are drug free. According to the NIJ, most of those tested were charged with street crimes, such as burglary, grand larceny and assault. The most frequently found drugs were marijuana, cocaine, heroin, PCP and amphetamines.

Incarcerated adults and youths report high levels of drug use. Among those incarcerated for violent crimes, one-third of state prisoners and more than one-third of the incarcerated youths said they had been under the influence of an illegal drug at the time of their offense. In addition major drug use (cocaine, heroin, PCP, LSD and methadone) is related to the number of prior convictions for state prisoners: The greater the use of major drugs, the more prior convictions the inmate was likely to report.

Drugs and guns have also been linked. When crack became a major drug of choice, those recruited to distribute it were mainly youths. Fearing for their safety because they often carried large quantities of money, these youths also carried guns. Youths are apt to resort to violence to settle arguments rather than resolving disputes verbally. When guns are available, the outcome can be deadly.

Summary

A major threat facing our nation today is gangs. Gangs and gang membership increased significantly between 2002 and 2008, and reporting agencies perceive the problem as worsening.

Distinguishing characteristics of gangs include criminal activity, organization, leadership, domain identification, use of symbols and a name. Young gang members are frequently victims of violence as well as offenders.

The most common reasons for joining a gang are for belonging, identity or recognition; protection; fellowship and brotherhood; or to make money. Broken families, unemployment, poverty and general despair lead young people to seek out economic opportunities frequently available through gang membership. However, family structure is probably the most important risk factor in the formation of a gang member.

Currently the most commonly used strategy to combat a gang problem is targeting gang hot spots, followed by targeting known offenders, use of informants, school resource officers and saturation patrol of targeted gang areas. The most effective strategies to combat gang violence were saturation patrols and targeting gang hot spots; identifying, tracking and targeting known gang members; zero tolerance initiatives; partnerships and multi-agency initiatives; task forces; and prosecution efforts

The Department of Justice's dual approach to combat gang violence focuses on robust enforcement—suppression—and on prevention programs. The OJJDP Comprehensive Gang Model focuses on five strategies: community mobilization, opportunities provision, social intervention, suppression, and organizational change and development (*Best Practices*, p.2).

Drug use and abuse pose another serious threat to our nation. In 1914 the federal government passed the Harrison Narcotics Act, which made the sale or use of certain drugs illegal. In most states narcotics and other dangerous drugs may not be used or sold without a prescription. Federal law prohibits sale or distribution not covered by prescription.

According to the *National Drug Threat Assessment 2009,* the five major problem drugs currently are cocaine, heroin, marijuana, methamphetamine and MDMA (Ecstasy). Marijuana is the most available and abused illegal drug in the United States. Arrest for possession of marijuana is the most frequent drug arrest.

Common effects of the various narcotics and other dangerous drugs include: (1) they are mind altering, (2) they may become addicting—either physically or psychologically, and (3) overdosage may result in convulsions and death.

The core components of the national drug control strategy are (1) stopping drug use before it starts—prevention, (2) healing America's drug users—treatment, and (3) disrupting the market—law enforcement efforts. The third component, crime control, includes enforcement at the local level and source control at the national and international level.

Discussion Questions

1. How have gangs influenced American pop culture?
2. Are there gangs in your area? If so, in what criminal activities are they involved?
3. What do you think might be done to reduce the gang problem? Is a hard or soft approach to gang activity the best approach to curtail criminal activity?

4. Which drugs pose the greatest problem for law enforcement?
5. What are the pros and cons of legalizing drugs?
6. If drugs were legalized, how would this affect street gangs or organized crime?
7. What is the best approach to combat drugs?
8. Should nonviolent drug offenders be incarcerated or be diverted to treatment or some other form of community corrections?
9. Which poses the greater threat: gangs or drugs?
10. What law enforcement strategies might work equally well in suppressing gangs and drugs?

Gale Emergency Services Database Assignments

- Use the Gale Emergency Services Database to help answer the Discussion Questions as appropriate.
- Using the Gale Emergency Services Database, search for articles on *alcohol and teen drinking*. Find one article to outline, and be prepared to discuss your findings with the class.
- Using the Gale Emergency Services Database, find the article "Street Gangs: Lessons From a Task Force": http://find.galegroup.com/gps/retrieve.do?contentSet=IAC-Documents&resultListType=RESULT_LIST&qrySerId=Locale%28en%2C%2C%29%3AFQE%3D%28ke%2CNone%2C12%29street+gangs%24&sgHitCountType=None&inPS=true&sort=DateDescend&searchType=BasicSearchForm&tabID=T003&prodId=IPS&searchId=R1¤tPosition=2&userGroupName=cpg3&docId=A159228744&docType=IAC&contentSet=IAC-Documents

  Assignment: Read the case study in this assignment. Be prepared to discuss in class.
- Using the Gale Emergency Services Database, find the article "Combating Gangs: The Need for Innovation (Strategies to Prevent Crimes Perpetrated by Street Gangs)": http://find.galegroup.com/gps/retrieve.do?contentSet=IAC-Documents&resultListType=RESULT_LIST&qrySerId=Locale%28en%2C%2C%29%3AFQE%3D%28ke%2CNone%2C12%29street+gangs%24&sgHitCountType=None&inPS=true&sort=DateDescend&searchType=BasicSearchForm&tabID=T003&prodId=IPS&searchId=R1¤tPosition=5&userGroupName=cpg3&docId=A20564017&docType=IAC&contentSet=IAC-Documents

  Assignment: Read the article and identify two to three strategies that the article highlights in combating gang related crime. Be prepared to discuss these strategies with the class.
- Using the Gale Emergency Services Database, find the article "Graffiti Paint Outs (Alleviation of the Graffiti Problem in Los Angeles, California)": http://find.galegroup.com/gps/retrieve.do?contentSet=IAC-Documents&resultListType=RESULT_LIST&qrySerId=Locale%28en%2C%2C%29%3AFQE%3D%28ke%2CNone%2C12%29street+gangs%24&sgHitCountType=None&inPS=true&sort=DateDescend&searchType=BasicSearchForm&tabID=T003&prodId=IPS&searchId=R1¤tPosition=7&userGroupName=cpg3&docId=A13421825&docType=IAC&contentSet=IAC-Documents

Assignment: Read and be prepared to discuss the methods highlighted in the article to alleviate gang graffiti.

- Using the Gale Emergency Services Database, find the article "Connecting Drug Paraphernalia to Drug Gangs": http://find.galegroup.com/gps/retrieve.do?contentSet=IAC-Documents&resultListType=RESULT_LIST&qrySerId=Locale%28en%2C%2C%29%3AFQE%3D%28ke%2CNone%2C11%29gangs+drugs%24&sgHitCountType=None&inPS=true&sort=DateDescend&searchType=BasicSearchForm&tabID=T003&prodId=IPS&searchId=R2¤tPosition=1&userGroupName=cpg3&docId=A98253652&docType=IAC&contentSet=IAC-Documents

  Assignment: Identify what the drug paraphernalia and drug gang connections are in this article. What is the Shop Light Investigation? Be prepared to discuss in class.

Internet Assignments

Select two assignments to complete.

- Search for the key words *youth gangs*. Locate information on gangs in the United States and in foreign countries. Outline the similarities and differences between these gangs. Be prepared to discuss your findings with the class.
- Go to http://www.whitehousedrugpolicy.gov and outline the *president's drug policy*. Be prepared to share and discuss your outline with the class.
- Go to http://www.zonezero.com/exposiciones/fotografos/rodriguez for a photographic history of *gang life* seen from the street. Take notes on this photo essay, and be prepared to share your notes with the class.
- Go to http://www.usdoj.gov/ndic and find the National Drug Intelligence Center's *State Drug Threat Assessments*. Find your state and outline the assessment for your state.

References

Basich, Melanie. "Are Gang Members Hopeless Cases?" *Police*, May 2009, pp.21–22.

Bell, Kerryn E. "Gender and Gangs: A Quantitative Comparison." *Crime & Delinquency*, July 2009, pp.363–387.

Best Practices to Address Community Gang Problems: OJJDP's Comprehensive Gang Model. Washington, DC: National Youth Gang Center, June 2008.

Bjerregaard, Beth. "Gang Membership and Drug Involvement: Untangling the Complex Relationship." *Crime & Delinquency*, January 2010, pp.3–34.

Booth, William, and Forero. "Plying the Pacific, Subs Surface as Key Tool of Drug Cartels." *Washington Post*, June 6, 2009, p.A1.

Dawe, Brian. "Prison Gang: An Overview." *American Cop Magazine*, November/December 2009, pp.16–17.

Decker, Scott." "Dr. Scott Decker Explains the Importance and Structure of a Comprehensive Gang Strategy." In *Gang Violence: The Police Role in Developing Community-Wide Solutions*. Washington, DC: Police Executive Research Forum, February 2010, pp.16–18.

Decker, Scott H.; Katz, Charles M.; and Webb, Vincent J. "Understanding the Black Box of Gang Organizations: Implications for Involvement in Violent Drug Sales, and Violent Crime & Delinquency, January 2008, pp.153–172.

Delaney, Tim. *American Street Gangs*. Upper Saddle River, NJ: Pearson Prentice Hall, 2006.

"Domestic 'Meth' Production Rising, Drug Intelligence Center Reports." *Criminal Justice Newsletter*, January 15, 2009, pp.4–5.

Egley, Arlen, Jr.; Howell, James C.; and Moore, John P. "Highlights of the National Youth Gang Survey." Washington, DC: OJJDP Fact Sheet, March 2010. (NCJ 229249)

Esbensen, Finn-Aage. "Evaluating GREAT: A School-Based Gang Prevention Program." *NIJ Journal*, 2004. (NCJ 198604)

Esbensen, Finn-Aage. *Preliminary Short-term Results from the Evaluation of the G.R.E.A.T. Program*. December 2008. Retrieved from http://www.iir.com/nygc/publications/2008-12-esbensen.pdf

Fields, Gary. "White House Czar Calls for End to 'War on Drugs'." *The Wall Street Journal*, May 14, 2009. Retrieved from http://online.wsj.com/article/SB124225891527617397.html

Fine, John Christopher. "Street Gangs on the East Coast." *9-1-1 Magazine*. November/December 2009, pp.16–22.

Gang Violence: The Police Role in Developing Community-Wide Solutions. Washington, DC: Police Executive Research Forum, February 2010.

Griffith, David. "Finding a Cure for a Cancer." *Police*, March 2009a, p.14.

Griffith, David. "Police Readers Say 'Don't Legalize.'" *Police*, June 2009b, p.14.

Griffith, David. "Rethinking D.A.R.E." *Police*, August 2009c, p.8.

Hill, Karl G.; Lui, Christina; and Hawkins, J. David. *Early Precursors of Gang Membership: A Study of Seattle Youth*. Washington, DC: Office of Juvenile Justice and Delinquency Prevention, Juvenile Justice Bulletin, December 2001. (NCJ 190106)

Johnson, Gene. "U.S.–Canada Drug Smugglers Have Easy Access to Aircraft." *PoliceOne.com News*, August 3, 2009. Retrieved from http://www.policeone.com/drug-interdiction-narcotics/articles/1862065-U-S-Canada-drug-smugglers-have-easy-access-to-aircraft/

Johnston, Lloyd D.; O'Malley, Patrick M.; Bachman, Jerald G.; and Schulenberg, John E. *Monitoring the Future*. Bethesda, MD: National Institute on Drug Abuse, 2010.

Kaplan, J. *Heroin*. Washington, DC: National Institute of Justice, Crime File Study Guide. U.S. Department of Justice, no date.

Laine, Russell B. "A Crisis We Must Confront." *The Police Chief*, April 2009, p.6.

Lessons from the Battle over D.A.R.E.: The Complicated Relationship between Research and Practice. Washington, DC: Bureau of Justice Assistance, 2009.

Marizco, Michael. "Border Epidemic?" *Law Enforcement Technology*, February 2009, pp.40–47.

Maxson, Cheryl L.; Hennigan, Karen M.; and Sloane, David C. "It's Getting Crazy Out There: Can a Civil Gang Injunction Change a Community?" *Criminology and Public Policy*, August 2005, pp.577–606.

McGloin, Jean M. *Street Gangs and Interventions: Innovative Problem Solving with Network Analysis*. Washington, DC: Office of Community Oriented Policing Services, no date. (NCJ 211933)

National Drug Threat Assessment 2009. Washington, DC: National Drug Intelligence Center, October 2010. Retrieved from http://www.usdoj.gov/ndic/products.htm

National Gang Threat Assessment 2009. Washington, DC: National Gang Intelligence Center, January 2009. Retrieved from http://www.justice.gov/ndic/pubs32/32146/32146p.pdf

National Youth Gang Survey Analysis 2009. Washington, DC: National Youth Gang Center. Retrieved from http://www.nationalgangcenter.gov/Survey-Analysis

O'Neil, Ann. "Stakes Rise as Drug War Threatens to Cross Border." CNN.com/crime. May 18, 2009. Retrieved from http://www.cnn.com/2009/CRIME/05/18/mexico.us.cartels/

Page, Douglas. "Scanner Yields Instant Meth Presence." *Law Enforcement Technology*, August 2009, pp.46–51.

Petrocelli, Joseph. "Graffiti." *Police*, March 2008, pp.18–19.

Petrocelli, Joseph. "Clandestine Meth Labs" *Police*, January 2009, pp.14–17.

"Racial Justice." New York Civil Liberties Union Web Site, 2010. Retrieved October 25, 2010, from http://www.nyclu.org/issues/racial-justice/stop-and-frisk-practices

Rose, Rebecca M. "Combating Methamphetamine Abuse." Washington, DC: BJA Fact Sheet, October 2009. (FS 000318)

Scoville, Dean. "Chronic Confusion." *Police*, June 2009, pp.53–54.

Stockton, Dale. "A Clear & Present Danger." *Law Officer Magazine*, June 2009, p.8.

Taniguchi, Travis A.; Eengert, George F.; and McCord, Eric S. "Where Size Matters: Agglomeration Economies of Illegal Drug Markets in Philadelphia." *Justice Quarterly*, December 2009, pp.670–694.

Taylor, Terrance J. "The Boulevard Ain't Safe for Your Kid . . . Youth Gang Membership and Violent Victimization." *Journal of Contemporary Criminal Justice*, May 2008, pp.125–136.

Timoney, John E. "Ending the 'War on Drugs': This Will Not Be a Walk in the Park." *Subject to Debate*, May 2009, p.2.

Tita, George, and Ridgeway, Greg. "The Impact of Gang Formation on Local Patterns of Crime."

Journal of Research in Crime and Delinquency, May 2007, pp.208–237.

Walker, Samuel; Spohn, Cassia; and DeLone, Miriam. *The Color of Justice: Race, Ethnicity, and Crime in America*, 4th ed. Belmont, CA: Wadsworth Publishing Company, 2007.

Watkins, Thomas. "Use of Twitter, Facebook Rising among Gang Members." *The Huffington Post*, February 2, 2010. Retrieved from http://www.huffingtonpost.com/2010/02/02/gangs-use-of-twitter-facebook_n_445551.html

Wingfield, Nick, and Scheck, Justin. "Push for Looser Pot Laws Gains Momentum." *The Wall Street Journal*, January 15, 2010. Retrieved from http://online.wsj.com/article/SB10001424052748704381604575005333978437228.html?KEYWORDS=%22push+for+looser+pot+laws%22

Cases Cited

Chicago v. Morales, 527 U.S. 41 (1999)
United States v. Bajakajian, 524 U.S. 321 (1998)
United States v. Ursery, 518 U.S. 267 (1996)

Additional Resources

Following are gang Web sites recommended for additional study:

- *Gangs and Security Threat Group Awareness:* http://www.dc.state.fl.us/pub/gangs/index.html
  This Florida Department of Corrections Web site contains information, photographs and descriptions on a wide variety of gang types, including Chicago- and Los Angeles–based gangs, prison gangs, nation sets and supremacy groups.
- *Gangs or Us:* http://www.gangsorus.com
  This site offers a broad range of information, including a state-by-state listing of all available gang laws, gang identities and behaviors applicable to all areas of the United States as well as links to other sites that provide information to law enforcement, parents and teachers.
- *Southeastern Connecticut Gang Activities Group (SEGAG):* http://www.segag.org
  This coalition of law enforcement and criminal justice agencies from southeastern Connecticut and New England provides information on warning signs that parents and teachers often observe first, along with a large number of resources and other working groups that are part of nationwide efforts to contain gang violence.
- *National Gang Crime Research Center (NGCRC):* http://www.ngcrc.com
  This nonprofit independent agency carries out research on gangs and gang members and disseminates the information through publications and reports.

CHAPTER 10

Terrorism and Homeland Security

Where the stakes are the highest, in the war on terror, we cannot possibly succeed without extraordinary international cooperation. Effective international police actions require the highest degree of intelligence sharing, planning and collaborative enforcement.

—Barack Obama

© Joel Gordon

The September 11, 2001, attack on the World Trade Center in New York. On this fateful Tuesday, the United States became violently aware of its vulnerability to terrorism, as two jetliners full of passengers and fuel were turned into missiles and flown into the Twin Towers. A third plane struck the Pentagon. A fourth crashed in a Pennsylvania field, short of its intended target, because of the heroic efforts of the doomed passengers aboard. Currently, the national threat level in the airline sector remains at orange, or High.

Do You Know . . .

- What most definitions of terrorism include?
- What three elements are common in terrorism?
- What domestic terrorist groups exist in the United States?
- What motivates most terrorist attacks?
- What methods terrorists may use?
- What weapons of mass destruction include?
- What federal office was established as a result of 9/11?
- What the lead federal agencies in combating terrorism are?
- What major act was legislated as a result of 9/11? How it enhances counterterrorism efforts by the United States?
- What the keys to successfully combating terrorism are?
- What local law enforcement responsibilities in homeland security involve?
- What the first line of defense against terrorism is?
- What two concerns are associated with the current "war on terrorism"?
- What dual challenges are facing law enforcement?

Can You Define?

asymmetric warfare
bioterrorism
contagion effect
cyberterrorism
deconfliction
jihad
red teaming
SAR
sleeper cell
terrorism

INTRODUCTION

The "war on drugs" has been a top priority since the 1970s; however, on September 11, 2001 (9/11), as a result of the terrorist attacks on America, this priority changed. The war on drugs, at least for the moment, has taken a backseat to the war on terrorism, as both the FBI and the U.S. Customs Service have made terrorism their top priority: "Terrorism is the most significant national security threat our country faces. The FBI counterterrorism goal is specific and compelling—it must prevent, disrupt and defeat terrorist operations before attacks occur" (*Strategic Plan*, 2004–2009, p.26).

The horrific events of that September day necessarily added a new dimension to American policing. Experience now tells us that the first responders to any future terrorist incidents will most assuredly be local police, fire and rescue personnel. As a result, law enforcement officials must now strategically rethink public security procedures. Completed and attempted terrorist attacks present a significant, difficult challenge for law enforcement: "We must now make sure that our law enforcement agencies and officers are prepared to combat not only criminals but also terrorists. The keys to success in this battle are cooperation, communication, and intelligence sharing" (Carroll, 2010, p.6).

An internal Homeland Security Threat Assessment for 2008 to 2013 reports that terrorism threats will be driven by instability in the Middle East and Africa, quoting Michael Chertoff's year-end address in December 2009: "The threat of terrorism and the threat of extremist ideologies has not abated. This threat has not evaporated, and we can't turn the page on it" ("DHS Forecasts Top Security Threats for the Next Five Years," 2009, p.2).

THE CHAPTER AT A GLANCE

This chapter begins by defining terrorism and explaining the nature of asymmetric warfare. Next, the classification of terrorist acts as either domestic or international is presented, followed by an examination of the various underlying motivations for terrorism. Next is a look at the evolution of terrorism and the methods terrorists use. This is followed by a discussion of the U.S. response to the attacks on September 11, 2001, and the critical role of local law enforcement in the national response to terrorism, including officers' role as first responders and investigators of terrorist acts, as well as a discussion of terrorists as criminals. The chapter then examines two major concerns related to that war: erosion of civil liberties and retaliation against people of Middle Eastern descent. The chapter concludes with a look at the dual challenges facing law enforcement today—crime and homeland security.

TERRORISM DEFINED

Terrorism is nothing new and has existed since the beginning of recorded history. Nonetheless, it can be difficult to define:

> Terrorism has been described variously as both a tactic and strategy; a crime and a holy duty; a justified reaction to oppression and an inexcusable abomination. Obviously, a lot depends on whose point of view is being represented. . . .
>
> There are three perspectives of terrorism: the terrorist's, the victim's, and the general public's. The phrase "one man's terrorist is another man's freedom fighter" is a view terrorists themselves would accept. Terrorists do not see themselves as evil. They believe they are legitimate combatants, fighting for what they believe in, by whatever means possible. A victim of a terrorist act sees the terrorist as a criminal with no regard for human life. The general public's view is the most unstable. The terrorists take great pains to foster a "Robin Hood" image in hope of swaying the general public's point of view toward their cause. This sympathetic view of terrorism has become an integral part of their psychological warfare and needs to be countered vigorously ("What Is Terrorism?," n.d.).

Even within the U.S. government, agencies having different functions in the battle against terrorism use different definitions, with no single definition universally accepted. The Terrorism Research Center defines **terrorism** as "the use of force or violence against persons or property in violation of the criminal laws of the United States for purposes of intimidation, coercion or ransom." This is similar to definition used by the FBI, which is stated in the *Code of Federal Regulations*: "Terrorism is the unlawful use of force or violence against persons or property to intimidate or coerce a government, the civilian population, or any segment thereof, in furtherance of political or social objectives" (28 C.F.R. Section 0.85, p.iii).

terrorism
"The use of force or violence against persons or property in violation of the criminal laws of the United States for purposes of intimidation, coercion or ransom."

Most definitions of *terrorism* include the systematic use of physical violence, either actual or threatened, against noncombatants to create a climate of fear and cause some religious, political or social change.

The U.S. Code Title 22 defines *terrorism* as the "premeditated, politically motivated violence perpetrated against non-combatant targets by subnational groups or clandestine agents, usually intended to influence an audience."

Three elements of terrorism are (1) it is criminal in nature, (2) targets are typically symbolic and (3) the terrorist actions are always aggressive and often violent.

A fourth characteristic of terrorism is that it is often an effective tactic for the weaker side in a conflict against a much more powerful adversary, giving terrorism a distinct asymmetric slant.

ASYMMETRIC WARFARE

"Desert Storm in 1991 was the last conventional war fought by the United States when it pushed Iraqi forces out of Kuwait," says Young (2008). He cites defense analyst Brannon as noting, "Despite lessons from Vietnam and elsewhere, our military has been almost singularly obsessed across-the-board with fighting another conventional military that would line up on the battlefield and face us and fight that way." But things have changed.

The Terrorism Research Center notes that the September 11 terrorist attacks marked "the precipitating moment of a new kind of war that will define a new century. This war will be fought in shadows, and the adversary will continue to target the innocent and defenseless." In Iraq, Afghanistan and other trouble spots around the globe, "the U.S. military has been confronted by guerrilla—so called 'asymmetrical'—warfare. Instead of confronting regular armies, American troops now typically face insurgents and terrorists who fight with whatever they have" (Young, 2008).

asymmetric warfare

Conflict in which a much weaker opponent takes on a stronger opponent by refusing to confront the stronger opponent head on.

Asymmetric warfare is described as "leveraging inferior tactical or operational strength against the vulnerabilities of a superior opponent to achieve disproportionate effect with the aim of undermining the opponent's will in order to achieve the asymmetric actor's strategic objectives" (McKenzie, 2001). In this new kind of warfare, a weaker group strikes at a superior group not by attacking head on but rather by attacking areas where the stronger adversary least expects to be hit, causing great psychological shock. Asymmetric warfare gives power to the powerless and destroys the stronger adversary's ability to use its conventional weapons. Because of the secretive nature and small size of terrorist organizations, they often offer opponents no clear organization to defend against or to deter ("What Is Terrorism?"). Asymmetric warfare often involves the use of **sleeper cells**, groups of individuals designed to "sleep" or stay hidden until they are called to action.

sleeper cell

A group of terrorists who blend into a community.

Asymmetric conflict confers coercive power with many of the advantages of military force at a fraction of the cost. A prime example was the use by al Qaeda terrorists of box cutters to convert airplanes into weapons of mass destruction, costing billions of dollars of losses to the U.S. economy and tremendous loss of life—all at an estimated cost to the terrorists of $500,000.

CLASSIFICATION OF TERRORIST ACTS

The FBI categorizes terrorism in the United States as either international or domestic terrorism.

International Terrorism

International terrorism is foreign-based or directed by countries or groups outside the United States against the United States. The FBI divides international terrorism into three categories. The first threat is foreign state sponsors of international terrorism using terrorism as a tool of foreign policy, for example, Iraq, Libya and Afghanistan. The second threat is formalized terrorist groups, such as Lebanese Hezballah, Egyptian Al-Gam'a Al-Islamiyya, Palestinian HAMAS and Osama bin Laden's al Qaeda. The third threat comes from loosely affiliated international radical extremists who have a variety of identities and travel freely in the United States, unknown to law enforcement or the government.

According to the Proteus Trend Series, *55 Trends Now Shaping the Future of Terrorism* (Cetron and Davies, 2008, pp.15–16), "Militant Islam continues to spread and gain power:

- Muslim lands face severe problems with religious extremists dedicated to advancing their political, social and doctrinal views by any means necessary.
- According to the American intelligence community, al Qaeda was more powerful in 2007 than it had been before the so-called 'war on terror' began—more dangerous even than it had been when it planned the attacks of September 11, 2001.
- American support for Israel has also made the United States a target for Muslim hatred."

For at least the next two decades, Western society, especially the United States, must expect more and more violent acts of terrorism: "Europe faces a significant homegrown Muslim extremist movement, and the United States may do so in the near future, due largely to waves of immigration since the 1980s which have made Islam the fastest-growing religion in both regions. This must be taken seriously since, for the first time, a Muslim country, Pakistan, has nuclear weapons" (Cetron and Davies, 2008, p.16).

On February 23, 1998, Osama bin Laden declared **jihad**, a holy war, on the United States, calling on every Muslim to comply with God's order to kill Americans and having publicly stated that his global terrorist groups intend to kill four million Americans, including one million children. Osama bin Laden was put on the FBI's 10 Most Wanted List in connection with the August 7, 1998 bombings of U.S. embassies in Dar Es Salaam, Tanzania; and Nairobi, Kenya:

jihad
A holy war.

> The FBI's greatest concern currently is the threat from al-Qaeda attack cells, which retain the ability to inflict serious harm with little or no warning. These cells maintain strict operational and communications security with militant Islamic groups and mosques in the United States to avoid drawing attention to themselves. Al-Qaeda

> will continue efforts to acquire and develop various WMD (biological, chemical, radiological and nuclear) and will continue to favor sensational attacks. . . .
>
> HAMAS and Hizballah also have an extensive presence in the United States, and have the ability to carry out attacks domestically. Up until 9/11, Hizballah had killed more Americans than any other terrorist organization.
>
> The events of 9/11 shifted the FBI's focus to international terrorist groups operating inside the United States, but not to the exclusion of domestic groups that threaten the safety of our citizens. The threat of domestic terrorists launching large-scale attacks to inflict mass casualties is low compared to that of international terrorist groups, due, in part, to longstanding efforts to disrupt and dismantle these groups. The most significant threat over the next five years will continue to be the "lone wolf" terrorist (Cetron and Davis, 2008, pp.26–27).

One "lone wolf" incident occurred on Christmas Eve 2009, when Umar Farouk Abdulmultallab, a Nigerian national living in the United Kingdom, boarded a U.S. airliner in Amsterdam and tried to blow it up as it landed in Detroit. Abdulmultallab claimed connections with al Qaeda's affiliates in Yemen, who have in turn claimed credit for his attack:

> Al-Qaida's shocking ambitious strategy to exhort, inspire, train and dispatch terrorists from around the world to wage war on and in the United States would blur the distinction between the frontline and the home front. It would end the idea of war as the work of a single hostile nation or alliance of nations. It would finish the notion that armies were made up mainly of soldiers from one nation under the control of one, or any, government. Al-Qaida's terrorist operatives would comprise many nationalities. They would come at the United States from all directions. Some would be homegrown (Jenkins, 2009).

Homegrown Terrorists

Straw (2010a, p.47) points out, "In the years following 9/11, it was first thought that radical jihad was unlikely to find fertile ground in the United States, where the Muslim population is among the most integrated and assimilated in the world. But the more recent events are driving home the message that it only takes a few homegrown jihadis to create a serious threat." He also quotes Homeland Security Secretary Janet Napolitano's public acknowledgment: "Home-based terrorism is here. And, like violent extremism abroad, it will be part of the threat picture that we must now confront" (Straw, 2010a, p.47).

There has been notice of a trend in transnational Islamist terrorism, with growing domestic radicalization appearing in the United Kingdom, France, Germany, Australia and other countries, and security forces in all these countries routinely emphasize that the greatest threat they face is "homegrown terrorism" (Chalk, 2010). This trend appears to be continuing in the United States. Recent examples of alleged homegrown terrorists include Nidal Malik Hasan, the Virginia-born Army major who reportedly yelled "Allahu Akbar," an Islamic exclamation meaning "Allah is the Greatest," as he went on a murderous shooting rampage at Ft. Hood, Texas, which took the lives of 13 Americans and injured another 31 (French, 2009). Another example is naturalized U.S. citizen of Pakistani descent,

Faisal Shahzad, accused of the failed Times Square bombing attempt in May 2010. The following notable events occurred in 2009 and signal the rising threat of homegrown Muslim extremism in the United States (Rotella, 2009):

- There were major arrests of Americans accused of plotting with al Qaeda and its allies, including an Afghan American charged in a New York bomb plot described as the most serious threat in this country since the 9/11 attacks.
- Authorities tracked other extremism suspects joining foresight networks, including Somali Americans going to the battlegrounds of their ancestral homeland and an Albanian American from Brooklyn who was arrested in Kosovo.
- The FBI rounded up homegrown terrorism suspects in Dallas, Texas; Detroit, Michigan; and Raleigh, North Carolina, saying it had broken up plots targeting a synagogue, government buildings and military facilities.

Although these "homegrown terrorists" often lack the training and resources to attack high-profile, well-protected facilities, they are perhaps the most difficult to detect:

> First, they usually have no prior attachment to extremism and, hence, typically exist below the "radar" screen of law enforcement and intelligence agencies. This makes them extremely difficult to track and preempt. Second, they are unpredictable because their actions are neither defined nor bounded by the organizational constraints that are normally imposed on members of more structured terrorist groups.
>
> Third, while they lack the ability to hit so-called "hard" targets decisively, they are perfectly able to attack the plethora of "soft" venues that abound, like shopping malls, cinemas, mass surface transportation, restaurants and office complexes.
>
> Fourth, in the cases of religious "converts," the desire to contemplate extreme violence is likely to be especially strong as this may well be viewed as the most visible way of demonstrating and validating their Islamist credentials. Finally, they can greatly inflate the perceived threat of militant extremism because their actions are specifically directed against places central to day-to-day lives of ordinary citizens (Chalk, 2010).

In addition to detecting these "international" terrorists who are within the United States, law enforcement is tasked with the challenges presented by domestic terrorists, a challenge since the formation of the Ku Klux Klan.

Domestic Terrorism

The FBI defines *domestic terrorism* as "activities that involve acts dangerous to human life that are a violation of the criminal laws of the United States or of any state; appear to be intended to intimidate or coerce a civilian population; to influence the policy of a government by mass destruction, assassination, or kidnapping; and occur primarily within the territorial jurisdiction of the United States" [18 U.S.C. § 2331 (5) (p.iv)]. However, it expanded its definition of domestic terrorism in an article, "Domestic Terrorism in the Post-9/11 Era," (2009) stating,

"The threat of domestic terror—Americans attacking Americans based on U.S.-based extremist ideologies—is alive and well. Today's domestic terror threats run the gamut from hate-filled White supremacists . . . to highly destructive ecoterrorists . . . to violence-prone anti-government extremists. . . to radical separatist groups."

Domestic terrorist groups include White supremacists, Black supremacists, militia groups, other right-wing extremists, left-wing extremists, pro-life extremists, animal rights activists and environmental extremists.

According to the FBI ("Domestic Terrorism in the Post-9/11 Era," 2009), "As with all forms of extremism, preventing homegrown attacks before they are hatched is our overriding goal. It's an especially tall order given the civil liberties we all enjoy as American citizens, including the right to free speech. Hate and anger are not crimes; neither are hard-line and poisonous ideologies. It's only when actions by groups or individuals cross the line into threats, the actual use of force of violence, or other law-breaking activities that we can investigate."

Domestic terrorist groups have been in the news for decades. However, one particular type of group—militia groups—has been gaining national attention because their efforts to regroup and strengthen have led some experts to fear their numbers could grow rapidly (Sullivan, 2009). The Southern Poverty Law Center (SPLC), an organization that tracks such trends, reports, "The number of extremist groups in the United States exploded in 2009 as militias and other groups steeped in wild, antigovernment conspiracy theories exploited populist anger across the country and infiltrated the mainstream" ("New SPLC Report," 2010). Potok (2010, p.137) states, "The anger seething across the American political landscape—over racial changes in the population, soaring public debt and the terrible economy, the bailouts of bankers and other elites, and an array of initiatives—goes beyond the radical right. . . . Sixty-one percent of Americans believe the country is in decline according to a recent NBC News/Wall Street Journal poll. . . . Just a quarter think the government can be trusted . . . . The signs of growing radicalization are everywhere."

There has been tremendous growth in the number of anti-immigrant vigilante groups, with approximately 136 new groups formed during 2009, an increase of nearly 80 percent (Potok, 2010). Furthermore, "So-called 'Patriot' groups—militias and other organizations that see the federal government as part of a plot to impose 'one-world government' on liberty-loving Americans—came roaring back after years out of the limelight" (Potok, 2010).

In 2009 a Midwest Christian militia, the Hutaree, preparing for the Antichrist war, were conspiring to kill a police officer and then attack the ensuing funeral using homemade bombs, in the hopes of killing more law enforcement personnel. The Michigan-based group planned to use the attack on police as a catalyst for a larger uprising against the government ("Christian Militia Charged with Police-Killing Plot," 2010). However, "The militia group's poor operational security mitigated the threat they posed" (Burton and West, 2010). Authorities had been gathering information about the Hutarees for more than a year, as the militia's Web site offered photos of members, dates of scheduled meetings and postings by members and visitors. This "spectacular" failure to maintain isolation by the militia allowed authorities to penetrate its circle and maintain surveillance quite readily. When the Hutarees identified police officers as their target, they became an easy target for federal law enforcement agencies.

A joint anti-terrorism task force consisting of the FBI, the U.S. Bureau of Alcohol, Tobacco, Firearms and Explosives (ATF), and state and local police raided Hutarees groups from March 27 to March 29, making nine arrests, mainly in southeastern Michigan, near the Ohio border (Burton and West, 2010). On March 29, 2010, these nine individuals were indicted. Their cases are pending as this text goes to press.

The Lone Offender

Similar to international terrorism, domestic terrorism is often committed by a "lone wolf" offender. The FBI ("Domestic Terrorism," 2009) cautions, "One particularly insidious concern that touches all forms of domestic extremisms is the lone offender—a single individual driven to hateful attacks based on a particular set of beliefs without a larger group's knowledge or support. In some cases, these lone offenders may have tried to join a group but were kicked out for being too radical or simply left the group because they felt it wasn't extreme or violent enough. We believe most domestic attacks are carried out by lone offenders to promote their own grievances and agendas."

The lengthy bombing spree of the Unabomber as well as the pipe bomb explosions in Centennial Olympic Park during the 1996 Summer Olympic Games highlight the threat of the lone bomber with a deep hatred of something or someone. Motivations behind terrorism vary considerably.

MOTIVATIONS FOR TERRORISM

According to the Terrorist Research Center ("Goals and Motivations of Terrorists," n.d.), a terrorist group seeks to:

- Produce widespread fear.
- Obtain worldwide, national, or local recognition for its cause by attracting the attention of the media.
- Harass, weaken, or embarrass government security forces so that the government overreacts and appears repressive.
- Steal or extort money and equipment, especially weapons and ammunition vital to the operation of the group.
- Destroy facilities or disrupt lines of communication to create doubt that the government can provide for and protect its citizens.
- Discourage foreign investments, tourism, or assistance programs that can affect the target country's economy and support of the government in power.
- Influence government decisions, legislation, or other critical decisions.
- Free prisoners.
- Satisfy vengeance.
- Turn the tide in a guerrilla war by forcing government security forces to concentrate their efforts in urban areas. This allows the terrorist group to establish itself among the local populace in rural areas.

Most terrorist acts result from dissatisfaction with a religious, political or social system or policy and frustration resulting from an inability to change it through acceptable, nonviolent means.

Religious motives are seen in Islamic extremism. Political motives include such elements as the Red Army Faction. Social motives are seen in single-issue groups such as antiabortion groups, animal rights groups and environmentalists.

Ecoterrorism is typically perpetrated by domestic groups consisting of environmental extremists who resort to violence to meet their objectives. Examples include break-ins and release of animals in research facilities, and violent protesting. Narco-terrorism includes both international and domestic groups that exploit drug trafficking to fund their terrorist objectives. Narco-terrorism also includes violence used by drug traffickers against government agencies to influence and stop the government's efforts in the war on drugs.

THE EVOLUTION OF TERRORIST IDEOLOGY

The ideological development of terrorism may go through a four-stage process as illustrated in Figure 10.1. This ideological transformation, referred to as radicalization, can occur through several mechanisms, such as by having direct contact with terrorists either within the United States or abroad, through contact with other radicals via the Internet, or by undergoing a process of self-radicalization (Sullivan and Barrett, 2010).

One challenge to law enforcement is understanding the process that leads a person from being merely sympathetic to extremist rhetoric to one who is willing to engage in suicide bombing. Although many people never make that leap, some are transformed in a matter of months (Sullivan and Barrett). Consider the case of Colleen LaRose, the Pennsylvania woman who allegedly met violent jihadists

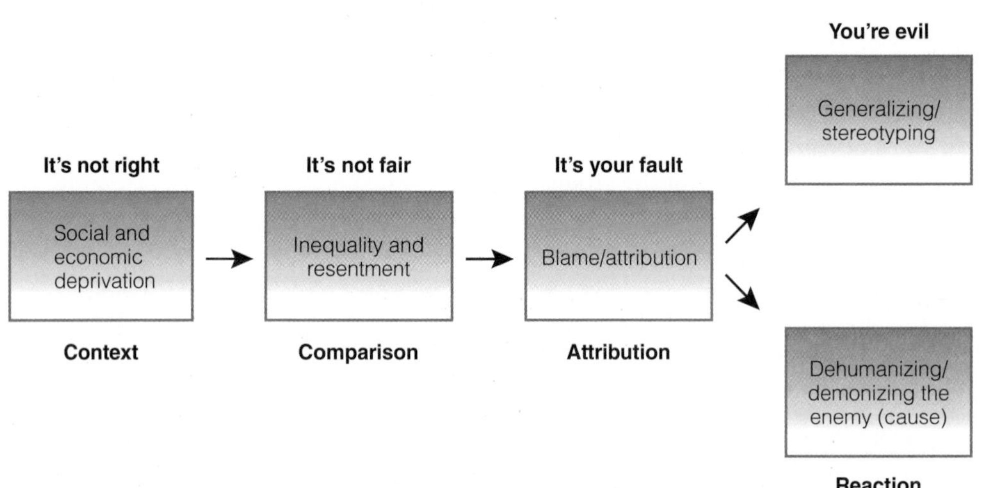

FIGURE 10.1 The Process of Ideological Development

SOURCE: Randy Borum. "Understanding the Terrorist Mind-Set." *FBI Law Enforcement Bulletin*, July 2003, p.9.

online under the name "Jihad Jane" and became radicalized in only a few months. A June 2008 YouTube video showed the blond, green-eyed Muslim convert saying she was "desperate to do something somehow to help" ease the suffering of Muslims (Sullivan and Barrett). Options for the "something" abound.

METHODS USED BY TERRORISTS

Terrorists may use arson, explosives and bombs; weapons of mass destruction (biological, chemical or nuclear agents); and technology; as well as kidnapping, hostage-taking and murder.

Although bombing has historically been the most common terrorist method used, armed attacks have occurred more frequently in recent years, as illustrated in Figure 10.2.

Arson, Explosives and Bombs

Of the previously listed methods, some experts suggest that incendiary devices and explosives are most likely to be used because they are inexpensive and easy to make. Noting the devastation caused by improvised explosive devices (IEDs) in Iraq, Afghanistan and elsewhere, Corderre and Register (2009, p.38) contend, "By far the most dangerous emerging threat to our homeland defense is the criminal

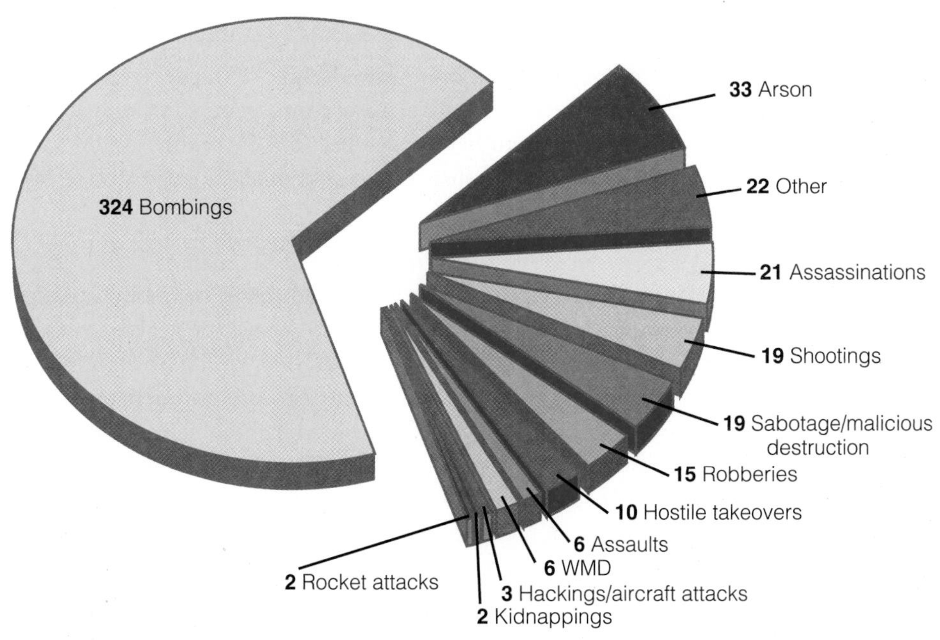

• Figure includes the events of September 2001, which are counted as one terrorist incident.

FIGURE 10.2 Terrorism by Method, 2008

SOURCE: *2008 Report on Terrorism*. Washington, DC: National Counterterrorism Center, April 30, 2009, p.28.

and terrorist use of [IEDs]. Cheap, lethal, and low-tech, the IED has been the weapon of choice for foreign terrorists since the first World Trade Center attack and for domestic terrorists since the Oklahoma City bombing in 1995. From Madrid to London, Bali to Mumbai, and Baghdad to Kabul, the IED is a global tactical and strategic threat to Americans and our allies." During the first six months of 2009, the average number of monthly IED events outside of Iraq and Afghanistan was 305 (Corderre and Register, 2009, p.41).

Directions for making pipe bombs and other incendiary devices can be found on the Internet. From 1978 to 1996 Theodore Kaczynski terrorized the country as the Unabomber, through a string of 16 mail bombings that killed three people, apparently in protest against technology. Ramzi Ahmed Yousef, found guilty of masterminding the first World Trade Center bombing in 1993, declared that he was proud to be a terrorist and that terrorism was the only viable response to what he saw as a Jewish lobby in Washington. The car bomb used to shatter the Alfred P. Murrah Federal Building in 1995 was Timothy McVeigh's way to protest the government and the raid on the Branch Davidians at Waco. In 2002 Lucas Helder terrorized the Midwest with 18 pipe bombs placed in mailboxes across five states, leaving antigovernment letters with the bombs. Six exploded, injuring four letter carriers and two residents. And the most horrific act of terrorism against the United States occurred on September 11, 2001, when two airplanes were used as missiles to explode the World Trade Center twin towers, another plane was used as a missile to attack the Pentagon, and a fourth plane crashed in a Pennsylvania field before it could reach its intended target.

Suspicious Packages Although it is not uncommon for a law enforcement officer to be dispatched to a suspicious package, unattended bag or other such items, these calls are potentially lethal. If an officer suspects that the call involves an IED, the officer should (1) move to an area not in direct line of sight of the device, (2) move away from glass and parked vehicles, (3) move away from secondary hazards such as electricity and gas, (4) move behind hard cover and (5) set cordons at 100 yards for items carried by hand, 200 yards for suspect cars and small vans and 400 to 800 yards for suspect large vehicles.

Suicide Bombers Potential suicide terrorists may come from different backgrounds and different age groups and may be male or female, educated or uneducated, an upstanding citizen or a deviant. Most suicide terrorists believe the act makes them martyrs and ensures them a place in their version of heaven. Their families are usually held in reverence and taken care of financially. Suicide bombers try to kill as many people as possible and often have a well-oiled machine behind them that relies on a recruitment procedure using the values of the Muslim community and a religious justification.

Suicide bombers can be extremely difficult, if not impossible, to thwart, given their determination to serve their cause and the fact that many have already endured significant loss in their lives. Consider the Black Widow terrorists, also known as Shahidka, who are Islamic Chechen female suicide bombers, many of whom have been widowed by Russian forces in Chechnya.

A consideration in thwarting suicide bombers is the use of K-9s. Dogs can detect 19,000 types of explosives, making them more effective at catching potential suicide bombers than are security cameras or random suspect searches.

Weapons of Mass Destruction (WMD)

Law enforcement agencies use the term *CBR* as shorthand for chemical agents (C), biological agents (B) and radiation exposure (R) from nuclear weapons.

Weapons of mass destruction include biological, chemical and nuclear agents.

Nuclear, biological and chemical agents are also referred to as NBC agents. Of the three, chemical devices are most likely to be used because the raw materials are easy to get and easy to use; bioterrorism is the next most likely terrorist act to occur, although these two methods fall a distant second and third place to the use of explosives. Figure 10.3 presents the most likely to least likely terrorist threats; Figure 10.4 illustrates the level of impact by the weapon used.

Biological Agents **Bioterrorism** involves such biological WMD as anthrax, botulism, smallpox, salmonella, natural poisons and viruses. The Central Intelligence Agency (CIA) reports that at least 10 countries are believed to possess or to be conducting research on biological agents for use as WMDs.

bioterrorism
Involves such biological weapons of mass destruction (WMDs) as anthrax, botulism and smallpox to cause fear in a population.

In October 2001 a photo editor in Florida died from inhalation of anthrax. Several weeks later, anthrax-laced letters were delivered to several major media networks and numerous government offices around Washington, DC. Environmental sampling also indicated massive amounts of anthrax spores at several post offices and mailroom facilities. In all, 5 Americans died and 17 more became seriously ill in what has been, to date, the worst biological attack in U.S. history. The FBI's investigation of the terrorism—code-named Amerithrax—was one of the largest, most complex criminal investigations in the history of law enforcement. When a major breakthrough in the case was announced in August 2008, the prime suspect, Dr. Bruce Ivins, took his own life before charges could be filed against him. The case was officially closed on February 19, 2010.

Especially susceptible to bioterrorism are the nation's food and water supply. *Agroterrorism* refers to attacks on our nation's "soft" agricultural heartland and

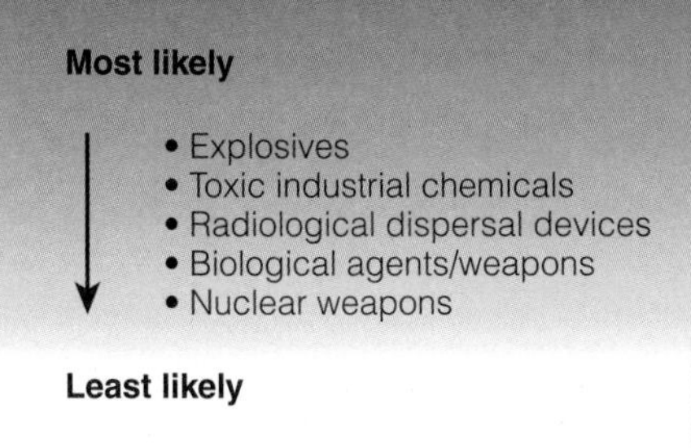

FIGURE 10.3 Terrorist Threats from Most Likely to Least Likely

SOURCE: Melissa Reuland and Heather J. Davis. *Protecting Your Community from Terrorism: Strategies for Local Law Enforcement, Volume 3: Preparing for and Responding to Bioterrorism.* Washington, DC: Community Oriented Policing Services Office and the Police Executive Research Forum, September 2004, p.7. Reprinted by permission of the Police Executive Research Forum.

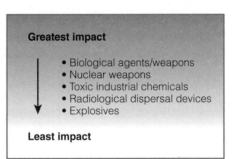

Greatest impact

- Biological agents/weapons
- Nuclear weapons
- Toxic industrial chemicals
- Radiological dispersal devices
- Explosives

Least impact

FIGURE 10.4 Level of Impact by Weapon Used

SOURCE: Melissa Reuland and Heather J. Davis. *Protecting Your Community from Terrorism: Strategies for Local Law Enforcement, Volume 3: Preparing for and Responding to Bioterrorism.* Washington, DC: Community Oriented Policing Services Office and the Police Executive Research Forum, September 2004, p.8. Reprinted by permission of the Police Executive Research Forum.

tainting of the nation's food supply. Some experts, however, suggest it is unlikely terrorists would target our water supply, with two options of "poisoning the well": physically damaging the plant or introducing an agent into the water stream. Although the first option is very possible given the antiquated condition of most of America's government-owned utilities, such an action would simply result in a large-scale investigation while affected citizens used bottled water or other sources of clean water. The second option is poisoning the water system; however, the odds of poisoning a small segment of a community, much less an entire system, is slim.

Chemical Agents The Aum Shinrikyo attack in the Tokyo subway in 1995 focused the security industry's efforts on detecting and mitigating chemical agent threats. That incident confirmed what those in this industry had long feared. A non-state entity could manufacture a viable chemical agent and deliver it in a public location. Unfortunately, anyone with access to the Internet can obtain the chemical formula for sarin in less than 40 minutes through a Web search and can produce it inexpensively.

Law enforcement officers should be aware of toxic industrial chemicals and military weapon agents such as hydrogen cyanide, arsine, chlorine and ammonia, which can all be easily obtained.

Nuclear Agents Making a radiological dispersal device (RDD), or dirty bomb, is not hard. The U.S. Nuclear Regulatory Commission (NRC) reports that approximately 375 devices of all kinds containing radioactive material are reported lost or stolen each year.

A new technology involves detectors that can decipher between deadly radiation in nuclear weapons and harmless radiation carried by patients involved in recent medical procedures. The technology is part of the $30 million Securing the Cities Initiation, a partnership between the DHS and local law enforcement. The goal is to ban nuclear weapons from New York by creating a 50-mile protective perimeter.

A WMD Team Local law enforcement agencies should consider selecting and training officers to form a WMD team. The officers' time is not devoted solely to the unit, but they are ready if a need for their skills arises. Adequate personal protective equipment (PPE) for investigators involved in bioterrorism incidents is vitally important, and a well-implemented PPE program protects the protectors and results in no "blue canaries."[1]

Technological Terrorism

Modern societies are susceptible to two methods of technological terror. The first is using weapons of mass destruction or converting an industrial site–such as a chemical plant—into a massively lethal instrument through sabotage. The other method is to attack a source that supplies technology or energy. Either type of attack could be catastrophic. Ironically, the U.S. success with technology makes the

---

[1]A reference to the practice of coal miners releasing a canary into mine shafts to see if the shafts are safe. If the canary dies, more ventilation is needed. Police officers who walk unwittingly into hazardous situations and die are sometimes referred to as *blue canaries*.

country vulnerable to attacks on technology and by technology. If a terrorist group could shut off U.S. energy, it could close down major portions of the economy. One crucial form of technologic terrorism is **cyberterrorism**, defined by the FBI as "terrorism that initiates, or threatens to initiate, the exploitation of or attack on computerized information systems." Cyberterrorism can have critical impact on our infrastructure, economy and national security.

cyberterrorism

"Terrorism that initiates, or threatens to initiate, the exploitation of or attack on computerized information systems."

Mazzetti (2010) reports that Dennis Blair, director of national intelligence, began his annual threat testimony before Congress by stressing the growing risk of a crippling attack on telecommunications and other computer networks, as an increasingly sophisticated group of enemies had "severely threatened" the country's sometimes fragile information infrastructure, with malicious and extraordinarily sophisticated cyber activity occurring on an unprecedented scale. Blair urged lawmakers to see the surge in cyber attacks, including the penetration of Google's servers from inside China, as a "wake-up call" for those who dismissed the threat of computer warfare.

Dewar (2010, p.35) cautions, "Critical infrastructure is a 'good' target for cyber terrorists because most sectors are relatively exposed, vast, interconnected, and unprotected." He explains that centers of electronic information typically have two targets: data systems and control systems, both of which police departments use. A cyber attack will do one or more of the following to the target systems: steal data, disrupt or damage data, deny access to data or access to computers, spread disinformation or shut down control systems. Any such actions could be disastrous for an agency.

Straw (2010b, p.24) reports, "Recent months have seen news about the global cyber threat environment go from bad to worse." He reports on a study by a tech security firm, McAfee, working with the Center for Strategic and International Studies, which surveyed IT professions from 600 companies in 24 countries. They found that attacks are growing not only in severity but also in volume, and to a shocking degree. At the same time already inadequate security efforts have been compromised by economic recession and resulting funding cuts.

Data may be stolen, and it may be corrupted, with some in the industry likening these attacks to "death by a thousand cuts": "We're bleeding data, intellectual property, information and source code, bit by bit" (Mueller, 2010). Stolen information can be used to exploit finances or to disrupt large financial, medical and government institutions.

Cyber attacks also threaten our national security, as hackers actively target our government networks, with the information bought and sold by anyone, anywhere in the world (Mueller, 2010). Cyber attacks are usually subtle and may go unnoticed for a long time, allowing the devastation to grow.

Kidnappings and Hostage-Takings

Much more open methods used by terrorists are kidnappings and hostage-takings. The Terrorist Research Center explains how kidnapping and hostage-taking are used by terrorists to establish a bargaining position and elicit publicity: "Kidnapping is one of the most difficult acts for a terrorist group to accomplish, but, if . . . successful, it can gain terrorists money, release of jailed comrades, and publicity for an extended period. [Unlike kidnapping,] hostage-taking involves the seizure of a facility or location and the taking of hostages . . . [to provoke] a confrontation with authorities. It forces authorities to either make dramatic decisions or to comply with the terrorist's demands. It is overt and designed to attract and hold media attention. The terrorists' intended target is the audience affected by the hostage's confinement, not the hostage" ("Types of Terrorist Incidents," n.d.).

THE U.S. RESPONSE TO 9/11—DETECT, PREPARE, PREVENT, PROTECT, RESPOND AND RECOVER

Although the methods used by terrorists have not changed much over the years, the U.S. response to the threat of terrorism has changed drastically since the 9/11 attacks. The *Federal Bureau of Investigation Strategic Plan 2004–2009* (p.1) declares, "The events of September 11th have forever changed our nation and the FBI. Since that terrible day, the FBI's overriding priority has been protecting America by preventing further attacks." In their list of priorities, that is number one (p.9). Priority 9 is to support federal, state, local and international partners: "To achieve its mission, the FBI must strengthen three inextricably linked core functions: intelligence, investigations and partnerships . . . Partnerships are essential if the FBI is to effectively address evolving threats that are too complex or multi-jurisdictional for one agency to handle alone. To achieve its vital mission, the FBI is dependent upon the goodwill, cooperation and expertise of our local, state, federal and international partners" (p.19).

The Department of Homeland Security

On October 8, 2001, President George W. Bush signed Executive Order 13228 establishing the Department of Homeland Security (DHS).

As a result of 9/11 the Department of Homeland Security was established, reorganizing the departments of the federal government.

The mission of the DHS is "to develop and coordinate the implementation of a comprehensive national strategy to secure the United States from terrorist threats or attacks." The organization of the DHS is shown in Figure 10.5.

At the federal level, the FBI is the lead agency for responding to acts of domestic terrorism. The Federal Emergency Management Agency (FEMA) is the lead agency for consequence management (after an attack). The Department of Homeland Security (DHS) serves in a broad capacity, facilitating collaboration between local and federal law enforcement to develop a national strategy to detect, prepare for, prevent, protect against, respond to and recover from terrorist attacks within the United States.

The DHS has outlined a six-point agenda:

1. Increase overall preparedness, particularly for catastrophic events.
2. Create better transportation security systems to move people and cargo more securely and efficiently.

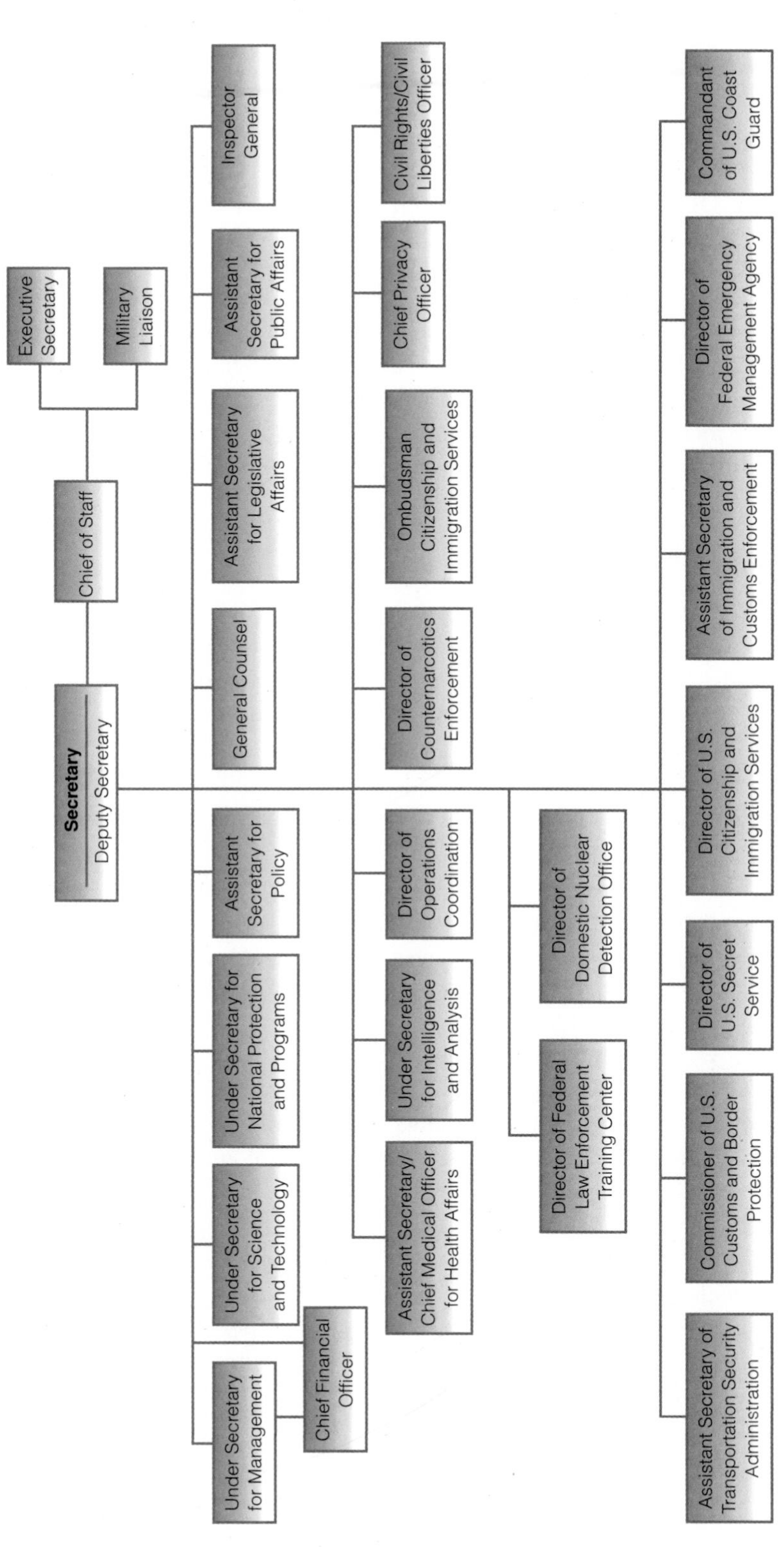

FIGURE 10.5 Organizational Chart for the Department of Homeland Security

SOURCE: Department of Homeland Security, www.dhs.gov.

3. Strengthen border security and interior enforcement and reform immigration processes.
4. Enhance information sharing with our partners.
5. Improve DHS financial management, human resource development, procurement and information technology.
6. Realign the DHS organization to maximize mission performance.

Each initiative is discussed in this chapter.

The DHS also has a program called the Commercial Equipment Direct Assistance Program (CEDAP) that awards free equipment to local police departments. Such equipment can be used for communications interoperability, information sharing and chemical detection as well as sensor devices and personal protective equipment. The focus is on a regional response.

Another effort to enhance national security was passage of the USA PATRIOT Act.

The USA PATRIOT Act

On October 26, 2001, President Bush signed into law the Uniting and Strengthening America by Providing Appropriate Tools Required to Intercept and Obstruct Terrorism (USA PATRIOT) Act, giving police unprecedented ability to search, seize, detain or eavesdrop in their pursuit of possible terrorists.

The USA PATRIOT Act significantly improves the nation's counterterrorism efforts by

- Allowing investigators to use the tools already available to investigate organized crime and drug trafficking.
- Facilitating information sharing and cooperation among government agencies so they can better "connect the dots."
- Updating the law to reflect new technologies and new threats.
- Increasing the penalties for those who commit or support terrorist crimes.

The USA PATRIOT Act also included money laundering provisions and set strong penalties for anyone who harbors or finances terrorists. In addition, the PATRIOT Act established new punishments for possessing biological weapons and made it a federal crime to commit an act of terrorism against a mass transit system.

After nearly a yearlong debate pitting Democrats against Republicans and Republicans against the White House, Congress voted to renew the USA PATRIOT Act. The Senate cleared the measure by a vote of 90–10, the House by a vote of 280–13. The renewed act included provisions to strengthen port security and made it a criminal offense to impede law enforcements' efforts to board vessels.

Increased Border Security

Enhancing security at our nation's borders is a fundamental step in keeping our citizenry safe, and the immigration issues has become an increasingly hot topic as border states, namely Arizona, grapple with rising numbers of illegal immigrants. The Department of Homeland Security's U.S. Visitor and Immigrant Status

Indicator Technology (US-VISIT) program seeks to enhance the security of our citizens and visitors, facilitate legitimate travel and trade and ensure the integrity of our immigration system The program requires visitors to submit to inkless finger scans and digital photographs, allowing Customs and Border Protection officers to determine whether the person applying for entry is the same one who was issued a visa by the State Department. Biometric and biographic data is checked against watch lists of suspected foreign terrorists and databases of sexual predators, criminals wanted by the FBI and people previously deported. The program was implemented in January 2004.

Border security has been further strengthened under the Western Hemisphere Travel Initiative (WHTI), an initiative that resulted from the Intelligence Reform and Terrorism Prevention Act of 2004 and requires U.S. and Canadian travelers to present a passport or other document denoting identity and citizenship when entering the United States. WHTI went into effect for air travel in January 2007 and for land and sea travel June 1, 2009 ("Western Hemisphere Travel Initiative," 2009).

The goal of WHTI is to facilitate entry for U.S. citizens and legitimate foreign visitors, while strengthening U.S. border security. Standard documents allow the DHS to quickly and reliably identify a traveler: "The WHTI will greatly simplify the number of documents that immigration officials have to scrutinize. It will also mean that the documents needed to enter the United States will be far harder to counterfeit, alter or obtain by fraud than the documents previously required for entry. This will make it more difficult for criminals, illegal aliens and militants to enter the United States, but it will by no means make it impossible" (Burton, 2009).

The National Incident Management System (NIMS)

Although most emergency situations are handled locally, when there is a major incident help may be needed from other jurisdictions, the state and the federal government. The National Incident Management System (NIMS) was developed in 2004 so responders from different jurisdictions and disciplines can work together better to respond to natural disasters and emergencies, including acts of terrorism. Input was obtained from first responders; tribal officials; cities, counties and townships; territories; states; and the federal government.

Since 2006 the NIMS was reviewed to incorporate best practices and lessons learned from the 2001 terrorist attacks and from the 2005 hurricane season. A wide range of feedback was incorporated, but no major policy changes were made in the core components of NIMS. According to the *National Incident Management System* (2008),

> The *National Incident Management System* (NIMS) provides a systematic, proactive approach to guide departments and agencies at all levels of government, nongovernmental organizations, and the private sector to work seamlessly to prevent, protect against, respond to, recover from, and mitigate the effects of incidents, regardless of cause, size, location, or complexity, in order to reduce the loss of life and property and harm to the environment (p.1). . . .

What NIMS Is:

A comprehensive, nationwide, systematic approach to incident management, including the Incident Command System, Multiagency Coordination Systems, and Public Information.

A set of preparedness concepts and principles for all hazards.

Essential principles for a common operating picture and interoperability of communications and information management.

Standardized resource management procedures that enable coordination among different jurisdictions or organizations.

Scalable, so it may be used for all incidents (from day-to-day to large-scale).

A dynamic system that promotes ongoing management and maintenance.

What NIMS Is NOT:

A response plan.

Only used during large-scale incidents.

A communication plan.

Only applicable to certain emergency management/incident response personnel.

Only the Incident Command System or an organization chart.

A static system (p.6).

Two key principles of NIMS are flexibility and standardization. While providing the flexibility to respond to any emergency, large or small, NIMS also provides the standardization required for interoperability and coordination of personnel and resources. Five core components make up the system: (1) preparedness, (2) communications and information management, (3) resource management, (4) command and management and (5) ongoing management and maintenance (*National Incident Management System*, p.7). NIMS is intended to work in conjunction with the National Response Framework.

The National Response Framework (NRF)

The *National Response Framework* (NRF) provides the "nuts and bolts" for implementing NIMS. This comprehensive, national, all-hazards approach was written for government executives, private-sector business and nongovernmental leaders and emergency management practitioners. The NRF retains the same core components of NIMS and is built around five principles: (1) engaged partnerships; (2) tiered response; (3) scalable, flexible, adaptable operational capabilities; (4) unity of effort through unified command; and (5) readiness to act (*National Response Framework*, 2008). Another initiative to enhance homeland security is the *National Response Plan*.

The National Response Plan

NIMS and NRF outline how to handle disasters, whereas the *National Response Plan* (NRP) defines the federal government's role in responding to domestic emergencies. The NRP assumes that incidents are typically managed best at the lowest possible geographic, organizational or jurisdictional level. However, since large natural and human-caused disasters can overwhelm state and local governments, the federal government must play a large role in disaster response. Each of the preceding initiatives depends upon information sharing and intelligence.

Intelligence Gathering and Sharing

Communication should be the number-one priority in any terrorist-preparedness plan, and it is also number one in collaboration among local, state and federal law enforcement agencies. An extremely valuable resource for investigators is the Regional Information Sharing Systems (RISS) program, which assists state and local agencies by sharing information and intelligence regarding terrorism.

It is not sufficient to simply gather data. It must be analyzed and shared systematically with neighboring law enforcement agencies, different levels of law enforcement (i.e., local, state and federal) and other institutions, such as schools, hospitals, city departments and motor vehicle divisions.

A distinction is made between *information* and *intelligence*, with intelligence broadening to become organized information that has been analyzed, evaluated and distributed to meet the needs of a particular enterprise. The application of such information in efforts to combat terrorism can be visualized as an intelligence cycle (see Figure 10.6). In a threat-driven environment, *intelligence requirements*—identified information needs, or what must be known to safeguard the nation—are what drive investigations. Identified information needs depend on a plan to gather and apply information.

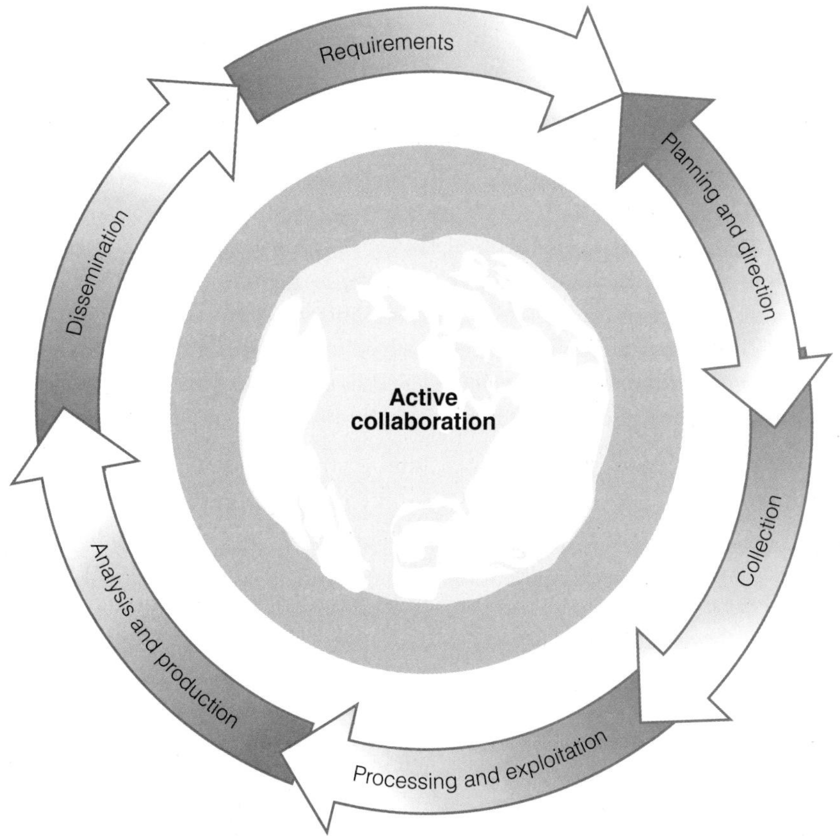

FIGURE 10.6 The Intelligence Cycle

SOURCE: Stephen A. Loyka, Donald A. Faggiana and Clifford Karchmer. "Protecting Your Community from Terrorism: The Strategies for Local Law Enforcement." *The Production and Sharing of Intelligence, Volume 4.* Washington, DC: Community Oriented Policing Services Office and the Police Executive Research Forum, February 2005, p.35.

Interoperability Continuum

Limited leadership, planning and collaboration among areas with minimal investment in the sustainability of systems and documentation → High degree of leadership, planning and collaboration among areas with commitment to and investment in sustainability of systems and documentation

Governance	Individual agencies working independently	Informal coordination between agencies	Key multi-discipline staff collaboration on a regular basis	Regional committee working within a statewide communications interoperability committee	
Standard operating procedures	Individual agency SOPs	Joint SOPs for planned events	Joint SOPs for emergencies	Regional set of communications SOPs	National incident management system integrated SOPs
Technology — Data elements	Swap files	Common applications	Custom-interfaced applications	One-way standards-based sharing	Two-way standards-based sharing
Technology — Voice elements	Swap radios	Gateway	Shared channels	Proprietary shared systems	Standards-based shared systems
Training and exercises	General orientation on equipment and applications	Single agency tabletop exercises for key field and support staff	Multi-agency tabletop exercises for key field and support staff	Multi-agency full functional exercises involving all staff	Regular comprehensive regionwide training and exercises
Usage	Planned events	Localized emergency incidents	Regional incident management	Daily use throughout region	

FIGURE 10.7 Interoperability Continuum

SOURCE: http://www.safecomprogram.gov/NR/rdonlyres/54F0C2DE-FA70-48DD-A56E-3A72A8F35066/0/Interoperability_Continuum_Brochure_2.pdf.

SAFECOM is a communications program within the Office for Interoperability and Compatibility (OIC) that provides research, development, testing and evaluation, guidance, tools and templates on communications-related issues to local, tribal, state and federal emergency response agencies working to improve emergency response and enhance interoperability ("About SAFECOM," 2010). Figure 10.7 illustrates the complexities involved in interoperability.

The *National Emergency Communications Plan* is another such effort to enhance the sharing of information through interoperability.

The National Emergency Communications Plan (NECP) The DHS National Emergency Communications Plan (NECP) is a strategy that "sets goals and identifies key national priorities to enhance governance, planning, technology, training and exercises, and disaster communications capabilities. The NECP provides recommendations, including milestones to help emergency response providers and relevant government officials make measurable improvements in emergency communications over the next three years. The goals include that by 2013, 75 percent of all agencies are able to demonstrate response-level emergency communications within one hour for routine events involving multiple jurisdictions and within 3 hours for a significant event" (Careless, 2009, p.30). The NECP is designed to ensure that the numerous statewide interoperability efforts currently being undertaken integrate seamlessly into a coherent national system and provides realistic deadlines for implementing changes and tracking progress (Careless).

The National Information Sharing Strategy (NISS) Yet another initiative to enhance information sharing is the FBI's *National Information Sharing Strategy* (NISS) (2008), the result of the FBI's commitment to share timely, relevant, *actionable* intelligence to the widest *appropriate* audience. "The FBI is required to effectively balance the need to effectively and securely share information with its responsibility to protect sources, investigative operations, national security information, and the privacy and civil liberties of U.S. persons" (p.2). This dual charge partially explains lack of information sharing between local jurisdictions and the FBI and how such lapses contribute to incidents such as that which occurred at Ft. Hood.

Addressing Obstacles to Intelligence Sharing

Two barriers to effective exchange of intelligence are interoperability issues, already discussed, and lack of deconfliction protocols. A **deconfliction** protocol essentially provides guidelines to avoid conflict, jurisdictional squabbles and archaic rules that prevent cooperative working relationships with local, regional, tribal and federal law enforcement.

deconfliction
Avoiding conflict.

The keys to combating terrorism lie with the local police and the intelligence they can provide to federal authorities, how readily information is shared between agencies at different levels and the interoperability of communications systems should an attack occur.

The community can also be instrumental in providing information, especially in those communities in which community policing is used. Figure 10.8 illustrates a model to help local police implement their new antiterrorism responsibilities.

THE CRITICAL ROLE OF LOCAL LAW ENFORCEMENT IN HOMELAND SECURITY

Homeland security issues will have a tremendous impact on policing during the next several decades: "Law enforcement will be expected to divide its current efforts focused on the traditional core mission of policing because it has augmented the existing job with the added expectation by the populace to develop prevention measures for domestic/homeland security" (Cetron and Davies, 2008, p.16). The *2010 Program Plan, Section 8*, "Countering Terrorism and Domestic Emergencies," reports, "Within the span of one week in September 2009, three separate plots to attack four U.S. cities (Dallas, Texas; Denver, Colorado; New York City; and Springfield, Missouri) were uncovered and neutralized through effective partnerships and activities designed to fight terrorism. These incidents offer dramatic evidence that threats from international and domestic terrorists have not diminished in the 8 years since the attacks of September 11, 2001." The successful neutralizing of the plots is also testimony to the importance of vigilance at the local level and the sharing of information. Of utmost importance are local law enforcement officers.

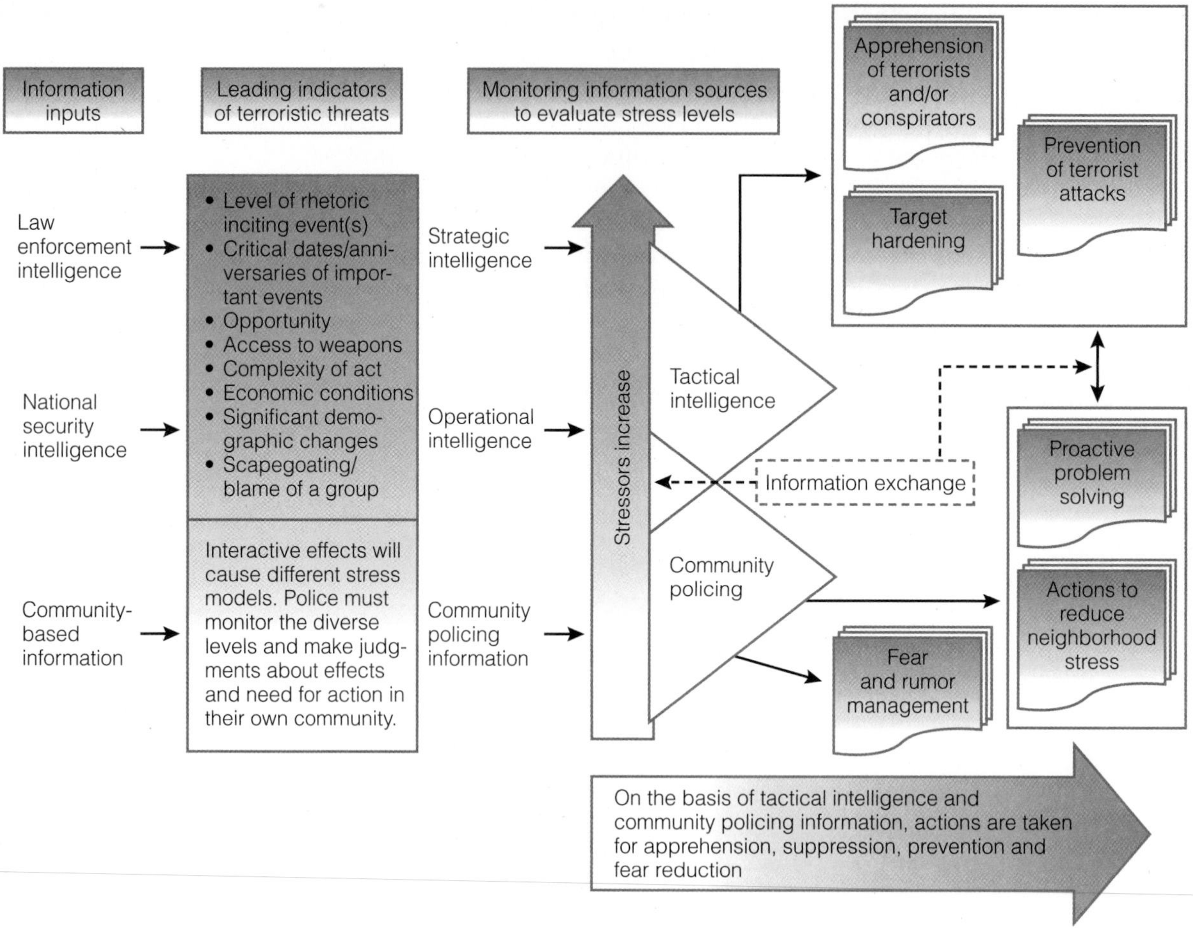

Information inputs
Leading indicators of terroristic threats
Monitoring information sources to evaluate stress levels

Law enforcement intelligence
National security intelligence
Community-based information

- Level of rhetoric inciting event(s)
- Critical dates/anniversaries of important events
- Opportunity
- Access to weapons
- Complexity of act
- Economic conditions
- Significant demographic changes
- Scapegoating/blame of a group

Interactive effects will cause different stress models. Police must monitor the diverse levels and make judgments about effects and need for action in their own community.

Strategic intelligence
Operational intelligence
Community policing information

Stressors increase

Tactical intelligence
Community policing
Information exchange

Apprehension of terrorists and/or conspirators
Target hardening
Prevention of terrorist attacks
Proactive problem solving
Actions to reduce neighborhood stress
Fear and rumor management

On the basis of tactical intelligence and community policing information, actions are taken for apprehension, suppression, prevention and fear reduction

FIGURE 10.8 Implementation Model

SOURCE: David L. Carter and Richard N. Holden. "Terrorism and Community Security." *Local Government Police Management*, 4th ed., edited by William A. Geller and Darrel W. Stephens. Washington, DC: International City/County Management Association, 2003, p.307. Reprinted with permission of the International City/County Management Association, 777 North Capitol Street, NE, Suite 500, Washington, DC. 2002. All rights reserved.

Local police officer responsibilities related to homeland security include:

- Knowing the enemy, what to look for and being vigilant.
- Completing suspicious activity reports (SARs) and sharing information.
- Taking all possible steps to prevent a terrorist attack.
- Preparing themselves, the department and their community for an attack, should one occur, through education and training.
- Responding to an attack.
- Investigating any attack.

Knowing the Enemy and Being Vigilant—Prevention

The preceding discussions provide basic information about terrorism with which all local law enforcement officers should be familiar.

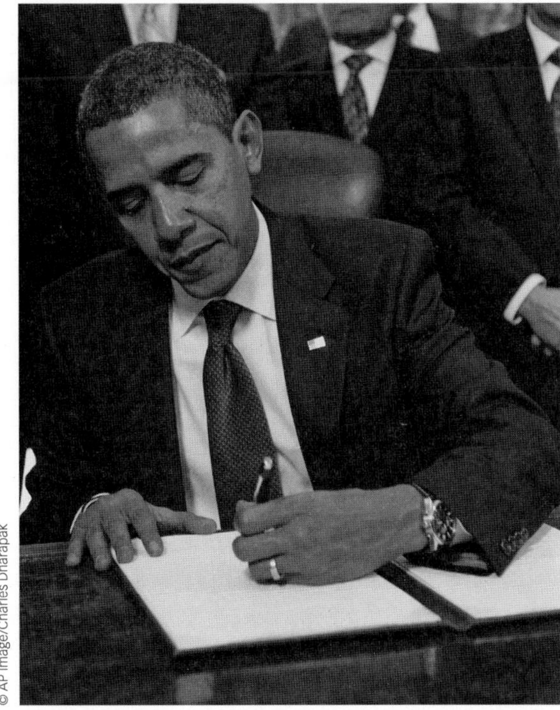

© AP Image/Charles Dharapak

President Barack Obama signs an executive order closing the prison at Guantanamo Bay, Thursday, January 22, 2009, in the Oval Office of the White House in Washington.

The first line of defense against terrorism is the patrol officer in the field.

Law enforcement officers must be aware of the possibility for contact with terrorists at any time during their normal course of duty. Many of the 9/11 hijackers had contact with law enforcement officers in various parts of the country. For example, on September 9, 2001, Ziad Jarrah, hijacker of the plane that crashed in Shanksville, Pennsylvania, was stopped by police in Maryland for speeding, was issued a ticket and released. In August 2001, Hani Hanjour, hijacker and pilot of the plane that crashed into the Pentagon, was stopped by police in Arlington, Virginia, issued a ticket for speeding and released.

Completing Suspicious Activity Reports (SARs) and Sharing Information

The Nationwide Suspicious Activity Reporting Initiative (NSI) (2010) is a collaborative effort among federal, state, local and tribal government agencies with counterterrorism responsibilities. The NSI establishes a replicable process whereby suspicious activity report (**SAR**) information can be shared to help detect and prevent terrorism-related criminal activity: "The SAR process engages a largely untapped resource: 800,000 law enforcement officers nationwide. SAR processes are designed to work for law enforcement agencies of all sizes" (Colwell and Kelly, 2010, p.65).

SAR

Suspicious activity report. Contains information documented by local law enforcement that can be shared with other law enforcement agencies to help detect and prevent terrorism-related criminal activity:

DHS Secretary Napolitano reports that her agency is collaborating with the IACP and others on a nationwide SARs initiative, which will help train frontline officers to recognize and document activities possibly linked to terrorism-related crime across the United States (Napolitano, 2010). As part of this program, intelligence regarding threats to the homeland are provided to police departments across the country: "Already those cities participating in the suspicious activity reporting pilot are better able to identify and address emerging crime trends" (Colwell and Kelly, 2010, p.66).

SARs are vetted by regional Joint Terrorism Task Forces (JTTFs) for consideration of a potential nexus to terrorism and possible criminal investigation. However, SARs have also heightened civil libertarians' concerns amid a series of revelations during the past year about political activities that some law enforcement agencies have already singled out (Straw, 2009, p.22). Preserving civil liberties is discussed later in the chapter.

Preparing—the Agency and the Community

The 9/11 attacks undoubtedly shifted the priorities of policing. Law enforcement agencies must not, however, let the "war on terrorism" tempt them into abandoning or diminishing community policing efforts in favor of a return to the traditional model of policing with its paramilitary emphasis.

The successful detection and prevention of terrorism depends on information, and a community–police relationship based on mutual trust is most likely to uncover matters helpful in identifying prospective terrorists. Information citizens provide officers on their beat can be invaluable.

One of the most important responsibilities of local law enforcement is to be certain they are prepared to respond to an emergency. However, it is not sufficient to merely have carefully thought-out plans for responding to a terrorist attack. The plans must also be practiced.

Practicing the Response

The NIMS provides a framework for local plans. Departments should also become familiar with the different state and federal emergency plans and resources to make their community safer.

First responders should practice their response regularly in multiagency exercises to ensure good liaison between the agencies and that commanders are familiar with their counterparts in other agencies.

Departments might borrow from the military a useful training technique known as red teaming, which the military uses in war-game scenarios whereby they assume the position of their opposing forces in a simulated conflict to detect weaknesses in the military force. In the business world, **red teaming** refers to an independent peer review of abilities, vulnerabilities and limitations. Applied to homeland security, red teaming involves thinking or acting like a terrorist in an effort to identify security weaknesses and potential targets.

red teaming

An independent peer review of abilities, vulnerabilities and limitations; applied to homeland security, involves thinking or acting like a terrorist in an effort to identify security weaknesses and potential targets.

In March 2008, the Los Angeles Police Department (LAPD) implemented a National Counter-Terrorism Academy (NCTA) initiative, a pilot program for state and local law enforcement that includes both public and private partnerships to assist in training public safety. One of the training programs used by the NCTA is

Hydra, a high-tech immersive training simulator designed in the United Kingdom and used to train public safety command-level officers in dealing with large-scale disasters such as earthquakes, riots, police shootings and terrorist attacks, among other scenarios. Hydra trains and tests a student's real-time decision-making skills as applied to events such as large-scale disasters or terrorist attacks and provides learning scenarios that are as close to the real thing as possible.

There are 53 other Hydra training centers around the world; however, LAPD is currently the only one in the United States. The LAPD likens this training to the flight simulator training used by pilots, noting that Hydra is specific to public safety and emergency management scenarios. The LAPD also views this training as a possible supervisor training tool.

An important part of being prepared is assessing what types of terrorist attacks might be likely—what the vulnerabilities of a given community are.

Assessing Risks and Identifying Potential Terrorist Targets

Potential targets might be a transit system hub, a chemical storage warehouse or high-level government officials' residences. Although jurisdictions necessarily focus efforts on protecting logical, high-profile targets for terrorist attacks, soft targets should not be overlooked. Soft targets, those that are relatively unguarded or difficult to guard, include shopping malls, subways, trains, sporting stadiums, theaters, schools, hospitals, restaurants, entertainment parks, compressed gas and oil storage areas, chemical plants, pharmaceutical companies and many others.

The *National Infrastructure Protection Plan* (NIPP) (2009) provides a coordinated approach to critical infrastructure and key resource protection roles and responsibilities for federal, state, local, tribal and private sector security partners. This national plan can serve as a guide for communities to assess their unique infrastructure risks and how to address them. Figure 10.9 illustrates the NIPP Risk Management Framework.

A tool available to law enforcement agencies across the country is the Community Vulnerability Assessment Methodology (C-VAM), a back-to-basics approach that identifies a community's weaknesses by using a detailed, systematic analysis of the facilities and their relationship to each other. This initiative examines a community as a whole to help departments focus resources and funds on the

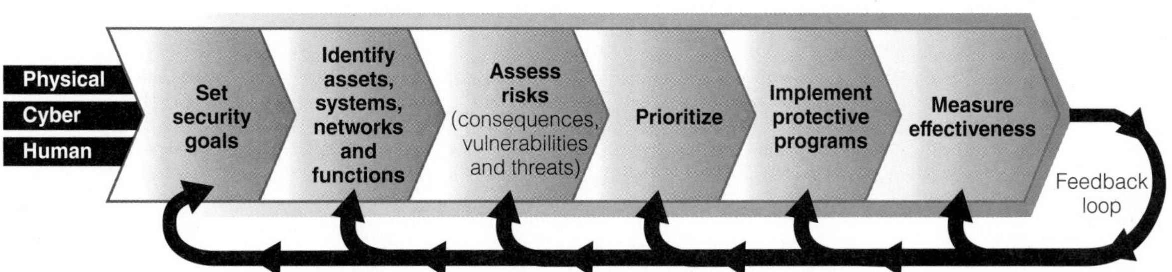

FIGURE 10.9 NIPP Risk Management Framework

SOURCE: *National Infrastructure Protection Plan*, Washington, DC: Department of Homeland Security, 2009, p.4.

areas needing them most. It uses a performance-based system to calculate how effective a community's current physical protection systems are against likely threats.

A variety of other risk-assessment tools and seminars have been developed to help communities gauge and respond to potential vulnerabilities in their local infrastructure. The Department of Homeland Security has identified 17 forms of infrastructure a jurisdiction must consider when soliciting grant monies from DHS.

Developing an awareness of community vulnerabilities is a vital step for law enforcement agencies taking a proactive stance toward terrorism.

Being Proactive and Forming Partnerships

As with gangs, drug dealers and cartels, domestic violence and other areas of concern to law enforcement, a proactive approach to terrorism is needed.

Success in terrorism prevention might be enhanced by cultivating numerous community information sources such as Neighborhood Watch; hotels; real estate agents; storage facilities; fraternal, social and civic clubs; colleges and universities; business managers; transportation centers and tourist attractions; major industrial enterprises; schools; health care providers; bar and liquor stores; licensing and permit agencies; delivery services; department of public works employees and refuse haulers; housing managers; meter readers—and the list goes on.

The extent of the preceding list illustrates how broad a community's information network can be for law enforcement officers faced with tackling terrorism and makes clear that the police are most certainly not "in this alone." The private sector is a vital part of the front line of homeland security efforts and is crucial to identifying and locating terrorists, as well as disrupting terrorist networks.

Another important partnership already briefly mentioned is the media.

The Role of the Media in the War on Terrorism The Terrorism Research Center suggests, "Terrorism and the media have a symbiotic relationship. Without the media, terrorists would receive no exposure, their cause would go ignored, and no climate of fear would be generated. Terrorism is futile without publicity, and the media generates much of this publicity."

Television and terrorism are closely related because terrorists feed television's need for drama and television gives terrorists a means to communicate. The mass media can become a force multiplier because reporting can increase the psychological aura surrounding terrorist events. This raises the question of the **contagion effect**; that is, does the coverage of terrorism inspire more terrorism? It is in effect, contagious. This controversial issue leads to discussions about censorship in the war on terrorism.

contagion effect
Media coverage of terrorism inspires more terrorism.

Law enforcement agencies attempting to engage the community in a collective effort to fight terrorism must at some level be aware of the negative undercurrent that exists among segments of society regarding the actions of the government, largely perpetuated by the media.

RESPONDING TO TERRORIST ATTACKS

America's first line of defense in any terrorist attack is the "first responder," the local police, firefighters and emergency medical professionals. Properly trained, they have the greatest potential to save lives and limit destruction. Key to their success is interoperability among those first responders. Lack of such interoperability was devastatingly obvious during the 9/11 attacks. However, when Hurricane Katrina hit the Gulf Coast in August 2005, the lack of progress in addressing communication problems was again underscored, as radio transmissions were hindered because the storm's winds toppled towers.

SAFECOM, a communications program of the DHS for OIC, is aimed at improving interoperable communications by working with federal partners to provide research, development, testing, evaluation, guidance, tools and templates on communications-related issues to local, state and federal public safety agencies.

Officers should be thoroughly familiar with their response plans and should practice, practice, practice. They might also consider enlisting the aid of Citizen Corps, the arm of the USA Freedom Corps that provides opportunities for civilians who want to make their communities more secure. Since Citizen Corps was introduced to the country in 2002, the Web site has received more than 1.6 million hits from Americans from all 50 states and all U.S. territories. More than 15,000 volunteers are looking to be trained to assist the first responders in the event of a terrorist attack. In addition, more than 5,000 potential volunteers have expressed an interest in joining the Medical Reserve Corps in their communities.

INVESTIGATING TERRORIST ACTS

When attacks are not prevented, they must be thoroughly investigated. Fortunately, investigating terrorism has many similarities with investigating any other kind of criminal activity. Several lessons learned from the war on drugs can help in the war on terrorism. For example, both "wars" involve covert illegal activities calling for sophisticated undercover operations. Both have domestic and international fronts. In addition, both require coordination between various agencies and information sharing with partners within this country and globally.

One starting point for investigating terrorist attacks is to determine how the attack was funded because this often involves criminal activity.

Funding Terrorism

Money is needed to carry out terrorism—for weapons and for general operating expenses. Many terrorist operations are financed by charitable groups and wealthy Arabs sympathetic to the group's cause. Terrorist groups commonly collaborate with organized criminal groups to deal drugs, arms and, in some instances, humans. To finance their operations, terrorist groups smuggle stolen goods and contraband, forge documents, profit from the diamond trade and engage in extortion and protection rackets. Terrorists also generate income by offering their security services to narcotics traffickers.

Trafficking in illicit goods and commodities by terrorists and their supporters is a critical element in generating funds. Members of both Hezbollah and HAMAS have established front companies and legitimate businesses in the cigarette trade in Central and South America. In other fundraising efforts, terrorists conspire with cargo theft rings to obtain commodities to sell on the black market.

Fraud has become increasingly common among terrorists, as a way to generate revenue and as a way to gain access to their targets. Fraudulently obtained drivers' licenses, passports and other identification documents are often found among terrorists' belongings.

CAREER PROFILE

Rich Philipps (CSI Team—Roseville, CA, Police Department)

I was in college when I chose a career in law enforcement. I worked for the UCLA Police Department as a community service officer (CSO) and eventually became the hospital security manager for the Medical Center. My wife and I left the Los Angeles area in 1989 and relocated to northern California. In early 1993 I began working for the Roseville Police Department, where I am currently employed as a Police Scene Technician.

I was originally hired at the Roseville PD as a CSO—a civilian position that takes reports and investigates property-related crimes. Shortly thereafter, I was assigned to the Property and Evidence Lab and immediately developed an interest in crime-scene investigation. I attended a basic crime-scene investigation course in 1996 and began processing a wider variety of crime scenes. I was assigned to the Traffic Unit in 2000 to investigate traffic collisions. During this assignment, I became a member of the Major Accident Investigation Team (MAIT) and further developed scene-processing skills while responding to numerous fatal vehicle collision investigations. I was also called on to assist in processing homicides, suicides, robberies and a variety of assaults.

In 2004 I became a member of our department's crime scene investigation (CSI) team. The day after the team was formed, we responded to an attempted murder and subsequent arson; our team was off and running! Since the inception of the CSI Team, I have continued to receive specific forensic training to keep up with the changing demands of crime-scene investigation. The team approach to crime-scene processing identifies and utilizes specialty skills like photography; latent-fingerprint lift techniques; use of alternate light sources to identify trace evidence, blood and fluids; stain swabbing for DNA; and diagramming to process and preserve scene evidence. While I have performed all these roles, my primary assignments are scene management, photography and diagramming.

One of the biggest challenges a crime-scene investigator faces is maintaining the integrity of the scene. Advances in DNA processing over the past 10 years, while undoubtedly improving our abilities to examine evidence to solve crimes, have also brought a significant potential for cross-contamination. For example, in addition to all of the legitimate police personnel who need to view a crime scene during an investigation, contamination may be introduced by minute details, as might happen if the same fingerprint brush (or other equipment that may transfer DNA) is used to process different areas within the scene. Another big challenge involves the dynamic nature of forensic processing.

Changes in technology allow for much more advanced, accurate and detailed processing. The use of lasers, digital cameras, variable-spectrum lighting sources, total station measuring devices and computer software, and the constant refinement of techniques make continuing education a must. Sometimes, though, the best techniques or equipment are developed impromptu in the field by technicians who experiment because they are not satisfied with an existing method. Necessity really is the mother of invention. Most of the techniques and equipment used on the television series *CSI* demonstrate the most innovative forensic processing skills. Some of these techniques and equipment are used by CSI technicians at the scene, but much of the technical analysis is done in a lab by a criminalist. Of course in the real world we rarely solve whodunit-type crimes in one hour!

CSI is definitely involved in major terrorist cases. Usually the FBI oversees the processing, and the scene is divided up into many smaller scenes to be processed by smaller CSI groups comprising federal and local law enforcement agencies. As an example, a good friend and colleague of mine, who retired from the FBI after 30-plus years and was on their evidence response team (ERT), processed the Oklahoma City bombing, the first World Trade Center bombing, the Unabomber's cabin and numerous terrorist bombings worldwide. I have completed an FBI post-blast evidence recovery school and am on a national database of forensic processors to potentially be deployed in the event of a critical incident involving explosives.

There are several avenues to pursue a career as a crime-scene technician. A college degree in forensics, biology, chemistry or criminal justice is preferred and may qualify a candidate for a lab-based criminalist position. However, the best qualification of a field crime-scene technician is passion. If you can obtain any position with a law enforcement agency and are willing to intern as a crime-scene technician while performing your other job duties, my experience has taught me that you have a good chance of obtaining a full-time position. This job is challenging, stressful, often tedious, rarely glamorous (as portrayed on TV) and almost always in conflict with your personal schedule, but it is the most rewarding job I have ever had. One person in the private sector once told me, "Most of us just work for money. You work for something much more meaningful."

TERRORISTS AS CRIMINALS

The importance of knowing one's enemy cannot be overemphasized. One critical dimension of this knowledge is differentiating the street criminal from the terrorist. Terrorists operate with different motivations, have different objectives and use much deadlier weapons than the typical street criminal does. Most terrorists are first-timers. In addition, terrorists seek wide-scale damage, whereas criminals seek gain. Another crucial difference is that, with terrorists, it is more often a matter of life and death—it's kill or be killed, not capture and convict. The fight against terrorism has blurred the line between crime and war, drawing law enforcement directly into the war.

A documented nexus exists between traditional crime and terrorism, involving fraudulent identification, trafficking in illegal merchandise and drug sales as means to terrorists' ends. Many organized crime investigations lead back to terrorism cases.

Law enforcement officers should stay alert for routine crimes serving as red flags to possible terrorist planning, including any of the following products being produced, stored or sold in large quantities: bleaching products, chlorine products and cleaning solutions, crowd/riot control sprays, disinfectants, drain cleaners, dyes, fertilizers, fumigation products, fungicides, galvanizing solutions, herbicides, insecticides, metal polishes, organic chemicals, pesticides, pharmaceuticals, photographic solutions, plastics/polymers, solvents and weed killers. Other things for officers to consider are prowling reports, burglaries, thefts, missing inventory and suspicious new applicants for employment.

Law enforcement is charged with being an active participant in the war on terror, so officers must also be aware of and sensitive to concerns regarding individuals' rights and privacy.

CONCERNS RELATED TO THE WAR ON TERRORISM

The DHS recognizes the importance of preserving liberty and privacy in this country, but the public expects law enforcement to deal with the terrorist threat. Former DHS Secretary Michael Chertoff once said, "Law enforcement must adapt and be practical to ensure we preserve what is the most basic civil right, which is the right not to be blown up."

Two concerns related to the "war on terrorism" are that civil liberties may be jeopardized and that people of Middle Eastern descent may be discriminated against or become victims of hate crimes.

Concern for Civil Rights

The first guiding principle of the Department of Homeland Security is to protect civil rights and civil liberties: "We will defend America while protecting the freedoms that define America. Our strategies and actions will be consistent with the individual rights and liberties enshrined by our Constitution and the Rule of Law. While we seek to improve the way we collect and share information about terrorists, we will nevertheless be vigilant in respecting the confidentiality and protecting the privacy of our citizens. We are committed to securing our nation while protecting civil rights and civil liberties" (*Securing Our Homeland*, p.6).

Civil libertarians are concerned that valued American freedoms will be sacrificed in the interest of national safety. For example, the Justice Department has issued a new regulation giving itself the authority to monitor inmate–attorney communications if "reasonable suspicion" exists that inmates are using such communications to further or facilitate acts of terrorism. However, criminal defense lawyers and members of the American Civil Liberties Union (ACLU) have protested the regulation, saying it effectively eliminates the Sixth Amendment right to counsel because, under codes of professional responsibility, attorneys cannot communicate with clients if confidentiality is not assured. The ACLU has vowed to monitor police actions closely to see that freedoms protected under the Constitution are not jeopardized.

Retaliation or Discrimination against People of Middle Eastern Descent

Another concern is that some Americans may retaliate against innocent people of Middle Eastern descent, many of whom were either born in the United States or are naturalized citizens. To prevent racial profiling or discrimination against Arab Americans, local law enforcement might increase communication and develop person-to-person contacts, create a community liaison position to work with the Arab American community and recruit more Arab Americans into law enforcement.

An example of the FBI's increased efforts to reach out to community leaders is seen in the Minneapolis, Minnesota, area, where young Somali American men have disappeared and are believed to have gone to Somalia to fight with militants. An FBI spokesperson reported that since the disappearances of the young men, the bureau has worked to expand relationships with community elders, religious leaders and others active in the local Somali populations, estimated to be about 80,000: "We want to make them feel comfortable with us. We want them to come forward with concerns about their young people. We share the same concerns. We want to help, and we need people with concerns to come forward with information" (Baldor, 2009).

Pressure on such communities comes from many directions. Many U.S. Muslims consider the government response to terrorism, such as the U.S. Terrorist Act of 2001 and the USA PATRIOT Act, as infringing on their individual civil liberties. Law enforcement officials have voiced concerns that the estimated population of between 2 and 3 million Muslims living in the United States could be a source of "violent Islamist extremism" (Stainbrook, 2010, p.32). At the same time, American Muslim communities are under extraordinary pressures including negative media attention and additional precautions in the travel industry. Law enforcement officers at all levels can address such pressures assertively and compassionately by working with Muslim communities, focusing on three broad categories (Stainbrook):

- Direct police–community engagement strategies
- Indirect police–community engagement strategies
- Media communications strategies

Local police departments are the key to outreach efforts. They might use as their model the FBI's outreach philosophy and perspective, as voiced by Hovington (2010), chief of the FBI's Community Relations Unit: "As a special agent, I can attest that an individual's understanding and perception of the FBI can make everything we do easier or harder. As we see more instances of individuals in the United States being radicalized to commit violent acts, our efforts to build understanding and trust become more critical than ever." It must be kept in mind, however, that although radicalization is a growing concern, the overwhelming majority of Muslim Americans are loyal, law-abiding citizens (Hovington).

Closely related concerns are the rights of citizens detained as enemy combatants and the rights of detained foreign nationals. In *Hamdi v. Rumsfeld* (2004), the Supreme Court ruled that a citizen detained in the United States as an enemy combatant must be afforded the opportunity to rebut such a designation. Petitioner Hamdi was captured in an active combat zone in Afghanistan following the September 11, 2001, attack on the United States and surrendered an assault rifle. The U.S. District Court found that the declaration from the Defense Department did not support Hamdi's detention and ordered the government to turn over numerous materials for review. The U.S. Court of Appeals for the Fourth Circuit reversed, stressing that, because it was undisputed that Hamdi was captured in an active combat zone, no factual inquiry or evidentiary hearing allowing Hamdi to rebut the government's assertions was necessary. A 6–3 Supreme Court decision vacated and remanded, concluding that Hamdi should have a meaningful opportunity to offer evidence that he was not an enemy combatant.

In *Rasul v. Bush* (2004), the Supreme Court ruled that U.S. courts have jurisdiction to consider challenges to the legality of the detention of foreign nationals captured in Afghanistan in a military campaign against al Qaeda and the Taliban regime that supported it. The petitioners, 2 Australians and 12 Kuwaitis, were being held in Guantanamo Bay, Cuba, without charges. These and other legal issues regarding civil rights will be debated as the country seeks to balance the need for security with civil rights.

A FINAL CONSIDERATION—THE DUAL CHALLENGE

As Bratton cautions, "The threat of terrorism is clearly not going away, and while we have been very fortunate there has not been a successful effort since 9/11, every indication is that these attacks are going to increase, and in fact, that they will occur" (Wyllie, 2010). The irony, of course, is that because of counterterrorism efforts, there have been no successful attacks on U.S. soil, at least of the magnitude of the 9/11 attacks, in nearly nine years, leading some administrators down a dangerous path of complacency in thinking that they can, or should, cut back the resources allocated to this issue. In these trying economic times, when governments must decide how to direct and spend limited resources, it is tempting to divert funding away from counterterrorism to the everyday issues of crime and disorder.

The dual challenges in combating violence facing law enforcement are countering terrorism while continuing to address crime and disorder.

Wyllie, citing the adage "the squeaky wheel gets the grease," contends that "the squeaky wheel is increasing gang activity and the day-to-day holdups of liquor stores and what have you—that is the typical plague on our streets." Nonetheless. "Over the past year, on at least eight occasions, people linked to radical Islamic thought attempted or carried attacks on targets in the U.S. The list includes the failed Christmas Day bombing on a Detroit-bound airliner, the shooting rampage at Ft. Hood in Texas, three bomb plots foiled by the Federal Bureau of Investigation last September, and a handful of earlier plots broken up last spring and summer" (Johnson, 2010). The car-bomb attempt in New York's Times Square in May 2010 could have resulted in a major disaster had it not been discovered. The United States must remain vigilant about terrorism, while responding to the myriad challenges of gangs, drugs, violent crime and the increasingly serious illegal immigration issue.

Summary

The threat of terrorism has become a reality in the United States. Most definitions of *terrorism* have common elements, including the systematic use of physical violence, either actual or threatened, against noncombatants to create a climate of fear to cause some religious, political or social change. Three elements of terrorism are (1) it is criminal in nature, (2) targets are typically symbolic and (3) the terrorist actions are always aggressive and often violent.

The FBI, the lead agency for responding to terrorism, classifies terrorist acts as either domestic or international. Domestic terrorist groups include White supremacists, Black supremacists, militia groups, other right-wing extremists, left-wing extremists, pro-life extremists, animal rights activists and environmental extremists. Most terrorist acts result from dissatisfaction with a religious, political or social system or policy and frustration resulting from an inability to change it through acceptable, nonviolent means. Terrorists may use arson, explosives and bombs; weapons of mass destruction (biological, chemical or nuclear agents); and technology; as well as kidnapping, hostage-taking and murder. Weapons of mass destruction include biological, chemical and nuclear agents.

As a result of 9/11 the Department of Homeland Security (DHS) was established, reorganizing the departments of the federal government. At the federal level, the FBI is the lead agency for responding to acts of domestic terrorism. The Federal Emergency Management Agency (FEMA) is the lead agency for consequence management (after an attack). The DHS serves in a broad capacity, facilitating collaboration between local and federal law enforcement to develop a national strategy to detect, prepare for, prevent, protect against, respond to and recover from terrorist attacks within the United States.

The USA PATRIOT Act significantly improves the nation's counterterrorism efforts by

- Allowing investigators to use the tools already available to investigate organized crime and drug trafficking.
- Facilitating information sharing and cooperation among government agencies so they can better "connect the dots."
- Updating the law to reflect new technologies and new threats.
- Increasing the penalties for those who commit or support terrorist crimes.

The keys to combating terrorism lie with the local police and the intelligence they can provide to federal authorities, how readily information is shared between agencies at different levels and the interoperability of communications systems should an attack occur. Local police officers' responsibilities related to homeland security include knowing the enemy, what to look for and being vigilant; completing suspicious activity reports (SARs) and sharing information; taking all possible steps to prevent a terrorist attack; preparing themselves, the department and their community for an attack, should one occur, through education and training; responding to an attack; and investigating any attack. The first line of defense against terrorism is the patrol officer in the field.

Two concerns related to the "war on terrorism" are that civil liberties may be jeopardized and that people of Middle Eastern descent may be discriminated against or become victims of hate crimes. The dual challenges in combating violence facing law enforcement are countering terrorism while continuing to address crime and disorder.

Discussion Questions

1. Which is the greater threat—domestic or international terrorism? Why?
2. Does your police department have a counterterrorism strategy in place? If so, what is it?
3. What can an average citizen who is not involved in public safety do to help the war on terror? Do you think we each have a civil responsibility to contribute, or is it primarily the responsibility of our government?
4. Do you feel Americans have become complacent about terrorism?
5. What provision of the USA PATRIOT Act do you think is most important?
6. What barriers to sharing information among the various local, state and federal agencies do you think are most problematic?
7. How do terrorist groups use the media to meet their objectives?
8. Should Americans expect to give up some civil liberties to allow law enforcement officers to pursue terrorists?
9. What problems or obstacles will local and state law enforcement agencies face in an effort to shift some resources toward homeland security?
10. What is local and state law enforcement doing in an effort to combat terrorism?

Gale Emergency Services Database Assignments

- Use the Gale Emergency Services Database to help answer the Discussion Questions as appropriate.
- Using the Gale Emergency Services Database, find the article, "Valuable Lessons Learned at an International Counter Terrorism Forum": http://find.galegroup.com/gps/retrieve.do?contentSet=IAC-Documents&resultListType=RESULT_LIST&qrySerId=Locale%28en%2C%2C%29%3AFQE%3D%28ke%2CNone%2C9%29terrorism%24&sgHitCountType=None&inPS=true&sort=DateDescend&searchType=BasicSearchForm&tabID=T003&prodId=IPS&searchId=R1¤tPosition=1&userGroupName=cpg3&docId=A205577030&docType=IAC&contentSet=IAC-Documents

  Assignment: Read the article and outline some of the lessons learned in this forum. Be prepared to discuss this in class.

- Using the Gale Emergency Services Database, find the article, "State and Local Law Enforcement: Contributions to Terrorism Prevention": http://find.galegroup.com/gps/retrieve.do?contentSet=IAC-Documents&resultListType=RESULT_LIST&qrySerId=Locale%28en%2C%2C%29%3AFQE%3D%28ke%2CNone%2C9%29terrorism%24&sgHitCountType=None&inPS=true&sort=DateDescend&searchType=BasicSearchForm&tabID=T003&prodId=IPS&searchId=R1¤tPosition=7&userGroupName=cpg3&docId=A196055257&docType=IAC&contentSet=IAC-Documents

  Assignment: Read the article and be prepared to discuss Joint Terrorism Task Forces with the class.
- Using the Gale Emergency Services Database, find the article, "Software for Homeland Security & Terrorism Response (Protecting Our Homeland)": http://find.galegroup.com/gps/retrieve.do?contentSet=IAC-Documents&resultListType=RESULT_LIST&qrySerId=Locale%28en%2C%2C%29%3AFQE%3D%28ke%2CNone%2C9%29terrorism%24&sgHitCountType=None&inPS=true&sort=DateDescend&searchType=BasicSearchForm&tabID=T003&prodId=IPS&searchId=R1¤tPosition=16&userGroupName=cpg3&docId=A194548370&docType=IAC&contentSet=IAC-Documents

  Assignment: Be prepared to discuss the software that is examined in this article and how it benefits law enforcement. Also, research other computer software technology that is emerging for law enforcement to use in combating terrorism.
- Using the Gale Emergency Services Database, find the article, "Demand of Police Services in a WMD Incident (Weapons of Mass Destruction)": http://find.galegroup.com/gps/retrieve.do?contentSet=IAC-Documents&resultListType=RESULT_LIST&qrySerId=Locale%28en%2C%2C%29%3AFQE%3D%28ke%2CNone%2C9%29terrorism%24&sgHitCountType=None&inPS=true&sort=DateDescend&searchType=BasicSearchForm&tabID=T003&prodId=IPS&searchId=R1¤tPosition=41&userGroupName=cpg3&docId=A177274846&docType=IAC&contentSet=IAC-Documents

  Assignment: Outline some of the demands discussed in this article and be prepared to share your outline with the class.
- Using the Gale Emergency Services Database, find the article, "Countering Violent Islamic Extremism: A Community Responsibility": http://find.galegroup.com/gps/retrieve.do?contentSet=IAC-Documents&resultListType=RESULT_LIST&qrySerId=Locale%28en%2C%2C%29%3AFQE%3D%28ke%2CNone%2C9%29terrorism%24&sgHitCountType=None&inPS=true&sort=DateDescend&searchType=BasicSearchForm&tabID=T003&prodId=IPS&searchId=R1¤tPosition=55&userGroupName=cpg3&docId=A172599466&docType=IAC&contentSet=IAC-Documents

  Assignment: Describe how this article highlights the responsibility of citizens as well as public safety in regards to Homeland Security and the War on Terror, and be prepared to discuss your findings with the class.

- Using the Gale Emergency Services Database, find the article, "Homeland Security: All Day, Everyday: Grant Funding & Ground-Breaking Legislation Help Secure One of the Nations' Busiest Seaports": http://find.galegroup.com/gps/retrieve.do?contentSet=IAC-Documents&resultListType=RESULT_LIST&qrySerId=Locale%28en%2C%2C%29%3AFQE%3D%28ke%2CNone%2C17%29homeland+security%24&sgHitCountType=None&inPS=true&sort=DateDescend&searchType=BasicSearchForm&tabID=T003&prodId=IPS&searchId=R2¤tPosition=142&userGroupName=cpg3&docId=A167512504&docType=IAC&contentSet=IAC-Documents

  Assignment: After reading this article, identify how Homeland Security also involves the nation's seaports. Be prepared to discuss the improvements made in seaport security and the methods used to assist public safety.

Internet Assignments

Select two assignments to complete.

- Go to the Web sites of the DEA (www.dea.gov), the FBI (www.fbi.gov), the Department of Justice (www.usdoj.gov) and the Department of the Treasury (www.ustreas.gov) and note how the different agencies are addressing the issue of *terrorism*. How do their focuses differ?
- Search for *USA PATRIOT Act* (2001). List specific applications of the act to law enforcement practices and explain how they might differ from conventional practices. Do you believe the phrase "extraordinary times demand extraordinary measures" justifies "bending the rules," so to speak, in the war on terrorism? In other words, do the ends justify the means? Should law enforcement be permitted to use roving wiretaps and to breach privileged inmate–attorney communication in the name of national security, or is this the beginning of the end of our civil liberties?
- Go to the Department of Justice Web site devoted to the USA PATRIOT Act and list the myths the site dispels.
- Go to http://www.policeforum.org and find "Local Law Enforcement's Role in Preventing and Responding to Terrorism." Read and outline the article.
- To learn what the U.S. Department of Homeland Security is doing to keep America safe, go to http://www.ready.gov/ and outline what this site says.
- Go to the Terrorism Research Center's Web site, http://www.terrorism.com/ and select one of the links related to the U.S. Homeland Attack on 9/11.
- Go to the Counterterrorism Training and Resources Web site at http://www.counterterrorismtraining.gov and outline what resources are available for local police departments.
- Go to the Center for Domestic Preparedness (CDP) at http://cdp.dhs.gov/ and outline what this site says regarding weapons of mass destruction.

References

"About SAFECOM." Washington, DC: Office for Interoperability and Compatibility (OIC), 2010. Retrieved from http://www.safecomprogram.gov/SAFECOM/about/default.htm

Baldor, Lolita C. "Study: Terror Fight Must Include Battle of Ideas." *The Washington Post*. Retrieved February 26, 2009, from http://www.washingtonpost.com/wp-dyn/content/article/2009/02/26/AR2009022600322

Burton, Fred. "Practical Implications of the WHTI." *PoliceOne.com News*, June 2, 2009. Retrieved from http://www.policeone.com/federal-law-enforcement/articles/1838441-Practical-implications-of-the-WHTI/

Burton, Fred, and West, Ben. "Analyzing the Hutarees: Lessons from a Failed Plot." *PoliceOne.com News*. Retrieved April 1, 2010, from http://www.policeone.com/terrorism/articles/2033393-Analyzing-the-Hutarees-Lessons-from-a-failed-plot/

Careless, James. "National Emergency Communication Plan (NECP)." *Law and Order*, November 2009, pp.30–31.

Carroll, Michael J. "Information Sharing Is Key to Fighting Terrorism." *The Police Chief*, February 2010, p.6.

Cetron, Marvia J., and Davies, Owen. *55 Trends Now Shaping the Future of Policing*. Carlisle Barracks, PA: Proteus USA, 2008.

Chalk, Peter. "Below the Radar," RAND Newsroom Commentary, March 18, 2010. Retrieved from http://www.rand.org/commentary/2010/03/18/NYT.html

"Christian Militia Charged with Police-Killing Plot." *PoliceOne.com News*, March 29, 2010. Retrieved from http://www.policeone.com/patrol-issues/articles/2030977-Christian-militia-charged-with-police-killing-plot/

Colwell, Lee, and Kelly, Dennis. "Suspicious Activity Reporting: An Overview for Chiefs—Engaging Untapped Local Law Enforcement and Private Industry Capabilities to Fight Crime and Terrorism." *The Police Chief*, February 2010, pp.64–74.

Corderre, Michael, and Register, Michael. "Fighting Back against IEDs." *Police*, September 2009, pp.38–41.

"Countering Terrorism." Washington, DC: Office of Justice Programs Program Plan, Section 8, 2010. Retrieved from http://www.ojp.gov/ProgramPlan/section8.htm

Dewar, John. "Cyberterrorism Attacks on Police Departments." *The Police Chief*, March 2010, pp.34–37.

"DHS Forecasts Top Security Threats for the Next Five Years." *Security Director News*, February 2009, pp.2, 9.

"Domestic Terrorism in the Post-9/11 Era." Washington, DC: FBI Headline Archives, September 7, 2009. Retrieved from http://www.fbi.gov/page2/sept09/domesticterrorism090709.html

Federal Bureau of Investigation Strategic Plan 2004–2009. Published November 2007. Retrieved from http://www.fbi.gov/stats-services/publications/strategic-plan/?searchterm=strategic plan

French, Glenn. "Terrorism Strikes, U.S. Law Enforcement Responds." *PoliceOne.com News*, November 6, 2009. Retrieved from http://www.policeone.com/active-shooter/articles/1962819-Terrorism-strikes-U-S-law-enforcement-responds/

"Goals and Motivations of Terrorists." Terrorism Research Center, no date. Retrieved October 25, 2010, from http://www.terrorism-research.com/goals/

Hovington, Brett. "Congressional Testimony." March 17, 2010. Retrieved from http://www2.fbi.gov/congress/congress10/hovington031710.htm

Jenkins, Brian Michael. "How a Decade of Terror Changed America." RAND Newsroom Commentary, December 30, 2009. Retrieved from http://www.rand.org/commentary/2009/12/30/SPH.html

Johnson, Keith. "Attempts Suggest Shift to Small-Scale Strikes." *The Wall Street Journal*, May 3, 2010. Retrieved from http://online.wsj.com/article/SB10001424052748703969204575220473875597084.html?KEYWORDS=%22Attempts+Suggest+Shift+to+Small-Scale+Strikes%22

Mazzetti, Mark. "Senators Warned of Terror Attack on U.S. by July." *The New York Times*, February 3, 2010.

McKenzie, Kenneth F., Jr. "The Rise of Asymmetric Threats: Priorities for Defense Planning." In *QDR 2001, Strategy Driven Choices for America's Security*, Michele A. Flourney, ed. Washington, DC: National Defense University Press, 2001, p.76.

Mueller, Robert S., III. "Congressional Testimony, January 20, 2010." Retrieved from http://www2.fbi.gov/congress/congress10/mueller012010.htm

Napolitano, Janet. "Meeting the Homeland Security Needs of State, Local, and Tribal Law Enforcement." *The Police Chief*, February 2010, p.26.

National Emergency Communications Plan. Washington, DC: Department of Homeland Security, 2008. Retrieved from http://www.safecomprogram.gov/SAFECOM/natlemergencycommplan/

National Incident Management System. Washington, DC: Homeland Security, December 2008.

National Information Sharing Strategy. Washington, DC: Federal Bureau of Investigation, August 2008.

National Infrastructure Protection Plan. Washington, DC: Department of Homeland Security, 2009. Retrieved from www.dhs.gov/nipp

National Response Framework. Washington, DC: Department of Homeland Security, January 2008. Retrieved from http://www.fema.gov/pdf/emergency/nrf/nrf-core.pdf

Nationwide Suspicious Reporting Initiative (NSI): Technical Implementation Options. Washington, DC: Office of the Director of National Intelligence, March 2010.

"New SPLC Report: 'Patriot' Groups, Militias Surge in Number in Past Year." Montgomery, AL: Southern Poverty Law Center, March 2, 2010. Retrieved from http://www.splcenter.org/get-informed/news/splc-report-number-of-patriot-groups-militias-surges-by-244-in-past-year

Potok, Mark. "Rage on the Right: The Year in Hate and Extremism." *Intelligence Report*, Spring 2010. Retrieved from http://www.splcenter.org/get-informed/intelligence-report/browse-all-issues/2010/spring/rage-on-the-right

Rotella, Sebastian. "U.S. Sees Homegrown Muslim Extremism as Rising Threat." *L.A. Times*, December 7, 2009. Retrieved from http://articles.latimes.com/2009/dec/07/nation/la-na-us-radicalization7-2009dec07

Securing Our Homeland. Washington, DC: U.S. Department of Homeland Security, no date.

Stainbrook, Mark G. "Reaching Out: Policing with Muslim Communities in the Age of Terrorism." *The Police Chief*, April 2010, pp.32–40.

Straw, Joseph. "Connecting the Dots, Protecting Rights." *Security Management*, August 2009, pp.22–24.

Straw, Joseph. "The Evolving Terrorist Threat." *Security Management*, April 2010a, pp.47–55.

Straw, Joseph. "Yet Another Cyber 'Wake-Up Call.'" *Security Management*, April 2010b, pp.24–33.

Sullivan, Eileen. "Officials See Rise in Militia Groups across U.S." *The Huffington Post*, August 12, 2009. Retrieved from http://www.huffingtonpost.com/2009/08/12/officials-see-rise-in-mil_n_257128.html

The Terrorism Research Center, no date. Retrieved from http://www.terrorism.com/index.php

"Types of Terrorist Incidents." Washington, DC: Terrorism Research Center, no date. Retrieved from http://www.terrorism-research.com/incidents/

Western Hemisphere Travel Initiative (WHTI). Washington, DC: Department of Homeland Security, 2009. Retrieved from http://www.dhs.gov/files/programs/gc_1200693579776.shtm

"What Is Terrorism?" Washington, DC: Terrorism Research Center, no date. Retrieved October 25, 2010, from http://www.terrorism-research.com

Wyllie, Doug. "American Policing in the Next Decade: A Conversation with Chief Bill Bratton." *PoliceOne.com News*, April 30, 2010. Retrieved from http://www.policeone.com/patrol-issues/articles/2056048-American-policing-in-the-next-decade-A-conversation-with-Chief-Bill-Bratton/

Young, Jeffrey. "Pentagon Sets 'Asymmetric' Warfare as High Priority." *VOA News*, December 15, 2008. Retrieved from http://www.voanews.com/english/news/a-13-2008-12-15-voa44-66620102.html

Cases Cited

Hamdi v. Rumsfeld, 542 U.S. 507 (2004)

Rasul v. Bush, 542 U.S. 466 (2004)

CHAPTER 11

Issues Concerning Police Conduct

> No one is compelled to choose the profession of a police officer, but having chosen it, everyone is obliged to perform its duties and live up to the high standards of its requirements.
>
> —Calvin Coolidge

© AP Images/Beth A. Keiser

Abner Louima, left, who was tortured in a police station bathroom in 1997, stands with his attorney Johnnie Cochran, right, during a news conference in New York on July 12, 2001. Louima was arrested in a brawl outside a Brooklyn nightclub and taken to the 70th Precinct stationhouse, where one officer sodomized Louima with a broomstick while other officers looked on. Louima sued for $155 million, claiming that officers conspired to create a "wall of silence and lies to obstruct justice." Louima received $8.7 million in a settlement with the city of New York—the most it has ever paid to a police brutality victim.

Do You Know . . .

- Whether police discretion is positive or negative?
- Whether discrimination or disparity may account for any disproportionality?
- What immigration issues law enforcement faces?
- When force should or should not be used?
- If use-of-force continuums have outlived their usefulness? If they should be included in use-of-force policies? And if they increase liability exposure?
- What level and amount of force is allowed in those cases where police are authorized to use it?
- What six less-lethal options are commonly available to law enforcement officers?
- If use of deadly force is justifiable?
- If officers criminally charged in a use-of-force case retain their constitutional rights?
- The effectiveness or safety level of high-speed police pursuits?
- Whether civil liability is of much concern for modern police agencies and officers?
- What the key elements of police corruption are?
- What three ethics-check questions are?
- What three areas can enhance police integrity and reduce corruption?

Can You Define?

continuum of compromise
corruption
deadly force
discrimination
disparity
ethics
excessive force
excited delirium
exculpatory evidence
force
***Garrity* protection**
ghosting
homophobia
integrity
less-lethal force
liability
litigaphobia
pursuit
racial profiling
reasonable force
287(g)

INTRODUCTION

Policing faces several vital issues in the 21st century. Some have existed for decades; others are relatively new. Each "Do You Know" presents more than facts—each presents major issues that face policing because the questions have no correct answers. They are controversial. Notice also that some subjects, such as discretion, have been introduced earlier.

THE CHAPTER AT A GLANCE

This chapter focuses on issues related to how officers behave on the job, beginning with a brief review of police discretion. Next is a look at the critical issue of discrimination in enforcing the law based on a subject's gender, class or race, and how discrimination differs from disparity. Then the chapter discusses police use of force, police pursuits and civil liability issues associated with specific police conduct. The chapter concludes with a look at the issues of officer corruption, ethics and integrity.

DISCRETION

Discretion has been a theme throughout this text. Just as citizens can decide to obey the laws or not, police agencies and their officers can decide which offenses to actively seek to control and which offenses to simply ignore, which services to provide and at what level. Police discretion can become an issue of controversy when claims of discrimination arise.

Police discretion is the freedom of an agency or individual officer to choose to act or not. Whether such discretion is positive or negative is an issue.

Discretion might be viewed on a continuum from low to high. Low-discretion situations include those involving routine activities such as executing a search warrant, responding to a citizen complaint or seeing an obvious violation of the law, for example, a motorist running a red light. The officer usually need not ponder what action to take. High-discretion situations, in contrast, are less clear cut, for example, responding to a call from a citizen reporting a fight going on next door. Upon arrival, the officers must determine what the situation is and sort out who is the victim and who is the perpetrator, or if both are at fault. The high-discretion incidents invite both intentional and unintentional abuses of discretionary police power.

One of the most important discretionary options police officers have is whether to arrest someone. If the decision is to arrest, then the discretionary power of the prosecutor comes into play.

The ability to use discretion is, indeed, a vital element of contemporary American policing, not to mention the entire criminal justice system, and is at the heart of the issues discussed in this chapter. Any discussion of discretion would be incomplete without recognizing the awesome power of citizen discretion.

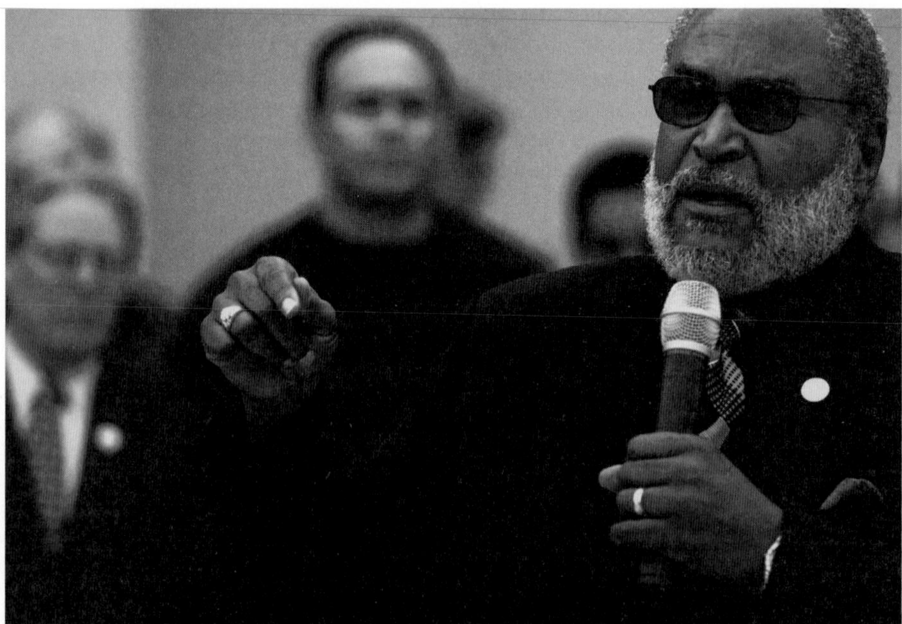

Mel Mason, Civil Rights Coalition Chairman, speaks at a press conference in Castroville, California, on December 26, 2009, to discuss excessive force complaints against the Monterey County (California) Sheriff's Office.

The less serious a crime is to the public, the less pressure is placed on police for enforcement. In addition, the wishes of complainants greatly influence police selective enforcement, often more than any other factor. Police discretion is frequently at the center of issues involving discrimination, racial profiling, use of force and pursuit.

DISCRIMINATION OR DISPARITY IN POLICING: GENDER, CLASS AND RACE ISSUES

The guarantee of equal protection under the law to all citizens is a fundamental principle of our democracy. When officers fail to treat citizens equally because of economic status, race, religion, sex or age biases, discrimination occurs. ***Discrimination*** is showing a preference in treating individuals or groups or failing to treat equals equally, especially illegal unequal treatment based on race, religion, sex or age. Some male traffic officers, for example, are known to issue warnings to females who violate traffic laws and to issue tickets to males for the same violation. Is this a matter of discrimination or of disparity? ***Disparity*** refers to a simple difference, not necessarily caused by any kind of bias. For example, if there are more male drivers and if they more frequently break traffic laws, the difference in the number of traffic tickets issued to male drivers would be a function of disparity, not discrimination. Another simple example: In a high school, most students will be between 16 and 18 years of age; this reflects disparity, not discrimination.

discrimination

Showing a preference in treating individuals or groups or failing to treat equals equally, especially illegal unequal treatment based on race, religion, sex or age.

disparity

A simple difference, not necessarily caused by any kind of bias.

This same issue arises when the numbers of individuals involved in the criminal justice system are examined. Are more minorities arrested, processed and sentenced to prison because of discrimination or because they commit crimes in disproportionate numbers because of numerous economic and social factors discussed in Chapter 3? The issue of disproportionate minority confinement (DMC) was elevated by Congress when it required that all states receiving formula grants address DMC among detained and confined youth (Solar and Garry, 2009, p.1). Under the Juvenile Justice and Delinquency Prevention Act of 2002, if a state fails to address the overrepresentation of minority youth in the juvenile justice system, the Office of Juvenile Justice and Delinquency Prevention (OJJDP) may withhold 20 percent of the state formula grant allocation for the following year. Disparity and discrimination, as related to racial and ethnic minorities, has been described as existing along a discrimination-disparity continuum between the extremes of systematic discrimination and pure justice, as illustrated in Figure 11.1 (Walker et al., 2007, p.18).

There is much controversy about whether study results indicate a pattern of systematic *discrimination* or a *disparity* that is related to other factors such as involvement in crime.

Gender Issues

The differential treatment of men and women by police is seldom raised as an issue. Why is it that so many more men than women are arrested and incarcerated? Are women better drivers and, therefore, get stopped less for traffic violations? Are women less violent? Do women commit fewer crimes? Or are women given preferential treatment? Limited research has addressed this issue.

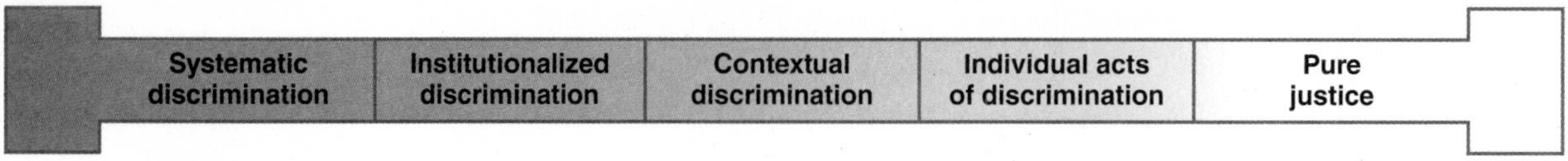

Systematic discrimination	Institutionalized discrimination	Contextual discrimination	Individual acts of discrimination	Pure justice

Definitions

Systematic discrimination—
Discrimination at all stages of the criminal justice system, at all times, and all places.

Institutionalized discrimination—
Racial and ethnic disparities in outcomes that are the result of the application of racially neutral factors, such as prior criminal record, employment status and demeanor.

Contextual discrimination—
Discrimination found in particular contexts or circumstances (for example, certain regions, particular crimes, or special victim-offender relationships).

Individual acts of discrimination—
Discrimination that results from the acts of particular individuals but is not characteristic of entire agencies or the criminal justice system as a whole.

*Pure justice—*No racial or ethnic discrimination at all.

FIGURE 11.1 Discrimination—Disparity Continuum

SOURCE: Walker/Spohn/Delone. **ACP The Color of Justice*, 3e. © 2004 (p.401) Wadsworth, a part of Cengage Learning, Inc. Reproduced by permission. www.cengage.com/permissions

homophobia

A fear of gays and lesbians.

A gender-related issue that lacks research is that of police attitudes toward homosexual individuals. Friction between the police and the homosexual community has been reported since the 1960s. What limited research is available has suggested police officers exhibit higher levels of **homophobia** than do other sectors of society; that is, they are fearful of gays and lesbians. Based on such data, a line might then be drawn connecting homophobic officers to greater instances of discriminatory policing. Such officers may even engage in discrimination unconsciously. However, the increasing number of openly gay police officers may help heighten departmental sensitivity to this issue. Again, however, as research has not explored this topic, such correlations and expectations remain purely speculative.

Class Issues

Another area receiving limited attention is discriminatory policing based on a person's economic level. More than a half century ago, in *Griffin v. Illinois* (1956), Justice Hugo Black declared, "There can be no equal justice where the kind of trial a man gets depends on the amount of money he has." To many people, the O. J. Simpson double-murder trial was a blatant example of unlimited financial resources being able to "buy" a not-guilty verdict.

At the law enforcement level, those who are poor are much more likely to come to the attention of the police simply because they are on the streets more than are those who are not poor. Many are homeless, and some of their behaviors, such as sleeping on park benches, have been made illegal, changing a social problem into a law enforcement problem. And if a poor person does have a vehicle, it is often in need of repair, resulting in the person being ticketed for faulty equipment.

Many poor people travel by mass transit—frequent targets of police sweeps for drugs. In West Palm Beach, bus sweeps over a 13-month period netted 300 pounds of cocaine, 800 pounds of marijuana, 24 handguns and 75 suspected drug "mules." In *Florida v. Bostick* (1991), a 28-year-old Black man, Terrance Bostick, on his way from Miami to Atlanta, was asleep on a bus that had stopped in Ft. Lauderdale. Police officers boarded to work the bus looking for drugs. Wearing raid jackets with the Broward County Sheriff's Office insignia and displaying badges, the officers, one holding a gun, awakened Bostick and asked to search his bag. Bostick agreed, and the officers found a pound of cocaine. Had Bostick been traveling in a private vehicle instead of a public transit vehicle, it is much more likely his illicit drugs would have gone undiscovered.

Bostick was convicted, and on appeal the case found its way to the Florida Supreme Court, which overturned the conviction. His lawyer argued that given the circumstances, most reasonable people would not feel free to ignore the police's request. Further, no reasonable person would agree to allow a search of a bag containing cocaine. The case then went to the Supreme Court, which overturned the Florida Supreme Court decision. The consequence of this ruling is that police can conduct dragnet-like searches of buses and trains, settings where it is difficult for any citizen to refuse cooperation.

An additional factor that may contribute to higher levels of criminal activity among economically disadvantaged social classes is the lack of collective efficacy in many poor neighborhoods. *Collective efficacy* refers to the shared level of trust among residents in a neighborhood, including their expectations of social control and their capacity to wield some degree of control over what happens in their own community (Walker, 2006). Research has shown that neighborhoods with high collective efficacy have lower crime rates than do similarly poor neighborhoods with little or no sense of collective efficacy (Walker, 2006, p.295).

Racial Issues

When people hear the word *discrimination*, they most commonly place it within the context of race. Allegations of racial discrimination and its correlation to DMC have become an increasingly scrutinized topic in criminal justice. Sorting out whether DMC results from discrimination or disparity is a difficult task. Unnever et al. (2009, p.378) reanalyzed the Richmond Youth Project data used by criminologist Travis Hirschi to refute the strain theory that discrimination might contribute to the delinquency of African American youths and found that perceived discrimination is a "robust predictor of delinquent involvement." This hypothesis, that *perceived* discrimination is a potential source of crime, has important implications: "Negative relations that stem from perceived racial discrimination are consequential, fostering crime and, as the research shows, a range of problem outcomes. At the same time, positive social relationships—close bonds to family and schools—may be a conduit for coping with discrimination. They may insulate against crime by providing social support" (Unnever et al., 2009, p.401). Unnever et al. (p.404) conclude, "African American adolescents living in disenfranchised areas may find themselves being raised by parents with less personal 'social capital' to effectively racially and culturally socialize their children. The end result of this process is African American adolescents with low self-efficacy, weak ties with conventional institutions and ineffective coping styles to mitigate the noxious effects of racial discrimination."

Research by Ousey and Lee (2008) focused on racial disparity rather than discrimination in social control in an effort to explain arrest rate inequality. They evaluated the mediating factors in the racial threat and benign neglect models and link racial disparities to opportunities for bias that result from residential segregation and variations in police discretionary authority across crime types. The racial threat theory suggests that an encroachment of Blacks threatens Whites' economic and political standing, so Whites exert social control to quell the minority group threat, spending more money on policing and corrections. The benign neglect theory suggests that police pay less attention to make fewer arrests for nonviolent crime or to crimes that have no complaining victims or witnesses.

Data analysis from 136 cities revealed two key findings: " First, an uneven distribution of Blacks and Whites is associated with higher arrest disparities for drug and weapons arrest, but not with violent or property crime arrest disparities. Second, there is little evidence in support of the venerable racial threat or benign neglect explanatory frameworks" (Ousey and Lee, 2008, p.322). The results suggest that dissimilarity in the distribution of Blacks and Whites can set the stage for implicit or explicit biases that lead to racially disparate arrest rates as a reflection of police discretion in arrest decisions (Ousey and Lee).

Discrimination based on a person's race has come to the forefront of policing in the issue of racial profiling.

racial profiling

Any police-initiated action that relies on the race, ethnicity or national origin rather than on the behavior of an individual for the police to believe a particular individual is engaged in criminal activity.

Racial Profiling **Racial profiling** refers to any police-initiated action that relies on the race, ethnicity or national origin rather than on the behavior of an individual for the police to believe a particular individual is engaged in criminal activity. The practice of racial profiling is illegal, and is typically addressed in department policy that requires officers to refrain from engaging in it. The Police Executive Research Forum (PERF) replaces the term *racial profiling* with *racially biased policing*, stating that use of the word *profiling* creates confusion about an "otherwise legitimate policing term." Racial profiling was introduced in Chapter 5 in connection with traffic stops. Research on racial disparity, not discrimination, in traffic stops at both the micro (individual) and macro (agency) level revealed the following results:

> The microlevel analysis of individual stops confirmed racial disparity in the frequency of traffic stops as well as in subsequent police treatments. Blacks were overrepresented and other racial and ethnic groups were underrepresented in traffic stops, with a greater disparity in investigatory stops. The macrolevel analysis found that the likelihood of being stopped and being subjected to unfavorable police treatment (e.g., arrest, search, and felony charge) was greater in beats where more Blacks or Hispanics resided and/or more police force was deployed, consistent with the racial threat or minority threat hypothesis. These findings imply that racial disparity at the level of individual stops may be substantially explained by differential policing strategies adopted for different areas based on who resides in these areas. (Roh and Robinson, 2009, p.137)

These findings, which run counter to those of Ousey and Lee, have important implications for problem-solving policing and hot spot policing. At the macrolevel, areas with more frequent traffic stops and more negative outcomes were spatially clustered and the majority of the clusters spatially coincided with minority residential areas and police resource concentration areas: "No matter what the reason is, there exist racially or ethnically minority communities where social problems are concentrated. And these communities often constitute hot spots of crime and disorder, which draw greater attention from police agencies, and consequently invite more intensive law enforcement activities. The problem-oriented policing strategy, accompanied by scientific analyses (e.g., hot spot analysis and crime analysis) is widely understood by police administrators to maneuver police resources more efficiently and effectively" (Roh and Robinson, 2009, p.162).

Lundman and Kowalski (2009) looked at research on the differences in the disproportionate number of Blacks compared with Whites in traffic stops for speeding (15 mph or more over the speed limit) to determine whether there were differences in speeding *behavior* grounded in race and ethnicity. Lundman and Kowalski also conducted their own research on speeding in 55-mph and 65-mph speed zones. Some previous studies as well as their own research suggest that Black drivers were more likely to speed in 65-mph speed zones than Whites were. Lundman and Kowalski (p.504) suggest that the charge of racial discrimination implied in the phrase "Driving While Black" might be partially explained by a more accurate phrase "Speeding While Black," implying disparity rather than discrimination. Doubtless this controversy will continue. Whatever view one takes on police actions against minorities, racial discrimination in the form of racial profiling is to be avoided.

Avoiding Charges of Racial Profiling The roots of racial profiling can be traced back to the pre–Civil War era, when police agencies were expected to enforce slavery laws, and for another century thereafter in enforcing segregation laws (Bratton, 2009, p.87). This legacy engendered in African American populations a distrust and, in some cases "outright hatred of the police" (Bratton, 2009, p.87). During the last several decades of the 20th century, police have focused efforts on handling the violent crime and drug crises: "The unfortunate reality is that crime and disorder in our country are concentrated in poorer neighborhoods, and often the poorest neighborhoods are minority neighborhoods" (Bratton, p.87). When police institute hot spot policing, it makes the agency the "flash point" for racial tension because it involves getting into the middle of discord and strife:

> Because police agencies are inherently in the thick of things, I believe that there is no type of government agency that has a greater opportunity to have a positive impact in minority communities. If we "get it right," we can not only work to ameliorate the legacy of difficult relations between police and racial minorities, we can establish ourselves as the branch of government that takes the lead in effecting positive change on racial issues.
>
> By "getting it right," I mean finding ways to reduce the violence and fear that is so prevalent in many of our minority neighborhoods. I mean policing consistently, compassionately, and constitutionally, and adopting the principles of community policing. (Bratton, 2009, p.88)

To avoid charges of racial profiling, officers must focus on a person's *behavior* in their "profiling." Many departments are training officers in behavior pattern recognition (BPR), a technique originated in Israel and used to look at how an individual behaves in an airport environment, as a way of determining potential threats. Other departments are training all airport employees in suspicious passenger observation techniques, to look for passengers who are acting out of the ordinary or display certain behavioral or observational cues. Are they wearing a warm coat on a hot day? Are they sweating or nervous when they come to the airport security checkpoint? Do they have no luggage or carry ons?

Another way to avoid charges of racial profiling is to focus on intelligence regarding known or suspected terrorists, the quality and quantity of which has changed dramatically since 9/11. Intelligence operations are controversial, partly because of concern that in the zeal to prevent terrorism, citizens' civil rights will be abridged. Further controversies involve concerned citizens' and civil rights groups' fears that law enforcement agencies will gather and keep information about citizens who have not committed crimes but are exercising their civil rights on controversial issues.

Data Collection Many departments are approaching claims of racial profiling through data collection. However, data collection and effective analysis can be costly. In addition, all policies and procedures and all training materials should be reviewed for bias, and citizens should be involved in both the review and the data collection and analysis.

Resistance against legislation mandating data collection may result in *balancing*, unfairly stopping unoffending motorists to protect officers from the "statistical microscope" individually or collectively. The rationale is simple. If an officer stops a minority driver, he or she has to stop a certain number of White drivers to make the numbers come out right. This results in a great deal of unproductive work and opens the door to citizen complaints, and this type of response is still a form of racial profiling—stopping White drivers to balance out minority stops. **Ghosting**, falsifying patrol logs, might also occur to make the numbers come out right.

ghosting

Falsifying patrol logs to make the numbers come out right in response to alleged racial profiling practices.

The Immigration Issue Racial profiling has become embroiled in the immigration issue as well.

Give me your tired, your poor,
Your huddled masses yearning to breathe free,
The wretched refuse of your teeming shore,
Send these, the homeless, tempest-tost to me,
I lift my lamp beside the golden door!

These are the immortal words of poet Emma Lazaras that appear at the base of the Statue of Liberty in New York. These words once reflected a welcoming philosophy of a country developed largely by immigrants.

Today immigration issues challenge our past beliefs and, some would say, the future of America. An estimated 11 to 12 million illegal immigrants reside in this country and have become an increasing focus of controversy. The economy, possibly racism and the 9/11 attack on America, carried out by hijackers who entered the country on student or tourist visas, contribute to the changing political climate. Americans recognized the porous borders and lax enforcement of immigration laws as security threats, and in Congress both parties have pushed for a tougher line. Several challenges facing law enforcement agencies in jurisdictions with large immigrant populations include (Lysakowski et al., 2009, p.3)

- Large numbers of people who do not speak English well (or at all).
- Immigrants' reluctance to report crime.
- Fear of police.
- Effects of federal law enforcement actions.
- Confusion about whether and to what extent local police enforce immigration laws.
- Misunderstandings based on cultural differences.
- Personal interaction between immigrants and police officers that damage good will and trust.

The Department of Homeland Security (DHS) Immigration and Customs Enforcement (ICE) delegates federal immigration enforcement to state and local law enforcement agencies through its authority under section 287(g) of the *Immigration and Nationality Act*. The program, called **287(g)** for the section of the law authorizing it, is intended to help local law enforcement agencies assist in enforcing immigration laws. Although the law has been on the books for years, the first time it was used was in 2002. As of February 2009, 950 law enforcement officers in 23 states had been trained by ICE and 67 law enforcement officers in 23 states were participating in the program. The program has been criticized by civil liberties groups, Hispanic citizens and congressional auditors. Some organizations and individuals have charged the program with promoting racial profiling ("Governments 287(g) Program Criticized in Hearings in House," 2009, pp.5–7).

287(g)
The section of the *Immigration and Nationality Act* delegating federal immigration enforcement to state and local law enforcement agencies

A report issued by the DHS, *The Performance of 287(g) Agreements* (2010, p.1.) states, "We observed instances in which ICE and participating law enforcement agencies were not operating in compliance with the terms of the agreements. We also noted several areas in which ICE had not instituted controls to promote effective program operations and address related risks." The report, coming out of the Office of the Inspector General of DHS, makes 33 specific recommendations to strengthen management controls and improve its oversight of 287(g).

In testimony on immigration enforcement issues, the problems associated with the 287(g) program were voiced: "Increased political pressure on local law enforcement to reduce undocumented immigration, coupled with the federal deputation of local police to enforce federal immigration statutes, is jeopardizing sound and well-established policing practices. Community policing requires active community engagement, which is predicated on trust. For community engagement to flourish, the public must trust the police. It is nearly impossible to gain the required trust to make community policing a reality in places where the community fears the police will deport them, or deport a neighbor, friend or relative" ("Immigration Enforcement," 2010, p.6).

Thus although ICE is clearly charged with dealing with illegal immigrants, the question remains whether the regular beat cop patrolling the streets and responding to calls for service should be responsible for this task as well. Generally, if there is an issue over an illegal person status, it is referred to ICE or to U.S. Citizenship and Immigration Services (USCIS) to deal with. Another question is whether local law enforcement agencies in general have the resources to address this task. The immigration issue is such a considerable challenge that not even a federal agency completely dedicated to it can keep a good handle on it. Outside major and large departments, most police agencies in the country lack the resources to deal with this issue.

The immigration issue centers on whether police officers should be enforcers of immigration laws or should seek to build trust with immigrants as advocated by community policing.

A survey conducted by the Police Executive Research Forum (PERF) and reported in *Police Chiefs and Sheriffs Speak Out on Local Immigration Enforcement* (2008, p.11) found that most state and local jurisdictions lacked written policies on immigration. It also found that 57 percent of respondents believed that if local police enforced immigration laws, illegal immigrants would be even less likely to report being a victim of crime (p.15). Top concerns about enhanced local enforcement were insufficient personnel (65%), undermined trust between the department and the immigrant community (61%), insufficient resources (60%), and insufficient jail space (51%).

Constitutional interpretation also struggles with how to respond. The Fifth and Fourteenth Amendments do not protect citizens alone from arbitrary or unjust government actions. Rather, the amendments use the broader term *persons*.

The Supreme Court has held that whether people are considered legal or otherwise, government does not have a legitimate interest in denying certain services. Laws requiring a one-year waiting period before new legal residents could receive welfare benefits were struck down in *Shapiro v. Thompson* (1969). In *Plyler v. Doe* (1982), the Court held that a Texas law denying public education to children of illegal immigrants was unconstitutional. And in *Sugarman v. Dougall* (1973) and *Hampton v. Mow Sun Wong* (1976), the Court held that state and federal laws barring resident aliens from employment in the federal competitive civil service were illegal.

An amended Arizona law passed in 2010 allows police to verify individual's citizenship status based on reasonable suspicion or probable cause during stops, detainments or arrests. It is a misdemeanor crime to not have proper documentation. The law, which will go into effect in the summer of 2010 as this text goes to press, has caused a whirlwind of national controversy regarding civil liberties and the Fourth Amendment. It is being challenged by several states and will perhaps be challenged by the federal government. Arizona Governor Jan Brewer signed the immigration "papers" bill in response to ongoing issues with illegal immigrants within the state including increasing violent crime involving illegal immigrant, especially gang members and drug dealers, and the lack of federal intervention in helping address these issues. Critics say the law will lead to racial profiling, whereas supporters contend it involves no racial profiling and is needed to crack down on the rising levels of violent crime attributed to illegal immigrants ("Holder: Feds May Sue," 2010).

Profiling as a Legitimate Law Enforcement Tool A central problem with racial profiling is that *profiling* has been a valuable tool in policing for decades. At airports, law enforcement and security personnel are taught to watch for certain traits—paying for a ticket in cash, no luggage, Middle Eastern descent, nervousness and so on—to alert them to drug dealers or potential terrorists. Thus it might be appropriate to change the name of "profiling" to "building a case," with race simply part of most suspect descriptions.

The courts are generally supportive of race being included as one of several factors used to identify suspects. In *United States v. Weaver* (1992) a Drug Enforcement Administration (DEA) officer stopped and questioned Arthur Weaver because he was a roughly dressed, young Black male on a direct flight from Los Angeles to Kansas City who walked rapidly from the airport toward a cab, had two carry-on bags and no checked luggage, and appeared nervous. Weaver was carrying drugs and was arrested, but he challenged the legality of the officer's intervention. The Eighth Circuit Court of Appeals upheld the officer's conduct, explaining,

> Facts are not to be ignored simply because they may be unpleasant—and the unpleasant fact in this case is that he [the DEA agent] had knowledge, based upon his own experience and upon the intelligence reports he had received from Los Angeles authorities, that young male members of the African American Los Angeles gangs were flooding the Kansas City area with cocaine. To that extent then, race, when coupled with the other factors [the agent] relied upon, was a factor in the decision to approach and ultimately detain [the suspect]. We wish it were otherwise, but we take the facts as they are presented to us, not as we would wish them to be.

Despite such court support, officers must be educated on how to avoid unintentional racial profiling based on personal bias. It might be best to avoid the term *racial profiling* because profiling has a legitimate place in law enforcement, and replace it with *racially biased policing*, which has no place in law enforcement.

In addition to racial profiling, disparities have been found in other areas of the criminal justice process. Closely related to the issue of racially biased policing is the perception that police use force more often with minorities than with Whites. Indeed, police use of force on any citizen can become an issue.

USE OF FORCE

English philosopher Herbert Spencer proclaimed in 1851, "Policemen are soldiers who act alone; soldiers are policemen who act in unison." As solitary soldiers the police are justified in using force when required to control crime and keep the peace in our society: "No other enforcement task is more difficult or more demanding personally and professionally than to use force only at the right time, in the right way, and for the right reason" (Means and Seidel, 2010, p.18). The International Association of Chiefs of Police (IACP) defines **force** as "that amount of effort required by police to compel compliance from an unwilling subject." When most people think of "use of force," they envision some type of active, hands-on, or physical tactic. However, it is important to recognize that mere officer presence is, in itself, a *use of force* in that most citizens, when in the presence of a uniformed officer, will act lawfully.

force
Action taken to compel an individual to comply with an officer's request.

 If there is no physical resistance, no physical force should be used.

Five recognized and accepted purposes, commonly referred to as the "rules of engagement," justify the legitimate use of force (Cope and Callanan, 2009):

- *Self defense*—a right common to all people.
- *Defense of others*—a duty assigned to police personnel.
- *Effectuate an arrest*—a vested authority granted by law.
- *Prevent an escape*—a vested authority granted by law.
- *Overcome resistance*—a vested authority granted by law.

Of these five rules of engagement, the fifth rule is the most common reason police use force (Cope and Callanan, 2009).

Force includes any physical, psychological or verbal contact between police officers and citizens. It may involve an officer pushing, grabbing, kicking or hitting a citizen. Force also includes police-dog bites, unconsciousness-rendering holds, handcuffs and leg restraints, chemical agents (pepper spray, Cap-Stun), electrical devices (TASER) and a firearm pointed in a citizen's direction or the threat to carry out any of these types of force. The killing of a subject by an officer is the most extreme use of police force, and deadly force is used as a last resort. In certain circumstances, however, the first action may be the last resort.

A study conducted in Canada looked at the use and relative risk of five major force options: empty-hand control techniques, baton, OC spray, conducted energy weapons and lateral vascular neck restraint ("New Study Ranks Risks," 2008). The study analyzed 562 use-of-force events involving officer arrests of resistant subjects over a 2-year period in Calgary (population: more than a million) and found,

- Conducted energy weapons were the most frequently deployed of the five options, used with 48.2 percent of resistant arrestees. About 1 percent of resistant arrestees were hospitalized, about 12 percent needed minor outpatient

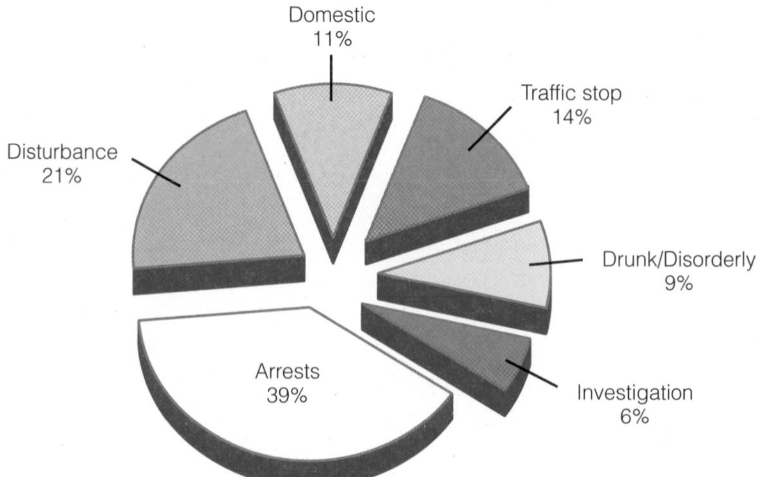

FIGURE 11.2 Percent of Officer Use of Force by Circumstance of Encounter (1999–2000)

SOURCE: *Police Use of Force in America 2001.* Alexandria VA: International Association of Chiefs of Police, 2001, p.ii. Reprinted by permission.

treatment, and more than 42 percent had only minor injuries. Nearly 45 percent sustained no injuries, and there were no fatalities.

- Empty-hand controls were applied in 38.5 percent. Four percent of arrestees were hospitalized, nearly 14 percent required outpatient aid, and almost 50 percent had minor injuries. Among officers, 1 percent required hospitalization, 4.5 percent needed outpatient aid, and nearly 17 percent had minor injuries.
- Batons, used in 5.5 percent of force-involved arrests, caused the greatest rate of higher-level injury. Fewer than 39 percent remained uninjured. Of the officers involved, 13 percent required outpatient treatment and 16 percent sustained minor injuries.
- OC, used in roughly 5 percent of force-involved arrests, produced the lowest rate of injury; more than 80 percent sustained no injury.
- Out of more than 827,000 police–public interactions, the 562 instances that involved use of force represented less than 1 percent (.07 percent) of the total.

The final item emphasizes how infrequently force is used in police-citizen encounters, yet biased reporting of such events has led to widespread public misperception of such force being used routinely. The study results also reveal that police departments must seek alternatives to the baton if they hope to reduce the frequency and seriousness of injuries sustained by both citizens and officers.

Literature reviews have reported that use of force is most likely to occur when the suspect shows signs of alcohol or drug intoxication or engages in hostile behavior. Other studies of use-of-force incidents have identified as contributing factors inappropriate demeanor by lower or marginalized social groups.

Gender and Use of Force

Research shows that female officers are less likely to use excessive or deadly force. Furthermore, a study conducted by the Los Angeles Police Department found that female officers are often better able than male officers are to de-escalate potentially violent or aggressive situations through their presence and use of interpersonal skills, thus reducing the need to employ physical force (Tuomey and Jolly, 2009, p.69), It might also be kept in mind that many offenders and citizens in general may not perceive female officers to be as great a threat as male officers and, consequently, may not exhibit the type of behavior that often leads officers to use more aggressive types of compliance control.

The Use-of-Force Continuum

The amount of force used can be placed on a continuum: no physical force (used with a cooperative person), to ordinary force (used with a person who is resisting), to extraordinary force (used with a person who is assaultive). One use-of-force continuum is shown in Figure 11.3.

Not all continuums used by police are consistent with the one illustrated in Figure 11.3. Many departments have begun moving away from a straight-line continuum to a circular one, partly because of criticism that the former option suggests a linear progression to how force must be applied but that, in reality, incidents

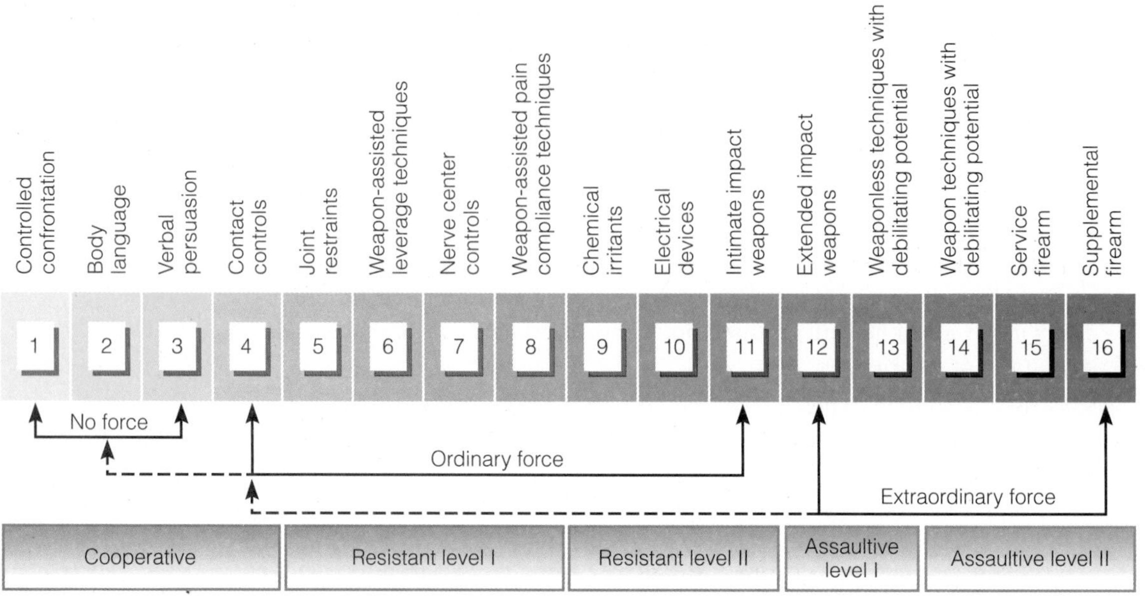

FIGURE 11.3 Use-of-Force Continuum

SOURCE: Adapted from G. Connor. "Use of Force Continuum: Phase II." *Law and Order*, March 1991, p.30. Reprinted by permission of *Law and Order* magazine.

are rarely linear and that officers may need to skip past a few "steps" to achieve immediate control. Such an unrealistic expectation or standard may leave an officer open to a lawsuit. Depending on the totality of the circumstances, officers may find themselves suddenly at the "end" of the continuum, needing to use deadly force to handle the existing threat. Thus, to address concerns over the nonlinear application of use of force and remove the unrealistic expectation that force application must progress through a predetermined set of stages to reach a particular level, many departments are now using a circular use-of-force, as shown in Figure 11.4.

Three questions surround these continuums (Peters and Brave, 2006, pp.8–9).

Controversy regarding use-of-force continuums involves (1) whether they have outlived their usefulness, (2) whether they should they be included in use-of-force policies and (3) whether they increase liability.

First, have they outlived their usefulness? Force continuums were developed by trainers in the 1960s. Since then more than 50 such continuums have been developed; many are complex and ambiguous, while others are deceptively simple. Some argue that force continuums are still necessary, but others feel they are as outdated as city call boxes.

Second, should use-of-force policies include such continuums? Critics say including a force continuum in an agency's use-of-force policy is like mixing oil with water. The Fourth Amendment reasonableness clause does not require that officers use the least intrusive means. The landmark case on use of force, *Graham v. Connor* (1989), is broad and favors police officers, considering numerous factors that continuums do not. For example, many continuums depict only the relationship

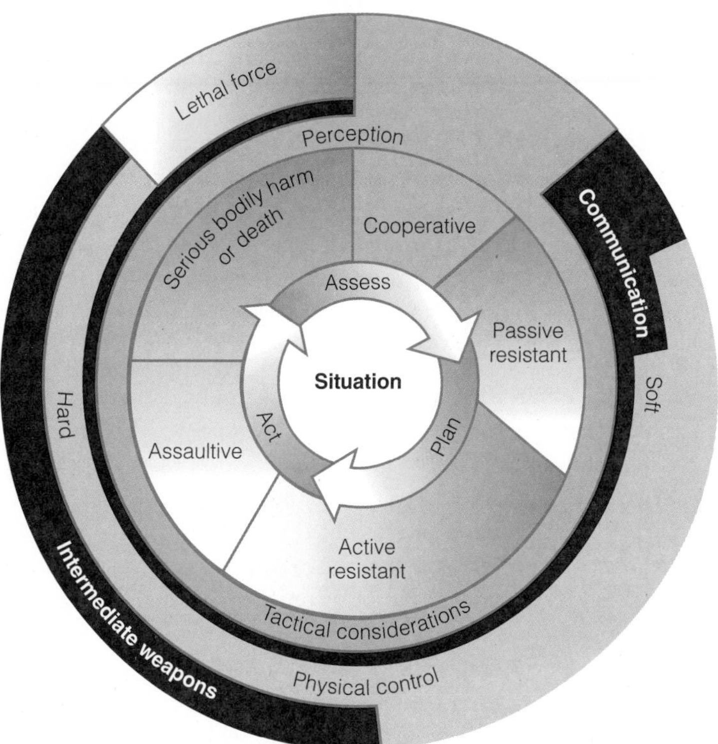

The officer continuously assesses the situation and selects the most reasonable option relative to those circumstances as perceived at that point in time.

FIGURE 11.4 Circular Use-Of-Force

SOURCE: Courtesy of City of Ottawa and Ottawa Police Services.

between the subject's current behavior (actively resisting, for example) and the officer's force response.

Third, do force continuums increase liability exposure? Those who want to abolish any kind of measured response (what force continuums are designed to do) are often looking for a way to avoid losses in litigation. Others contend that abolishing continuums is not going to change anything. The U.S. Department of Justice's Civil Rights division has urged agencies to adopt a progressive-force continuum and train all officers in it. Use-of-force policies create consistency and provide a training standard. Such a continuum should include *all* types of force used by an agency, including firearms, pepper spray, batons and canines. Each agency should address these three questions when deciding whether a use-of-force continuum fits their department. Use of force policies should also consider a department's response to the relatively rare instance of sudden in-custody death.

Sudden In-Custody Death

The media have different names for the cause of death of a person being restrained while being arrested: excited delirium, restraint asphyxia, positional asphyxia and "in-custody death" syndromes. Each year people die suddenly while restrained, most of whom were being arrested after a violent police encounter. It is uncertain how many restraint-related sudden deaths occur annually, but it may range between 50 and 125 per year, with some estimates higher.

Definitions According to the World Health Organization, *sudden death* refers to cardiorespiratory collapse occurring within 24 hours of the beginning of symptoms. Others define it as cardiorespiratory collapse occurring within 1 hour of the onset of symptoms. *In-custody death* has many definitions. Technically, anyone who dies in prison is "in custody." A *sudden in-custody death* refers to any *unintentional* death that occurs while a subject is in police custody.

Restraint Asphyxia Research shows that a sudden in-custody restraint death is a statistically rare event given the annual number of police-citizen contacts (Ross, 2010). Using Department of Justice statistics, it is estimated that a sudden restraint in custody death has about a .000005 percent likelihood of occurrence. Even so, the tension between science, the use of force and the law is high in such deaths: "Medical experts will attempt to prove that the cause of death resulted from a theory of 'positional or restraint asphyxia as a result of prone restraint. The claim is that placing the subject in the prone position for control and restraint and/or the weight applied to the back of the subject during restraint interfered with the mechanics of ventilation, causing asphyxia, and death" (Ross).

Other studies, however, do not support the contention that ventilation is significantly compromised by such positional restraints, whether in a prone or hogtied position, with or without weight on the back: "Other factors such as excited delirium, drug intoxication, mental illness, stress, trauma, and catecholamine hyperstimulation, are considered to be factors playing the most significant role in these sudden deaths" (Ross).

Drug Abuse and Sudden Death A study analyzed 668 sudden deaths during a 32-month period, and found no indication that police tactics or equipment caused the fatalities. Sudden deaths in the general population are often related to cocaine abuse in at least 3 of every 100 cases. Even occasional "recreational" cocaine users increase their risk of sudden death as a result of prone restraint. The same risk likely pertains to use of methamphetamine ("New Study: Cocaine Abuse," 2010).

excited delirium

Identified by such behaviors as being extremely agitated, threatening violence, talking incoherently, tearing off clothes and requiring four or five officers to restrain the individual.

Excited Delirium Death **Excited delirium** (ED) refers to a psychological and physical meltdown, sometimes resulting in death. The subject's behavior indicates the syndrome. Among the characteristics of a person with excited delirium are unbelievable strength, imperviousness to pain, ability to effectively resist multiple officers over an extended time, hyperthermia (temperatures from 105 to 119 degrees Fahrenheit), sweating, bizarre and violent behavior, aggression, hyperactivity, extreme paranoia, incoherent shouting or nonsensical speech, hallucinations, confusion or disorientation, grunting or animal-like sounds while struggling, foaming at the mouth, drooling and dilated pupils. Physical restraint compounds these effects. The suspect is likely to be near complete exhaustion despite the behaviors exhibited. The typical excited delirium death involves the subject slipping into a state of sudden tranquility, either during or after the struggle.

Lewinski, executive director of the Force Science Institute, reports on a growing body of evidence that supports the existence of excited delirium, despite skepticism by some people in the medical profession and activist groups who are suspicious of the police ("Research Roundup," 2009). In fact, a special investigative task force of the American College of Emergency Physicians has formally declared, "The violent and sometimes lethal phenomenon known as 'excited delirium' really does exist" ("Emergency Docs," 2009). However, even with an extensive autopsy, there is no definitive way to prove someone died of excited delirium.

The incident report of any sudden in-custody death should describe the suspect's behavior precisely. It should also describe the restraints used, if any, as well as how many officers were involved in subduing the suspect.

Although officers are authorized to use force, including deadly force, they must use only that level and amount of force *reasonably* necessary to accomplish a legitimate law enforcement objective.

Reasonable Force

reasonable force
Force no greater than that needed to achieve the desired end.

What constitutes **reasonable force** was established in *Graham v. Connor* (1989). In this case, Graham, a diabetic, asked a friend to drive him to a store for some orange juice to counteract an insulin reaction. The friend agreed, but when Graham entered the store, he saw a long checkout line and, concerned about the delay, hurried out of the store to ask the friend to take him someplace else. Officer Connor, seeing Graham hastily enter and leave the store, grew suspicious and followed their car. Half a mile from the store, Connor made an investigative stop. Although the friend told Connor that Graham was simply suffering from a "sugar reaction," the officer ordered the two men to wait while he found out what, if anything, had happened at the store. When the officer returned to his patrol car to request backup, Graham got out of the car and passed out on the curb.

Moments later a number of other officers arrived on the scene. One officer rolled Graham over on the sidewalk and cuffed his hands tightly behind his back, ignoring the friend's pleas to get Graham some sugar. Several officers then lifted Graham up, carried him over to the friend's car, and placed him face down on its hood. Regaining consciousness, Graham asked the officers to check his wallet for a diabetic decal. One officer told him to "Shut up," and shoved Graham's face against the hood of the car. Four officers grabbed Graham and threw him headfirst into the police car. Another friend of Graham's brought some orange juice to the car, but the officers refused to let him have it. Finally Officer Connor received a report that Graham had done nothing wrong at the store, and the officers drove him home and released him.

During this encounter Graham sustained a broken foot, cuts on his wrists, a bruised forehead and an injured shoulder. He also claimed to have developed a loud, permanent ringing in his right ear. Graham filed a lawsuit under 42 U.S.C. § 1983 against the individual officers involved in the incident, alleging they had used excessive force in making the investigatory stop. The Court, however, ruled that the officers did not use excessive force, explaining,

> The calculus of reasonableness must embody allowance for the fact that police officers are often forced to make split-second judgments—in circumstances that are tense, uncertain, and rapidly evolving—about the amount of force that is necessary

> in a particular situation. . . . The reasonableness of a particular use of force must be judged from the perspective of a reasonable officer on the scene, rather than with the 20/20 vision of hindsight.

The *Graham* Court listed four factors against which an officer's actions must be measured: (1) the immediate threat of serious physical harm to the officer or others; (2) the degree to which the situation is tense, uncertain and rapidly evolving; (3) the nature of the crime at issue; and (4) whether the subject is resisting arrest or attempting to evade arrest by flight.

Excessive Force

excessive force
Force beyond that which is reasonably necessary to accomplish a legitimate law enforcement purpose.

The IACP defines **excessive force** as "the application of an amount and/or frequency of force greater than that required to compel compliance from a willing or unwilling subject."

Excessive force is synonymous with police brutality. An extreme example of such unprofessional conduct was the brutalization of Abner Louima, a Haitian immigrant who was sodomized at the police department with a broomstick. Louima received an $8.7 million settlement because of the incident.

Research from the National Center for Women and Policing (NCWP) has found that female police officers are substantially less likely than are their male counterparts to be involved in problems of excessive force. Data from the NCWP indicates women currently comprise about 13 percent of the total sworn personnel in large metropolitan departments, but only 5 percent of citizen complaints for excessive force and 2 percent of the sustained allegations involve female police officers. Female officers also account for only 6 percent of dollars paid out in court judgments and settlements for excessive force among large police agencies Complaints about excessive force sometimes involve less-lethal force.

Less-Lethal Force

less-lethal force
Force that has less potential for causing death or serious injury than do traditional tactics.

As law enforcement technology expands, a wider variety of response options are becoming available to officers. For instances where an increased level of force is necessary but deadly force is too extreme, there are now a variety of **less-lethal force** alternatives. Common less-lethal options include Mace, CN and CS tear gas, oleoresin capsicum (OC) pepper spray, projectile launchers and specialty impact munitions such as beanbags, flexible baton rounds designed to deliver blunt trauma, and conducted energy devices (CEDs) such as the TASER. Capture nets are another less-lethal option, but they are difficult to deploy inside buildings or if a suspect is near a wall or other obstacle. In addition, once a suspect is ensnared, handcuffing and searching are difficult if not impossible.

Six options for controlling a suspect with less-lethal force are (1) verbal/visual management of the scene, (2) empty-hand control, (3) restraints, (4) aerosols, (5) impact weapons and (6) electronic control devices (ECDs).

A *PoliceOne* poll conducted in February 2010 asked officers what kind of less-lethal weapon they last deployed and found that 58 percent replied "TASER." This was followed by OC (28 percent), baton (9 percent), 40mm (3 percent) and beanbag (2 percent) (Hawkes, 2010).

Restraints No matter what other nonlethal control options a department provides, officers will always receive some means of restraining people, most typically handcuffs. However: "Improper or sloppy use of handcuffs, and sometimes failure to use them at all, has probably gotten more officers hurt and killed than any other commonly used law enforcement tool" (Ashley, 2007, p.72). Also, if an officer applies cuffs and fails to double-lock them, they may continue to tighten on a subject's wrists until the situation has progressed to a medical one, requiring treatment of the subject by a health care provider and additional paperwork for the officer, not to mention possible civil liability.

Aerosols Chemical agents such as CS and CN (tear gas) are less-lethal weapons effective for crowd control. Another effective chemical agent is OC or pepper spray. In many departments' force options, pepper spray is allowed when verbal commands are ineffective, even before control holds and impact weapons are suggested. Current efforts to increase airline security include arming sky marshals with pepper-ball guns that incapacitate a subject yet, unlike conventional bullets, will not puncture the plane's fuselage.

Impact Weapons Specialty impact munitions (SIMs) are excellent tools for quelling rioting crowds and taking down armed emotionally disturbed persons. Among the less-lethal projectiles are rubber buckshot, rubber balls, rubber slugs and beanbags. However, some beanbag rounds and rubber bullets can cause serious injuries.

Electronic Control Devices Electronic control devices (ECDs) are also referred to as stun guns, electromuscular devices (EMDs), electronic immobilization devices (IMDs) and conducted energy devices (CEDs). A national survey conducted by PERF and Dr. Geoffrey Alpert of the University of South Carolina found that 69 percent of police agencies had deployed CEDs by 2008, compared with 53 percent in 2005, and use of OC had declined from 93 percent in 2005 to 87 percent in 2008 and the use of batons had been cut nearly in half over the same time period ("Survey by PERF," 2009). Research has demonstrated that CEDs can help significantly lower the injury rate to both suspects and police officers: "Overall . . . the use of CEDs is associated with a 70 percent reduction in the chances of an *officer* being injured compared to agencies that do not use CEDs. And the odds of a *suspect* being injured are reduced by more than 40 percent in CED agencies compared to non-CED agencies" ("Major Research Study by PERF," 2009, pp.4–5).

Safety concerns surround the use of CEDs, with some media stories reporting incidents of heart attacks and other detrimental health impacts resulting from contact with such devices. However, an interim report by the National Institute of Justice states, "Although exposure to CED is not risk free, there is no conclusive medical evidence within the state of current research that indicates a high risk of serious injury or death from the direct effects of CED exposure. Field experience with CED use indicates that exposure is safe in the vast majority of cases. Therefore, law enforcement need not refrain from deploying CEDs, provided the devices are used in accordance with accepted national guidelines" (*Study of Deaths*, 2008, p.3). Such guidelines have been jointly issued by PERF, the National

Sheriffs' Association (NSA) and the Bureau of Justice Statistics (BJS) ("PERF, NSA and BJA Issue Report and Guidelines," 2009, pp.3–4).

The best-known CED, in use for nearly 30 years, is the TASER, an acronym for Thomas A. Swift Electric Rifle (named after Tom Swift in the popular children's adventure series of the 1920s and 1930s). Field data collected by TASER International indicates that use of their less-lethal devices has significantly reduced the number of officer and suspect injuries, decreased the use of lethal force and contributed to substantial liability savings (*TASER® Electronic Control Devices (ECDs): Field Data and Risk Management*, 2009).

In *Bryan v. McPherson* (2009), a case that has drawn recent national attention, the U.S. Court of Appeals for the Ninth Circuit ruled that use of a TASER on a bizarrely behaving, but nonthreatening, driver is excessive force. Even though the case controls law only in the Ninth Circuit (Alaska, Arizona, California, Hawaii, Idaho, Montana, Nevada, Oregon, and Washington), it provides judicial guidance to law enforcement as well as to other courts throughout the country. Following is a description of the circumstances of the incident in which Bryan was tazed (Means and McDonald, 2010, p.52):

> Carl Bryan's day began with a series of mishaps, including a trek to Los Angeles to retrieve his car keys, a speeding ticket, and a second encounter with police for failing to wear his seatbelt. When stopped, Bryan stepped out of the car wearing only his boxer shorts and tennis shoes, and stood on the side of the road non-compliantly yelling gibberish and hitting his thighs. His "bad day" culminated when Officer McPherson "shot Bryan with his TASER gun." Bryant was immobilized by the jolt and fell face forward onto the asphalt, breaking four of his front teeth.

The *Bryan* court, using *Graham v. Connor* as precedent, evaluated the use of force for reasonableness by examining four core factors: "(1) whether the suspect poses an immediate threat to the safety of the officers or others; (2) whether the suspect is actively resisting arrest; (3) the severity of the crime at issue; and (4) whether the suspect is attempting to evade arrest by flight" (Brave and O'Linn, 2010, p.12). The court concluded that Bryan was stopped for a seat belt violation, was not a dangerous felon, was not a flight risk, did not offer resistance at all, and was not an immediate threat being unarmed, wearing only boxer shorts, standing 15 to 25 feet away, and was, at most, a disturbed, upset young man not threatening anyone. In addition, the officer failed to warn Bryan that noncompliance would lead to Bryan being shot with a CED, and the officer did not consider other available tactics.

Sanow (2010, p.6) warns, "The courts are, indeed, raising the bar on use of less-lethal force against non-compliant, but non-threatening subjects. Forget using the TASER on people who refuse to get on the ground during an arrest or who are fleeing. If the subject is passively resistant, any use of a TASER whatsoever is becoming seen as 'unreasonable.' TASER misuse is, simply put, the use of excessive force, period." In addition, policy makers should be aware of a study by the New York City Police Department that identified predictors of TASER effectiveness: "Findings indicate that several factors are associated with reduced effectiveness, including suspect body weight (more than 200 pounds), drug and alcohol use, physical violence and close distance (3 feet or less) between the officer and the suspect" (White and Ready, 2010, p.70).

Every agency that uses electronic control weapons should have a comprehensive policy providing specific information as to the placement of the device on an approved use-of-force continuum. In addition, each agency should require a report to be initiated each time the device is used regarding the nature of its deployment.

Compliance tools, as less-lethal options are commonly called, give officers more options for controlling a situation before it escalates to a deadly force incident: "Having a less lethal option available means you can start at a lower level on the use-of-force continuum and possibly end a confrontation without resorting to lethal force. It's a good option to have" (Basich, 2009, p.30).

Less-Lethal Can Still Be Lethal Debate has centered over the terminology applied to these weapons—should they be called *less-than-lethal*, *less-lethal*, *defensive*, *intermediate* or something else? Some use-of-force experts prefer the term *less-lethal* to *less-than-lethal* because of liability implications and misrepresentation of a weapon's lethality. What does *less-lethal* mean? Can someone be less dead? The terms *less-lethal* and *less-than-lethal* create a trap for police officers and the agencies they serve and can be used for them or against them depending on the situation. The weapons might be called an intermediate weapon or a defensive weapon instead. Whatever term is used, it must be recognized that many of these alternatives *can* cause death.

Although officers acknowledge the fatal possibilities that may accompany use of less-lethal force, at times officers are justified in using force they *know* will likely result in a subject's death. As Basich (2010, p.51) cautions, "Sometimes officers take too many chances to employ less-lethal munitions or tactics and actually put themselves in undue danger. We always say, 'never bring a beanbag to a gunfight.' If the suspect has a firearm, in most situations, I would think less-lethal weapons are not appropriate."

Deadly Force

Although definitions vary among jurisdictions, **deadly force** is generally defined as "any force that can reasonably be expected to cause death or serious bodily injury." The authority to use deadly force is an awesome responsibility. When considering the justifiable use of deadly force, two interrelated rights are important: the legal right to use such force and the moral right compelling the officer to do so.

deadly force

Any force that can reasonably be expected to cause or is intended to cause death or serious physical injury.

State legislators have generally given the police broad discretion in this area, with most politicians fearful of being labeled as "soft on criminals" if they do otherwise. Many state statutes authorize use of deadly force to prevent commission of a felony. Yet, to balance the legal and moral rights involved, several states have adopted penal codes that do not rely solely on a crime being classified as a felony. They focus instead on the danger the suspect poses to the officer and society.

Justification for use of deadly force must consider the legal right and the need to apprehend the suspect compared with the arresting officer's safety and the value of human life.

The landmark Supreme Court ruling, *Tennessee v. Garner* (1985), bars police from shooting to kill fleeing felons unless there is an imminent danger to life. This ruling invalidated state laws (passed in almost half the states) that allowed police officers to use deadly force to prevent the escape of a suspected felon.

The case involved a 1974 incident in which a Memphis police officer shot and killed an unarmed 15-year-old boy fleeing from the police after having stolen $10 in money and jewelry from an unoccupied home. The officer testified that he shot the boy to prevent him from escaping. He had been trained to do so, and Tennessee law permitted him to do so. The Supreme Court ruled that the Tennessee "fleeing felon" statute was unconstitutional because it authorized use of deadly force against unarmed fleeing suspects who posed no threat to the officer or third parties. In effect, taking a life is a "seizure," which the Fourth Amendment states must be reasonable.

The Contagious Fire Phenomenon *Contagious fire* can be defined as "the phenomenon that occurs when one officer shoots, causing other officers to have a proclivity to also shoot, even if they are unaware for the justification for shooting" (Joyner, 2010). Most officers find the term offensive because it is frequently misused to describe an officer-involved shooting (OIS). Joyner (2010) stresses, "A number of officers firing their weapons should *not* be described as 'contagious fire' if each individual officer perceived a threat and made a reasonable deadly force decision based on that threat. . . . When politicians claim that it's unacceptable for over 50 shots (or some other arbitrary number) to be fired, they're wrong. It's completely acceptable, and necessary, for survival, to shoot more than 50 rounds if the threat continues to exist."

Research shows that, on average, "extra shots" are generally beyond an officer's control and are more likely to be an involuntary reaction under stress than a conscious decision without malicious motivation (Lewinski and Hudson, 2003). Further research shows that officers may "reasonably" fire six rounds or more into suspects who are initially standing and then begin falling and who, in fact, may already be mortally wounded. The average suspect took 1.1 seconds to fall, during which time four shots *per officer* could be fired ("Excessive Shots," 2010).

A summary of the law on the use of force is given in Table 11.1.

Shooting of Unarmed Suspects When police shoot an unarmed suspect, the public is often outraged. Some question why the officer could not just shoot the suspect in the knee. However, officers need to ask themselves if they can be reasonably sure the suspect is unarmed or if the suspect could take the officer's weapon.

Conditioned Hesitation Many factors can lead to an officer hesitating in a kill zone, and any such hesitation in a crisis can potentially cost an officer's life. Factors contributing to the problem include training, the officer's level of physical fitness, the officer's mind-set and attitudes, suspect/subject factors and fear.

K-9s as Deadly Force Dogs have been of tremendous help to law enforcement officers in locating and apprehending criminal suspects. This use, however, often requires the dog to apply force, at the handler's command, on the suspect and thus falls under the Fourth Amendment's requirement of reasonableness. Several court

TABLE 11.1 Summary of the Law on the Use of Force

Situation	Less-Than-Deadly Force	Deadly Force
In self-defense or in the defense of others	"The use of (reasonable) force upon or toward another person is justified when the actor (reasonably) believes that such force is immediately necessary for the purpose of protecting himself or herself (or another) against the use of unlawful force by such other person on the present occasion."[a]	"The use of deadly force is not justified . . . unless such force is necessary to protect . . . against death, serious bodily harm, kidnapping, or sexual intercourse compelled by force or threat."[b]
In the defense of property	"Only such degree of force or threat thereof may intentionally be used as the actor reasonably believes is necessary to prevent or terminate the interference."[c]	Under the old common law, deadly force could be used in the defense of property. All states now forbid the use of intentional deadly force in the defense of property.
To apprehend a person who has committed a crime	"When an officer is making or attempting to make an arrest for a criminal offense, he is acting for the protection of public interest and is permitted even greater latitude than when he acts in self-defense, and he is not liable unless the means which he uses are clearly excessive."[d]	*Misdemeanor: NEVER* *Fleeing Felon:* Deadly force could be used when officers "have probable cause . . . to believe that the suspect (has committed a felony and) poses a threat to the safety of the officers or a danger to the community if left at large." *Tennessee v. Garner*
To stop a person for investigative purposes when only "reasonable suspicion" exists	Only such force that is reasonable and necessary under the circumstances that then exist.	NEVER
Disciplining children (corporal punishment)	Only parents and other people having a status of in loco parentis to a child may use reasonable force "reasonably believed to be necessary for (the child's) proper control, training, or education."[e] Other persons (such as strangers or neighbors) may not discipline a child.	NEVER

[a] Sections 3.04(1) and 3.05(1) of the Model Penal Code.

[b] Section 3.04(2)(b) of the Model Penal Code.

[c] Section 939.49(1) of the Wisconsin Statutes.

[d] Restatement of Torts, Section 132(a).

[e] Restatement of Torts, Section 147(2), as quoted by the U.S. Supreme Court in *Ingraham v. Wright*, 429 U.S. 975, 97 S.Ct. 481 (1976).

SOURCE: Gardner/Anderson. *Criminal Law*, 7E. © 2000 (p.127) Wadsworth, a part of Cengage Learning, Inc. Reproduced by permission. www.cengage.com/permissions

decisions around the country have indicated that law enforcement–trained K-9s are to be considered a less-lethal alternative—and safer—means of applying force.

Use of Force and Race Research on the relationship between race and support for police use of force found that the race of the offender influences Blacks' approval for the use of force by police, but does not affect Whites' approval: "Whites were equally likely to approve of police using force if the offender was a Black teenager or a White teenager. In contrast, and consistent with expectations, the race of the offender had a significant impact on Blacks' support for police of force. Blacks were much less likely to approve of police using force when the offender was

CAREER PROFILE

Dan Wise (K-9 Officer)

Throughout my life, I have been encouraged to perform tasks to the best of my ability and to do the right thing. As a child, I would watch television programs and movies that contained a strong "good-guy" role. I remember watching the sheriffs of western towns and big city detectives, all doing their best to stop crime and catch the "bad guy." As early as age 6 I was recorded as having expressed a desire to be a police officer, but it wasn't until I was 14 that I became resolute in that choice. I was still unsure as to the specific direction in law enforcement that I wanted to travel; all I knew was that I wanted to become a police officer.

As the years went by my desire and education in law enforcement led me toward the state police. The department had a good reputation for officers that were well respected by both citizens and criminals. Once I learned of the pay and benefits offered by different agencies, my criteria for employment narrowed significantly. During my senior year in college, I was required to choose a department at which to serve a four-month internship. I chose the Decatur, Illinois, Police Department (DPD) because of its location in the state, the opportunity it offered for me to experience many sides of policing and its strong reputation. During my internship I tested with the department and grew fond of what Decatur had to offer me. The summer after my internship was completed, I was hired by the DPD, yet at that time I was still uncertain as to what direction I wanted to go with my career.

During my first five years I was able to become a field training officer and an instructor in defensive tactics and firearms. I was also exposed to the K-9 program. After training and assisting the K-9 teams with their various activities, I knew that my desire was to be a K-9 handler, a position that I have now held for almost eight years.

As a K-9 handler, I am assigned to third shift (11 P.M.–7 A.M.). My duties include responding to all violent or forcible felonies, any situation in which the dog's scenting ability would assist with the apprehension of a suspect (tracking and building searches) or the locating of evidence. K-9s can be trained to accomplish many different tasks. Our department's K-9s are trained to detect four different types of narcotic odors, track on any type of surface, perform evidence searches, search buildings for suspects and apprehend suspects. The K-9 teams perform many public demonstrations that showcase the K-9's abilities and allow for positive contact with citizens. All K-9 handlers are expected to board and care for the K-9 at their home. Routine training and visits to the vet are also part of the expected duties. We are compensated for the extra time spent on care for the animal. A specially equipped squad car is assigned as a take-home vehicle due to the on-call status of all handlers regardless of the time of day or night.

My current K-9 partner's name is "Dutch," and he is a 3 and a half-year-old Belgian Malinois. I have been partnered with him for 2 and a half years. Departments usually start to train a K-9 when it is 1 to 2 years old. All good K-9s will like to do whatever the given task because they are working for their reward. They should not see a job and slowly start to do it because they have to. They should all be eager and excited every time you get them from the kennel or the squad car. I treat my dog as a tool. I take care of him and do all that I can to keep him in good shape, but I realize he could get hurt. I have a wife, two children and bills every month to pay. Dutch is there to do what I can't and to take the risks that I shouldn't have to take. I like my dog a lot, but he will never be treated as a pet until the day he is retired. If your K-9 gets rewarded for looking cute or watches TV with you all night, then why would he want to work as hard when he is actually deployed? Dutch has limited contact with my family—it's a good relationship with them, but *limited* is the key word. A good "working dog" of any kind will always be treated in such a fashion.

Over the years I have trained with many departments and assisted with the training of several K-9s from beginning to end. During this time I have discovered many challenges to being a good K-9 handler. First and foremost is training. Many K-9 handlers don't realize the amount of on- and off-duty time and effort required to develop and maintain a good, consistent and reliable partner. It is easy to routinely train with the same people under the same conditions or to slack off when training is available. But the end result will only be too obvious when the K-9 is deployed.

Consistent training under various conditions will develop you and your partner's experience and stamina for the most difficult of deployments. When lives are potentially at stake, don't let the lack of quality training be the reason for failure. Every time the K-9 locates what it is supposed to be searching for, count that as a personal success. Some of the most fulfilling moments I have experienced have been when the K-9 does the seemingly impossible. Locating an Alzheimer patient when hope was lost, finding the evidence when officers had already looked or catching the bad guy that was supposed to be long gone. Self-pride and a little friendly rivalry with other K-9 handlers has always been my biggest motivator.

The ability to educate yourself about working dogs can often be as close as your local kennel club, Schutzhund club or dog obedience school. Once you have made contacts within the K-9 world, you can better decide if becoming a K-9 handler is the right direction for your career.

a Black teenager than when the offender was a White teenager" (Johnson and Kuhns, 2009, p.615).

Gau et al. (2010, p.27) studied the impact of race on police use of the TASER and found a moderate relationship, with Hispanic suspects being twice as likely as Whites to have TASER used against them: "Hispanic ethnicity, although not the primary determinant of TASER use, proved to increase the likelihood that a suspect would be subdued with a TASER."

Avoiding Use-of-Force-Related Problems

Means and Seidel (2010, pp. 18–20) identify four keys to navigating the complex interplay of law, human nature, interpersonal communication, physical ability and specific weapon proficiencies:

> Key #1—Interpersonal skills and emotional management. Interpersonal communications skills often do succeed in de-escalating volatile situations and frequently allow officers to gain voluntary compliance. When problems are solved without the need for force, everybody wins. Even in those cases where tactical communication fails and force is used, the genuine pre-force attempt to manage behavior with verbal techniques puts the subsequent use of force in the best possible light.
>
> Key #2—Assuring the legal validity of core transactions. When there is a "problem" with a use-of force involvement, it is rare that the amount of force used by the officer is the cause of the problem. Far more typically, the issue is some legal flaw in the transaction itself—the thing the officer is doing in the first place. It turns out that the cure for most use-of-force problems is found in proper training and supervision in matters of arrest and detention and of search and seizure.
>
> Key #3—Maintaining proportionality and managing force escalations. Use-of-force policy and training models should deal with the increasing complexity of weapon systems in the field. Use-of-force policy should resist the simplistic nature of giving pat guidance. Policy that is rich with multiple, well-described scenarios that consider the full range of "objectively reasonable" officer responses are a viable alternative to sterile models that do not represent the dynamic nature of use-of-force decision making.
>
> Key #4—Avoiding peripheral poisonings. Correct use-of-force cases can be poisoned by pre- or post-force officer behaviors or reputations or behavior during a force incident that has nothing to do with the force itself. Laughing and joking about hurting or killing people—as if it would be great fun—can come back to officers and agencies whether it occurs before or after a force incident. Name-calling or verbal abuse during a force transaction can alter witness perceptions negatively.

Officers' Rights in Use-of-Force Lawsuits

Kruger (2009, p.12) warns, "Because use-of-force incidents, particularly those involving a firearm, have the potential to subject officers to criminal investigation, officers involved in such incidents will be concerned about protecting their individual constitutional rights, such as the right against compelled self-incrimination, the right to counsel and the right to be free from unreasonable search and seizure." Although police have a public duty to assist in a criminal investigation of a use-of-force incident, they do not give up their constitutional rights in such an investigation. Because of this, two parallel investigations are usually conducted, one to determine the facts of the case and the other as a criminal investigation.

Two well-known Supreme Court cases address the Fifth Amendment issue in the public workplace: *Garrity v. New Jersey* (1967) and *Gardner v. Broderick* (1968). In both cases, officers were forced to choose between waiving their right to remain silent and retaining their jobs (Kruger, 2009). In *Garrity*, the Court held that states cannot use incriminating statements of employees obtained when employees are threatened with job loss in subsequent criminal proceedings: "When an officer is compelled (ordered under threat of discipline) to produce information (statement, report or answer to questions), the information produced is protected from use against the officer in a criminal proceeding, if the officer invokes the protection of the Fifth Amendment. The employer is prohibited from compelling (ordering under threat of discipline) the officer to waive assertion of the protection of the Fifth Amendment. The information may only be used against the officer in an internal proceeding. The *Garrity* right must be interpreted as consisting of two principles, protection for an officer and prohibition against an employer" ("Quick Reference Guide," 2009). Commonly referred to as the ***Garrity* protection**, this ruling means employers can insist that officers provide information for the administrative investigation, but must be told that they retain their constitutional rights and that any information so provided cannot be used if a criminal proceeding is brought against the officer.

Garrity protection

Employers can insist that officers provide information for an administrative investigation, but must be told that they retain their constitutional rights and that any information so provided cannot be used if a criminal proceeding is brought against the officer.

Garrity was upheld in *Gardner v. Broderick*: "We now hold the protection of the individual under the Fourteenth Amendment against coerced statements prohibits use in subsequent criminal proceedings of statements obtained under threat of removal from office, and that it extends to all, whether they are policemen or other members of our body politic."

Police officers involved in use-of-force incidents retain their constitutional rights against unreasonable search and seizures (Fourth Amendment), against self-incrimination (Fifth Amendment) and for legal representation (Sixth Amendment).

POLICE PURSUITS

One controversial type of force used by police is pursuit, which may result in injury or death for fleeing suspects, pursuing officers or innocent bystanders. Vehicle pursuits can be extremely dangerous activities for law enforcement: "Pursuits are particularly unique in that their dangers are often aimed directly at innocent victims; studies suggest that more than 300 civilians are killed each year in police vehicle pursuits" (Yates, 2009).

According to Nugent et al. (n.d., p.iv), "Police throughout the country engage in hundreds of high-speed automobile chases every day. Enough of these result in serious property damage, personal injury, and death to make police pursuit a major public concern." **Pursuit** is defined as: "An active attempt by a law enforcement officer on duty in a patrol car to apprehend one or more occupants of a moving motor vehicle, providing the driver of such vehicle is aware of the attempt and is resisting apprehension by maintaining or increasing his speed or by ignoring the law enforcement officer's attempt to stop him" (Nugent et al., n.d., p.1).

pursuit

An active attempt by a law enforcement officer on duty in a patrol car to apprehend one or more occupants of a moving motor vehicle, providing the driver of such vehicle is aware of the attempt and is resisting apprehension by maintaining or increasing his speed or by ignoring the law enforcement officer's attempt to stop him.

Although this definition limits pursuits to actions involving vehicles and, indeed, most people think of high-speed vehicle chases when they hear a pursuit is in progress, the majority of "pursuits" are on foot. Few departments have policies on foot pursuits and even fewer train in this area, instead focusing primarily on the execution and hazards of high-speed vehicle pursuit and whether such a pursuit should even be initiated.

To Pursue or Not to Pursue

The controversy over pursuits ranges from those who say pursuits should be banned totally, to those who say pursuits should only be allowed under certain circumstances, to those who say pursuits should be left to the discretion of the officer involved in the incident. The basic dilemma of pursuits is whether the benefits of potential apprehension outweigh the risks posed to police officers, the public and the suspects. Lum and Fachner (2008, p.4) explain, "Perhaps the most compelling, ongoing and logical reason for law enforcement's continued interest in high-speed vehicular pursuits has been its concern in balancing the values of crime control and offender apprehension with ensuring the safety of all parties who potentially might be involved—police officers, suspects, victims, bystanders and the public."

 High-speed pursuits are both effective and dangerous.

Because of the high probability of damage to property and people not connected with the pursuit, many advocate discontinuing a policy of police pursuit. In fact, liability concerns have led many departments across the nation to adopt "no pursuit" policies. Suspects who flee the police can be caught later without the risks of a high-speed pursuit. Other people, however, contend that police pursuit serves a vital purpose, arguing that if lawbreakers knew they could simply drive away and the police would not pursue, why would anyone ever stop? Many believe that with proper policies and increased officer training, pursuits should be allowed to continue.

Since the 1960s, researchers have focused on two opposing positions in this debate—first, support for pursuit because of the need to enforce laws and apprehend violators, and second, opposition to pursuit because of the risk to public safety. Three aspects of pursuit are agreed upon by law enforcement: (1) pursuits are dangerous, (2) pursuits must be controlled and (3) involvement in a pursuit increases the participants' adrenaline and excitement.

Pursuit Policies

As noted, pursuit policies range from a total ban on them to allowing officers complete discretion. Most policies suggest that factors to be considered include the offense, traffic conditions and weather conditions. Many departments' pursuit policies include use of a pursuit continuum, similar to those established for use of force. Figure 11.5 illustrates a pursuit continuum going from simply trailing a suspect vehicle to ramming and use of firearms, depending on the known threat posed by the suspect as indicated by the behavior observed.

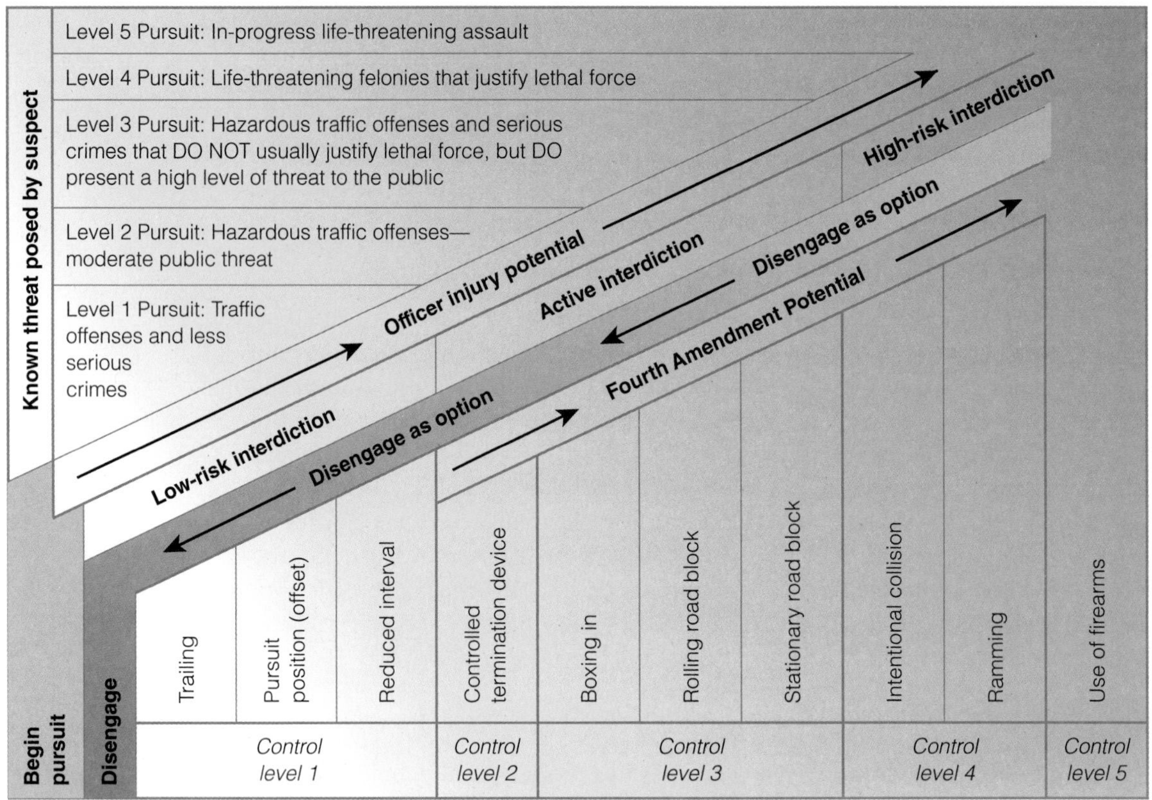

FIGURE 11.5 Pursuit Management Continuum

SOURCE: Steven D. Ashley. "Pursuit Management Implementing a Control Continuum." *Law and Order*, December 1994, p.60. Reprinted by permission.

Notice in Figure 11.5 that "disengage as an option" is always present along the continuum. Such continuums make sense considering a large number of pursuits result from minor traffic law violations. Despite the possibility of such pursuits ending in a collision, the fact also remains that many pursuits result in the arrest of a felon.

Many pursuit policies use situational elements as the determining criteria in whether to initiate a pursuit, differentiating between serious offenses where officers have little or no discretion and a sworn duty to act and minor offenses where pursuit may be more discretionary. Two classes of pursuit should be considered in the policy: imperative (Class I) and elective (Class II), the differences between which are explained in Figure 11.6.

Agencies often employ technology to make high-speed pursuits safer or eliminate them altogether. The most popular options are spike strips (tire-puncturing devices) and retractable barrier strips that can be remotely deployed so they affect only the subject's vehicle. Other technology may also reduce the risks of high-speed pursuits, including global positioning systems (GPS) tracking systems, aircraft intervention, vehicle-to-vehicle communication technology and traffic-light warning systems to shut down an intersection through which the pursuit might pass.

Class I: Imperative
(Armed escapee/reckless drunken driver)

Sworn duty requires a danger to be stopped

"I believe safety is at serious risk, and my duty requires me to act."

Reasonable belief that the pursuit does not further increase the danger

"My pursuit is not increasing the danger."

But pursuit must be abandoned when the pursuit itself becomes more dangerous than the original incident

"I will abandon pursuit because the danger is increasing."

Class II: Elective
(Driver fails to stop for minor traffic violation)

Lawful reason to stop

"I have a lawful right to stop this driver."

Reasonable belief that the pursuit does not seriously endanger the public

"My pursuit is not endangering the public."

But pursuit must be abandoned when the risk of pursuit poses a serious danger

"I will abandon pursuit because there is a serious danger."

FIGURE 11.6 Imperative vs. Elective Police Pursuit

SOURCE: Phil Wright and Les McCarthy. "Why Do We Make Pursuit Policies?" *The Police Chief*, July 1998, p.52. Reprinted by permission.

Another tactic used to end a pursuit is the PIT maneuver, which only trained officers are authorized to use. PIT is known by several different names but is an acronym for the precision immobilization technique (PIT), a method used to turn an offender's car sideways with a goal of having it lose control and come to a stop safely.

In addition to sound pursuit policies, departments must provide training in use of the policy as well as in executing it. Without such training, departments increase their vulnerability to lawsuits.

Liability in Police Pursuits

Because so many police vehicle pursuits end in crashes, and some in fatalities, lawsuits are inevitable. Departments can, however, minimize the risk of lawsuits by creating a pursuit policy that balances the need to apprehend offenders in the interest of justice with the need to protect citizens from the risks associated with such pursuits. Departments must also know what limitations and allowances state and federal statutes provide.

County of Sacramento v. Lewis (1998) set the standard for liability in police pursuits. In this case, 16-year-old Philip Lewis was a passenger on a motorcycle driven by 18-year-old Brian Willard. When Willard committed a traffic violation, a Sacramento County sheriff's deputy tried to stop the motorcycle, but the driver sped away. The deputy followed, and during the pursuit, the chase reached speeds of as much as 100 miles per hour. The pursuit ended when the motorcycle tipped over and Lewis was struck and killed by the patrol car. The Ninth Circuit Court ruled that the deputy was liable for Lewis's death by showing "deliberate indifference to, or reckless disregard for, a person's right to life and personal security."

The Supreme Court, however, overturned this ruling and held, "Only conduct that shows an intent on the part of the officer to cause harm unrelated to the legitimate object of making the arrest will meet the test of shocking and arbitrary conduct actionable as a deprivation of substantive due process." As a result of *Lewis*, in high-speed vehicle pursuit cases, Section 1983 liability ensues only if the conduct of the officer "shocks the conscience." The lower standard of "deliberate indifference" does not apply.

For more than half a century, the Supreme Court has applied a "shocks-the-conscience" test to analyze claims similar to the one made in this case, and the Court considers *Rochin v. California* (1952) to be the benchmark case explaining this standard. In the years between *Rochin* and *Lewis*, the Court explained that conduct that "shocks the conscience" is conduct so brutal and offensive that it does not comport with traditional ideas of fair play and decency. Through this ruling, the Supreme Court recognizes that law enforcement officers are not to blame for police pursuits and therefore should not be held liable for accidents that result from them. "The fault lies with drivers who endanger their own lives and the lives of others by fleeing police. The driver who fails to stop and elects to flee is the one responsible for placing his or her life in danger, placing the officers' lives in danger and is a menace to the civilian population."

In *Scott v. Harris* (2007), the Supreme Court, relying heavily on in-car camera video evidence, held that police officers may use potentially deadly force to end a high-speed chase of a suspect whose actions put the public at risk. The case involved Deputy Scott's decision to end a chase by ramming the back of Harris's Cadillac, sending Harris' car down an embankment. The car flipped and Harris, then 19, was left a quadriplegic. He sued, claiming the drastic action taken by the deputy that led to the paralysis violated his constitutional rights. Scott, claiming immunity, said his actions were warranted because of the danger Harris posed to pedestrians, other drivers and police officers. Despite the Court's ruling, officers may still be sued civilly under state statutes for wrongful death.

CIVIL LIABILITY

As discussed, many aspects of police work (e.g., use of force, high-speed pursuits) leave officers and their departments vulnerable to possible lawsuits. Searches and arrests have the potential for lawsuits, as do failures to investigate or arrest. **Liability** is a legal obligation incurred for an injury suffered or complained of that results from failure to conduct a specific task or activity within a given standard. As discussed in Chapter 2, the U.S. Constitution and the Bill of Rights define the civil rights and civil liberties guaranteed each citizen by the government. Other civil rights protections with specific relevance to law enforcement are granted under 42 U.S.C. § 1983.

liability

A legal obligation incurred for an injury suffered/complained about that results from failure to conduct a specific task/activity within a given standard.

Civil liability suits, however, have not always been an issue for law enforcement. Until 1978, a public entity was not a "person" who could abuse official power and authority to deprive constitutionally protected civil rights or act in a conspiracy to violate otherwise constitutionally protected rights. This changed in 1978 when the Supreme Court decided *Monell v. New York City Department of Social Services*. This case and several subsequent cases effectively removed the absolute sovereign immunity previously enjoyed by governmental entities and their employees.

Today concern for civil liability is quite evident in law enforcement agencies' policies and practices.

"Lawsuit paranoia" has also been called **litigaphobia**, or the fear of litigation. Fear of being sued can cause confusion regarding which action to take in a given situation—the "damned if you do, damned if you don't" dilemma. As an example, for a while citizens in need of lifesaving assistance were filing and winning lawsuits against those who responded to their needs for injuries sustained during the assistance or for other more ludicrous reasons. People grew reluctant to "get involved," and lawsuits were then filed for failure to assist. To protect well-intentioned assistants, Good Samaritan laws were passed that required a showing of gross, wanton or willful negligence before someone could be sued.

litigaphobia
Fear of a lawsuit.

A police duty more commonly the subject of lawsuits is making arrests. High-risk warrantless arrest situations include drunk and disorderly arrests, escalating to excessive force claims and arrests under pro-arrest domestic violence statutes. In contrast is the officer sued for failing to arrest. This most often occurs when an officer fails to arrest an intoxicated driver.

Investigative procedure is another area of police work commonly brought up in lawsuits. Almost every investigation gives officers discretion to decide what evidence should be included in prosecutor reports and warrant applications and what evidence should be omitted. *Brady v. Maryland* (1963) places on a prosecutor an affirmative constitutional duty to disclose **exculpatory evidence** (favorable to the accused) to a defendant: "We now hold that the suppression of evidence by the prosecution of evidence favorable to an accused upon request violates due process where the evidence is material either to guilt or to punishment, irrespective of the good faith or bad faith of the prosecution."

exculpatory evidence
Evidence favorable to the accused.

> Leaving out exculpatory evidence may lead to liability for false arrest, malicious prosecution, and illegal search and seizure claims. To support such liability claims, a plaintiff must show that the affiant knowingly and deliberately, or with reckless disregard for the truth, omitted facts that are material or necessary to a finding of probable cause (*Franks v. Delaware*, 1978).

The constitutional protections extended to police officers while performing their duties "under color of law" were affirmed in *Saucier v. Katz* (2001). Katz, president of Defense of Animals, attempted to confront then–Vice President Gore during an appearance by Gore with a banner that read, "Please Keep Animal Torture Out of Our National Parks." The military police, charged with keeping protestors at bay, had been alerted to the probable presence of Katz, and Officer Saucier and a sergeant picked Katz up and delivered him to a military vehicle.

Katz claimed he was "thrown" into the vehicle and had to catch himself to avoid being injured. Katz filed an excessive-force suit against Saucier. The District Court denied Saucier qualified immunity, and at the Ninth Circuit of Appeals, Saucier fared no better. However, the Supreme Court overturned the Ninth Circuit Court's holding.

The Supreme Court held that courts must take a two-step approach: The first inquiry must be whether a constitutional right would have been violated on the facts alleged; second, assuming the violation is established, the question of whether the right was clearly established must be considered on a more specific level. The Court explained that the privilege of qualified immunity is "an immunity from suit rather than a mere defense to liability; and like an absolute immunity, it is effectively lost if a case is erroneously permitted to go to trial. . . . We repeatedly have stressed the importance of resolving immunity questions at the earliest possible stage in litigation." In other words, the court is to resolve the issue of qualified immunity early and not put an officer through an entire trial.

Lawsuits and SWAT

SWAT teams should avoid unnecessarily damaging property. In *United States v. Ramirez* (1998) the Supreme Court held that causing unnecessary property damage could be a separate Fourth Amendment violation in and of itself: "A warrant could be valid, the entry could be valid and the evidence lawfully seized, but if a SWAT team breaks more windows and doors than are viewed as reasonable to effect the warrant, the department and its members can be subjected to a federal civil rights lawsuit."

Officer ignorance and disrespect for diversity may also lead to civil lawsuits. Chances of a lawsuit increase when officers fail to understand those who are different from themselves—different race, culture or background. Chances also increase when officers deal with persons with mental illness. Sound policies and effective training are among the many ways departments can reduce officers' civil liability.

Reducing Civil Liability

When police chiefs were asked what steps could prevent lawsuits, the most frequent answers were treating people fairly, better training, better supervision, better screening and early identification of problem officers—in that order. To help with the increasing tangle of legal issues, many police agencies now employ part- or full-time legal advisors.

Although many departments cannot afford permanent, in-house legal counsel, it is vital that they develop a sound working relationship with such an advisor. Another way departments are reducing civil liability is by modifying administrative policy decisions.

One possible way to reduce the risk of a lawsuit is to apologize. Although lawyers caution against admitting anything and never apologizing, anecdotal evidence and recent research suggest they are wrong. Consider, for example, a police chief who went to the home of bereaved parents whose daughter was struck and killed by a police vehicle responding at excessively high speed to a call for service. After the chief's visit, in which he offered expressions of regret and condolences, the parents decided a lawsuit was unnecessary. They felt there was no need to teach police a lesson because police "knew they were wrong" and "a lawsuit won't bring our daughter back." Their desire for revenge against police abated. Data from empirical research suggests an apology can prevent loss (Wright and Means, 2006).

As discussed in Chapter 7, community policing takes a proactive approach to combating crime and other problems that plague a community by encouraging and supporting partnerships between law enforcement agencies and officers and the citizens and organizations within the community they serve. This fundamental shift in policing philosophy is still resisted by some agency administrators who are skeptical about the effectiveness and benefits of such an approach.

A critical factor in reducing lawsuits is for officers to articulate, explain and justify their actions in their incident reports, especially use-of-force reports: "A failure to adequately do so can lead to release of a suspect, civil liability or, in the extreme, criminal charges" (Dwyer, 2010).

While agencies and their officers continue to struggle with the question "Is it legal?," another question often posed is "Is it ethical?"

CORRUPTION, ETHICS AND INTEGRITY

Several commissions have examined police corruption, beginning with the 1890s Lexow and Mazet commissions and the 1910s Curan Committee to handle corruption in the New York City Police Department (NYPD). The 1931 Wickersham Commission report documented corruption and brutality in the criminal justice system throughout the United States. The 1960s Knapp Commission again uncovered bribery and kickbacks throughout the NYPD. In 1974 the Philadelphia police were accused of engaging in criminal practices throughout the force. In the 1980s more than 70 Miami police officers were arrested for serious acts of corruption.

In 1993 the Mollen Commission report again found large-scale corruption in the NYPD, including extortion, bribery and theft. From 1993 to 1995 more than 50 New Orleans police officers were arrested, indicted or convicted on charges including rape, aggravated battery, drug trafficking and murder. The Christopher Commission, investigating the Los Angeles Police Department after the Rodney King beating, found that significant numbers of LAPD officers "repetitively use excessive force against the public and persistently ignore the written guidelines of the department regarding force." In the late 1990s the Rampart Commission again found serious problems within the LAPD.

What Constitutes Corruption?

Corruption is "a violation of integrity through the abuse of one's role or position or the influencing of a person in authority either for personal benefit or the benefit of another" (Vernon, 2009, p.68). Corruption occurs when an officer misuses authority for personal gain, including accepting gratuities.

corruption
When an officer misuses authority for personal gain, including accepting gratuities.

The key elements of corrupt behavior are that the conduct (1) is prohibited by law or rule, (2) involves misuse of position and (3) involves a reward or personal gain for the officer.

One or more of the following factors are usually involved in the personal lives of officers involved in corruption: lack of legitimate accomplishments, anger at being a victim of the system, lack of character, lack of team spirit, short-term goal orientation, lack of knowledge or greed (Vernon, 2009). Trautman (2009), director of the National Institute of Ethics, gives four reasons good cops do unethical things: "They lie to themselves with excuses; they experience momentary selfishness; they just make a bad decision; and they are afraid of 'being ostracized' for doing the right thing."

Although accepting discounts, gratuities and free service are usually not considered forms of corruption, "looking the other way" when crimes are committed or cash payments are made to police officers are quite another matter. It is a serious issue when an officer accepts an outright bribe to refrain from making an arrest or imposing a fine. Another form of extremely serious police corruption occurs when officers appropriate material or money that comes into their possession in the line of duty, for example, detectives dividing their "scores" of narcotics and cash, sometimes amounting to thousands of dollars, or property being taken from the property room and then mysteriously "disappearing."

The Knapp Commission, in its 1972 investigation of corruption among New York City police, distinguished between "grass eaters" and "meat eaters," with the grass eaters being officers who passively accepted gratuities offered to them, in contrast to the meat eaters who aggressively solicited payments. The commission also discovered another problem—officers who were not directly involved in corruptive practices but who tolerated or ignored such activities by their colleagues, thereby allowing an environment of corruption to flourish.

History has shown that some police officers have come to value results over duty and principle, and the standard measurement of good police work has become goal achievement, with all else being secondary. This tendency to place ends over means is one reason corruption can arise and perpetuate, but the problem is much more complex.

Of extreme concern is corruption at our borders: "While it's true that the most common acts of border corruption involve drug trafficking and human smuggling, a single incident of the wrong person getting into the country could result in a catastrophe. . . A corrupt officer might believe that he or she is accepting a bribe in return for allowing a carload of illegal immigrants to enter the country, when these individuals may actually be hard-core gang members or terrorists. A corrupt officer could knowingly or unknowingly allow entry of a truck, rail car, ship or airplane carrying weapons of mass destruction, chemical or biological weapons, or bomb-making materials. ("Combating Border Corruption: Locally and Nationally," 2010).

The Corruption Continuum Just as with the use of force and pursuits, a continuum exists to describe the transition from honest to corrupt cop—the **continuum of compromise**, illustrated in Figure 11.7. Something seemingly insignificant can put an officer on a slippery slope of compromised behavior, leading to major crimes. The "slippery slope" often begins with an officer accepting gratuities or tokens of appreciation.

continuum of compromise

Describes the transition from honest to corrupt cop; the slippery slope often begins with an officer accepting gratuities or tokens of appreciation.

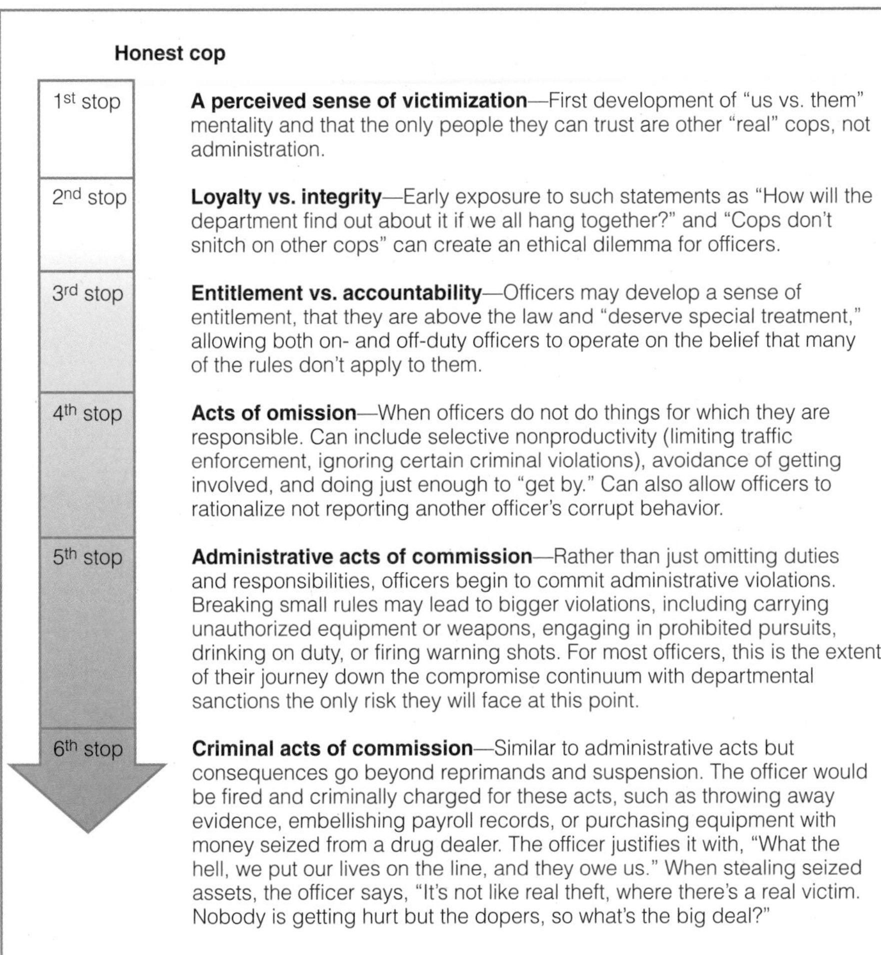

Honest cop
1st stop
A perceived sense of victimization—First development of "us vs. them" mentality and that the only people they can trust are other "real" cops, not administration.
2nd stop
Loyalty vs. integrity—Early exposure to such statements as "How will the department find out about it if we all hang together?" and "Cops don't snitch on other cops" can create an ethical dilemma for officers.
3rd stop
Entitlement vs. accountability—Officers may develop a sense of entitlement, that they are above the law and "deserve special treatment," allowing both on- and off-duty officers to operate on the belief that many of the rules don't apply to them.
4th stop
Acts of omission—When officers do not do things for which they are responsible. Can include selective nonproductivity (limiting traffic enforcement, ignoring certain criminal violations), avoidance of getting involved, and doing just enough to "get by." Can also allow officers to rationalize not reporting another officer's corrupt behavior.
5th stop
Administrative acts of commission—Rather than just omitting duties and responsibilities, officers begin to commit administrative violations. Breaking small rules may lead to bigger violations, including carrying unauthorized equipment or weapons, engaging in prohibited pursuits, drinking on duty, or firing warning shots. For most officers, this is the extent of their journey down the compromise continuum with departmental sanctions the only risk they will face at this point.
6th stop
Criminal acts of commission—Similar to administrative acts but consequences go beyond reprimands and suspension. The officer would be fired and criminally charged for these acts, such as throwing away evidence, embellishing payroll records, or purchasing equipment with money seized from a drug dealer. The officer justifies it with, "What the hell, we put our lives on the line, and they owe us." When stealing seized assets, the officer says, "It's not like real theft, where there's a real victim. Nobody is getting hurt but the dopers, so what's the big deal?"

FIGURE 11.7 The Continuum of Compromise

SOURCE: Adapted from Kevin M. Gilmartin and John J. Harris. "The Continuum of Compromise." *The Police Chief,* January 1998, pp.25–28. Reprinted by permission. Copyright held by The International Association of Chiefs of Police, Inc. Further reproduction without express written permission is prohibited.

A model of circumstantial corruptibility considers the motivation of both the giver and the receiver of an exchange, no matter what the value of that exchange (see Figure 11.8). A giving exchange is a voluntary act of offering something of value without any expectation of reciprocity. The receiver, exerting no influence on the giver, accepts the gift. As long as the giver and receiver continue to assume these roles, corruption does not occur.

How Corruption Arises and Perpetuates

Every occupation has a learning process or socialization to which its new members are subjected. The socialization process makes most newcomers in the occupation adopt the prevailing rules, values and attitudes of their colleagues. Often, however,

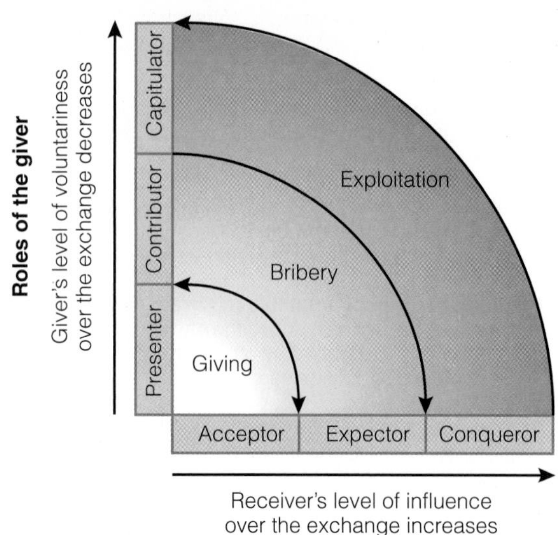

FIGURE 11.8 A Model of Circumstantial Corruptibility

SOURCE: Brian L. Withrow and Jeffrey D. Dailey. "A Model of Circumstantial Corruptibility." *Police Quarterly,* June 2004, p.171. Reprinted by permission.

some existing informal rules and attitudes are at odds with the formal rules and attitudes society as a whole expects members of the occupation to follow. Officers may be taught to plant evidence, lie in court, shake people down or beat them up.

The Slippery Slope The slippery slope of corruption posits that police corruption begins with a lowering of ethical expectations and values to attain a gratuity of minor value, for example, accepting a free cup of coffee. Although this action in itself is most likely harmless and inconsequential as a corrupting force, it may over time produce a snowball effect, leading an officer to accept gratuities of larger magnitude. Furthermore, such practices often lead those providing the "freebies" to expect preferential treatment by recipient officers.

Noble Cause and Ends Versus Means Another facet of unethical behavior concerns the noble cause corruption dilemma, in which officers believe unlawful means are justified when the result is the protection of human life or some other noble cause. Unquestionably, law enforcement officers face difficult decisions daily.

Because officers are granted awesome coercive authority, it is imperative that they exercise their power responsibly and ethically. When confronted with the "really bad guys," it may be tempting to take advantage of this power and the discretion granted to administer "street justice." It takes moral courage and strong ethical principles to resist the "ends justifying the means" pitfall.

Above the Law The public understands that the police are granted special privileges and exceptions from obeying the law. Officers can exceed speed limits, violate traffic controls and carry concealed weapons in the line of duty. During the socialization process, some officers receive the message they are special and above the law. However, "equality under the law" is the foundation of the American criminal justice system. Officers who believe they are above the law subvert the essence of our criminal justice system.

Bad Apples or a Bad Barrel? Often the argument is heard that just as a few "bad apples" can ruin the entire barrel, so a few bad cops can ruin the entire department. Managers must examine their department and find ways to promote integrity and ethical behavior that adheres to this higher standard. Research has found that when the "brass" ignores bad cops, a culture of corruption begins to flourish in the department.

The Code of Silence Another reason corruption can exist is the "code of silence." Police loyalty, the "blue wall" or the "code of silence" has forced many officers to jeopardize their careers and their liberty to cover up another officer's misconduct. However, as Hubbard (2009, p.50) offers, "Should you have to arrest another officer, or call attention to dishonesty or corruption—*you did not cause the problem.* It was the deliberate, conscious choice of that individual that caused the problem. You're merely the one who had the guts to shine a light on it and say, 'Not on my watch.'"

How Police Learn about Ethics

Ethics involves moral behavior, doing what is considered right and just. Police managers may provide ethical leadership by helping officers develop their ethical decision-making skills: "Law enforcement does a shameful job of preparing cops to make difficult ethical decisions. This is particularly tragic considering the fact that virtually every time an officer is justifiably fired or arrested it resulted from a bad ethical decision. An ethical dilemma, such as whether or not to be totally honest with your sergeant about a mistake you made, can be a career-ending moment" (Trautman, 2009). PERF held a town hall meeting focusing on sanctions against officers who lie. Among the comments made by chiefs were the following ("PERF's Town Hall Meeting," 2009):

ethics
Involves moral behavior, doing what is considered right and just; the rules or standards governing the conduct of a profession.

> Cops have been getting a pass on lying for a long time (Boston commissioner Davis, p.1).
>
> Our officers realize lying for a colleague puts them at risk (Nashville Chief Serpas, p.2).
>
> No more leniency in minor cases (Aurora, Colorado, Chief Oates, p.3).
>
> I'm tired of hiding liars I can't fire (Montgomery County, Maryland, Chief Manger, p.3).
>
> Little lies are like broken windows (retired Minneapolis chief Olson, p.5).
>
> Lying officers cost us big money—and our credibility (Toronto Chief Blair, p.5).

The IACP has developed a code of ethics and "Police Code of Conduct" to guide police administrators and officers through the ethical standards expected. These codes include the primary responsibilities of a police officer, how the duties are to be performed, use of discretion, use of force, confidentiality, integrity, cooperation with other police officers and agencies, personal-professional capabilities and even private life. The Law Enforcement Code of Ethics is on the book Web site.

One simple adage might serve as a starting point for a discussion on ethics: "There is no right way to do a wrong thing" (Blanchard and Peale, 1988, p.9). Three questions can be used as personal "ethics checks" (Blanchard and Peale, 1988, p.20).

Three ethics-check questions are

- Is it legal?
- Is it balanced?
- How will it make me feel about myself?

The Importance of Police Integrity and Core Virtues

integrity

A series of concepts and beliefs that provide structure to an agency's operation and officers' professional and personal ethics, including, but not limited to, honesty, honor, morality, allegiance, principled behavior and dedication to mission.

Integrity, the most important quality a police officer can possess, is a series of concepts and beliefs that provide structure to officers' professional and personal ethics. These concepts and beliefs include honesty, honor, morality, allegiance, principled behavior and dedication to mission. Avoiding bad behavior is not the same as having integrity any more than avoiding grammatical errors can make one a Pulitzer prize–winning author. Having integrity is more than simply playing by the rules. To develop officers with integrity, police departments need a formal code of ethics as well as a statement of core values. Many internal and external forces interact to influence police integrity. The dynamics of these forces are illustrated in Figure 11.9.

Building an Ethical Department

Given the wide variety of forces influencing officer integrity, the challenge of building an ethical police department has never been greater. For administrators struggling to build an ethical department, it may come as small consolation to know that although corruption has been a persistent problem in American policing, it is not a unique phenomenon, nor is it one that can ever be beaten down completely and permanently. While acknowledging that corrupt officer behavior will likely never be eradicated entirely, administrators must not stop trying to achieve an ethical department. To help in this effort, administrators should focus on three areas to enhance police integrity.

Three areas in which to enhance police integrity and reduce corruption are

- The applicant selection process
- Consistent reinforcement of values through training and professionalization
- Anticorruption posture of checks and balances

In the applicant selection process, prior behavior, arrest records, drug use and integrity must be aggressively researched. Consistent reinforcement of values is also vital. Department personnel should regularly discuss and analyze conduct standards to strengthen their understanding of and commitment to such principles. Management's most important task is to create an environment in which every police officer can perform with integrity and professionalism. In an anticorruption posture of checks and balances, management can reinforce integrity, detect corruption and limit the opportunity for wrongdoing. The chief sets the

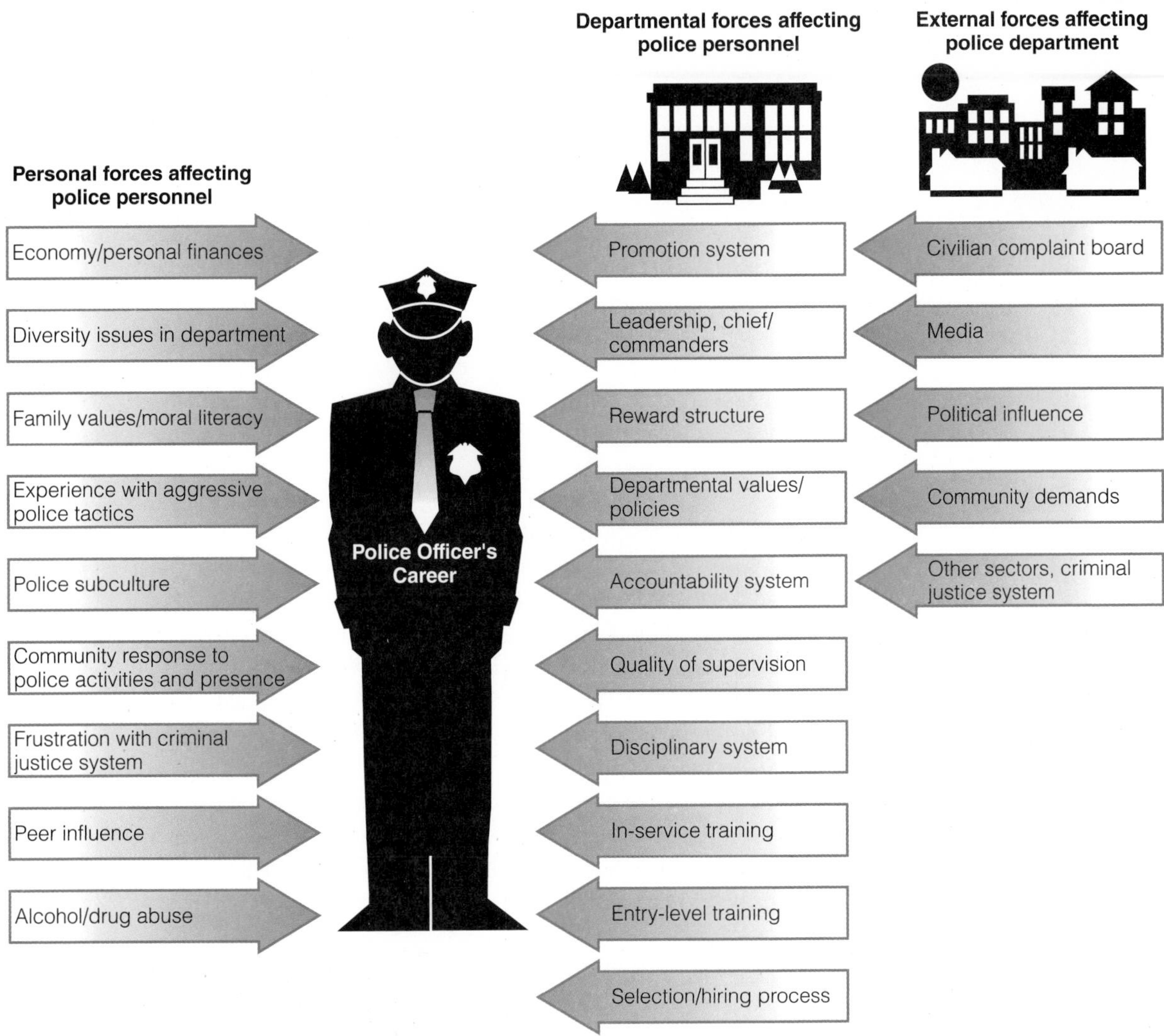

FIGURE 11.9 Dynamics of Police Integrity

SOURCE: *Police Integrity: Public Service with Honor.* Washington, DC: National Institute of Justice, January 1997, p.92.

level of integrity for the entire department. Supervisors provide leadership and guidance when needed.

When allegations of officer misconduct arise, the internal affairs (IA) division is called in to investigate one of its own. IA is the division of a police department that investigates internal issues that relate to crime, corruption, and policy violations. This division holds licensed officers accountable for actions and maintains a department's professional standards. Investigations are conducted by licensed peace officers who answer to high-level police administrators, and sometimes to civilian review boards.

As agencies seek to build ethical departments and officers with integrity, the National Institute of Ethics may be of assistance. Information about this organization may be found at http://www.ethicsinstitute.com.

Summary

Policing faces several vital, often controversial, issues in the 21st century, some of which have existed for decades, whereas others are relatively new. One of the most controversial issues surrounds police discretion, the freedom of an agency or individual officer to choose whether to act. Whether such discretion is positive or negative is a matter of debate.

Closely related to discretion is the issue of discrimination versus disparity. Minorities are arrested, stopped and questioned, and shot and killed by the police out of proportion to their representation in the population. There is much controversy about whether study results indicate a pattern of systematic *discrimination* or a *disparity* related to other factors such as poverty, socioeconomic class and involvement in crime.

The immigration issue centers on whether police officers should be enforcers of immigration laws or should seek to build trust with immigrants as advocated by community policing.

Use of force has been an issue of increasing concern for police agencies. When making an arrest, if there is no physical resistance, no physical force should be used. Controversy regarding use-of-force continuums involves whether they have outlived their usefulness, whether they should be included in use-of-force policies and whether they increase liability. Although officers are authorized to use force, including deadly force, they must use only that level and amount of force *reasonably* necessary to accomplish a legitimate law enforcement objective. Six options for controlling a suspect with nonlethal force are verbal/visual management of the scene, empty-hand control, restraints, aerosols, impact weapons and electronic control devices (ECDs). Justification for use of deadly force must consider the legal right and the need to apprehend the suspect compared with the arresting officer's safety and the value of human life. Police officers involved in use-of-force incidents retain their constitutional rights against unreasonable search and seizures (Fourth Amendment), against self-incrimination (Fifth Amendment) and for legal representation (Sixth Amendment).

One form of use of force is the police pursuit. High-speed pursuits are both effective and dangerous. They also raise serious liability issues. Today concern for civil liability is quite evident in law enforcement agencies' policies and practices.

The issues of corruption, ethics and integrity are also of concern. The key elements of corrupt behavior are that the conduct (1) is prohibited by law or rule, (2) involves misuse of position and (3) involves a reward or personal gain for the officer. Three ethics-check questions are: (1) Is it legal? (2) Is it balanced? (3) How will it make me feel about myself? Three areas in which to enhance police integrity and reduce corruption are the applicant selection process, consistent reinforcement of values through training and professionalization and an anticorruption posture of checks and balances.

Discussion Questions

1. Are police officers allowed too much discretion? Why is discretion a necessary element of policing? Or is it?
2. Do you see any problems with use-of-force continuums or pursuit continuums?
3. Should officers and their departments be shielded from civil liability as was previously allowed under "sovereign immunity"? Why or why not?
4. What roles can K-9s assume in dealing with fleeing suspects?

5. Do you believe the phrase "excessive force" has different meanings to different people in the criminal justice system? If so, why?
6. Do you think profiling is necessary and justified for the sake of national security?
7. Do you think chemical agents are appropriate to use in dealing with uncooperative, violent suspects?
8. Because pursuits are one of the most dangerous aspects of law enforcement, both to police and the general public, do you think police pursuits should be abolished completely?
9. What is the most important characteristic of police integrity?
10. How prevalent do you think corruption is in law enforcement agencies?

Gale Emergency Services Database Assignments

- Use the Gale Emergency Services Database to help answer the Discussion Questions as appropriate.
- Use the Gale Emergency Services Database to research *police pursuits*. Many standards are recommended in dealing with police pursuits. Outline these and pick one standard you feel could be the best with the least officer liability.
- Use the Gale Emergency Services Database to find the article "Use of Deadly Force to Prevent Escape": http://find.galegroup.com/gps/retrieve.do?contentSet=IAC-documents&resultListType=RESULT_LIST&qrySerId=Locale%28en%2C%2C%29%3AFQE%3D%28ke%2CNone%2C17%29police+discretion%24&sgHitCountType=None&inPS=true&sort=DateDescend&searchType=BasicSearchForm&tabID=T003&prodId=IPS&searchId=R1¤tPosition=1&userGroupName=cpg3&docId=A15353041&docType=IAC&contentSet=IAC-Documents

  Assignment: Read the article and identify the importance of discretion on this topic. Be prepared to discuss police discretion in class.
- Use the Gale Emergency Services Database to find the article "Use of Force Policies and Training: A Reasoned Approach": http://find.galegroup.com/gps/retrieve.do?contentSet=IAC-Documents&resultListType=RESULT_LIST&qrySerId=Locale%28en%2C%2C%29%3AFQE%3D%28ke%2CNone%2C22%29use+of+force+continuum%24&sgHitCountType=None&inPS=true&sort=DateDescend&searchType=BasicSearchForm&tabID=T003&prodId=IPS&searchId=R2¤tPosition=3&userGroupName=cpg3&docId=A93915942&docType=IAC&contentSet=IAC-Documents

  Assignment: Summarize this assignment and be prepared to discuss *Graham v. Connor* and its relation to the use of force in policing.
- Use the Gale Emergency Services Database to find the article "The Role of Race in Law Enforcement: Racial Profiling or Legitimate Use?": http://find.galegroup.com/gps/retrieve.do?contentSet=IAC-Documents&resultListType=RESULT_LIST&qrySerId=Locale%28en%2C%2C%29%3AFQE%3D%28ke%2CNone%2C16%29racial+profiling%24&sgHitCountType=None&inPS=true&sort=DateDescend&searchType=BasicSearchForm&tabID=T003&prodId=IPS&searchId=R3¤tPosition=7&userGroupName=cpg3&docId=A81223386&docType=IAC&contentSet=IAC-Documents

Assignment: Read this article and be prepared to debate racial profiling in depth, including consideration of arguments on its legitimate use.

- Use the Gale Emergency Services Database to find the article "Evidence-Based Decisions on Police Pursuits: The Officer's Perspective": http://find.galegroup.com/gps/retrieve.do?contentSet=IAC-Documents&resultListType=RESULT_LIST&qrySerId=Locale%28en%2C%2C%29%3AFQE%3D%28ke%2CNone%2C15%29police+pursuits%24&sgHitCountType=None&inPS=true&sort=DateDescend&searchType=BasicSearchForm&tabID=T003&prodId=IPS&searchId=R4¤tPosition=1&userGroupName=cpg3&docId=A221649832&docType=IAC&contentSet=IAC-Documents

  Assignment: Outline this article and be ready to discuss this topic from a police officer's perspective.

- Use the Gale Emergency Services Database to find the article "Repairing Broken Windows" (Police Corruption): http://find.galegroup.com/gps/retrieve.do?contentSet=IAC-Documents&resultListType=RESULT_LIST&qrySerId=Locale%28en%2C%2C%29%3AFQE%3D%28ke%2CNone%2C17%29police+corruption%24&sgHitCountType=None&inPS=true&sort=DateDescend&searchType=BasicSearchForm&tabID=T003&prodId=IPS&searchId=R5¤tPosition=4&userGroupName=cpg3&docId=A72299788&docType=IAC&contentSet=IAC-Documents

  Assignment: Examine police corruption as described in this article and identify prevention methods that are outlined. Be prepared to discuss this in class.

Internet Assignments

- Use the Internet to research *corruption in law enforcement*. Note the many uncomplimentary articles. Do these articles give you the idea there is another side to some police officers? Explain.
- Download *Racially Biased Policing* at http://www.PoliceForum.org and outline one chapter. Be prepared to share your outline with the class.

References

Ashley, Steve. "What Gets You Sued Gets You Hurt." *Law Officer Magazine*, February 2007, pp.72–75.

Basich, Melanie. "Less Lethal Force." *Police*, September 2009, pp.30–33.

Basich, Melanie. "Not Going for the Kill." *Police*, March 2010, pp.44–51.

Blanchard, Kenneth, and Peale, Norman Vincent. *The Power of Ethical Management.* New York: Fawcett Crest, 1988.

Bratton, William. "Stepping Up to Racial Issues." In *Leadership Matters*, edited by Craig Fischer, Washington, DC: Police Executive Research Forum, 2009, pp.87–89.

Brave, Michael, and O'Linn, Mildred K. "*Bryan v. McPherson*—A New Standard for the Use of Electronic Control Devices?" *The Police Chief*, February 2010, pp.22–23.

"Combating Border Corruption: Locally and Nationally." Washington, DC: Federal Bureau of Investigation, Headline Archives, May 7, 2010.

Cope, Curtis J., and Callanan, Joe. "Understanding the Objectively Reasonable Standard—Overcome Resistance." *LawOfficer.com*, June 17, 2009. Retrieved from http://www.lawofficer.com/article/tactics-and-weapons/understanding-objectively-reas-4

Dwyer, Terrence P. "Police Liability and Litigation." *Police One.com News*, May 7, 2010. Retrieved from http://www.policeone.com/pc_print.asp?vid=2059075

"Emergency Docs on Excited Delirium: 'Yes, It's for Real!'" Mankato, MN: Force Science Research Center, Transmission #136, November 6, 2009.

"'Excessive' Shots and Falling Assailants: A Fresh Look at OIS Subtleties." Mankato, MN: Force Science Research Center, Transmission #144, March 3, 2010.

Gau, Jacinta M.; Mosher, Clayton; and Pratt, Travis C. "An Inquiry into the Impact of Suspect Race on Police Use of Tasers." *Police Quarterly*, March 2010, pp.27–48.

"Government's 287(g) Program Criticized in Hearings in House." *Criminal Justice Newsletter*, March 2, 2009, pp.5–7.

Hawkes, Andrew. "Keeping Your Less Lethal Options Open." *PoliceOne.com News*. February 16, 2010. Retrieved from http://www.policeone.com/police-products/less-lethal/TASER/articles/2001750-Keeping-your-less-lethal-options-open/

"Holder: Feds May Sue over Arizona Immigration Law." *CNN Politics*, May 9, 2010. Retrieved from http://edition.cnn.com/2010/POLITICS/05/09/holder.arizona.immigration/index.html

Hubbard, Bill. "Whatcha Gonna Do? Ethical Quandaries." *American Cop Magazine,* November/December 2009, pp.46–50.

"Immigration Enforcement." *Subject to Debate*, February 2010, p.6.

Johnson, Devon, and Kuhns, Joseph B. "Striking Out: Race and Support for Police Use of Force." *Justice Quarterly*, September 2009, pp.592–623.

Joyner, Chuck. "Fighting the Contagious Fire Phenomenon." *PoliceOne.com News*, January 29, 2010. Retrieved from http://www.policeone.com/pc_print.asp?vid=1996906

Kruger, Karen J. "When Public Duty and Individual Rights Collide in Use-of-Force Cases. *The Police Chief*, February 2009, pp.12–14.

Lewinski, Bill, and Hudson, Bill. "Reaction Times in Lethal Force Encounters. Time to Start Shooting? Time to Stop Shooting? The Tempe Study." *The Police Marksman*, September/October 2003, pp.26–29.

Lum, Cynthia, and Fachner, George. *Police Pursuits in an Age of Innovation and Reform.* Alexandria, VA: International Association of Chiefs of Police, September 2008.

Lundman, Richard J., and Kowalski, Brian R. "Speeding While Black? Assessing the Generalizability of Lange et al.'s (2001, 2005) New Jersey Turnpike Speeding Survey Findings." *Justice Quarterly*, September 2009, pp.504–527.

Lysakowski, Matthew; Pearsall, Albert Antony III; and Pope, Jill. *Policing in New Immigrant Communities.* Washington, DC: Office of Community Oriented Policing, June 2009.

"Major Research Study by PERF Indicates That CEDs Can Reduce Injuries to Police and Suspects, But PERF Continues to Urge Caution." *Subject to Debate*. September 2009, pp. 1, 4–5.

Means, Randy, and McDonald, Pam. "Taser and the 9th Circuit Decision." *Law and Order*, April 2010, pp.52–56.

Means, Randy, and Seidel, Grea. "Keys to Winning with Use of Force: A Four-Step Plan." *Tactical Response*, March–April 2010, pp.18–20.

'"New Study: Cocaine Abuse and Sudden Death." Mankato, MN: Force Science Research Center, Transmission #143, February 11, 2010.

"New Study Ranks Risks of Injury from 5 Major Force Options." Mankato, MN: Force Science Research Center, Transmission #102, July 18, 2008.

Nugent, Hugh; Connors, Edward F., III; McEwen, J. Thomas; and Mayo, Lou. *Restrictive Policies for High-Speed Police* Pursuits. Washington, DC: National Institute of Justice, no date. (NCJ 122025)

Ousey, Graham C., and Lee, Matthew R, "Racial Disparity in Formal Social Control: An Investigation of Alternative Explanations of Arrest Rate Inequality." *Journal of Research in Crime and Delinquency*, August 2008, pp.322–355.

"PERF, NSA and BAJ Issue Report and Guidelines on Use of CEDs in Custodial Settings." *Subject to Debate*, August 2009, pp.3–4.

"PERF's Town Hall Meeting in Denver Focuses on Sanctions against Officers Who Lie." *Subject to Debate*, October 2009, pp.1–7.

The Performance of 287(g) Agreements. Washington, DC: Department of Homeland Security, Office of Inspector General, March 2010.

Peters, John G., and Brave, Michael A. "Force Continuums: Three Questions." *The Police Chief*, January 2006, pp.8–9.

Police Chiefs and Sheriffs Speak Out on Local Immigration Enforcement. Washington, DC: Police Executive Research Forum, April 2008.

"Quick Reference Guide to the *Garrity* Right." Redford, MI: Police Officers Association of Michigan, 2010.

Retrieved from http://www.poam.net/blog/quick-reference-guide-to-the-garrity-right/

"Research Roundup: Latest on Tasers, Arrest-Related Deaths, Excited Delirium." Mankato, MN: Force Science Research Center, Transmission #127, July 20, 2009.

Roh, Sunghoon, and Robinson, Matthew. "A Geographic Approach to Racial Profiling: The Microanalysis and Macroanalysis of Racial Disparity in Traffic Stops." *Police Quarterly*, June 2009, pp.137–169.

Ross, Darrell L. "Science, Liability, Use of Force, and Restraint Asphyxia." *PoliceOne.com News*, January 22, 2010. Retrieved from http://www.policeone.com/pc_print.asp?vid=1996241

Sanow, Ed. "Taser Misuse Train Better!" *Law and Order*, April 2010, p.6.

Solar, Mark, and Garry, Lisa M. "Reducing Disproportionate Minority Contact: Preparation at the Local Level." *DMC Disproportionate Minority Contact*. Washington, DC: Office of Juvenile Justice and Delinquency Prevention, September 2009.

Study of Deaths Following Electro Muscular Disruption: Interim Report. Washington, DC: National Institute of Justice, June 2008.

"Survey by PERF and University of South Carolina Shows Rapid Increase in CED Deployments." *Subject to Debate*, December 2009, pp.1, 6.

TASER® Electronic Control Devices (ECDs): Field Data and Risk Management. TASER International, March 3, 2009. Retrieved from http://www.taser.com/company/pressroom/Documents/Injury%20Reduction%20Stats%20PUBLIC%2003%2005%2009.pdf

Tuomey, Lianne M., and Jolly, Rachel. "Step up to Law Enforcement: A successful Strategy for Recruiting Women into the Law Enforcement Profession." *The Police Chief*, June 2009, pp.68–73.

Trautman, Neal. "Surviving Ethical Dilemmas." *LawOfficer.com*, June 13, 2009. Retrieved from http://www.lawofficer.com/article/needs-tags-columns/surviving-ethical-dilemmas

Unnever, James D.; Cullen, Francis T.; Mathers, Scott A.; McClure, Timothy E.; and Allison, Marisa C. "Racial Discrimination and Hirschi's Criminological Classic: A Chapter in the Sociology of Knowledge." *Justice Quarterly*, September 2009, pp.378–409.

Vernon, Bob. "Corruption: A Personal, Incremental Struggle." *Law Officer Magazine*, August 2009, pp. 68–70.

Walker, Samuel. *Sense and Nonsense about Crime and Drugs: A Policy Guide*, 6th ed. Belmont, CA: Thomson Wadsworth, 2006.

Walker, Samuel; Spohn, Cassia; and DeLone, Miriam. *The Color of Justice: Race, Ethnicity, and Crime in America*, 4th ed. Belmont, CA: Wadsworth Publishing Company, 2007.

White, Michael D., and Ready, Justin. "The Impact of the Taser on Suspect Resistance: Identifying Predictors of Effectiveness." *Crime & Delinquency*, January 2010, pp.70–102.

Wright, Kim, and Means, Randy. "Should Law Enforcement Agencies Apologize for Mistakes?" *The Police Chief*, February 2006, pp.8–9.

Yates, Travis. "Analysis of the IACP Report: 'Police Pursuits in an Age of Innovation and Reform.'" *PoliceOne.com News*, February 23, 2009. Retrieved from http://www.policeone.com/pc_print.asp?vid=1800003

Cases Cited

Brady v. Maryland, 373 U.S. 89 (1963)
Bryan v. McPherson, 608 F.3d 614 (9th Cir. 2010)
County of Sacramento v. Lewis, 523 U.S. 833 (1998)
Florida v. Bostick, 501 U.S. 429 (1991)
Franks v. Delaware, 438 U.S. 154 (1978)
Gardner v. Broderick, 392 U.S. 273 (1968)
Garrity v. New Jersey, 385 U.S. 493 (1967)
Graham v. Connor, 490 U.S. 386 (1989)
Griffin v. Illinois, 351 U.S. 12 (1956)
Hampton v. Mow Sun Wong, 426 U.S. 88 (1976)
Ingraham v. Wright, 430 U.S. 651 (1977)
Monell v. New York City Department of Social Services, 436 U.S. 658 (1978)
Plyler v. Doe, 457 U.S. 202 (1982)
Rochin v. California, 342 U.S. 165 (1952)
Saucier v. Katz, 533 U.S. 194 (2001)
Scott v. Harris, 550 U.S. 372 (2007)
Shapiro v. Thompson, 394 U.S. 618 (1969)
Sugarman v. Dougall, 413 U.S. 634 (1973)
Tennessee v. Garner, 471 U.S. 1 (1985)
United States v. Ramirez, 523 U.S. 65 (1998)
United States v. Weaver, 966 F.2d 391 (8th Cir. 1992)

CHAPTER 12

Becoming a Law Enforcement Professional

The only place success comes before work is in the dictionary.

—Vince Lombardi

Graduates of the 36th Alaska Law Enforcement Training class stand at attention during their graduation ceremony at the Sheldon Jackson College Hames P.E. center in Sitka, Alaska, Thursday Nov. 16, 2006. Thirty-one graduated from the 14-week course. Graduates work as municipal police officers, state troopers, fire marshals and other law enforcement officers in towns across the state.

Do you know . . .

- What qualities are essential for good police officers?
- What the benefits of racially balanced and integrated police departments are?
- What advantages exist for law enforcement agencies that hire and retain more women?
- What steps are usually involved in officer selection?
- What basic requirements officer candidates must meet?
- Whether a college education is required of most police officer candidates?
- If police officers are required to live in the same community in which they work?
- What most physical fitness tests evaluate?
- What information is sought during interviews?
- What occurs during the background investigation?
- What is most important in the medical examination?
- What legal considerations in hiring practices are mandated by the Equal Employment Opportunity Act and the Americans with Disabilities Act?
- What the length and purpose of probation are?
- What two areas related to training are most commonly involved in civil lawsuits?
- What keys to avoid civil liability related to training are?
- How stressful police work may be?
- What common sources of stress are?
- What the primary purpose of unions is?
- How unions are viewed by line officers and administrators?
- Whether moonlighting is accepted?
- What accreditation is and whether it is worth the time and expense?
- What the three key elements of professionalism are?

Can you define?

accreditation
affirmative action
bona fide occupational qualification (BFOQ)
burnout
burst stress
collective bargaining
credentialing
critical incident
due diligence
Firefighter's Rule
moonlighting
negligent hiring
posttraumatic stress disorder (PTSD)
reverse discrimination
sexual harassment
situational testing
split-second syndrome
vicarious liability

INTRODUCTION

Today's law enforcement agencies seek a new breed of officer—a balance of brawn and brains—one who possesses the physical qualities traditionally associated with policing, such as strength and endurance, and the emotional and intellectual characteristics needed to effect public order in an ever-changing and increasingly diverse society. "People skills" have become a critical tool for law enforcement officers, as have technology skills.

For years society has sought more effective law enforcement and a criminal justice system to meet its needs. At the same time criminologists, psychologists, sociologists, police practitioners and scientists have worked to solve America's crime problem. Despite some disillusionment and cynicism, progress has been made.

The most visible signs of progress in the vast criminal justice system have been in the field of law enforcement, and the most notable advancement in this field has been the professionalization of the police officer. This is partly because 80 to

90 percent of most police agencies' budgets are allocated for personnel; therefore, agencies are demanding higher quality performance from their personnel. This is sometimes difficult to obtain, however, because most police departments are understaffed. The attrition rate throughout the United States—approximately 100,000 officers per year—compounds this problem and creates a constant demand for training.

An equally important force behind the professionalization of the police officer is the realization that, to a large degree, the future success of law enforcement is contingent on its police officers' quality and effectiveness, their status in the community and their ability to serve the community's residents. Women and members of minority groups are now considered necessary and valuable members in most departments. Although members of minority groups and women have had a long, difficult battle in achieving equal employment rights, excellent opportunities exist today for all who are interested in a law enforcement career.

THE CHAPTER AT A GLANCE

This chapter begins with some suggestions about how to evaluate and select a law enforcement agency for employment. This is followed by a look at recruiting and selection and the federal guidelines and regulations affecting employment, including the Equal Employment Opportunity Act, affirmative action initiatives and the Americans with Disabilities Act. After examining who is selected and how, the chapter turns to what happens next, typically probation and training. The importance of retaining officers is discussed, including how factors such as salary, benefits, promotional opportunities, stress and burnout affect officer retention. This is followed by a look at some controversial areas in law enforcement, including unions, moonlighting and accreditation. The chapter concludes with a discussion of law enforcement as a profession.

EVALUATING AND SELECTING AN AGENCY FOR EMPLOYMENT

Before an agency can screen and select an officer candidate, the candidate must first select the agency. This is done by researching the available options, assessing one's own professional goals and then evaluating and selecting specific agencies to apply to. Several factors are important to those seeking employment in law enforcement, including, but not limited to, the advantages and disadvantages of the following:

- Employment with municipal, county, state or federal agencies
- Working in a small, medium or large agency
- Working in an environment with a high rate of crime versus an environment with little crime and therefore limited police enforcement activity
- Working in a community where one was raised or currently resides

Other factors to consider include the salary, pension and fringe benefits; the opportunities to work varied assignments in the broad spectrum of law enforcement; department morale and reputation; and the potential for promotion. What are the agency's current needs? Is there a hiring freeze? Does it have serious budget constraints?

Often, interested applicants may request, either in person at the department, over the phone or online, a fact sheet containing a brief job description, the salary range and fringe benefits, and an application. Applicants may also be notified of the time and location of the next written examination or hiring opportunity.

How does a law enforcement candidate find an open position to evaluate? If the law enforcement agencies in the area are progressive, they will have a successful recruiting program. Many departments also recruit online by posting job openings on their Web sites. Although all departments seek "the best" candidates to hire, they must first specify which characteristics are most important.

Desired Qualities of Law Enforcement Officers

If citizens were asked what traits they felt were desirable in police officers, their responses would be considerably different, perhaps something like this: Police officers should be able to work under pressure, to accept direction, to express themselves orally and in writing. They should have self-respect and the ability to command respect from others. They should use good judgment, and they should be considerate, compassionate, dependable, enthusiastic, ethical, fair, flexible, honest, humble, industrious, intelligent, logical, motivated, neat, observant, physically fit, prompt, resourceful, self-assured, stable, tactful, warm and willing to listen and to accept change.

Furthermore, with our society becoming increasingly diverse, the ideal officer would be able to police without bias or discrimination and be sensitive to the needs and concerns of various populations within a community. Unfortunately, no one has all these traits, but the more of these traits police officers have, the more effective they will be in dealing with the citizens of the community as well as lawbreakers.

In most states, law enforcement candidates must also be U.S. citizens and must meet rigorous physical and personal qualifications. Personal qualities, such as honesty, good judgment and a sense of responsibility, are especially important.

Qualities of a good police officer include reliability, leadership, judgment, persuasiveness, communication skills, initiative, integrity, honesty, ego control, intelligence, sensitivity and problem-solving ability.

Finding qualified individuals is no easy task. Recruiting, screening and selecting candidates are continuous, critical functions of all police agencies.

Finding Qualified Applicants

The generational transition currently under way and at the center of the workforce crisis that existed before the economic crisis changed the picture drastically resulted from the convergence of two trends: the growing number of aging baby boomers and the much smaller cohort of younger people, the generation Xers, who follow behind them. Members of the 102 million–strong millennial

CAREER PROFILE

Jennifer Molan (Sergeant, Dakota County Sheriff's Office, Minnesota)

When I was a young girl, I would play "Cagney & Lacey" with my best friend. We would bike through our neighborhood pretending to fight crime and solve serious criminal cases. Years later, I found myself still interested in law and order. When I entered college, I dreamt of being a criminal attorney. During my junior year, I completed an internship with a nonprofit organization that monitored domestic assault court cases and, at that point, realized I needed more out of my career. I began searching for an opportunity to be part of the criminal justice community.

A classmate had told me about a volunteer opportunity with the Minneapolis (Minnesota) Police Department. I sought more information, and within a few months I was a Minneapolis reserve police officer. I spent several years volunteering by directing traffic, passing out community bulletins, driving in parades and assisting the police department with their needs. I quickly obtained the rank of corporal. Although it was a nice title, at that time it had little meaning to me. My responsibilities didn't change, and I knew I was still seeking more.

After completing my undergraduate degree, I started working full time as a Detention Deputy for the Hennepin County Sheriff's Office, the largest Sheriff's Office in Minnesota, booking in over 50,000 inmates a year. During my two years there, I learned an incredible amount. I saw people in their worst state. I saw the effects that drugs and alcohol can have on people. I saw how incarceration can destroy a family and ruin friendships. Shortly before taking another job, I became a field training officer (FTO) and was responsible for training future detention deputies. This was a big responsibility and my first real taste of leadership.

The experience I gained while working for the Hennepin County Sheriff's Office helped me get my first licensed peace officer job. In 2001, I began working for the Dakota County Sheriff's Office (Dakota County is the third largest county in Minnesota). I worked a short six weeks in the court security division before being assigned as a school resource officer (SRO) at a school for children with emotional and behavioral disorders. My first day at the school was a real eye opener. The school had three "bouncers," whom I quickly got to know, as they became my lifeline. I often found myself having to physically restrain students. Despite the hard working conditions, this was one of the most rewarding assignments in my career. I had the opportunity to investigate all sorts of crimes within the school and the community. I was also able to make good connections with staff and students. I truly had the best of both worlds during the four years I worked as an SRO. I spent the cold Minnesota winters working in the school and the nice enjoyable summers assigned to the patrol division.

After years of working in the schools, I was temporarily promoted to an investigator and assigned to the Minnesota Gang Strike Force, spending three years on a multi-jurisdictional task force responsible for investigating all types of gang crimes throughout the state and learning an incomprehensible amount about the inner workings of criminal investigations. While assigned to the Minnesota Gang Strike Force, I worked closely with the Bureau of Alcohol, Tobacco and Firearms (ATF) to help create a joint statewide task force responsible for investigating several hundred "smash and grab" burglaries involving the theft of tobacco products. As a result of the work of this task force, Minnesota saw a substantial decrease in tobacco store burglaries.

Just before my tenure at the Gang Strike Force was going to come to an end, I was again promoted to detective, working in general investigations with the Dakota County Sheriff's Office. I was responsible for investigating all types of crimes and worked closely with other detectives and agencies on everything from simple thefts to complex homicides. I received specialized training in crime scene investigating, child sexual assault interviews, homicide investigations, and interviews and interrogations.

During my years with the Dakota County Sheriff's Office I sought out several special assignments. I spent five years as a police explorer advisor and was responsible for teaching youth interested in law enforcement careers about the ins and outs of being a patrol officer. I was also a member of the sheriff's office underwater search and recovery dive team. At the request of the Dakota County Attorney's Office, I co-developed a youth accountability program for first-time juvenile property offenders. I teach this class three times a month to youth offenders and their parents. The class focuses on helping teens live a crime-free life.

During my time at the Minnesota Gang Strike Force, I also returned to school to seek a masters degree. During my masters program, I took some great classes that helped me find myself as an officer. After completing several leadership and ethics course, I aspired to hold a leadership role in the Dakota County Sheriff's Office. Shortly after finishing my masters degree, I applied for a sergeant position within the department. After sending in my résumé, taking a written exam and surviving two interviews, the sheriff selected me to be a sergeant in the detention services division.

Today, I am the supervisor of the prisoner transport division and occasionally supervise the court security division. I am the only licensed female supervisor within the Dakota County Sheriff's Office and supervise a staff of up to twenty. I am also the child safety coordinator and am responsible for alcohol and tobacco compliance. I am confident that my education, experience and confidence helped me to get to where I am today. I truly believe the field of law enforcement involves lifelong learning, and I encourage you to continue to learn every day and take advantage of the opportunities that life presents you.

generation (born between 1982 and 2002) have yet to fully affect the law enforcement workplace, but they will be the majority of new police officers and deputies hired in the coming decade.

Although law enforcement agencies typically say recruitment is among their most pressing issues, Alan Deal, of the California Peace Officers Standards and Training (POST) Commission, told the RAND Summit on Police Recruitment and Retention that they do not typically make it a priority. They are hindered by a lack of strategic planning for recruitment, a lack of understanding of the market, and advertising and marketing methods that are out of touch and out of date for today's potential market. Traditional advertising and marketing are unlikely to overcome these problems (Wilson and Grammich, 2009, p.16).

Finding qualified police recruits became tougher after September 11, 2001 (9/11) because the expansion of federal law enforcement has created more options for people interested in the field. Many candidates recruited for policing in the past are now being successfully recruited by other agencies (Pearsall and Kohlhepp, 2010, p.128). In addition, the wars in Iraq and Afghanistan have led many public-service minded people to join the military. Figure 12.1 illustrates the competition local law enforcement agencies face in recruiting candidates.

Yet another contributor to the reduction in qualified applicants may be the negative publicity over high-profile incidents of racial profiling and excessive use of force among police.

When force numbers need to be increased, organizations tend to lower their standards and hire the needed numbers, sacrificing quality for quantity. For example, some departments have relaxed standards for prior drug use to expand the pool

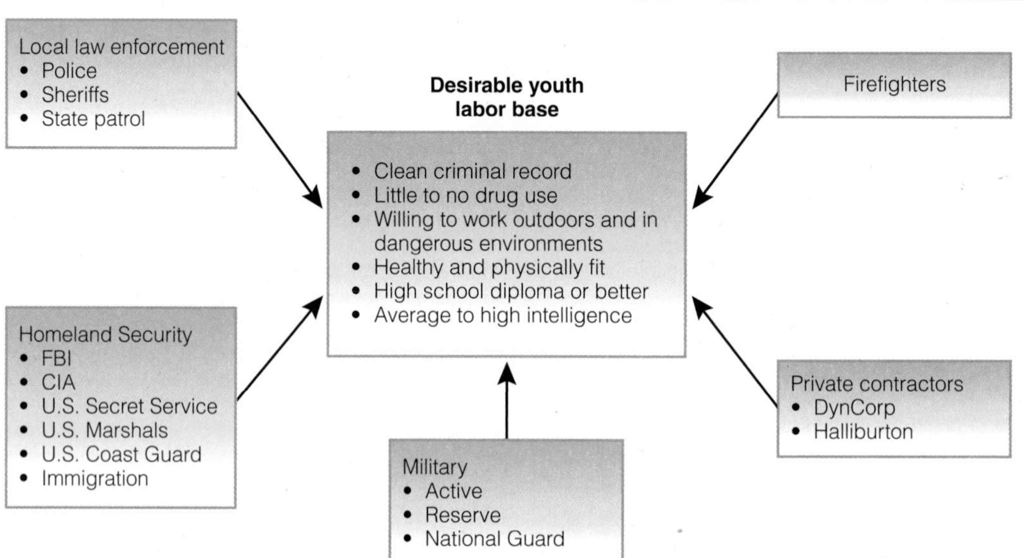

FIGURE 12.1 Sources of Competition against Local Law Enforcement Agencies for Suitable Applicants

SOURCE: Jeremy M Wilson and Clifford A. Grammich. *Police Recruitment and Retention in the Contemporary Urban Environment: A National Discussion of Personnel Experiences and Promising Practices from the Front Lines.* RAND Center on Quality Policing and the Community Oriented Policing Services, Department of Justice, © RAND Corporation, 2009, p.3.

of applicants. In some agencies the window of past drug use has shifted from the past three to five years to within the last year or six months. In some departments physical screening standards have changed from "pass/fail" to "close enough" if the candidate is within a certain range, as agencies believe they can get candidates to the desired fitness level once they are in the academy and participating in a physical training program (Schreiber, 2009, pp.15–16).

Other Recruiting Challenges

In addition to falling numbers of applicants, departments face other recruiting challenges, such as appealing to a new generation of applicants, dispelling misconceptions of the real job caused by the mass entertainment media and understanding that law enforcement has changed from the traditionally blue-collar job to a challenging profession requiring technical skills. In a strong economy, veteran officers and good potential candidates may be lured away from public police by the private sector and the potential for better pay. Compounding the recruiting challenge is the high attrition rate currently sweeping through the nation's police agencies, as baby boomers approach retirement. Furthermore, increased educational requirements in many jurisdictions have limited the pool of eligible candidates from which to choose.

An important recruiting challenge is the need for those who see policing as a calling, not just a job, and who can be trusted to enforce the law without violating it themselves. Finding that ideal police recruit, one who seeks a long-term career as one of society's peacekeepers, is increasingly difficult.

Recruiting Strategies

Most departments recruit through traditional avenues such as handouts, media advertisements (newspapers, radio, TV), job fairs and visits to colleges. In addition, many agencies use their Web sites to provide information about the agency, job opportunities, how to apply and the like. The International Association of Chiefs of Police (IACP) has a job Web site, http://careercenter.discoverpolicing.org, where departments list job openings for a fee. Job searches, however, are free. Referral incentives are also being used. Some departments have had success with offering current officers a bonus for recruiting a candidate who makes it through the academy.

Some departments are focusing on recruiting second-career officers. For example, a recent rookie class in the Appleton (Wisconsin) Police Department included a car salesman, a former teacher, a juvenile counselor, a dental technician, a nurse, a paramedic, a businessman and an assistant district attorney.

Nevertheless, colleges remain a fundamental source of police recruits. One way departments are avoiding the obstacle of recruiting inexperienced college graduates is by accessing participants in the College Law Enforcement Internship Program. Although specific programs vary, student interns are generally placed with an agency and must complete a certain number of credit hours per term.

Table 12.1 shows the various recruitment techniques used and their perceived effectiveness. The most frequently used recruitment technique was word-of-mouth. Whichever avenues an agency selects for recruiting officer candidates, the target audience should be diverse.

TABLE 12.1 Recruitment Techniques and Their Perceived Effectiveness

Technique	Number Using	% Using	Average Effectiveness Rating (0 to 9)
Word-of-mouth	118	95.0	6.83
Newspaper ads	103	83.1	5.38
Community college	89	71.8	5.62
Internet	78	62.9	4.64
Personnel listings	76	61.3	4.13
Auxiliary/reserve force	71	57.3	5.32
Job fairs	61	49.2	2.89
Police Corps	44	35.5	2.73
Radio/TV ads	34	25.4	.85

NOTE: Survey respondents were encouraged to select all recruitment techniques used by their agencies; therefore, percentages do not equal 100.

SOURCE: Douglas L. Yearwood. "Recruitment and Retention of Police Officers in North Carolina." *The Police Chief*, March 2004, p.43. Reprinted by permission. Copyright held by The International Association of Chiefs of Police, Inc. Further reproduction without express written permission is prohibited.

The IACP and the Bureau of Justice Assistance (BJA) have created a Web-based recruiting resource, DiscoverPolicing.org, which launched in 2008 and offers a combination of clear, accurate information on law enforcement careers and a central platform for hiring agencies to connect with applicants throughout the country. It is fast becoming the "premier destination" for law enforcement job seekers and hiring agencies (Kohlhepp and Phillips, 2009, p.46).

The Law Enforcement Recruitment Toolkit

The IACP has also developed a recruitment toolkit for law enforcement to assist local law enforcement recruitment efforts. The toolkit has four main sections: Police Recruitment: Foundation Concepts, Recruiting for Diversity, Agency Collaboration in Police Officer Recruitment and Selection, and Community Partnerships in Police Recruitment. The following information is from the first section of *Law Enforcement Recruitment Toolkit*, (2009): "Foundation Concepts." Recruiting for diversity follows this discussion. The importance of partnerships with other agencies as well as with the community has been noted throughout the text.

At least five factors hinder police recruitment: (1) unfavorable demographic and social trends including the aging of our population and declining birthrates have resulted in smaller cohorts between ages 21 and 35, the target age for new officers; (2) lack of diversity in some police departments, with the underrepresentation of minorities and women creating a shortage of role models for recruiting these populations; (3) unattractiveness of paramilitary organization, with the media and some recruiters leading potential recruits to believe a police career consists primarily of thrill-filled days engaged in high-risk endeavors; (4) intense competition for candidates (previously discussed); and (5) bureaucratic and burdensome personnel regulations with applicants sometimes subjected to repeated visits to participate in stages of the selection cycle. A "superbly qualified" candidate may be lost to another employer that is able to test and assess the candidate and make a firm job offer in less time (*Law Enforcement Recruitment Toolkit*, 2009, pp.5–7). This happens frequently with very good candidates.

Numerous strategies are recommended to improve recruitment (*Law Enforcement Recruitment Toolkit*, 2009, pp.7–14):

- Collaborate with other police agencies, engage the community, and improve relations with external human resource offices and elected officials
- Streamline the recruitment and selection process
- Involve everyone in the department in recruitment but put someone in charge of recruiting
- Tell the police story, enhance Web outreach, enlist the support of the media
- Reach out to the young; hire younger—and older, as well as transitional workers
- Mentor applicants through the process.

The second section of the IACP's tool kit addresses the challenge of recruiting for diversity.

Recruiting for Diversity

Diversity is vital to law enforcement's continued success: "We have learned that to be effective, police cannot operate alone; they require the active support and assistance of their communities. Central to maintaining that support is the recognition that law enforcement agencies must reflect the diversity of the communities they serve. Every day, our officers come into contact with individuals from different cultural backgrounds, socioeconomic classes, religions, sexual orientations, and physical and mental abilities. Each of these groups brings a different perspective to police community relations and, as a result, our officers must be prepared to respond to each group in the appropriate fashion" (*Law Enforcement Recruitment Toolkit*, 2009, p.32).

Of special concern is the apparent low interest among women and minorities in police work. Many police leaders suspect that women see law enforcement as a male-dominated profession that does not welcome women, that they may face sexual harassment or be ostracized and stereotyped, that they may have difficulty being promoted or obtaining the more prestigious assignments, and that a police career may be incompatible with raising a family. Minorities may associate police work with civil rights abuses from the past, as well as present-day bias, including racial and ethnic profiling. Recent immigrants may be suspicious of police in this country because police in their countries are corrupt or frequently use excessive force (*Law Enforcement Recruitment Toolkit*, 2009, p.33).

To attract more diverse recruits, agencies have started to advertise in a different light, portraying the many aspects of police work such as participating in community policing events, assisting those in need and working with youth in schools. Many departments have ads showing minorities and women in higher-level positions.

A racially balanced and integrated police department fosters community relations and increases police effectiveness.

Recruiting Minorities To gain the community's general confidence and acceptance, police departments seek personnel to represent the community. An integrated department helps reduce stereotyping and prejudice. Minority officers provide a department with an understanding of minority groups, their languages and their subcultures, all with practical benefits to successful law enforcement. For example, a police officer who speaks Spanish can help prevent conflicts between the police and the community's Spanish-speaking residents. A minority officer may also have insight into a particular population's cultural or behavioral idiosyncrasies, such as the reluctance of those in the Asian community to report victimization to the police. Unfortunately, it can be difficult for departments to find qualified recruits who reflect the ethnic or racial composition of their jurisdictions. Efforts to step up the reputation of law enforcement in such communities can encourage young citizens in these areas to consider policing as a future career.

Although many minorities view police as the "enemy" and would never consider joining their ranks, others view law enforcement as a way to a better life. An African American police lieutenant from Atlanta explains why he became a police officer: "You got out of my neighborhood without ending up dead or in prison by either becoming a minister or a cop. I always fell asleep in church so I decided to become a cop."

Several incidents have challenged the fragile cooperation that law enforcement and Muslims nationwide are struggling to create. Without the Muslim community's cooperation, the FBI, sheriffs and police chiefs believe they will never penetrate the world of homegrown Islamic extremists and potential terrorists they are convinced are out there. Muslim leaders say they want to help. In jurisdictions with large Muslim populations, recruiting Muslim officers is a giant step in bridging the gap.

Another issue related to minority officers is where they should be assigned. Many believe that minority neighborhoods should be policed by officers of the same background. Others, however, view this as a form of segregation. In addition to minorities, another group gaining representation in law enforcement is women.

Recruiting Women

The Uniform Crime Report showed that in 2007 women occupied about 11.8 percent of all sworn positions and 18.3 percent of the positions in our country's largest cities. In addition, the Bureau of Labor Statistics reports that in 2007 women held 13.7 percent of first-line police supervisory positions and 23.2 percent of criminal investigative positions. Data from 2007 and 2008 suggest a combined total of almost 100,000 female sworn officers nationwide are employed in federal, state and local law enforcement agencies (Langton, 2010). It is reasonable to anticipate that within 20 years women will hold at least 40 percent of sworn positions in many departments (Orrick, 2009. p.31).

Studies show that women perform as well as men in police work, are less apt to use excessive force, can help implement community-oriented policing and can improve an agency's response to violence against women. In addition, an increased female presence among officers can reduce problems of sex discrimination and harassment and foster policy changes that benefit all officers.

Despite the many benefits women officers bring to law enforcement, they still are not accepted in some departments. The growing presence of females in a traditionally male-dominated profession can undoubtedly lead to conflict between the genders.

So what can departments do to improve their recruitment efforts? The emphasis on upper-body strength often washes out qualified candidates, especially women, even though a survey of law enforcement agencies found physical ability to be the *least* important of 10 dimensions of "being a successful peace officer." The highest-ranking characteristic was integrity.

One barrier preventing women from considering a career in law enforcement is the absence of female role models and mentors working in police positions. If women are in the rank and file, candidates should be encouraged to talk to them about this subject. An agency that allows sexual harassment will have little chance of increasing the number of women officers and is likely to face a lawsuit. Sexual harassment is discussed with retention later in the chapter. Once an agency has identified and recruited potential candidates, the question becomes, Who to hire?

THE IMPORTANCE OF HIRING WELL

The hiring process is so critical in law enforcement partly because of **vicarious liability**, which refers to the legal responsibility one person has for the acts of another. Managers, the entire agency and even the jurisdiction served may be legally responsible for the actions of a single officer. *Vicarious* means "taking the place of another thing or person, substituting for." Law enforcement officers have always been responsible for their individual wrongdoings, criminally or civilly. Civil liability most frequently involves violation of the Civil Rights Act, specifically Statute 42 of the U.S. Code, Section 1983, discussed in Chapter 2. The act states that anyone acting under the authority of law who violates another person's constitutional rights can be sued. In 1978 in *Monell v. New York City Department of Social Services*, the Supreme Court ruled that local municipalities were also liable under Section 1983 (Title 42, U.S.C.).

vicarious liability

The legal responsibility one person has for the acts of another; managers, the entire agency and even the jurisdiction served may be legally responsible for the actions of a single officer.

It is now accepted that local government may be responsible for the wrongdoing of a subordinate enforcing a local ordinance, regulation or policy. In cases in which law enforcement managers directed, ordered or participated in the acts, they are equally liable. Additionally, if upper-level managers are negligent in hiring, assigning, training, retaining, directing or entrusting, they may be liable even if they were not present.

Negligent-hiring litigation is becoming more common. Law enforcement managers and supervisors have been held liable for negligence in hiring personnel unqualified or unsuited for law enforcement work. Negligent-hiring cases allow evidence about a person's past negligence and reputation, items typically not admissible in court proceedings. As such, liability in negligent-hiring cases can be tremendous, and the results are often disastrous. Most of these cases involve failure to use an adequate selection process or to check for prior offenses or misconduct.

negligent hiring

Negligence in hiring personnel unqualified or unsuited for law enforcement work.

THE SELECTION PROCESS

A person wanting to become a police officer must usually go through several steps in the selection process, often referred to as the *multiple hurdle procedure.* Although procedures differ greatly from agency to agency, several elements are common to most selection processes.

Police officer selection usually includes

- A formal application and résumé.
- A written examination.
- A physical fitness test.
- A psychological examination.
- At least one oral interview, possibly more.
- A thorough background investigation.
- A medical examination.

The order in which these steps occur may vary from department to department. Figure 12.2 illustrates a typical selection process. Failure at any point in the selection process may disqualify a candidate.

The Formal Application—Basic Requirements to Become a Police Officer

Usually a police officer candidate completes a formal application, which includes driving record; any criminal record; visual acuity; physical, emotional and mental condition; and education. Most police agencies and civil service commissions accept applications even when no openings are listed. It is common to submit a résumé with the application. The application is placed on file, and when an examination is to be conducted, the applicant is notified by mail or phone.

Most law enforcement agencies require that a police officer

- Be a U.S. citizen.
- Have or be eligible for a driver's license in the state.
- Not have been convicted of a felony.

Requirements related to education and residency are also frequently stated.

Education Educational requirements for officers have long been a source of controversy in law enforcement. Opinions differ greatly about how much education a police officer candidate should have or how much should be a prerequisite for advancement. In some states, such as Minnesota, a two-year college degree is required for licensure. Standards for promotion commonly include completion of a 4-year degree.

The most common reason for not requiring higher education is the fear the requirement would be challenged in court or through labor arbitration. A landmark case was *Griggs v. Duke Power Company* (1971), in which Griggs, an African American employee, claimed that Duke's intradepartmental transfer policy requirement of having a high school diploma and passing two aptitude tests

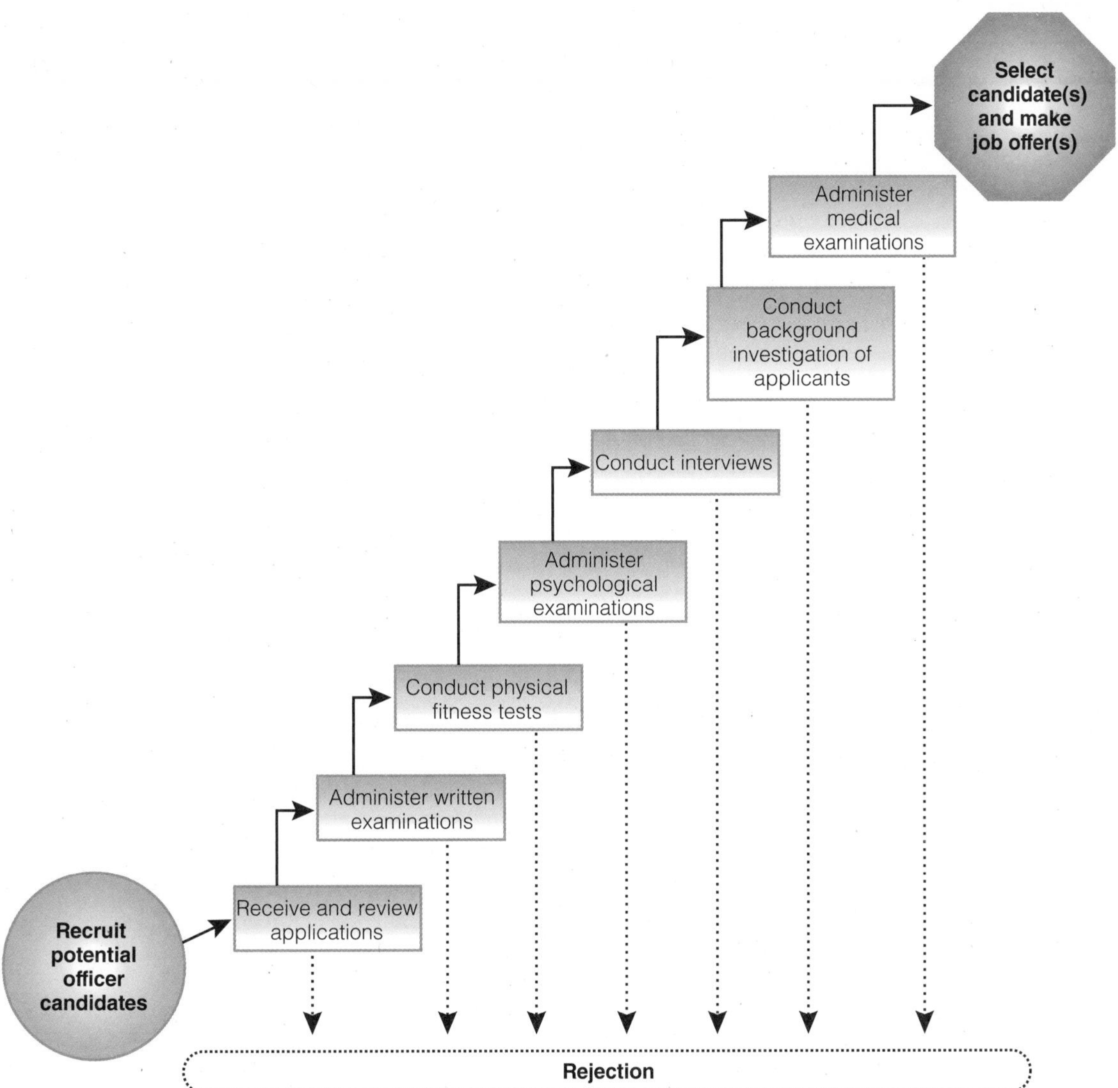

FIGURE 12.2 Typical Selection Process

SOURCE: Adapted from HARR/HESS *Careers in Criminal Justice and Related Fields*, 6E. © 2010 Wadsworth, a part of Cengage Learning, Inc. Reproduced by permission. www.cengage.com/permissions.

discriminated against African American employees in violation of Title VII of the 1964 Civil Rights Act. A district court dismissed Griggs' claim, and an appellate court ruled there was no discrimination. The Supreme Court, however, disagreed, holding that the Duke's standardized testing requirement, which was neither directed nor intended to measure an employee's ability to learn or perform a particular job or category of jobs within the company, prevented a disproportionate number of African American employees from being hired by, and advancing to higher-paying positions within, the company. The Court concluded that purpose of these requirements was to illegally protect the company's long-standing policy of giving job preferences to its White employees.

Most police agencies require a minimum of a high school education or equivalency certificate, and some require a two- or four-year degree. Many police agencies are now requiring some college education for employment or promotion. Limited empirical evidence exists about whether such education helps officers perform better.

The debate about how important education is for police started in 1905 when August Vollmer began his career in law enforcement administration in Berkeley, California, and back in 1931 a special presidential commission recommended that every officer have the minimum of a bachelor's degree for entry into the field.

The basic issue is this: Does more "formal" education make for better police officers? The topic has been the source of litigation. For example in *Davis v. City of Dallas* (1985) the department's requirement that applicants have completed 45 semester hours of college credit with a "C" average was challenged. In this case the court ruled in favor of the police department:

> The City introduced evidence which supports the educational requirement. Numerous nationwide studies have examined the problem of setting the education requirement for police departments with favorable conclusions. A college education as a condition of hiring as a police officer has been recommended by the National Commission on Law Observance in 1931; by the President's Commission on Law Enforcement and Commission on Intergovernmental Relations in 1971; by the American Bar Association in 1972; and by the National Advisory Commission on Criminal Justice Standards and Goals in 1973. Defendant's experts established the relationship between college education and performance of police officers. A study by one expert relied upon factual data from two large metropolitan areas that took two years to complete, showing significantly higher performance rates by college-educated officers. A persuasive point was made that a high-school diploma today does not represent the same level of achievement which it represented 10 years ago.

Proponents of higher education for officers contend college-educated officers are less biased, less authoritarian and less likely to use force than are non–college-educated officers. Advocates of advanced learning also believe college-educated officers hone their ability to flexibly handle difficult situations and develop an increased empathy and tolerance for minorities and persons with different lifestyles and ideologies. Completing occupation-specific courses provides a more complete understanding of the "big picture" of the criminal justice system and a better appreciation for the prosecutorial, court and corrections roles. Furthermore, the entire college experience allows time for the individual to mature and develop a general sense of responsibility.

Henson et al. (2010, p.5) collected data on 486 officers hired between 1996 and 2006 by a Midwestern police department to examine characteristics related to academy success as well active police service. The researchers found that most demographic and experience variables did not predict academy or active service success. However, Whites and those scoring highest on the civil service exam consistently performed better on multiple academy outcome measures than their counterparts. Further, those scoring higher on overall academy success measures generally received better evaluations from their superiors. Most importantly, for this discussion, their results showed that higher education is *not* related to any of the measures of academy or on-the-job success used in their analysis. The researchers (p.20) speculate that the two variables consistently related to the academy success measures—race and civil service exam scores—may be masking an effect of socioeconomic status and that police academy training curriculum may favor the values and characteristics of White males and a middle-class bias. Unlike race, gender was not related to academy performance. The study concluded that one of the best criteria for police departments to base hiring decisions on may be high civil service scores (Henson et al., 2010, p.21).

Researchers Rydberg and Terrill (2010, p.92) looked at two medium-sized cities and the impact of higher officer education on three key decision-making points: arrest, search, and use of force. The analysis found that college education did not influence the probability of an arrest or search but did significantly reduce the amount of force used. Rydberg and Terrill (p.113) note, however, that their findings do not warrant a reversal of the National Academies Panel on Police Policy and Performance's statement that there was not enough quality evidence to recommend a college education requirement for employment as a police officer.

Despite all the supposed advantages, many contend that good officers could be lost if educational levels are set too high. Critics of a college education requirement assert college graduates would be unlikely to seek employment in law enforcement, particularly women and minority college graduates, which would undermine the progress being made in recruiting them.

Some police chiefs believe that too much education makes social service officers of personnel who ought to be fighting crime in the streets. Others feel that requiring a degreed officer to perform such mundane tasks as issuing traffic tickets and parking tickets, making money runs and carding juveniles in liquor stores is demeaning. These opponents contend that such routine tasks soon diminish the highly educated officer's interest in law enforcement, which leads to greater job dissatisfaction, increasing turnover rates and higher hostility levels toward non–college-educated officers. Critics of required higher education assert that the skills effective officers need can be learned only on the street, not in a classroom.

All controversy aside, the trend in today's law enforcement agencies appears to be supportive of high education standards for officers.

Research looked at the question "Are street smarts better than book smarts?" and found that officers with bachelor of science degrees were below the average in frequency of commendations and above the average in the negative work habits of traffic collisions, sick-time use and discipline. Officers with bachelor of arts degrees, in contrast, were above the average in the frequency that they received commendations and below the average in traffic collisions, sick-time use and frequency of discipline.

Figure 12.3 illustrates the number of commendations per officer by type of college degree. As seen, those with associate of applied science, associate of science and bachelor of science degrees received, on average, fewer commendations than did officers holding associate of arts, bachelor of arts or master of arts degrees or those officers who had completed only high school and held no college degree.

A partial explanation offered for this disparity is that a bachelor of arts degree emphasizes problem solving, develops understanding of how perceptions influence behavior, increases a person's comfort with ambiguity and assumes the

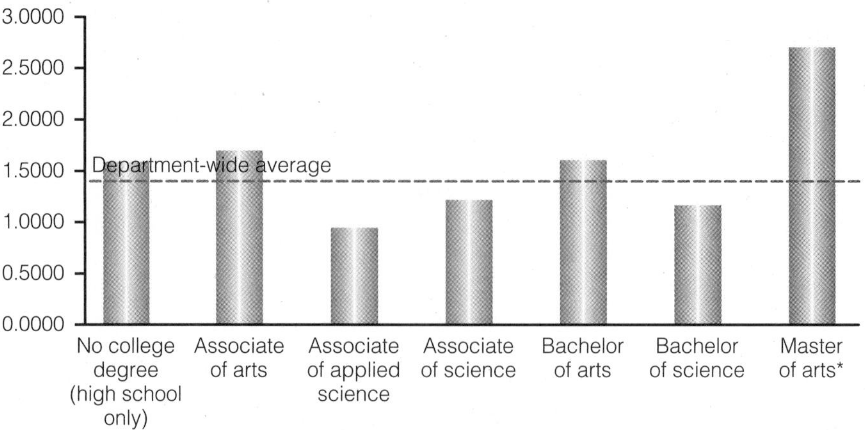

*Officers who had master of science (two) or doctor of philosophy (one) degree were statistically insignificant.

FIGURE 12.3 Commendations per Officer, September 1999–September 2002, by Type of College Degree

SOURCE: Mathew D. Bostrom. "The Influence of Higher Education on Police Officer Work Habits." *The Police Chief*, October 2005, p.24. Reprinted by permission. Copyright held by The International Association of Chiefs of Police, Inc. Further reproduction without express written permission is prohibited.

things going on in the world are fluid and interrelated. Officers with a bachelor of science degree, in contrast, tend to be rewarded for collecting verifiable facts and drawing conclusions based on those facts. The difference between the types of degrees might reflect the type of person who chooses to pursue a bachelor of arts degree rather than a bachelor of science degree.

Residency Requirements Over the years cities and municipalities have waived residency requirements to obtain better candidates. Though residency is still generally not required, some cities are again beginning to accept only candidates who reside within their boundaries. Alternately, some agencies are providing free residency in government-funded housing as a benefit to attract qualified candidates, particularly in low-income areas where recruiting tends to be more challenging.

It is usually preferred and sometimes required that police officers live in the community they serve.

Sometimes compromises have been made whereby candidates are given one year to move into the community they serve. City and municipal politicians feel that by living in the community, police officers become more closely identified with that community, more sensitive to its crime problems and more willing to participate in community activities.

Local residency is particularly important for departments instituting community policing. In addition, politicians' self-interests dictate that their police officers live in the community so they can contribute their fair share of taxes. Some officers, however, may not be able to afford the cost of housing in the community they serve. Another issue with such residency requirements is that officers' families may be targeted for victimization in high-crime or otherwise unsafe areas. Thus there are many arguments on both sides of the coin related to residency requirements.

The Written Examination

Some departments use a civil service examination. Others use examinations designed specifically for their department. In either case the examinations do not usually test knowledge of police work or procedures but rather various abilities and aptitudes. Their primary function is to screen out those who lack the "basic material" to be a police officer.

Written examinations are usually in multiple-choice format and last two to three hours. They may test spelling, grammar and mathematical ability. They may also test reasoning ability, problem solving, reading comprehension, interpersonal communications skills or ability to process information.

Increasingly departments are looking at how well an applicant can write. Although report-writing skills can be taught, they do take time to develop and master. A recruit who already possesses strong written communication skills can help a hiring manager decide between two or more otherwise equally qualified candidates.

Critics, however, claim written exams cannot measure common sense and penalize those who do not test well. Such tests may also inadvertently "weed out" candidates who possess other valuable skills that cannot be measured on paper. Another downside to written exams is the potential for adverse impacts against minority applicants and those for whom English is not their primary language.

Most written examinations are a straight pass/fail situation, serving as an entry into the next phase of the selection process. Some agencies, however, factor the score on this examination into their final selection decision. Many reference books and study guides are available to help candidates prepare for written law enforcement examinations. Those candidates who do well on the written test go on to physical fitness testing.

Physical Fitness Tests

Most police departments require physical fitness tests of applicants. Physical fitness tests determine a candidate's coordination and muscular strength and ascertain whether the candidate is in good physical condition. The type of test varies with police agencies throughout the country.

A candidate may be required to run a designated number of yards and while doing so hurdle a 3-foot barrier, crawl under a 24-inch bar, climb over a 4- or 6-foot wall with both hands on top of the wall and sprint the remaining distance—all within a designated time monitored by a police officer with a stopwatch. Candidates may also be required to climb ropes or fire ladders and do chin-ups or push-ups.

Most agencies use one of two types of fitness tests: the physical qualifications test (PQT) and the job standards test (JST), with some agencies using a combination of the two. The PQT usually uses timed minimum standards, adjusted for age and gender, for such activities as sit-ups, pushups and a run. The JST, as the name implies, uses job-related activities. The New York Police Department (NYPD) test items, for example, include (1) a barrier surmount to replicate a street condition, (2) a stair climb to replicate chasing someone, (3) a physical restraint simulation to replicate efforts in restraining a person, (4) a pursuit run to replicate dexterity

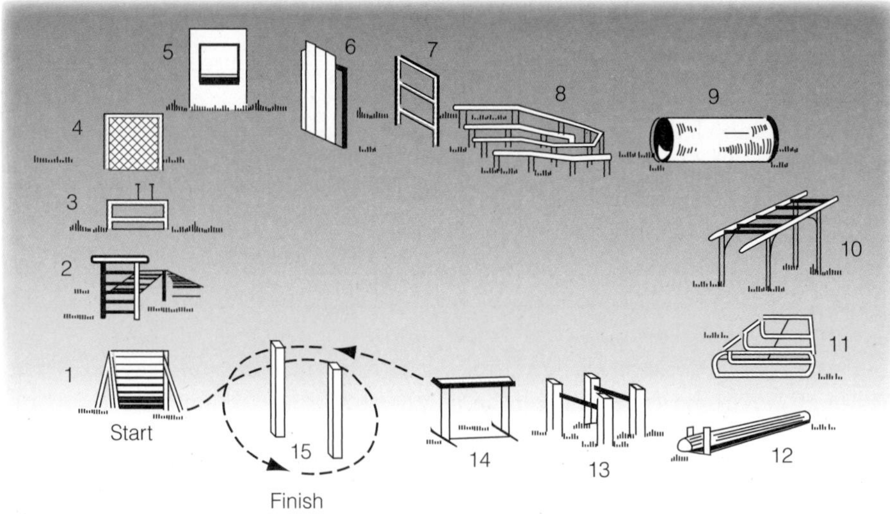

1) Start – 6' Wall
2) Ladder climb – Run across flat landing and down ramp
3) Hurdle – Use hands only!
4) Chain link fence climb – Reach, lift and climb over fence
5) Window climb through
6) Wooden gate – Open fence gate door, go through and close door
7) Hurdle – Climb over
8) Running maze – Enter at left. DO NOT touch siding!
9) Tunnel crawl – Crawl through. DO NOT dive!
10) Hand bar walk – Reach with hands, walk across
11) High stepper – Lift feet high
12) Log walk – Slanted, walk across
13) Horizontal hand walk – Use hands, push off ground and walk across bars
14) Short wall – Jump up and over
15) Pole run – Run to your right, go $1\frac{1}{2}$ times around. DO NOT touch poles!

FINISH

FIGURE 12.4 Physical Fitness Course

SOURCE: Criminal Justice Institute, Broward Community College, Ft. Lauderdale, FL. Reprinted by permission.

efforts, (5) a victim rescue to replicate a rescue in an emergency and (6) repeated firing of a gun (Gotay, 2010, p.33).

Figure 12.4 illustrates the physical fitness course used at the Criminal Justice Institute of Broward Community College in Ft. Lauderdale, Florida.

Physical fitness tests evaluate a candidate's coordination, speed and strength. The most common physical fitness tests are similar to military obstacle courses that must be completed within a designated time.

Psychological Testing

Psychological tests are administered to determine if the person is emotionally suited for a career in law enforcement. Employers use psychological tests to learn about the applicant's present state of mind, what is important to that person and how that person is likely to respond to certain stimuli.

Psychological tests commonly used during officer selection include the Minnesota Multiphasic Personality Inventory–2 (MMPI–2), the California Psychological Inventory (CPI), the Myers-Briggs Type Indicator™, the Watson-Glaser Critical Thinking Appraisal and the Strong Interest Inventory. The MMPI–2 is one of the most widely used, best-known tools for measuring psychological pathology. This test helps identify and avoid hiring of those prone to irresponsible, unsafe, counterproductive behavior. The test complies with the federal Civil Rights Act and EEOC but must be administered post-offer and be interpreted by a qualified psychologist.

The Interview

The interviewing board usually consists of three to five skilled interviewers knowledgeable in their fields. They may be staff officers from the agency doing the hiring or from other agencies, psychologists, sociologists or representatives of a community service organization. The entire interviewing board may consist of members of a police or civil service commission. In smaller jurisdictions oral boards are sometimes replaced by an interview with the mayor, a member of the city council or the chief of police.

Interviews are used to evaluate an applicant's appearance, alertness, communication ability, social adaptability, judgment, emotional stability, and interest in and suitability for the job.

Interviews, whether structured or unstructured, are designed to elicit answers revealing the candidates' personalities and suitability for police work, not to determine their technical knowledge in the police field. Candidates should be prepared to answer questions such as

- Why do you want to be a police officer?
- What have you done to prepare for a career in law enforcement?
- What do you believe are the causes of crime?
- How do you feel about community policing?
- What is the last book you have read?
- What was your favorite subject in school?
- When did you last get drunk?
- Why did you select this department to apply to?

Interviews also test a candidate's ability to use good judgment in specific situations. For example:

- A person is standing on the corner making a speech regarding the overthrow of the government. He is drawing a crowd, and a certain amount of animosity is being shown toward the speaker, indicating future trouble. How would you handle this situation?
- You are working radar, and you clock the mayor going 39 mph in a 30-mph zone. How would you handle this situation?

The interview usually lasts about 30 minutes. The same questions are posed to each candidate to allow comparison of answers. After the interview, each candidate's qualifications are evaluated, and the candidate is given an overall rating, which is combined with the scores of the other examinations to yield a composite (total) score.

The Background Investigation

The applicant's background is a critical factor, and the background investigation serves two vital purposes: (1) it examines and verifies the past work and educational record of the candidate, and (2) it determines if anything in the candidate's background might make him or her unsuitable for police work.

The extensiveness of the background investigation is limited only by the number of candidates being investigated and time available. Normally all information given by the applicant on the personal history sheet must be verified. Birth and age records are verified through vital statistics, and driving records are verified through the driver's license bureau. Adverse driving records containing drunken driving, driving after suspension or revocation of license, or a consistent pattern of moving violations may cause disqualification.

Candidates are fingerprinted, and the prints are sent to the FBI to determine if the candidate has a criminal record. The candidate's criminal record is also checked at the local and state levels, usually through fingerprints, name and date of birth. Juvenile records are normally discounted unless a person has committed a heinous crime.

Ironically, because of the transient nature of our population, individuals wanted on a warrant in one part of the country have applied for a police officer's position in another part of the country. The criminal record check has sometimes resulted in their apprehension. Most states have passed laws making it difficult, if not impossible, for ex-offenders to acquire employment as police officers.

Military records are usually checked to verify service and eligibility under the veteran's preference acts of some states. The check also determines if the candidate was involved in any court-martials or disciplinary actions.

All personal and professional references listed on the history sheet are interviewed. Interviewing of references is sometimes criticized because candidates obviously will list only those who see them favorably; however, these references may lead to others who know the candidates and have a different view of them. When candidates list out-of-town references, letters or questionnaires are usually mailed.

Previous employers are contacted to verify the applicant's work record. An inability to hold continuous employment may indicate trouble getting along with supervisors. A high absentee rate may indicate lack of interest or initiative or health problems.

The financial status of the candidate is also determined, usually through a credit records check. Those whose expenditures exceed their total incomes may be candidates for bankruptcy or bribery. Good credit indicates the person can live within his or her means and possesses self-control. The candidate may be required to submit a financial statement.

Educational records from high school, college and any other schools attended are usually checked through personal contact. The education record may indicate interests, achievements, accomplishments and social lifestyle while attending school.

The scholastic record reflects intelligence and study habits. Any degrees, certificates of achievement or awards are usually noted.

Polygraph examinations are growing in popularity as tools to verify information from background investigations, with most police departments currently using this test. Although some states have banned their use for preemployment purposes, in those states where it is used, it is necessary to determine why it is being given. Some departments use the polygraph extensively, especially if they have many transient applicants from other parts of the country. Some agencies use it to determine if the candidate has ever engaged in criminal activity and was ever apprehended. Some want to know if the candidate has any sexually deviant behaviors. Others use it to verify the information the candidate has given on the application and history sheet.

The background investigation includes

- Verification of all information on the application and history sheet.
- Check of driving record.
- Fingerprinting and a check of any criminal record.
- Check of military records.
- Interviews with personal references, acquaintances, past employers, neighbors and teachers.
- Check of financial status.
- Check of any pending litigation.
- Check of past performance at schools and previous jobs.

The American Society for Industrial Security (ASIS) International has published *Preemployment Background Screening Guideline* (2006) for establishing *due diligence* in its hiring process: "**Due diligence** is the attention and care that a reasonable person exercises under the circumstances to avoid harm to other persons or their property. Failure to make this effort is considered negligence" (p.8). The *Guideline* (p.9) goes on to define *negligent hiring* as "The failure to use reasonable care in the employee selection process, resulting in harm caused to others. Employers have a legal duty not to hire people who could pose a threat of harm to others, which can include everything from slight to fatal bodily injury, theft, arson, or property damage." To maximize due diligence and minimize claims of negligent hiring, it is suggested that, at minimum, a background check include verification of the Social Security Number, the address history, a countywide felony/misdemeanor record search, a driver's license search and education verification (*Preemployment Background Screening Guideline*, p.39). Figure 12.5 provides a sample preemployment background screening flow chart.

due diligence

The attention and care a reasonable person exercises under the circumstances to avoid harm to other persons or their property; failure to make this effort is considered negligence.

Testing or Assessment Centers

Some police departments use a testing or assessment center in the selection process. Used by corporate America for more than six decades, assessment centers were first used by law enforcement agencies during the mid-1980s to help with promotional decisions. Today such testing centers offer many benefits to agencies when selecting and promoting law enforcement personnel. For example, many of these centers put candidates through video-based simulations or scenarios to evaluate

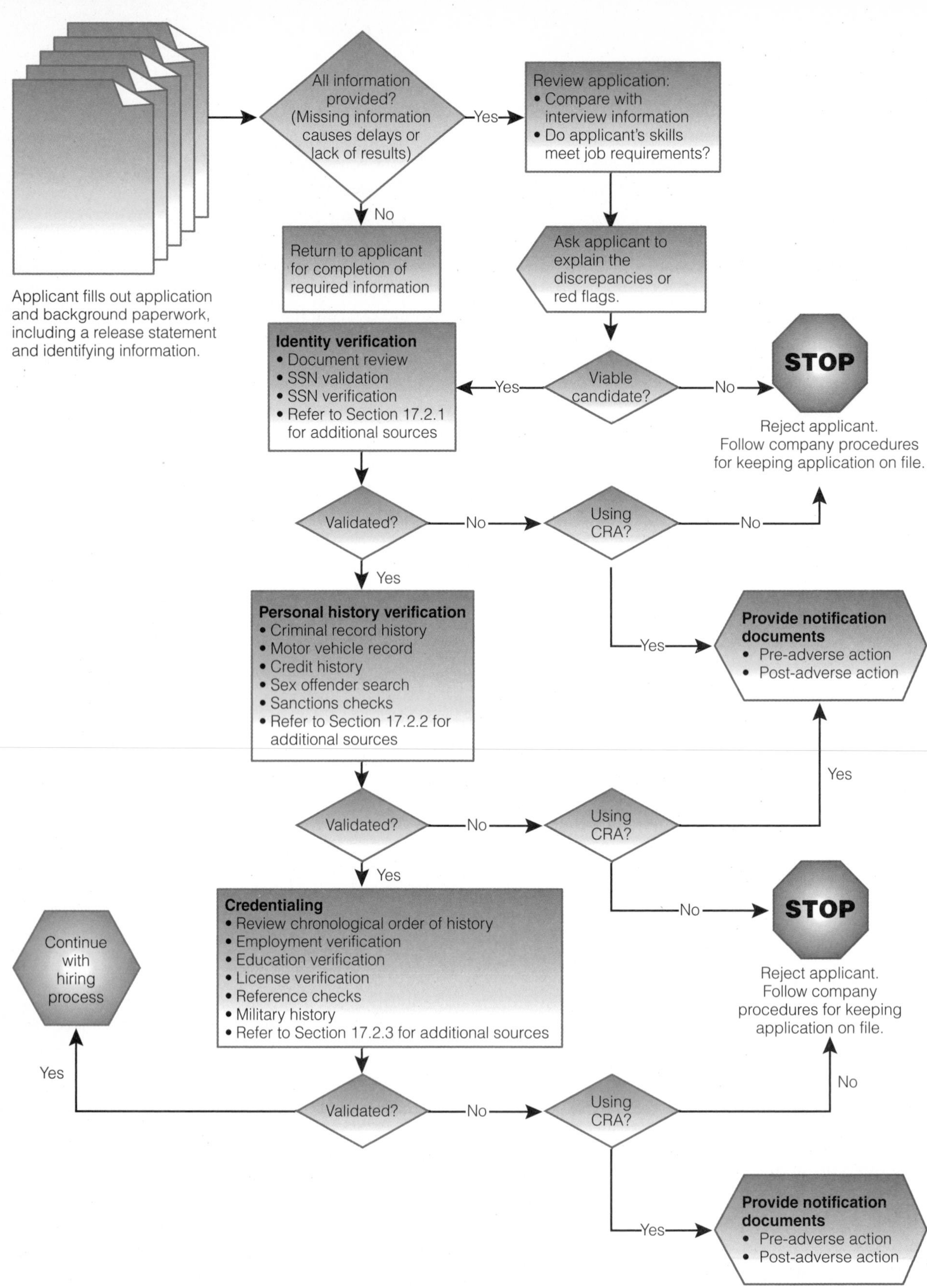

FIGURE 12.5 Sample Preemployment Background Screening Flow Chart

SOURCE: ASIS Preemployment Background Screening Guideline. Fairfax, VA: American Society for Industrial Security (ASIA) International, 2006, p.41.

individual judgment, cognitive decision making and physical reflexes. Such job-related simulation exercises, also called **situational testing**, are designed to assess a candidate's qualifications and suitability for a law enforcement position.

situational testing

Job-related simulation exercises to assess a candidate's qualifications and suitability for a law enforcement position.

The Medical Examination

Medical requirements vary from jurisdiction to jurisdiction, but the purpose is the same. With the current emphasis on health care, more importance is placed on the medical examination. Citizens, concerned that police officers may retire early because of poor health, are demanding physically fit officer candidates. The medical standards usually include a variety of factors with some—vision, hearing and the cardiovascular-respiratory system—being more important than others.

Good eyesight is of great importance. Candidates who wear glasses that correct their vision to 20/20 can qualify in most departments. Likewise, candidates who wear hearing aids that correct their hearing to meet the agency's requirements can qualify.

Because of job stress and the hypertension that often accompanies it, the cardiovascular system is thoroughly checked. The respiratory and cardiovascular systems play a critical role in fitness. To a great degree, endurance, the ability to continue exertion over a prolonged time, is directly related to the capacity of the cardiovascular-respiratory system to deliver oxygen to the muscles.

Vision, hearing and the cardiovascular-respiratory system are of prime importance in the medical examination.

Other medical factors often tested are the ratio of total cholesterol to HDL cholesterol (which identifies cardiovascular risk factors), blood pressure, smoking status, drug use and blood sugar level for diabetes. A physician who feels a candidate has a functional or organic disorder may recommend disqualification.

The Final Result

After all required tests are completed, they are analyzed, and a composite score is given for each candidate. A list is made of eligible candidates, and they are called as openings occur. Some larger police departments keep their eligibility lists for one to two years, depending on civil service requirements or other requirements mandated by states or municipalities. Many of the same methods used during the initial hiring process are used for promotional testing as well.

FEDERAL GUIDELINES AND REGULATIONS

The basic rule of thumb is that all requirements must be clearly job related. A **bona fide occupational qualification (BFOQ)** is one that is reasonably necessary to perform the job. It may on the surface appear to be discrimination. For example in law enforcement, applicants may be required to have normal or correctable-to-normal hearing and vision because these attributes are required to perform the job.

bona fide occupational qualification (BFOQ)

Skill or knowledge that is reasonably necessary to perform a job and, consequently, may be a requirement for employment.

Equal Employment Opportunity Act

In 1964 Congress enacted the Omnibus Civil Rights Law, of which Title VII concerned employment opportunities and prohibited discrimination based on sex, race, color, religion or national origin. The law also established the Equal Employment Opportunity Commission (EEOC) as its administrator. This law affected only private business, not state and local governments, and therefore had little impact on police agency practices.

However, in 1972 Congress passed the Equal Employment Opportunity Act, which modified Title VII to include state and local units of government. This law was passed because six years after the EEOC published guidelines for employment and promotion testing, few state or local central personnel selection agencies had taken positive steps to meet the guidelines.

The 1972 Equal Employment Opportunity Act prohibits discrimination due to sex, race, color, religion or national origin in employment of any kind, public or private, local, state or federal.

The EEOC legislation restricts the type of information that can be gathered from job applicants and requires all questions posed to applicants to be relevant to the job for which the applicant is applying. The following information cannot be asked about on application forms or during interviews: race or color, religion, national origin, age, marital status or ages of children, or if the person has ever been arrested. Applicants may be asked if they have ever been convicted of a crime and, if so, when and where it took place. Questions about education and experience are largely unrestricted.

Affirmative Action

affirmative action

Results-oriented actions taken to ensure equal employment opportunity.

The Affirmative Action Amendment (signed by President Richard Nixon in 1973) further strengthened the power of the EEOC. **Affirmative action** refers to special endeavors by employers (including law enforcement agencies) to recruit, hire, retain and promote minority group members and to eliminate past and present employment discrimination.

reverse discrimination

Giving preferential treatment in hiring and promoting to women and minorities to the detriment of White males.

Affirmative action is more than simply not discriminating during hiring—it is actively favoring women and minorities. Though the increases in the number of women and minorities in law enforcement agencies across the country are to be applauded, problems still exist. Sometimes these advancements are made at the expense of others—most notably White males. This is referred to as **reverse discrimination**—giving preferential treatment in hiring and promoting to women and minorities to the detriment of White males.

The Supreme Court has held that mandatory quotas established to meet an affirmative action plan's racially motivated goals are unlawful and thereby unconstitutional under federal law. In *Griggs v. Duke Power Company* (1971), the Court ruled that racially based quotas violated federal law. In the 2002–2003 term the Supreme Court handed down two landmark decisions regarding affirmative action. In *Grutter v. Bollinger* (2003), the Supreme Court upheld the University of Michigan's law school admissions' racially based affirmative action plan that permitted race to be one factor used in the admissions process. However, in *Gratz v. Bollinger* (2003), it declared the University of Michigan's undergraduate admissions program unlawful because it made race a "final and critically decisive factor and used a point system in which the race of an undergraduate applicant was factored into the final score upon which final admission was predicated.

Title VII of the Civil Rights Act of 1964 prohibits two types of employment discrimination, whose prohibitions sometimes conflict with each other. The first type of prohibited discrimination is *disparate impact*, which refers to an employer's policy or practice that results in an unintentional, disproportionately negative effect on minorities. The second type is *disparate treatment*, which is intentional discrimination based on race, color, religion, sex or national origin. The second type is quite easy to recognize and avoid. Disparate impact is a different story because it is truly unintentional. A claim of disparate impact may be defended against by showing that the policy or practice is "job related for the position in question and consistent with business necessity": "Even if an employer's policy or practice has a disproportionate adverse impact on minorities, the policy or practice may nonetheless be lawful if the employer can establish its job-relatedness and business necessity" (Means and McDonald, 2009, p.21). The recent Supreme Court case of *Ricci v. DeStefano* (2009) dealt with a claim of reverse discrimination. Although the case involved firefighters, it applies equally to law enforcement:

> The city of New Haven, CT decided not to certify two promotional exams it had administered to it firefighters because the White and Hispanic candidates outperformed the Black candidates.
>
> The city's refusal to certify the test results denied the White and Hispanic firefighters who passed the exams the possibility of promotion. They filed this lawsuit alleging that the city's decision to discard the test results was based on the racial disparity of the test scores and was unlawful racial discrimination. The United States Supreme Court agreed with them, ruling that the city's refusal to certify the tests because of the racially divided scores was unjustified racial discrimination, violating Title VII of the Civil Rights Act of 1964. . . .
>
> The city of New Haven found itself in the precarious position of having to choose between certifying the exam results, permitting the disproportionate adverse effect on its Black candidates (disparate impact), and refusing to certify the exam results, an intentional race-based decision that would deny the White and Hispanic candidates promotions (disparate treatment). In its attempt to avoid liability for disparate impact discrimination, the city used race as the determining factor in its decision to throw out the test results, thereby committing disparate treatment discrimination. . . .
>
> The question for the Court then was whether it is permissible to commit one form of discrimination in an effort to avert potential liability for another form of discrimination. The Court's answer was a somewhat qualified "no." The Court explained that the mere fear of litigation is not sufficient to justify the race-based decision to reject the test results. (Means and McDonald, 2009, pp.18, 21–22)

Justice David Souter contended that the situation put New Haven in a "damned-if-you-do-damned-if-you-don't" predicament. Managers in law enforcement are all too familiar with such predications, but decisions must be made.

This issue has separated Whites from minorities, men from women and the advocates of affirmative action from those who believe in a strict "merit" principle for employment and advancement. The majority position has been summarized as a concern that for every deserving minority group member who is provided a job or promotion through preferential quotas, a deserving, and often more qualified, nonminority person is deprived of a job or promotion. A growing number of majority member workers are complaining bitterly about their own civil rights being abridged, and some are filing reverse-discrimination suits in court. Such suits, however, are not always easily won. In fact, the courts themselves have been deeply divided over the constitutionality of the reverse discrimination that some believe is implicit in minority quotas and double standards.

Frequently those who might be beneficiaries of affirmative action do not welcome it, as noted by a veteran female sergeant who is Hispanic and one-quarter Navajo and was "deeply insulted" when her department instituted an affirmative action program: "The assumption is that I am incompetent and inferior to White males, therefore rendering me incapable of succeeding on my own merit. That assumption is degrading and undermines my morale and incentive to compete. My peers will not respect me because they will assume that I have accomplished everything through means of affirmative action. The public will have less respect for me for the same reasons. You don't eliminate discrimination by practicing discrimination" (Oglesby, 2002).

Americans with Disabilities Act

Further complicating the selection and employment process is the Americans with Disabilities Act (ADA), which President George H. W. Bush signed into law in July 1990. The purpose of this civil rights law is to guarantee equal opportunity to jobs for qualified individuals with disabilities. The Americans with Disabilities Amendments Act (ADAA), which went into effect January 1, 2009, provided new definitions and broadened the group of individuals eligible for protection under the "regarded as" clause of the ADA. What effect the changes will have on police departments is not yet known, but experts agree that an increase in the number of ADA-related lawsuits is likely to result (Collins, 2009, p.12).

The Americans with Disabilities Act (ADA) of 1990 prohibits discrimination in employment based on a disability.

Conditions excluded from protection include current use of illegal drugs, compulsive gambling, kleptomania, pyromania, sexual behavior disorders and dysfunctions, pedophilia, voyeurism, exhibitionism and psychological disorders caused by current use of illegal drugs.

During the application process, the ADA prohibits employers from asking any questions or conducting any medical examinations that would identify applicants with disabilities or the nature and extent of such disabilities. Tests for use of illegal drugs are not considered medical examinations under the ADA. Employers can ask preemployment questions about the applicants' ability to perform essential job-related tasks.

PROBATION AND TRAINING

Unfortunately, many departments stress the physical aspects of policing and weapons skills without emphasizing that communication is usually an officer's most valuable weapon. Some states have mandated that recruits must be given from 240 to 400 hours of police training within one year of employment. One year is also the usual length of time officers are placed on probation.

The probationary period is a trial period, usually one year, during which the officer is observed while obtaining training and applying this training on the streets.

Police officers may obtain their training in a state police academy, a city academy or a specialized rookie school. The basic training of police officers varies with each jurisdiction and its needs, but most officers will be trained in constitutional law; laws of arrest, search and seizure; and in the various requests for service, such as accident investigation, crisis intervention and first aid.

While in training, recruits may be required to return to the department and spend a specified number of hours on street patrol. Some jurisdictions alternate their training periods every two weeks, allowing an officer to apply on the street what was learned in basic recruit school.

While on the street, the recruits ride with a field training officer or FTO, usually a sergeant, who monitors their movements and helps them apply principles learned in rookie school. While in school the officers are evaluated and tested by their instructors, who periodically send progress reports to the chief. After completing training new recruits continue to ride with one or more training officers who evaluate their street performance. Officers typically ride with an FTO anywhere from 2 to 4 months and train directly with another officer out on the field before going out on their own. The training consists of phases that begin with the probationary officer observing the FTO, and ends with the FTO "shadowing" the probationary officer.

Following successful completion of the probationary period, new recruits are full-fledged police officers. After probation some states license the person to be a police officer. Legislatures in many states have adopted standards for police officers that must be met to satisfy the state's training requirements for licensing.

States have also mandated a certain amount of in-service training to keep the license current. Many of these in-service training requirements revolve around the behavioral sciences to give police officers a better understanding of the entire criminal justice system. Guest speakers from the corrections system, the court system and, on many occasions, minority groups present their philosophy and objectives to police officers.

Preparatory police academies have been proposed as an alternative approach to law enforcement recruitment and training. Other training opportunities include national scholarship programs similar to the military's Reserve Officer Training Corps (ROTC).

Training and Civil Liability

Civil lawsuits related to training and law enforcement commonly fall into two categories: failure-to-train litigation and civil liability for injuries sustained during training.

Failure-to-Train Litigation The landmark case in failure-to-train suits is *City of Canton, Ohio v. Harris* (1989). Geraldine Harris was arrested by the Canton police and taken to the police station. When they arrived at the station, the officers found her on the floor of the patrol wagon and asked if she needed medical attention. Her reply was incoherent. While inside the station, she fell to the floor twice, so the officers left her there to avoid her falling again. No medical assistance was provided. She was released to her family, who called an ambulance. She was hospitalized for a week with severe emotional illness and received treatment for a year. She sued the city for failure to provide adequate medical attention while she was in custody. She won, with the Supreme Court ruling that a municipality might be held liable for deliberate indifference for failure to train.

However, the rather amorphous "deliberate indifference" standard has been replaced by the ruling in *Brown v. Bryan* (2000), in which the Supreme Court refused to consider the county's appeal concerning municipal liability for failure to train. In *Brown*, the sheriff testified he did not have sufficient funds to conduct training. The county ended up paying $642,300 for the failure-to-train claim.

The Supreme Court, in *Board of County Commissioners v. Brown* (1997), suggests liability for failure to train *a single officer*. Lawyers routinely begin their investigation by requesting the training records and evaluations of an officer being civilly sued. The plaintiff's attorneys will search individual defendant officers' training records

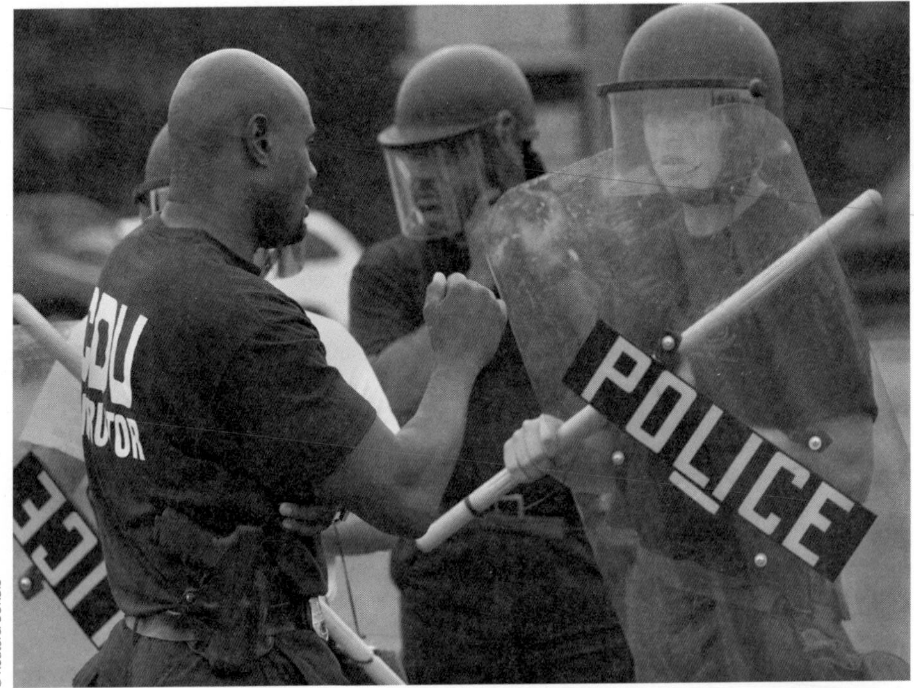

A civil disturbance unit (CDU) police officer (left) trains other members of the Washington, DC, police force at the Metropolitan Police Training Center in Lorton, Virginia. Officers must receive ongoing, in-service training to keep their skill levels up, particularly for those tasks and scenarios that are not part of their daily routine.

to find some deficiency related to their client's claimed injury and hire some expert to identify these training deficiencies.

Among the most common actions and incidents leading to a lawsuit against an officer and agency are officer-involved shootings, use of force, pursuits, police vehicle accidents, detentions, arrests, searches, special weapons and tactics (SWAT) operations and K-9 operations.

Keys to avoiding civil liability related to training are to provide first-rate training, to thoroughly document such training and to require thorough reports on any incident that could lead to a lawsuit.

Civil Liability for Injuries Sustained during Training Police trainers usually cannot be held civilly liable for trainees' injuries during training. This exemption is based on the legal defenses known as the *Firefighter's Rule* and *assumption of risk*. The **Firefighter's Rule** states that a person who negligently starts a fire is not liable to a firefighter injured while responding to the fire. This rule has long been fully applicable to police officers if an officer is injured confronting a risk or conduct that occasioned his or her response or presence. The *assumption-of-risk* defense bars liability if a person is injured as a result of the normal dangers associated with an activity a person voluntarily engages in, for example, extreme sports.

Firefighter's Rule

A person who negligently starts a fire is not liable to a firefighter or other public officer injured while responding to the fire.

RETENTION

The process of recruiting, selecting and training new officers is expensive and time consuming, and the problem intensifies with the loss of more experienced officers. It is costly to lose officers, and in time, agencies with higher turnover and therefore less experienced officers also often suffer reduced productivity, lower quality service delivery, more frequent complaints and more lawsuits.

Law enforcement agencies throughout the country are experiencing increased rates of staff turnover, a problem approaching critical levels for many agencies. Although overall attrition rates are not unusually high (less than 8 percent), unanticipated vacancies cause difficulty for about half of agencies.

Agencies are not the only ones who suffer when officers leave. Police recruits who voluntarily resigned within the first 16 months experienced conflict and cognitive dissonance when their academy training, field training and police work were "inconsistent with or contradictory to" their sense of self and their belief about what police work should be. In addition, for female recruits, gender discrimination was part of their decision to resign. When employees leave, replacement costs can include separation costs, recruitment costs, selection costs, new-employee costs and other "soft" costs when departments must stack calls and forgo proactive policing. Failure to retain an officer can end up costing $100,000 in additional costs to a department (Wilson and Grammich, 2009, p.19).

Why Officers Leave

Supervisors should recognize when an officer may be considering other employment. Most employees send subtle clues. These may occur during transitional phases in their lives, such as the birth of a child, a child's graduation from high school or college, divorce or purchase of a new home. Other possible signs include

- Expressing prolonged disappointment about being passed over for transfer or promotion.
- Having a close friend who goes to another job and who is perceived as having better opportunities.
- Reviewing their own personnel and training records to update their résumés.
- Making inquiries of human resources about early retirement or transfer of benefits (Orrick, 2008, p.182).

A participant at the Summit on Police Recruitment and Retention noted that officers leave either for external or internal reasons (Orrick, 2008). External reasons relate to the economy and better compensation or opportunities elsewhere. Internal reasons relate to what the department offers, with the "single greatest influence" being the officer's immediate supervisor: "People don't quit their jobs; they quit their bosses." Other reasons suggested by the participants include uncompetitive salary, lack of career growth, unmet job expectations, inadequate feedback, insufficient recognition, or lack of training for career growth (Wilson and Grammich, 2009, p.19).

Salary and Benefits

Salaries among police departments in the country have little uniformity. A variety of factors influence a police officer's salary, such as the community's ability to pay, the cost of living in the area and the prevailing wages of similar police departments in surrounding areas.

Normally, position-classification plans are implemented under a personnel ordinance or department rule book. Steps on the salary scale are established in each position classification. New recruits start at the bottom of the salary scale and receive increment raises after six months and each succeeding year until they reach their maximum salary, usually after three to five years. They obtain more salary only if granted a cost-of-living raise; however, a promotion to the next rank would bring them into a higher salary bracket. Sergeants, lieutenants, captains and chiefs all have minimum and maximum starting levels, with the top salary usually reached after three years in the position.

To compensate those who do not attain a rank during their police careers, many police departments have adopted longevity plans whereby nonranking officers receive a certain percentage more of their salaries after the 10th year, the 15th year and so on. This seniority system has been attacked, however, on the grounds that it discourages initiative and further education. Some agencies offer education pay or increased salary for having completed a college degree.

When salary schedules are formulated, such fringe benefits as hospitalization and dental plans, insurance, vacation, sick leave and holidays are all considered. Police officers' indirect benefits from their employers are estimated to be approximately 33 percent, comparable to what business and industry currently allow their employees. In addition to the more common benefits of paid holidays and

TABLE 12.2 Retention Techniques and Their Perceived Effectiveness

Technique	Number Using	% Using	Average Effectiveness Rating (0 to 9)
Annual pay increase irrespective of performance	101	81.5	5.9
Education/training agency expense	95	76.6	5.6
Promotions	86	69.4	4.5
Annual pay increase performance-based	82	66.1	5.6
Formal awards, recognition	80	64.5	4.2
Assigned favorable work shift	75	60.5	5.2

Note: Survey respondents were encouraged to select all recruitment techniques used by their agencies; therefore, percentages do not equal 100.

Source: Douglas L. Yearwood. "Recruitment and Retention of Police Officers in North Carolina." *The Police Chief,* March 2004, p.46. Reprinted by permission. Copyright held by The International Association of Chiefs of Police, Inc. Further reproduction without express written permission is prohibited.

vacations, personal and family sick leave, and medical and dental insurance, other benefits a department might provide include a uniform and clothing allowance, child care, life insurance, disability insurance, hospitalization insurance, workman's compensation, military leave, deferred compensation, college incentive pay, tuition reimbursement, a retirement fund, a pension plan and a credit union.

Retention techniques and their perceived effectiveness are shown in Table 12.2.

Policies vary regarding how to pay officers for overtime on the job, going to court while on duty, attending required training sessions while off duty and being called back to duty in an emergency. Some departments pay overtime; others give compensatory time off. Police departments may belong to unions that bargain for them. Usually all conditions of employment are clearly spelled out in their contracts.

Elimination of Sexual Harassment

Sexual harassment has become an issue of concern because of the rising number of women in law enforcement and the resistance to change by many officers from the "old school" in the traditionally male-dominated occupation. In addition the number of sexual harassment cases has been increasing, and the monetary awards have been sometimes shocking.

Sexual harassment is prohibited by Title VII of the 1964 Civil Rights Act, which states, "It is unlawful for any employer to discriminate against any individual with respect to his compensation, terms, conditions or privileges of employment, because of such individual's race, color, religion, sex, or national origin." Most state laws also prohibit sexual harassment.

The federal government defines **sexual harassment** as "unwelcome sexual advances, requests for sexual favors, and other verbal or physical conduct of a sexual nature" ("Preventing Sexual Harassment," n.d., p.1).

sexual harassment

Has two conditions: (1) It must occur in the workplace or an extension of the workplace (department sanctioned), and (2) it must be of a sexual nature that does not include romance or that is not of a mutually friendly nature; the harassment must be unwelcome, unsolicited and deliberate.

There are two legally recognized types of sexual harassment. One type, *quid pro quo harassment*, usually involves a supervisor's demand for sexual favors from an employee in return for a job benefit. The National Center for Women and Policing Web site explains that *quid pro quo* harassment means that a person is asked to perform sexual acts in return for a job benefit. For example, "If you engage in some type of sexual behavior for me, I will let you pass probation," or get a promotion, get a good performance evaluation, not be written up for doing something wrong, and so on.

The second type, *hostile-environment harassment*, as the name implies, involves a hostile environment (whether created by co-employees or by supervisors). According to the National Center for Women and Policing, "A hostile environment consists of unwelcome sexual behavior, such as jokes, cartoons, posters, banter, repeated requests for dates, requests for sexual favors, references to body parts, or physical touching that has the purpose or effect of unreasonably interfering with an individual's work performance or creating an intimidating, hostile, or offensive working environment. Isolated acts that are not severe will not rise to the level of a hostile environment." Two conditions determine liability for employers in cases of hostile-environment sexual harassment: (1) The employer knew or should have known about the harassment, and (2) the employer failed to take appropriate corrective action.

Many female officers are reluctant to report sexual harassment, well aware of the common perception among male officers that women are overly sensitive and prone to emotionalism. For females who have struggled to overcome this stereotype, filing a sexual harassment complaint means risking further alienation by their peers.

Although extensive evidence exists that sexual harassment has permeated even the most professional police agencies, administrators remain reluctant to acknowledge its presence and often exhibit surprisingly cavalier attitudes toward the problem. Preventing sexual harassment from occurring is the best strategy for handling the issue.

A twist in the problem of sexual harassment is same-sex sexual harassment, which, according to the EEOC, is also actionable. The EEOC *Compliance Manual* (§ 615.2[b][3]) states that "the victim does not have to be of the opposite sex from the harasser. Since sexual harassment is a form of sex discrimination, the crucial inquiry is whether the harasser treats a member or members of one sex differently from members of the other sex." The Supreme Court ruling in *Oncale v. Sundowner Offshore Services, Inc.* (1998) expanded the definition of illegal same-sex harassment.

All officers, males and females alike, must protect their interests and help eradicate sexual harassment that threatens to undermine the effectiveness of policing. It can most certainly be a cause of stress.

Stress and Burnout

No discussion of retention would be complete without recognizing the highly stressful nature of this profession. Police officers deal with crisis daily, usually that of someone else. Sometimes, however, the demands of the roles and how they are expected to be performed create enough stress to put police officers themselves into a crisis situation.

A police officer's job is highly stressful and may result in a personal crisis for the officer.

Stress can be either positive or negative. Dr. Hans Selye (1907–1982), known as the "father of the stress field," first defined *stress* as the nonspecific response of the body to any demand placed on it. He later said stress was simply the wear and tear caused by living.

The excitement/stress of police work is one important reason people enter the profession. Unfortunately much of the stress experienced by police officers and, indeed, the general population, is negative.

Stress may also be acute or chronic. Acute stress is temporary and often positive. It keeps a person alert and focused. Chronic stress, in contrast, is continuous and can be debilitating. Everyone experiences stressors in their lives. Hess and Orthmann (2012, p.402) observe, "Some common stress producers of daily living are changing relationships, a lifestyle inconsistent with values (too committed), money problems (credit-card debt, poor investments), loss of self-esteem (falling behind professionally, accepting others' expectations), and fatigue or illness (poor diet, lack of sleep or lack of exercise)."

Stress comes from several sources, many work related.

Stress commonly arises from change and uncertainty, shift work, lack of control and pressure.

Change and uncertainty are an unavoidable part of life and of law enforcement. Officers responding to a call often have no idea what awaits. They may be unsure of who they can trust or believe. *Lack of control* may be seen when law enforcement officers apprehend suspects they believe to be guilty and see these suspects not prosecuted or found not guilty. Officers must work with assigned partners they did not select. They must be polite to surly citizens.

Shift work is another area that can cause stress, especially if shifts change or rotate constantly. Two-thirds of patrol officers and administrators have different shift preferences, and this same number (65 percent) prefers longer, 10-hour workdays. *Pressure* is also abundant in law enforcement, with work overloads, paperwork, sometimes-unrealistic expectations from the public and the responsibility to protect life and property and to preserve "the peace." The need for hyper-vigilance creates a constant level of stress. Officers never know when they might face a **critical incident**, an event that elicits an overwhelming emotional response from those witnessing it. This can result in **burst stress**, that is, having to go immediately from relative calm to high-intensity, sometimes life-threatening activity. This is closely related to what Fyfe (1986) refers to in his classic split-second syndrome that affects police decision making in crisis. The **split-second syndrome** asserts that if a person has intentionally or unintentionally provoked or threatened a police officer, at that instant the provoker rather than the police should be viewed as the cause of any resulting injuries or damages. In such situations, all that can reasonably be asked is that officers respond quickly and that a high percentage of inappropriate decisions should be expected and accepted.

As they wage war on crime and violence, law enforcement personnel may have a problem similar to that experienced by military combat personnel. During

critical incident
An event that elicits an overwhelming emotional response from those witnessing it.

burst stress
Having to go immediately from relative calm to high-intensity, sometimes life-threatening activity.

split-second syndrome
Asserts that if a person has intentionally or unintentionally provoked or threatened a police officer, at that instant the provoker rather than the police should be viewed as the cause of any resulting injuries or damages.

World War I, soldiers were *shell-shocked*. In World War II, they suffered from *combat fatigue* and *battle stress*. Psychologists came to realize that officers involved in major catastrophes such as earthquakes, fires, rapes and terrorist attacks could experience similar stress disorders, currently referred to as **posttraumatic stress disorder (PTSD)**, a clinical name associated with a debilitating condition suffered by Vietnam War veterans. An estimated one-third of law enforcement officers in the United States suffer from PTSD. Symptoms included diminished responsiveness to their environment, apathy, disinterest, pessimism and diminished sex drive.

posttraumatic stress disorder (PTSD)

A psychological illness that happens after a highly stressful event or series of events, commonly associated with shooting incidents.

Other sources of stress are not as obvious as the preceding. Law enforcement has many other "hidden stressors." One such insidious stressor is isolation—long hours spent alone on patrol; set apart from the rest of society by a uniform; and being held to a higher, almost nonhuman, standard than the general public. Adding to this sense of isolation is the daily interaction with the "criminal element" and routine exposure to the worst of the human condition—violence, death, pain, loss, poverty, drug addiction and lies, lies, lies. Over time, the effects of such stressors may spill over into officers' personal lives, leading them to distrust even their own family and friends, which, in turn, causes greater alienation.

Another hidden stressor is the unspoken, perhaps subconscious, double standard many citizens hold regarding the law, their personal freedoms and the responsibilities of the police. Examples of some of the mixed messages officers receive from the public include these: "Stop those crazy drivers from speeding through my neighborhood. But you'd better not give me a ticket for rushing home." Or, "Get tough on drunk drivers—they should have the book thrown at them. But I know I'm competent to drive after a night of bar-hopping with my friends." Or, "Keep us safe. But don't invade our privacy."

Many studies have been conducted on the types and effects of stress on police officers. Table 12.3 ranks, in descending order, those factors officers view as causing the greatest amount of personal stress. In general, job-related stressors have the greatest negative impact, with external factors interspersed along the continuum, and organizational stressors, as a whole, falling near the lower end of the spectrum.

If the stresses become great enough, officers may burn out. Being aware of and reducing stressors can prevent officer **burnout**: "Burnout has occurred in a person who is 'used up or consumed by a job,' made listless through overwork and stress. Burnout results from long-term, unmediated stress. . . . Those most likely to experience burnout are those who are initially most committed. You cannot burn out if you have never been on fire" (Hess and Orthmann, 2012, pp.418–419). Symptoms of burnout include lack of enthusiasm and interest, decreased job performance, temper flare-ups and a loss of will, motivation or commitment (Hess and Orthmann, 2012).

burnout

A psychological state that occurs when someone is made exhausted and listless and rendered unserviceable or ineffectual through overwork, stress or intemperance.

Strategies for reducing stress and avoiding burnout include physical exercise, proper nutrition, adequate sleep, social outlets, relaxation techniques and time management. Many police departments are recognizing the hazards of stress for their officers and are taking steps to reduce or eliminate the causes over which they have control.

Long-term stress is destructive and may be fatal in police work. In addition, police divorce is at double the national average, and as many as 25 percent have

TABLE 12.3 Police Officer Stressors Ranked by Mean Scores

	Organizational	Job-Related	External	SD
Fellow officers being injured or killed		54.42		31.04
Public criticism of police			53.62	29.85
Family demands			51.36	31.09
Making important on-the-spot decisions		49.39		26.99
Fellow officers not doing their job		48.57		30.52
Responding to a felony in progress		43.33		29.30
Incompatible partner		41.13		35.10
Job conflict with rules (i.e., by the book vs. the situation)		40.70		29.41
Exposure to death		37.88		27.29
Sustaining a serious physical injury on the job		37.73		29.55
Threat of lawsuit			37.00	34.42
Situations requiring use of force		36.53		30.69
Assignment of increased responsibility	35.98			26.91
Transfer to another assignment area	35.01			30.85
Department/unit reorganization	33.62			26.87
Promotion competition	33.30			33.48
Racial conflicts			33.20	30.21
Subject of internal affairs investigation	28.79			33.54
Shift work		27.38		32.99
Undercover work		22.45		26.26
Personal thoughts of suicide*			9.56	21.35
Scales total/means			36.81	18.04
		37.93		18.25
	33.10			20.35
Total index 35.43				16.80

*Although not significant among the stressors, 20% of respondents (i.e., 210 officers) indicated having some thoughts of suicide during the previous 12 months, and 7% (i.e., 73 officers) specified that it had caused them moderate or high levels of stress.

SOURCE: Luis Garcia, Dale K. Nesbary, and Joann Gu. "Perceptual Variations of Stressors Among Police Officers during an Era of Decreasing Crime." *Journal of Contemporary Criminal Justice*, February 2004, pp.33–50. Reprinted by Permission of SAGE Publications.

alcohol abuse problems. Some of the danger signs that an officer might be slipping emotionally include compulsive drinking or dependency on meds or distancing or isolating themselves from family, friends and social events. Avoiding usual recreational activities, neglecting regular workouts, experiencing financial problems, extreme emotional outbursts on and off the job or blowing up over nothing can also be warning signs.

UNIONS

Another way in which officers seek to protect their interests is by establishing police labor unions and other local employee organizations. Police labor unions have played an active role in law enforcement and have provided numerous benefits to police officers. A union, in the broadest context, is any group authorized to represent the members of the law enforcement agency in negotiating such matters as wages, fringe benefits and other conditions of employment. A union shop is an agency where people must belong to or join the union to be hired. Most police officers are currently members of local employee organizations and are not directly enrolled in a national labor union.

In 2007 legislation was introduced requiring every state to have a minimum level of bargaining standards, but it stalled in committee. On January 9, 2009, a similar bill, H.R.413, the Public Safety Employer-Employee Cooperation Act, passed the House of Representatives by an overwhelming majority, but has failed in the Senate. Basically, H.R.413 would federalize state and local government labor-management relations, depriving them of what many in law enforcement believe is the needed flexibility to manage their public safety operations as they choose.

The bill, as submitted to the 111th Congress, is "to provide collective bargaining rights for public safety officers employed by states or their political subdivisions" ("Text of H.R.413," p.1). On March 10, 2010, hearings were held by the Subcommittee on Health, Employment, Labor, and Pensions, and then the bill was submitted to the House Committee on Education and Labor. As of October 27, 2010, questions related to the bill were still being posted on GovTrack.us ("Overview, 2010"). This Web site reports that as of December 2009, the bill is supported by the Fraternal Order of Police University and College Law Enforcement Association, the American Federation of Teachers and the International Association of Fire Fighters who have collected 103 times the financial support as those who oppose it—$4,844,829 compared with $47,109. Those opposing the bill include Tea Party Patriots, the National Right to Work Legal Defense Foundation, and the National Institute for Labor Relations Research. In addition, the IACP's legislative representative, Mays (2009, p.12) reports that the IACP "strongly opposes" the legislation.

The primary purpose of unions is to improve employment conditions through collective bargaining.

collective bargaining
The process whereby representatives of employees meet with representatives of management to establish a written contract that sets forth working conditions for a specific time, usually one to three years.

Collective bargaining is the process whereby representatives of employees meet with representatives of management to establish a written contract that sets forth working conditions for a specific time, usually one to three years. The contract deals with wages and benefits and with hours of work and overtime, grievance procedures, disciplinary procedures, health and safety, employees' rights, seniority and contract duration. Most states have laws restricting officers from going on strike.

The Fraternal Order of Police (FOP) was founded in 1915 and is the world's oldest, largest and most influential sworn law enforcement officer's organization. It has more than 310,000 members in more than 2,100 lodges. According to its Web site, it is the "voice of law enforcement professionals . . . committed to improving the working conditions of law enforcement."

For many law enforcement agencies, unions are a positive force; for others, they create problems and dissension; and in yet others, they are nonexistent.

One frequent objection to unions is the tactics commonly employed, including slowdowns, "sickouts" and strikes. Although it is generally illegal for most public employees to strike, strikes by law enforcement officers have occurred in San Francisco, Tucson and Oklahoma City. Some of the strikes lasted only a few days, but others lasted weeks. In some instances strikers lost their jobs, but in other instances they obtained raises. Contemporary unions, however, typically adhere to a "no strike clause" because police are essential to public safety.

Other objections raised against unions include the fear that the law enforcement administrators and public officials who unionized police employees could abuse their collective bargaining power and that specific aspects of administration, such as transfers and promotions, could become bound up in arbitration and grievance procedures. Many administrators see the union as interfering with their leadership and with the officers in the ranks. In addition, police unions have resisted changes in law enforcement organizations and techniques that affect their membership. For example, the unions have opposed attempts to shift from two-person to one-person patrol cars. Unions have also objected to efforts to hire civilians in clerical positions, and they have resisted affirmative action efforts, seeking to maintain the status quo rather than to increase recruitment of women and minorities.

Line officers usually favor unionization because it gives them collective bargaining power with the administration. Administrators, however, disapprove of some union tactics and feel unionization limits their power and authority.

Unions are strongest in the northeast and on the West Coast. The International Union of Police Associations (IUPA) began in 1978 as the only union exclusively designed for law enforcement personnel and, as of June 2001, there were 4,000 police unions in the United States with 225,000 sworn law enforcement members and 11,000 retired members.

The National Association of Police Organizations (NAPO) is a coalition of police unions and associations across the country that seeks to advance the interests of law enforcement officers through legislative and legal advocacy, political action and education. "Founded in 1978, NAPO is now the strongest unified voice supporting law enforcement officers in the United States. NAPO represents more than 2,000 police unions and associations, 241,000 sworn law enforcement officers, 11,000 retired officers and more than 100,000 citizens who share a common dedication to fair and effective crime control and law enforcement" ("Welcome to NAPO," 2010).

One highly debated issue related to union membership is who should belong. What ranks should be included? Should managers and supervisors belong to the same union as patrol officers? Another topic of concern to unions and their members is the growing presence of private police forces.

MOONLIGHTING

Moonlighting, working at a part-time job while fulfilling the obligations of a full-time position, has been a source of controversy in the police field for many years and falls within a gray area some departments prefer to avoid.

moonlighting

Working at a second, part-time job while fulfilling the obligations of a full-time position.

 Moonlighting is controversial and is handled differently in different departments.

Most police departments restrict the type of work that can be done and the number of hours an officer can work while off duty. Some cities allow their police officers to work off duty in only police-related areas; others allow them to work in only non–police-related areas. While allowing police officers to work off duty has definite advantages, disadvantages also exist, and most cities and municipalities have developed policies that place limits on the officer's off-duty time. Policies on moonlighting address issues such as how to obtain permission for off-duty work, what types of off-duty jobs are not permitted and so on. Policies must also adhere to the Fair Labor Standards Act (FLSA) rules concerning moonlighting officers and the conditions attached to dual employment, joint employment, "special-detail" work and "volunteer" work. Standards regarding secondary employment of police officers are among the 439 standards outlined by the Commission on Accreditation for Law Enforcement Agencies (CALEA) for agencies seeking accreditation.

ACCREDITATION

accreditation

Being approved by an official review board as meeting specific standards.

"**Accreditation** is a progressive and time-proven way of helping law enforcement agencies calculate and improve their overall performances. The foundation of accreditation lies in the promulgation of standards containing a clear statement of professional objectives. Participating agencies conduct a thorough self-analysis to determine how existing operations can be adapted to meet these objectives. When the procedures are in place, a team of trained assessors verify that applicable standards have been successfully implemented. The process culminates with a decision by a committee that the agency has met the requirements for accreditation" ("Accreditation," 2008, p.342).

CALEA was formed in 1979 to develop a set of law enforcement standards and to establish and administer a *voluntary* process through which agencies could demonstrate that they meet professionally recognized criteria for excellence in management and service delivery. The commission is the combined effort of the IACP, the National Organization of Black Law Enforcement Executives (NOBLE), the National Sheriffs' Association (NSA) and the Police Executive Research Forum (PERF). Members of these four organizations direct approximately 80 percent of the law enforcement community in the United States. The first law enforcement agency was accredited in 1984, and since that time participation has grown to more than 1,000 agencies. Of agencies with 300 or more officers, 50 percent are participating in the accreditation process (Cordner and Hartley, 2010, p.1).

 The goal of the Commission on Accreditation for Law Enforcement Agencies (CALEA) is to develop professional standards and to administer a voluntary accreditation process. Controversy exists regarding the value of such accreditation.

The CALEA standards address nine major law enforcement subjects: (1) roles, responsibilities and relationships with other agencies; (2) organization, management and administration; (3) personnel structure; (4) personnel process; (5) operations; (6) operational support; (7) traffic operations; (8) prisoner and court-related activities;

and (9) auxiliary and technical services. The goals of these standards are to help law enforcement agencies (1) strengthen crime prevention and control capabilities, (2) formalize essential management procedures, (3) establish fair and nondiscriminatory personnel practices, (4) improve service delivery, (5) solidify interagency cooperation and coordination and (6) boost citizen and staff confidence in the agency.

CALEA's accreditation process consists of five phases: (1) the application, (2) self-assessment, (3) on-site assessment, (4) commission review and (5) maintaining compliance and re-accreditation.

For agencies willing to meet the challenge, accreditation may provide the following benefits:

- A set of clear, written policies and procedures so every employee knows what's expected
- Assurance that department operations are consistent with current professional standards
- Greater accountability within the agency and higher morale
- Improved management/union relations
- Enhanced defense against citizen complaints and lawsuits, and reduced litigation costs
- Controlled liability insurance costs and discounts from insurance carriers
- Increased professionalism, an enhanced reputation for the department and greater community advocacy
- Increased support of government officials bolstered by their confidence in the agency's ability to operate efficiently and meet community needs
- Greater justification for resource and budget requests
- A proven management system of written directives, sound training, clearly defined lines of authority, and routine reports that support decision making and resource allocation
- A better-managed agency

Sylvania Township, Ohio, has about 28,000 residents and is policed by 47 sworn officers assisted by 16 civilian staff. Having become accredited, the department does not expect to derive all the potential benefits discussed. It hopes to achieve reduced liability, management and department stability, a current and complete set of written directions, reduced costs, and continuity for the future, recognizing that change will and should occur. Its chief of police cautions, "CALEA is not a panacea for all the ills of a department. It is one step that a department can take to ensure compliance with the highest standard of the law enforcement profession" (Metzger, 2010, p.27).

Many agencies report a decline in legal actions against them once they become accredited. Despite these potential benefits, accreditation does have critics. A pool of randomly selected law enforcement agencies indicated five major arguments against accreditation: (1) too expensive, (2) too time consuming, (3) dubious benefits, (4) hard to justify to community government and (5) department administration does not believe in it. Table 12.4 summarizes the results of a survey of law enforcement administrators on the perceived benefits of accreditation.

TABLE 12.4 Perceived Benefits of Accreditation

Statement	Agreed	Disagreed	Unsure
Accreditation is more a status symbol or public relations tool than it is a valuable process.	53%	21%	26%
Accreditation has an appreciable impact on how well an agency performs.	54%	31%	15%
Accreditation does establish accountability within the office.	60%	28%	12%
Accreditation establishes uniformity in service delivery.	44%	32%	24%
Accreditation promotes efficient and effective administration and deployment of personnel.	36%	32%	32%
Accreditation provides stronger defense against lawsuits.	44%	40%	16%
Accreditation improves employee morale.*	24%	32%	44%

*Most significant finding

SOURCE: Adapted from Arthur G. Sharp. "Accreditation: Fact or Fixture?" *Law and Order*, March 2000, p.93.

Although criticism of the accreditation process is not new and controversy has surrounded such standards from the start, much of the debate in recent years has centered on whether these standards facilitate or inhibit the implementation of community policing.

Accreditation requires law enforcement agencies to document their policies. Community policing requires agencies to engage the community in a process of evaluating what ought to be documented. Both ask participants to take a critical look at the status quo.

credentialing

Process whereby individual police officers are evaluated and approved by the National Law Enforcement Credentialing Board (NLECB) as meeting certain standards.

Another approach being used to ensure accountability is police **credentialing**, a process whereby individual police officers are evaluated and approved by the National Law Enforcement Credentialing Board (NLECB) as meeting certain standards. The NLECB was established by the FOP and is supported by other law enforcement groups. A three-year study established national standards to evaluate officers, including disciplinary record, community service and post-academy education and training. Officers must submit evidence of meeting the standards and are then allowed, for a fee, to take a three-hour test consisting of 200 multiple-choice items.

Acceptance of credentialing is not automatic. Critics point out that there has never been agreement on just what constitutes an "outstanding police officer." Nor is there agreement that this can be ascertained through a multiple-choice test. In addition, there is no limit on the number of times an officer can pay the fee and take the same test over. A further obstacle is that historically most state-level Peace Officers Standards and Training (POST) boards have been reluctant to recognize any training or certification other than their own. Whether credentialing will become nationally recognized remains to be seen.

Another approach to demonstrate competence in a given area is certification. Officers might become certified in using various forms of less-lethal weapons, radar, batons and so on. Certification is an important tool for officers and agencies wishing to enhance their professionalism.

POLICE PROFESSIONALISM

Throughout this text policing has been referred to as a profession; however, whether law enforcement technically qualifies as a profession is controversial. Part of the problem is that definitions of professionalism vary. To some, *professional* means simply an important job or one who gets paid, as opposed to an *amateur*. Sociologists, however, have identified certain elements that qualify an occupation as a profession.

Sociological Elements of Professionalism

Three key elements of professionalism are (1) specialized knowledge, (2) autonomy and (3) a service ideal.

Specialized Knowledge The time when someone could walk into a police department, fill out an application and be hired is gone in most parts of the country. Many departments now require a two-year college degree, and some require a four-year degree. In addition to a college degree, many departments require that applicants complete skills training. As noted, most larger departments also have their own rookie schools or academies where new police officers learn what is expected in a particular agency. As technology advances and as criminals become more sophisticated, more knowledge and training are expected to be required.

Autonomy *Professional autonomy* refers to the ability to control entrance into the profession, to define the content of the knowledge to be obtained and to be responsible for self-monitoring and disciplining. In addition the autonomy of a profession is usually authorized by the power of the state; for example, physicians, dentists, lawyers and teachers are licensed by the state. These professions are, in effect, legalized monopolies.

Law enforcement does fit the criterion of professional autonomy in that requirements to be a police officer are usually set by the legislature. The growth in the number of POST boards throughout the country to oversee the profession attests to this fact.

A Service Ideal The third element of a profession, a service ideal, requires that members of the profession follow a formal code of ethics and be committed to serving the community. In this area police officers qualify as professionals, provided the department stresses the public servant aspects of police work.

The Final Analysis—Does Law Enforcement Qualify?

In most states, the minimum education requirement to enter law enforcement has gone unchanged for decades. Although a college degree requirement has been advocated since the 1967 President's Commission, no states currently meet this goal. Many departments, however, do require a four-year degree. Some states, such as Minnesota, require a two-year associate's degree to enter law enforcement, whereas other states, such as Wisconsin, simply require candidates to have completed a certain number of college credits to qualify for licensure, all steps in the right direction.

Summary

Valid recruitment, screening, testing and selection procedures must be used to assure that only well-qualified candidates are hired as law enforcement officers. Qualities of a good police officer include reliability, leadership, judgment, persuasiveness, communication skills, initiative, integrity, honesty, ego control, intelligence, sensitivity and problem-solving ability. Individuals possessing such skills are sought through a careful selection procedure.

Agencies are also seeking to hire more minorities and women. A racially balanced and integrated police department fosters community relations and increases police effectiveness. Studies show that women perform as well as men in police work, are less apt to use excessive force, can help implement community-oriented policing and can improve an agency's response to violence against women. In addition, an increased female presence among officers can reduce problems of sex discrimination and harassment and foster policy changes that benefit all officers.

Police officer selection usually includes a formal application and résumé; a written examination; a physical fitness test; a psychological examination; at least one oral interview, possibly more; a thorough background investigation; and a medical examination. Most agencies require that a police officer candidate be a U.S. citizen or be in the process of acquiring citizenship and have or be eligible for a driver's license in the state; most require that officers not have been convicted of a felony. Most police agencies require a minimum of a high school education or equivalency certificate, and some require a two- or four-year degree. Many police agencies are now requiring some college education for employment or promotion. Limited empirical evidence exists about whether such education helps the officers perform better. Regarding residency, it is always preferred and sometimes required that police officers live in the community they serve.

Because fitness is an important quality of law enforcement officers, physical fitness tests are used to evaluate a candidate's coordination, speed and strength. The most common physical fitness tests are similar to military obstacle courses that must be completed in a designated time. The candidate also undergoes an oral interview to evaluate appearance, alertness, communication ability, social adaptability, judgment, emotional stability, and interest in and suitability for the job. The background investigation includes verification of all information on the application and history sheet; a check of driving record; fingerprinting and a check of any criminal record; a check of military records; interviews with personal references, acquaintances, past employers, neighbors and teachers; a check of financial status; a check of any pending litigation; and a check of past performances at schools and previous jobs. Finally, a medical examination is conducted to assess the candidate's vision, hearing and cardiovascular-respiratory system.

In addition to local and state requirements for recruitment and selection of police officers, certain federal guidelines and regulations must be met. Most important are the 1972 Equal Employment Opportunity Act, which prohibits discrimination due to sex, race, color, religion or national origin in employment of any kind, public or private, local, state or federal; and the Americans with Disabilities Act (ADA), which prohibits discrimination in employment based on a disability.

Once candidates have passed all tests in the selection process, they usually enter a one-year probationary period during which they are observed while obtaining training and while applying this training on the streets. Civil lawsuits related to training and law enforcement commonly fall into two categories: failure-to-train litigation and civil liability for injuries sustained during training. Keys to avoiding civil liability related to training are to provide first-rate training, to thoroughly document such training and to require thorough reports on any incident that could lead to a lawsuit.

A police officer's job is highly stressful and may result in a personal crisis for the officer. Stress commonly arises from change and uncertainty, shift work, lack of control and pressure. The primary purpose of unions is to improve employment conditions through collective bargaining. Line officers usually favor unionization because it gives them collective bargaining power with the administration. Administrators, however, disapprove of some union tactics and feel unionization limits their power and authority. Many agencies permit their officers to moonlight in private security and other fields. Moonlighting is controversial and is handled differently in different departments.

The issues of accreditation and police professionalism are additional topics of controversy. The Commission on Accreditation for Law Enforcement Agencies was formed to develop professional standards and to administer a voluntary accreditation process, although controversy exists over the value of such accreditation. The three key elements of professionalism are (1) specialized knowledge, (2) autonomy and (3) a service ideal.

Discussion Questions

1. What is the most common reason for rejection during the selection process?
2. What are the requirements to be eligible for a peace officer license in your state? Does your local jurisdiction have additional requirements?
3. How does stress affect a police officer, personally and professionally?
4. Compare and contrast the advantages and disadvantages to police officers for living within the community in which they work. Does one outweigh the other?
5. Should there be an educational requirement to work as a peace officer? Why or why not?
6. Is there still a glass ceiling for women and minorities in the law enforcement profession?
7. Is accreditation worth the expense and effort? What are some drawbacks?
8. How does recruiting the Generation Y-ers (aka Millennials) differ from efforts to recruit previous generations into the field of law enforcement?
9. Do you support or oppose union membership? Why?
10. Do you consider law enforcement a profession? What about the entire criminal justice field?

Gale Emergency Services Database Assignments

- Use the Gale Emergency Services Database to help answer the Discussion Questions as appropriate.
- Using the Gale Emergency Services Database, find the article "Establishing the Validity of Employment Standards": http://find.galegroup.com/gps/

retrieve.do?contentSet=IAC-Documents&resultListType=RESULT_LIST&qrySerId=Locale%28en%2C%2C%29%3AFQE%3D%28ke%2CNone%2C13%29police+hiring%24&sgHitCountType=None&inPS=true&sort=DateDescend&searchType=BasicSearchForm&tabID=T003&prodId=IPS&searchId=R1¤tPosition=5&userGroupName=cpg3&docId=A17482641&docType=IAC&contentSet=IAC-Documents

Assignment: Read and summarize the purpose of this article.

- Using the Gale Emergency Services Database, find the article "Police Recruitment: Today's Standard – Tomorrow's Challenge": http://find.galegroup.com/gps/retrieve.do?contentSet=IAC-Documents&resultListType=RESULT_LIST&qrySerId=Locale%28en%2C%2C%29%3AFQE%3D%28ke%2CNone%2C18%29police+recruitment%24&sgHitCountType=None&inPS=true&sort=DateDescend&searchType=BasicSearchForm&tabID=T003&prodId=IPS&searchId=R2¤tPosition=5&userGroupName=cpg3&docId=A13421839&docType=IAC&contentSet=IAC-Documents

  Assignments: Identify the demographic changes, recruitments strategies, and future needs for quality personnel recruitment and retention outlined in the article and be prepared to discuss these topics in class.

- Using the Gale Emergency Services Database, find the article "Study: Officer's Shift, Gender Affect Stress": http://find.galegroup.com/gps/retrieve.do?contentSet=IAC-Documents&resultListType=RESULT_LIST&qrySerId=Locale%28en%2C%2C%29%3AFQE%3D%28ke%2CNone%2C13%29police+stress%24&sgHitCountType=None&inPS=true&sort=DateDescend&searchType=BasicSearchForm&tabID=T003&prodId=IPS&searchId=R5¤tPosition=1&userGroupName=cpg3&docId=A190015464&docType=IAC&contentSet=IAC-Documents

  Assignment: Identify how gender and shift work effect police officer stress. Be prepared to compare and contrast stress in relation to shift work and gender in a class discussion.

- Using the Gale Emergency Services Database, find the article "Negative Influences of Police Stress": http://find.galegroup.com/gps/retrieve.do?contentSet=IAC-Documents&resultListType=RESULT_LIST&qrySerId=Locale%28en%2C%2C%29%3AFQE%3D%28ke%2CNone%2C13%29police+stress%24&sgHitCountType=None&inPS=true&sort=DateDescend&searchType=BasicSearchForm&tabID=T003&prodId=IPS&searchId=R6¤tPosition=5&userGroupName=cpg3&docId=A92285044&docType=IAC&contentSet=IAC-Documents

  Assignment: Read and outline the article, and be prepared to discuss some of the negative influence of stress on police officers.

- Using the Gale Emergency Services Database, find the article "Preferences In Hiring & Promotion: Courts Impose Heightened Scrutiny" (Employment Discrimination): http://find.galegroup.com/gps/retrieve.do?contentSet=IAC-Documents&resultListType=RESULT_LIST&qrySerId=Locale%28en%2C%2C%29%3AFQE%3D%28K0%2CNone%2C25%29police+affirmative+action%24&sgHitCountType=None&inPS=true&sort=Date

Descend&searchType=BasicSearchForm&tabID=T003&prodId=IPS&search Id=R9¤tPosition=1&userGroupName=cpg3&docId=A16548142& docType=IAC&contentSet=IAC-Documents

Assignment: Read the related case law within the article and be prepared to discuss the positives and negatives of affirmative action.

Internet Assignments

- Using the key words *police stress*, research the reasons law enforcement officers become stressed. Do any of them surprise you? What, if any, suggestions are given to prevent or reduce such stress?
- Go to the Web site of a law enforcement department and find starting salary and benefit figures for an officer *with* a college degree and one *without* a degree. Bring your data to class and calculate a mean (average) and median figure for the departments surveyed.

References

"Accreditation." In *Police Chiefs Desk Reference*, 2nd ed. Alexandria, VA: International Association of Chiefs of Police and the Bureau of Justice Assistance, 2008, pp.342–343.

Collins, John M. "Americans with Disabilities Amendments Act: What It Means for Law Enforcement Agencies." *The Police Chief*, January 2009, pp. 32–33.

Cordner, Gary, and Hartley, Craig. "Smaller Agency Accreditation: Realistic, Valuable, Evolving." *Big Ideas*, Spring 2010, pp.1–4.

Fyfe, James J. "The Split-Second Syndrome and Other Determinants of Police Violence." In *Violent Transactions*, edited by Anne Campbell and John Gibbs. New York: Basic Blackwell, 1986.

Gotay, Alberto. "Predictive Models for Police Physical Tests." *Law and Order*, February 2010, pp.32–35.

Henson, Billy; Reynes, Bradford W.; Klahm, Charles F. IV; and Frank, James. "Do Good Recruits Make Good Cops? Problems Predicting and Measuring Academy and Street-Level Success." *Police Quarterly*, March 2010, pp.5–26.

Hess, Kären M., and Orthmann, Christine Hess. *Management and Supervision in Law Enforcement*, 6th ed. Clifton Park, NY: Delmar/Cengage Publishing, 2012.

Kohlhepp, Kim, and Phillips, Tracy. "DiscoverPolicing.org: A Nationwide Online Recruiting Resource for the Law Enforcement Profession." *The Police Chief*, January 2009, pp.46–47.

Langton, Lynn. *Women in Law Enforcement, 1987–2008*. Washington, DC: Bureau of Justice Statistics Crime Data Brief, June 2010. (NCJ 230521)

Law Enforcement Recruitment Toolkit: COPS/IACP Leadership Project. Arlington, VA: The International Association of Chiefs of Police, June 2009.

Mays, Meredith. "Collective Bargaining Legislation Still Looming." *The Police Chief*, October 2009, p.12.

Means, Randy, and McDonald, Pam. "New Haven Firefighters Case. . . 'Reverse' Discrimination: The Final Answer?" *Law and Order*, September 2009, pp.18–22.

Metzger, Robert W. "One Department's Experience: CALEA Accreditation." *The Police Chief*, March 2010, pp.20–27.

Oglesby, Denise Chavez. Statement regarding affirmative action written for this text and updated in 2002.

Orrick, W. Dwayne. "A Best Practices Guide for Recruitment, Retention and Turnover in Law Enforcement." In *Police Chiefs Desk Reference*, 2nd ed. Alexandria, VA: International Association of Chiefs of Police and the Bureau of Justice Assistance, 2008, pp.172–183.

Orrick, W. Dwayne. "Recruiting Female Candidates." *Law and Order*, December 2009, pp.30–36.

"Overview." GovTrack.us. Retrieved from http://www.govtrack.us/congress/bill.xpd?bill=h111-413

Pearsall, Albert Antony III, and Kohlhepp, Kim. "Strategies to Improve Recruitment." *The Police Chief*, April 2010, pp.128–130.

Preemployment Background Screening Guideline. Alexandria, VA: American Society for Industrial Security (ASIS) International (ASIS GDL PBS 09 2006).

"Preventing Sexual Harassment." St. Paul, MN: Equal Opportunity Division, Department of Human Relations, no date.

Rydberg, Jason, and Terrill, William. "The Effect of Higher Education on Police Behavior." *Police Quarterly*, March 2010, pp.92–120.

Schreiber, Sara. "From a Face to a Force." *Law Enforcement Technology*, March 2009, pp.10–19.

"Text of H.R.413: Public Safety Employer-Employee Cooperation Act of 2009." GovTrack.us. Retrieved from http://www.govtrack.us/congress/bill.xpd?bill=h111-413

"Welcome to NAPO," 2010. Retrieved from http://www.napo.org/

Wilson, Jeremy M., and Grammich, Clifford A. *Police Recruitment and Retention in the Contemporary Urban Environment: A National Discussion of Personnel Experiences and Promising Practices from the Front Lines.* Santa Monica, CA: The RAND Center on Quality Policing, the Community Oriented Policing Services Office and the National Institute of Justice, 2009.

Cases Cited

Board of County Commissioners v. Brown, 520 U.S. 397 (1997)

Brown v. Bryan, 219 F.3d 450 (5th Cir. 2000)

City of Canton, Ohio v. Harris, 489 U.S. 378 (1989)

Davis v. City of Dallas, 777 F.2d 205 (5th Cir. 1985)

Gratz v. Bollinger, 539 U.S. 244 (2003)

Griggs v. Duke Power Company, 401 U.S. 424 (1971)

Grutter v. Bollinger, 539 U.S. 306 (2003)

Monell v. New York City Department of Social Services, 436 U.S. 658 (1978)

Oncale v. Sundowner Offshore Services, Inc., 523 U.S. 75 (1998)

Ricci v. DeStephano, 557 U.S. ___ (2009)

COURTS AND CORRECTIONS: LAW ENFORCEMENT'S PARTNERS IN THE CRIMINAL JUSTICE SYSTEM

The criminal justice system comprises three major components: law enforcement, courts and corrections. Each component acts independently and interdependently as the total system functions. What happens in one component directly affects the other two components. If law enforcement arrests and elects to process thousands of suspects, this could create a problem with overcrowded dockets in the courts. Likewise, if the courts sentence thousands of defendants, the correctional system can become overcrowded, resulting in early release of prisoners and a potential problem for law enforcement. Figure IV.1 illustrates the normal flow of the criminal justice process and what occurs in each of the three major components.

Further complicating our criminal justice system is the existence of a separate but parallel juvenile justice system. Within the law enforcement component, juveniles may be assigned to a separate division or may be handled by all officers. In addition,

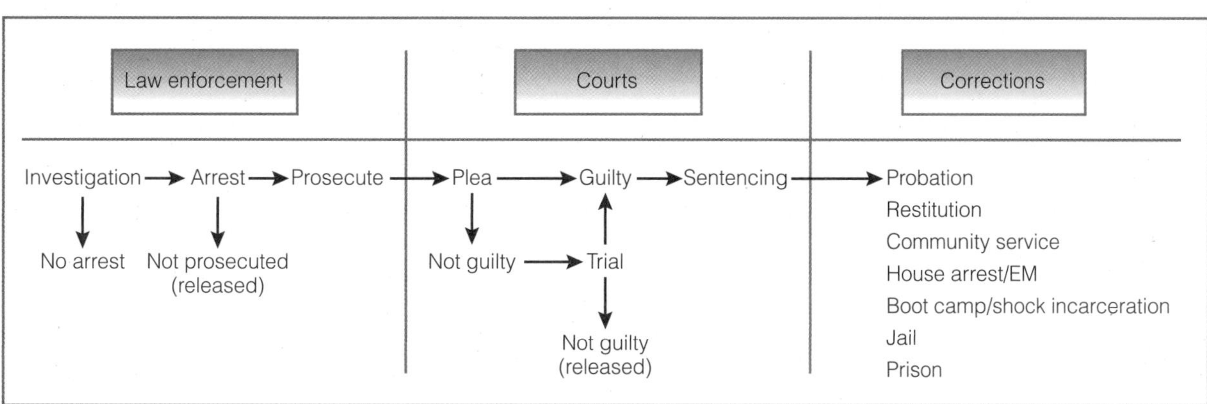

Note: This is an oversimplification to illustrate the key events in a person's "journey" through the criminal justice system.

FIGURE IV.1 The Criminal Justice Process

states vary in the age establishing juvenile status. In many instances, older juveniles may be transferred into the adult system.

The first three sections of this text explored the law enforcement component of the criminal justice system. This final section presents basic information about the other two components of the system with which law enforcement interacts: courts (Chapter 13) and corrections (Chapter 14).

CHAPTER 13

U.S. Courts

Justice is truth in action.
—Disraeli

© Glow Images / Alamy

The Supreme Court Building, constructed between 1932 and 1935, was designed on a scale in keeping with the importance and dignity of the Court and the judiciary as a coequal, independent branch of the federal government and as a symbol of "the national ideal of justice in the highest sphere of activity." Despite its role as a coequal branch of government, the Supreme Court was not provided with a building of its own until 1935, the 146th year of its existence. At the laying of the cornerstone for the building on October 13, 1932, Chief Justice Charles Evans Hughes stated, "The Republic endures and this is the symbol of its faith."

DO YOU KNOW . . .

- What the typical hierarchy is within the state court system? The federal court system?
- What was established by the Juvenile Court Act of 1899?
- How juvenile court differs from adult court?
- What the adversary system requires?
- Who the key players in the judicial process are?
- What the dual role of the prosecutor is?
- What the critical criminal justice stages are?
- What purpose a preliminary hearing serves?
- What alternatives to trial are?
- What the most important rule for officers' testifying in court is?
- How the defense attorney may attempt to discredit the testimony of a police officer?
- How officers can avoid objections to their testimony?

Can You Define?

acquittal
adjudication
adversary system
appellate jurisdiction
arraignment
bench trial
complaint
cross-examination
***de minimus* communication**
discovery process
diversion
hung jury
impeach
judicial waiver
jurisdiction
jurisprudence
no bill
nolo contendere
one-pot approach
original jurisdiction
parens patriae
petition
plea bargaining
preliminary hearing
preponderance of the evidence
presumption of innocence
***pro bono* work**
reasonable doubt
R.P.R.d
standing mute
venue
voir dire
the well
writ of certiorari
writ of habeas corpus

INTRODUCTION

Police officers must become familiar with our courts, as well as each step of the criminal justice process, because they may find themselves playing important roles in this component of the criminal justice system. They must also be familiar with criminal jurisprudence. **Jurisprudence** is the science or philosophy of law in a given area, or a department of law.

jurisprudence

The science or philosophy of law in a given area; a department of law.

First, just as law enforcement officers are the "gatekeepers" or the criminal justice system, using their discretion about who to arrest, prosecutors are the "gatekeepers" to the judicial system, using their discretion to determine who to charge and bring to trial. Friction may occur between officers and prosecutors when they disagree whether a case is strong enough to bring to trial.

Second, if the case does go to trial, officers are frequently called on to testify. Therefore, officers should be familiar with the courtroom itself as well as how it operates and their role as government witnesses. They should also recognize the various levels of courts, the dual (federal and state) organization of our judicial system, and that they, or at least their reports, could end up in the U.S. Supreme Court.

In addition, officers may find themselves frustrated by actions taken by the courts unless they understand the restrictions under which the courts operate. For example, the Sixth Amendment requires that suspects be given a "speedy" trial. This may force law enforcement to hasten its investigations or even to lose valuable evidence if officers detain a suspect for an unreasonable time. Pretrial release may anger police as may plea bargains in which they have no say. Especially frustrating for officers is when defendants are found not guilty because of a technicality, often the result of some unintentional but unconstitutional action of an officer.

Finally, prisoners released on parole and defendants sentenced to or released on probation are of concern. Although the corrections portion of the criminal justice system is technically responsible for these individuals, in reality these parolees and probationers are living within some local department's jurisdiction where officers are charged with "keeping the peace." The Bureau of Justice Statistics reports that at year end 2008 nearly 5.1 million adults were under community supervision; 84 percent were probations (Glaze and Bonczar, 2009, p.1). A sentence of probation may anger and frustrate law enforcement officers who worked the case and see such sentences as contributing to the "revolving door" of the criminal justice system. Law enforcement catches the "bad guys," and the system lets them go. The role of law enforcement in community supervision is discussed in Chapter 14.

jurisdiction
The geographic area within which a court (or public official) has the right and power to operate; also refers to individuals and subjects over which a court has the right and power to make binding decisions.

THE CHAPTER AT A GLANCE

This chapter begins with an overview of the court systems in the United States, including state court systems, the juvenile court, the federal court system, the Supreme Court and several specialized courts, including problem-solving courts. Next the adversary system and its key players—the defendant, the prosecutor, the defense attorney and the judge—are introduced. This is followed by a description of the critical stages in the criminal justice system. Because not all cases result in a court trial, alternatives to such a trial are discussed next, including diversion and plea bargaining. This is followed by a description of the typical trial. The chapter concludes with discussions of the police officer's role in the courts and courtroom security.

THE COURT SYSTEM: AN OVERVIEW

U.S. courts operate within a highly structured framework that may vary greatly from state to state. Many dualities exist within this framework. One such duality is their **jurisdiction**, which refers to a geographic area and to a court's authority to try, or adjudicate, a case or to hear an appeal, the duality being that of original versus appellate jurisdiction. A court with **original jurisdiction** has the authority to try cases, whereas a court with **appellate jurisdiction** has the authority to hear an appeal to set aside a conviction without holding a trial. In some cases, a court has both types of jurisdiction, for example, the U.S. Supreme Court.

Adjudication is the process of judicially deciding a legal case. A court with authority to adjudicate cases is often called a *trial* court, and because such courts are often the first to record the proceedings, they are also referred to as *courts of record*. A *court of last resort* refers to the highest court to which a case may be appealed. Further complicating our court system is the duality of an adult and a

original jurisdiction
A court's power to take a case, try it and decide it; in contrast to an appellate court that hears appeals to the decisions of the original court.

appellate jurisdiction
A higher court with the power to hear and decide an appeal to the decision of an original court without holding a trial.

adjudication
The process of judicially deciding a legal case.

TABLE 13.1 Overview of Court Structure in the United States

Federal	State
Hears cases everywhere in the United States	Important variations from state to state
Decides 46,000 criminal cases a year	State felony filings outnumber federal by 87 to 1
U.S. Supreme Court	**Supreme Court**
Most powerful court in the world	Typically has almost total control over cases to be heard
Virtually complete control over cases it hears	Major policymaker for the state
Decisions have completely changed the criminal justice system	Final decider of questions of state law
Hears only a handful of state criminal cases	Decides a handful of criminal appeals
U.S. Courts of Appeals	**Court of Appeals or Appeals Court**
Twelve circuits are organized regionally	Thirty-nine states have intermediate courts of appeals
Must hear all requests for review	Must hear all requests for review
Last stop for the vast majority of defendants convicted in federal court	One in 16 appellants wins a significant victory
U.S. District Court	**District, Superior, or Circuit Court**
Eighty-nine courts in the continental United States	Organized by county (or groups of counties)
Criminal cases: drugs, fraud, and embezzlement	Criminal cases: burglary, theft, drugs, murder, robbery, rape
Civil cases: civil rights, federal statutes, diversity of citizenship	Civil cases: automobile accidents, divorce, contract, probate
U.S. Magistrate Court	**Municipal, City or Justice of the Peace Court**
Responsible for preliminary stages of felony cases	In rural areas, judges may be nonlawyers
Hears a fair volume of minor crimes on federal property	Handles preliminary stages of felony cases
Has responsibility (but not authority) over habeas corpus petitions	Criminal cases: petty theft, public drunkenness, disturbing the peace, disorderly conduct
	Civil cases: small claims

SOURCE: David W. Neubauer. *America's Courts and the Criminal Justice System*, 8th ed. Belmont, CA: Wadsworth Publishing Company, 2005, p.54.

juvenile court system, as well as that of felony courts and misdemeanor court, both discussed later in the chapter.

The most obvious duality, however, is the system of state and federal courts. Table 13.1 compares the federal and state court systems.

The State Court System

Each state's constitution and statutory law establish its court structure. Consequently great variety exists in the types of courts established, the names by which they are known and the number of levels in the hierarchy.

The hierarchy at the state level often goes up from courts of special or limited jurisdiction called justice of the peace (J.P.) courts, to trial courts or original and general jurisdiction courts (including probate court, municipal court, county court, circuit court, district court and superior court), to intermediate appellate courts, to the state supreme court.

Most cases originate in a municipal or county court, and it is in such courts that most law enforcement officers are called upon to testify. Although municipalities and counties are self-governed and have their own courts, they need to comply with state and federal laws. In some states, cases may be appealed to an intermediate appellate court. In every state, the state supreme court is the court of last resort at this level. Figure 13.1 illustrates the state court system. Cases may progress beyond this point, however, into the federal court system. Before looking at the adult federal system, consider the juvenile courts existing within each state.

Juvenile Courts

For more than a century the United States has had a court system, separate from the adult criminal court, to deal with juveniles. In 1899 Illinois passed the Juvenile Court Act, creating the first juvenile court in Cook County and beginning an era of social jurisprudence. The court's primary purpose was to help wayward children become productive community members. The act, however, also gave expanded jurisdiction to the juvenile court in handling those youths who broke the law and in regulating the treatment and control of dependent, neglected and delinquent children.

The Juvenile Court Act equated poor and abused children with delinquent and criminal children and provided that they be treated in essentially the same way, establishing a **one-pot approach**.

one-pot approach
Equating poor and abused children with delinquent and criminal children and treating them in essentially the same way.

Most juvenile courts today have this same dual charge.

The Chicago legislation grew out of the efforts of civic-minded citizens who saw the inhumane treatment of children confined in police stations and jails. The legislation included many characteristics of our current juvenile courts, including a separate court for juveniles, separate and confidential records, informal proceedings and the possibility of probation. The act was also grounded in the English common-law doctrine of ***parens patriae***—that the state was responsible for the general protection of all people within its jurisdiction who could not protect themselves, including children.

parens patriae
The right of the government to take care of minors and others who cannot legally take care of themselves.

Historically juvenile courts have been informal, private, non-adversarial systems that stress rehabilitation rather than punishment of youths.

Juvenile courts vary from state to state, but most begin with some sort of intake, usually starting a **petition**—a document alleging a juvenile is a delinquent, status offender or dependent and asking the court to assume jurisdiction of the child. It is the formal process for bringing a matter before the juvenile court. Often the petition originates with a law enforcement agency, but it can come from another source, such as social services. The intake or initial screening is usually controlled and supervised by the juvenile court.

petition
In the juvenile justice system, a document alleging a juvenile is a delinquent, status offender or dependent and asking the court to assume jurisdiction of the child.

At the *adjudication hearing* (comparable to the preliminary hearing in the adult system), the youth is questioned about the alleged offense. If the evidence is insufficient, the petition may be dismissed. If enough evidence exists that the child is delinquent, a court date is set for the disposition hearing (comparable to the trial in the adult system).

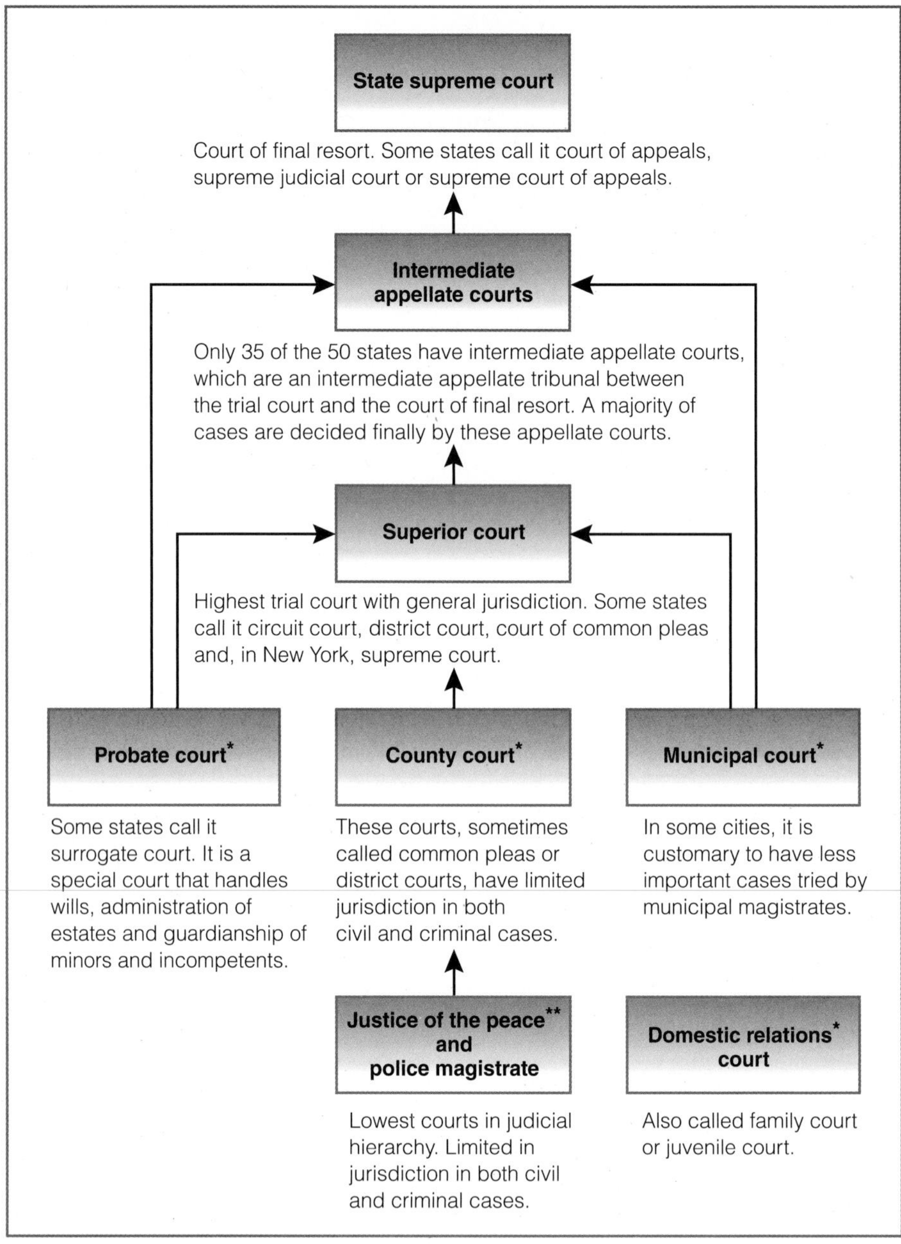

State supreme court
Court of final resort. Some states call it court of appeals, supreme judicial court or supreme court of appeals.
Intermediate appellate courts
Only 35 of the 50 states have intermediate appellate courts, which are an intermediate appellate tribunal between the trial court and the court of final resort. A majority of cases are decided finally by these appellate courts.
Superior court
Highest trial court with general jurisdiction. Some states call it circuit court, district court, court of common pleas and, in New York, supreme court.
Probate court*
County court*
Municipal court*
Some states call it surrogate court. It is a special court that handles wills, administration of estates and guardianship of minors and incompetents.
These courts, sometimes called common pleas or district courts, have limited jurisdiction in both civil and criminal cases.
In some cities, it is customary to have less important cases tried by municipal magistrates.
Justice of the peace** and police magistrate
Domestic relations* court
Lowest courts in judicial hierarchy. Limited in jurisdiction in both civil and criminal cases.
Also called family court or juvenile court.

*Courts of special jurisdiction, such as probate, family or juvenile courts, and the so-called inferior courts, such as common pleas or municipal courts, may be separate courts or part of the trial court of general jurisdiction.
**Justices of the peace do not exist in all states. Where they do exist, their jurisdictions vary greatly from state to state.

FIGURE 13.1 State Judicial System

SOURCE: American Bar Association. *Law and the Courts.* Chicago: American Bar Association, 1974, p.20. Updated information provided by West Publishing Company.

Courtesy, History Colorado, BFP-Lindsey, Benjamin (Juvenile Court)

Judge Benjamin Lindsey presided in juvenile court in Denver, Colorado, from 1900 to 1927. His court stressed a caring approach "in the best interests of the child."

At the *disposition hearing*, the judge has several alternatives. Based on the findings of the investigation, the judge may place the youth on probation or in a foster home, release the child to the parents, commit the child to an institution or make the child a ward of the court. Serious juvenile offenders may be committed to mental institutions, reformatories, prisons, and county and state schools for delinquents. Some cities, such as New York and Chicago, have set up youth courts that are adult courts using the philosophy of juvenile courts. These youth courts usually confine their hearings to misdemeanors. The usual sequence of events within the juvenile court is illustrated in Figure 13.2.

The Federal Court System

 The federal court system has three tiers: district courts, appellate courts and the U.S. Supreme Court.

The three-tiered federal court system is illustrated in Figure 13.3. A state may be divided into federal districts (91 districts in 50 states), and several states may fall within a circuit (11 circuits plus a DC circuit).

The Supreme Court

The U.S. Supreme Court is presided over by nine justices appointed by the president of the United States, subject to Senate confirmation. The president also appoints a chief justice, who assigns the cases to the other justices. Most have been

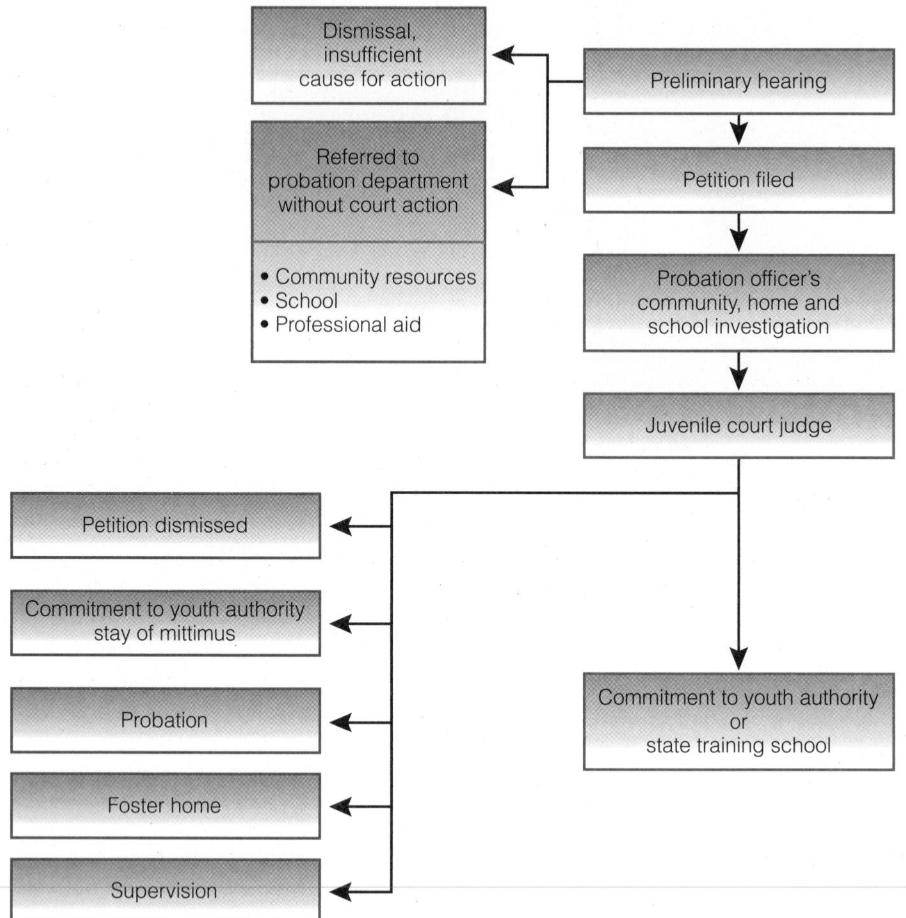

FIGURE 13.2 Juvenile Court Responsibility

SOURCE: Reprinted by permission. Copyright held by The International Association of Chiefs of Police, Inc. Further reproduction without express written permission is prohibited.

lawyers from the upper class and have been White, male, Protestant and graduates of prestigious universities. More than half were judges before their appointments. The first Black Supreme Court justice was Thurgood Marshall, appointed in 1967. Sandra D. O'Connor was the first woman Supreme Court justice, appointed in 1981. Sonia Sotomayor, an associate justice appointed in 2009 by President Barack Obama, is the first Hispanic person to hold the position of Supreme Court justice.

The Constitution established tenure for "life on good behavior." Therefore, the only way to remove a justice is through impeachment unless voluntary retirement can be obtained. When the Supreme Court decides to hear a case, it grants a **writ of certiorari**, which is a request for a transcript of the proceedings of the case for review. When the Supreme Court rules on a case, the ruling becomes precedent, commonly referred to as a landmark decision, which must be honored by all lower courts. The use of precedent in the legal system gives the Supreme Court power to influence and mold the everyday operating procedures of the police.

writ of certiorari

A request for a transcript of the proceedings of a case for review; granted when the Supreme Court decides to hear a case.

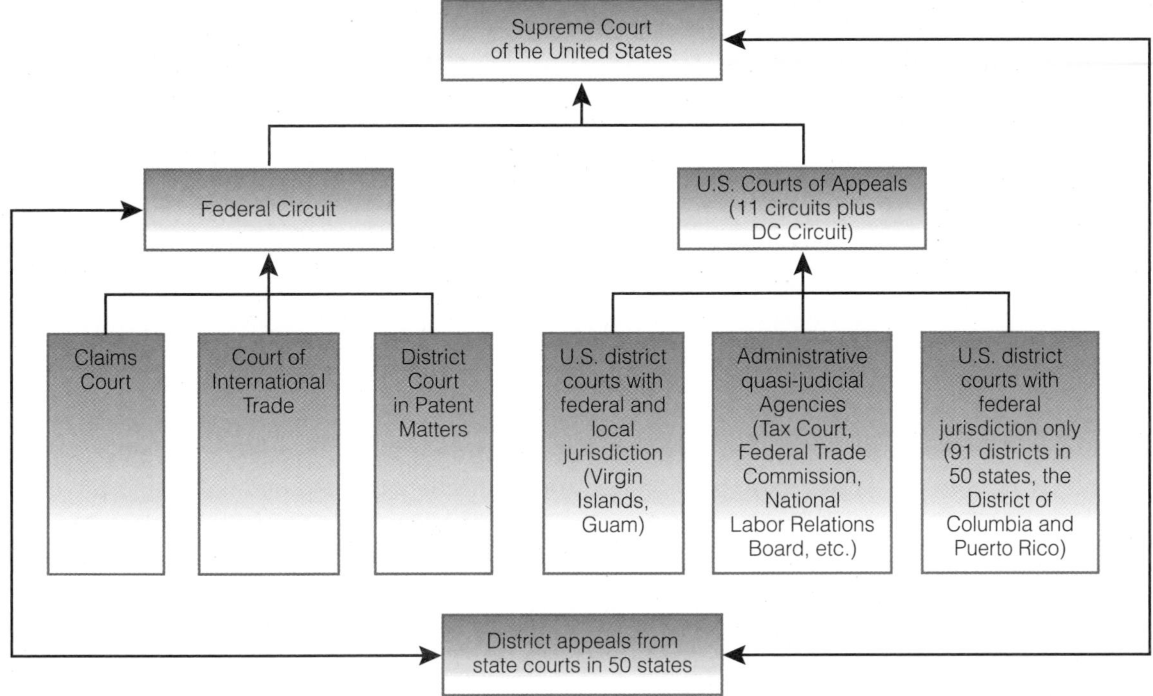

FIGURE 13.3 Federal Judicial System

SOURCE: American Bar Association. *Law and the Courts.* Chicago: American Bar Association, 1974, p.21. Updated information provided by the Federal Courts Improvement Act of 1982 and West Publishing Company.

SENNA/SIEGEL. *Introduction to Criminal Justice,* 7E. © 1996, p.21. Wadsworth, a part of Cengage Learning, Inc. Reproduced by permission. www.cengage.com/permissions

SPECIALIZED COURTS

Specialized courts have developed to address specific criminal justice cases. It is hoped these alternatives to the traditional courtroom will dispense more equitable justice as applied to particular issues. Among the specialized courts are tribal courts; community courts; problem-solving courts such as drug courts, DWI courts, domestic violence courts, mental health courts, homeless courts, reentry courts and juvenile courts.

Tribal Courts

The tribal court system includes trial and appellate courts, as well as specialized civil, criminal, family, healing and wellness, juvenile and drug courts. These courts hear cases pertaining to Native American law that affect both Native Americans and non–Native Americans living or operating a business within the jurisdiction of a Native American government.

Community Courts

Community courts are neighborhood based and seek to solve local problems. They bring together local resources and create problem-solving partnerships with community groups, government agencies and social service providers.

Similar to other collaborative justice courts, community courts aim to improve efficiency in judicial proceedings, match sanctions and services to offenders, and build bridges between public and private agencies that serve offenders. Community courts focus on quality-of-life crimes and on cleaning up neighborhoods that are deteriorating from crime and neglect.

In many community courts, police officers participate in court-run panels to discuss the impact of low-level crime on local neighborhoods where they explain the strategies they apply to these vexing problems and answer questions from community members and offenders (Doniger, 2009). The *Annual Report of the Center for Court Innovation* (2009, p.7) provides an example of the growing support for community courts: "A community survey conducted annually in Red Hook, Brooklyn, found that 94 percent of residents feel positively about having a community court in their neighborhood—a dramatic turnaround from the days before the Red Hook Community Justice Center opened, when only 12 percent expressed support for local courts." The report (p.8) notes that by the end of 2009 there were over 70 community courts in operation around the globe based on the model created by the Center for Court Innovation.

Problem-Solving Courts

Problem-solving courts seek to achieve tangible outcomes for victims, offenders and society. These include reduction in recidivism, reduced stays in foster care for children, increased sobriety for addicts, reentry courts for prior offenders and healthier communities. Problem-solving courts rely on the active use of judicial authority to solve problems and to change the behavior of litigants. These courts do not pass cases off—to other judges, probation departments or community-based treatment programs. Judges at problem-solving courts stay involved with cases throughout the post-adjudication process.

Problem-solving courts use a collaborative approach, relying on both government and nonprofit partners. They promote reform outside the courtroom as well as within. Problem-solving courts vary greatly in their approach, but they have in common the fact that they were born out of frustration, both within the court system and among the public, with the enormous number of cases that seem to cycle repeatedly through the courts repeatedly disposed of but not resolved.

Initially, problem-solving courts were thought of as separate entities with separate calendars, staffs and services as well as their own tenets. Then, in the late 1990s practitioners began to emphasize the courts' similarities, reflected in the emergence of the term itself. As Wolf (2007, pp.1, 3) explains:

> It was New York State Chief Judge Judith S. Kaye who gave national prominence to the term in a 1999 column in *Newsweek* when she explained that drug treatment courts, community courts, and domestic violence courts shared three important principles: a belief that courts can and should play a role in trying to solve the problems that are fueling caseloads; a belief that outcomes—not just process and precedent—matter; and a recognition that the coercive power of courts can change people's behavior.
>
> In 2000, the Conference of Chief Justices and Conference of State Court Administrators gave a joint seal of approval to the term "problem-solving courts,"

> and, even more significantly, they called for "the broad integration over the next decade of the principles and methods employed in the problem-solving courts into the administration of justice." The American Bar Association passed a similar resolution in 2002.
>
> Since then, literature has begun to emerge focusing on the general value of "problem-solving principles" and ways these principles can be transferred to traditional courts. The six principles of problem-solving justice are (1) enhanced information, (2) community engagement, (3) collaboration, (4) individualized justice, (5) accountability and (6) outcomes.
>
> The general thrust of the literature is that the future of problem solving may involve both specialized courts and the broad application of problem-solving principles into traditional courtrooms.

Outcomes are process results that are evaluated through the active and ongoing collection and analysis of data. Such measured outcomes are "crucial tools for evaluating the effectiveness of operations and encouraging continuous improvement" (Wolf, 2007, p.2).

Because there are more than 3,000 specialized problem-solving courts nationwide, a set of universal performance indicators is a useful tool by which to judge the effectiveness of such courts. These performance indicators can be arranged into three organizing principles (Porter et al., 2010, pp. iii–iv):

- Problem-Solving Orientation, including individualized screening and problem assessment resulting in individualized treatment or service mandate, direct engagement of participants/litigants, a focus on outcomes with the court retaining participants/litigants
- Collaboration within the justice system, with social service providers and with the community
- Accountability by insisting on regular and rigorous compliance monitoring—and clear consequences for non-compliance—the justice system can improve the accountability of offenders. It can also improve the accountability of service providers by requiring regular reports on their work with participants.

The most well-known and researched specialized courts are the drug courts.

Drug Courts Drug courts are community-based courts designed to reflect community concerns and priorities, access community resources and seek community participation and support. Although the structure, scope and target populations of drug courts vary from one jurisdiction to another, the goals remain the same: to reduce recidivism and substance abuse and rehabilitate participants. By providing drug treatment to offenders as soon as they enter the court system, instead of waiting until they have passed into the correctional component of criminal justice, drug courts have taken quite a different path from traditional court processes. Estimates cite over 1,500 adult drug courts and almost 500 juvenile drug courts in this country, serving more than 70,000 offenders at any given time. The limited research on drug courts is "generally positive" ("Study Finds Ohio's Adult and Juvenile Drug Courts Reduce Recidivism," 2009, p.51).

DWI Courts As with drug courts, driving while intoxicated (DWI) courts are being established to protect public safety and to reduce recidivism by attacking the root cause of impaired driving—alcohol and substance abuse. The mission of sobriety and DWI courts is to hold offenders accountable for their actions, change their behavior to end the cycle of recidivism and alcohol abuse, treat the victims of DWI offenders fairly and justly and educate the public about the benefits of DWI courts.

Domestic Violence (DV) Courts According to the Center for Court Innovation, an important part of domestic violence court involves putting victims in touch immediately with social services. Victim safety is the cornerstone of domestic violence courts. Every victim should be given immediate access to an advocate who can assist with safety planning and explain court procedures. In addition to providing services, victim advocates should keep victims informed about the status of their cases. A basic element of domestic violence courts is tight judicial monitoring of convicted offenders.

Mental Health Courts According to the Bureau of Justice Assistance, "Mental health courts (MHCs) are a new and rapidly expanding phenomena. In 1997 only four MHCs existed in the country. As of June 2005, there are approximately 125 operational courts in 36 states" (*Mental Health Courts*, n.d.). Modeled after drug courts, MHCs practice therapeutic jurisprudence, often altering the traditional dynamics of the courtroom. For example, in some courts prosecutors and defense lawyers come together to discuss their common goals for each defendant. The main goal of such courts is to interrupt the "revolving door" for those with mental health problems from street to court to cell and back again without ever receiving support and services. The courts are also a response to the overrepresentation of people with mental illness in the criminal justice system. All mental health courts are voluntary.

Homeless Courts Homeless courts help homeless defendants resolve outstanding misdemeanor criminal cases. In the Homeless Court Program, the traditional court sanctions of fines, public work service and custody are replaced with alternative sentencing. The defendants learn life skills, address chemical dependency through Alcoholics Anonymous or Narcotics Anonymous meetings, take computer and literacy classes, train or search for employment, receive counseling or perform volunteer work.

Reentry Courts A relatively recent specialized court is the reentry court, of which there are presently at least two dozen throughout the country (Hamilton, 2010, p.iii). Reentry courts serve parolees before their release from incarceration by working with correctional staff to develop detailed profiles of participating inmates that include information about medical status (including mental health), addiction, criminal involvement, living arrangements, vocational skills and family composition. The profile is used to customize a treatment and supervision plan. After parolees are released, the court helps their reintegration by helping them find jobs, secure housing, remain drug-free and assume family and person responsibilities.

Hamilton reports on a quasi-experimental research design from a pool of 20,750 parolees released in Manhattan from November 2002 through February 2008. The researchers selected 317 parolee participants in the Harlem Parole

Reentry Court and matched them with 637 parolees placed in traditional supervision, tracking these subjects over three years from their release. The researchers found that reentry court parolees were less likely to be rearrested or reconvicted.

Teen Courts/Youth Courts Teen courts, also called youth courts and peer courts, are designed to address a variety of youthful problem behaviors, such as underage drinking, substance abuse, truancy and related status offenses. The goal is to rehabilitate and help youths pursue a path that leads them to becoming more responsible, productive citizens. Goodwin et al. (n.d., p.49) describe the Teen Court Program as a "community-based intervention/prevention program designed to provide an alternative response for the juvenile justice system for first-time, nonviolent, misdemeanor juvenile offenders, in which community youths determine the appropriate sanctions for the offender. The program will hold youthful offenders accountable and provide educational services to offenders and youth volunteers in an effort to promote long-term behavioral change that leads to enhanced public safety."

Youth volunteers, supervised by adult volunteers, work as bailiffs, clerks, jury and judges, questioning the offender, debating and imposing sentences. The goal is to intervene in early antisocial, delinquent and criminal behaviors to prevent escalation of such behaviors. At its core, youth court has two main goals: (1) response to the behavior, with behavioral consequences such as restitution, community service and personal restrictions, as well as the implied threat that failing to follow through will bring severe consequences and (2) building youth responsibility (Garrett, 2009, p.46). Studies show a low recidivism rate—less than 13 percent—among teen participants (Garrett, 2009, p.47).

Juvenile Drug Courts and Gun Courts Like the adult court, the juvenile court also has a drug court component. A recent addition to the courts available for youths is the gun court. A gun court is a problem-solving court that intervenes with youths who have committed gun offenses that have not resulted in serious physical injury. Most juvenile gun courts are short-term programs that augment rather than replace normal juvenile court proceedings (*Gun Court*, 2007).

Waiver to Adult Court When juveniles commit a series of serious crimes or a single particularly violent crime, juvenile courts can declare them to be under the jurisdiction of the adult (criminal) court. This **judicial waiver** allows juvenile court judges to transfer cases based on a juvenile's age, type of offense, prior record and dangerousness. This is also known as binding over, transferring or certifying juvenile cases to criminal courts. Such juveniles are then charged and required to appear in adult criminal court. Other juvenile transfer mechanisms include *prosecutorial waiver* (or direct file), where the prosecutor has the discretion to charge a youth as an adult, and *legislative waiver* (or statutory exclusion), whereby the state legislature delineates a list of offenses and offender characteristics that provide for the automatic transfer of a youth to adult criminal court, absent any type of judicial oversight. The age at which youths come under the jurisdiction of the criminal courts varies from state to state, ranging from age 16 to 19.

judicial waiver

The juvenile court waives jurisdiction and transfers a case to criminal court; also known as binding over, transferring or certifying juvenile cases to criminal courts.

Having looked at the organizational structures of our various court systems, next turn your attention to a concept on which our entire criminal justice system rests: the adversary system.

THE ADVERSARY SYSTEM

Our criminal justice system is based on an **adversary system**—the accuser versus the accused.

Our adversary criminal justice system requires the accuser to prove beyond a reasonable doubt to a judge or jury that the accused is guilty of a specified crime.

Presumption of innocence means that the accused is assumed innocent until proof to the contrary is clearly established. On the side of the accused are the defendant and the defense attorney. On the side of the accuser is the citizen (or victim), the prosecutor and the police officer. They bear the burden of proof.

An impartial judge or jury hears both sides of the controversy and then reaches a decision whether the accuser has proven the accused guilty beyond a **reasonable doubt**, that state of a case in which, after comparing and considering all the evidence, the jurors cannot say they feel an abiding conviction of the truth of the charge; jurors are morally uncertain as to the truth of the charges.

Reasonable doubt is a more stringent evidentiary standard than that required in a civil trial, where a mere **preponderance of the evidence** is standard. The preponderance of the evidence standard simply means it is more likely than not, based on the bulk of the evidence, that the plaintiff's version of the case holds up. Table 13.2 illustrates the various evidentiary standards of proof or degrees of certainty required in varying circumstances.

adversary system

The criminal justice system used in the United States that puts the accuser versus the accused; the accuser must prove that the one accused is guilty.

presumption of innocence

The accused is assumed innocent until proof to the contrary is clearly established.

reasonable doubt

That state of a case in which, after comparing and considering all the evidence, the jurors cannot say they feel an abiding conviction of the truth of the charge; moral uncertainty of the truth of the charges.

preponderance of the evidence

The greater weight of the evidence; one side is more credible than the other; standard of proof used in civil trials.

TABLE 13.2 Evidentiary Standards of Proofs—Degrees of Certainty

Standard	Definition	Where Used
Absolute certainty	No possibility of error; 100 percent certainty	Not used in civil or criminal law
Beyond reasonable doubt; moral certainty	Conclusive and complete proof, without leaving any reasonable doubt as to the guilt of the defendant; allowing the defendant the benefit of any possibility of innocence	Criminal trial
Clear and convincing evidence	Prevailing and persuasive to the trier of fact	Civil commitments, insanity defense
Preponderance of evidence	Greater weight of evidence in terms of credibility; more convincing than an opposite point of view	Civil trial
Probable cause	U.S. constitutional standard for arrest and search warrants, requiring existence of facts sufficient to warrant that a crime has been committed	Arrest, preliminary hearing, motions
Sufficient evidence	Adequate evidence to reverse a trial court	Appellate review
Reasonable suspicion	Rational, reasonable belief that facts warrant investigation of a crime on less than probable cause	Police investigations
Less than probable cause	Mere suspicion; less than reasonable to conclude criminal activity exists	Prudent police investigation where safety of an officer or others is endangered

SOURCE: SENNA/SIEGEL. *Introduction to Criminal Justice,* 7E. © 1996, p.391. Wadsworth, a part of Cengage Learning, Inc. Reproduced by permission. www.cengage.com/permissions

KEY PLAYERS IN THE JUDICIAL PROCESS

Key players in the judicial process include the defendant, prosecutor, defense attorney, judge and jury.

The Defendant

Everyone, including a person suspected of committing a crime, has certain rights that must be protected at all stages of the criminal justice process. Defendants have all the rights set forth in the Bill of Rights. They may waive these rights, but if they do, the waiver should be in writing because proof of the waiver is up to the police officer or the prosecution. The police officer must be able to show that all rights have been respected and that all required procedures have been complied with.

The Fifth Amendment guarantees due process: notice of a hearing, full information regarding the charges made, the opportunity to present evidence before an impartial judge or jury and the right to refrain from self-incrimination. The Sixth Amendment establishes the requirements for criminal trials, including the right to a speedy public trial by an impartial jury and the right to have a lawyer. The Eighth Amendment forbids excessive bail and implies the right to such bail in most instances.

The criminal justice system is sometimes criticized when a defendant is found not guilty because of a technicality. Even though a person confesses to a hideous crime, if he or she was not first told of his or her rights and allowed to have a lawyer present during questioning, the confession is not legal. As noted by the Supreme Court in *Escobedo v. Illinois* (1964), "No system of criminal justice can or should survive if it comes to depend for its continued effectiveness on the citizens' abdication through unawareness of their constitutional rights. No system worth preserving should have a fear that if an accused is permitted to consult with a lawyer, he will become aware of and exercise these rights. If the exercise of constitutional rights will thwart the effectiveness of a system of law enforcement, then there is something very wrong with that system."

The Prosecutor

A prosecutor is an official elected to exercise leadership in representing the government and, therefore, the people in the criminal justice system. Prosecutors may be city, county, state, commonwealth or district attorneys or solicitors. They are usually elected to a two- or four-year term at the state level. At the federal level, they are appointed by the president.

The prosecutor chooses the cases to be prosecuted, selects the charges to be brought into court, recommends the bail amount required for pretrial release, approves any plea bargains and recommends sentences. Researchers Shermer and Johnson (2010, p.242) studied the subtle but important influences that extralegal offender characteristics play in discretionary federal prosecutorial charging decisions and found, "Despite public concern, widespread prejudices do not seem to dominate prosecutorial decision making at the federal level." One notable exception was that females were especially likely to receive charge reductions compared with males.

Prosecutors also determine law enforcement priorities and are key in determining how much, how little and what types of crimes the public will tolerate. They serve the public interest and consider the public's need to feel secure, its sense of how justice should be carried out and the community's attitude toward certain crimes. Sometimes a case becomes so well publicized that the prosecutor is forced to "do something about it" or face defeat in the next election.

Prosecutors are also the legal advisors for police officers; they decide what cases should be prosecuted and how. They rely heavily on police officers' input in determining if a case should be brought to court. Often, however, misunderstanding and even ill will results when a prosecutor refuses a police officer's request for a complaint because of insufficient evidence or some violation of a criminal procedure, such as an illegal arrest. Plea bargaining may also cause ill will between a prosecutor and a police officer.

Because both police officers and prosecutors are striving for the same end—justice—they should be familiar with each other's problems. Police officers, for example, should understand what the prosecutor can and cannot do, which types of cases are worth prosecuting and the need for and advantages of plea bargaining in certain situations. Prosecutors, on the other hand, should be sensitive to the police officers' objections to legal technicalities and excessive paperwork and should include police officers in plea bargaining when possible or, at the least, inform them when such bargaining has occurred. It is important to remember that the police are a part of the prosecutor's team, and vice versa.

Prosecutors perform one other critical function in the criminal justice process. They are responsible for protecting the rights of all involved, including the suspect. In essence they have a dual responsibility. On the one hand, they are the leaders in the law enforcement community, the elected representatives of the public and the legal advisors to the police. On the other hand, they are expected to protect the rights of persons accused of crimes. In *Berger v. United States* (1935), Justice George Sutherland defined the prosecutor's responsibility as being "the representative not of an ordinary party to a controversy, but of a sovereignty whose obligation to govern impartially is as compelling as its obligation to govern at all; and whose interest, therefore, in a criminal prosecution is not that it shall win a case, but that justice shall be done."

Prosecutors have the dual function of leading the law enforcement community while protecting the rights of the accused.

Some prosecutors are teaming up with citizens in the overall community justice movement.

The Defense Attorney

The defense attorney represents the accused in court. Lawyers who represent the accused have the same duties and obligations whether privately retained, serving as a legal aid in the system or appointed by the court. They investigate the circumstances of the cases and explore facts relevant to their clients' guilt or innocence. Defense attorneys try to uncover evidence for their clients' defenses to present in court.

Most criminal cases are assigned to public defenders or to a few private lawyers who handle such cases. Public defenders are full- and part-time lawyers hired by the state or county government to represent people who cannot afford to hire a lawyer. Many lawyers donate time to represent the indigent, called ***pro bono* work**.

pro bono work

Work done for free; lawyers volunteer their time to be public defenders.

Judges

Although most people think of trial judges when they hear the word *judge*, many different kinds of judges exist. If a person comes to trial, he or she will already have encountered certain levels of the court system and judges acting within that system. The various types of judges and the functions they serve depend on the court to which they are appointed.

Judges have many important functions throughout the entire judicial process and can exercise great discretion by accepting or rejecting pleas; deciding in preliminary hearings if evidence is sufficient to justify prosecution or dismissing the charges; determining whether to grant bail, and if so, how much; deciding whether

CAREER PROFILE

Marsh Halberg (Attorney)

When you are in law school, all of your friends and family will keep asking you the same question, "What type of law do you want to practice?" My stock answer was always, "I don't know—anything but criminal law." I now look back on that response and chuckle. For more than 30 years I have practiced criminal law as an assistant county attorney, city prosecutor, federal public defender and private defense attorney. The lesson is that life will take unexpected turns as your life unfolds.

What I learned while going to law school is that the great majority of practicing attorneys sit behind desks all day long drafting or reviewing documents. I am very much a "people person," and being buried behind paperwork would be a slow death for me. The reality is that most cases never go to trial. If ever you do get to trial in a civil lawsuit, many times those cases will be heard before a judge and not a jury.

A criminal practice, by contrast, has a large volume of files that pass across your desk. Because there is such a high volume of cases, the chances for going to trial increase. Being able to be in a courtroom every day, negotiating or trying cases, was far more appealing to me than the other areas of law.

When I first got out of law school I had what I thought was a strong résumé. However, I found a job market flooded with new lawyers looking for work. I went to numerous interviews but found myself not landing the job based upon the stiff competition. I was loading trucks for UPS and started to think the whole investment in law school was a serious mistake. Then, over the course of three weeks, I had three job offers to pick from. One offer was being a civil attorney at a big law firm; the second was being a contract negotiator for a corporation; and the third was to be an assistant county attorney.

I decided I could always go from being a trial lawyer to a contract negotiator, but I would never go from being a negotiator to a trial lawyer. Also, the thought of working for a big, ostentatious law firm did not fit my personality.

I became an assistant county attorney for Carver County. I tried my first two jury trials during the first month of employment. I proceeded over the next several years to try an average of two jury trials a month, making numerous mistakes but honing my trial skills.

I decided to leave government practice for the better income that private practice would bring. I found a great job working with a 15-attorney law firm in Minneapolis. I contracted with the City of Edina to do their prosecution work. In the Minneapolis metropolitan area, many communities contract with private law firms to be their prosecutors on a contract basis. As such, over the next 20 years I prosecuted part-time and was able to do criminal defense work in other jurisdictions where there was not a conflict.

I had a wonderful opportunity to see both sides of criminal law and handle cases both as a prosecutor and defense lawyer. My criminal defense practice began to grow, and it became difficult to "serve two masters." I felt uncomfortable trying to be a stern prosecutor in the morning and then trying to seek lenient sentences in the afternoon. I decided I needed to pick one side or the other and felt it would be a great challenge to try to start a criminal defense law firm with some of my friends whose abilities I respected.

In 2005 I started a criminal law firm with my partners handling only criminal defense cases. It has been a great experience to now be in a situation to control my work environment, taking the cases I choose and practicing in an area that I have now been doing now for over 30 years.

to grant delays; presiding over the trial; giving the jury instructions; and imposing the sentence if a defendant is found guilty. Judicial discretion, however, can also lead to a significant amount of sentencing disparity.

Having looked at the nature of the adversary system and most of the key players, now consider the critical steps normally involved in the criminal justice process.

CRITICAL STAGES IN THE CRIMINAL JUSTICE PROCESS

The law on the books and the law in action relating to the critical stages in the criminal justice process are illustrated in Figure 13.4.

The criminal justice process consists of the steps that occur between and including the filing of a complaint through the acquittal or sentencing of an offender. An **acquittal** is a formal certification by the court stating that the accused is found "not guilty" of the crimes he or she has been charged with. The charges are dropped and the defendant is released. At various points along the way, a case may be dismissed, as illustrated in Figure 13.5.

acquittal

A formal certification by the court stating that the accused is found "not guilty" of the crimes he or she has been charged with; the charges are dropped and the defendant is released.

The criminal justice process consists of several critical stages: complaint or charge, warrant, arrest, booking, preliminary hearing, grand jury hearing, arraignment, trial and sentencing.

Usually the criminal justice process begins when a police officer or a citizen approaches the prosecutor to obtain a complaint. A formal **complaint**, also called the charge, is a legal document drawn up by a prosecutor that specifies the alleged crime and the supporting facts providing probable cause.

complaint

A legal document drawn up by a prosecutor that specifies an alleged crime and the supporting facts providing probable cause.

The police officer or citizen then presents the complaint to a judge and, in the judge's presence, swears to the accuracy of the content of the complaint and signs a statement to that effect. If the judge concurs with the charge, he or she grants an arrest warrant ordering the police to arrest the suspect.

The arrest may occur at several points throughout the criminal justice process. For example, it may have occurred without a complaint or warrant if the crime was committed in the presence of the arresting officer. The prosecutor also may choose to present the case to a grand jury for indictment before arresting a suspect.

After suspects are taken into custody, they are booked at the police station or they are transported directly to the county jail and booked and processed in there; that is, they are formally entered into the police records system. The suspect is photographed and fingerprinted. The prints are placed on file with the FBI in Washington, DC, and the suspect has a police arrest record.

Bail and Writ of Habeas Corpus

Usually one right of the accused is the right to be released from custody, in keeping with the legal premise that a person is innocent until proven guilty. After the formal booking process is completed, the suspect is usually entitled to be released on bail or *released* on his or her own *personal recognizance* (**R.P.R.d**) if the crime

R.P.R.d

Release on one's own personal recognizance.

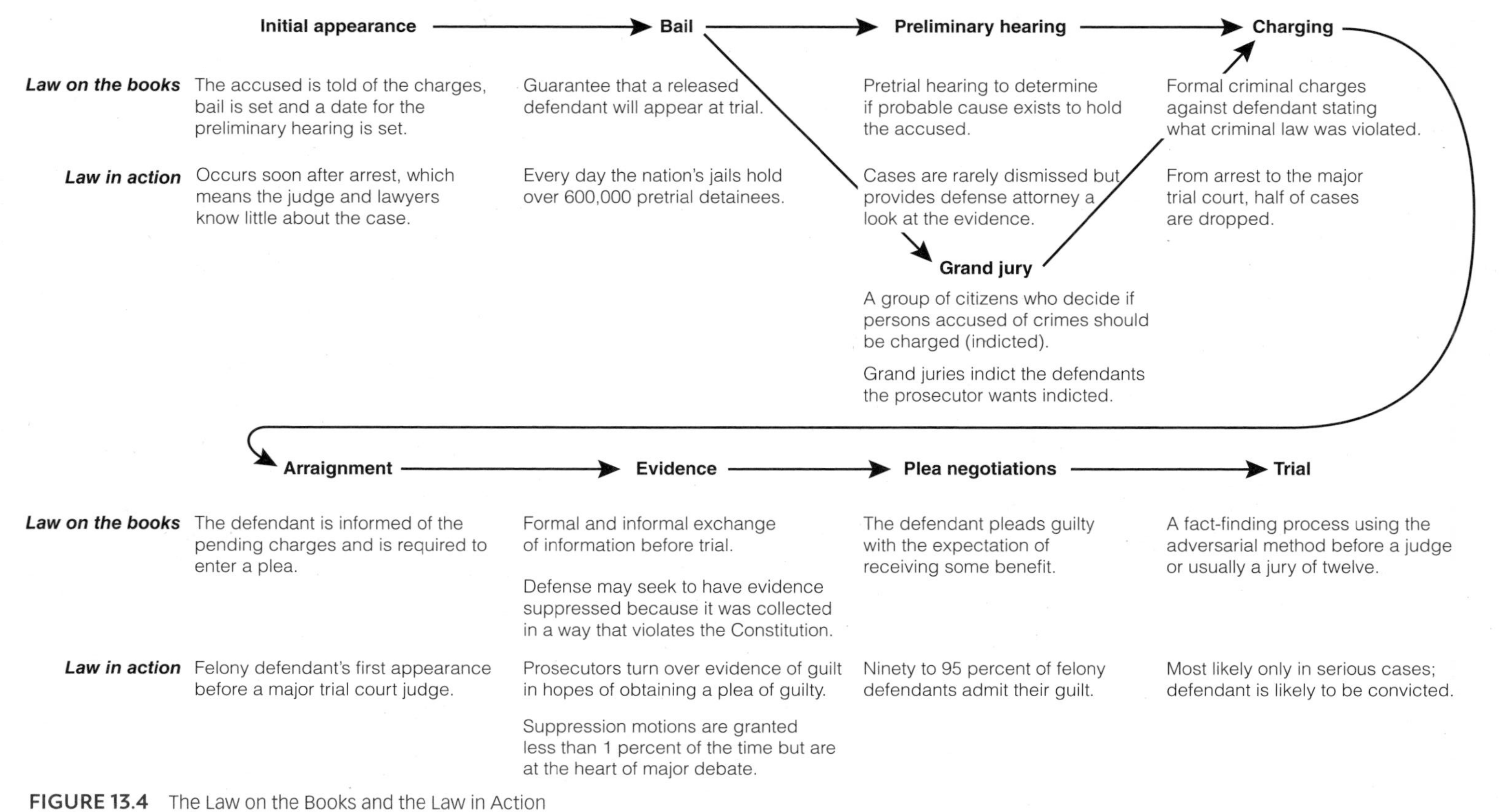

Initial appearance
Bail
Preliminary hearing
Charging
Law on the books
The accused is told of the charges, bail is set and a date for the preliminary hearing is set.
Guarantee that a released defendant will appear at trial.
Pretrial hearing to determine if probable cause exists to hold the accused.
Formal criminal charges against defendant stating what criminal law was violated.
Law in action
Occurs soon after arrest, which means the judge and lawyers know little about the case.
Every day the nation's jails hold over 600,000 pretrial detainees.
Cases are rarely dismissed but provides defense attorney a look at the evidence.
From arrest to the major trial court, half of cases are dropped.
Grand jury
A group of citizens who decide if persons accused of crimes should be charged (indicted).
Grand juries indict the defendants the prosecutor wants indicted.
Arraignment
Evidence
Plea negotiations
Trial
Law on the books
The defendant is informed of the pending charges and is required to enter a plea.
Formal and informal exchange of information before trial.
Defense may seek to have evidence suppressed because it was collected in a way that violates the Constitution.
The defendant pleads guilty with the expectation of receiving some benefit.
A fact-finding process using the adversarial method before a judge or usually a jury of twelve.
Law in action
Felony defendant's first appearance before a major trial court judge.
Prosecutors turn over evidence of guilt in hopes of obtaining a plea of guilty.
Suppression motions are granted less than 1 percent of the time but are at the heart of major debate.
Ninety to 95 percent of felony defendants admit their guilt.
Most likely only in serious cases; defendant is likely to be convicted.

FIGURE 13.4 The Law on the Books and the Law in Action

SOURCE: Adapted from David W. Neubauer. *America's Courts and the Criminal Justice System*, 8th ed. Belmont, CA: Wadsworth Publishing Company, 2005, p.9. Reprinted by permission.

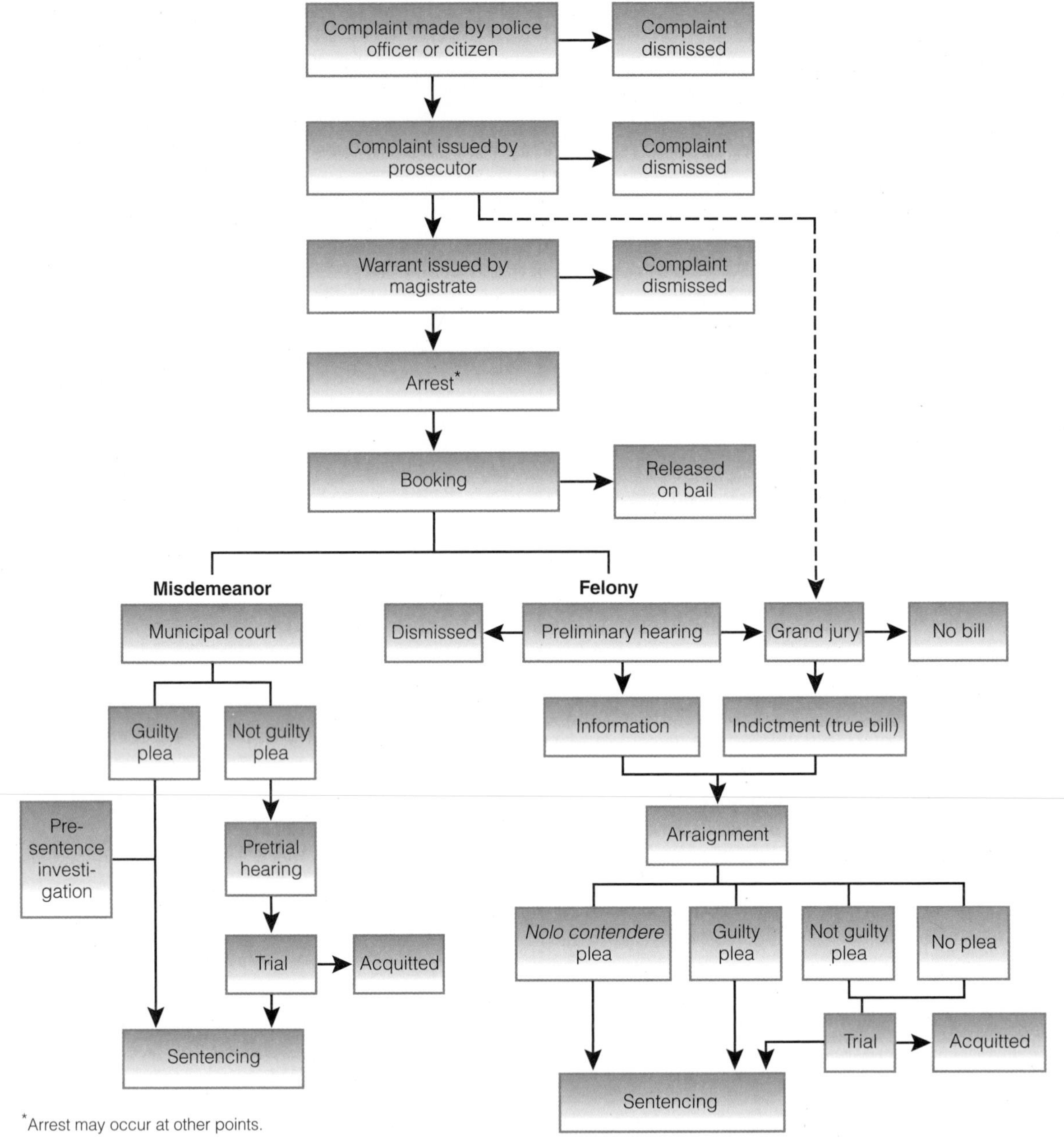

FIGURE 13.5 The Criminal Justice Process from Complaint to Disposition

is a misdemeanor or released on a writ of habeas corpus or bond if the crime is a felony.

The judge decides how much bail is reasonable as a deposit to bring the defendant back into court if released. Some defendants use a person or company that pays the bail for the defendant for an additional fee, typically a percentage of the amount of bail. Critics argue that bail bonding discriminates against poor defendants and allows wealthy defendants to buy their way out of jail.

Periodically a person in jail may be released on a **writ of habeas corpus**—a legal court order literally meaning "bring forth the body you have"—which commands that a person being held be brought forth immediately. This means of determining whether the jailing of the suspect is legal is used primarily when the justice process moves slowly and a prisoner is detained for an unreasonable time before the court appearance. Most states have guidelines as to how long a person may be jailed before being charged, being released or making a court appearance. These guidelines range from 36 to 72 hours, taking into consideration Sundays and holidays.

writ of habeas corpus

A legal court order literally meaning "bring forth the body you have," which commands that a person being held be brought forth immediately.

The Preliminary Hearing

In the **preliminary hearing**, the judge determines whether probable cause exists for believing that an offense has been committed and that the accused committed it. Most statutes and rules of criminal procedure require a preliminary hearing to be held within a "reasonable time."

preliminary hearing

That stage in the judicial system seeking to establish probable cause for believing that an offense has been committed and that the accused committed it, thus preventing persons from being indiscriminately brought to trial.

The preliminary hearing seeks to establish probable cause to prevent people from being indiscriminately brought to trial.

The judge in a preliminary hearing is not bound by the rules of evidence that ordinarily control a trial. The prosecutor need only establish probable cause, not prove beyond a reasonable doubt that the crime was committed.

In reality the preliminary hearing is often a mini-trial where the defense obtains as much information as possible to strengthen its case. Both prosecution and defense often use this stage of the criminal justice process for tactical purposes. In some instances overwhelming evidence may lead to a guilty plea or to a request for plea bargaining.

The **discovery process** requires that all pertinent facts on both sides be made available before the trial. Used properly the discovery process reduces questions of probable cause and other questions normally brought out in a preliminary hearing and encourages more final dispositions before trial, thereby saving court time. Available to both the prosecution and defense attorneys, it eliminates surprise as a legitimate trial tactic. The outcome of a preliminary hearing may be to (1) dismiss the charges, (2) present an information and bind the defendant over to a higher court or (3) send the case to a grand jury.

discovery process

A system that requires all pertinent facts be made available to the prosecutor and the defense attorney before the trial.

The Grand Jury

The U.S. Constitution requires an indictment by a federal grand jury before trial for most crimes against federal law. The consideration of a felony charge by a grand jury is not a trial. Only the prosecution's evidence is usually presented and considered. Contrary to the popular portrayal of grand juries on television and in movies, suspected offenders are usually not heard nor are their lawyers present to offer evidence on their behalf.

A grand jury meets in secret sessions and hears from witnesses to and victims of a crime. Like a preliminary hearing, it determines only whether enough evidence exists to accuse a person of a crime. In some states, by statute, a grand jury can hear evidence from suspects. However, the person being considered for indictment must sign a waiver of immunity and agree to answer all questions even though the testimony might be incriminating and may be used against them in a criminal trial. Their lawyers are not allowed to be present.

After the grand jury receives all testimony and evidence, it deliberates. If the majority of the grand jurors (or a specified number) agree that the person is guilty of a crime, they instruct the prosecutor to prepare an indictment specifying all the facts of the case. Grand juries may also issue what is called a **no bill**, meaning the jurors believe there is no criminal violation.

no bill

Issued by a grand jury if it decides that no crime has been committed.

The Coroner's Jury

Coroners investigate violent deaths where suspicion of foul play exists. By law coroners may conduct autopsies to determine the cause of death, and they may conduct inquests. The coroner's jury usually consists of six members. In some states the coroner's jury system has been abandoned and its functions are performed by a professional medical examiner.

The Arraignment

arraignment

A court procedure whereby the accused is read the charges against him or her and is then asked how he or she pleads.

standing mute

Refusing to answer as to guilt or innocence at an arraignment; entered as a "not guilty" plea.

nolo contendere

"I will not contest it." A defendant's plea of "no contest" in a criminal case; it means he or she does not directly admit guilt but submits to sentencing or other punishment.

When defendants are charged with a felony, they must personally appear at an **arraignment**. As in the preliminary hearing, they are entitled to counsel. The procedures of the arraignment vary by state, but generally defendants appear before the court; are read the complaint, information or indictment; and if they have not received a copy, they are given one. They then enter a plea.

Defendants have several alternatives when they appear for the formal arraignment. **Standing mute**, that is, refusing to answer, is entered by the judge as a not guilty plea. ***Nolo contendere*** means "no contest." By entering a plea of *nolo contendere*, defendants, in effect, throw themselves on the court's mercy. A *guilty plea* means the accused admits the charge or a lesser charge agreed to in plea bargaining. *Not guilty* means the accused denies the charge. Some states require defendants to automatically plead not guilty to such capital crimes as first-degree murder. Durose et al. (2009) report that 94 percent of felony offenders sentenced in 2006 pleaded guilty.

If defendants plead guilty or *nolo contendere*, a sentencing time is set. Usually a presentence investigation is ordered to determine if probation is warranted. If defendants make no plea or plead not guilty, they have the choice of a trial by a judge or by a jury. If defendants wish a jury trial, the case is assigned to the court docket and a date set.

Omnibus Hearing

An omnibus hearing is a pre-trial hearing that typically occurs immediately after a person's arraignment. The purpose of this hearing is to determine if the evidence in the case is admissible in court. This includes testimony, which may require that police officers involved in the incident be present. Both the prosecutor and the defense attorney attend this hearing to discuss the pre-trial matters regarding the case.

Before looking at the trial itself, next consider some alternatives to a trial.

ALTERNATIVES TO A TRIAL

Before cases go to court, defense attorneys may explore the possibility of diverting the case from the criminal justice system or seeking a plea bargain.

Diversion

diversion
Bypassing the criminal justice system by assigning an offender to a social agency or other institution rather than trying him or her in court.

Diversion is a discretionary decision that can occur at many points as the case progresses through the criminal justice process. For example, a police officer diverts when he or she assumes custody of an intoxicated person and releases that person to the custody of family or a detoxification center. Likewise a prosecutor who delays prosecution while a defendant participates in psychiatric treatment diverts. In both cases a discretionary decision is made that there is a more appropriate way to deal with the defendant than to prosecute.

Diversion provides justice system decision makers expanded options with which to respond to criminal behavior. Diversion can be a valuable tool for helping low-level or first-time offenders stay out of the formal court system and link them to supervised services, such as drug treatment. This population of offenders who need treatment might be better served outside the traditional court setting. Ways in which diversion might work include

- Charges are not pressed as long as the defendant fulfills the requirements of the diversion program (e.g., attends a set number of classes or performs a certain number of hours of community service)
- A charge is brought and suspended until the defendant fulfills program requirements
- A defendant enters a guilty plea, which is then dismissed once he or she completes the program requirements ("Using Diversion as Part of a Problem-Solving Strategy," 2010, p.1)

In advocating diversion for petty crimes, a report by the National Association of Criminal Defense Lawyers (NACDL), *Minor Crimes, Massive Waste: The Terrible Toll of America's Broken Misdemeanor Courts* (Boruchowitz, 2009, p.1) states, "The explosive growth of misdemeanor cases is placing a staggering burden on America's courts. Defenders across the country are forced to carry unethical caseloads that leave too little time for clients to be properly represented. As a result, constitutional obligations are left unmet and taxpayers' money is wasted."

The NACDL undertook a comprehensive examination of misdemeanor courts across the country and concluded that they are "incapable of providing accused individuals with the due process guaranteed them by the Constitution. As a result, every year literally millions of accused misdemeanants, overwhelmingly those unable to hire private counsel and disproportionately people of color, are denied their constitutional right to equal justice."

Twenty years ago the National Advisory Commission on Criminal Justice Standards and Goals set a caseload limit of 400 misdemeanors for full-time public defenders, and in 2007 the American Council of Chief Defenders also recommended that defenders handle no more than 400 misdemeanors per year: "Despite these standards, across the country, lawyers who are appointed to represent people charged with misdemeanors have caseloads so overwhelming that they literally have only minutes to prepare each case" (Boruchowitz, 2009, p.21). Even at the set standard of 400 cases per year, the attorney would have only 6 hours to prepare the case. The NADCL report (Boruchowitz, 2009, p.15) quotes a deputy public advocate from Kentucky as saying, "The dirty little secret of the criminal justice system is that most eligible people do not get defenders." The report also recommends to divert all misdemeanants who do not threaten public safety and impart penalties that are less costly than a court trial to taxpayers (p.1).

What accounts for this impossible overload? One possible cause is overcriminalization and the zealous enforcement of crimes that were once simply deemed undesirable behavior and punished by a fine, such as leash laws for pets, seatbelt laws, turnstile jumping, fish and game violations, laws against riding bicycles on the sidewalk, and similar minor offenses (Boruchowitz, 2009, pp.25–26). Another possible source of case overload is the movement toward proactive policing and the efforts of many jurisdictions to crack down on incivilities that may have previously gone unenforced.

As might be expected, diversion has its opponents, including many in law enforcement. Some feel this is "letting criminals off easy." However, major benefits can result, including saving court time; avoiding the stigma of conviction, particularly for first-time offenders; providing treatment for offenders whose criminal activity is the result of an addiction or disorder; allowing offenders to repay society through community service or other work programs; and easing overcrowding in correctional facilities. In today's economy, criminal justice policies and practices must be based on sound use of cost-benefit ratios and direct limited resources to where they will be most effective and provide the greatest return on investment.

The burgeoning caseloads facing most courts put pressure on everyone involved in the courtroom work group—defenders, prosecutors and judges—to resolve cases quickly. How? Commonly through plea bargaining.

Plea Bargaining

plea bargaining
A legal negotiation between the prosecutor and the defense lawyer or the defendant to reach an agreement or compromise that avoids a court trial, conserving time and expense.

Plea bargaining is legal negotiation between the prosecutor and the defense lawyer or the defendant to reach an agreement or compromise that avoids a court trial, conserving time and expense. Most studies on plea bargaining have one common thread—the percentage of defendants pleading guilty in federal and state criminal cases has remained typically high. Actually, most cases—nearly 95 percent by some estimates—are disposed of through plea bargaining, not by court trial.

Basically plea bargaining involves compromises and promises, with prosecutors having great discretion in plea negotiations with defendants. From the prosecutor's perspective, a plea bargain might mean that if a series of charges had been filed, the defendant would be charged with only one; all other charges would be dismissed. It might also mean the prosecutor would reduce a charge if only one charge had been filed. A charge of burglary might be reduced to breaking and entering, which carries a lesser penalty. In many jurisdictions across the country, the courtroom work group has reached a mutual understanding about the "going rate" for particular offenses, meaning if one knows the seriousness of the top charge or crime involved and the defendant's prior criminal record, the outcome of the plea bargain can be predicted with a high degree of regularity (Walker, 2006, p.171). Although the "going rate" may vary from jurisdiction to jurisdiction, there is little denying the pervasiveness of such dispositional consensuses among courtroom work groups nationwide, to the point that these shared perspectives about what a case is "worth" mean that little "bargaining" actually needs to occur (Walker).

Social scientists and legal scholars have debated whether this dominant method for disposing of cases is suitable, with most academics and policy makers supporting the position that the system is in dire need of reform (Bowen, 2009, p.3). A review of the literature suggests that the focus of reform should be on achieving a better balance of power between the prosecution and the defense. (The enormous power of the prosecutor has been discussed.)

One approach to achieving this balance of power is through the creation of an early plea unit (EPU) where nondrug felony plea negotiations take place (Bowen, 2009). These highly formalized, rationalized units handle negotiations institutionally separate from the trying of cases. A prosecuting attorney and a plea-negotiating attorney meet independently of the trial attorneys. Prosecutors charge conservatively, and the defense attorney knows what to expect. If their clients plead guilty, the low range of the appropriate sentence will likely be recommended.

The most common type of plea is that arranged for those accused of a misdemeanor to plead guilty at their first appearance, without benefit of an attorney. "Prosecutors use one-time only plea offers to force early pleas. Judges utilize bail determinations and the threat of pretrial incarceration to encourage early pleas. Defenders, if they are even involved, note that a better deal might not come along and that they have no time to fully investigate the client's case. As a result, an extraordinary number of misdemeanor defendants plead guilty at their first appearance in court whether or not they committed the crime. . . . Often in misdemeanor courts, defendants are not informed of their right to counsel under the Sixth Amendment, or are coerced into waiving counsel to avoid having to spend additional time in jail awaiting the appointment. Sometimes they are even required to pay an application fee in order to obtain the counsel that is guaranteed by the Constitution" (Boruchowitz, 2009, p.2). Further, in some states defendants are usually told they must talk to a prosecutor about the case and get a plea offer before they are allowed to have a lawyer appointed. No matter what the plea offers, in millions of cases, defendants are deprived of their right to a trial.

THE TRIAL

The trial is the climax in the criminal justice procedure. How well the police have investigated the case, compiled evidence and reported it, and dealt with the victim and witnesses are weighed in the courtroom. The trial also tests how well the prosecutor prepared the case.

The key figures in the trial are the judge, members of the jury, the defendant and defense attorney(s), the prosecuting attorney(s), police officer(s) and witnesses. The judge has charge of the trial and decides all matters with respect to the law. He or she also ensures that all rules of trial procedure are followed. If a defendant chooses to waive a jury and appear before the judge only, it is called a **bench trial**.

bench trial

When a defendant chooses to waive a jury and appear only before a judge.

The jury—people selected by law and sworn to examine the facts and determine the truth—decides all matters of fact. The trial begins with the jury selection. Before a jury can be assembled, the geographic location of the trial, called the **venue**, must be determined. A trial's venue is usually the same area in which the offense occurred. However, if a case has received such extensive publicity that picking an impartial jury from the local population is impossible, the trial may be moved to another part of the state, a process called a *change of venue.*

venue

The local area where a case may be tried; it is usually required that the trial for an offense be held in the same area in which the offense occurred.

Jury Selection

Safeguards built into the jury selection process protect the defendant's rights and ensure the public that justice is done. Trial jurors are selected at random from voting or motor vehicle records or telephone directories by district or superior court judges or the commissioners of the county board. The defense attorney and then the prosecuting attorney question each person about his or her qualifications to be a juror in this case. The judge may also question the prospective jurors. The random selection of potential jurors and the careful questioning of each, called **voir dire**, helps ensure selection of 6 or 12 fair and impartial jurors.

voir dire

The random selection of potential jurors and the careful questioning of each.

Some critics of the present jury system claim that our legal system has gotten too complex for the average person to render a fair decision. Others contend the media and the movie industry's portrayal of the criminal courtroom has given the public unrealistic expectations of how the process should work. (Recall the CSI effect from Chapter 6.) Some advocate replacing the present system with a three-judge tribunal.

Testimony

After the jury is selected and instructed by the judge, opening statements are presented. The prosecutor informs the jury of the state's case and how he or she intends to prove the charges against the defendant. The defense lawyer makes an opening statement in support of the accused or may waive this opening statement.

The prosecutor then presents evidence and the witness testimony, attempting to prove a crime has been committed and that the defendant did it. Through **cross-examination** the defense attorney tries to discredit prosecution witnesses, the evidence and the testimony of the police officers.

cross-examination

Questioning of an opposing witness in a trial or hearing.

Closing Statements and Jury Deliberation

After all testimony has been given, the jury hears the closing statements—a contest in persuasion first by the prosecution, stating that the jury should render a guilty verdict, then by the defense attorney, concluding that the defendant is surely innocent or at least not proven guilty beyond a reasonable doubt.

After the closing statements, the judge reads the instructions to the jury. This includes an explanation of the crime, what elements constitute the crime, alternate charges and the concepts of presumption of innocence and reasonable doubt. The jurors then retire behind closed doors to deliberate their findings. They can return one of three findings: guilty, not guilty or no verdict. *No verdict* simply means that no agreement can be reached; this is also sometimes known as a **hung jury**.

hung jury

A jury that cannot reach a decision; the result is a "no verdict" decision that can result in a retrial.

After the jury has come to a decision, the judge is notified and the jury returns to the courtroom. With everyone present the jury foreperson announces the verdict. Jurors may then be polled as to how each voted and asked if the verdict read by the foreperson is the verdict of the juror. If the finding is guilty, the defendant may either be sentenced immediately or be given a sentencing date. If found not guilty, he or she is set free. If a hung jury results, the defendant may be retried at the prosecutor's discretion.

Sentencing

Sentences for people convicted of crimes vary considerably from lenient to extremely severe penalties, from probation to many years in prison or even death. In many jurisdictions the court has the authority to set, within limits established by state statute, both maximum and minimum sentences. Judges have a host of intermediate choices available, as shown in Figure 13.6. In 2006 an estimated 69 percent of all persons convicted of a felony in state courts were sentenced to a period of confinement—41 percent to state prison and 28 percent to local jails (Durose et al., 2009).

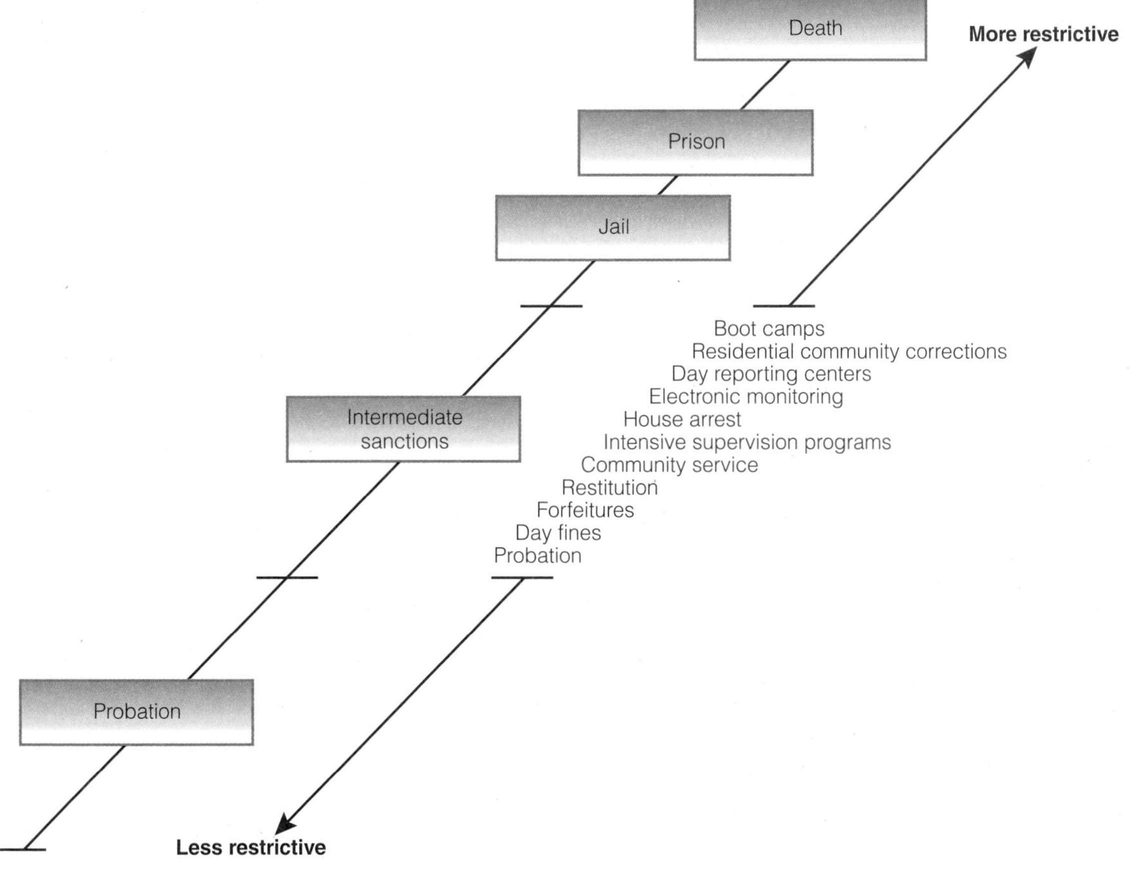

FIGURE 13.6 The Sentencing Continuum

SOURCE: Norman A. Carlson, Kären M. Hess and Christine M. H. Orthmann. *Corrections in the 21st Century: A Practical Approach.* Belmont, CA: West/Wadsworth Publishing Company, 1999, p.101. Reprinted by permission.

Sentencing Guidelines The Federal Sentencing Guidelines set out a uniform sentencing policy for defendants convicted of felonies and serious misdemeanors in the federal system. The guidelines are intended to alleviate sentencing disparities that research has indicated are prevalent in the existing sentencing system. The sentences are based primarily on two factors: the offense level and the defendant's criminal history. These guidelines are advisory only, both at the state and federal level. To pass a prison sentence, a judge cross-references the offense level with the criminal history on the guideline table to determine the recommended number of months to be served. Some circumstances, considered mitigating factors, warrant giving the lowest number of months, for example, if a defendant has been cooperative with the government, takes responsibility or shows remorse. Other circumstances, known as aggravating factors, warrant giving the maximum recommended sentence, for example, the offense being gang-related or a hate crime.

Research on whether the sentencing guidelines achieved their stated purpose of uniformity in federal sentencing and reduced inter-judge disparity in sentencing found "mixed support" for the claim that the guidelines produced uniformity in sentencing decisions (Anderson and Spohn, 2010, pp.386–387). The study found that the prison sentences offenders received depended to some extent on the judge who heard the case. Three offender characteristics had differential effects on the sentences imposed, with female offenders, employed offenders and offenders released before sentencing receiving lesser sentences (Anderson and Spohn).

Doerner and Demuth (2010) used data compiled by the U.S. Sentencing Commission to study the effects of the extralegal characteristics of race/ethnicity, gender and age on sentencing and found that particularly harsh sentences were focused on a narrow segment of the defendant population—young, Black males. The researchers findings also support a growing body of literature that, like Black defendants, Hispanic defendants may be "disadvantaged" within state and federal court systems (Doerner and Demuth, p.23).

Three-Strikes Laws, Mandatory Minimums and Truth-in-Sentencing In the effort to crack down on crime and get tough on criminals, sentences for repeat offenders and those convicted of certain crimes have become tougher. One popular sentencing reform has been "three-strikes" laws, first enacted in California, which require judges to impose life sentences on offenders who commit their third felony. Yet another get-tough-on-crime reform is the mandatory minimum sentences for certain offenses, most notably drug and weapons offenses. Truth-in-sentencing laws aim to restrict or stop early-release practices and keep offenders incarcerated for the duration of their sentences.

Such legislation, however, is being criticized for its inability to achieve the desired results and its significant contribution to prison overcrowding.

Mandatory minimums have also been blamed for filling up the nation's prisons with nonviolent offenders more in need of treatment than incarceration. Such sentencing schemes are falling out of favor with many judges.

Case Review and Appeal

To ensure that justice is served, the court system provides for a judicial review of cases and for a person convicted to appeal the conviction in most instances. Once the sentence has been passed, the corrections component of the justice system—the final stage in the administration of U.S. criminal justice—takes over, as discussed in Chapter 14.

THE POLICE OFFICER IN COURT

Almost all officers have a day in court. Because of overloaded court dockets, cases usually come up well after the officers' investigations; therefore, officers must refer to their reports and their original notes to refresh their memories. A court appearance is an important part of any police officer's duty. All elements of the investigation are brought together at this point: the report, the statements of the witnesses, the evidence collected and possibly even a confession.

The prosecution needs to establish the elements of the crime by testimony of witnesses, physical evidence, documents, recordings or other admissible evidence. This information usually comes from police officers, their recollections, notes and reports. The prosecutor works with police officers in preparing and presenting the arguments for the prosecution.

A Denver police officer testifies during the trial of a man charged with second-degree murder in the death of a Denver detective and attempted first-degree murder and assault in the wounding of another detective. The officer on the witness stand was one of the first officers to arrive at the scene of the shootings. Despite the highly emotional nature of the testimony, officers must maintain truthfulness when testifying in court.

Preparing a Case for Prosecution

Preparation plays the biggest part in an officer's success on the witness stand. The more prepared they are, the more confident they will appear—and be—in front of the jury, and the less likely they will fall victim to the many ploys the defense may use.

The prosecution must prove the case *beyond a reasonable doubt*—the degree of proof necessary to obtain a conviction. To assist in this effort, officers should:

- Review and evaluate all evidence, positive and negative, and the chain of custody.
- Review all reports on the case.
- Prepare witnesses.
- Hold a pretrial conference with the prosecutor.

At the pretrial conference all evidence is reviewed. Especially important is a review of any digital evidence because the defense is likely to attack it as having been manipulated in some way (*Digital Evidence in the Courtroom*, 2007). The strengths and weaknesses of the case are discussed, as is the probable line of questioning by the prosecutor and the defense. The prosecutor may be able to offer insights into the style of the defense attorney as well as the judge hearing the case. If witnesses are included in the pretrial conference, officers should listen carefully to what each witness says because during the trial, the judge may exclude all witnesses from the courtroom except the person testifying. For this same reason, officers should also review the case with other officers who are going to testify.

Shortly before the trial, officers again review their notes and final report and confirm that the physical evidence is being taken to the courtroom and will be available for the prosecuting attorney when needed. They also confirm that laboratory technicians are available to appear when necessary.

Appearing as a Witness

Most police departments have regulations regarding attire when officers appear in court. Some departments specify that officers should appear in uniform. The wearing of service weapons in the courtroom is governed by jurisdictional policy. Some areas require uniformed officers to wear their firearms visibly; others dictate that a weapon should not be visible. If an officer wears other attire, such as a suit, policy may set forth that a weapon may be concealed under the suit jacket, with the police badge right next to it.

Officers should not discuss the case while waiting in the hallway to testify, or joke with the defense attorney, even if on good terms with them. If a juror or another witness hears an officer's statements, the officer may have created grounds for a mistrial. It is not possible for officers to avoid all contact with jurors, and chance contacts—passing in the hall or crowded in an elevator—may be unavoidable. In such instances, ***de minimus* communication**, that is, a simple hello or giving directions, is allowable. It is important that officers not appear aloof or unfriendly.

de minimus communication

A simple hello or giving directions.

The most important rule for testifying in court is to always tell the truth.

Officers who tell the truth do not have to worry about being tripped up on cross-examination, being contradicted or not having their testimony corroborated by other witnesses. In addition, at the end of their testimony, when the last question has been answered, the jury must find them *credible*, that is, believable.

It is imperative that police officers take seriously the role of witness and the duty of testifying for successful conclusion of their cases and for their own reputations. During their careers, officers may testify on many occasions and will develop reputations—whether good or bad—among judges, prosecutors and regular defense attorneys. Members of the courtroom work group often learn the reputations of the local police officers regarding their effectiveness on the witness stand. If the police officer has a strong professional and credible reputation, there is a likelihood that the defense may not even pursue a trial if they can plea a better deal. However, the testimony of officers who have poor reputations or are new tends to be challenged more often.

Testifying under Direct Examination

First impressions are critical. When an officer's name is called, he or she should answer "Here" or "Present" and move directly to the front of the courtroom, going behind the attorneys. Officers should never walk in front of the judge, between the judge and the attorney's tables. This area, called the **well**, is off-limits and is to be entered only if the judge so directs or permission is granted. Traditionally, the area was a sword's length and was intended for the judge's protection.

well
The area between the judge and the attorney's tables; this area is off-limits and is to be entered only if a judge so directs or permission is granted.

Notes or a report should be carried in a clean manila file folder in the left hand so the right hand is free for taking the oath. If the reports are bulky, many experts on testifying recommend placing them under the witness chair until needed. Officers must avoid making inadmissible statements including opinions and conclusions (unless the witness is qualified as an expert), hearsay, privileged communications and statements about character and reputation, including the defendant's criminal record.

The prosecutor will determine the line of questioning. Prosecutors may point out any problems with the case. Officers should be supportive because they are on the same team.

Officers should

- Speak clearly, firmly and with expression.
- Answer questions directly. Do *not* volunteer information.
- Pause briefly before answering.
- Refer to their notes if they do not recall exact details.
- Admit calmly when they do not know an answer.
- Admit any mistakes they make in testifying.
- Avoid police jargon, sarcasm and humor.

Testifying under Cross-Examination

Recall the earlier description of the adversary system. It is understandable why an investigator would consider the defense attorney's cross-examination an attack on the prosecution's case. Officers should be aware of tactics the defense attorney may use to **impeach** (discredit) them.

impeach
Discredit.

During cross-examination the defense attorney may

- Be disarmingly friendly or intimidatingly rude.
- Attack an officer's credibility and impartiality.
- Attack an officer's investigative skill.
- Attempt to force contradictions or inconsistencies.
- Ask leading questions or deliberately misquote an officer's statement.
- Ask for a simple answer to a complex question.
- Use the silent treatment.

The defense attorney can be extremely friendly, hoping to put officers off guard by making the questioning appear to be just a friendly chat. The attorney may praise an officer's skill in investigation and lead him or her into boasting or a show of self-glorification that will leave a bad impression on the jury. The "friendly" defense attorney may also try to lead officers into testifying about evidence of which they have no personal knowledge. This error will be immediately exposed and officers' testimony tainted, if not completely discredited.

At the opposite extreme is the defense attorney who appears outraged by officers' statements and goes on the attack immediately. This kind of attorney appears excited and outraged, as though the trial is a travesty of justice. A natural reaction to such an approach is for officers to exaggerate their testimony or lose their temper, which is exactly what the defense attorney wants. If officers show anger, the jury may believe they are more interested in obtaining a conviction than in uncovering the truth.

The defense attorney may also try to confuse or discredit a police officer by (1) rapid-fire questioning, (2) establishing that the officer wants to see the defendant found guilty, (3) accusing the officer of making assumptions or (4) implying that the officer does not want anyone else to know what is in his or her notes.

An example of a defense team able to discredit a police officer was seen in the O. J. Simpson trial when defense attorneys were able to challenge the testimony given by former Los Angeles Police Department Detective Mark Fuhrman—causing him to assert his Fifth Amendment right against self-incrimination.

To avoid objections to testimony, officers should avoid conclusions and nonresponsive answers and should answer yes-or-no questions with "yes" or "no."

Expert Testimony

Rule 702 of the Federal Rules of Evidence states, "If scientific, technical or other specialized knowledge will assist the trier of fact to understand the evidence or to determine a fact in issue, a witness qualified as an expert by knowledge, skill, experience, training or education, may testify thereto in the form of an opinion or otherwise, if (1) the testimony is based upon sufficient facts of data, (2) the testimony is the product of reliable principles and methods, and (3) the witness has applied the principles and methods reliably to the facts of the case."

Daubert v. Merrell-Dow Pharmaceuticals, Inc. (1993) established standards for the admission of expert testimony in federal courts. Under *Daubert*, an expert's testimony must be specialized and relate directly to some fact at issue in the case. Officers who qualify as experts in an area are allowed to give opinions and conclusions, but the prosecution must qualify the officer as an expert on the stand. The prosecution must establish that the person has special knowledge that others of moderate education or experience in the same field do not possess. To qualify as an expert witness, one must have as many of the following as possible:

- Present or prior employment in the specific field
- Active membership in a professional group in the field
- Research work in the field
- An educational degree directly related to the field
- Direct experience with the subject if not employed in the field
- Papers, treatises or books published on the subject or teaching experience in it

Police officers can become experts on sounds, firearms, distances, lengths of time, visibility problems and so on simply through years of experience in police work. Other areas, such as firearms identification, drug recognition, fingerprint classification and handwriting analysis, require specialized training. Just who qualifies as an expert is not always clear, and different qualifications may exist for scientific and nonscientific evidence.

After Testifying

Officers should not leave the stand until instructed to do so by the counsel or the court. Officers who are in the courtroom at the time of the verdict must show neither approval nor disapproval at the outcome. If they have been credible witnesses and told the truth, win or lose in court, they have done their job and should not take the outcome personally.

The complainant should be notified of the disposition of the case. A form such as the one shown in Figure 13.7 is frequently used.

Before concluding this chapter, it is prudent to briefly consider the topic of courtroom security because it can affect police officers in several ways, whether they are working security detail in a courtroom or attending trial in uniform.

COURTROOM SECURITY

Court security is a relatively new concept that has resulted from several high-profile incidents of courthouse violence and shootings. In many major and established courtrooms, licensed deputies serve as professional security forces to secure the main entrances to the court house. Visitors and court employees passing through such entrances are screened in a manner very similar to that conducted by airport security, with much of the same technology used for screening items and detecting weapons and other contraband, such as explosives.

The following extract is a brief document made available by the National Sheriffs' Associations pertaining to the history and evolution of courtroom security:

Case disposition report

Date disposition made: 4–25–20 D.R. #: 97–1002
Date of incident: 2–10–20 Type of incident: Burglary

Disposition:
(x) Case clearance
(x) Property recovered
( ) Disposition of property: (x) Owner ( ) Police evidence
( ) Other
If Other specify type:

Victim: (If runaway juvenile or missing adullt, disregard this section)
Name Jerome Slater Address 3041 Harding, Edina, Minnesota

Suspect(s):

	Name	Arrested?	BCPD I.D. #
No. 1:	John Toben	Yes	20146
No. 2:	William Moss	Yes	20147
No. 3:			

Property recovered:

Item	Description	Value
Item no. 1:	One Car Radio, Sears	$87.00
Item no. 2:	One Car Battery, Sears	60.00
Item no. 3:	Micro Wave Oven-GE	250.00
Item no. 4:	One 17" TV-Sears Solid State	350.00

Recovering agency: Edina Police Department Total value recovered property: $747.00

Cancellations: (Specify date, time, agency and officer receiving cancellation and officer making cancellation)

NCIC:
Other agencies: Hennepin County Sheriffs Office
Other agencies:

Officer making disposition:
Supervisor approving:
Details: Full recovery of property

FIGURE 13.7 Case Disposition Notice

The security in the courtroom and the courthouse varies considerably throughout the United States. In some states the Sheriff is mandated to "attend court"; in some states no one is assigned the task. In some jurisdictions the Sheriff has assumed the responsibility because he is the most logical choice and best prepared for the duty, while in a few instances responsibility for court security is divided or not clearly defined. One form that has shown success is when all stakeholders have established a courthouse security committee. An example of committee participants where the sheriff has statutory responsibility would be the Sheriff, Chief Judge, Commissioners or County Board Members, facility or maintenance manager, and other elected or appointed officials that occupy the court facility. The participants best decide the makeup of a committee, and the general concept is to involve everyone that has a responsibility in the court facility. This involvement allows for the security to be addressed from all vantage points and allows incorporation into design of new facilities, upkeep and efficient coverage of existing facilities, and permits those responsible for the protection of the facility a "seat at the table."

In 1994 the National Sheriffs' Association published the results of a two-year study relating to the security in the nation's state and local courts. This study became a national reference for the improvement of court security. The National Sheriff's Association served as a consultant to the United States Marshals Service in the development and training of court security professionals. The evidence is that since the 1980s up to the present, the perpetrators of court violence are ever changing and employing all methods of disruptions. Intimidation, actual violence within the courthouse and courtrooms, explosives set outside and inside, and since September 2001 the new threat of terrorist attack by individuals merely wishing to inflict destruction on American soil have been added to this mix of violence.

Recent past events involving the judiciary and all its stakeholders clearly demonstrate the need to assess the vulnerability of judges, staffs, witnesses, and the general citizenry who utilize the courthouse and all the public offices that are located in our nation's courthouses. Added to this equation is the increasing occurrence of violence within the workplace. Incidents involving employees, customers, and the relationship mix that is brought to the workplace has increased the need for a well-trained security staff and an informed and trained support staff. Security is no longer protecting the court; it has expanded to a situation that courthouses and their immediate areas now need a security component that can only best be described as a police district in and of itself functioning as any unit with the duty to serve and protect.

Summary

Our judicial system operates at both the state and federal levels. The hierarchy at the state level often goes up from courts of special or limited jurisdiction called justice of the peace (J.P.) courts, to trial courts or original and general jurisdiction courts (including probate court, municipal court, county court, circuit court, district court and superior court), to intermediate appellate courts, to the state supreme court. The federal court system has three tiers: district courts, appellate courts and the U.S. Supreme Court.

A specialized type of court is the juvenile court. The Juvenile Court Act equated poor and abused children with delinquent and criminal children and provided that they be treated in essentially the same way, establishing a one-pot approach. Historically, juvenile courts have been informal, private, non-adversarial systems that stress rehabilitation rather than punishment of youths.

Our criminal justice system is based on the adversary system, which requires that the accuser prove beyond a reasonable doubt to a judge or jury that the accused is guilty of a specified crime. Key players in the judicial process include the defendant, prosecutor, defense attorney, judge and jury. Prosecutors have the dual function of leading the law enforcement community while protecting the rights of the accused. The criminal justice process consists of several critical stages: complaint or charge, warrant, arrest, booking, preliminary hearing, grand jury hearing, arraignment, trial and sentencing. The preliminary hearing seeks to establish probable cause to prevent people from being indiscriminately brought to trial. Before cases go to court, defense attorneys may explore the possibility of diverting the case from the criminal justice system or seeking a plea bargain.

Police officers' testimony at the trial is of great importance. The most important rule for testifying in court is to always tell the truth. Officers should be aware of tactics the defense attorney may use to impeach (discredit) them. During cross-examination the defense attorney may

- Be disarmingly friendly or intimidatingly rude.
- Attack an officer's credibility and impartiality.
- Attack an officer's investigative skill.
- Attempt to force contradictions or inconsistencies.
- Ask leading questions or deliberately misquote an officer's statement.
- Ask for a simple answer to a complex question.
- Use the silent treatment.

Other tactics often used by defense attorneys to confuse or discredit a police officer who is testifying include (1) rapid-fire questioning, (2) establishing that the officer wants to see the defendant found guilty, (3) accusing the officer of making assumptions or (4) implying that the officer does not want anyone else to know what is in his or her notes. To avoid objections to testimony, officers should avoid conclusions and nonresponsive answers and answer yes-or-no questions with "yes" or "no."

Discussion Questions

1. Is the jury system really fair?
2. Should the police be consulted when plea bargaining is used?
3. Is our system truly an adversary system when the prosecutor also has to protect the accused's rights?
4. Do you feel diversion is an acceptable alternative in some instances? If so, when? If not, why?
5. Does your community use any form of community prosecution or community courts? If so, what?
6. Do you feel the process of justice should be the same for juveniles as it is for adults?
7. If you were accused of a crime, would you prefer a trial with or without a jury?
8. Is there a better system than the jury system?
9. Does an acquittal mean the investigator failed?
10. How prevalent do you believe "testilying" (not telling the truth) is by law enforcement officers?

Gale Emergency Services Database Assignments

- Use the Gale Emergency Services Database to help answer the Discussion Questions as appropriate.
- Using the Gale Emergency Services Database, find articles on *restorative justice*. Find and outline at least two articles on the subject. Be prepared to discuss your outlines with the class.

- Using the Gale Emergency Services Database, find the article "Taking on Testilying: The Prosecutor's Response to In-Court Police Deception": http://find.galegroup.com/gps/retrieve.do?contentSet=IAC-Documents&resultListType=RESULT_LIST&qrySerId=Locale%28en%2C%2C%29%3AFQE%3D%28K0%2CNone%2C22%29police+court+testimony%24&sgHitCountType=None&inPS=true&sort=DateDescend&searchType=BasicSearchForm&tabID=T002&prodId=IPS&searchId=R1¤tPosition=1&userGroupName=cpg3&docId=A56952271&docType=IAC&contentSet=IAC-Documents

  Assignment: Read the text and examine the problem of "testilying." Outline the article's major points and be prepared to discuss this issue in class.

- Using the Gale Emergency Services Database, find the article "Juvenile Mental Health Court Opens in Cleveland": http://find.galegroup.com/gps/retrieve.do?contentSet=IAC-Documents&resultListType=RESULT_LIST&qrySerId=Locale%28en%2C%2C%29%3AFQE%3D%28ke%2CNone%2C14%29court+violence%24&sgHitCountType=None&inPS=true&sort=DateDescend&searchType=BasicSearchForm&tabID=T004&prodId=IPS&searchId=R2¤tPosition=1&userGroupName=cpg3&docId=A178758362&docType=IAC&contentSet=IAC-Documents

  Assignment: Read the article and identify the goal of this specialized court, paying attention to the statistics referenced in it. Do you think court resources that are directed to crime this specific is good or bad? Why or why not? Be prepared to discuss and defend your position in class.

- Using the Gale Emergency Services Database, find the article "Supreme Court Cases 2008-2009 Term" (Legal Digest): http://find.galegroup.com/gps/retrieve.do?contentSet=IAC-Documents&resultListType=RESULT_LIST&qrySerId=Locale%28en%2C%2C%29%3AFQE%3D%28ke%2CNone%2C29%29supreme+court+law+enforcement%24&sgHitCountType=None&inPS=true&sort=DateDescend&searchType=BasicSearchForm&tabID=T003&prodId=IPS&searchId=R3¤tPosition=1&userGroupName=cpg3&docId=A209698194&docType=IAC&contentSet=IAC-Documents

  Assignment: Read this article and identify two or more court cases that affect law enforcement. Be prepared to discuss your findings in class.

- Using the Gale Emergency Services Database, find the article "Teen Court": http://find.galegroup.com/gps/retrieve.do?contentSet=IAC-Documents&resultListType=RESULT_LIST&qrySerId=Locale%28en%2C%2C%29%3AFQE%3D%28ke%2CNone%2C15%29juvenile+courts%24&sgHitCountType=None&inPS=true&sort=DateDescend&searchType=BasicSearchForm&tabID=T003&prodId=IPS&searchId=R4¤tPosition=2&userGroupName=cpg3&docId=A19545727&docType=IAC&contentSet=IAC-Documents

  Assignment: Read this article and be prepared to explain in class how juvenile courts differ from adult courts. Also, be prepared to discuss if you support having the courts separated or unified. Why or why not?

- Using the Gale Emergency Services Database, find the article "The Boundaries of Plea Bargaining: Negotiating the Standard of Proof": http://find.galegroup.com/gps/retrieve.do?contentSet=IAC-Documents&resultListType=RESULT_LIST&qrySerId=Locale%28en%2C%2C%29%3AFQE%3D%28ke%2CNone%2C15%29plea+bargaining%24&sgHitCountType=None&inPS=true&sort=DateDescend&searchType=BasicSearchForm&tabID=T002&prodId=IPS&searchId=R7¤tPosition=7&userGroupName=cpg3&docId=A178186954&docType=IAC&contentSet=IAC-Documents

  Assignment: Read and summarize this article. Be prepared to discuss this in detail in class.

 Internet Assignment

- Research televising courtroom cases on the Web and find at least two articles to outline. What are the pros and cons associated with this practice? What are the various legal considerations and challenges involved? Be prepared to discuss your findings with the class.

References

Anderson, Amy L., and Spohn, Cassia. "Lawlessness in the Federal Sentencing Process: A Test for Uniformity and Consistency in Sentence Outcomes." *Justice Quarterly*, June 2010, pp.362–393.

Annual Report of the Center for Court Innovation. New York: Center for Court Innovation, 2009.

Boruchowitz, Robert C.; Brink, Malia N.; and Dimino, Maureen. *Minor Crimes, Massive Waste: The Terrible Toll of America's Broken Misdemeanor Courts*. Washington, DC: National Association of Criminal Defense Lawyers, April 2009.

Bowen, Deirdre M. "Calling Your Bluff: How Prosecutors and Defense Attorneys Adapt Plea Bargaining Strategies to Increased Formalization." *Justice Quarterly*, March 2009, pp.2–29.

Digital Evidence in the Courtroom: A Guide for Law Enforcement and Prosecutors. Washington, DC: National Institute of Justice, January 2007.

Doerner, Jill K., and Demuth, Stephen. "The Independent and Joint Effects of Race/Ethnicity, Gender and Age on Sentencing Outcomes in U.S. Federal Courts." *Justice Quarterly*, February 2010, pp.1–27.

Doniger, Kate. "Inspiring the Judiciary: Community Courts Adapt Community Policing Principles." *Community Policing Dispatch*, February 2009.

Durose, Matthew R.; Farole, Donald; and Rosenmerkel, Sean P. "Felony Sentences in State Courts, 2006." Washington, DC: Bureau of Justice Statistics, December 30, 2009. (NCJ 226846)

Garrett, Ronnie. "A Jury of Their Peers." *Law Enforcement Technology*, July 2009, pp.44–50.

Glaze, Lauren E., and Bonczar, Thomas P. *Probation and Parole in the United States, 2008*. Washington, DC: Bureau of Justice Statistics Bulletin, December 2009. (NCJ 228230)

Goodwin, Tracy; with Steinhart, David J.; and Fulton, Betsy A. *Peer Justice and Youth Empowerment: An Implementation Guide for Teen Court Programs*. Washington, DC: U.S. Department of Transportation, National Highway Traffic Safety Administration; American Probation and Parole Association; and the U.S. Department of Justice, Office of Juvenile Justice and Delinquency Prevention, no date.

Gun Court. Washington, DC: Office of Juvenile Justice Delinquency Prevention, 2007.

Hamilton, Zachary. *Do Reentry Courts Reduce Recidivism? Results from the Harlem Parole Reentry Court*. New York: Center for Court Innovation, March 2010.

Mental Health Courts: A National Snapshot. Washington, DC: Bureau of Justice Assistance, no date.

Porter, Rachel; Rempel, Michael; and Mansky, Adam. *What Makes a Court Problem Solving?* Universal Performance Indicators for Problem-Solving Justice. New York: Center for Court Innovation, February 2010.

Shermer, Lauren O'Neill, and Johnson, Brian D. "Criminal Prosecutions: Examining Prosecutorial Discretion and Charge Reductions in U.S. Federal District Courts." *Justice Quarterly*, June 2010, pp.394–430.

"Study Finds Ohio's Adult and Juvenile Drug Courts Reduce Recidivism." *Criminal Justice Research Review*, January/February 2009, pp.51–52.

"Using Diversion as Part of a Problem-Solving Strategy." New York: Center for Court Innovation and the Bureau of Justice Assistance, 2010. Retrieved from Problemsolvingjustice.org

Walker, Samuel. *Sense and Nonsense about Crime and Drugs: A Policy Guide*, 6th ed. Belmont, CA: Thomson Wadsworth, 2006.

Wolf, Robert W. *Don't Reinvent the Wheel.* New York: Center for Court Innovation and the Bureau of Justice Assistance, 2007. Retrieved from Problemsolvingjustice.org

Cases Cited

Berger v. United States, 295 U.S. 78 (1935)

Daubert v. Merrell-Dow Pharmaceuticals, Inc., 509 U.S. 579 (1993)

Escobedo v. Illinois, 378 U.S. 478 (1964)

CHAPTER 14

Corrections

> The fact that so many Americans, including hundreds of thousands who are a threat to no one, are incarcerated means that something is wrong with our criminal justice system and the way we deal with both dangerous criminals and those whose behavior we simply don't like.
>
> —David Keene

Prisoners in one of the Marion County (Indiana) Lockup cells, CM-D, sleep on the floor. Numerous jurisdictions across the country face the issue of overcrowding, with inmate populations near or beyond their intended capacities. Many corrections departments have been using some form of early release to reduce the number of inmates.

Do You Know . . .

- What *corrections* refers to?
- What role law enforcement plays in the correctional system?
- What the primary purposes of corrections are?
- What two conflicting views of criminality compete?
- What four ideologies have developed and with which model each is associated?
- What correctional alternatives to incarceration are being used in the United States?
- Who John Augustus was and what he contributed to corrections?
- How jail differs from prison?
- What term the American Correctional Association recommends replace the term *prison guard*?
- What two philosophies are evident in U.S. prisons?
- How parole differs from probation?
- What factors can facilitate reentry and reduce recidivism?
- What correctional alternatives are available for juveniles?
- What intermediate sanctions are available for juveniles?

Can You Define?

aftercare
boot camp
deterrence
general deterrence
incapacitation
incarceration
intermediate sanctions
just deserts
justice model
lex talionis
medical model
parole
probation
recidivism
rehabilitation
restitution
retribution
shock incarceration
specific deterrence

INTRODUCTION

Corrections is that portion of the criminal justice system charged with carrying out the sentences of our courts. To the public, the term *corrections* is almost synonymous with punishment. It was not until 1954 that the American Prison Association changed its name to the American Correctional Association, reflecting a fundamental paradigm shift in the philosophy of handling those who break the law. Not only was punishment a valid objective but so too was the rehabilitation, or correction, of persons found guilty of crime. However, recidivism rates reveal that all too frequently this does not happen.

Corrections refers to the programs, services, agencies and institutions responsible for supervising individuals charged with or convicted of crimes.

Since the 1960s, corrections has been greatly influenced by several "environments" in addition to the criminal justice system of which it is a part. These environments are illustrated in Figure 14.1.

The pattern of crime to prison to parole to crime and back to prison *ad infinitum* describes what has become called the "revolving door of criminal justice," a loop involving all three components of the justice system. The Bureau of Justice Statistics (BJS) reports that more than 700,000 individuals will be released from

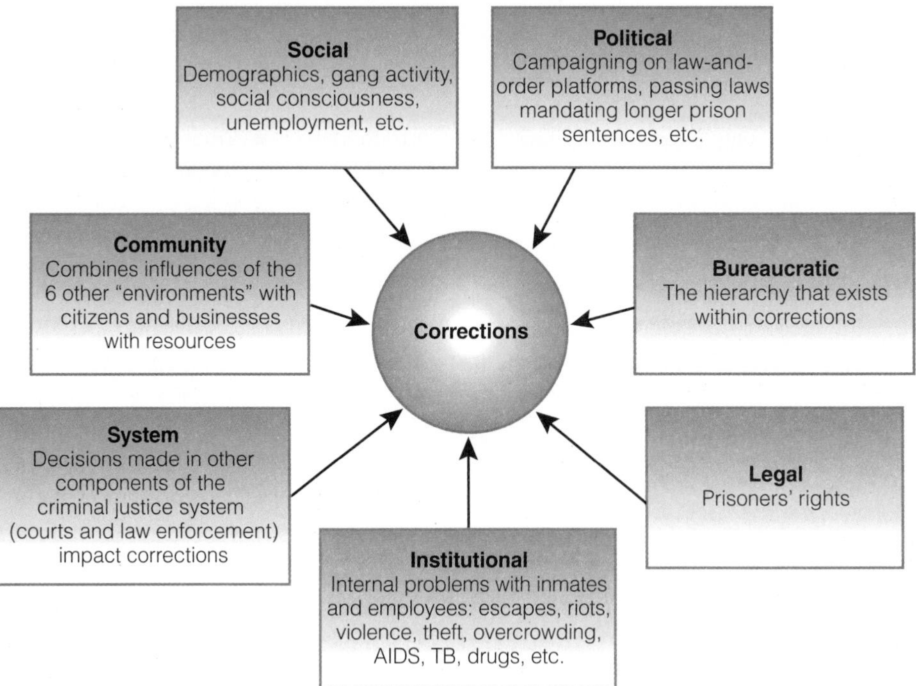

FIGURE 14.1 Environments that Influence Corrections

U.S. state and federal prisons each year, quadruple the number released 30 years ago. At year-end 2008, nearly 5.1 million adults were under community supervision, the equivalent of 1 in every 45 adults in the country. Probationers represented the majority (84 percent), parolees accounted for the remaining 16 percent (Glaze and Bonczar, 2009). In addition, BJS estimates that each year 13 million individuals leave the nation's jails.

If past BJS statistics hold true, more than two-thirds of those released from prison will be arrested for new offenses within three years, and more than 50 percent will return for committing new crimes or for violating conditions of their supervision: "The release and recidivism statistics are not surprising to policing professionals. They only confirm what law enforcement officers have believed all along: that they are arresting and rearresting the same individuals in their jurisdictions time and again" (Jones and Flynn, 2008, p.26).

Law enforcement officers' arrest decisions directly affect who may end up in corrections. Officers are also key partners in reentry efforts, including pretrial supervision, probation and parole.

Too often these offenders have a substance abuse problem or are mentally ill and did not receive appropriate treatment during their incarceration. Jails report inmates with mental illness being booked into the facility as many as 30 to 40 times during a 10-11 year span. One jail reported that a 52-year-old man with mental illness was arrested 300 times during a 20-year period (Gelman, 2010, p.22).

THE CHAPTER AT A GLANCE

This chapter begins with a discussion of the development of corrections and its theoretical roots, including the purposes it has meant to serve through the years. This is followed by an overview of contemporary corrections and a discussion of pretrial services and detention. Then the correctional alternatives available in the community—the intermediate sanctions short of incarceration—are examined, including probation. Next, incarceration and parole are discussed, followed by a look at the role of police in probation and parole, the various community-based reintegration programs that are available, and the issue of recidivism. Then the controversial debate between the death penalty and life without parole is explored. The chapter concludes with a discussion of reentry and a brief look at the juvenile correctional system.

THE DEVELOPMENT OF CORRECTIONS

Throughout history, society has dealt with lawbreakers in many ways and has emphasized different goals and methods to accomplish those goals. The pendulum has swung from seeking pure revenge to viewing criminals as being ill and in need of treatment. It has swung from very public punishment, such as floggings and hangings, to very private punishment, such as solitary confinement (see Figure 14.2). As the pendulum swings, the primary purposes to be served by corrections also shift. No matter where emphasis is placed, however, corrections generally serves four basic, often overlapping, purposes.

The primary purposes of corrections are retribution, deterrence, incapacitation and rehabilitation.

This simple statement belies the complexity of the issues. What purpose or purposes corrections *should* serve has been and continues to be the subject of heated debate.

Retribution is punishment for the sake of punishment and was most prevalent in ancient societies, existing in such approaches as just deserts and *lex talionis*. **Just deserts** means individuals "get what's coming to them." ***Lex talionis*** is a closely related concept based on the notion of "an eye for an eye." Retribution is probably the oldest of the four purposes, a principle dating back at least to biblical times, as found in the Old Testament of the Christian Bible: "Life shall go for life, eye for eye, tooth for tooth, hand for hand, foot for foot" (Deut. 19:21).

retribution
Punishment for the sake of punishment; revenge.

just deserts
Retribution; individuals "get what's coming to them."

lex talionis
An eye for an eye.

Retribution has its roots in the classical theory developed by Italian criminologist Cesare Beccaria (1738–1794), which held that people are rational and responsible for their acts. Recall that the classical theory sees people as free agents with free will. In other words, people commit crimes because they want to.

Criminals must repay society for breaking the law. The just deserts approach to corrections was influenced by Andrew von Hirsch's *Doing Justice*, published in 1976. In this work, von Hirsch contends that criminals should be punished for actions they have already committed, not for what they might do in the future or what others might do without the example of what happens to those who break

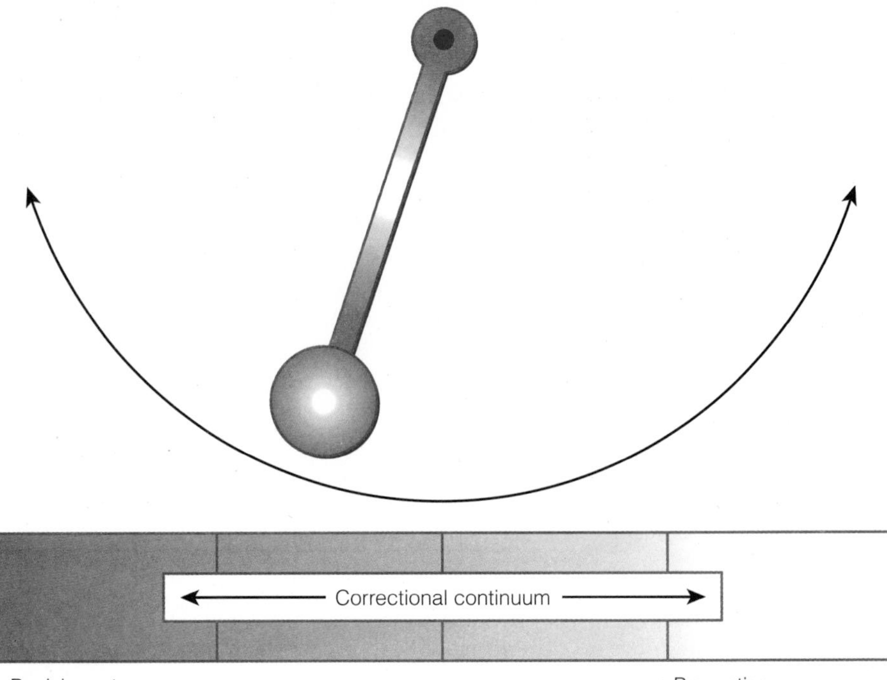

FIGURE 14.2 The Pendulum Effect

restitution

Compensating or making up for loss, damage or injury; requiring an offender to repay the victim or the community in money or services.

deterrence

Sees corrections as a way to prevent future criminal actions; tries to show offenders that the price of committing crimes is too great.

specific deterrence

Deterrence aimed at offenders; attempts to make the consequences of committing crime so severe that when offenders return to society, they will not commit crime.

general deterrence

Deterrence to serve as an example to others of the consequences of crime.

incapacitation

Making it impossible for offenders to commit further offenses.

the law. Retribution focuses almost exclusively on the crime itself rather than on the offender's needs or those of the community. It is almost entirely reactive. More recently retribution has come to include **restitution**, whereby an offender reimburses the victim, most often with money and occasionally with services.

Deterrence sees corrections as a way to prevent future criminal actions, a more functional, proactive view. It is intended to show offenders and would-be offenders that the price for committing crimes is too steep. The pain is greater than the gain. Deterrence aimed at individual offenders is called **specific deterrence**, which tries to make the consequences of committing crime so severe that when offenders return to society, they will not reoffend. Deterrence that serves as an example to society of the consequences of crime is called **general deterrence**. One corrections issue that tests the effectiveness of deterrence is capital punishment. Does the threat of losing one's own life deter a potential murderer? This sensitive and highly controversial issue is discussed later in the chapter.

Incapacitation refers to making it impossible for offenders to commit further offenses. Incapacitation can take many forms. One of the earliest forms was banishment, also referred to as social death. Some people feel this is the ultimate punishment, more devastating than being executed. In preliterate societies, offenders were often cast out from the village. More recently England banished its outlaws and undesirables to Australia and then to the United States.

Other forms of incapacitation make it physically impossible for a criminal act to be repeated. A thief whose hands are cut off will not easily steal again. A castrated male will be unable to rape again. An incarcerated child molester will not be able to abuse children while in prison. And a murderer who is executed will kill no more. Currently, the most common method of incapacitation is incarceration. The most extreme form of incapacitation is capital punishment.

Rehabilitation sees the purpose of corrections to be clear from its name—to *correct* deviant behavior. Rehabilitation is proactive in that it focuses on the future needs of offenders, as well as the needs of the community to which the offenders may return. Voltaire expressed belief in the rehabilitation of offenders when he said, "The punishment of criminals should be of use—when a man is hanged he is good for nothing." Another proponent of this function of corrections was former Chief Justice Warren Burger, who stated, "When society places a person behind walls and bars, it has a moral obligation to take reasonable steps to try to work with that person and render him or her better equipped to return to a useful life as a member of society."

rehabilitation
Correcting deviant behavior.

Rehabilitation rests on the positivist theory of Cesare Lombroso (1835–1909), who saw criminals as "victims of society" and of their own biological, sociological, cultural and physical environments. The problem of **recidivism**, or offenders returning to crime, raises questions about whether corrections can effectively rehabilitate offenders. Closely related to this purpose is the goal of reintegrating offenders into society as productive, law-abiding citizens.

recidivism
Repeated or habitual offending.

For centuries this clash between the classic and the positivist view of criminality has resulted in fervent debate centered on who or what is responsible for crime and how society should deal with those who break the law.

Two Conflicting Views of Corrections

The classical view holds that humans have free will and are responsible for their own actions. It focuses on crime. The positivist view holds that humans are the product of environmental and cultural influences. It focuses on the criminal.

Although the classical and positivist views exist at opposite ends of the continuum of correctional thought, both have made significant contributions to the field. The classical view, in focusing on crime, encouraged due process of law and endorsed restrictions on the arbitrary use of judicial authority. The positivist view, by focusing on the criminal, helped advance experimental methods of research in the field of criminology.

Most people do not believe exclusively in one view or the other but see some combination of free will and determinism governing human behavior. Most also, however, tend to place greater credence in one view than the other, and this directly influences how they view crime and criminals, as well as what they consider to be the primary purpose of corrections. These differing views have resulted in two distinct models: the *medical model* and the *justice model*, summarized in Table 14.1.

medical model
In corrections, assumes criminals are victims of society and need to be "cured."

justice model
Assumes offenders are self-directed, acting on free will and responsible for their crimes.

The **medical model** assumes offenders are victims of society and their environment who need to be cured. The **justice model** assumes offenders are self-directed, acting on free will and responsible for their crimes. Although the table

TABLE 14.1 Comparison of the Medical versus the Justice Model

Issue	Medical Model 1930–1974	Justice Model 1974–Present
Cause of crime	Disease of society or of the individual	Form of rational adaptation to societal conditions
Image of offender	Sick, product of socioeconomic or psychological forces beyond control	Capable of exercising free will; of surviving without resorting to crime
Object of correction	To cure offender and society; to return both to health; rehabilitation	Humanely control offender under terms of sentence; offer voluntary treatment
Agency/institution responsibility	Change offender, reintegrate back into society	Legally and humanely control offender; adequate care and custody; voluntary treatment; protect society
Role of treatment and punishment	Voluntary or involuntary treatment as means to change offender; treatment is mandatory, punishment used to coerce treatment, punishment and treatment is viewed as same thing	Voluntary treatment, only; punishment and treatment not the same thing: punishment is for society's good, treatment is for offender's good
Object of legal sanctions (Sentence)	Determine conditions which are most conducive to rehabilitation of offender	Determine conditions which are just re: wrong done, best protect society and deter offender from future crime
Type of sentence	Indeterminate, flexible; adjust to offender changes	Fixed sentence (less good time)
Who determines release time?	"Experts" (parole board for adults, institutional staff for juveniles)	Conditions of sentence as interpreted by Presumptive Release Data (PRD) formula

SOURCE: From PACE. *Community Relations Concepts,* 4E. © 2003, p.101. Delmar Learning, a part of Cengage Learning, Inc. Reproduced by permission. www.cengage.com/permissions.

includes only portions of the 20th and 21st centuries, societies throughout the ages have vacillated from one model to the other, with intermediate models in between, as reflected in the correctional ideologies that parallel them.

CORRECTIONAL IDEOLOGIES AND MODELS

The complexity of corrections is evident in the interrelatedness of correctional ideologies. Understanding these ideologies is important to understanding the current state of corrections and the problems and issues facing it, for these ideas are historically conditioned and change, partly because of matters unrelated to criminal justice policy or practice (for example, the 1960s youth culture and the civil rights movement). A specific purpose or philosophy of punishment becomes more or less attractive to society as it considers these complex sets of ideas. Thus, the rhetorical strategies of one era differ from those of another—"penitentiaries" give way to "reformatories," and "big houses" or "prisons" give way to "correctional institutions." Most of the ideologies applied to correctional actions over the years fall into one of four categories.

The four basic ideologies underlying corrections are punishment, control, treatment and prevention.

These ideologies may overlap; for example, some forms of punishment might also be perceived as methods of control.

Punishment and the Justice Model

 Punishment is associated with the *justice* model.

In a *punishment ideology*, punitive actions of various forms can serve several purposes previously discussed. The most common purpose is retribution, vengeance or "getting even." The fundamental principle underlying the justice model is that society has a duty to punish those who break its laws and that this threat of punishment is vital in implementing the law.

Another common reason for using punishment is for deterrence. As behavior modification experts stress, to be effective, the negative consequences for a negative act must be immediate, certain and personal. These conditions are readily observable as one trains a pet or raises a child. Unfortunately, our criminal justice system has numerous loopholes (lack of certainty) and usually moves slowly (lack of immediacy), greatly reducing the effectiveness of the punishment. These conditions may partially account for the reasoning of police or corrections officers who "dispense their own justice" rather than relying on the system.

A third purpose of punishment is incapacitation, previously discussed. Banishing or incarcerating offenders makes them incapable of doing further harm to society.

Control and the Custodial Model

 Control is associated with the *custodial* model.

The *control ideology* and its resulting custodial model is the least complex and often most prevalent. The focus is on the present and on the immediate need to restrain the behavior of those convicted of crimes. Correctional officers often have all they can do simply to maintain control over their institutions. Punishing those who fail to comply may be one extremely important means of doing so and may be counterproductive to the other, more humanitarian purposes often set forth for corrections. Many critics of our prisons contend that they are nothing more than human warehouses, violent places of confinement.

Treatment and the Medical Model

 Treatment is associated with the *medical* model.

The *treatment ideology* views offenders as capable of rehabilitation. Although many criticize this ideology as being "soft" on criminals, it has room for punishment, unlike the punishment ideology that leaves little room for treatment. This model parallels the steps taken by a physician dealing with an ill patient: examine, diagnose, prescribe, treat and follow up.

The Prevention Ideology and the Reintegration Model

 Prevention is associated with the *reintegration* model.

The *prevention ideology* considers both the offender and the offender's environment. A goal of both the punishment and treatment models is to *prevent* further offenses.

Throughout the course of criminal justice evolution in the United States, these ideologies have shaped how offenders are dealt with at the corrections stage of the process.

CORRECTIONS TODAY: AN OVERVIEW

"Americans deserve criminal justice policies that keep them safe. They want serious, violent, and chronic criminals put in prison. At the same time, a majority of Americans support cost-effective strategies for dealing with offenders who pose less risk to the community" ("Corrections and Public Safety," 2010). To meet both goals, the Pew Center on the States (PCS) seeks to help states advance sound sentencing and corrections policies and practices that protect public safety, hold offenders accountable and control corrections spending.

PCS conducts credible research, brings together diverse perspectives and analyzes states' experiences to determine what works and what does not. The Center works with a wide variety of partners to identify and advance nonpartisan, pragmatic solutions for pressing problems affecting Americans.

In 2006 the PCS launched the Public Safety Performance Project to help states advance fiscally sound, data-driven sentencing and corrections policies and practices that protect public safety, hold offenders accountable and control costs. The PCS reports that corrections is the fastest expanding major segment of state budgets, being second only to Medicaid in growth as a share of state expenditures during the past two decades. State corrections costs now top $50 billion annually and consume one in every 15 discretionary dollars (*One in 31: The Long Reach of American Corrections*, 2009, p.1). *One in 31* (pp.1–3) provides the following explanation:

> The remarkable rise in corrections spending wasn't fate or even the natural consequence of spikes in crime. It was the result of state policy choices that sent more people to prison and kept them there longer. The sentencing and release laws passed in the 1980s and 1990s put so many more people behind bars that last year the incarcerated population reached 2.3 million and, for the first time, one in 100 adults was in prison or jail.
>
> The escalation of the prison population has been astonishing, but it hasn't been the largest area of growth in the criminal justice system. That would be probation and parole—the sentenced offenders who are not behind bars.
>
> With far less notice, the number of people on probation or parole has skyrocketed to more than 5 million, up from 1.6 million just 25 years ago. This means that 1 in 45 adults in the United States is now under criminal justice supervision in the community, and that combined with those in prison and jail, a stunning 1 in every 31 adults, or 3.2 percent, is under some form of correctional control. The rates are drastically elevated for men (1 in 18) and Blacks (1 in 11) and are even higher in some high-crime inner-city neighborhoods.

> Probation and parole, the dominant community corrections programs, have had larger population growth than prisons, but far smaller budget growth. Looking at a handful of states that were able to provide long-term spending figures, seven times as many new dollars went to prisons as went to probation and parole. And while fewer than one out of three offenders is behind bars, almost nine out of 20 corrections dollars are spent on prisons.
>
> Incarceration understandably costs more. Prisons must house, feed and provide medical care to the most dangerous offenders. But the price gap is nevertheless staggering: on average, the daily cost of supervising a probationer in fiscal 2008 was \$3.42; the average daily cost of a prison inmate, \$78.95, is more than 20 times as high. . . .
>
> "Focus must be placed on locking up the most dangerous people instead of diverting time and money to incarcerate the wrong people" (U.S. Sen. Jim Webb) . . .
>
> After an extraordinary quarter-century expansion of American prisons, one unmistakable policy truth has emerged: We cannot build our way to public safety.
>
> Serious, chronic and violent offenders belong behind bars, for a long time, and the expense of locking them up is justified many times over. But for hundreds of thousands of lower-level inmates, incarceration costs taxpayers far more than it saves in prevented crime. And new national and state research shows that we are well past the point of diminishing returns, where more imprisonment will prevent less and less crime. . . .
>
> Rather than trying to weather the economic storm with short-term cost saving measures, policy leaders should see that as a chance to retool their sentencing and corrections systems. If we had stronger community corrections, we wouldn't need to lock up so many people at such a great cost. By redirecting a portion of the dollars currently spent on imprisoning the lowest-risk inmates, we could significantly increase the intensity and quality of supervision and services directed at the same type of offenders in the community.[1]

The fundamental driver of correctional costs is the number of people incarcerated in jails or prisons and the number in the community under pretrial, probation or parole supervision (Innes, 2010b, p.32). In 1980 the count was about 1.84 million compared with today, 30 years later, with the count at more than 7.5 million. Based on a U.S. population of 303 million, the U.S. incarceration rate is 762 inmates per 100,000. By comparison, according to the most recent available estimates, the world incarceration rate is 145 inmates per 100,000. No other country has a higher incarceration rate than the United States.

While incarceration rates and costs rise, the crime rate has been dropping. The FBI reports, "Preliminary data indicates that, for the third year in a row, the rate of violent crime in the United States is down. It appears that property crime also declined for the seventh straight year" (*Crime in the United States 2009, Preliminary Annual Uniform Crime Report, January through December*, 2010). Proponents of the "get tough" approach may point to decreasing crime rates as evidence that locking up more people can reduce crime and enhance public safety, but empirical data has yet to positively document a causative relationship.

---

[1]SOURCE: *One in 31: The Long Reach of American Corrections.* Washington, DC: The Pew Charitable Trusts, March 2009."

The National Institute of Corrections (NIC) has been exploring the possibility of dramatically reducing the total correctional population—in half, through the Norval Morris Project. (Morris was instrumental in founding NIC and was a guiding influence as a charter member of the NIC Advisory Board until his death in 2004.) An initial, dramatic reduction in the total corrections population might seem unrealistic; cutting the correctional population in half would return it to where it was in 1988 (Innes, 2010a, p.33). That year marked the end of an eight-year period of rapid growth during which the correctional population doubled from 1.8 million in 1980 to 3.8 million. "In theory, if the correctional population could double in eight years, it ought to be able to halve in eight years. If corrections could safely build up to meet the challenge in the 1980s, it ought to be able to safely build down to meet the new challenge of today" (Innes, p.33).

A starting point to reducing correctional populations is more effective pretrial services.

PRETRIAL SERVICES/DETENTION

Pretrial services, no matter how brief the detention, provide a window of opportunity. From the moment an offender is arrested and charged with a crime, offender assessment should begin to determine what level of supervision and services are required. Although reentry usually refers to inmates being released from prison, it also includes millions of offenders who leave the nation's jails each year, *before* their trial: "The sheer number of offenders cycling through local jails provides a great opportunity for community supervision, diversion and treatment that may interrupt criminal behavior. Focusing on the transition from jail to the community after any length of confinement creates a platform to decrease the collateral consequence of the arrest" (Stevenson and Legg, 2010, p.104). Such collateral consequences include being removed from family and perhaps the loss of a job. In our criminal justice system, those charged with a crime are presumed to be innocent until found guilty. In most instances, they also have the right to bail to ensure their appearance in court.

Diversion

Diversion was introduced in the last chapter. During the pretrial assessment, it might be determined that the appropriate services are available in the community and that offenders, adults and juveniles, might be better served by appearing before an alternative sentencing court such as a drug court or guided into existing treatment options for drug problems or mental illness.

Travis et al. (2009, p.39) looked at 20 studies on the effectiveness of drug treatment programs in reducing recidivism and found that in-prison drug treatment and drug treatment in jail resulted in quite a similar reduction in recidivism, with 6.9 percent and 6.0 percent reductions, respectively. Drug treatment in the community, however, had much better results, with a 12.4 percent reduction in recidivism. Another study of the effect of residential and nonresidential drug treatment on recidivism among drug-involved probationers found, "Compared to those receiving no treatment, those receiving nonresidential treatment took longer to fail or recidivate. However, those receiving residential treatment did not differ from those who received no treatment in time to failure. In the treatment-only model, nonresidential treatment participants took longer to fail than their matched residential treatment counterparts" (Krebs et al., 2009, p.442). For many suspects, beginning a drug treatment program rather than merely sitting in jail while awaiting trial makes sense.

INTERMEDIATE SANCTIONS/COMMUNITY CORRECTIONS

Intermediate sanctions, also called *community corrections*, exist along a continuum of increasing control and are tougher than traditional probation but less restrictive and costly than imprisonment (recall Figure 13.6 from the last chapter). Community corrections includes any activities in the community aimed at helping offenders become law-abiding citizens and requires a complicated interplay among judicial and correctional personnel from related public and private agencies, law enforcement agencies, citizen volunteers and civic groups.

intermediate sanctions

Sanctions that are tougher than traditional probation but less stringent and less expensive than imprisonment.

Alternatives to incarceration include straight fines and day fines, forfeiture, restitution, community service, intensive supervision, house arrest and electronic monitoring, day reporting centers, residential community corrections and probation.

Day fines differ from straight fines in that they are based on an offender's daily income and ability to pay. *Forfeiture* also imposes a financial penalty on offenders by seizing their illegally used or acquired property or assets. *Restitution* has become an increasingly common criminal sanction, often imposed as a condition of probation, whereby an offender reimburses a victim, most often with money though occasionally with services. *Community service*, like restitution, is usually imposed not as a sole penalty but as a condition of probation. Community service often requires the offender to perform unpaid labor to pay a debt to society, with assignments ranging from cleaning litter along roadsides to janitorial work in churches or schools to serving as a volunteer in a hospital or rehab center.

Intensive supervision programs (*ISPs*), also called *intensive supervised probation*, involve more supervision and greater restrictions than standard probation does. ISPs emphasize offender control and surveillance rather than treatment and rehabilitation. Although no single specific model exists for ISPs, common elements found in the various programs across the country include frequent personal contacts between the probation officer and the offender; strict enforcement of conditions, such as curfews, and random drug and alcohol testing; fulfillment of restitution and community service obligations; mandatory employment; participation in treatment programs or educational classes; routine checks of local and state arrest records; and house arrest and electronic monitoring. Interestingly, several studies have found that the increased supervision and surveillance involved in ISPs leads to increased levels of probation violations. This suggests that the more one looks for something, the more likely it is one will find it.

House arrest, also known as *home confinement* or *home detention*, requires offenders to remain in their homes during specified times and to adhere to a strict curfew. Probation officers may monitor those under house arrest by random calls and home visits, or they may rely on technology to help keep track of offenders through electronic monitoring (EM). Such monitoring allows the release of defendants charged with more serious offenses. Global positioning systems (GPS) capabilities add another layer of public safety: "Commended for its enhanced surveillance capabilities or 'eyes in the skies,' GPS-EM has become the alternative sanction of choice for a number of populations, including sex offenders, domestic violence offenders and high-risk pretrial populations" (Stevenson and Legg, 2010, p.106).

Day reporting centers (*DRCs*) are nonresidential facilities where offenders must appear daily. First used in the United States during the 1970s for juvenile offenders and deinstitutionalized mentally ill persons, day reporting centers today serve as an alternative to jail or prison. Although the emphasis at DRCs is on helping offenders find jobs, a variety of counseling and treatment programs are often also available.

For those offenders for whom live-in sanctions are more appropriate, *residential community corrections* are available—an alternative just a step away from incarceration. These residences provide a semisecure correctional environment within the community while addressing the dual objectives of community protection and offender reintegration. Such centers may take many forms, including halfway houses, prerelease centers, transition centers, work furlough and community work centers, community treatment centers and restitution centers. Offenders may live either part-time or full-time at these facilities, depending on the conditions set forth by the court.

Consider next the most common form of community corrections—probation.

PROBATION

Probation is the oldest community-based correctional program and the most common alternative to a jail or prison sentence. Probation provides a foundation on which to build a wide range of community-based services. The American Correctional Association (ACA) defines **probation** as "a court-ordered disposition alternative through which an adjudicated offender is placed under the control, supervision, and care of a probation field staff member in lieu of imprisonment, so long as the probationer meets certain standards of conduct." A major benefit of probation is that it allows offenders to remain in the community, able to maintain important family ties and fulfill vital work, family and community obligations.

probation

The conditional suspension of a sentence of a person convicted of a crime but not yet imprisoned for that crime; the defendant is placed under the supervision of a probation officer for a set period and must meet specific conditions.

John Augustus, the Father of Probation

John Augustus (1784–1859) was a prosperous Boston shoemaker with several employees in his shop. One August morning in 1841 he was in court when a wretched-looking man was brought in and charged with being a drunkard. Knowing the man would most likely be sentenced to prison, Augustus felt a better alternative existed. Augustus spoke briefly with the man and then provided the man's bail on the provision that the man sign a pledge to never drink spirits again and to return to court at a set time as a reformed man.

For the next 18 years, Augustus attended court and provided bail for drunkards and prostitutes. Initially he and his wife took them into their home. Later they established a House of Refuge. Augustus's actions are viewed as the origin of probation and community-based corrections.

John Augustus is known as the father of probation and an originator of community corrections.

From 1841 to 1851 Augustus provided bail for more than a thousand men and women, some as young as 8 years old.

Who Gets Probation?

The court considers the presentence investigation (PSI) report and state statutes in determining if an offender should be put on probation, but some statutes involving mandatory sentences preclude the option. Probation is most often used with first-time offenders, property offenders, low-risk offenders and nonviolent offenders, such as those convicted of white-collar crimes.

Conditions of Probation

Conditions of probation vary depending on the nature of the offense and the court's goals. The general purpose of probation is to help offenders maintain law-abiding behavior through supervision. Some courts are more treatment oriented in assigning conditions, whereas other courts are more punitive. One universal condition for all probationers is to obey the law. Other conditions may include adherence to a curfew, maintaining steady employment or refraining from engaging in a specific employment or occupation, completing prescribed educational or vocational training, meeting family responsibilities, staying away from certain types of people or places, abstaining from drug and alcohol use, abiding by firearms possession restrictions, performing community service and making restitution.

Probation and Punishment

As noted earlier, behavior modification experts stress that to be effective, punishment must be swift, certain and personal. Probation is certainly personal, but it is usually neither swift nor certain. Often it is perceived as "getting a break." New research on Hawaii's Opportunity Probation with Enforcement (HOPE) program shows that HOPE probationers were significantly less likely to be arrested for a new crime, to use drugs and to have their probation revoked. As a result, HOPE participants also served or were sentenced to an average of 48 percent fewer days in jail and prison. The HOPE program, launched in 2004, identifies probationers at high risk of violating the conditions of their community supervision and aims to deter them from using drugs and committing crimes with frequent and random drug tests backed up by swift, certain and short jail stays ("'Swift and Certain' Sanctions in Probation Are Highly Effective: Evaluation of the HOPE Program," 2010).

The one-year randomized controlled trial conducted by Pepperdine University and the University of California, Los Angeles, found that HOPE probationers were:

- 55 percent less likely to be arrested for a new crime.
- 72 percent less likely to use drugs.
- 61 percent less likely to skip appointments with their supervisory officer.
- 53 percent less likely to have their probation revoked.

The Growing Use of Probation

The first state to implement a formal probation program was Massachusetts in 1878. By 1927 juvenile probation programs were operating in every state, but it was not until 1957 that every state was providing similar services for adult offenders. Probation is now the fastest-growing sentencing alternative in the United States. The increased use of this disposition has led to an overload on the probation system and has fueled the increasing demand for an effective network of diversionary community-based programs known as intermediate sanctions. Often standard probation is combined with forms of intermediate punishment to increase the level of punishment and restriction imposed on the offender.

For violent offenders and those whose crimes are particularly severe or habitual, community corrections is often not an appropriate alternative. For these offenders, incarceration is a more likely sentence.

INCARCERATION

incarceration Being confined in jail or prison.

Many types of correctional facilities exist for the **incarceration** (confining) of offenders. The primary goal of these correctional institutions is to protect society. Secondary goals may be to deter, rehabilitate and reintegrate offenders into society. Although corrections tries to rehabilitate offenders, conditions cannot be such that the prison is a pleasant place to be. Inmates should dread a return. Unfortunately, however, too often our correctional institutions do not rehabilitate but actually contribute to and reward criminal behavior.

The type of correctional institution in which an offender is incarcerated usually depends on the type of crime committed and the offender's past record. Incarceration options include local and county jails and state and federal prisons.

Jails

Jails are an important part of the U.S. criminal justice system and go by a variety of names, including houses of detention and houses of corrections, but their definitions are generally the same. A jail is a place of confinement, typically administered by local law enforcement, although occasionally by a regional or state law enforcement agency.

Jails serve the dual function of (1) detaining individuals waiting to appear before the court, either for trial (preconviction) or for sentencing (post conviction) and (2) holding those sentenced to a year or less of incarceration. Although jails vary considerably in their management and operational philosophies, the basic responsibilities of jail personnel remain constant, including the intake and classification of inmates, orientation of new residents, transportation of inmates between the jail and court and the release of inmates.

Jail operations are a complex endeavor, considering the myriad services required, the detailed staffing needs, the potential civil liability issues presented by the ever-rotating inmate population, and the continuously dwindling budgets: "The typical county jail operation serves as the critical workflow hub and clearing house for all aspects of local or regional criminal justice activities. Courts, probation, district attorney, public defender, state parole, and street and highway patrol elements all rely upon and filter their 'work product' through the county jail. Take a county jail out of service and watch as the many and varied cogs and gears of law enforcement and criminal justice grind to a sudden and chaotic halt" (Fawell, 2010, p.94).

Jails differ from lockups in that lockups, commonly located in city halls or police stations, are temporary holding facilities, authorized to hold individuals for a maximum of 48 hours. Jails differ from prisons in that prisons are state or federally administered and hold only those convicted of a crime and sentenced, not those awaiting trial or sentencing.

Jail differs from prison in that its inmates are there for shorter terms, usually for less serious crimes. They are usually the responsibility of local or county law enforcement.

According to the BJS, the nation's local jail population has *declined* for the first time since 1982 when the federal government began keeping count. At midyear 2009 more than 42 percent of local jail inmates were White, more than 38 percent were Black, and more than 16 percent were Hispanic. The capacity for all jails nationwide reached 849,544 beds at midyear 2009, up more than 2,000 beds from 12 months earlier. Local jails admitted an estimated 12.8 million inmates during the 12-month span ending June 30, 2009 (Yost, 2010). In addition, at midyear 2008, a total of 2,135 inmates were confined in Indian country jails, a 1.3 percent *decrease* from the previous year (Minton, 2009, p.1).

The turnover rate of the jail population is relatively high, with offenders being booked and released and coming and going much more often than do inmates in prison.

Issues Facing Jails Today With jails receiving perhaps more attention today than ever before, the number of issues concerning jails is quite extensive, ranging from overcrowding to high suicide rates to accreditation and privatization of jail facilities. Issues of concern vary slightly between state and federal jail facilities, including overcrowding, assaults, rape, inmate suicide and inmate rights. In addition to increases in their own populations, jails are expected to shoulder the overflow from crowded prisons.

Staffing shortages are also a critical issue facing jail administrators. Turnover frequently leaves jail administrators scrambling to fill positions, and the quality of applicants has often left much to be desired. Because jails are typically a low priority for funding, staff positions at jails have not always attracted highly qualified applicants. Additionally, the levels of burnout and stress experienced in corrections lead to high turnover.

The other major type of correctional institution in the United States, where the inmates *have* been convicted of a crime, is the prison.

Prisons

Prisons are often what come to people's minds when they think of *corrections*. A prison is administered by a warden or superintendent and holds convicted offenders sentenced to more than one year of incarceration. Just as the United States has both a state and federal court system, it also has a state and federal prison system. Since 1930 the federal Bureau of Prisons (BOP), an agency within the Department of Justice, has been the authority charged with running our nation's federal facilities, which house those convicted of federal offenses.

The word *prison* usually conveys a mental picture of rows of cage-like cells several levels high, crowded mess halls and a "yard" where prisoners engage in physical activities, organized and not so organized, all patrolled by tight-lipped, heavily armed guards. Although perhaps once accurate, this image no longer typifies many modern prisons. In keeping with their new image, the American Correctional Association passed a resolution regarding terminology.

The American Correctional Association recommends that the term *correctional officer* replace the term *guard*.

At year end 2008, federal and state correctional facilities held more than 1,610,446 prisoners, an increase of 0.8 percent, the second year of decline in the *rate* of growth and the slowest overall growth in eight years (Sabol et al., 2009, p.1). These statistics "give fresh evidence that the field may be undergoing a historic transformation," with the growth of correctional populations stalling (Innes, 2010a, p.92). Because these figures are based on 2008 data and are more than a year old, the incarcerated populations may be continuing to shrink.

Prisons may be punitive or treatment oriented. Punitive-oriented prisons are more formal and rigid, with an emphasis on obedience. Obedience is sought through negative incentives. Treatment-oriented prisons are more informal and flexible, with positive incentives for good behavior.

For the first time in nearly 40 years, the number of state prisoners in the United States has *declined*, according to "Prison Count 2010." As of January 2010, there were 1,404,053 persons under the jurisdiction of state prison authorities, 4,777 fewer than on December 31, 2008, marking the first year-to-year drop in the nation's state prison population since 1972. Although the study showed an overall decline, it revealed great variation among jurisdictions. The prison population declined in 26 states, while increasing in 24 states and in the federal system.

In the past few years, several states have enacted reforms designed to get taxpayers a better return on their public safety dollars. These strategies include:

- Diverting low-level offenders and probation and parole violators from prison.
- Strengthening community supervision and reentry programs.
- Accelerating the release of low-risk inmates who complete risk reduction programs.

CAREER PROFILE

Norman A. Carlson (Federal Bureau of Prisons)

Like many individuals who spend their careers in corrections, I became involved in the field by accident rather than by design. While a junior in college, I decided to change my major from business to sociology, primarily because of an outstanding young professor who taught the introductory course in the Department of Sociology. He stimulated my interest and thinking in criminal justice and juvenile delinquency, areas I had never previously considered.

During my senior year, about to graduate with a degree in sociology, I began to think seriously about the future, particularly as it related to employment opportunities. Recognizing that the demand for individuals with undergraduate degrees in sociology was rather limited (then, as it is now), I decided to go on to graduate school. While in graduate school, my faculty advisor at the University of Iowa suggested that I consider spending time working as a correctional officer at the Iowa State Penitentiary and writing a required major paper on the experience. That initial three-month exposure to corrections as an officer in a state prison was the beginning of a 30-year career with the Federal Bureau of Prisons.

What I enjoyed most about the field of corrections was its dynamic nature—that the challenges, problems and opportunities were constantly changing. In a very real sense, the issues I faced daily were rarely the same as those I had encountered previously. That made for an exciting and stimulating career in an area the public knows little about. Unlike many other occupations, corrections can never be described as being dull, boring or routine.

I began in the federal system as a caseworker at the U.S. Penitentiary, Leavenworth, Kansas, where I was responsible for 500 convicted offenders. After several years, I was promoted and transferred to the Federal Correctional Institution, Ashland, Kentucky. Later, I was transferred to the Federal Bureau of Prisons headquarters in Washington, DC, where I spent the remainder of my career working in several different positions. During 1970, I was appointed director of the Bureau by the attorney general and remained in the position until my retirement in 1987.

As director, I was responsible for the management and administration of all federal prisons and jails in the United States. While it was a difficult, challenging and, at times, frustrating position, I thoroughly enjoyed what I did and wouldn't trade the opportunities and experiences with anyone. During that time, there was considerable controversy in the country as to the basic purpose or objective of incarceration. Was it intended to incapacitate, deter, punish or rehabilitate offenders? That controversy carried over into the Congress, where members expressed vastly different views on the topic. Several specific legislative proposals were introduced that illustrated the divergent viewpoints. One proposal would have eliminated the Federal Bureau of Prisons entirely and relied on community-based programs for virtually all federal offenders. Another congressman introduced a bill that would have given the bureau a desolate island in the Aleutian chain for conversion into a large, self-contained colony for all federal offenders. Fortunately, neither proposal gained support, but they serve to illustrate the differing views on the topic.

As I look back on my career, the highlight was clearly the opportunity of working with a group of well-trained and dedicated staff who shared a commitment to manage institutions that were safe and humane and provided opportunities for offenders to change their behavior. With the active support of the Congress, we developed an excellent staff-training program for all employees. We were also able to build a number of new institutions based on the concept of maximizing staff/inmate interaction and expanding direct supervision. Community-based programs were also developed to assist offenders in making the transition back to society when they are released from confinement.

While corrections will undoubtedly always be a controversial topic, it will also continue to provide a stimulating and rewarding opportunity for students interested in careers in criminal justice. For those who want to make a real difference in society, the field provides a unique challenge.

Issues in Prisons As with jails, our nation's prisons face several issues, the most critical of which is overcrowding. Overcrowded prisons suffer because of stretched or insufficient resources and place added stress on management and staff, who struggle to maintain order in facilities holding more inmates than they were designed for. Debate exists whether such overcrowding contributes to higher levels of violence or increased spread of illness. Research suggests that prison overcrowding adversely affects both institutional management and employee satisfaction. Overcrowding may be linked to violent deaths, suicide, psychiatric commitments and disciplinary infractions. Prison crowding has also led to numerous lawsuits filed by prisoners claiming inhumane confinement and other violations of their Eighth Amendment right against cruel and unusual punishment. Various methods have been used to alleviate the pressures of overcrowding, including constructing more prisons.

Other issues facing prisons include:

- Continued inward flow of contraband, such as drugs.
- Assaults and rapes.
- Prison gangs—virtually every correctional system in the nation has had some experience with prison gangs and the violence in which they engage.
- Criminalizing environment—socialization that occurs in prison may draw offenders away from a community's values and norms and strengthen their criminal tendencies. This phenomenon, which Clemmer (1971) identified as *prisonization*, leads prisoners to identify with and learn to coexist with other criminals and lose touch with any conventional values they may have had on the outside.
- Privatization—the provision of correctional services by organizations outside the governmental framework, either nonprofit or for profit, remains highly controversial.

Although proponents contend privatization will streamline and reduce the costs of corrections to the community, critics argue that private prisons, motivated by the "bottom line," will cut corners, from cheaper, inferior construction materials to hiring inexperienced personnel, making decisions that enhance profits at the expense of security, quality of service and the rights and well-being of inmates.

Regardless of whether an offender is housed in a public or private correctional facility, the reality for most inmates is that one day they will be released.

PAROLE

parole

A release from prison before a sentence is finished; continued release depends on good behavior and reporting to a parole officer; the most frequent type of release from a correctional institution.

Parole is the conditional release from prison before the expiration of the sentence and the period of supervision in the community following this release. It is the most frequent type of release from a correctional facility. At year-end 2008, 828,169 adults were on parole or mandatory conditional release following a prison term (Glaze and Bonczar, 2009, p.1).

Parole differs from probation in that a person who is paroled has spent some time serving a prison sentence. It is similar to probation in that both require supervision of the offender and set up certain conditions the offender must meet.

Administratively, parole, like law enforcement, is part of the executive branch of government; probation is under the courts and part of the judicial branch of government. Paroling authorities include parole board chairs, board members and executive staff. Paroling authorities are appointed in some states and elected in others. Often these individuals have no background in law or corrections. Nonetheless they are a critical factor in reentry efforts. "When paroling authorities understand the full breadth of the functions and requirements of their position, they become better equipped to address their responsibilities with insight" (Banks, 2010, p.94). In fact, Paparozzi and Guy (2009, p.397) call paroling authorities the "lynchpin to evidence-based practices and prisoner reentry." They (p.399) note that these authorities significantly influence the flow of inmates in and out of prisons through their four main functions: (1) making release and revocation decisions, (2) setting requirements for conditional liberty, (3) framing policies and practices related to parole supervision and (4) recommending sentencing policies and new legislation.

Factors influencing whether a person serving a sentence is eligible for or, indeed, is granted parole include the type of offense committed, the offender's prior record, state statutes, the inmate's behavior while incarcerated, participation in programs, whether the inmate has a plan for life on the outside and if the inmate poses any public risk. In some jurisdictions parole is prohibited by statute for certain crimes. In other jurisdictions, however, people sentenced to prison are immediately eligible for parole. The type of parole release or reentry program granted depends on the inmate's individual needs and the variety of programs offered in a particular area. Common release programs include furloughs, work release, educational release and halfway houses.

Conditions of parole typically include regular meetings between the parolee and the parole officer, a requirement to acquire and hold a job, a promise to act lawfully, a restriction on leaving the county or state without permission, a prohibition on purchasing or using a firearm and submission to random or routine drug testing. Violation of the conditions of parole typically sends the offender back to prison.

Parole has had many advocates and critics over the years. Proponents assert parole plays an important role in relieving the pressures of our overcrowded prisons, while opponents claim parole lets offenders off by shortening their stay behind bars and exposes the public to criminals who have not yet paid their debt or who still pose a threat to society.

The parole process is not perfect, so many states have chosen to abolish it. However, many states still rely on parole to return inmates to society. In fact, in California, once inmates have served their original sentences, they are automatically released and placed on parole, usually for three years, including those who are potentially dangerous to society and others who may not need any supervision (Mandelstam, 2009, p.122).

In 2008 the National Institute of Justice released *Parole Violations and Revocations in California*, considered the "largest, most comprehensive study of parole violations and revocations ever conducted" (Mandelstam, 2009, p.122). The researchers studied the behavior of every adult on parole in California during 2003 to 2004, recording the behavior of 254,468 parolees weekly. About half the parolees in the study had at least one violation report, and nearly one-quarter had multiple reports (Grattet, Petersilia and Lin, 2008). More than one-third of the violations were for noncriminal (technical) violations such as missing appointments or absconding. As for the personal characteristics of parolees, the strongest predictor of violation was the number of times the parolee had been in prison as an adult, and the risk for all types of violations was highest during the first six months on parole. Intensity of supervision did not deter violation; in fact, more intensive supervision increased the likelihood of all types of violations, probably because the offenders were being watched so closely.

As for parole agents' characteristics, neither their age nor length of time on the job was related to risk violation, but gender did play a role, with female agents more forgiving of low-level offenses such as drug use, and male agents being more forgiving of absconding. Finally, parolees who lived in economically disadvantaged neighborhoods were more likely to abscond but were at no greater risk for other violations. Where substance abuse and mental health treatment were available, low-level criminal violations were less likely.

Once an inmate is released, it is the parole officer's (PO) task to supervise the parolee. How the PO responds to violations is critical because, as noted, one-third of those on parole are returned to custody after having committed a technical violation. Researchers at the University of Cincinnati evaluated the effect of Ohio's progressive sanction grid (Martin and Van Dine, 2008). This matrix allows multiple sanctions before parole is revoked, including more restrictive conditions on parole, increased structured supervision, substance testing and monitoring, reprimands and halfway house placement. The study found that using the violation grid significantly reduced reliance on revocation hearings and sanctions, keeping offenders out of jails. In addition, offenders were less likely to return to prison for technical violations.

States with large numbers of parolees face many challenges, including a system that may not be responsive to identifying parolees' risks and needs, time-consuming and costly parole violation hearings, an overuse of expensive custody sanctions rather than treatment, and issues of fairness and proportionality (Fialkoff, 2009). The Ohio parolee study and the California probationer study could have implications for the country as a whole (Fialkoff).

POLICE, PROBATION AND PAROLE

The American Probation and Parole Association (APPA) vision statement reads, "We see a fair, just and safe society where community partnerships are restoring hope by embracing a balance of prevention, intervention and advocacy." This vision statement aligns well with the community policing philosophy: "Community policing promotes organizational strategies that support the systematic use of partnerships and problem-solving techniques that proactively address the immediate conditions that give rise to safety issues such as crime, social disorder and fear of crime."

Carl Wicklund, Executive Director of the APPA, notes the similarities between their vision statement and that of the Office of Community Oriented Policing Services (COPS) and questions why so few collaborations exist between them, then offers as a possible reason the fact that their approaches to public safety may appear to be diametrically opposed. Police spend much of their time getting offenders off the street while probation and parole officers try to keep these same offenders in the community: "Ultimately both law enforcement and probation and parole officers are responsible for keeping these offenders from committing new crimes and, consequently, creating new crime victims" (Wicklund, 2010). The importance of partnerships has been stressed throughout this text and continues to be extremely important in establishing relationships between law enforcement and probation and parole. Police and correctional officers need to recognize each other's role in reentry and work together, rather than seeing their goals as being at odds. It benefits the officers, the offenders and society when reentry is successful.

COMMUNITY-BASED REINTEGRATION PROGRAMS

Traditional community-based institutional programs aimed at reintegrating offenders into society include halfway houses and restitution centers. As the name implies, halfway houses are community-based institutions for people who are halfway into prison, that is, on probation, or halfway out of prison, that is, on or nearing parole. Halfway houses typically provide offenders with a place to live, sleep and eat. Counselors help offenders return to society and transition back to normal life, sometimes helping them find suitable jobs or providing transportation to jobs.

A restitution center differs from a halfway house in that at the restitution center, offenders work to partially repay their victims. Like the halfway house, restitution centers offer an alternative to prison, either for those halfway into or halfway out of prison.

Several other approaches to reintegrating offenders into society have been used, with varying degrees of success. Three common reintegration methods are furloughs, work release and study release. In all cases the possibility of escape from the directives of the criminal justice system must be considered.

Furloughs are short, temporary leaves from a prison or jail, supervised or unsupervised, although generally the latter, often used as positive motivators for good behavior. Work and study release are also positive motivators for good behavior that help reintegrate offenders into society. Often such programs are conducted through halfway houses or through local jails.

The conditions of furloughs, work release and study release programs are usually explicit and rigid. For example, a strict curfew may be established, going into a bar may be prohibited and associating with known criminals may be forbidden. People on work programs usually have their pay closely controlled. They may be required to pay a portion of their room and board, and, if married, to send part of their earnings to their dependents.

RECIDIVISM

Recidivism is usually defined as one or more arrests of a returning prison inmate over three years. BJS data reveal the three-year recidivism rate for individuals leaving state prisons is more than two-thirds. The rate of failure, defined by rearrest, is significantly higher in the first few months following release, with 30 percent of all arrests during the entire three-year period occurring within the first six months. Consequently, "It is a simple, but revolutionary concept: front-load reentry services and align resources to match the risk" (Travis et al., 2009, p.39).

Nowhere is the issue of recidivism of greater concern than when considering how to handle offenders who have committed heinous and violent crimes. Because the general population and the courts agree such offenders should not be returned to society, the question then becomes a matter of life versus death: Should we keep these offenders locked up forever (life) or execute them (death)?

DEATH ROW VERSUS LIFE WITHOUT PAROLE

Many brutal methods have been used throughout history to execute condemned criminals, including being buried alive, thrown to wild animals, boiled in oil, stoned, stretched on a rack, disemboweled and beheaded. Capital punishment in the United States "evolved" as society searched for more humane ways of killing its condemned—from hangings in the early years, to the first electrocution in 1890, the invention of the gas chamber in 1923, the use of a firing squad and finally the adoption of lethal injections in 1977. Today, lethal injection is the predominant method of execution in the United States, used in 37 states. In 2008, 37 inmates were executed, 36 by lethal injection; 1 by electrocution. Of those executed, all were men, 20 were White and 17 were Black. During 2009, 11 states executed 52 inmates, 12 more than the number executed in 2008 (Snell, 2009).

At year-end 2008, 38 states and the federal government had laws authorizing capital punishment. Following the Court's ruling in *Roper v. Simmons* (2005), 18 states and the federal government have set 18 as the minimum age at which an offender can be eligible for a death sentence. However, 14 states have statutes specifying an age of eligibility between 14 and 17, and 6 states have no specified minimum age of eligibility for imposition of a capital sentence (p.4).

As correctional philosophies and practices fluctuate, and the pendulum swings from punishment to rehabilitation and back, so too do attitudes concerning capital punishment. Gallup polls conducted between 1936 and 2006 show support for the death penalty reached its lowest point in 1966 (42 percent favored it) and peaked in 1994, with 80 percent favoring capital punishment for someone convicted of murder.

Supporters of capital punishment see it as both a deterrent and as a form of retribution. Whether the threat of the death penalty deters others from murder is questionable, however. According to the Death Penalty Information Center, the states with the fewest executions since 1976, the Northeast region with 4 executions, had the lowest murder rate during that time (4.2 percent). States in the West had 67 executions and a murder rate of 4.8. Those in the Midwest had 141 executions and a 4.8 murder rate. However states in the South had more than 1,000 executions, accounting for 82 percent of the total, and a murder rate of 6.6. During that period, the national murder rate was 5.4 ("Geography and the Death Penalty," 2010).

Supporters also assert that imprisoning for life those convicted of capital crimes will only further burden an already overcrowded prison system. Those who argue against the death penalty contend it is morally reprehensible and self-defeating, sending the message that "it's okay to punish an act of killing with an act of killing." Some opponents assert that such state-sanctioned killings cheapen the value of human life and dull society to issues concerning intentional death. Others criticize the disparity shown by the court when deciding who should receive capital punishment. Indeed several studies have shown that the financial status of the offender, the location of the offense and the races of the victim and offender are factors in determining who receives a death sentence. Another disparity concerning the death penalty centers on the gender of the offender—women are conspicuously absent on death row.

Many opponents to capital punishment suggest life without parole (LWOP) as a suitable alternative, bolstering their argument by citing the potential good the inmate might do if allowed to live, including providing restitution to the victim's family and participating in the rehabilitation of other inmates. Many death row inmates actually consider LWOP a worse alternative than execution, saying they would rather be put to death than rot behind bars for the rest of their lives, which may last decades.

Given the relatively young age at which many murderers commit their crimes and the likelihood these prisoners will spend many years behind bars if given LWOP, concern about the cost to warehouse these criminals has become another issue of the debate. Capital punishment proponents estimate that at $10,000 to $20,000 a year, a 20-year-old who lives 60 years in prison would cost society more than $1 million. However, dollar estimates for executions that include the full cost of appeals are also often in the millions.

Debate has also erupted over the possibility of innocent people being executed. According to the Center on Wrongful Convictions (CWC) at Northwestern University's School of Law (2006):

> Proponents of the death penalty have asserted that it has not been proven that an innocent person has been executed in the United States since the death penalty was restored in the mid-1970s following *Furman v. Georgia*. That is true only according to the proponents' definition of innocence.
>
> They define an innocent person as someone whose innocence has been officially exonerated, either by a court or admission by the prosecutor. Under that operative definition, innocence has never been established because the criminal justice process officially ends with execution. There simply is no process for post-execution exoneration.
>
> However, at least 38 executions have been carried out in the United States in face of compelling evidence of innocence or serious doubt about guilt. While innocence has not been proven in any specific case, there is no reasonable doubt that some of the executed prisoners were innocent. (Center on Wrongful Convictions, 2006)

Since capital punishment was restored in 1972 following the Supreme Court's decision in *Furman v. Georgia*, the CWC has identified and analyzed 86 cases in which the defendants (84 men and 2 women) had been sentenced to death but were later legally exonerated based on strong claims of actual innocence. The CWC's analysis revealed that, of the 86 legally exonerated individuals, eyewitness testimony, whether mistaken or perjured, had played a role in the convictions of 46 of them (53.5 percent), making eyewitness error the leading cause of wrongful conviction. Figure 14.3 shows the various causes of wrongful convictions by percentage.

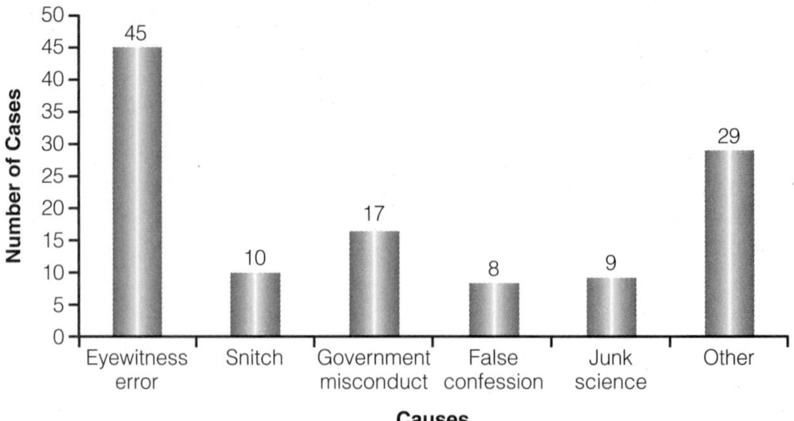

FIGURE 14.3 Causes of Wrongful Convictions

Note: Nearly half of the cases included more than one reason for a wrongful conviction. Therefore the total of the cases in the chart equals more than 86.

SOURCE: Rob Warden, with research by Shawn M. Armbrust and Jennifer Linzer. *How Mistaken and Perjured Eyewitness Identification Testimony Put 46 Innocent Americans on Death Row: An Analysis of Wrongful Convictions Since Restoration of the Death Penalty Following* Furman v. Georgia. Chicago, IL: Center on Wrongful Convictions, Northwestern University School of Law. Presented May 2, 2001 at Andrews University–Berrien Springs, Michigan.

As DNA evidence becomes increasingly used and reliable, the number of exonerations is likely to increase exponentially.

Many argue that the potential for even one mistake should be reason enough to abolish capital punishment. Others, however, assert that to abolish the death penalty out of fear of error is to second-guess the integrity of the system or to undermine the very credibility of our criminal justice system. The controversy regarding capital punishment and life without parole is likely to continue. There is little doubt, however, that capital punishment is the ultimate form of retribution.

Unless offenders die in prison, whether by natural causes at the end of lengthy life sentences, through execution, or from some other cause short of their release, they will eventually be returned to society. This reentry occurs for the vast majority of people who serve a period of incarceration. Thus reentry is a critical stage in the criminal justice process.

REENTRY

Historically, many correctional departments operated as independent, somewhat secretive entities. Today, however, that cloak of autonomous reticence has been largely stripped away because it has been increasingly clear that partnerships among various criminal justice agencies is a necessary ingredient in improved public safety: "As correctional departments around the country expand upon their mission of public safety to incorporate a greater emphasis on reducing recidivism through successful prisoner reentry, partnerships with law enforcement agencies and community service providers have become even more critical" (Wall and

Poole, 2008, p.30). For prisoner reentry to be effective, the following assumptions are important:

- Prisoner reentry is a statewide issue.
- The current approach to corrections is costly and the outcomes are not great.
- Solutions do not lie solely within correctional departments.
- Both human services and law enforcement must join together with corrections.
- Communication and data-sharing are essential.
- Success can (and should) be measured (Wall and Poole, 2008, p.31).

"Evidence shows that citizens most susceptible to criminal behavior are those in the greatest need of job skills, employment, housing, health care, transportation and addiction treatment. . . .These individuals may receive various agency services before, during or after being charged or convicted as criminal offenders. With no program established to coordinate the expenditure of community resources on these individuals, jurisdictions can often only provide inmates with a disjointed delivery of services at best" (Barbee, 2010, p.152).

The National Institute of Corrections (NIC) has proposed a new approach to reentry: The Transition from Jail to the Community (TJC) initiative takes a broader approach that is based on risk and need assessment, predicated on evidence-based practices and committed to collaboration with community-based services as equal partners. The model allows officials to target their resources on offender criminogenic needs (Barbee, 2010).

In recognizing the need for a new approach to reentry efforts, the BOP is shifting its principal release preparation efforts from a program or process-centered model to a skills- or competency-based model. The federal system, the largest correctional system in the United States and serving a population of more than 207,000 as of July 2009, releases about 45,000 inmates per year back to U.S. communities (Breazzano, 2009, p.50). In shifting its emphasis from clinical assessment and program participation to a competency-based assessment, the BOP believes that offender reentry can achieved more successfully and efficiently if these components are implemented:

- Identification of the core skills needed for successful offender reentry
- An objective assessment of those skills and continual measurement of the skills acquisition, rather than simple program completion
- Linkage of programs to specific reentry skills
- Allocation of resources to those inmates with the greatest skill deficiencies and hence, the greatest risk of recidivism
- Information sharing and the building of community collaborations for a holistic approach to transitioning offenders (Breazzano, 2009, p.51)

One area frequently neglected is the ability for individuals to obtain access to Medicaid and Social Security disability benefits: "Hundreds of thousands of people with mental illness are released each year without the ability to pay for needed health and behavioral health treatment and medications. Without medication and comprehensive services to address housing and mental health and substance abuse treatment needs, people with mental illness have a greater risk of violation and rearrest" (Dennis and Abreu, 2010, p.83). The Social Security Administration's Supplemental Security Income (SSI) program focuses limited local and state resources on people with the highest needs and on people who use a disproportionate amount of unreimbursed services in the community.

Next, consider briefly the area of juvenile corrections.

JUVENILE CORRECTIONS

Of the estimated 100,000 juveniles residing in detention centers each day, less than a third have been arrested for violent crimes. Approximately two in three juveniles have been detained for nonviolent and nonserious offenses, at least in terms of public safety, such as status offenses (running away, truancy, etc.), property damage and nonviolent drug or alcohol violations. Despite a substantial investment in detaining juveniles, all too often none of the primary objectives of confinement—rehabilitating the offender and protecting the community—is achieved. An estimated 50 to 80 percent of youth released from juvenile facilities are rearrested within three years (Katz and Bonham, n.d., p.32).

Correctional alternatives for juveniles also include probation, intermediate sanctions, incarceration and, in some states, the death penalty, although probation is by far the most frequent disposition in juvenile delinquency cases.

The primary focus of juvenile corrections has traditionally been, and continues to be, rehabilitation. Figure 14.4 shows the various correctional avenues for juvenile offenders, providing a sense of the emphasis placed on correcting deviant behavior in youths.

Perhaps one of the most crucial areas of juvenile justice is correctly assessing where to place juveniles who are brought into the system. A mounting body of evidence has shown that incorrect assessment and placement of a youthful offender can actually worsen his or her antisocial behavior and decrease the chances of successful rehabilitation. Thus, many jurisdictions are critically reevaluating how and where they place juveniles among the variety of correctional alternatives available.

Intermediate Sanctions for Juveniles

Intermediate sanctions for juvenile offenders include shelters; ranches, forestry camps and farms; group homes; and halfway houses. Juveniles requiring greater supervision and more security may be placed in correctional facilities such as detention centers, training schools, boot camps or residential facilities.

The philosophy behind community-corrections programs for juveniles is based on the need to integrate rather than isolate offenders. It is believed that isolating juvenile offenders from their normal social environment may actually encourage development of a delinquent orientation, thus furthering delinquent behavior. Community-based corrections includes both nonresidential and residential alternatives.

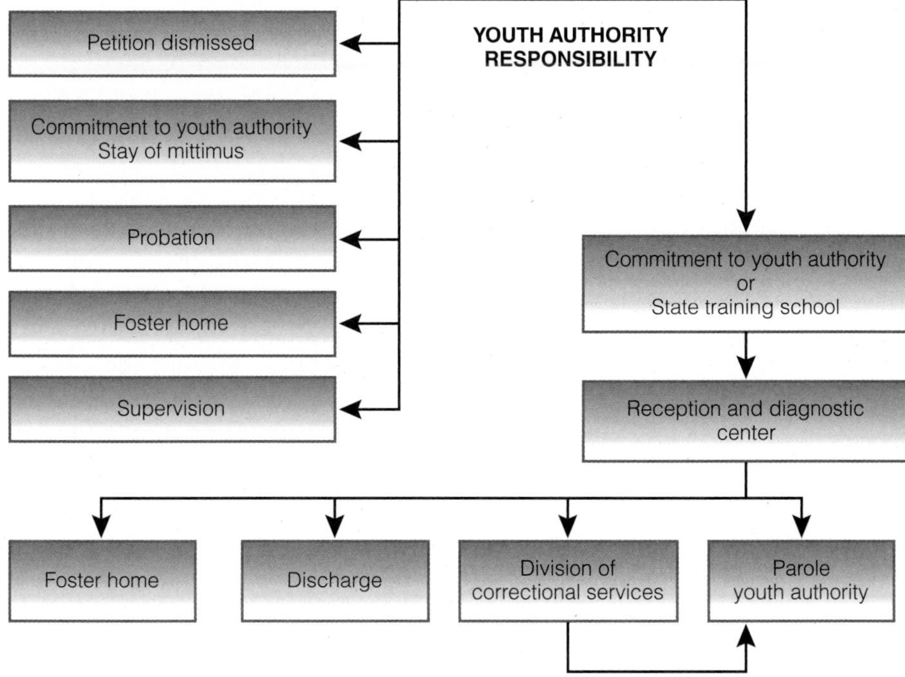

FIGURE 14.4 Youth Authority Responsibility

SOURCE: Reprinted by permission. Copyright held by The International Association of Chiefs of Police, Inc. Further reproduction without express written permission is prohibited.

A wide variety of *nonresidential corrections programs* exist, including community supervision, family crisis counseling, proctor programs and service-oriented programs such as recreational programs, counseling, alternative schools, employment training programs, and homemaking and financial planning classes. Another alternative is the nonresidential day treatment program. Many state and local governments are turning to day treatment alternatives for delinquent juveniles because they appear to be effective and are less costly than residential care. Alternatives might include evening and weekend reporting centers, school programs and specialized treatment facilities. Such programs can provide education, tutoring, counseling, community service, vocational training and social and recreational events.

Such programs tend to be successful because they can focus on the family unit and the youth's behavior in the family and the community. They are also effective from a legal standpoint in those states that require that youths be treated in the least restrictive environment possible.

Other nonsecure facilities—correctional farms, ranches and camps for youths—are usually located in rural areas. These facilities are an alternative to confinement or regimented programs. The programs with an outdoor or rural setting encourage self-development, provide opportunities for reform and secure classification of juveniles according to their capabilities. Close contact with staff and residents instills good work habits. Yet another alternative is a boot camp.

boot camp

Patterned after the traditional military boot camps for new recruits, a system of incarceration for youths that stresses strict and even cruel discipline, hard work and authoritarian decision making and control by a drill sergeant; also called *shock incarceration*.

shock incarceration

Patterned after the traditional military boot camps for new recruits, a system of incarceration for youths that stresses strict and even cruel discipline, hard work and authoritarian decision making and control by a drill sergeant; also called *boot camp*.

Boot Camps

For some offenders, community corrections are not the answer. One alternative is **boot camp**, also known as **shock incarceration.** If a judge rules shock incarceration the appropriate sentence, the offender has a choice: consent to the placement and serve a relatively shorter sentence (typically 90 to 180 days) or refuse and be placed in prison to serve a longer sentence.

The dual goals of boot camps are to rehabilitate offenders and reduce prison overcrowding. Structured after the military boot camp, strict discipline and physical labor are elements of many shock incarceration programs. Education and behavior modification are also common elements of shock incarceration programs.

In considering research on the effectiveness of boot camps, one should keep in mind that most boot camps are selective about who they accept, limiting admission to first-time, nonviolent offenders who have no psychological problems and are not suicide risks.

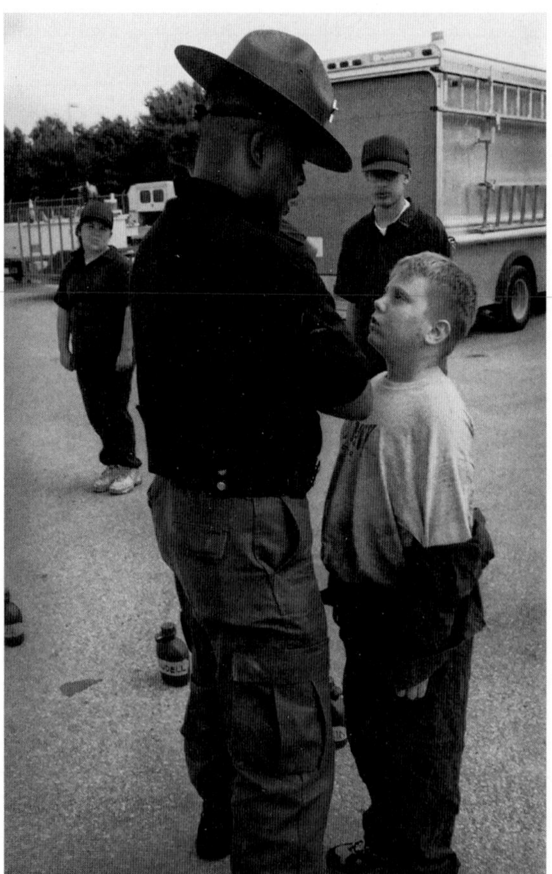

© Joel Gordon

A juvenile boot camp drill instructor disciplines a juvenile offender. Shock incarceration has been criticized as an inappropriate correctional alternative for youth on the grounds that it models aggressive behavior and focuses too much on physical conditioning and not enough on building the cognitive/behavioral skills necessary for making better life choices.

Residential Placement

During the early 1990s, tough-on-crime legislators turned to the juvenile justice system, with the majority of states lowering the minimum age for youth to be tried as adults or increasing the kind of crimes that land them in the adult system or placing them in residential facilities for youths. However, between 1997 and 2008 the juvenile arrest rate has fallen a significant 33 percent (Richmond, 2010). States throughout the country are quietly shuttering dozens of reformatories and adopting softer treatment policies. For example, in Ohio the number of juvenile offenders plummeted by nearly half during the past two years, causing the state to close three facilities. California closed a youth institution near Los Angeles that had been in operation for more than a hundred years. The result is that the number of juveniles in state institutions has dropped by 26 percent between 2000 and 2008, from about 109,000 to 80,000. In 2008, 263 juvenile offenders were in placement for every 100,000 juveniles in the general population (Sickmund, 2010, p.1).

The Office of Juvenile Justice and Delinquency Prevention (OJJDP) conducts a biannual Juvenile Residential Facility Census (JRFC). According to this census, 44 percent of juvenile facilities were publicly operated and held 69 percent of juvenile offenders (Hockenberry et al., 2009, p.2). The OJJDP also conducts a Survey of Youth in Residential Placement (SYRP), which describes the characteristics of youths' perceptions of the conditions of their confinement; their needs and the services they received; and their experiences of victimization in placement. Among the key findings of this survey were the following (Sedlak and McPherson, 2010):

- Overall, youth in custody are lukewarm in their ratings of staff. Youth in unlocked units are more than twice as likely to live in units with good youth-staff relations (26 percent versus 12 percent). Those in locked units are almost twice as likely to live where youth-staff relations are poor (53 percent versus 28 percent).
- Nearly one-third professed some gang affiliation, and 60 percent reported gangs in their facilities.
- Seventy-five percent said they received a copy of the facility's rules when they arrived, and 90 percent said they understood them; 68 percent felt the rules were applied equally to all residents.
- One-half reported that staff apply punishment without cause, and more than one-third claim staff use unnecessary force. Youth in locked units have more negative views of fair and reasonable treatment in all categories compared with youth in units that are staff secure during the day.
- Group punishment was experienced by 49 percent, 43 percent experienced removal of special privileges, 26 percent had been placed in their rooms, 24 percent were placed in solitary confinement, 23 percent were given extra work, and 20 percent were removed to another facility.

Aftercare

As in adult corrections, a major focus in juvenile corrections is reentry after being placed in nonresidential or residential care. Referred to as **aftercare**, it is important to begin aftercare efforts as early as possible, continuing through community

aftercare

In juvenile corrections, the focus on reentry into the community, which should be a focus through a juvenile's involvement in the system; usually the weakest component of the system.

corrections efforts as well as incarceration and continuants after their completion. It is similar to parole in the adult system.

Aftercare is often the weakest component of juvenile corrections. Barriers to success include lack of housing and educational options, limited interpersonal and life skills and education, mental health or substance abuse problems, and lack of community support. The school is a critical institution in aftercare for many offenders.

Two key components of aftercare are that offenders receive services and supervision and that they receive intensive intervention while incarcerated, during transition into the community and while under community supervision. More than 15 years ago, researchers Altschuler and Armstrong (1994) described an intensive aftercare program (IAP) model designed to make the process of transitioning confined youth back into the community more successful. The IAP model is based on five underlying principles:

1. Preparing youth for progressively increased responsibility and freedom in the community
2. Facilitating youth-community interaction and involvement
3. Working with both the offender and community support systems on qualities needed for constructive interaction and the youths' successful return to the community
4. Developing new resources and supports where needed
5. Monitoring and testing the youth's and the community's ability to work productively together (*Intensive Aftercare Program* [IAP], n.d.).

Recently, efforts have been made to adapt the traditional IAP model for use with girls in the juvenile justice system, incorporating the comprehensive, theoretically grounded approach to reentry with compatible "best practices" for female juvenile offenders that emphasize individualized treatment plans and consistent relationships throughout the treatment process (Ryder, 2008, p.54).

Summary

Corrections is that portion of the criminal justice system that carries out the court's orders. It includes the programs, services, agencies and institutions responsible for supervising individuals charged with or convicted of crimes. Law enforcement officers' arrest decisions directly affect who may end up in corrections. Officers are also key partners in reentry efforts, including pretrial supervision, probation and parole.

The primary purposes of corrections are retribution, deterrence, incapacitation and rehabilitation. These purposes reflect two conflicting views of criminality. The classical view holds that humans have free will and are responsible for their own actions. It focuses on crime. The positivist view holds that humans are the product of environmental and cultural influences. It focuses on the criminal.

The four basic ideologies underlying corrections are punishment, control, treatment and prevention. Punishment is associated with the justice model, control with the custodial model, treatment with the medical model and prevention with the reintegration model.

Alternatives to incarceration include straight fines and day fines, forfeiture, restitution, community service, intensive supervision, house arrest and electronic monitoring, day reporting centers, residential community corrections and probation. John Augustus is known as the father of probation and an originator of community corrections.

Many offenders, especially repeat offenders, are sentenced to correctional institutions, jails or prisons. Jail differs from prison in that its inmates are there for shorter terms, usually for less serious crimes. Jails are usually the responsibility of local or county law enforcement. The American Correctional Association recommends that the term *correctional officer* replace the term *guard*.

Prisons may be punitive oriented or treatment oriented. Punitive-oriented prisons are more formal and rigid, with an emphasis on obedience. Obedience is sought through negative incentives. In contrast, treatment-oriented prisons are more informal and flexible, with positive incentives for good behavior.

Most people sentenced to jail or prison become eligible for parole. Parole differs from probation in that a person who is paroled has spent some time serving a prison sentence. It is similar to probation in that both require supervision of the offender and set up certain conditions that the offender must meet.

Correctional alternatives for juveniles also include probation, intermediate sanctions, incarceration and, in some states, the death penalty, although probation is by far the most frequent disposition in juvenile delinquency cases. Intermediate sanctions for juvenile offenders include shelters; ranches, forestry camps and farms; group homes; and halfway houses. Juveniles requiring greater supervision and more security may be placed in correctional facilities such as detention centers, training schools and boot camps.

Discussion Questions

1. Which of the four purposes of corrections do you feel is most important?
2. What impacts have "get-tough" and "three-strikes" laws had on corrections?
3. Which environment do you think has the greatest influence on corrections today: social, political, bureaucratic, legal, community, institutional or system? The least?
4. Should drug users be put in prison even though violent offenders are granted early release due to prison overcrowding?
5. What are your views on capital punishment? A sentence of life without parole? Which would be the harsher sentence?
6. Should juveniles who commit violent offenses be handled as adults and judged in the criminal justice system?
7. Why do you think the United States has the highest incarceration rate and number of people behind bars?
8. Does your community use any forms of community corrections? If so, what are they?
9. How can corrections, which includes probation and parole, work better with law enforcement to achieve the common goal of public safety?
10. Should law enforcement play a greater role in corrections?

Gale Emergency Services Database Assignments

- Use the Gale Emergency Services Database to help answer the Discussion Questions as appropriate.
- Using the Gale Emergency Services Database, find articles on *capital punishment*. Outline one article in favor of and one article opposed to this form of "corrections," and be prepared to discuss your findings with the class.
- Using the Gale Emergency Services Database, find the article "Corrections: A Victim of Situational Ethics": http://find.galegroup.com/gps/retrieve.do?contentSet=IAC-Documents&resultListType=RESULT_LIST&qrySerId=Locale%28en%2C%2C%29%3AFQE%3D%28ke%2CNone%2C22%29history+of+corrections%24&sgHitCountType=None&inPS=true&sort=DateDescend&searchType=BasicSearchForm&tabID=T002&prodId=IPS&searchId=R3¤tPosition=2&userGroupName=cpg3&docId=A20517100&docType=IAC&contentSet=IAC-Documents

  Assignment: Read and outline some of the obstacles corrections have faced throughout history. Be prepared to discuss this topic in class.
- Using the Gale Emergency Services Database, find the article "Punishment For Profit: Private Prisons/Public Concerns": http://find.galegroup.com/gps/retrieve.do?contentSet=IAC-Documents&resultListType=RESULT_LIST&qrySerId=Locale%28en%2C%2C%29%3AFQE%3D%28ke%2CNone%2C22%29history+of+corrections%24&sgHitCountType=None&inPS=true&sort=DateDescend&searchType=BasicSearchForm&tabID=T002&prodId=IPS&searchId=R3¤tPosition=3&userGroupName=cpg3&docId=A18861021&docType=IAC&contentSet=IAC-Documents

  Assignment: Read the article and identify the main points. What is your opinion on the private versus public prisons? Compare and contrast the positives and negatives of both, and be prepared to discuss your perspectives with the class.
- Using the Gale Emergency Services Database, find the article "Prisons: Partners with the Community": http://find.galegroup.com/gps/retrieve.do?contentSet=IAC-Documents&resultListType=RESULT_LIST&qrySerId=Locale%28en%2C%2C%29%3AFQE%3D%28ke%2CNone%2C19%29correctional+system%24&sgHitCountType=None&inPS=true&sort=DateDescend&searchType=BasicSearchForm&tabID=T003&prodId=IPS&searchId=R4¤tPosition=8&userGroupName=cpg3&docId=A15140120&docType=IAC&contentSet=IAC-Documents

  Assignment: How does the example in this article differ from other prison facilities? Identify several reasons and be prepared to discuss them in class.
- Using the Gale Emergency Services Database, find the article "Corrections": http://find.galegroup.com/gps/retrieve.do?contentSet=EBKS&resultListType=RESULT_LIST&qrySerId=Locale%28en%2C%2C%29%3AFQE%3D%28K0%2CNone%2C21%29correctional+programs%24&sgHitCountType=None&inPS=true&sort=Relevance&searchType=BasicSearchForm&tabID=T001&prodId=IPS&searchId=R5¤tPosition=1&userGroupName=cpg3&docId=CX3441000037&docType=EBKS&contentSet=EBKS

Assignment: Read the article and identify one topic to discuss in detail in class. Be prepared to provide in-depth details on that topic as well as your personal thoughts, feelings and opinions.

- Using the Gale Emergency Services Database, find the article "Boot Camp for Prisoners": http://find.galegroup.com/gps/retrieve.do?contentSet=IAC-Documents&resultListType=RESULT_LIST&qrySerId=Locale%28en%2C%2C%29%3AFQE%3D%28ke%2CNone%2C10%29recidivism%24&sgHitCountType=None&inPS=true&sort=DateDescend&searchType=BasicSearchForm&tabID=T003&prodId=IPS&searchId=R6¤tPosition=15&userGroupName=cpg3&docId=A15140126&docType=IAC&contentSet=IAC-Documents

  Assignment: Read and outline this article, paying particular attention to data regarding how boot camps affect recidivism. Be prepared to share your outline and findings with the class.

- Using the Gale Emergency Services Database, find the article "A Comparison of Sexual Coercion Experiences Reported by Men and Woman in Prison": http://find.galegroup.com/gps/retrieve.do?contentSet=IAC-Documents&resultListType=RESULT_LIST&qrySerId=Locale%28en%2C%2C%29%3AFQE%3D%28ke%2CNone%2C7%29prisons%24&sgHitCountType=None&inPS=true&sort=DateDescend&searchType=BasicSearchForm&tabID=T003&prodId=IPS&searchId=R8¤tPosition=14&userGroupName=cpg3&docId=A172050807&docType=IAC&contentSet=IAC-Documents

  Assignment: What are some of the statistics regarding this matter that the article reveals? How has the U.S. government, along with correctional institutions, responded to this problem? Identify some ways this issue is being dealt with and be prepared to discuss your response in class.

Internet Assignment

- Research *community justice* on the Web at http://www.communityjustice.org. Outline at least two references.

References

Altschuler, D. M., and Armstrong, T. L. *Intensive Aftercare for High-Risk Juveniles: A Community Care Model.* Washington, DC: Office of Juvenile Justice and Delinquency Prevention, 1994.

Banks, Cathy. "NIC Publications Address Parole Competencies." *Corrections Today*, February 2010, pp.94–95.

Barbee, Jim T. "Transitioning from Jail to the Community: NIC's Response." *Corrections Today*, April 2010, pp.152–153.

Breazzano, DonaLee. "The Federal Bureau of Prisons Shifts Rentry Focus to Skills-based Model." *Corrections Today*, December 2009, pp.50–57.

Center on Wrongful Convictions, Northwestern University School of Law. Retrieved from http://www.law.northwestern.edu/cwc/

Center on Wrongful Convictions. "Executing the Innocent." Chicago, IL: Northwestern University School of Law, 2006. Retrieved from http://www.law.northwestern

.edu/wrongfulconvictions/issues/deathpenalty/executinginnocent/

Clemmer, Donald. "The Process of Prisonization." In *The Criminal in Confinement*, edited by Leon Radzinowicz and Marvin Wolfgang. New York: Basic Books, 1971, pp.92–93.

"Corrections and Public Safety." Washington, DC: The PEW Center on the States, 2010.

Crime in the United States 2009, Preliminary Annual Uniform Crime Report, January through December. Washington, DC: Federal Bureau of Investigation, May 24, 2010.

Dennis, Deborah, and Abreu, Daniel J. "Access to Benefits Enables Successful Reentry." *Corrections Today*, April 2010, pp.82–85.

Fawell, Sean. "Coordinating Jail Workflows and Information in Your Facility and Beyond." *Corrections Today*, April 2010, pp.94–99.

Fialkoff, David. "Standardizing Parole Violation Sanctions," *NIJ Journal*, June 2009. (NCJ 226873)

Gelman, Diane. "Managing Inmates with Mental Illness," *Corrections Today*, April 2010, p.22.

"Geography and the Death Penalty," Washington, DC: Death Penalty Information Center, June 10, 2010. Retrieved from http://www.deathpenaltyinfo.org/

Glaze, Lauren E., and Bonczar, Thomas P. "Probation and Parole in the United States, 2008," Washington, DC: Bureau of Justice Statistics Bulletin, December 2009. (NCJ 228230)

Grattet, Ryken; Petersilia, Joan; and Lin, Jeffrey. *Parole Violations and Revocations in California.* Washington, DC: U.S. Department of Justice, October 2008.

Hockenberry, Sarah; Sickmund, Melissa; and Sladky, Anthony. Juvenile Offenders and Victims: National Report Series, *Juvenile Residential Facility Census 2006: Selected Findings.* Washington, DC: Office of Juvenile Justice and Delinquency Prevention, December 2009. (NCJ 228128)

Innes, Christopher A. "Is There a Corrections Bubble?" *Corrections Today*, February 2010a, pp.92–93.

Innes, Christopher A. "The Simple Solution for Reducing Correctional Costs," *Corrections Today*, February 2010b, pp.32–34.

Intensive Aftercare Program (IAP). Sacramento, CA: The Center for Delinquency & Crime Policy Studies (CDCPS), California State University, no date.

Jones, Justin, and Flynn, Edward. "Cops and Corrections: Reentry Collaborations for Public Safety." *Corrections Today*, April 2008, pp.26–29.

Katz, Joanne, and Bonham, Gene. *Effective Alternatives to Incarceration: Police Collaborations with Corrections and Communities.* Washington, DC: Office of Community Oriented Policing Services, no date.

Krebs, Christopher P.; Strom, Kevin J.; Koetse, Willem H; and Lattimore, Pamela K. "The Impact of Residential and Nonresidential Drug Treatment on Recidivism among Drug-Involved Probationers: A Survival Analysis." *Crime & Delinquency*, July 2009, pp.442–471.

Mandelstam, Janet. "California Study Looks at Factors Leading to Parole Revocation." *Corrections Today*, October 2009, pp.122–123.

Martin, Brian, and Van Dine, Steve. *Examining the Impact of Ohio's Progressive Sanction Grid, Final Report.* U.S. Department of Justice, October 2008.

Minton, Todd D. *Jails in Indian Country, 2008.* Washington, DC: Bureau of Justice Statistics Bulletin, December 2009. (NCJ 228271)

One in 31: The Long Reach of American Corrections. Washington, DC: The Pew Charitable Trusts, March 2009.

Paparozzi, Mario A., and Guy, Roger. "The Giant That Never Woke: Parole Authorities as the Lynchpin to Evidence-Based Practices and Prisoner Reentry." *Journal of Contemporary Criminal Justice*, November 2009, pp.397–411.

"Prison Count 2010: State Population Declines for the First Time in 38 Years." Washington, DC: The Pew Charitable Trusts, March 16, 2010.

Richmond, Todd. "States Closing Youth Prisons as Arrests Plunge." The Associated Press, June 8, 2010. Retrieved from http://www.journal-news.com/news/nation-world-news/states-closing-youth-prisons-as-arrests-plunge-749339.html?cxtype=rss_nation-world

Ryder, Judith. "Revamping the Altschuler and Armstrong Intensive Aftercare Program for Use with Girls in the Juvenile Justice System." *Criminal Justice Research Review*, March/April 2008, pp.54–57.

Sabol, William J.; West, Heather C.; and Cooper, Matthew. "Prisoners in 2008." Washington, DC: Bureau of Justice Statistics Bulletin, December 2009. (NCJ 228417)

Sedlak, Andrea J., and McPherson, Karla S. *Conditions of Confinement: Findings from the Survey of Youth in Residential Placement.* Washington, DC: Office of Juvenile Justice and Delinquency Prevention, Juvenile Justice Bulletin, May 2010. (NCJ 227729)

Sickmund, Melissa. *Juveniles in Residential Placement 1997–2008.* Washington, DC: Office of Juvenile Justice and Delinquency Prevention Fact Sheet, February 2010. (NCJ 229379)

Snell, Tracy L. "Capital Punishment, 2008-Statistical Tables," Washington, DC: Bureau of Justice Statistics, December 3, 2009. (NCJ 228662).

Stevenson, Ben, and Legg, Shaunda. "The First Responders in the Reentry Process." *Corrections Today*, April 2010, pp.104–107.

"'Swift and Certain' Sanctions in Probation Are Highly Effective: Evaluation of the HOPE Program." Washington, DC: National Institute of Justice, April 23, 2010.

Travis, Jeremy; Crayton, Anna; and Mukamal, Debbie A. "A New Era in Inmate Reentry." *Corrections Today*, December 2009, pp.38–41.

Wall, Ashbel T., II, and Poole, Tracey Z. "Partnerships with Local Law Enforcement and Community Agencies: A Critical Component to Successful Prisoner Reentry Initiatives." *Corrections Today*, April 2008, pp.30–37.

Wicklund, Carl. "Police and Probation and Parole—A Relationship." *Community Policing Dispatch*, June 2010.

Yost, Pete. "Emptier Cells: Jail Population Declines for First Time Since '82." Associated Press, June 3, 2010. Retrieved from http:://www.boston.com/news/nation/washington/articles/2010/06/03/jail_population_declines_for_first_time_since_82/

Cases Cited

Furman v. Georgia, 408 U.S. 238 (1972)

Roper v. Simmons, 543 U.S. 551 (2005)

APPENDIX A

State Hate Crimes/Statutory Provisions

Alabama–Idaho

	AL	AK	AZ	AR	CA	CO	CT	DC	DE	FL	GA	HI	ID
Bias-Motivated Violence and Intimidation	✓	✓	✓		✓	✓	✓	✓	✓	✓	✓		✓
Civil Action				✓	✓	✓	✓	✓		✓	✓		✓
Criminal Penalty	✓	✓	✓		✓	✓	✓	✓	✓	✓	✓		✓
Race, Religion, Ethnicity[1]	✓	✓	✓		✓	✓	✓	✓	✓	✓			✓
Sexual Orientation			✓		✓		✓	✓	✓	✓			
Gender		✓	✓		✓			✓					
Other[2]	✓	✓	✓		✓			✓	✓				
Institutional Vandalism	✓		✓	✓	✓	✓	✓	✓	✓	✓	✓	✓	
Data Collection[3]			✓		✓		✓	✓		✓			✓
Training for Law Enforcement Personnel[4]			✓		✓								

Illinois–Missouri

	IL	IN	IA	KS	KY	LA	ME	MD	MA	MI	MN	MS	MO
Bias-Motivated Violence and Intimidation	✓		✓		✓	✓	✓	✓	✓	✓	✓	✓	✓
Civil Action	✓		✓			✓			✓	✓	✓		✓
Criminal Penalty	✓		✓		✓	✓	✓	✓	✓	✓	✓	✓	✓
Race, Religion, Ethnicity[1]	✓		✓		✓	✓	✓	✓	✓	✓	✓	✓	✓
Sexual Orientation	✓		✓		✓	✓	✓		✓		✓		
Gender	✓		✓			✓	✓			✓	✓	✓	
Other[2]	✓		✓			✓	✓		✓		✓		
Institutional Vandalism	✓	✓		✓	✓	✓	✓	✓	✓	✓	✓	✓	✓
Data Collection[3]	✓		✓		✓	✓	✓	✓	✓	✓	✓		
Training for Law Enforcement Personnel[4]	✓		✓		✓	✓			✓		✓		

Montana–Pennsylvania

	MT	NE	NV	NH	NJ	NM	NY	NC	ND	OH	OK	OR	PA
Bias-Motivated Violence and Intimidation	✓	✓	✓	✓	✓		✓[5]	✓	✓	✓	✓	✓	✓
Civil Action		✓	✓		✓					✓	✓	✓	✓
Criminal Penalty	✓	✓	✓	✓	✓		✓	✓	✓	✓	✓	✓	✓
Race, Religion, Ethnicity[1]	✓	✓	✓	✓	✓		✓	✓	✓	✓	✓	✓	✓
Sexual Orientation		✓	✓	✓	✓		✓					✓	
Gender		✓		✓	✓		✓		✓				
Other[2]		✓	✓	✓	✓		✓				✓		
Institutional Vandalism	✓		✓		✓	✓		✓		✓	✓	✓	✓
Data Collection[3]		✓	✓		✓						✓	✓	✓
Training for Law Enforcement Personnel[4]												✓	

Rhode Island–Wyoming

	RI	SC	SD	TN	TX	UT	VT	VA	WA	WV	WI	WY
Bias-Motivated Violence and Intimidation	✓		✓	✓	✓[6]	✓[7]	✓	✓	✓	✓	✓	
Civil Action	✓		✓	✓			✓	✓	✓		✓	
Criminal Penalty	✓		✓	✓	✓	✓	✓	✓	✓	✓	✓	
Race, Religion, Ethnicity[1]	✓		✓	✓			✓	✓	✓	✓	✓	
Sexual Orientation	✓			✓			✓		✓		✓	
Gender	✓						✓		✓	✓		
Other[2]	✓						✓		✓	✓	✓	
Institutional Vandalism	✓	✓		✓	✓			✓	✓		✓	
Data Collection[3]	✓				✓			✓	✓			
Training for Law Enforcement Personnel[4]	✓								✓			

[1]The following states also have statutes criminalizing interference with religious worship: CA, DC, FL, ID, MD, MA, MI, MN, MS, MO, NV, NM, NY, NC, OK, RI, SC, SD, TN, VA, WV.

[2]"Other" includes mental and physical disability or handicap (AL, AK, AZ, CA, DC, DE, IL, IA, LA, ME, MN, NE, NV, NH, NJ, NY, OK, RI, VT, WA, WI), political affiliation (DC, IA, LA, WV) and age (DC, IA, LA, VT).

[3]States with data collection statutes that include sexual orientation are AZ, CA, CT, DC, FL, IL, IA, MD, NV, OR, and WA; those that include gender are AZ, DC, IL, IA, MN, WA.

[4]Some other states have regulations mandating such training.

[5]New York State law provides penalty enhancement limited to the crime of aggravated harassment.

[6]The Texas Statute refers to victims selected "because of the defendant's bias or prejudice against a person or group."

[7]The Utah Statute ties penalties for hate crimes to violations of the victim's constitutional or civil rights.

SOURCE: Anti-Defamation League, 2001. Accessed from http://www.adl.org/99hatecrime/provisions.asp. Reprinted by permission.

APPENDIX B

Victim and Witness Services

	Stage One: Emergency Response	Stage Two: Victim Stabilization	Stage Three: Resource Mobilization	Stage Four: After Arrest
When:	First contact after crime	On scene, or upon report, or within 48 hours After victim reacts to trigger events	Until resolution of victimization experience	First contact after arrest
Who:	*By telephone:* 911 operator Crisis line Family and friends *Face-to-face:* On-scene crisis intervener Law enforcement Family and friends Public	Crisis counselors Law enforcement patrol and investigators Family and friends	Victim service providers Law enforcement Compensation programs Family or friends	Prosecutors Victim service providers Law enforcement Family and friends
What:	Trauma assessment Physical first aid Emotional first aid Crisis intervention Protection from further harm	*Crisis counselors or law enforcement:* Stabilizing interviews Crisis counseling Conflict management Shelter, transportation or protection Criminal justice orientation Referrals *Family and friends:* Personal assistance Emotional first aid Companionship and reassurance	*Victim services:* Outreach Supportive counseling Information, referrals *Aid with:* Financial claims Landlords, creditors Employers Property return Legal referrals Crime, violence, substance abuse information Advocacy *Law enforcement:* Fast property return Information, referrals *Compensation:* Outreach Assistance with claims Emergency aid *Family and friends:* Information Understanding Aid with crime prevention Advocacy	*Prosecutors* *Information on:* Justice process Case status Reparations *Consultations on:* Charging decisions Release conditions Diversion Case scheduling *Aid with:* Restitution Intimidation reports Protection orders Relocation *Victim services:* Start/continue Stage 1–3 services Aid with media Supportive counseling *Law enforcement:* Protection order, bail enforcement Relocation *Family and friends:* Support in system
Rights:	Protection Information Dignity and compassion	Protection Information Dignity and compassion	Protection Information Reparations Property/employment Dignity and compassion	Protection Information Counsel Reparations Property/employment Due process Dignity and compassion

Stage Five: Pre-Court Appearance	Stage Six: Court Appearance	Stage Seven: Before Case Disposition	Stage Eight: After Case Disposition
When: Before any appearance	**When:** Day of hearing or trial	**When:** After verdict or entry of guilty plea	**When:** After disposition
Who: Prosecutors Victim service providers Family and friends	**Who:** Prosecutors Judiciary Victim service providers Family or friends	**Who:** Judiciary Probation Prosecutors Victim service providers Family and friends	**Who:** All corrections agencies Victim service providers Prosecutors Judiciary Family and friends
What: *Prosecutors:* Enforcement of protection orders, bail Protection of victim names, addresses *Information on:* Justice process Case status scheduling, continuances Testifying and the courtroom Consultation on plea Aid with landlord, creditor, employer Support on due process claims *Victim Services:* Start/continue Stage 1–4 services Justice orientation Aid with media Aid with victim impact statements Aid with transportation, child care, creditors, etc. *Family and friends:* Support in court	**What:** *Prosecutors:* Protection from intimidation, media intrusion Aid with transportation, child care, creditors, etc. Consultation on unexpected events Aid with witness fees Aid with due process claims *Judiciary:* Ban badgering by defense, media Let victims, family attend all proceedings Provide information about court process *Victim service providers:* Start/continue Stage 1–5 services Help prosecutor provide services *Family and friends:* Support in court	**What:** *Judiciary:* Ban badgering by defense, media Allow victim impact statement, allocation Order restitution for all damages Address victim concerns at hearing *Probation:* Information on verdict, sentencing hearing Consultation on victim impact statement, restitution claims Explore VORP option *Prosecutor:* Parallel services with probation *Victim services:* Start/continue Stage 1–6 services Help prosecutor, probation provide services Information, referrals on civil entitlement *Family and friends:* Provide victim impact information Support in court	**What:** *Probation:* Administer VORP Offender status info Enforce conditions, restitution orders *Corrections:* Offender status information Teach "victim impact" Enforce restitution *Parole:* Notice on hearings Allow victim input Order/enforce restitution, protection *Prosecution:* Invite victim input in revocation hearings *Judiciary:* Enforce conditions *Victim service providers:* Advocacy with, support to, others Start/continue Stage 1–7 services *Family or friends:* Ongoing support Protection of victim from further intimidation or harassment Provide victim impact information
Rights: Protection Information Counsel Reparations Property/employment Due process Dignity and compassion	**Rights:** All victim rights involved	**Rights:** All victim rights involved	**Rights:** All victim rights engaged

SOURCE: Julie Esselman Tome and Daniel McGillis. *Serving Crime Victims and Witnesses*, 2nd edition. Washington, DC: National Institute of Justice, February 1997, pp.6–7.

APPENDIX C

Strategies for Your Agency to Ensure Language Access

- Determine the languages spoken in your jurisdiction by collecting demographic data from local and federal sources.
- Undergo a planning process to develop a language access policy and protocol guidance.
- Educate all agency personnel about language access and how to utilize agency language assistance services.
- Recruit bilingual personnel and offer a base pay increase for staff who pass a proficiency exam.
- Provide bilingual personnel with police interpreter training.
- Encourage officers and civilian staff to use their language skills.
- Train staff on how to effectively work with "ad hoc," volunteer, and professional interpreters during an interaction with an LEP (Limited English Proficiency) individual.
- Deploy bilingual personnel to areas with high numbers of LEP residents.
- Use bilingual civilian staff to conduct community outreach and build relationships between your department and immigrant and LEP residents.
- Translate signage and documents that communicate vital information to the public into the most prevalent languages spoken by LEP community members.
- Notify the public about your agency's language access policy and language assistance resources.
- Pool resources and leverage assets with other agencies and services in your city or county.

GLOSSARY

The number following the definition refers to the chapter(s) in which the term is introduced. Definitions of specific crimes are from the Federal Bureau of Investigations Uniform Crime Reports.

accreditation—Being approved by an official review board as meeting specific standards. (12)

acquittal—A formal certification by the court stating that the accused is found "not guilty" of the crimes he or she has been charged with; the charges are dropped and the defendant is released. (13)

actus reus—A guilty, measurable act, including planning and conspiring. (2)

adjudication—The process of judicially deciding a legal case. (13)

administrative services—Those services such as recruiting, training, planning and research, records, communications, crime laboratories and facilities, including the police headquarters and jail. (4)

administrative warrant—Official permission to investigate the cause of a fire after the fire has been extinguished. (8)

adversary system—The criminal justice system used in the United States that puts the accuser versus the accused; the accuser must prove that the one accused is guilty. (13)

affidavit—A statement reduced to writing and sworn to before a judge or notary having authority to administer an oath. (8)

affirmative action—Results-oriented actions taken to ensure equal employment opportunity. (12)

aftercare—In juvenile corrections, the focus on reentry into the community, which should be a focus through a juvenile's involvement in the system; usually the weakest component of the system. (14)

aggressive patrol—Uses crime statistics to plan shift and beat staffing, providing more coverage during times of peak criminal activity and in high-crime areas; designed to handle problems and situations requiring coordinated efforts; also called *directed patrol.* (5)

American creed—The belief in individual freedom. (2)

American Dream—Belief that anyone who works hard and is willing to sacrifice for a while can be successful. (7)

appellate jurisdiction—A higher court with the power to hear and decide an appeal to the decision of an original court without holding a trial. (13)

arraignment—A court procedure whereby the accused is read the charges against him or her and is then asked how he or she pleads. (13)

arrest—The taking of a person into custody by the actual restraint of the person or by his or her submission to the custody of the officer so that he or she may be held to answer for a public offense before a judge. (8)

arson—Intentionally damaging or destroying, or attempting to damage or destroy, by means of fire or explosion the property of another without the consent of the owner or one's own property, with or without the intent to defraud. (3)

assault—An unlawful attack by one person upon another for the purpose of inflicting severe bodily injury. (3)

asymmetric warfare—Conflict in which a much weaker opponent takes on a stronger opponent by refusing to confront the stronger opponent head on. (10)

ballistics—A science dealing with the motion and effects of projectiles such as bullets and bombs. (6)

battery—Physical assault. (3)

bench trial—When a defendant chooses to waive a jury and appear only before a judge. (13)

Bill of Rights—The first 10 amendments to the U.S. Constitution. (2)

bioterrorism—Involves such biological weapons of mass destruction (WMDs) as anthrax, botulism and smallpox to cause fear in a population. (10)

Bloods—Well-known African American gang; rivals of the Crips. (9)

bona fide occupational qualification (BFOQ)—Skill or knowledge that is reasonably necessary to perform a job and, consequently, may be a requirement for employment. (12)

boot camp—Patterned after the traditional military boot camps for new recruits, a system of incarceration for youths that stresses strict and even cruel discipline, hard work and authoritarian decision making and control by a drill sergeant; also called *shock incarceration*. (14)

Bow Street Runners—The first English detective unit; established in London by Henry Fielding in 1750. (1)

bowling-alone phenomenon—Refers to a striking decline in social capital and civic engagement in the United States. (7)

broken-window phenomenon—Maintains that if a neighborhood is allowed to run down, it will give the impression that no one cares and crime will flourish. (7)

***Buie* sweep**—A quick check of closets or behind doors to see if anyone who may pose a threat is present. (8)

burglary—An unlawful entry into a building to commit a theft or felony. (3)

burnout—A psychological state that occurs when someone is made exhausted and listless and rendered unserviceable or ineffectual through overwork, stress or intemperance. (12)

burst stress—Having to go immediately from relative calm to high-intensity, sometimes life-threatening activity. (12)

carjacking—Stealing a car from the driver by force. (3)

case law—A collection of summaries of how statutes have been applied by judges in various situations; the precedents established by the courts. (2)

chain of custody—Documenting who has had possession of evidence from the time it was discovered and taken into custody until the present time. (6)

civil injunction—A court order prohibiting a person or group from engaging in certain activities. (9)

civil law—All restrictions placed upon individuals that are noncriminal in nature; seeks restitution rather than punishment. (2)

civil liberties—An individual's immunity from governmental oppression. (2)

civil rights—Claims that citizens have to the affirmative assistance of government. (2)

classical theory—Theory developed by eighteenth-century Italian criminologist Cesare Beccaria that sees people as free agents with free will; people commit crimes because they want to. (3)

collective bargaining—The process where tatives of employees meet with representat agement to establish a written contract that sets forth working conditions for a specific time, usually one to three years. (12)

common law—In England, the customary law set by judges as disputes arose; the law in force before and independent of legislation. (2)

community era—(1980–present) The third era of policing; characterized by authority coming from community support, law and professionalism; provision of a broad range of services, including crime control; decentralized organization with more authority given to patrol officers; partnerships with the community; and use of foot patrol and a problem-solving approach. (1)

community policing—A philosophy that emphasizes a problem-solving partnership between the police and the citizens in working toward a healthy, crime-free environment; also called *neighborhood policing*. (4, 7)

complainant—The person reporting the offense. (6)

complaint—A legal document drawn up by a prosecutor that specifies an alleged crime and the supporting facts providing probable cause. (13)

CompStat policing—A method of management accountability and a philosophy of crime control. (7)

conflict theory—Contends that certain behaviors are criminalized to keep the dominant class in power. (2)

consensus theory—Holds that individuals within a society agree on basic values, on what is inherently right and wrong. (2)

consent—To agree; to give permission; voluntary oral or written permission to search a person's premises or property. (8)

constable—An elected official of a hundred, responsible for leading the citizens in pursuit of any lawbreakers; the first English police officer and, as such, in charge of the weapons and horses of the entire community. (1)

constitution—A system of fundamental laws and principles that prescribe the nature, functions and limits of a government or other body; the basic instrument of government and the supreme law of the United States; the written instrument defining the power, limitations and functions of the U.S. government and of each state. (2)

contagion effect—Media coverage of terrorism inspires more terrorism. (10)

contamination—The introduction of something foreign into the scene, moving items at the scene or removing evidence from it. (6)

continuum of compromise—Describes the transition from honest to corrupt cop; the slippery slope often begins with an officer accepting gratuities or tokens of appreciation. (11)

contraband—Anything illegal to import, export, produce or possess, such as heroin or a machine gun. (8)

corpus delicti—Literally, the body of the crime itself—the distinctive elements that must exist for a particular crime to be proven. (2)

corruption—When an officer misuses authority for personal gain, including accepting gratuities. (11)

crack—A form of cocaine available at greatly reduced costs. (9)

credentialing—Process whereby individual police officers are evaluated and approved by he National Law Enforcement Credentialing Board (NLECB) as meeting certain standards. (12)

crime control—Emphasizes collective needs of society and the idea that all offenders should receive the harshest penalty allowed by law. (2)

crime scene investigation (CSI)—As a noun, is a specialized unit that focuses on the discovery, investigation, and collection of evidence of a crime; CSI as a verb is a highly methodological way of evidence collection that leads to information about a crime, including the identification and conviction of suspects. (6)

criminal intent—A resolve, design or mutual determination to commit a crime, with full knowledge of the consequences and exercise of free will; the *mens rea* or, literally, the "guilty mind." (2)

criminal law—The body of law that defines crimes and assigns punishments for them. (2)

criminal sexual conduct (CSC)—Encompasses all sex crimes regulated by law, including rape and other minor sexually deviant related behaviors. (3)

criminalistics—A branch of forensic science that deals with physical evidence related to a crime, including fingerprints, firearms, tool marks, blood, hair, documents and other types of physical evidence. (6)

Crips—Gang with the reputation of being the toughest African American gang in Los Angeles; rivals of the Bloods. (9)

critical incident—An event that elicits an overwhelming emotional response from those witnessing it. (12)

cross-examination—Questioning of an opposing witness in a trial or hearing. (13)

curtilage—That portion of property associated with the common use of land—for example, buildings, sheds and fenced-in areas. (8)

custody—State of being kept or guarded, or being detained. (8)

cyberterrorism—Terrorism that initiates, or threatens to initiate, the exploitation of or attack on computerized information systems. (10)

dark figure of crime—The actual, unknown number of crimes being committed. (3)

de facto arrest—Occurs when officers who lack probable cause to arrest take a suspect in for questioning; officers' actions have the appearance of an arrest—that is, the suspect is not free to leave. (8)

***de minimus* communication**—A simple hello or giving directions. (13)

deadly force—Any force that can reasonably be expected to cause or is intended to cause death or serious physical injury. (11)

deconfliction—Avoiding conflict. (10)

delinquency—Actions or conduct by a juvenile in violation of criminal law or constituting a status offense; an error or failure by a child or adolescent to conform to society's expectations of social order. (3)

demographics—Refers to the characteristics of the individuals who live in a community, including a population's size, distribution, growth, density, employment rate, ethnic makeup and vital statistics such as average age, education and income. (7)

detention—Occurs when an officer has said or done something that would cause reasonable innocent persons to believe they are not free to disregard the police presence and go about their business; must be justified by reasonable suspicion; the higher standard of probable cause is not constitutionally required for detention. (8)

determinism—Regards crime as a consequence of many factors, including population density, economic status and the legal definition of crime. (3)

deterrence—Sees corrections as a way to prevent future criminal actions; tries to show offenders that the price of committing crimes is too great. (14)

differential response strategies—Suiting the response to the call. (5)

diffusion of benefits—Crackdowns can reduce crime and disorder outside the target area or reduce offenses not targeted in the crackdowns. (5)

directed patrol—Uses crime statistics to plan shift and beat staffing, providing more coverage during times of peak criminal activity and in high-crime areas; designed to handle problems and situations requiring coordinated efforts; also called *aggressive patrol.* (5)

direct victims—Those who are initially harmed by injury, death or loss of property as a result of crimes committed; also called *primary victims.* (3)

discovery crimes—Illegal acts brought to the attention of the victim and law enforcement after the act has been committed—a burglary, for example. (6)

discovery process—A system that requires all pertinent facts be made available to the prosecutor and the defense attorney before the trial. (13)

discretion—The freedom of an agency or individual officer to make choices as to whether to act; freedom to act or judge on one's own. (4)

discrimination—Showing a preference in treating individuals or groups or failing to treat equals equally, especially illegal unequal treatment based on race, religion, sex or age. (11)

disparity—A simple difference, not necessarily caused by any kind of bias. (11)

diversion—Bypassing the criminal justice system by assigning an offender to a social agency or other institution rather than trying him or her in court. (13)

DNA profiling—Uses the material from which chromosomes are made to positively identify individuals; no two individuals except identical twins have the same DNA structure. (6)

double jeopardy—Unconstitutionally being tried for the same crime more than once. (2)

drug-defined offenses—Illegal acts involving drugs; that is, the crime occurs as a part of the drug business or culture, for example, marijuana cultivation or cocaine distribution. Also called *systemic offenses.* (9)

drug-related offenses—Illegal acts in which the effect of a drug is a contributor, such as when a drug user commits crime because of drug-induced changes in physiological functions, cognitive ability and mood, or in which the need for the drug is a factor, as when a drug user commits crime to obtain money to buy drugs. (9)

dual motive stop—When the officer has an ulterior motive for the stop; also called a *pretext stop.* (5)

due diligence—The attention and care a reasonable person exercises under the circumstances to avoid harm to other persons or their property; failure to make this effort is considered negligence. (12)

due process of law—Embodies the fundamental ideas of American justice expressed in the Fifth and Fourteenth Amendments, requiring the fundamental principles of fairness and justice to prevail during judicial proceedings. (2)

ecclesiastical law—Law of the church. (2)

8% problem—A group of repeat offenders dramatically different from those who are arrested only once; account for a disproportionate amount of youth crime. (3)

elements of the crime—The distinctive acts making up a specific crime; the elements make up the *corpus delicti* of the crime. (2)

E911 (enhanced 911)—Requires wireless carriers to identify the location of the caller to within 125 meters at least two thirds of the time. (4)

entrapment—Occurs when a government agent induces someone to commit a crime that is not normally considered by the person for the purpose of prosecuting that person. (8)

environmental anomalies—Unusual activities that warrant further investigation. (5)

equity—A concept requiring that the "spirit of the law" takes precedence over the "letter of the law." (2)

ethics—Involves moral behavior, doing what is considered right and just; the rules or standards governing the conduct of a profession. (11)

evidence-based policing (EBP)—Takes what has been shown, through scientific research, to be effective and applies it to real-world policing. (7)

excessive force—Force beyond that which is reasonably necessary to accomplish a legitimate law enforcement purpose. (11)

excited delirium—Identified by such behaviors as being extremely agitated, threatening violence, talking incoherently, tearing off clothes and requiring four or five officers to restrain the individual. (11)

exclusionary rule—A U.S. Supreme Court ruling that any evidence seized in violation of the Fourth Amendment will not be admissible in a federal or state trial. (8)

exculpatory evidence—Evidence favorable to the accused. (11)

exigent circumstances—The same as emergency situations. (8)

extra patrol—Typically used when a specific type of crime has occurred several times in a certain area, or if there is a high probability that a crime might occur. (5)

federalism—A principle whereby power is shared by the national government and the states. (2)

felony—A major crime—for example, murder, rape, arson; the penalty is usually death or imprisonment for more than one year in a state prison or penitentiary. (2)

field identification—At-the-scene identification, made within a reasonable time after a crime has been committed. (6)

field inquiry—Briefly detaining or stopping persons to determine who they are or what they are up to. (8)

field services—The operations or line divisions of a law enforcement agency, such as patrol, traffic control, community service, and investigation. (4)

Firefighter's Rule—A person who negligently starts a fire is not liable to a firefighter or other public officer injured while responding to the fire. (12)

first-degree murder—Willful, deliberate and premeditated (planned) taking of another person's life. (3)

foot patrol—Consists of officers walking a "beat" and responding to incidents on foot. (5)

force—Action taken to compel an individual to comply with an officer's request. (11)

forced entry—An announced or unannounced entry into a dwelling or a building by force for the purpose of executing a search or arrest warrant to avoid the needless destruction of property, to prevent violent and deadly force against the officer and to prevent the escape of a suspect. (8)

forensic science—The study of evidence for the purpose of answering legal questions. (6)

Frankpledge system—Norman modification of the tithing system requiring loyalty to the king's law and mutual local responsibility in maintaining the peace. (1)

frisk—A patting down or minimal search of a person to determine the presence of a dangerous weapon. (8)

fusion center—An effective, efficient mechanism to exchange information and intelligence, maximize resources, streamline operations and improve the ability to fight crime and terrorism by merging data from a variety of sources. (7)

gang—A group of people who form an allegiance for a common purpose and engage in unlawful or criminal activity. (9)

***Garrity* protection**—Employers can insist that officers provide information for an administrative investigation, but must be told that they retain their constitutional rights and that any information so provided cannot be used if a criminal proceeding is brought against the officer. (11)

gateway theory—Contends that marijuana use leads to use of harder drugs. (9)

general deterrence—Deterrence to serve as an example to others of the consequences of crime. (14)

ghosting—Falsifying patrol logs to make the numbers come out right in response to alleged racial profiling practices. (11)

graffiti—Writing or drawing on buildings and walls; a common form of communication used by gang members to mark their territory; sometimes called the newspaper of the street. (9)

homicide—The willful killing of a human by another human; also called *murder.* (3)

homophobia—A fear of gays and lesbians. (11)

hot spots—Specific locations with high crime rates. (5)

hue and cry—A shout by a citizen who witnessed a crime, enlisting the aid of others in the area to chase and catch the offender; may be the origin of the general alarm and the citizen's arrest. (1)

hundreds—Groups of 10 tithings. (1)

hung jury—A jury that cannot reach a decision; the result is a " no verdict" decision that can result in a retrial. (13)

identity theft—A crime involving misappropriation of names, social security numbers, credit card numbers or other pieces of personal information for fraudulent purposes. (3)

image—How one is viewed; the concept of someone or something held by the public. Police image results from the media's portrayal of police and from everyday contacts between individual police officers and citizens. (4)

immediate control—Within a person's immediate reach; also called *wingspan.* (8)

impeach—Discredit. (13)

implied consent laws—Laws stating that any person driving a motor vehicle is deemed to have consented to a chemical test of the alcohol content of his or her blood if arrested while intoxicated; refusal to take such a test can be introduced in court as evidence. (5)

incapacitation—Making it impossible for offenders to commit further offenses. (14)

incarceration—Being confined in jail or prison. (14)

incident—An isolated event that requires a police response. (7)

incident-driven policing—Where calls for service drive the department; a reactive approach with emphasis on rapidity of response. (5)

incivilities—Visible signs of people not caring about their community, for example, broken windows, unmowed lawns, piles of accumulated trash, litter, graffiti, abandoned buildings, rowdiness, drunkenness, fighting and prostitution. (7)

incorporation doctrine—Holds that only those provisions of the Bill of Rights fundamental to the American legal process are made applicable to the states through the due process clause; also called *selective incorporation*. (2)

indicted—Formally charged with a specific crime by a grand jury, based on probable cause. (2)

indigent—Destitute, poverty-stricken, with no visible means of support. (2)

indirect victims—All other community members who may be threatened or fearful as a result of the commission of crime; can include family, relatives, friends, neighborhoods, the entire community and even police officers who must deal with the aftermath of violent crimes, such as battered children and grisly deaths; also called *secondary victims*. (3)

inevitable discovery doctrine—Holds that illegally obtained evidence may be admitted at trial if the prosecution can prove that the evidence would have been discovered sooner or later (inevitably). (8)

informant—Person who furnishes information concerning accusations against another person or persons, but who did not witness the offense. (6)

inspection warrant—See *administrative warrant*. (8)

instruments of a crime—The means by which a crime is committed or the suspects or victims transported, for example, gun, knife, burglary tools, car, truck. (8)

integrated patrol—An operational philosophy that combines community-based policing with aggressive enforcement and provides a balanced, comprehensive approach to addressing crime problems throughout an entire jurisdiction rather than merely in targeted areas within a community. (7)

intelligence-led policing (ILP)—A methodical approach to prevent, detect and disrupt crime, including terrorist activities. (7)

integrity—A series of concepts and beliefs that provide structure to an agency's operation and officers' professional and personal ethics, including, but not limited to, honesty, honor, morality, allegiance, principled behavior and dedication to mission. (11)

interdiction—Cutting off or destroying a line of communication—in the case of drug control, halting the flow of drugs into the United States. (9)

intermediate sanctions—Sanctions that are tougher than traditional probation but less stringent and less expensive than imprisonment. (14)

interoperability—The capacity of various telecommunications and computing devices to "talk" to each other. (4)

interrogate—To question a suspect. (6)

interview—To question a witness or person with information relating to an incident. (6)

investigatory stop—The simple act of stopping someone based on reasonable suspicion, alternately called a *field inquiry*, a *threshold inquiry* or, most commonly, a *Terry stop*. (8)

involvement crimes—Illegal acts discovered while being committed. (6)

jihad—A holy war. (10)

judicial waiver—The juvenile court waives jurisdiction and transfers a case to criminal court; also known as binding over, transferring or certifying juvenile cases to criminal courts. (13)

jurisdiction—The geographic area within which a court (or public official) has the right and power to operate; also refers to individuals and subjects over which a court has the right and power to make binding decisions. (13)

jurisprudence—The science or philosophy of law in a given area; a department of law. (13)

just deserts—Retribution; individuals "get what's coming to them." (14)

justice model—Assumes offenders are self-directed, acting on free will and responsible for their crimes. (14)

justifiable homicide—Includes killing in self-defense or in the defense of another person if the victim's actions and capability present imminent danger of serious injury or death. (3)

landmark decision—A judicial ruling that significantly alters or affects existing law and guides future decisions on the same issue. (2)

larceny-theft—The unlawful taking and removing of the property of another with the intent of permanently depriving the legal holder of the property. (3)

law—A body of rules for human conduct enforced by imposing penalties for their violation. (1)

Leges Henrici—A document that made law enforcement a public matter and separated offenses into felonies and misdemeanors. (1)

less-lethal force—Force that has less potential for causing death or serious injury than do traditional tactics. (11)

lex talionis—An eye for an eye. (1, 14)

liability—A legal obligation incurred for an injury suffered/complained about that results from failure to conduct a specific task/activity within a given standard. (11)

litigaphobia—Fear of a lawsuit. (11)

magistrate—A judge. (8)

Magna Carta—A decisive document in the development of constitutional government in England that checked royal power and placed the king under the law (1215). (1)

mala in se—"Bad in itself," a crime such as murder or rape so offensive that it is obviously criminal. (2)

mala prohibita—"Bad because it is forbidden," a crime that violates a specific regulatory statute and would not usually be considered a crime if no law prohibited it, for example, certain traffic violations. (2)

manslaughter—Accidentally causing the death of another person; no malice, intent, hatred, ill will or disregard for the lives of others is involved. (3)

medical model—In corrections, assumes criminals are victims of society and need to be "cured." (7, 14)

mens rea—Guilty intent; literally "a guilty mind." (2)

meta-analysis—Provides a rigorous, objective, and quantitative strategy to make effective use of an existing body of research, even when the results seem inconsistent and inconclusive. (7)

methamphetamine—A powerful stimulant emerging as a major problem for law enforcement because of its tendency to invoke violence in the user. (9)

misdemeanor—A minor offense—for example, breaking a municipal ordinance, speeding; the penalty is typically a fine or a short imprisonment, usually less than one year, in a local jail or workhouse. (2)

modus operandi (MO)—A method of criminal attack specific to an individual offender, which can be used to help identify a suspect. (6)

monikers—Street names of gang members. (9)

moonlighting—Working at a second, part-time job while fulfilling the obligations of a full-time position. (12)

motive—Reason for doing something. (2)

motor vehicle theft—The unlawful taking or stealing of a motor vehicle without the authority or permission of the owner; includes automobiles, trucks, buses, motorcycles, motorized boats and aircraft. (3)

mules—Individuals who smuggle cocaine for professional drug dealers; often tourists or students. (9)

murder—See *homicide*. (3)

negligent hiring—Negligence in hiring personnel unqualified or unsuited for law enforcement work. (12)

negligent homicide—An accidental death that results from the reckless operation of a motor vehicle, boat, plane or firearm. (3)

nightcap warrants—Nighttime search or arrest warrants. (8)

no bill—Issued by a grand jury if it decides that no crime has been committed. (13)

no-knock search warrant—Authorization by a magistrate upon the issuance of a search warrant to enter a premise by force without notification to avoid the chance that evidence may be destroyed if the officers' presence was announced. (8)

nolo contendere—"I will not contest it." A defendant's plea of "no contest" in a criminal case; it means he or she does not directly admit guilt but submits to sentencing or other punishment. (13)

one-pot approach—Equating poor and abused children with delinquent and criminal children and treating them in essentially the same way. (13)

open fields doctrine—Holds that land beyond what is normally associated with use of that land, that is, undeveloped land, can be searched without a warrant. (8)

ordinances—Local laws or regulations. (2)

organizational culture—Any group demonstrating specific patterns of behavior that distinguish it from others within a society; policing has been referred to as "The Blue Brotherhood." (4)

organized crime—A continuing criminal conspiracy seeking high profits with an organized structure that uses fear and corruption. (3)

original jurisdiction—A court's power to take a case, try it and decide it; in contrast to an appellate court that hears appeals to the decisions of the original court. (13)

paradigm—A way of thinking, of viewing the world. (1)

parens patriae—The right of the government to take care of minors and others who cannot legally take care of themselves. (13)

parish—The area in which people who worshipped in a particular parish church lived. (1)

parish constable system—An early system of law enforcement used primarily in rural areas. (1)

parole—A release from prison before a sentence is finished; continued release depends on good behavior and reporting to a parole officer; the most frequent type of release from a correctional institution. (14)

participatory leadership—Each individual has a voice in decisions, but top management retains the ultimate decision-making authority. (7)

pat down—An exploratory search of an individual's clothing; the "search" phase of a stop and frisk. (8)

petition—In the juvenile justice system, a document alleging a juvenile is a delinquent, status offender or dependent and asking the court to assume jurisdiction of the child. (13)

phishing—A form of Internet fraud in which criminals use technology to misrepresent themselves and mask their true identity from others, in an attempt to acquire personal or financial gain; also called *spoofing*. (3)

plain feel/touch doctrine—Related to the plain view doctrine; an officer who feels/touches something suspicious during the course of lawful activity can investigate further. (8)

plain view—Evidence that is not concealed and is seen by an officer engaged in a lawful activity; what is observed in plain view is not construed within the meaning of the Fourth Amendment as a search. (8)

plea bargaining—A legal negotiation between the prosecutor and the defense lawyer or the defendant to reach an agreement or compromise that avoids a court trial, conserving time and expense. (13)

police authority—The right to direct and command. (4)

police power—The power of the federal, state or municipal governments to pass and enforce laws to regulate private interests, to protect the health and safety of the people, to prevent fraud and oppression and to promote public convenience, prosperity and welfare. (2)

political era—(1840–1930) The first era of policing; characterized by authority coming from politicians and the law, a broad social service function, decentralized organization, an intimate relationship with the community and extensive use of foot patrol. (1)

positivist theory—Theory developed at the turn of the century by Italian criminologist Cesare Lombroso that sees criminals as "victims of society" and of their own biological, sociological, cultural and physical environments. (3)

posttraumatic stress disorder (PTSD)—A psychological illness that happens after a highly stressful event or series of events, commonly associated with shooting incidents. (12)

preliminary hearing—That stage in the judicial system seeking to establish probable cause for believing that an offense has been committed and that the accused committed it, thus preventing persons from being indiscriminately brought to trial. (13)

preponderance of the evidence—The greater weight of the evidence; one side is more credible than the other; standard of proof used in civil trials. (13)

presumption of innocence—The accused is assumed innocent until proof to the contrary is clearly established. (13)

pretext stop—When an officer stops a vehicle for ulterior motives; also called a *dual motive stop*. (5)

primary victims—Individuals directly affected by an incident, such as the person who is robbed, burglarized or raped. (3)

proactive—Seeking to find the causes of crime and to rectify those problems, thereby deterring or even preventing crime; acting before the fact rather than reacting to something that has already occurred. (1)

probable cause—Reasonable grounds for presuming guilt; facts that lead a person of ordinary care and prudence to believe and conscientiously entertain an honest and strong suspicion that a person is guilty of a crime. (8)

probation—The conditional suspension of a sentence of a person convicted of a crime but not yet imprisoned for that crime; the defendant is placed under the supervision of a probation officer for a set period and must meet specific conditions. (14)

problem-solving policing—A departmental-wide strategy aimed at solving persistent community problems; police identify, analyze and respond to the underlying circumstances that create incidents. (7)

***pro bono* work**—Work done for free; lawyers volunteer their time to be public defenders. (13)

procedural criminal law—Laws specifying what must be proved and how, that is, legally within the constraints of the Constitution and the Bill of Rights. (2)

procedural due process—Deals with notices, hearings and gathering evidence in criminal matters. (2)

professional model—The style of policing used during the reform era, based on the philosophies of August Vollmer and O. W. Wilson. (1)

protective sweep—A quick and limited search of premises, incident to an arrest and conducted to protect police officers or others. (8)

public offense—Any crime; includes felonies and misdemeanors. (8)

public safety exception—Allows police officers to question suspects without first giving the *Miranda* warning if the information sought sufficiently affects the officers' or the public's safety. (8)

pursuit—An active attempt by a law enforcement officer on duty in a patrol car to apprehend one or more occupants of a moving motor vehicle, providing the driver of such vehicle is aware of the attempt and is resisting apprehension by maintaining or increasing his speed or by ignoring the law enforcement officer's attempt to stop him. (11)

racial profiling—Any police-initiated action that relies on the race, ethnicity or national origin rather than on the behavior of an individual for the police to believe a particular individual is engaged in criminal activity. (5, 11)

random patrol—Having no set pattern; by chance; haphazard. (5)

rape—Having sexual intercourse through force or threat of force; may be aggravated (the more violent offense), simple or statutory; also called *sexual assault.* (3)

rattle watch—A group of citizens patrolling at night and armed with rattles to call for help; used in New Amsterdam in the 1650s. (1)

reactive—Responding to crimes after they have been committed. (1)

reasonable—Sensible, justifiable and logical. (8)

reasonable doubt—That state of a case in which, after comparing and considering all the evidence, the jurors cannot say they feel an abiding conviction of the truth of the charge; moral uncertainty of the truth of the charges. (13)

reasonable force—Force no greater than that needed to achieve the desired end. (11)

reasonable suspicion—A legal standard defined in *United States v. Cortez* (1981) as "a particularized and objective basis for suspecting the particular person stopped of criminal activity"; also referred to as *arguable suspicion.* (8)

recidivism—Repeated or habitual offending. (14)

recidivist—One who habitually or repeatedly breaks the law. (3)

red teaming—An independent peer review of abilities, vulnerabilities and limitations; applied to homeland security, involves thinking or acting like a terrorist in an effort to identify security weaknesses and potential targets. (10)

reeve—The top official of a hundred. (1)

reform era—(1930–1980) The second era of policing; characterized by authority coming from the law and professionalism; crime control as the primary function of law enforcement; a centralized, efficient organization; professional remoteness from the community; and an emphasis on preventive motorized patrol and rapid response to crime. (1)

regulators—Respectable settlers of average or affluent means who joined others as vigilantes to attack and break up outlaw gangs and restore order in the 1760s. (1)

rehabilitation—Correcting deviant behavior. (14)

representing—Visually displaying an allegiance to a gang and commonly encompasses dressing to the "left" or "right" side of the body, depending on the particular gang. (9)

residual deterrence effect—The positive effects of crackdowns that continue after a crackdown ends. (5)

restitution—Compensating or making up for loss, damage or injury; requiring an offender to repay the victim or the community in money or services. (14)

restorative justice—Philosophical framework that focuses on crime as an act against another individual rather than against the state and focuses on the harm done and how that harm might be repaired; goal is to reconcile the needs of victims and offenders with the community's needs. (2)

retribution—Punishment for the sake of punishment; revenge. (2, 14)

retributive justice—System where a person who breaks the rules must pay; an eye for an eye. (2)

reverse discrimination—Giving preferential treatment in hiring and promoting to women and minorities to the detriment of White males. (12)

reverse 911 (R911)—As the name implies, allows agencies to alert the public in emergencies. (4)

riot act—An order permitting the magistrate to call in the military to quell a riot. (1)

ritualistic crime—An unlawful act committed during a ceremony related to a belief system; the crime, not the belief system, must be investigated. (3)

road rage—An angry, frequently violent response to an aggressive-driving incident; not the same as aggressive driving. (5)

robbery—Stealing anything of value from the care, custody or control of a person in his or her presence, by force or by the threat of force. (3)

roll call—The briefing of officers before their tour of duty to update them on criminal activity and calls for service. (4)

R.P.R.d—Release on one's own personal recognizance. (13)

SAR—suspicious activity report. Contains information documented by local law enforcement that can be shared with other law enforcement agencies to help detect and prevent terrorism-related criminal activity. (10)

SARA model—Four strategies used in problem-oriented policing: scan, analyze, respond, assess. (7)

saturation patrol—Involves an increased enforcement effort targeting a specific geographic area to identify and arrest impaired drivers. (5)

scienter—A degree of knowledge that makes an individual legally responsible for the consequences of his or her acts. (2)

search warrant—A judicial order directing a peace officer to search for specific property, seize it and return it to the court; it may be a written order or an order given over the telephone. (8)

secondary victims—Family members and friends of victims who also feel pain and suffering along with the victim; also called *indirect victims.* (3)

second-degree murder—The unpremeditated but intentional killing of another person. (3)

seizure—A forcible detention or taking of a person or property in an arrest. (8)

selective enforcement—Targets specific crashes or high-crash areas. (5)

selective incorporation—Holds that only those provisions of the Bill of Rights fundamental to the American legal process are made applicable to the states through the due process clause; also called the incorporation *doctrine.* (2)

sexual harassment—Has two conditions: (1) It must occur in the workplace or an extension of the workplace (department sanctioned), and (2) it must be of a sexual nature that does not include romance or that is not of a mutually friendly nature; the harassment must be unwelcome, unsolicited and deliberate. (12)

sheriff—The principal law enforcement officer of a county. (1)

shire-reeve—The top official of a shire (county); the forerunner of our county sheriff. (1)

shires—Counties in England. (1)

shock incarceration—Patterned after the traditional military boot camps for new recruits, a system of incarceration for youths that stresses strict and even cruel discipline, hard work and authoritarian decision making and control by a drill sergeant; also called *boot camp.* (14)

sinsemilla—A highly potent form of marijuana obtained from unpollinated female plants. (9)

situational testing—Job-related simulation exercises to assess a candidate's qualifications and suitability for a law enforcement position. (12)

skimming—Using a small, portable device that copies and stores data from debit and credit cards' magnetic strips. (3)

slave patrols—Special enforcement officers during the mid-1790s who were allowed to enter any plantation and break into slaves' dwellings, search slaves' persons and possessions at will and beat and even kill any slaves found violating the slave code. (1)

sleeper cell—A group of terrorists who blend into a community. (10)

social capital—The bond among family members and their immediate, informal groups as well as the networks tying individuals to broader community institutions, such as schools, civic organizations and churches, and to various levels of government, including the police. (7)

social contract—Provides that for everyone to receive justice, each person must relinquish some freedom. (7)

solvability factors—Factors affecting the probability of successfully concluding a case. (6)

span of control—The number of individuals or resources one supervisor can manage effectively during emergency response incidents or special events. (4)

specific deterrence—Deterrence aimed at offenders; attempts to make the consequences of committing crime so severe that when offenders return to society, they will not commit crime. (14)

split-second syndrome—Asserts that if a person has intentionally or unintentionally provoked or threatened a police officer, at that instant the provoker rather than the police should be viewed as the cause of any resulting injuries or damages. (12)

spoils system—A political system whereby "friends" of politicians were rewarded with key positions in the police department. (1)

spoofing—Uses technology to misrepresent a criminal and mask his or her true identity from others, in an attempt to acquire personal or financial gain; also called *phishing.* (3)

stacking—Gang members demonstrating and representing their own gang by throwing up visual hand signs. (9)

standing mute—Refusing to answer as to guilt or innocence at an arraignment; entered as a " not guilty" plea. (13)

status offenses—Crimes restricted to persons under the legal age—for example, smoking, drinking, breaking curfew, absenting from home, truancy, incorrigibility. (3)

statutory law—Law passed by a legislature. (2)

stop—Briefly detaining someone who is acting suspiciously; a stop is not an arrest. (8)

strict liability—Intent is not required; the defendant is liable regardless of his or her state of mind when the act was committed. (2)

substantive criminal law—Statutes specifying crimes and their punishments. (2)

substantive due process—Protects individuals against unreasonable, arbitrary or capricious laws and limits arbitrary government actions. (2)

suppressible crimes—Crimes that commonly occur in locations and under circumstances that provide police officers a reasonable opportunity to deter or apprehend offenders; includes robbery, burglary, car theft, assault and sex crimes. (6)

symbiotic relationship—Mutually dependent on each other. (7)

symbolic speech—Tangible forms of expression such as wearing buttons or clothing with political slogans or displaying a sign or flag; protected by the First Amendment. (2)

terrorism—The use of force or violence against persons or property in violation of the criminal laws of the United States for purposes of intimidation, coercion or ransom. (10)

***Terry* stop**—The simple act of stopping someone based on reasonable suspicion; alternately called an *investigatory stop*, a *field inquiry*, or a *threshold inquiry*. (8)

tithing—In Anglo-Saxon England, a unit of civil administration consisting of 10 families; established the principle of collective responsibility for maintaining law and order. (1)

tithing system—Established the principle of collective responsibility for maintaining local law and order by organizing families into groups of 10 families known as tithings. (1)

tort—A civil wrong for which the court seeks remedy in the form of damages to be paid. (2)

totality of circumstances—Considering all factors involved in a given situation. (6, 8)

turf—The geographic territory claimed by a gang. (9)

287(g)—The section of the *Immigration and Nationality Act* delegating federal immigration enforcement to state and local law enforcement agencies. (11)

typologies—Systematic classifications, as in styles of policing. (4)

venue—The local area where a case may be tried; it is usually required that the trial for an offense be held in the same area in which the offense occurred. (13)

vetted—Thoroughly checked out; verified. (6)

vicarious liability—The legal responsibility one person has for the acts of another; managers, the entire agency and even the jurisdiction served may be legally responsible for the actions of a single officer. (12)

victim impact statement (VIS)—A written or spoken statement detailing the medical, financial and emotional injuries resulting from a crime; the information is usually provided to a probation officer who writes a summary to be included in the defendant's presenting packet. (3)

victim statement of opinion (VSO)—A spoken or written statement to the judge in which victims tell the court their opinions on what sentence the defendant should receive; more subjective than the victim impact statement. (3)

vigilante—A person who takes the law into his or her own hands, usually in the absence of effective policing. (1)

voir dire—The random selection of potential jurors and the careful questioning of each. (13)

waiver—The voluntary giving up of a right. (8)

wannabees—Youths who dress and act like gang members and hang out on the fringes of the gang, hoping to be invited in some day. (9)

Watch and Ward—A system of law enforcement that was used to protect citizens 24 hours a day; the day shift was called the *ward* and the night shift was called the *watch*. (1)

well—The area between the judge and the attorney's tables; this area is off-limits and is to be entered only if a judge so directs or permission is granted. (13)

white-collar crime—Occupational or business-related crime; also called *economic crime*. (3)

wingspan—The area within a person's reach; also known as *immediate control*. (8)

writ of certiorari—A request for a transcript of the proceedings of a case for review; granted when the Supreme Court decides to hear a case. (13)

writ of habeas corpus—A legal court order literally meaning "bring forth the body you have," which commands that a person being held be brought forth immediately. (13)

xenophobia—Fear or hatred of strangers or foreigners. (3)

AUTHOR INDEX

T

U

V

W

Y

SUBJECT INDEX

D

E

F

G

O

P

T

U